Ireland
1905 – 1925

Volume 1

*Text
and
Historiography*

R Rees

Colourpoint

For Jean, Gordon and Clark

Published by Colourpoint Books
© R Rees 1998

6 5 4 3 2 1

Dr Russell Rees graduated in History
with honours at the University of
Ulster, Coleraine and his doctoral
thesis dealt with the relations
between Northern Ireland, the Irish
Free State and Britain in the period
1945-51. He is presently Head of
History at Omagh Academy, Co
Tyrone. He is co-author of a number
of school textbooks including
**Ireland and British Politics 1870-
1921** and **Union to Partition,
Ireland 1800-1921**.

Designed by Colourpoint Books
Printed by ColourBooks

**ISBN 1 898392 19 6 paperback
1 898392 40 4 hardback**

Colourpoint Books
Unit D5, Ards Business Centre
Jubilee Road
NEWTOWNARDS
County Down
Northern Ireland
BT23 4YH

Tel: (01247) 820505/819787 Ex 239
Fax: (01247) 821900
E-mail: Info@colourpoint.co.uk
Web-site: www.colourpoint.co.uk

*Cover Illustration:
Wreck of a train blown up by the
IRA near Newry in June 1921.
See also photo 43 between
pages 192 and 193.*

Contents

Acknowledgements

A few people in particular helped to make this book a reality. Professor Tony Hepburn, the author of Volume Two of this work, has been a long-time source of encouragement and inspiration. My publishers, Norman and Sheila Johnston, have been supportive, enthusiastic and patient. My colleague, Audrey Hodge, read much of the script and offered useful suggestions. Essential practical assistance was provided by Catriona Dickson who never hesitated to place the full resources of her organisation at my disposal.

Note on numbers in heavy type

The numbers in square brackets and heavy type [127] which appear throughout this book, refer to documents in Volume Two of this work – *Ireland 1905–25 Vol 2: The Documents* by A C Hepburn **ISBN 1 898 392 20 X** (pbk), **1 898 392 46 3** (hbk). Whilst Volume One stands in its own right, readers of this book will find their understanding of the period greatly enhanced by cross-referencing to Volume Two.

Maps

Illustrations (between pages 192 and 193)

Photo credits

Ireland

Union to rebellion

The Act of Union, which came into force on 1 January 1801, was Britain's solution to the Irish problem. It did not work. The Irish problem had forced itself onto the political agenda at Westminster following the rebellion in 1798. Perhaps as many as 50,000 had taken part in the rebellion, which had been orchestrated by the Society of United Irishmen. Formed in 1791, the United Irishmen initially aroused interest among northern Presbyterians who had been influenced by the radical ideas of the French Revolution. As their name implied, the United Irishmen hoped to bring together Irishmen of all religious persuasions, principally Catholics, Church of Ireland and Presbyterians, in pursuit of their demands for a series of moderate political reforms. This situation changed when Britain went to war with France in 1793. The United Irishmen were suppressed in 1794, and their chief strategist, Wolfe Tone, a Dublin born Protestant lawyer, was forced into exile in 1795 [1]. By this stage the United Irishmen had become more revolutionary and more anti–English in character. Under Tone's influence they sought French help to end British rule in Ireland and establish a republic along French lines.

Tone and the other Protestant leaders of the United Irishmen also believed that if a revolution was to be successful, it must have mass support, which in Ireland meant Catholic support. The prospects for this were encouraging. For some time unrest among the Catholic peasantry had been growing, and the United Irishmen hoped to exploit this rural agitation and win support for their cause. Their main efforts were directed at the Defenders, a secret society which had originated in Ulster and was pledged to defend Catholic interests [2]. Although the Defenders had also been influenced by the French Revolution, their growth in the 1790s owed much more to simple sectarianism. There had been a long history of sectarian trouble in the southern counties of Ulster, particularly in County Armagh, but in the 1790s serious violence occurred. The Defenders found themselves up against their Protestant equivalent, the Peep O'Day Boys, and clashes between the two groups became more frequent and more violent. Such violence was the result of a mixture of sectarian bitterness and economic competition as both Protestant and Catholic farmer-weavers in the densely populated county tried to dominate the lucrative linen trade. The most famous incident in this period of sectarian unrest took place in September 1795 at the Diamond, a crossroads near the village of Loughgall in County Armagh [3]. Here a mini-battle between Defenders and Peep O'Day Boys resulted in the deaths of about twenty Defenders, and following their victory the Protestants assembled in Loughgall where they formed the Orange Society, which later became known as the Orange Order. After the skirmish at the Diamond a determined campaign of intimidation, aimed at driving Catholics from Armagh and the neighbouring counties, was mounted. Against this background the leaders of the United Irishmen were able to exploit Catholic fears and persuade the Defenders to enter into an alliance. Only by cutting Ireland free from Britain, they argued, could Catholics be assured of protection.

Meanwhile, Tone had stepped up his efforts to win French help, and in December 1796 he accompanied a large French force which almost made a successful landing in County Cork. This episode greatly alarmed the government, and a decision to crack down on potential revolutionary elements was taken. The arrest of key leaders seriously weakened the United Irishmen. When the rebellion finally got under way in May 1798, it was a hopelessly disjointed affair. Government forces quickly overcame pockets of resistance around Dublin, and there were isolated skirmishes in those parts of Antrim and Down where radical Presbyterianism was at its strongest. Only in County Wexford did the rebellion make any headway, but here the campaign was sectarian in character and was marked by vicious atrocities. In the end the Wexford rebels were routed on Vinegar Hill in June 1798, as the government forces resorted to ferocious brutality. A small French expeditionary force landed in County Mayo in August, but it came too late to influence events.

The final chapter of the 1798 rebellion was played out in October when a French naval squadron of ten assorted ships was intercepted by the British off the Donegal coast. After a brief engagement the French surrendered and among the prisoners brought ashore was Wolfe Tone. The British government now had the high profile leader of the United Irishmen in custody, and they were determined to make an example of him. His trial in Dublin was a foregone conclusion. Tone was sentenced to death, but he managed to cheat the hangman by committing suicide in his prison cell. In crushing the insurgents, many of whom displayed incredible bravery, government forces used brutal but effective measures. Later, however, memories of this brutality influenced the way people viewed the rebellion. Indeed, the perception of the rising was to play a significant role in the development of Irish revolutionary Nationalism. The legacy of 1798 was a vague inspiration for future risings. Moreover, in Wolfe Tone, later generations could identify with a martyr who had given Irishmen the concept of a republic, with Ireland free from Britain.

In the aftermath of the rebellion the chief British concern was defence, because the events of 1798 had demonstrated that the threat of a French invasion was very real. England had been at war with revolutionary France for five years, and while English naval power kept the Channel free, there was a genuine fear that the French might exploit Irish hostility to England and use Ireland as a base to attack England. The rebellion of the United Irishmen reinforced such fears. The Westminster government also had to consider the internal situation in Ireland. Although the rebellion had been crushed and the United Irish movement broken, widespread disorder continued in the countryside. It was these circumstances that forced the British government, led by William Pitt (Pitt the Younger), to act decisively by proposing a legislative union between Britain and Ireland. The idea of a union had been under consideration at Westminster for some time, but the knowledge that such a proposal would provoke a storm of opposition from the Irish parliament meant that it had not been adopted.

Although the upheaval caused by the rebellion had given Pitt the opportunity to press the case for a union, it was recognised that the problem of convincing the Irish parliament that its interests would be best served by a union, would have to be overcome. The Irish parliament was dominated by the Protestant Ascendancy, an elite, Anglo-Irish, Protestant (Church of Ireland), landowning class. Many of the Ascendancy politicians were determined to keep their parliament in Dublin's College Green, and when the principle of the Union was debated in the Irish parliament in 1799, a narrow majority had voted against it. The Protestant gentry opposing the Union believed that it was not the best way to strengthen the connection between Britain and Ireland. Pitt approached the problem in two ways. Control of the patronage system allowed the government to create a number of new titles for Irish MPs and to compensate others who then threw their support behind the Union. More were persuaded, however, by Pitt's argument that a legislative union would offer the best hope of establishing peace and firm government in Ireland. In other words, only the Union could maintain the power and protect the privileges of the Protestant Ascendancy. Yet Pitt also hoped that the Act of Union would be accompanied by Catholic Emancipation. Since 1793, Catholics meeting the property qualification had the right to vote, but they were barred from holding political office and, crucially, they were not allowed to sit in parliament. Despite appeals by Pitt, the Protestant Ascendancy would not sanction Catholic Emancipation, and the measure was quickly dropped.

The Act of Union abolished the Irish parliament. Henceforth, Ireland was allowed to send 100 MPs to the House of Commons at Westminster, a figure which would later rise to 105, and 28 Irish peers and 4 bishops to the House of Lords. Ireland had received generous representation, more than twice as much as Scotland enjoyed, but other aspects of the new relationship between Britain and Ireland revealed that political integration was far from complete. Ireland had a Viceroy, a Chief Secretary and a peculiar administrative structure. The Viceroy, or Lord Lieutenant, had overall responsibility for the administration of Ireland. He spent most of the year in the Vice-Regal Lodge in the Phoenix Park and attended all the major state ceremonies. Indeed, as the century progressed, his role became an increasingly ceremonial one. The Chief Secretary dealt with Irish matters in parliament and frequently he occupied a seat in cabinet. When parliament was not in session, the Chief Secretary was often in Ireland, liaising with the Viceroy and working with officials in the drafting of Irish legislation. The difficulty of travel between London and Dublin during the nineteenth century, though rail travel was to ease this burden, made the job of Chief Secretary a very demanding one. With the Chief Secretary spending so much time in London a great deal of the administrative responsibility passed to his Under Secretary. He was the senior civil servant in Ireland and was responsible for overseeing the work undertaken by the various departments of the Irish administration. This was to become a daunting task because, by the end of the century, there were forty such departments with a total of 26,000 officials. Not surprisingly, the distinctive style of the Irish administration allowed it to function with a considerable degree of autonomy because, for the most part, Westminster's primary concern was to ensure that the Irish administration operated within a tight budget. Dublin Castle was the nerve centre of this separate administration, and for the first thirty years of the Union it was controlled by the Protestant Ascendancy. However, such were the differences between conditions in Ireland and Britain, that separate administrative arrangements may have been the only sensible approach.

Although the immediate impact of the Union on Irish life was negligible, there was no doubt that it had altered Britain's responsibilities. It also meant that Irish problems were transferred from Dublin to Westminster and, as the century progressed, these problems came to dominate British political life. Westminster's principal function after the Union was the maintenance of law and order in the country, and this required the permanent deployment of a large garrison in Ireland. Soon, the Protestant Ascendancy came to realise that their security depended on this British garrison. Within twenty years they were to become firm supporters of the Union, seeing it as their only protection against the Catholic majority in Ireland. At the same time, the leading figures among the Ascendancy class had little difficulty in adjusting to political life at Westminster.

Catholics, on the other hand, did not accept the Union. The failure to implement Catholic Emancipation had left Catholics with a serious grievance. This was particularly true for the politically conscious Catholic middle classes who were impatient for the granting of full civil rights. Later in the century, when Britain took its first tentative steps on the road to mass democracy, Catholics became more familiar with the concept of a majority, and they realised that in Ireland they constituted a very large majority. For most of these Catholics, however, the political changes brought about by the Union were of no consequence. Their concerns were more basic. The peasantry, eking out a precarious existence in rural Ireland, laboured under an unjust land system which gave them no rights. As it was the Catholic masses who suffered most from the social and economic crises of the nineteenth century, they naturally looked for one overriding reason to explain their predicament and, increasingly, the existence of the Union was held responsible for their troubles. Moreover, the struggle to improve their condition saw them challenge the power of the Protestant landowners, and this developed into an attack on the Union itself. Perhaps, more than any other factor, it was Westminster's reluctance to tackle the land issue that did most to weaken the Union.

Social and economic conditions differed in north-east Ulster. It was only in the Belfast area that large scale industrialisation developed in the nineteenth century. Initially, this was based on linen manufacturing but, in the second half of the century, shipbuilding and engineering became prominent. Northern Presbyterians, who benefited most from this industrial expansion, were convinced that Ulster's economic prosperity was totally dependent on the Union, because Britain supplied the raw materials and then purchased the finished products. Like the Protestant Ascendancy in the rest of Ireland, these northern Presbyterians saw the Union as vital. Thus the powerful desire to maintain the Union drew these two potentially hostile groups together. When Catholics looked at the economic impact of the Union, they took the opposite view. Whereas Protestants attributed economic progress to the link with Britain, Catholics blamed the Union for their lack of prosperity. Both were probably mistaken. Yet, if the Union made little actual difference to Ireland, its introduction had created a new fault line in Irish politics and made consensus more difficult to achieve. Either you were a supporter of the Union or an opponent.

This divergence, however, took time to materialise. Immediately after the Union, political life in Ireland was uneventful. The one exception came in 1803, when Robert Emmet led the remnants of the United Irishmen in another rebellion against British rule. Although the rising was nothing more than a brief skirmish on the streets of Dublin, its significance, building on the tradition of 1798, was its legacy to later generations of republicans. Emmet, a new martyr, had given a stirring oration at his trial, and the youthful, heroic and romantic image he left provided an inspiration for future revolutionary activity.

Emancipation and Repeal

For most Irishmen, however, politics were of little significance. What mattered were local issues, particularly landlord-tenant relations. During the first twenty years of the Union, Irish peasants looked to the agrarian secret societies to overcome their problems. Then, in 1823, a transformation in Irish politics took place with the founding of the Catholic Association. This was the brainchild of Daniel O'Connell, a Catholic lawyer from a County Kerry landowning family. Until O'Connell's move, the campaign for Catholic Emancipation had been a low key affair conducted by a small group of Catholic notables [4]. O'Connell sought a new strategy. He intended to create a mass movement using the organisation and manpower of the Catholic Church.

The first half of the nineteenth century witnessed the rapid expansion of the Catholic Church in Ireland, and contemporary observers made frequent references to the number of new church buildings under construction all over the country. The demand for extra priests, which this expansion had caused, meant that the new clergy were increasingly drawn from the lower social orders. Many were farmers' sons who showed more interest in politics and identified closely with their parishioners. This expanding clergy played a vital role in the Catholic Association, enthusiastically organising the campaign at local level and helping to turn the struggle for Emancipation into a truly popular cause.

Within twelve months of its formation the Catholic Association was booming, as the Catholic masses were drawn by O'Connell's charismatic leadership. At its height almost one million peasants were subscribing a penny a month, and this gave the movement great financial strength. Such huge interest and commitment was generated by the belief that the movement would not just campaign for Emancipation, but would aim to redress Catholic grievances in general, and thereby transform Irish society. Great meetings were organised throughout the country, at which O'Connell and his lieutenants denounced the Westminster government and demanded the immediate granting of Emancipation. For four years the government stood firm, but O'Connell finally brought matters to a head when he himself successfully contested the Clare by-election in July 1828. It was clear that if the British continued to resist the growing clamour for Emancipation, they risked the prospect of serious unrest in Ireland, or maybe even a new rebellion. Eventually, the government backed down and, by April 1829, Catholic Emancipation was law. Catholics could now take their seats in parliament and were entitled to hold all but a few of the highest offices of state. Having achieved its goal the Catholic Association dissolved itself.

The working of the Act of Union meant that O'Connell had to somehow cajole the parliament at Westminster into accepting Emancipation, and the manner in which this was achieved had a profound effect on the future shape of Irish politics. The campaign to win Emancipation had politicised the Catholic masses and laid the foundations for constitutional Nationalism. The Catholic Association had been used to launch a great popular crusade, ostensibly to deliver Emancipation, but with the underlying assumption that all Catholic grievances could be put right. O'Connell himself possessed deep liberal convictions and believed that governments could be moved by the power of public opinion. Yet in the last resort the British government had yielded on the Emancipation issue, because it feared that the mass agitation could develop into serious violence. The lesson drawn by later generations of Irish Nationalists was that Westminster would refuse all concessions to Ireland unless confronted by the threat of revolution.

The fact that the first mass movement in Irish politics was exclusively concerned with a Catholic grievance also influenced subsequent political developments. In order to create this mass movement it had been necessary for O'Connell to mix politics with religion, and this had aroused Protestant fears. Indeed, the transformation of Catholic politics in the 1820s, and the impact of the popular agitation with its powerful clerical influence, tended to reinforce the sectarian hostility between Catholics and Protestants, which had surfaced towards the end of the eighteenth century. On the other hand, O'Connell thought that if Catholic grievances could be dealt with, Catholic Ireland could become reconciled to the Union and, in time, Catholics would become loyal subjects. Protestants, of course, doubted this. These Irish Protestants claimed justification for their fears, when O'Connell followed up his Emancipation victory by demanding the repeal of the Union and the restoration of the Irish parliament. From the 1830s their position as a minority in Ireland was brought home to them in no uncertain terms and Protestants became increasingly defensive. Just as he had done with Emancipation, O'Connell forced the British establishment to look seriously at repeal. Yet, perhaps because the Irish leader consistently refused to spell out precisely what repeal would mean, neither of the two main parties at Westminster ever considered supporting repeal. Instead, it was assumed that repeal, if granted, would lead to the eventual separation of Britain and Ireland. O'Connell, however, probably intended that a new mechanism of government would operate, but the connection with Britain would remain.

At Westminster O'Connell established an alliance with the Whigs (the forerunners of the Liberal party) who had earlier backed Emancipation and, though not in favour of repeal, were known to be sympathetic to Irish demands. Evidence of the lack of support for repeal at Westminster came in 1834 when the measure was defeated in the House of Commons by 529 to 38, demonstrating conclusively that repeal could not be won by conventional parliamentary methods [5]. Accordingly, O'Connell dropped his demand for repeal in 1835 and entered into the alliance with the Whigs which was to last six years. In return for the support of O'Connell and his colleagues, the Whigs provided Ireland with a tithe settlement and a number of moderate reforms. When the Whigs lost power in 1841, O'Connell returned to the repeal campaign and the Loyal National Repeal Association was formed. Clearly, O'Connell was going back to the strategy of mass agitation which had delivered Catholic Emancipation. Although the new organisation was not an immediate success, it soon gathered momentum. That it did was due to two factors. Interest in repeal was awakened by the Young Ireland group, a splinter of the repeal movement. Its romantic and cultural Nationalism was similar to the variety which was exciting young intellectuals in contemporary Europe. The Young Irelanders articulated their views and ideas in a new newspaper, *The Nation*, which was first published in October 1842 and within a year was to claim a readership of almost 250,000. Perhaps even more crucially, in terms of re-creating the crusading zeal of the Emancipation campaign, the Catholic Church had, by 1843, thrown its weight behind the Repeal Association. This proved vital for O'Connell in the organisation of the famous 'monster meetings', a key tactic in the repeal campaign. In 1843, the year that O'Connell had predicted would be 'repeal year', these monster meetings attracted huge numbers of people, often in excess of 100,000, who heard the Irish leader take an increasingly uncompromising line with the British government.

Not surprisingly, O'Connell's violent language alarmed the Conservative government at Westminster, where it was feared that Ireland, yet again, might be on the brink of revolution. On this occasion, however, the government decided to meet the agitation head on. The greatest of the monster rallies had been scheduled for Clontarf on 8 October 1843, and the Prime Minister, Sir Robert Peel, not only banned the meeting, but flooded the Clontarf area with troops to uphold the ban. Fearing widespread disorder, O'Connell called off the meeting. The repeal campaign never recovered from this setback, and O'Connell actually found himself in jail for the greater part of 1844. On his release it was clear that a rift had developed between O'Connell and the Young Ireland group and, when O'Connell moved to rebuild the old Whig alliance late in 1845, this rift became deeper. The Young Irelanders were angry that O'Connell had opted to abandon the repeal agitation in favour of playing parliamentary politics at Westminster. At this point O'Connell, urged on by his son, decided to press the issue. When a showdown took place in the summer of 1846, the Young Irelanders were forced to withdraw from the Repeal Association. As the bulk of the repeal movement and the clergy remained loyal to O'Connell, it seemed that the small Young Ireland group was destined for the political wilderness. Yet within a few years famine was to make the Repeal Association irrelevant. By the time of his death in May 1847 O'Connell was only a shadow of the figure who had moulded the Catholic political nation. He had never recovered from the Clontarf episode when, on the brink of serious confrontation, he drew back from leading the Catholic masses in open defiance of the government. Thereafter, his close relationship with the Whigs proved counter-productive, as his pleas for action by the Whig administration during the famine were ignored.

Naturally, the Young Irelanders also found it difficult to make political headway during the famine. Their intellectual appeal, strongly influenced by European developments in the 1840s, had no relevance for the great bulk of the people whose real concerns were altogether more basic. And yet the Young Irelanders played a crucial role in the development of Irish Nationalism. The leading figure in the movement, Thomas Davis, a Protestant who had been a distinguished student at

Trinity College, was the first to construct a coherent theory of Irish nationality [6]. In the pages of *The Nation* he claimed that Ireland was a separate nation, distinct from England, with her own rich history, culture and language. Concerned about the growing identification between Irish Nationalism and Irish Catholicism, Davis argued for a new spirit of nationality which would embrace all of Ireland's creeds and classes. However, Davis's death in 1845 removed a moderating influence from the movement. Soon, it fell under the influence of John Mitchel, the son of an Ulster Presbyterian minister, and James Fintan Lalor, another Protestant radical, who blamed the landlord class for the famine [7,8]. The excitement aroused by the sequence of European revolutions in 1848 gave further encouragement to these extremists. When, in July 1848, the government took the decision to crack down on the movement, those Young Irelanders who had not been arrested staged a rebellion. It proved a disaster. No plans for an armed uprising had been made, and what transpired was a confused escapade which cannot really be described as a rebellion. The main action took place in a widow's cabbage garden in County Tipperary, where about fifty insurgents surrendered to armed police following a brief skirmish. On this occasion no one was executed, though the main leaders of the rising were arrested and sentenced to transportation. The timing of the rising had been disastrous.

After three years of famine there was no chance of popular support and this doomed the rising to failure. Still, while nothing had been achieved in the fiasco of 1848, the Young Irelanders left their mark on later generations [9]. Their clear enunciation of a new sense of nationality, in which differences between Ireland and England were emphasised, and the romantic idealism of their youthful leaders, gave Irish Nationalism new intellectual content. Moreover, the rebellion of 1848, despite its dismal failure, helped to ingrain the tradition of violent revolutionary Nationalism.

Famine

In the late 1840s, of course, the devastating impact of the potato famine overshadowed both repeal agitation and Young Ireland politics. The bare statistics give some idea of the scale of suffering. More than 800,000 died and close to 1,500,000 emigrated as a result of the famine. There had been earlier failures of the potato crop in the nineteenth century, notably in 1817 and 1822, when 50,000 people died, but what created the great natural disaster of the late 1840s was that the crop failed over the whole country and that this failure was repeated in successive years. Potato blight spread from North America to Europe and made its first appearance in Ireland in August 1845. By the end of the year the blight had spread to seventeen counties, but some of the crop had been harvested before the disease struck. Although distress was acute, no one died from starvation in the 1845-46 season, as nearly half of the country had escaped the blight. In 1846, however, the blight was much more widespread and the bulk of the crop was diseased. By 1847 the blight had receded, but as few seed potatoes were available, the acreage planted was much smaller than usual. This pattern was reversed in 1848 as Irish farmers planted a very large crop, but the blight returned and was just as widespread and virulent as it had been in 1846. Indeed, the catastrophe did not end in 1848, because the blight continued in some areas up to 1852. In this last stage those counties most affected were Tipperary, Clare and Kerry.

Since the Act of Union, the ultimate responsibility for the relief of famine in Ireland rested with the authorities in London. Overwhelmed by the sheer scale and intensity of the famine, the government was accused of neglect. Indeed, what was perceived as total disregard for the suffering in Ireland was to convince many Irishmen that while Ireland may have been part of the Union, she was by no means an equal partner. After all, the United Kingdom was at that stage the most advanced and the wealthiest country in the world and, if the will had existed, the government should certainly have had the capacity to provide effective famine aid. Recently, historians of the famine have pointed to the Belgian experience of 1867 when the government there, albeit reluctantly, imported large quantities of food and combined this with other effective relief measures to stave off famine. In fact, the initial response to the Irish famine by Peel's Conservative government was similar. Immediately, a special scientific commission was dispatched to investigate the cause of the blight. By November 1845 Peel had authorised the purchase of £100,000 worth of maize, or Indian corn, in the United States and had it shipped to Cork. The purpose of this was to control food prices in Ireland by releasing these extra supplies of grain onto the market when prices began to rise. However, the key element in Peel's strategy was the provision of employment on relief schemes, a traditional response which had proved effective when Ireland faced food shortages earlier in the century. These relief schemes provided very low wages, usually no higher than 8d a day, for men engaged on public works such as road building. Relief schemes were coordinated by local relief committees which had been encouraged by the government and, by the summer of 1846, there were more than 600 such committees. The disaster in Ireland also influenced Peel's decision to repeal the corn laws. This involved the removal of tariffs on grain imports which, in turn, reduced the price of bread. As a measure of famine relief, the repeal of the corn laws made little impact because, for the poorest people in Ireland, bread, even at a reduced price, was beyond their means.

The repeal of the corn laws was a highly controversial move which split the Conservative party and led to the downfall of the Peel administration. The new Whig government under Lord John Russell remained in power until the end of the famine in 1852. This change of government brought a change in famine relief policy, as the new administration scaled down the level of government aid. Rather than operating a two-pronged strategy of providing cheap food and giving employment on public works, the Whig government confined its activities to the public works. The result was disastrous, because, in the autumn of 1846, when the blight was reported as widespread, relief was actually being reduced. This change in policy can be attributed to the ideological thinking of the Whig party at the time. The key figures in the administration, as far as famine relief was concerned, were Sir Charles Wood, the Chancellor of the Exchequer, and Charles Trevelyan, a leading official at the Treasury. Both men were committed to the doctrine of laissez-faire, believing that the state should refrain, wherever possible, from interfering with market forces, which meant that food should be supplied by private enterprise. They also thought that the relief of distress in Ireland through the provision of employment on public works should be paid for by Irish landlords. This policy had dire consequences. Even those who had the good fortune to find employment on the relief schemes did not earn enough money to buy food in a period of rising prices. Moreover, the winter of 1846-47 was particularly severe, and this added to the difficulties facing the starving. Large numbers were now dying, mainly from famine related disease, and emigration began to rise sharply. It was obvious, even to the Whig government, that a new strategy was required.

By February 1847 indirect relief was responsible for the employment of some 750,000 on the various public works but, with famine continuing to rage, the government was forced to introduce a direct relief programme. Consequently, a network of soup kitchens was established throughout Ireland and, by the summer of 1847, an estimated 3 million were receiving free soup rations. In many of the poorest areas in the west of Ireland the whole population was dependent on the soup kitchens. It was decided that if further relief was required, it should be provided under the machinery of the Poor Law and financed by local rates. This, therefore, was the position as the famine entered its worst year. In 1848 the workhouses, which were designed to be as spartan as possible, were bursting with more than 100,000 inmates, while a further 800,000 were receiving outdoor relief in the form of food rations. The particularly savage impact of the famine in 1848, and the horrific conditions in which lives were lost, left a legacy of bitterness against England which was, of course, exploited later by extreme Nationalists.

In assessing the overall impact of the famine a number of factors need to be emphasised. Ireland had developed serious economic problems in the early decades of the nineteenth century as domestic industry was in decline everywhere except Ulster, leaving the bulk of the country almost totally dependent on agriculture. Despite these economic difficulties, population was rising rapidly and, in the early 1840s, it passed the 8 million mark. Moreover, there had been a huge increase in the rural population, and many of these young families were sustained by potatoes on marginal land. Much of this increase in rural population can be attributed to the excessive subdivision of the land, a practice which had been fairly widespread throughout the country, but was much more prevalent in the very poorest counties such as Donegal and Mayo. In such densely populated rural areas subsistence farming predominated, with the potato providing the means of subsistence. Yet, significantly, the rate of population growth was in decline after 1821, though the population total still rose.

This rapid increase in population had a decisive impact on Ireland's complex rural class structure. Beneath the landlord class came the 'strong' farmers with over thirty acres and the 'middling' farmers who rented farms of over fifteen acres. Both these groups of tenant farmers were dominant in the midlands and east of the country, where they concentrated on commercial farming based on grain production and cattle rearing. The next layer in Irish rural society was occupied by the smallholders of one to fifteen acres, and even within this very large group of smallholders it was possible to regard those with one to five acres as a distinct class. Beneath the smallholders came the cottier class, labourers who received their wages in land and were almost entirely dependent on potato cultivation. By 1845 the numbers of smallholders and cottiers outnumbered the farmers two to one. When the famine struck, it was these two bottom layers in rural society, especially the cottier class, which were hardest hit. As the western province of Connacht was dominated by this cottier economy and its subsistence agriculture, it was devastated by the impact of the potato blight. In addition to the catastrophic loss of life, the famine also led to the disappearance of many of these smallholdings, as the number of one to five acre farms quickly declined by almost two-thirds. At the same time, there was a sharp increase in farms over thirty acres, and one result of this consolidation process was that livestock farming replaced tillage in many areas. Yet the pattern of increased livestock production on medium-sized farms was already taking shape before the famine. Rather than viewing the famine as a watershed in Irish history, therefore, it seems more accurate to describe the famine as an accelerator of change, albeit a turbo-charged one, as patterns of slower population growth, the process of farm consolidation and the transition from arable to livestock farming had already made their mark in pre-famine Ireland. This was also true of emigration. Numbers departing on emigration ships were already significant before the famine, though no one could have predicted the scale of emigration, which reached a peak in 1851 and was to remain a significant feature for the next hundred years. Here, once again, the continuity with pre-famine Ireland needs to be stressed.

What of the landlords? In pre-famine Ireland about one-third of these were absentees who left the running of their estates to a manager. Another group could be considered 'improving landlords', as they encouraged better methods of cultivation and contributed to farm improvements and better housing. The majority, however, were concerned solely with maximising rent returns. Although there were many landlords who threw themselves into famine relief work, the callous attitude of the majority meant that the Irish placed the blame for the famine at the landlord's door. Yet these landlords were also hit by the famine. As rents fell and rates soared, many Irish landlords ran into economic difficulties and about ten per cent of them actually went bankrupt. Meanwhile, the strong Irish farmers, who had continued to prosper even during the famine years, did little to alleviate the suffering, as they concentrated on producing cereals and rearing cattle. Still, with communications so poor in Ireland, the suffering in the west must have seemed as remote to the prosperous farmers of the midlands and the east, as famine in Africa seems today. Of course, what made most impact in Ireland was the British government's apparent disregard for the plight of the famine victims. Even Peel, subsequently praised for his prompt response to the failure of the potato crop, did not believe that the government should take responsibility for feeding the population, but his successors in the Whig administration were even less inclined to be moved by Irish suffering. Their attitude was typified by Trevelyan's utter lack of sympathy for the Irish, whom he regarded as an inferior and indolent race. The idea, popular at the Treasury where Trevelyan held sway, that the famine was a calamity sent by God, seemed to vindicate the Malthusian prophecy that overpopulation would be balanced by some future scarcity of resources. Not surprisingly, the British government found Irish charges of negligence difficult to refute. Indeed, the emotional and psychological impact of the famine was such that when the next generation of Irishmen recalled the period, many were convinced that the government in London was guilty of genocide.

The Fenians

The famine had generated mass political bitterness in Nationalist Ireland, but it was to be some time before this feeling found political expression. The key figure in the murky world of post-famine revolutionary politics was James Stephens, a veteran of the 1848 rising. Though slightly wounded in the County Tipperary skirmish, Stephens had managed to escape to France, where he learned the art of revolutionary theory and the technique of the secret society. On returning to Ireland in 1856 he began a marathon 3,000 mile journey, mainly on foot, to assess the state of Irish national feeling. Despite an apathetic response from a people who were only slowly recovering from the upheaval of the famine, Stephens never lost hope and, in the complex web of Ireland's agrarian secret societies, he saw the potential for the creation of a popular Nationalist movement. These secret societies, whose members were often referred to as 'ribbonmen', operated in nearly every part of Ireland and offered protection to small farmers and peasants. In a Dublin backyard, on 17 March 1858, Stephens founded a new secret society, whose members took an oath to fight for an independent democratic Irish republic. This organisation later became known as the Irish Republican Brotherhood (IRB). Following the example of continental revolutionary movements, and mindful of the manner in which informers had undermined previous rebellions, this new oath-bound secret society operated through a sophisticated cell structure which worked well for a time.

In the autumn of 1858 Stephens travelled to the United States where, with John O'Mahony, another Young Ireland veteran, he formed the American wing of the movement, the Fenian Brotherhood. Soon, participants on both sides of the Atlantic were labelled 'Fenians'. Initially, support was stronger in the United States, where Irish-Americans formed their own communities, and were distinguished by their sometimes fanatical interest in politics back home. Many had, of course, direct experience of the famine, and the Fenian movement gave them an outlet for their anti-British feelings. Meanwhile, political life in Ireland was still dead ten years after the famine, and it was not until the funeral of another Young Irelander, Terence Bellew MacManus, in November 1861 that interest was rekindled. MacManus's body had been sent back to Ireland by American Fenians, and his funeral to Glasnevin cemetery was watched by a crowd of 12,000. Added publicity for this event came from a row between the Catholic Church and the Fenians, as the Archbishop of Dublin, Paul Cullen, not only refused to allow the body to lie in state in Dublin Cathedral, but also denounced all secret societies and their use of violence. At the eleventh hour a sympathetic priest agreed to conduct the funeral service, and out of this controversy the movement began to flourish. For the most part, the new Fenian activists were drawn from the petty bourgeoisie and tended to live in the more prosperous rural areas of Munster and Leinster. Typically, they were shopkeepers, publicans, schoolmasters, clerks and shoemakers, rather than peasants or small farmers, but they were never numerous [10]. In 1863 the Fenian leaders began spreading their ideas in the columns of their new newspaper, the *Irish People*.

The new paper carried reports of the American Civil War (1861-65) and, in 1864, Stephens took the opportunity to return to the United States and recruit for the

Fenian Brotherhood among the Union armies of the North. So successful was his campaign that by the end of the year he claimed to have 100,000 trained men ready to fight for Ireland. Stephens now planned to stage a rebellion in 1865 and, with the Civil War ending in May of that year, the prospect of a Fenian rising seemed closer. In fact, a number of Irish-American soldiers had made the journey to Ireland in preparation for a rising, but disaster struck in September 1865, when most of the Fenian leadership was arrested, following a tip-off from a British agent who had infiltrated the organisation. Stephens had managed to evade capture, but he was arrested two months later when he was betrayed by yet another informer. Then, in a dramatic twist, he was sprung from jail and smuggled out of Ireland to the United States. There he found Fenian activists in uproar at his refusal to instigate the long awaited rising. Consequently, he was deposed as leader and replaced by Colonel T J Kelly, a native of Galway and a veteran of the American Civil War, who sailed from New York in January 1867 determined to stage a rebellion in England where, he assumed, he was safe from arrest. In September 1867, however, Kelly and a companion were observed acting suspiciously in a Manchester doorway and were picked up by the police. Earlier in the year, the rising had at last begun in Ireland, but it proved to be a hopeless failure, as poorly armed bands in different parts of the country were quickly overcome by government forces. Yet the decisive moment in the rebellion of 1867 came when the unescorted prison van transporting Kelly was intercepted by a gang of about thirty Fenians under a Manchester railway arch. In the confusion a police sergeant inside the van was shot dead, and though Kelly and his accomplice were never recaptured, five of the gang were convicted of murder. Three of the five were subsequently executed, although none of them had fired the fatal shot, and these three are remembered as the 'Manchester Martyrs'.

Like previous rebellions the Fenian rising kept alive the tradition of violent revolutionary Nationalism. In Ireland great mock funerals were held for the 'Manchester Martyrs', and huge crowds turned out in solemn processions in various Irish cities. The fact that the rising had been a dismal failure was quickly forgotten, as most people in Ireland, even those who had little sympathy with Fenian ideas, found themselves identifying emotionally with the 'Manchester Martyrs'. Yet, what made the 1867 rebellion even more significant than earlier armed risings was the simple, but clear, rationale behind the decision to rebel. Though he had many faults, Stephens had helped to shape a revolutionary elite made up of petty bourgeois elements with a strong anti-establishment and anti-clerical streak. This group was dismayed to find post-famine society developing in a way which was inimical to revolution, and it was decided to stage a rebellion, even without popular support, to keep the ideal of a free Ireland alive for the next generation. Their action was to have a profound effect on the future struggle for this freedom.

Historiography

A bewildering range of material exists for the study of Irish history in the nineteenth century. For a clear and succinct view of Ireland in the first half of the century G O'Tuathaigh's, *Ireland before the Famine 1798-1848* (Dublin, 1972) remains a valuable work. O'Tuathaigh explains how, after 1800, it was natural for most Irishmen to trace all of Ireland's troubles to a single source — the Union with England, but notes that simultaneously the Protestant Ascendancy class came to regard the maintenance of the Union as essential to their privileged position in Irish society. On O'Connell, O'Tuathaigh stresses how the Catholic Church and the Catholic middle classes were not as firmly behind the repeal agitation, as they had been earlier in the struggle for Catholic Emancipation. Another good general account of the O'Connell years is provided by D G Boyce's, *Nineteenth-Century Ireland: The Search for Stability* (Dublin, 1990) which highlights O'Connell's belief that if Catholic grievances could be successfully redressed, then Catholics could be loyal subjects. The problem was, Boyce suggests, that Irish Protestants were not convinced by this, and the mass agitation directed by O'Connell increased sectarian tension over much of Ireland.

Looking at the impact of the rise in Catholic power under O'Connell, O MacDonagh's, *States of Mind: Two Centuries of Anglo-Irish Conflict 1780-1980* (London, 1983) argues that this gave rise to the specification and articulation of Ulster separateness. More detail on the situation in Ulster can be found in J Bardon's, *A History of Ulster* (Belfast, 1992) which shows that the famine was particularly severe in the southern counties of Cavan, Fermanagh and Monaghan. The radical and dissenting tradition within Ulster Protestantism is explored by F Campbell's, *The Dissenting Voice: Protestant Democracy in Ulster from Plantation to Partition* (Belfast, 1991). Above all, Campbell emphasises the diversity within the Protestant community, later criticising what he regards as the deficiencies of Unionism which failed to recapture the radical tradition. In particular, he highlights a speech made by Rev Henry Cooke to a crowd of 40,000 at Hillsborough in 1834, which he claims was the first occasion when extreme Toryism and Protestant fundamentalism came together successfully in a mass meeting [11].

The Young Irelanders come under the microscope in R Davis's, *The Young Ireland Movement* (Dublin, 1987). Davis points out how close the Young Irelanders were to O'Connell on a whole range of issues, thereby emphasising the continuity between Old Ireland and Young Ireland. The details of the Fenian rebellion are expertly recorded in R Kee's, *The Bold Fenian Men* (London, 1976), while R V Comerford's, *The Fenians in Context: Irish Politics and Society 1842-1882* (Dublin, 1985) does exactly as its title suggests. Comerford argues that for Fenianism to thrive it had to venture beyond the physical force tradition of republican mythology and engage in more mundane pursuits such as organising sporting and leisure activities. In the opening pages of *Nationalist Revolutionaries in Ireland 1858-1928* (Oxford, 1987), T Garvin highlights James Stephens's belief that post-famine society was developing in a way which was inimical to revolution and, therefore, a revolutionary elite, led by the new middle class or petty bourgeoisie, had to pass on the separatist ideal to the next generation "in defiance of social trends".

Whereas Boyce's history of nineteenth century Ireland is predominantly political in emphasis, J Lee's, *The Modernisation of Irish Society 1848-1918* (Dublin, 1973) also offers a brilliant analysis of social and economic developments. He begins by showing how six key factors: the changing rural class structure, rising age at marriage, declining marriage, declining birth rates, a static death rate and emigration all influenced post-famine society. Yet while this combination of factors was unique to Ireland, Lee stresses the marked regional fluctuations within Ireland. On Fenianism, he notes that no previous movement in Irish history, either Catholic or Protestant, relied so little on clerical support. He also points out the trend, later picked up and developed by Garvin, that the Fenian movement was particularly strong in places which had been devastated by the famine. A notable example was Skibbereen in West Cork.

An excellent general history is K T Hoppen's, *Ireland since 1800: Conflict and Conformity* (London, 1989). The book is divided into three sections: from the Union to the famine, from the famine to partition, and from partition to the present day. Each section has chapters on politics, society and religion, and in the first section Hoppen explores how the concerns of local people in the early nineteenth century impacted upon national politics. Though he never wanted to promote social revolution, Hoppen observes that O'Connell himself realised that the masses who supported Emancipation saw it as a door which would open up the prospect of better wages, lower rents and a host of other economic benefits. Yet O'Connell's appeal to Catholic Ireland could go unnoticed. Hoppen recounts how Young Ireland rebels on the run in 1848 came across places where O'Connell was virtually unknown. Another brief, but useful, general account of the material covered in the opening chapter is D McCartney's, *The Dawning of Democracy: Ireland 1800-1870* (Dublin, 1987). McCartney focuses on the people and describes how they rose to challenge the country's Unionist establishment. For those wanting much more detail on the same period W E Vaughan's (ed), *A New History of Ireland: Volume V, Ireland under the Union; I, 1801-1870* (Oxford, 1989) can be used selectively. Particularly good are the broad narrative chapters by S J Connolly and R V Comerford.

The great current debate in Irish historiography concerns revisionism. In general, what the revisionist historians have done is to change traditional assumptions of Nationalist thinking. Critics of revisionism, however, have noted that such interpretations have a definite political agenda, as they seek to undermine the claims of present day Nationalism by attacking its view of the past. The recent violence in Northern Ireland has made such arguments all the more heated. This view is articulated by D Fennell's essay, 'Against Revisionism', which appears in C Brady's (ed), *Interpreting Irish History: The Debate on Historical Revisionism* (Dublin, 1994). A counter view is provided by M Laffan in C Brady's (ed), *Ideology and the Historians: Historical Studies XVII* (Dublin, 1991) when he argues that it is the job of a professional historian to examine the past in a critical and objective manner. In this sense revisionism in Irish history merely brings the discipline into line with developments in other countries. The most controversial work in the revisionist debate is R F Foster's, *Modern Ireland 1600-1972* (London, 1988), a book which the author himself describes as a narrative with a level of interpretation. While it was very well received at the time of its publication, a number of historians later came to criticise the book. Probably the most distinguished and outspoken among the 'anti-revisionist' group is B Bradshaw who claims that Irish historiography took a wrong turn in the 1930s when it began along the revisionist road. In *Interpreting*

Irish History: The Debate on Historical Revisionism and in an interview he gave to History Ireland, Vol 1, No 1 (Spring 1993) Bradshaw argues that Foster has tried to depopulate Irish history of its Nationalist heroes. Yet despite all the criticism, *Modern Ireland 1600-1972* must be considered a masterly and entertaining survey. Foster claims that the Union made little difference to Ireland. Even before the famine Ireland faced serious economic troubles such as the scale of de-industrialisation outside Ulster, while the pattern of emigration was already fixed before 1841. Before the famine the cottiers and smallholders outnumbered the farmers two to one, with Foster concluding that a large percentage of the population was, therefore, 'at risk'. After the famine he points to the growing power of the Catholic Church, which was not only due to the trauma of the famine but also to the strengthening of the respectable or middling farmers at the expense of the less devout cottier class. The result was increased religious devotion and what Foster calls 'rural embourgeoisement'.

Nothing has stirred the revisionist debate more that the famine, and the 150th anniversary of the first appearance of the potato blight in Ireland has led to a number of new publications. Foster's views are questioned in C O'Grada's, *The Great Irish Famine* (Dublin, 1989) which used economic statistics to argue that the undoubted signs of economic progress in the decades prior to the famine, and the unlikelihood of a series of harvest failures like those of the late 1840s, left the Irish people, and by implication the British government, totally unprepared for the catastrophe when it occurred. Those seeking a clear summary of the various opinions can consult C Kinealy's article, 'Beyond Revisionism: reassessing the Great Irish Famine' in *History Ireland*, Vol 3, No 4 (Winter 1995). Taking the revisionists to task, Kinealy cites six factors which need consideration. Firstly, she argues that the scale of the famine must not be minimised, as it was unique in modern European history. Secondly, the inevitability of famine should not be assumed because, on the eve of the famine, Ireland had one of the healthiest populations in Europe. Thirdly, the issue of culpability should not be ignored. The British government overcame huge logistical problems to establish a network of soup kitchens feeding over three million people, but this emergency aid was withdrawn in the autumn of 1847 and, consequently, mortality increased sharply. Fourthly, Kinealy rejects the collective guilt theory that since the population of Ireland today is descended from the survivors of the famine, these Irish people should feel a sense of responsibility for the suffering. Fifthly, the claim that the British government possessed neither the political nor the practical ability to tackle the crisis is refuted. Examples are given showing how other European governments, less sophisticated than the British, coped with contemporary disasters. Finally, Kinealy questions the thesis which emphasises the continuity between the pre-famine and post-famine periods.

One final observation. Students will find the magazine *History Ireland*, which first appeared in the spring of 1993, an invaluable resource.

Chapter 2
Land and Politics

In December 1867 there was a sequel to the Fenian rising, when an attempt was made to spring a senior Fenian prisoner from Clerkenwell jail in London. A great hole was blasted in the prison wall, but such was the force of the explosion that twelve innocent Londoners were killed and many others were injured. This atrocity, coming so soon after the policeman's killing in Manchester, inflamed public opinion in England, where tough action was demanded against those suspected of involvement in such outrages. Yet these terrifying incidents in Manchester and London also thrust the Irish Question onto the political agenda at Westminster in a way that even O'Connell at the height of his powers had failed to achieve. As Ireland was part of the United Kingdom, Irish affairs had, of course, been routinely discussed at Westminster, but the activities of the Fenians, especially in England, gave such discussion new urgency. It was against this background that the Liberal party under William Ewart Gladstone came to power in 1868. A towering figure in European, as well as British, nineteenth century history, Gladstone turned his formidable intellect and great political experience to Irish affairs. Indeed, Gladstone viewed Ireland through the eyes of a European statesman. He had travelled widely and had learned at first hand just how much Europeans disapproved of English rule in Ireland. It was his duty, he believed, to remove these grievances, which had spawned Fenianism, and bring justice to Ireland. On receiving news of the Liberal election victory in December 1868, Gladstone uttered the famous words: "My mission is to pacify Ireland". This was to prove a very difficult assignment.

Gladstone began this task with two specific measures in mind. His first move was to disestablish the Church of Ireland which, by this stage, represented well under twenty per cent of the population. Disestablishment was bitterly attacked by the Protestant Ascendancy, who belonged to the Church of Ireland, and by Gladstone's Conservative opponents, who argued that he was tampering with the Union. Yet not only was the measure popular with the Catholic majority in Ireland, but it also helped to solidify the alliance between the Liberal party and the nonconformists in Britain, which Gladstone had considered essential following the extension of the franchise in 1867. However, the act which became law in 1869 fell well short of Gladstone's expectations. To meet Protestant protests the Church of Ireland was given generous financial compensation but, while the measure was of great symbolic significance, it did little to improve the material position of the average Catholic. His chief concern was landlord–tenant relations, and it was to the land issue that Gladstone next turned his attention. It was the intention of the 1870 Land Act to improve safeguards for tenants. The act legalised the 'Ulster Custom' wherever it existed, which enabled evicted tenants to be compensated for any improvements they had made to their holdings but, since those most likely to have made improvements were the more progressive and prosperous sort unlikely to be facing eviction, this part of the act made little impact. A further provision in the act stated that any tenant evicted for reasons other than non-payment of rent was to be compensated, but it proved very difficult to carry this out in practice. In real terms, therefore, both the 1869 Irish Church Act and the 1870 Land Act brought little improvement, but what this legislation did achieve was to signal a new approach by the authorities at Westminster. Gladstone had become convinced that only reform in Ireland could prevent a further rebellion.

Butt and Home Rule

Still, in Ireland itself, Gladstone's progressive steps were quickly forgotten, as he came under fire for his refusal to grant an amnesty to Fenian prisoners in English jails. The failure of the 1867 rising had persuaded Fenian activists to consider alternative methods for advancing the cause of an independent Irish republic, and one consequence of this was their open involvement in the amnesty movement. In addition, Fenians were now prepared to infiltrate all kinds of national movements, trying to use them for their own ends. Less conspiratorial, however, was their involvement in the 1869 Tipperary by-election, when the convicted Fenian prisoner, Jeremiah O'Donovan Rossa, was elected, though of course, as a convicted felon, he was immediately unseated and the movement was unable to take advantage of this shock victory. Yet Fenianism also brought another major Irish figure to prominence. From 1865 high profile Fenian prisoners had been defended by Isaac Butt, a distinguished Irish lawyer who in 1868 became President of the Amnesty Association, the organisation aimed at securing the early release of all Fenian prisoners. Butt was the son of a Church of Ireland rector in County Donegal, and before turning to the law this gifted intellectual was Professor of Political Economy at Trinity College. Earlier, he had been a Conservative MP from 1852 to 1865, but his association with the Fenian movement had influenced his political thinking. Butt had no sympathy with Fenian methods, though he had been impressed by their sincerity, and he believed that another rebellion would be a disaster for Ireland. At the same time, he was convinced that Westminster had mishandled and neglected Irish affairs [12].

So in May 1870 Butt, together with a small group of friends, organised a meeting in Dublin which led to the formation of the Home Government Association. Its purpose was to canvass support for a new federal relationship to be established between Ireland and Britain under which an Irish parliament would be set up to look after Irish affairs. Such a solution, Butt argued, would not only improve conditions in Ireland, where an Irish parliament would be more sensitive to Irish needs, but would also strengthen the Union between Britain and Ireland. Initial interest in the Home Government Association was confined to small sections of the Dublin middle class, though its ideas spread as members of the association contested a number of by-elections between 1870 and 1873. Involvement in rough and tumble Irish by-elections had seen candidates identify themselves with popular causes such as land reform, and this helped to arouse interest in the Home Rule idea. In November 1873, as a result of this increased interest, 900 delegates attended a conference in Dublin at which the Home Government Association was dissolved and a new Home Rule League was launched, again under Butt's leadership.

The Home Rule League faced an immediate challenge when a general election was called at the beginning of 1874. In this election the Home Rulers, as they became known, surprised themselves by winning 59 seats, mainly at the expense of the Liberals who at the previous general election in 1868, had won two-thirds of the Irish seats. However, these statistics were misleading. Some of these new Home Rule MPs were former Liberals who only adopted the Home Rule tag to ensure they retained their seats, while others were, at best, only lukewarm supporters of the Home Rule ideal. It was estimated that there were only twenty who could be described as genuine Home Rulers. Moreover, it quickly became apparent that the new Home Rule party in the House of Commons lacked organisation and suffered from ineffective leadership. Butt did not impose party discipline, even allowing his nominal Home Rule followers to sit on either side of the House. His approach at Westminster was one of gentle persuasion, as he set out to show English MPs that Home Rule for Ireland was the key to a better future. Unfortunately, when it became apparent that the new Conservative government led by Benjamin Disraeli cared little for Irish affairs, Butt was content to sit on the sidelines and not rock the parliamentary boat. Soon, his moderation and polite conduct at Westminster weakened what little authority he did exert over the Home Rule party. Indeed, his more active and less polite followers were becoming increasingly frustrated, as their attempts to introduce private members' bills dealing with Irish issues were consistently rejected. Consequently, a small group of Home Rulers, disillusioned by Butt's indecision and complacency, decided to pursue a new strategy which would force parliament to look seriously at Irish affairs. Thus the policy of 'obstruction' was inaugurated. This involved the deliberate abuse of the rules of procedure in the House of Commons for the purpose of delaying parliamentary business. By the summer of 1877 the systematic use of obstruction techniques brought proceedings in the House of Commons to a virtual standstill. Only about half a dozen Home Rulers were involved in the action but, by speaking for hours at a time, they were able to disrupt parliament in an unprecedented way, and in the process they aroused the fury of other MPs whose more gentlemanly pursuits were now severely limited by the long hours they had to endure in the House. Naturally, such actions made them extremely unpopular at Westminster, but by their cynical exploitation of parliament's own rules the obstructionists did succeed in forcing Westminster to deal with Irish affairs.

Parnell

Initially, the most prominent figure among the obstructionists was Joseph Biggar, the MP for Cavan. In 1874 Biggar had been allowed to join the Fenian Brotherhood, or IRB, and he was soon elevated to the Supreme Council, the governing body of the Fenian movement. Butt was horrified by Biggar's antics, but the Home Rule leader's appeals for a more restrained approach fell on deaf ears, as Biggar and his colleagues intensified their campaign. Among his collaborators one, in particular, stood out. Charles Stewart Parnell had entered parliament in April 1875 following his victory in the Meath by-election. To begin with, Parnell made little impact at Westminster, though in his short maiden speech he had made the determined pronouncement: "Ireland is not a geographical fragment. She is a nation". However, an exchange with the Chief Secretary for Ireland in 1876 drew him to the public's attention. Parnell startled the House when he interrupted the Chief Secretary who had just referred to the 'Manchester murders', saying that no murder had been committed in Manchester. For a young man determined to make his mark in politics the obstructionist tactics of Biggar had obvious attractions, and Parnell soon joined the small group holding up parliamentary business. Parnell ignored Butt's criticism that his actions were damaging Ireland's chances of reform, because he based his strategy on the belief that Ireland had to stand up to Britain in order to force concessions. Although Butt deplored obstruction, it proved popular back in Ireland, and by 1877 Parnell was being seen in some circles as a serious challenger to Butt's leadership of the Home Rule party. Butt believed that the Irish people were essentially conservative and had only dabbled in rebellion following years of Westminster misgovernment. If they were given fair treatment, he argued, they would see that their future lay in the connection with Britain.

Parnell, on the other hand, was driven by a strong anti-British feeling which was partly attributable to his family background. His great-grandfather, Sir John Parnell, had been a leading political figure in Ireland at the end of the eighteenth century when he had bitterly opposed the Act of Union. An even stronger influence seems to have been his American mother, herself the daughter of a famous American admiral who had fought against the British in the war of 1812. Mrs Parnell was an admirer of the Fenian movement and her extreme anti-English sentiments must have made some impact on her son. Perhaps even more significant in the development of his Irish Nationalist philosophy, however, were Parnell's own experiences in England, where he had received his education. At Cambridge, in particular, he observed at close quarters English arrogance and their assumption of superiority, and he did not like it. Undoubtedly, this influenced his thinking, but Parnell's experiences in England also gave him one great advantage. Parnell was never overawed or intimidated by the traditions and sheer charm of Westminster to which Butt and a host of other Irish politicians succumbed. Even before Butt's death in 1879, Parnell had become the effective leader of the Home Rule party. Tall, distinguished looking, aloof, proud and confident, Parnell had all the necessary qualities for leadership. The fact that he was a Protestant landlord of Anglo-Irish stock, owning some 5,000 acres in County Wicklow, who looked like an English gentleman and spoke with a precise English upper class accent, only added to the aura which quickly built up around Parnell. He would obviously present a more determined challenge to the British government, as he brought single-mindedness and real energy to the Home Rule cause, but he was also flexible enough to see how extra-parliamentary pressure could complement his work at Westminster.

The Land War

The opportunity to develop the Home Rule party into one with genuine popular appeal arrived with a new agricultural crisis which struck Ireland in the late 1870s. Indeed, it was against this worsening economic background that the ageing Butt's ineffective leadership was cruelly exposed. The quarter of a century after the famine was a period of rapid and generally progressive rural change. With prices running well ahead of rents Irish agriculture was flourishing, and the quality of life in rural post-famine Ireland improved considerably. By the late 1870s, therefore, expectations were high and rising, and this explains why the agrarian crisis came as such a huge shock. It began in 1877 when the weather destroyed much of the potato crop in the west. Through 1878 and 1879 there was no improvement, as Ireland experienced three successive wet and cold years. Contemporary reports from Ulster described how extensive areas of farmland in Armagh, Tyrone and Fermanagh were constantly flooded. The Irish farmer suffered in two ways. The unprecedented bad weather caused a sharp fall in potato and grain production while, simultaneously, greatly increased competition from America saw Irish grain prices plummet. Not surprisingly, hardest hit were the subsistence level farms in Connacht, where the prospect of another famine raised new fears. As thoughtless landlords continued to demand the payment of rents, evictions became commonplace. This trend was all the more devastating because, since the famine, evictions had been rare. With the situation in the west deteriorating, Michael Davitt, a native of County Mayo, returned home to assist with the organisation of tenant defence. Davitt had been born at the height of the famine in 1846 and had emigrated to Lancashire in 1851 following his family's eviction. In 1870 he was sentenced to fifteen years penal servitude for his part in a Fenian assassination plot [13]. On his release from Dartmoor, in December 1877, Davitt rejoined the Fenian movement and, in August 1878, he crossed to the United States where he sought to arouse American Fenian interest in the plight of the Irish tenant farmer. The key figure in Irish Fenian circles at the time was John Devoy, a prominent member of Clan na Gael, the American oath-bound organisation which had been founded in New York in 1867 with the aim of promoting revolution in Ireland.

Of more immediate significance, however, was the reaction of tenant farmers to the depression in Davitt's native Mayo. Reversing previous patterns in the west, Mayo had been extensively politicised during the 1874 general election when John O'Connor Power, a radical Home Ruler, was elected. O'Connor Power was, like Biggar, a Fenian who joined the small group of obstructionists at Westminster, though both men were expelled from the Supreme Council in 1877, because of their parliamentary activities. As agricultural conditions worsened in the late 1870s, it was O'Connor Power's election team which provided the strong local leadership capable of exploiting the situation on behalf of Mayo's poor tenant farmers. Even Davitt, when he toured Connacht in 1878, found grass roots sentiment far ahead of him on the land issue, though he quickly adjusted his thinking, sensing that events in the west were nearing a climax. He drew up resolutions for a demonstration at Irishtown, in Mayo, to demand justice for tenant farmers who were threatened with eviction [14].

The success of the Irishtown meeting, which drew a crowd of 10,000, also caught Parnell's attention. Previously, Parnell had been non-committal on the land question, contenting himself with rather ambiguous statements, but after Irishtown he realised that he had to gain control of the land agitation which was rapidly assuming a momentum of its own. Although he had been caught off guard by the speed of the deteriorating economic situation and the subsequent land agitation, Parnell was, to his credit, quick to see the potential in linking the socio-economic aim of land reform to the political aim of Home Rule. He agreed, therefore, to Davitt's request to speak at another major demonstration in Westport, County Mayo, on 8 June 1879. Here, in a defiant speech Parnell told the 8,000 demonstrators that tenants must not be evicted if they paid a fair rent, which had to be reduced in difficult years. If the landlords could not be persuaded to adopt a more common sense position on rents in hard times, tenants should resist evictions: "You must show the landlords that you intend to keep a firm grip on your homesteads and lands. You must not allow yourselves to be dispossessed as you were dispossessed in 1847".

By this stage Parnell was convinced that the land question could be the catalyst for genuine popular interest in Home Rule. Of course, he realised that his support for agrarian agitation, which could so easily career out of control, was a risky strategy, but if he was to generate popular support for Home Rule, he knew it was a risk he would have to take. In fact, following a meeting in Dublin a week before the Westport demonstration, Parnell had committed himself to a new informal alliance which was known as the 'New Departure' [15]. The New Departure idea was based on an offer of Clan na Gael support for Parnell, on the understanding that he demanded self government for Ireland and backed vigorous agitation on the land question. The changing circumstances in 1879 pushed the land issue into the equation and, at the crucial meeting in June, Parnell and Devoy were joined by Davitt. This signalled the alliance of constitutional Nationalism, Irish-American Fenianism and agrarianism, a combination which promised to advance the cause of Irish Nationalism in an unprecedented manner. Significantly, there was confusion over what the three men had agreed. Devoy always maintained that Parnell had committed himself to going beyond reform, while both Parnell and Davitt claimed that no such undertaking had been given. Despite this misunderstanding, Parnell made brilliant use of the New Departure.

In the autumn of 1879 Davitt founded the Land League and installed Parnell as President. The League had two aims. In the short term it wanted to stop evictions and reduce the rents paid to the landlords, while in the longer term it wanted to ensure that the tenants would replace the landlords as owners of the land. The new organisation had its roots in the agrarian secret societies, and though Parnell and the other leaders constantly urged their followers to adopt peaceful methods there were frequent acts of violence. Such was the extent of agrarian trouble that the period from 1879 to 1882 is described as the 'Land War'. In the west, in particular, the prospect of a new famine drove tenant farmers, who were threatened with bankruptcy and eviction, to engage in a series of outrages, collectively described by the authorities as 'agrarian crime'. Central to the Land League programme was its opposition to evictions and the mobilisation of public opinion against anyone prepared to take over an evicted tenant's holding. In September 1880 Parnell explained to an audience in

Ennis, County Clare, how this could be done [16]. Having advised his listeners to hold onto their homesteads and not to pay unfair rents, Parnell then told them that landgrabbers should be shunned by the rest of the community. This simple tactic of social ostracism was known as 'boycotting', and its effect was devastating. It was employed over huge areas of the country and was quickly extended to cover landlords and their agents, solicitors and anyone connected with the landlord interest. Despite the success of this moral force strategy, a ruthless campaign of agrarian violence was mounted, which included intimidation, arson, cattle-maiming and shootings. In 1880 there were some 2,500 agrarian outrages with the most active counties being Mayo, Galway and Kerry, but in the following year this figure almost doubled as evictions continued to increase [17].

The breakdown of law and order in the Irish countryside forced the British government to take action. A general election in 1880, at which the Home Rulers won 62 seats, saw Gladstone and the Liberals returned with a comfortable majority. Their response to agrarian unrest was a stick and carrot strategy of coercion and reform. Early in 1881, a Coercion Bill was passed and this led to the arrest of a number of prominent Land League leaders. By October 1881 Parnell himself was imprisoned in Kilmainham jail, following a deliberately provocative speech he had made in Wexford. The government followed up these arrests by banning the Land League. Parnell's imprisonment provoked a vicious reaction over many parts of rural Ireland, and the number of agrarian outrages soared. Politically, however, the Irish leader's arrest came just at the right time. With agrarian violence intensifying Parnell had been forced to take a more uncompromising line in order to placate his more militant followers in the Land League [18]. Now in jail, though he had the most comfortable cell and enjoyed many privileges, Parnell was seen as a martyr to the cause, and yet, as he was under arrest, he could not be held responsible for the spiralling violence during the winter of 1881-82. Privately, Parnell was unnerved by the slide into rural anarchy and was coming to the view that the Land League had served its purpose. On the government side, meanwhile, Gladstone was anxious that Parnell would use his influence to curb the agrarian violence in order to give the Liberals' 1881 Land Act a chance to operate. During its passage through the House of Commons Parnell and his colleagues had dismissed the Land Bill as inadequate, but the Irish leader conceded in private that it would bring short term relief to many tenants. Consequently, secret negotiations were conducted, and Parnell was released in May 1882 on the understanding that he and his lieutenants would call off the land agitation and co-operate in working the new Land Act. In return the Coercion Act would be repealed and fresh legislation passed to help those with heavy rent arrears. This agreement was known as the 'Kilmainham Treaty'.

The 1881 Land Act was a major piece of legislation. It conceded the long-cherished 'three Fs': fair rent; free sale; and fixity of tenure. Rents were fixed by judicial arbitration for periods of fifteen years and a tenant could not be evicted as long as he paid this rent. In addition, a tenant was entitled to sell his interest in the holding for the best price he could obtain. These measures introduced a major change in the system of land holding in Ireland. From 1881 a system of dual ownership operated between landlord and tenant, a development which would ultimately ease the transition to peasant proprietorship. It seemed that the Land League's most famous slogan, 'the land for the people', had been heard at Westminster, and though the legislation did not go as far as Parnell wanted, he could see its long term significance. As part of the Kilmainham Treaty the government had also promised to wipe out rent arrears. This was completed by the 1882 Arrears Act which provided £800,000 worth of relief for some 130,000 tenants who were behind with their rents. Undoubtedly, the Kilmainham Treaty was a good deal for Parnell, as his part of the bargain was confined to giving rather vague promises to discourage agitation. By early 1882, moreover, the crisis on the land was easing, as the worst effects of the agricultural depression had passed. Parnell was now certain that the time had come to change direction, and a grisly incident which took place in Dublin only days after his release from Kilmainham confirmed this view. On 6 May 1882 a new Chief Secretary, Lord Frederick Cavendish, arrived in Dublin to take over from W E Forster, who had resigned in protest at the Kilmainham Treaty. That evening Cavendish and his Under Secretary, T H Burke, were walking in Dublin's Phoenix Park when they were butchered to death by a gang using surgical knives. The attack was carried out by the Invincibles, a secret society which had broken away from the Fenian movement. So shocked was Parnell by this atrocity that he considered withdrawing from public life altogether, but he was dissuaded by Gladstone. His priority now would be *political* agitation, not *agrarian* agitation and, to confirm this, no attempt was made to revive the Land League. Instead, the Irish National League was established in October 1882 with the intention of advancing the Home Rule cause.

In fact, Gladstone's Land Act and the subsequent Arrears Act had already done much to sap the vitality of the Land League. Tenant farmers found that tribunals reduced their rents and the desperation which had fuelled the rural agitation largely disappeared. Yet this should not obscure the impact of the Land League, which has been described as the most remarkable mass movement in Irish history and one of the most effective instruments of rural agitation in nineteenth century Europe. Within eighteen months of its formation the Land League had 200,000 members but, unlike the O'Connellite movements earlier in the century, the League did not depend on clerical participation. This may also help to explain why the League successfully spread into Ulster, with some areas experiencing intense agrarian activity, as the call was made for Protestants and Catholics to unite on the land issue. In another sense the League achieved real cohesion, because there was little tension between town and country, as the petty bourgeoisie of the small town, who were, of course, dependent on agricultural prosperity for their livelihoods, often provided local leadership for the tenant farmers of the area. The League's main weapons were propaganda — with the provincial press, especially in the west, totally committed to the movement — and moral intimidation, which was most famously practised in the systematic use of the boycott. Yet the League also made use of violence. Though there were some highly publicised landlord murders and there were repeated outbreaks of cattle mutilation, the actual scale of violence has to be put in perspective, considering the level of rural agitation. In fact, only 67 murders occurred during the Land War of 1879-82, an indication that there was just enough serious violence to make intimidation extremely effective. For the first time, therefore, with the possible exception of the 1790s, large sections of the Irish population became involved in a campaign with revolutionary aims, which enjoyed a strong organisation and inspirational leadership.

The land agitation threw up a generation of very able leaders, many of whom went on to make their mark on national politics, but at the summit stood Parnell.

Early in 1880, Parnell had toured the United States with John Dillon, one of his most able lieutenants, and in two months a sum of $200,000 was raised to give the Land League a solid financial footing. Money continued to flow from America and much of this was used to support evicted tenants. In Ireland the speeches of this charismatic 'Englishman', who poured scorn on the English government, won him a huge personal following. Yet while he was certainly moved by the suffering of the peasantry, the agrarian agitation was, for Parnell, primarily a political weapon. He was, above all, a constitutionalist, a moderate restraining the more extreme Davitt, but one who could make maximum use of the veiled threat of agrarian violence. His great skill in balancing constitutionalism and revolutionary agrarianism, which allowed him to push constitutionalism to the limits, was only one of Parnell's many political gifts. The Land League allowed him to build up his own power base, and he used the relationship with the League to make his Home Rule party more militant. At the right moment, however, he displayed qualities of statesmanship which brought the Land War to an end on terms advantageous to the tenants. In addition, the ending of the Land War and the Kilmainham Treaty laid the foundations for an alliance at Westminster with Gladstone's Liberal party.

The drive for Home Rule

With the land issue beginning to resolve itself Parnell concentrated on the political aim of Home Rule and, with the aid of his new National League, Nationalism was properly organised at constituency level. This built on the success of the Land League which had done much to politicise rural Ireland. After all, it was a relatively straightforward task to link local demands to the national aim of self government. While Home Rule may have been regarded as a vague idea in rural Ireland, the claim that only an Irish parliament could solve Irish problems had obvious attractions. At this stage of his career Parnell proved brilliantly successful at grafting the political energy generated by the Land League onto the Home Rule party. Through the National League he gave a measure of freedom to his able lieutenants, who had been blooded during the Land War, and they helped to develop a new Nationalist momentum at local level. Many of these men were farmers and shopkeepers, and those who became MPs were paid out of party funds. Of crucial importance was the parliamentary pledge, introduced in 1884, which committed all Home Rule candidates to vote with the party on all occasions when the majority decided that the party should act in unison. These developments helped Parnell to hone the Irish Parliamentary Party (IPP), as it was now frequently called, into a superb political instrument.

Another significant event in the evolution of Irish Nationalism was the 1884 Reform Act which extended the franchise to the bulk of the Irish tenant farmers, raising the male electorate from 220,000 to 740,000. When a general election was called in November 1885, the National League was in a strong position to win the support of many of these first-time voters. By then the organisation had over 1,200 branches throughout Ireland. It was most active in the midland counties, where the strong farmer class was prominent, rather than the west, where the Land League had enjoyed so much support. Within a few years of the 1881 Land Act, it was apparent that this rural class had gained more benefit from the new legislation than any other. Another difference between the two movements was the attitude of the Catholic hierarchy. Although local priests were often active in Land League agitation, the hierarchy had been hesitant about lending its support to such a radical movement. With the formation of the National League, however, the church was brought firmly on board, with parish priests playing a key role at local level and the hierarchy adding its weight at national level. This was, of course, another example of the church following its flock. The Irish Home Rule party which emerged in the mid-1880s, therefore, was both bourgeois and Catholic.

By 1885 Parnell backed by his highly disciplined political machine had succeeded where Butt had failed [19]. The Irish Question was now a crucial issue in Westminster politics and both main parties, Liberals and Conservatives, had come to realise that a new approach was needed to break the discredited formula of conciliation and coercion. Gladstone believed that a bipartisan policy on Ireland could introduce changes which would increase the long term stability of the Union but, in mid-1885, neither of the two main parties were prepared to back Home Rule. Then, in June 1885, the Home Rule party demonstrated its power by voting with the Conservatives to turn the Gladstone government out of office. The new minority Conservative administration, under Lord Salisbury, immediately introduced a major piece of land legislation for Ireland, but it was not prepared to gamble on a high risk strategy by seeking a comprehensive political settlement. Still, what Parnell had achieved in 1885 was to manoeuvre the Irish party in between the Liberals and Conservatives, so that each of the two great parties might become dependent on Irish support, if they wanted to stay in government. Now Parnell might be able to play one party off against the other. With a general election taking place in November 1885, the Irish leader made his move by asking Gladstone to commit his party to support Home Rule in the new parliament. When Gladstone refused to be drawn, Parnell called on Irish voters in Britain to back Conservative candidates in the election. Estimates vary on the impact of Parnell's intervention, but even if it only cost the Liberals a handful of seats, it proved significant, because the Home Rule party emerged from the general election holding the balance of power at Westminster.

The first Home Rule Bill

The 1885 general election gave the Liberals 335 seats, the Conservatives 249 seats and the Home Rule party 86 seats. Parnell held the exact balance with his 86 seats, but while he was considering the best strategy for the new parliament, a bizarre incident took place which tied him to the Liberal party. On 17 December Gladstone's son disclosed to the press that his father had been converted to Home Rule, but at this point Gladstone was still hopeful that the Salisbury administration would take the lead on the Irish Question. When the Conservatives made it clear in the new parliament that they had no such intention, the Liberals and Irish combined to defeat the Salisbury minority government. If Salisbury had wanted to remain in government, he would have needed the support of the 86 Home Rulers, but to ensure this he would have had to introduce Home Rule. Not surprisingly, he was not prepared to take the risk and was happy to see the Liberals wrestle with the Irish Question. By February 1886 Gladstone was back as Prime Minister, and was soon involved in the preparations for a Home Rule Bill. The reasons behind Gladstone's conversion to Home Rule are complex. Undoubtedly, he had been influenced by Parnell's sense of purpose and determination, but Gladstone's conversion seems to have been a gradual process, as his frustration at both the failure and the embarrassment of coercion in Ireland had been growing steadily. Surprisingly, Ireland was one issue where the Liberal leader was stirred by emotion, and with his strong Christian morals telling him that he must do the right thing by Ireland, Gladstone was inexorably pulled in the direction of Irish self government. Moreover, he was concerned that the Irish Question was beginning to poison the political atmosphere in Britain, and only its political settlement could allow the resumption of normal, constructive politics at Westminster. Such speculation, however, should not ignore the simple fact that Gladstone's adoption of Home Rule coincided with the Irish party holding the balance of power at Westminster.

It should also be stressed that, at this late stage in his political career, Gladstone was displaying increasingly idiosyncratic tendencies, frequently wanting to surprise his followers by make unexpected moves. Indeed, his failure to consult senior Liberal colleagues on such a crucial decision angered a number of them and they refused to support Home Rule. The most significant of these was Joseph Chamberlain, a highly talented and ambitious politician, who had earlier achieved fame as the radical Lord Mayor of Birmingham. Chamberlain was sympathetic to Ireland and had already proposed a devolution scheme based on the extension of local government powers, but he was firmly opposed to Home Rule. He believed that the establishment of a separate Irish parliament and executive would destroy the Union and ultimately lead to the break up of the British Empire. Consequently, when Gladstone introduced his Home Rule Bill in April 1886, Chamberlain and his radical followers in the Liberal party were lined up against him. The new bill was also opposed by the right wing of the party which was equally concerned about the adverse effect Home Rule for Ireland might have on the Empire. Led by Lord Hartington, these old Whig elements in the party had little interest in Ireland, but they had been increasingly worried by Gladstone's thinking on a host of other issues. The reality, therefore, was that the right wing of the party was already wavering in its support for Gladstone, even before he introduced the Home Rule Bill on 8 April 1886 [20].

Although the first Home Rule Bill was rejected by the House of Commons, many historians agree that the bill's introduction marked Gladstone's finest hour. Arguing that his conversion to Home Rule was the next logical step in his evolving Irish strategy, the Liberal leader told the House of Commons that Westminster's attempts to govern Ireland by coercion had proved counter-productive and a new approach was required which would involve modifying the Act of Union. The details of the bill were complicated. It proposed that the new Irish legislature should be composed of two 'orders' which would sit together but could vote separately, thus allowing one order to veto any measure for a period of three years. The First Order was to consist of 103 members, 75 of whom would be elected, while the Second or Lower Order was to be composed of 204 members, 103 of whom would be the existing Irish MPs at Westminster. Even more complex were the plans for the division of responsibilities between Westminster and the new parliament in Dublin, though they were guided by the principle that the Irish parliament would be subject to the supremacy of the British parliament. Those powers reserved for Westminster included defence, foreign and colonial relations, customs and excise, trade and navigation, the posts and telegraphs, coinage and lighthouses, while the new Irish exchequer was to meet one-fifteenth of 'imperial' expenditure. Indeed, finance was at the heart of the Home Rule proposals and provision for law and order in Ireland was influenced by Gladstone's guiding financial principle of, wherever possible, cutting government spending. Initially, control of the Royal Irish Constabulary (RIC) would rest with Westminster but, in time, responsibility for this expensive service would pass to Dublin.

In retrospect, the first Home Rule Bill seems an extremely modest measure, with Westminster retaining control over such a wide range of services. In the framing of the bill it seemed that, if there were areas of doubt on how to separate imperial and local matters, the safe option would be taken and power would remain at Westminster. Yet Gladstone's greatest problem was how to handle the question of future Irish representation in the House of Commons. The real problem was that Irish MPs would continue to have an interest in general imperial topics, such as naval expenditure, and so, in theory, would need to retain their presence in the House of Commons. However, if they could also speak and vote on issues which related to purely English, Scottish or Welsh business, they then would have an unfair advantage over MPs from the mainland who, of course, could not discuss Irish domestic affairs. Indeed, such was the difficulty of distinguishing between matters of imperial and local concern that Gladstone proposed the exclusion of Irish MPs from Westminster altogether. While this solution might have been expected to appeal to British MPs tired of the Irish Question, it was attacked by the bill's critics as a first step towards complete separation. Gladstone was also aware that his proposal left him open to the charge of imposing taxation without granting representation and he agreed to reconsider the question, though the bill's defeat made this academic.

Many of the flaws in the bill might have been corrected had not the legislation been so hastily prepared. As it was, the opponents of Home Rule did not lack ammunition when the bill was debated. Their criticism fell into three broad categories, and these arguments were repeated with even greater vigour in the two subsequent attempts to pass Home Rule. Firstly, the Ulster issue was used to punch a hole in the argument that Ireland was a single unit. A few months earlier, in a speech made in Belfast's Ulster Hall, Lord Randolph Churchill, a leading Conservative, warned the new Liberal government that if it insisted on Home Rule for Ireland, then "Ulster will fight (and) Ulster will be right" [21]. During the great debate on the first Home Rule Bill, Churchill sought to explain why Ulster would be right. He argued that it would be unjust to leave Ulster Protestants, whose only crime was loyalty to Britain, to the mercy of their Irish Nationalist rivals who would dominate any Home Rule parliament. In taking this approach, Conservative critics of the bill were able to exploit fully the genuine concerns which Ulster Protestants felt about the prospects for their long term economic security and religious freedom under Home Rule. The Ulster issue was also central to Chamberlain's criticism of the bill, because he presented Ulster Protestants as part of the British Anglo-Saxon Protestant nation which was under threat from a hostile Irish Catholic nation. Chamberlain also articulated a second line of attack for the opponents of Home Rule. He argued that the limited powers on offer would never satisfy Irish Nationalists. Home Rule, therefore, would represent only the first installment in a process which would lead to the total separation of Ireland from Britain, and this, in turn, would have serious consequences for the unity of the British Empire.

With hindsight, it is difficult to see how such a modest measure could have generated such fears, but two points should be kept in mind. Firstly, opponents of the bill only had to cite some of Parnell's past speeches, which seemed to indicate that the achievement of Home Rule was a short term goal in the ultimate drive for total separation. Indeed, only in January 1885 in perhaps his most celebrated speech, though not one which really reflected his political thinking, Parnell alluded to such a strategy when he informed an audience in Cork: "No man has the right to set a boundary to the onward march of a nation. No man has a right to say: 'Thus far shalt thou go and no further' ". Secondly, it is worth remembering just how important the Empire was to the governing classes in late Victorian England and why, therefore, any move which posed even the slightest threat to the Empire had to be taken seriously. The final line of opposition to the first Home Rule Bill cast doubt on the readiness of the Irish for self government. Senior Tories, such as Lord Salisbury the party leader, never sought to disguise their belief that the Irish were an inferior race and incapable of self government. Moreover, the recent background of agrarian violence, which seemed to have been orchestrated by some of the Irish party's MPs, convinced those Tories worried about attacks on property, that a Home Rule administration would not enforce the law.

Early in the morning of 8 June 1886, the first Home Rule Bill was defeated on its second reading by 343 to 313, with 93 Liberals voting against the government. These Liberal dissidents were a mixture of Hartington's old Whig element on the right of the party and Chamberlain's radical followers. During the debate Parnell had given an undertaking that he accepted the bill as a final settlement, but this was not enough to convince the doubters. Despite the bill's defeat, which was not unexpected, Parnell had reason to be satisfied with his role in making Home Rule a live issue at Westminster. Moreover, the reaction to the bill in Ireland, where Parnell was personally credited with converting Gladstone and the Liberal party to Home Rule, was euphoric, and even the bill's defeat could not alter this upbeat mood. Home Rule, it seemed, was inevitable. Yet such a view failed to take sufficient account of the strength of Unionist opposition both in Ireland and Britain. Parnell certainly underestimated the depth of feeling among Ulster Protestants. In Belfast savage rioting had broken out a few days before the crucial vote on 8 June and it continued until mid-September. The city had a history of sectarian violence, but the tensions created by the Home Rule crisis suddenly exacerbated what was always a volatile situation. In fact, the death toll of around 50 for those summer months marked the worst period of violence experienced anywhere in Ireland in the nineteenth century [22].

Two days after the bill's defeat parliament was dissolved, but Gladstone's appeal to the electorate in the ensuing general election demonstrated conclusively that there was little popular support for Home Rule in Britain. The Conservatives won a landslide victory, as the Liberals were reduced to 191 seats, spending seventeen of the next twenty years out of office. An obvious conclusion to draw is that the adoption of Home Rule had seriously damaged the Liberal party and contributed to its eventual decline. The reality, however, was different. The 191 Gladstonians returned in July 1886 comprised a much more cohesive party than before, once it had been shorn of the Whig elements. Moreover, it appears that less than ten per cent of local activists felt sufficiently opposed to Gladstone's Irish policy to leave the party. For Parnell, the Liberals' election reverse left him with little alternative but to wait on the sidelines and prepare for more favourable circumstances. While the adoption of Home Rule by the Liberal party had been a great triumph for Parnell, he now had to acknowledge that the independent existence of the IPP, which had seen it turn the Liberals out of government in June 1885, followed by the Conservatives in January 1886, was at an end. Parnell's priority, therefore, was to preserve the Liberal alliance which would mean following a more moderate policy in Ireland. Politically, this would pose little difficulty, but the fact that Home Rule was not immediately attainable removed the need for caution on the land question.

By the end of the summer the prospect of agrarian extremism had resurfaced with the launch of the 'Plan of Campaign' in October 1886. In the previous year an agricultural depression had begun in Ireland which was probably more severe than that of 1879-80. As prices fell sharply, the usual pattern of rural crisis was beginning to repeat itself. Much lower incomes meant that many tenant farmers were struggling to meet rent payments and, consequently, evictions were on the increase. The Plan of Campaign was devised and implemented by three of Parnell's most able followers in the IPP — John Dillon, William O'Brien and Timothy Harrington. Its strategy was to use combined action by tenants on individual estates, where evictions were being carried out, in order to force local landlords to accept rent reductions. Tenants on an estate came together to calculate a fair rent based on the prevailing agricultural climate and offered this to the landlord. If this was refused, the money was then paid into an estate fund, usually looked after by the local priest, which was used to support those evicted for participating in the action. When this money was exhausted, it was agreed that the National League would maintain payments to the evicted tenants.

The impact made by the Plan of Campaign suffers in comparison to the achievements of the Land League. The Plan was never as widespread, with its actual operation confined to just over 100 estates in parts of the south and west between 1886 and 1890. Secondly, it never caught the public's imagination or generated the mood of defiance against landlordism which dominated the Irish countryside in the 1879-82 period. Finally, unlike the Land League, the Plan was never taken up as the official movement of the IPP. Indeed, most of the Irish party played a negligible role in the Plan, and it was left to Dillon and O'Brien to orchestrate the agitation. Though he was reluctant to criticise his lieutenants, Parnell had serious misgivings about this new wave of agrarian extremism. During the winter of 1886-87 the Irish leader had been ill and had taken no part in either the composition or the implementation of the Plan. His chief concern was the impact which the agitation would have on

English public opinion and, in particular, the damage this might cause to the alliance with the Liberals. When the Plan began to fizzle out through lack of finances in the summer of 1890, O'Brien's desperate pleas to Parnell for support were ignored. The Irish leader's priorities were clear. Firstly, Home Rule had to be secured, and only then could the land question be tackled.

Home Rule in crisis

Part of the problem facing Dillon and O'Brien, as they strove to secure Parnell's active support for the Plan of Campaign, was that during the period 1886–90 his visits to Ireland really only coincided with the grouse-shooting season. The bulk of his time was now spent with his mistress, Katherine O'Shea, with whom he lived in Eltham in south east London. While Parnell's total commitment to the aim of Irish self government was never in question, there is evidence that his personal life interfered with his leadership of the Irish party. He had first met Katherine O'Shea in 1880 and the two soon became lovers. Katherine was the wife of Captain William O'Shea, an arrogant and opportunistic member of the Irish party. By 1880 Katherine and William had effectively parted as husband and wife, and she was able to convince Parnell, though this seems to have been an easy task, that William had no objection to their relationship. The only problem was that the liaison had to be kept secret from Katherine's elderly, rich aunt, Mrs Benjamin Wood, who was expected to leave her favourite niece a large fortune. Parnell and Mrs O'Shea began to live together for short periods in 1881, and the couple's desire to see each other again may have been a factor in his acceptance of the Kilmainham Treaty, which had led to his release from prison in May 1882.

Although William O'Shea's relationship with Parnell worsened considerably between 1882 and 1885, he continued to acquiesce in his wife's affair, as he hoped that the Parnell connection might help him gain political office. Besides, if he remained married to Katherine, O'Shea could expect to share in Mrs Wood's bequest. In politics O'Shea was something of a maverick. His rejection of the parliamentary pledge in 1884 made it certain that he would not retain his parliamentary seat, and during 1885 he put increasing pressure on his wife and Parnell to secure an alternative seat. In February 1886 Parnell took an enormous risk by insisting that O'Shea be adopted as the party's candidate for the by-election in Galway City [23]. This infuriated a number of senior colleagues who were in open revolt and only reluctantly accepted Parnell's decision after he had made it a test of his leadership of the party. Yet despite the huge gamble taken on his behalf, O'Shea did not even vote for the Home Rule Bill and resigned his new seat in June 1886. Some of the leading figures in the party knew of Parnell's relationship with Mrs O'Shea, and a number must have suspected that he had been blackmailed by her husband.

Parnell had always kept his distance from his party colleagues, but in the years after 1886 he became increasingly aloof and inaccessible. While this enabled him to avoid implication in the revival of agrarian extremism directed by his younger, more radical acolytes, his long absences from Ireland also facilitated the emergence of a potentially hostile faction on the right of the party. The key figure in what could be described as the party's right wing was T M Healy who, ever since the rumpus over the Galway City candidature, was incensed by Parnell's autocratic leadership. From mid-1888 Healy's views were aired in the *Irish Catholic,* a new newspaper controlled by his friend and colleague, William Martyn Murphy. Yet such developments should not obscure the fact that Parnell's authority as leader of the Irish party was unassailable. Indeed, both his reputation and popularity were soon to reach new heights. Back in March 1887, *The Times* published the first in a series of articles on 'Parnellism and Crime', in which allegations of criminality were made against Parnell, the Land League and the Irish party. Then, on 18 April, the paper featured a facsimile letter, ostensibly written by the Irish leader, which suggested that his denunciation of the Phoenix Park murders had been hypocritical [24]. Although Parnell dismissed the letter as a fabrication, he himself did not respond to the general charge, linking him to such a famous and gruesome outrage, by suing *The Times*. Instead, he requested a Select Committee of the House of Commons to investigate the charges. This was rejected, but the House did establish a Special Parliamentary Commission, made up of three judges, to examine, not only *The Times's* letters, but Parnell's whole career during, and after, the Land War. The investigation dragged on through 1888 and into 1889 and, in the course of its lengthy proceedings, the facsimile letter, and others acquired by the newspaper, were exposed as forgeries. The forger, a Dublin journalist named Richard Pigott, fled the country after giving evidence, and within days shot himself in a Madrid hotel room. The episode cost *The Times* a catastrophic £200,000.

With his reputation enhanced and his authority now unquestioned, Parnell seemed at the height of his powers. Although the Special Commission continued to investigate the general charges of criminality and conspiracy, all attention was focused on the exposure of the Pigott forgeries. On Parnell's first appearance in the House of Commons after the forgery revelations, Gladstone led the Liberals in giving the Irish leader a standing ovation. Throughout 1888-89 Parnell had been increasingly fulsome in his praise of the Liberal party, confident that the Irish party's alliance with the Liberals would deliver Home Rule. The exposure of the Pigott forgeries in February 1889 had increased his stature, particularly among Liberal circles in England but, before the year was out, Parnell was in trouble over his relationship with Katherine. In December 1889 Captain O'Shea filed a petition for divorce, citing Parnell as co-respondent. The aunt had died in May 1889, leaving her fortune to Katherine and having the good sense to leave the spendthrift captain disappointed. Yet he was now able to ally himself with the other disgruntled relatives who hoped to benefit from the will. In a contest both his, and their, case would be helped if Katherine could be portrayed as a scheming mistress who had carried on an adulterous affair unknown to her innocent husband. Although the divorce suit had been filed in December 1889, the actual trial did not take place until the following November. In the meantime, Parnell was calmly assuring his colleagues that he would emerge from the episode with his reputation intact. It seems that Parnell and Katherine hoped to bribe O'Shea with a reported £20,000. Presumably, he would then have dropped his charges and allowed Katherine to bring counter-charges which would have resulted in a divorce, but leaving Katherine as the wronged party. Certainly, Parnell wanted a divorce so that he could marry Katherine. The problem, however, was that neither Parnell nor Katherine could raise the necessary money to buy off O'Shea. She had a fortune coming to her but, as the will was being contested, she was unable to get her hands on it. Consequently, the case came to court and though O'Shea admitted that he had known about the affair for some years, the details of the 'secret' liaison presented the two lovers in a squalid light.

Despite their obvious concern, the members of the Irish party met soon after the trial and unanimously re-elected Parnell as Chairman on 25 November 1890, in full knowledge of the divorce scandal. Yet what these Irish MPs did not realise was that on the previous day the Liberals had decided that if Parnell did not retire from politics, they would lose the next election and, therefore, Home Rule would be postponed indefinitely. So the Liberal party insisted that Parnell must go. It appears that Gladstone was prepared to see him carry on, but he was forced to issue the ultimatum once the nonconformist wing of the party made its position clear. Gladstone's intervention was to split the IPP. Between 1 and 6 December the Irish party debated the leadership question, which the Liberal party had posed, in Committee Room Fifteen of the House of Commons. Of the 86 MPs, just over 70 were available to take part in the crucial vote. The proceedings in Committee Room Fifteen allowed the abrasive Healy to indulge in bitter personal conflict but, while the debate was full of passion, there were relatively few comments about Parnell's personal life, though one Healy gibe almost raised tempers out of control. The key issue was the Irish party's relationship with the Liberals. Parnell's leading supporter, John Redmond, argued that the independence of the party was even more precious than the Liberal alliance. In reply, the anti-Parnellites, as they soon were named, insisted that the cause of Home Rule was greater than any individual and, at this stage, this cause depended on continued Liberal support. Ironically, while it was Parnell who had created the powerful, disciplined, independent party, it was also Parnell who had developed the new alliance with the Liberals and, more particularly, with Gladstone. Only the Liberals would pass Home Rule and, after 1886, the Liberal alliance was essential to the IPP. Moreover, Parnell had worked very hard to keep the partnership on track during the late 1880s. When the votes were cast, the party split in two with 27 supporting Parnell and 45 opposing him. The majority then withdrew and elected Justin McCarthy as their new leader. It has been estimated that if all the Irish MPs had been present, the vote would have been 54 to 32 in favour of the anti-Parnellites.

Arguing that he owed his position as leader to the people of Ireland and not to the Irish MPs, Parnell seemed remarkably unperturbed by the voting and he immediately carried the battle to Ireland. Maybe, if he had withdrawn from political life for a year or so, he could have returned to lead the party, but Parnell was not interested in such a compromise. On his return to Ireland he found that personal devotion in the country remained strong but, crucially, the Catholic Church, with its natural interest in the moral issue of his relationship with Mrs O'Shea, was to provide insurmountable opposition. The real test came with three by-elections held between December 1890 and July 1891 in North Kilkenny, Carlow and North Sligo [25]. In each case Parnell's candidate was soundly beaten in contests which were remembered for their unbridled ferocity. In this final phase Parnell appealed for electoral support to Fenian sympathisers and, while he stirred these more advanced Nationalists and retained solid support in the towns, he could not match the influence of the forces ranged against him. Yet it should not be assumed that his appeal to the 'hillside men' indicated that he was about to abandon peaceful politics. As he had shown during the turbulent years of the Land War, Parnell had been highly effective in pushing constitutionalism to the limit, and his speeches during these by-election campaigns can be read in this context. Throughout his career, of course, Parnell had never been afraid to use inflammatory language. A key difference in 1891 was that where bishops and priests had been active in his support from 1879 to 1882, they were now in opposition. Yet perhaps even more crucially, Parnell had abdicated the leadership of Irish Nationalism during the Plan of Campaign, and in the desperate circumstances of 1891 he was unable to recapture it.

What is undisputed is that in taking the fight to Ireland, Parnell displayed great physical courage and the real tenacity of purpose which had characterised his early political career. Indeed, his pride and undoubted stubbornness saw him reject the compromise painstakingly worked out by Dillon and O'Brien in the early weeks of 1891. By then, he was in very poor health, and many who remembered him from the previous decade were shocked by his appearance as he toured the country desperately trying to rouse the people. In June 1891 he had married Katherine, but their marriage was to be short-lived, as Parnell died in Brighton on 6 October 1891. His funeral, which was held in Dublin five days later, drew a crowd of 200,000. Undoubtedly, Parnell had made a major contribution to Irish Nationalism, but the manner of his downfall, the bitter struggle in Ireland and his premature and tragic death all added to the confusion concerning his legacy. In fact, Parnell was claimed as the inspiration behind both constitutional and revolutionary Nationalism by the next generation of Irishmen. His great achievement, of course, had been to bring Ireland within touching distance of Home Rule, and in doing so he had demonstrated all the qualities of the consummate political leader. His strategy was twin-edged, for he skillfully combined effective political pressure at Westminster, using a highly disciplined party, with agrarian agitation in the Irish countryside, which allowed the creation of a national movement based on the struggle for ownership of the land. Along the way, moreover, he had won the support of the Liberal party for Home Rule. Parnell's death did nothing to heal the split within the Irish party, and the faction fighting continued until the end of the century. To onlookers, the bitterness and hostility shown by former colleagues to each other only served to emphasise Parnell's pre-eminence over his bickering followers and increased the sense of guilt felt by many Irishmen about the manner of his downfall. The myth of the lost leader, hounded by the Catholic Church, betrayed by unworthy colleagues and disowned by his own people, was becoming embedded in the Irish psyche. Myth, of course, is not reality.

When the results of the 1892 general election were announced, the Parnellite rump found itself with only nine seats to the seventy-one held by the anti-Parnellites. Yet even these anti-Parnellite MPs did not comprise a uniform group as several factions vied for dominance. The removal of Parnell's authoritarian leadership had allowed internal divisions, sometimes prompted by personality clashes as well as genuine political differences, to multiply. The one bright spot for the divided Nationalist movement was Westminster where, following the general election, Gladstone returned as Prime Minister in August 1892, leading a minority administration which relied, once again, on the support of the IPP. Despite misgivings within his own party, Gladstone's commitment to Home Rule remained as strong as ever, and the second Home Rule Bill was introduced on 13 February 1893. The preamble to the new bill emphasised Westminster's supremacy over the Dublin parliament, and it specifically noted that foreign affairs, defence, trade and customs and excise would all remain under Westminster control. The main difference with the 1886 bill was the proposal that Irish MPs would continue to sit at Westminster, but their number would be reduced from the current 103 to 80. It was intended that the Irish MPs would be prevented from voting on bills pertaining exclusively to England, Scotland or Wales, but this restriction was dropped once it became clear that such a scheme was unworkable. This apart, the second Home Rule Bill was similar to its predecessor. It would establish an Irish parliament consisting of two chambers, with disagreements between the two Houses being settled by fresh elections or by the majority decision of both Houses sitting together. The Lower House would be composed of 103 members drawn from the existing Westminster constituencies. The Upper House would have 48 members elected for single member constituencies by voters who owned or occupied land of £200 annual valuation. Obviously, this restrictive property franchise had been designed to protect the landlord interest. Such safeguards, however, were dismissed as irrelevant by Unionist opponents of the bill. Indeed, the intensity of Unionist opposition went beyond anything seen in 1886.

The second Home Rule Bill was fought over, clause by clause, for 82 days, longer than any other bill in the nineteenth century. The key Unionist argument was simple: Home Rule, as it stood, would never satisfy Irish Nationalist aspirations and, consequently, would represent only a first installment on the road to full separation. The varied reaction of the Irish party to the second Home Rule Bill only confirmed Unionist suspicions. The much larger anti-Parnellite group gave a general welcome to the bill, stressing that it only required a few minor changes in the committee stage to be regarded as a final settlement of the Irish Question. For the anti-Parnellites, John Redmond echoed this sentiment when he spoke on the first reading, but later in the debate he offered a more realistic assessment, informing MPs that he saw the bill as nothing more than a provisional settlement. The inability of the Irish party to speak with one voice allowed Unionists to raise the old taunt that the Irish were still not fit for self government. Certainly, the Home Rule cause missed Parnell's leadership and authority, as his successors failed to take full advantage of the more favourable political climate which existed at Westminster in 1893. Gladstone had been the key figure in the cabinet committee which drafted the bill, and in his eighty-fourth year he had shown remarkable stamina in personally piloting the bill through each difficult stage in the House of Commons. It passed its second reading in April by a margin of 43 votes and, on its third reading, the government's majority was still over 30. Then on 8 September, the second Home Rule Bill was, as expected, defeated in the House of Lords by 419 to 41. Gladstone was prepared to take the issue to the country, but his cabinet colleagues were not so keen and the ageing leader accepted their decision. He resigned early in March 1894, and was replaced by Lord Rosebery who had been Foreign Secretary. Unlike Gladstone, Rosebery was a staunch imperialist who was not going to grasp the Home Rule nettle.

Constructive Unionism

While the Conservative party had been steadfast in its opposition to Home Rule, it had also demonstrated the ability to follow an imaginative Irish policy when in office. Of course, all Conservative thinking on Ireland was based on the belief that the Union between Britain and Ireland was sacrosanct, but within this framework there was scope for experimentation. The basic principle underlying this new approach was the assumption that, if a series of measures was introduced which improved the social and economic order in Ireland, then the demand for Home Rule would gradually fade away and the Union would be strengthened. The politician most associated with the early phase of what is called 'constructive Unionism' was Arthur Balfour, the nephew of Lord Salisbury. At first sight, Balfour seems an unlikely figure to be cast in the role of the party's Irish reformer. He had taken up his post as Chief Secretary for Ireland in March 1887, and his first task had been to determine the government's response to the Plan of Campaign. Balfour's reaction to agrarian violence was unequivocal. His reliance on coercion and the ruthless use of his own Crimes Act quickly earned him the title, 'Bloody Balfour', from his Irish enemies. Balfour's strategy was clear. Only when he had restored order in Ireland where, of course, respect for the law had never been a prominent feature in rural areas, would he consider drawing up measures to remove agrarian grievances. His determination to prosecute as criminals all of those involved in the Plan of Campaign, regardless of their position, led to the arrest and imprisonment of many prominent figures including a substantial number of MPs.

Yet, despite his concentration on law enforcement, Balfour was well aware that the agrarian unrest unleashed by the Plan of Campaign was based on the tenants' genuine grievances. Moreover, Balfour had some expertise on the land question owning, as he did, over 180,000 acres in Scotland and having first-hand knowledge of the terrible economic hardships which faced both tenants and cottiers on marginal land in the last quarter of the century. Of course, earlier Liberal administrations had responded to such grievances by introducing land legislation in 1870 and 1881, which offered some protection for the tenants. While Balfour accepted Gladstone's argument that the landlord system was the major cause of Irish alienation, he was a bitter critic of the 1881 Land Act, claiming that the 'dual ownership' which it established undermined the whole system of property rights. Balfour's thinking, however, was to evolve over the next few years, and by the time he had become Chief Secretary he was convinced that peasant ownership was the only realistic long term solution to the land question. The transfer of the land to the tenants, he thought, would eliminate rural unrest and gradually remove Irish disaffection with the Union.

An important marker in this respect had already been laid down by the Salisbury Conservative government in 1885. The Ashbourne Act, as it was usually known, was a modest, but significant, measure which firmly established the principle of land purchase. The Treasury allocated £5 million to provide loans to tenants wishing to purchase their holdings from landlords who had expressed a willingness to sell. Interestingly, Ashbourne, who was Lord Chancellor of Ireland, was one of the first to take advantage of the act's provisions when he sold land in County Meath. Of crucial importance to the tenants was the stipulation that no deposit was necessary, as all of the sale price could be borrowed from the government at four per cent interest repayable over 49 years. Further protection was made available to tenants under the 1887 Land Act, and in the following year Balfour's Land Purchase Act provided an additional £5 million under the terms of the Ashbourne Act. Balfour's major contribution to the land question came with the 1891 Land Purchase Act which provided an extra £33 million of funding. While this new piece of legislation enabled some 47,000 tenants to purchase their holdings, its overall impact fell well short of Balfour's expectations. So complicated were the regulations surrounding land purchase under this new scheme that many prospective buyers were discouraged and, by 1896, only £13.5 million had been advanced from the fund.

More successful was the second part of the 1891 act which established the Congested Districts Board. The board was an administrative agency which was given jurisdiction over some 3.5 million acres in the west of the country, covering the poorest parts of Donegal, Leitrim, Sligo, Mayo, Roscommon, Galway, Kerry and Cork. Balfour had recognised that the impoverished west required special treatment, and the board, which was staffed by men with detailed knowledge of conditions in the region, was charged with responsibility for promoting local industries and developing forestry and fishing. Crucially, the Congested Districts Board was given powers of compulsory purchase, which allowed it to amalgamate uneconomic small holdings into economically viable units. In addition, assistance with migration to these newly amalgamated holdings was made available and technical instruction to establish modern agricultural techniques was provided. The Congested Districts Board was successful in improving conditions in the west and, in time, its jurisdiction was expanded to include one-half of Ireland and one-third of the population. The board's achievements even won praise from key figures on the Irish agrarian left, such as John Dillon and Michael Davitt, who were renowned for their vigorous attacks on all aspects of government policy. When the Board was wound up in 1923, it had spent £2 million on land improvement, farm buildings and rural dwellings, while over 2 million acres had been purchased and redistributed.

Despite his success with the Congested Districts Board and in other areas such as the construction of a light railway system which improved communications in the west, Balfour was unable to overhaul the system of local government in Ireland. This had to wait until 1898 by which time Gerald Balfour, Arthur's younger brother, was Chief Secretary. Gerald had successfully carried through a Land Act in 1896 which provided additional funds for land purchase and removed some of the obstacles which had discouraged tenants from buying under the terms of the 1891 act. Two years later the younger Balfour broadened the thrust of constructive Unionism by carrying through the far-reaching Local Government Act which greatly increased the number of Nationalist representatives. The 1898 act removed the archaic Grand Juries, which had been dominated by the big landowners, and replaced them with county councils, urban district councils and rural district councils. These were elected on a wide franchise, which included women, and in addition to the local rates the new councils were eligible for Treasury grants. The impact of this democratisation of local government was dramatic. In the important new county council elections 551

Nationalist councillors were returned, leaving the Unionists with only 125 seats, 86 of them in Ulster. Similar percentages were recorded in elections for the other new local bodies with the result that, at a stroke, Unionist domination was replaced by Nationalist domination at local government level in the three southern provinces. The fears expressed by some Unionists that local government democratisation would be accompanied by administrative and financial chaos proved unfounded, as Nationalist councillors carried out their duties with great responsibility and played a crucial role in completing the smooth transition to the new system. At the same time, of course, the changes in local government opened up new opportunities in the Home Rule camp at grass roots level and provided valuable experience for this new breed of local politician.

The Balfours' achievements in Ireland did not end with the Local Government Act because, in 1899, Gerald Balfour carried through the legislation which established the Department of Agriculture and Technical Instruction. This had been a key objective in the Conservative government's Irish policy. Yet much of the credit for the establishment of this new board belonged to Sir Horace Plunkett, an able and innovative agricultural reformer. Plunkett was from a Protestant landowning family, and he had spent ten years ranching in Wyoming before returning to Ireland in 1889 to manage his father's estates in County Meath. In 1892, standing as a Unionist, he won South Dublin, but he did not conform to the Unionist stereotype. While he firmly rejected the belief that Home Rule would mean progress in Ireland, his analysis of the Irish Question led to the conclusion that the essential problem was economic, not political. In particular, he wanted to improve agriculture, arguing that this would not only bring material benefit to Ireland's farmers but would also help to restore their self-respect. Such improvement would require investment in new techniques and new machinery, and this had encouraged Plunkett to establish co-operative societies. This development led to the appearance of creameries all over the country, where new machinery allowed high quality butter to be produced from the milk supplied by local dairy farmers. By 1894 enough progress had been made to allow the creation of a national organisation which developed links between existing societies and spread the movement into new areas. This new body was the Irish Agricultural Organisation Society, and Plunkett acted as its first President [26].

While Plunkett was determined that the new co-operatives would keep outside politics, he himself was no stranger to political controversy. As a Unionist MP he had naturally attacked the Home Rule case, warning that self government would not improve Ireland's economic performance. Moreover, he had also lambasted the Catholic Church for its apparent lack of concern with Ireland's backwardness. Yet, at the same time, he was equally critical of his own landlord class, which had failed to provide an imaginative response to their country's economic problems, because, he assumed, their primary concern was to preserve the status quo in Ireland. Despite some rumblings, Plunkett retained his parliamentary seat at the 1895 general election, which had seen the Conservatives back in government with a comfortable majority. Plunkett believed that a long period of Conservative rule, in which the divisive issue of Home Rule would not surface, presented the ideal opportunity to focus on making real progress on non-political issues such as agriculture. With this in mind he pressed the leaders of the main Irish parties to come together and consider these matters, and he was successful in arousing interest among moderate sections of both Unionist and Nationalist opinion. This new group held its meetings during the parliamentary recess, hence the name 'Recess Committee', and in 1896 it issued, somewhat surprisingly, a unanimous report calling for government financial and administrative support to help in the development of Irish agriculture. Plunkett had been successful in spreading his ideas on the need for a major shake up in agriculture, and following the implementation of the Local Government Act the government acceded to the Recess Committee's wishes by passing an act in 1899 which created the Department of Agriculture and Technical Instruction. While the new department made a significant contribution to Irish economic life, its impact was less than Plunkett had envisaged. Still, he had demonstrated that the Conservative government was receptive to constructive suggestions from moderate opinion in Ireland, indicating that further progress on the land question was possible.

In November 1900 Gerald Balfour was succeeded at the Irish Office by George Wyndham. The new Chief Secretary had been close to the Balfours and, from the outset, it was clear that the general policy of constructive Unionism would be retained. Indeed, Wyndham was a more radical Conservative with an intense dislike of coercion and a deep sympathy for Irish Catholicism. As Arthur Balfour's private secretary he had accompanied the Chief Secretary on his tour of the west in 1890, and the poverty he had witnessed left a lasting impression. For Wyndham land purchase was the solution to the plight of the peasantry, and he was determined to revive the programme set in motion by the Balfours, but which was now in danger of petering out. Battling to overcome a hostile Treasury, Wyndham's first Land Bill had to be dropped in June 1902 when it came under fire from all sides.

By that stage agrarian unrest had resurfaced in the west of Ireland, and Wyndham was coming under pressure from cabinet colleagues and his own backbenchers to take a tough line [27]. Fortunately, a Protestant landlord, Captain John Shawe-Taylor, offered a way out of the impasse by proposing a round table conference at which representatives of both the landlords and the tenants could meet to seek a solution to the land question. Wyndham quickly endorsed the proposal and the Land Conference met on 20 December 1902. Crucially, John Redmond and William O'Brien supported the initiative and both participated in the Land Conference. In Unionist circles, however, there was less enthusiasm for Shawe-Taylor's proposal, but a number of landlords were persuaded to attend the conference. The most prominent of these was the Earl of Dunraven, an improving landlord from County Limerick, who acted as Chairman of the Land Conference. The discussions were remarkably productive and on 4 January 1903 the Land Conference published a unanimous report. Its main proposal was that the government should make available new funds, which would allow direct cash payments to be made to landlords. The buyers would be given easy repayment terms with annuities fixed at 3¼ per cent over 68½ years. The report did not propose compulsory selling, but stated that a generous level of state aid would ensure that each landlord was guaranteed a fair price [28].

Wyndham was now in a much stronger position to gain cabinet and Treasury approval than he had been in the previous year. The joint landlord-tenant recommendation revealed a new consensus of Irish opinion on the land problem and, significantly, Arthur Balfour, who was a keen supporter of the purchase initiative, had replaced Lord Salisbury as Prime Minister. In fact, the Land Conference report formed the crux of the 1903 Land Act, more commonly known as the Wyndham Act. Its impact was revolutionary. Landlords were encouraged to sell entire estates, with the Treasury providing £12 million in direct cash payments to these Irish landlords, and sales were to be made on any estate where three-quarters of the tenantry acquiesced. Before the Wyndham Act sales under previous legislation had dwindled alarmingly, as it seemed that those landlords interested in selling had already done so, but after 1903 there was a rush to sell. Between 1903 and 1920 nearly 9 million acres passed from the landlords to the new owner occupiers in nearly 300,000 sales. By the outbreak of the First World War approximately seventy per cent of Irish farmers owned their own holdings. In 1909 the Liberal government carried through a new Land Act which, in essence, tidied up the Wyndham Act. The principle of compulsion was now endorsed and further funds were made available.

The Wyndham Act had been the most significant piece of legislation in the constructive Unionist jigsaw, and it was to have serious implications for the development of both Irish Nationalism and Irish Unionism. Constructive Unionism had emerged in the late 1880s as the Conservative alternative to Gladstone's endorsement of Home Rule. In considering Irish policy, Conservative leaders were convinced that the strength of Irish Nationalism was due to the exploitation of widespread social and economic grievances by a minority of political extremists. In this sense politicians such as Salisbury viewed agrarian agitation as the kind of socialist challenge to property which was being seen in contemporary Europe. Arthur Balfour had been instrumental in initiating this new approach, firmly believing that a policy of conciliation in Ireland would erode support for Home Rule. It was Gerald Balfour who coined the phrase which best described this policy when, in a speech to his constituents in Leeds shortly after his appointment as Chief Secretary, he spoke of "killing Home Rule with kindness".

In the late 1890s the prospects for such a policy appeared bright. A huge Conservative majority existed at Westminster, Gladstone was out of the way and Irish Nationalism was bitterly divided, but it proved impossible to reconcile the deep divisions in Irish politics. This may have been achieved if the Conservative government had forged some sort of alliance with the conservative Catholic Church, which it might have done by establishing a Catholic university, but when the two Balfours and Wyndham raised this issue, it ran aground on the shore of Conservative indifference. Indeed it was this lack of active support in London, where politicians were so badly informed on Irish matters, which contributed to the ultimate failure of 'killing Home Rule with kindness'. In the end British attempts at large-scale reform, such as the democratisation of local government and the 1903 Land Act, probably strengthened Irish Nationalism, while simultaneously undermining the entrenched position of the Unionist landowning class [29]. While some historians argue that the ten years of Conservative rule from 1895 to the end of 1905 actually contributed to the growing polarisation in Irish politics, it has to be acknowledged that the progressive measures adopted by successive Tory administrations made a significant contribution to the modernisation of Irish society.

Historiography

An excellent starting point for the student of the issue of 'Land and Politics' in late nineteenth century Ireland remains F S L Lyons's, *Ireland since the Famine* (London, 1971). Lyons explains that Gladstone recognised that Irish opposition to English rule in Ireland, which in its most extreme form found expression in the Fenian rising, stemmed from genuine grievances that were the responsibility of the government at Westminster. He also highlights the symbolic significance of Irish legislation introduced by the first Gladstone government in 1869 and 1870, stressing that it signalled a new way of looking at Irish problems. On the origins of Home Rule Lyons points out that Butt's early Home Rule movement enjoyed the support of a significant number of Protestant Conservatives in Ireland, but they quickly disappeared as the Home Rule League opened the way for the rise of a politically active, and mainly Catholic, middle class. This point is repeated in Boyce's, *Nineteenth Century Ireland* which claims that the Home Rule League quickly became a natural home for the defence of Catholic interests. Lyons is also good at unravelling the complex background to the New Departure. He rejects the claim made by John Devoy that at his crucial meeting in Dublin with Davitt and Parnell in June 1879 an agreement was reached, whereby the campaign for land reform and Home Rule would only be the prelude to a much greater measure of freedom, which would be achieved, if necessary, by violent revolution. Lyons acknowledges that Devoy himself believed that such a commitment had been made, and this encouraged him to throw Clan na Gael's weight behind the New Departure, but concludes that Parnell, while he may have appeared sympathetic, would not have committed himself to future revolution.

In looking at the origins of agrarian unrest Foster's, *Modern Ireland* plays down the impact of rackrenting landlords and evictions. Rather, he argues that up until 1876 Irish farmers had been enjoying increasing prosperity and an improving standard of living, and the key motivation for the agrarian agitation which followed was the sudden check on rising expectations brought about by the agricultural depression of the late 1870s. Lee's, *The Modernisation of Irish Society* offers a sharp analysis of the critical 1879–82 period. Lee describes the Land League as the most remarkable movement in Irish history. It politicised the rural Irish and, unlike O'Connell's mass movement, it was not dependent on clerical participation. Taking a broader view, Lee claims that the Land League was the most effective instrument of rural agitation in nineteenth century Europe, while in Ireland itself, the League questioned the very legitimacy of landlordism. One of the reasons for its effectiveness was the lack of tension between urban and rural areas, as they often shared the same interests. Indeed, the League at local level was often led by the businessmen of the small towns who, of course, depended on a prosperous tenant farming class for their livelihoods.

Detailed information on Davitt's role in the League can be located in T W Moody's, *Davitt and the Irish Revolution 1846-82* (Oxford, 1982). In a vivid description of a typical Land League meeting, held in the open air, usually on a Sunday, Moody declares that such meetings in 1879 launched a dynamic new movement in which the large, enthusiastic crowds were full participants. Moody also charts the League's relationship with the Catholic Church, pointing out that the

Mayo Land League was led and inspired by laymen in the face of hostility or aloofness from most of the bishops, but with growing support from the lower clergy, especially the curates. By October 1879, however, a number of bishops openly supported the National Land League, though Moody argues that some did so, only when they realised that they would lose influence with the people, if they did not change their attitude to the land agitation. Still, some of the more conservative clerics, notably Archbishop McCabe, never dropped their opposition to the agitation. In his assessment of Davitt, Moody claims that by the autumn of 1879 he had begun to distance himself from his Fenian past, as his energies were fully absorbed by the open agrarian organisation. However, Moody's sympathetic treatment of Davitt, whom he describes as a social reformer, is attacked in Paul Bew's essay, 'Parnell and Davitt', which appears in the very useful D G Boyce and A O'Day's (eds), *Parnell in Perspective* (London, 1991). Bew emphasises Davitt's commitment to Fenianism, claiming that, while the Land League sought to smash Irish landlordism, its neo-Fenian leadership also wanted this to be a prelude to smashing the British link. In his first major publication, Bew's, *Land and the National Question 1858-1882* (Dublin, 1978) dealt with the coalition of Irish agrarian interests which made up the Land League. Initially, the large graziers and the smallholders joined forces against the landlord but, crucially, from the middle of 1880 the larger farmers pushed aside the smallholders' demands for land redistribution, to consolidate their position by securing the three Fs. Useful comments on the significance of the three Fs appear in MacDonagh's, *States of Mind*. He argues that the 1881 land legislation was an acceptance of co-ownership, which overturned the English view of property as a free contract, because the tenant could now assert his 'moral authority' by deciding what rent he could afford to pay. At the same time, MacDonagh draws attention to the predicament of the landowners who regarded the Land League as squeezing concessions, at their expense, out of the Westminster government.

In looking at the influence of the Irish Question at Westminster, N Mansergh's, *The Irish Question 1840-1921*, 3rd edition (London, 1975) stresses Gladstone's European credentials and notes how the embarrassment which Ireland caused England influenced his thinking. This notion, that it was the duty of Englishmen to remove Irish grievances, is taken up in D G Boyce's, *The Irish Question in British Politics 1868-1986* (London, 1988). Boyce argues that, by the mid-1880s, Gladstone had been convinced that British public opinion, by now sickened with coercion, was ready to take up the cause of Irish Home Rule. Boyce demonstrated how Gladstone made Home Rule the central party issue in British politics, but acknowledges that he believed in a bipartisan approach as the best route to a solution. The most original treatment of Gladstone's conversion to Home Rule can be found in A B Cooke and J R Vincent's, *The Governing Passion: Cabinet Government and Party Politics in Britain 1885-86* (Brighton, 1974) which claims that Gladstone's support for Home Rule was due to opportunism, rather than conviction. In particular, he wanted to outmanoeuvre Joseph Chamberlain and reunite the Liberal party under his own leadership, something which, of course, the Home Rule issue allowed him to achieve. This thesis is firmly rejected in J Loughlin's, *Gladstone, Home Rule and the Ulster Question 1882-93* (Dublin, 1986). Loughlin reminds us of Gladstone's great sense of justice and his distaste for coercion, adding that he was one of the few British politicians with any real grasp of Irish history. He stresses that Gladstone's view of Ireland under Home Rule was a highly conservative one, which envisaged the return of the landlords as Irish political leaders. Yet Loughlin also points out that the speed at which Gladstone took up the Home Rule cause was inexplicable. The reason, he argues, was that the Liberal leader mistakenly believed Ireland to be close to anarchy and on the verge of revolution, leaving no time to pursue a gradual approach. His real fear was that unchecked violence in Ireland would result in serious social disorder in England. Boyce's, *Nineteenth Century Ireland* observes that the Land League had seemed ready to instigate social revolution, but by tackling the land question the British government snuffed out this threat.

The most recent work, R Jenkins's, *Gladstone* (London, 1995) claims that the Liberal leader decided on Home Rule in mid–November 1885 when he was campaigning in Midlothian. The title of the chapter dealing with this — 'Slow Road to Damascus' — indicates Jenkins's view that Gladstone's conversion to the idea of Home Rule had been a slow process, rather than an opportunistic attempt to hang onto power, as his Conservative critics suggested.

On the prospects for Home Rule, Foster's, *Modern Ireland* describes the first Home Rule Bill as a non-starter, but an important marker. Lyons's, *Ireland since the Famine* emphasises just how modest were the proposals in the 1886 bill, adding "it requires an effort of the imagination to understand the uproar they caused at the time". Of course, one of the reasons for this uproar was the belief that the Irish could not be trusted to rule themselves, as the country, under a Home Rule parliament, would rapidly degenerate towards general lawlessness. This belief was partly attributable to the very strong feeling of Anglo–Saxon superiority which caused many important opponents of the bill to view the Irish as an inferior race, a theme that Loughlin explores fully. Central to the Unionist argument opposing Home Rule was the assumption that even a modest measure of self government for Ireland would lead to total separation and, ultimately, to the break up of the Empire. In assessing Joseph Chamberlain's decision to abandon a promising career in the Liberal party, Lyons acknowledges that his fear of the Empire disintegrating was genuine, but he judges that it was an exaggerated fear. Later, in his detailed biography, *Parnell* (London, 1977) Lyons concludes that if Home Rule had been successful, Parnell believed that Irish Nationalists would have established a conservative regime which would have worked constitutionally towards dominion status. Boyce's, *Nineteenth Century Ireland* deals effectively with the impact of the 1886 bill on Ulster, claiming that the threat of Home Rule made it easy for Unionism to appeal across the class divide. Details on the Belfast riots in 1886 are recorded in Bardon's, *A History of Ulster*.

An old, but important, book analysing the Home Rule party in the 1880s is C C O'Brien's, *Parnell and his Party* (Oxford, 1957). O'Brien argues that Parnell was not a leader who made or shaped events, but one who had the patience to wait on the turn of events. When he was sure what the people thought and desired, he proved very effective in articulating this. Focusing on the IPP itself, O'Brien analyses its development, looking closely at how it cultivated the Liberal alliance. This leads him to conclude that the decision to depose Parnell in Committee Room Fifteen was not a betrayal, but the logical outcome of the leadership which Parnell himself had given the party. In examining the level of support in Ireland itself for Home Rule, Loughlin's, *Gladstone, Home Rule and the Ulster Question* endorses the views expressed in K T Hoppen's, *Elections, Politics and Society in Ireland 1832-85*

(Oxford, 1984). Hoppen argues that in the nineteenth century local affairs, as opposed to national affairs, were more significant in determining political support. Therefore, the great upsurge in support for the IPP in 1885 really represented the desire of each county to have its interests aired at Westminster.

Lyons's, *Parnell* notes how Parnell failed to appreciate the depth of Irish Protestant fears over Home Rule. This view is echoed in P Bew's, *C S Parnell* (Dublin, 1980), a short, but very original, book. Bew is highly critical of Parnell's approach to northern Unionism, which he never really tried to understand. Great stress is also laid on Parnell's position as a southern Anglo-Irish Protestant landlord which, Bew claims, explains his social conservatism. For Parnell, Bew argues, a genuinely conservative settlement of the Irish Question required a Dublin parliament which would be controlled by the Protestant landlord class rather than the Catholic bourgeoisie. While he may exaggerate Parnell's conservative streak, Bew is right to conclude that, by fighting for Home Rule after 1882, the Irish leader steered Irish Nationalism away from agrarian revolution. Moreover, Bew agrees with Lyons's assessment that Parnell never came close to formulating a strategy to deal with Ulster Unionism. Instead, Parnell's concerns were with the future of southern Protestants. Bew's conclusion is supported in R Foster's essay, 'Parnell, Wicklow and Nationalism', which appears in D McCartney's (ed), *Parnell: The Politics of Power* (Dublin, 1991). Foster claims that Irish Toryism and Irish Nationalism were by no means incompatible, adding that a number of progressive landlords, albeit a minority, had by the 1880s come to view the policy of land reform and land purchase as their only hope of survival in a 'modern' Ireland. Parnell, Foster argues, always remained archetypally Anglo-Irish, something which his Wicklow background, with its particular English 'feel', helped to nurture.

The other essays in the McCartney volume are useful in analysing particular aspects of Parnell's career. L Geary's contribution, 'Parnell and the Irish Land Question', describes Parnell's attitude to the Plan of Campaign as one of "undisguised antipathy". This theme is developed in great detail in S Warwick-Haller's, *William O'Brien and the Irish Land War* (Dublin, 1990) which examines the plan in action, with a special focus on O'Brien's role. In her assessment of the plan's failure, Warwick-Haller also points to Parnell's indifference. Yet, while it did not make anything like the impact of the Land League, the Plan of Campaign did, she argues, help to win over Arthur Balfour and the Conservatives to the need for a comprehensive settlement of the land question. Parnell's fall is effectively dealt with in F Callanan's, *The Parnell Split* (Cork, 1992). In considering Parnell's appeal to the 'hillsides' Callanan claims that he was simply recasting the old argument that, if parliamentary Nationalism failed, physical force would take its place. This was not an endorsement of Fenianism, though it undoubtedly attracted Fenian support to the Parnellite cause, but a reaffirmation of the power of constitutional action which was made all the more effective by his strange rapport with Fenianism. Only Parnell could retain Fenian sympathy for the constitutional movement, which, of course, made it more effective at Westminster, but then only Parnell, among the leaders of constitutional Nationalism, could hope to keep Fenianism in check. Callanan concludes by suggesting that Parnell's desperate campaign to reassert his leadership in 1890-91 was not a "frenzied aberration", but was consistent with the principles he had proclaimed during his early political career. The role of the Catholic Church in Parnell's downfall is expertly chronicled in E Larkin's, *The Roman Catholic Church in Ireland and the Fall of Parnell 1888-91* (Liverpool, 1979) which stresses that the crucial blow was struck, not by the Catholic Church, but by the nonconformist wing of the Liberal party.

Details of the proposals in the second Home Rule Bill, which shows only minor changes from the 1886 bill, are laid out in G Morton's, *Home Rule and the Irish Question* (London, 1980). R C K Ensor's, *England 1870-1914* (Oxford, 1936) claims that, despite its crushing defeat in the House of Lords, the second Home Rule Bill was very significant, because it went through all the stages in the elected House and emerged a complete measure. It was, therefore, bound to be revived if, and when, a majority of the nation took the view that the Lords had, in 1893, used their veto unfairly. Loughlin's, *Gladstone, Home Rule and the Ulster Question* notes that, by 1892-93, Gladstone was more prepared to conciliate Ulster Protestant fears than he had been in 1886, but he found no sympathy for such an approach among Irish Nationalists.

On the development of constructive Unionism, the progressive policy followed by the Conservative government around the turn of the century, C B Shannon's, *Arthur J Balfour and Ireland 1874-1922* (Washington, 1988) highlights Balfour's role in laying the foundations for a new Tory approach to Ireland. Later, she shows how Balfour's support, as Prime Minister, was crucial to Wyndham's land legislation in 1903. P Travers's, *Settlements and Divisions: Ireland 1870-1922* (Dublin, 1988) argues that constructive Unionism was a diverse movement combining British government policy and the wishes of progressive Irish landlords who were seeking a new accommodation with Nationalist Ireland. Constructive Unionism, Travers claims, was similar to the 'new conservatism' then prevalent in contemporary Europe, particularly Bismarck's Germany. Foster's, *Modern Ireland* rejects the idea that constructive Unionism had been carefully planned to undermine support for Home Rule. Instead, it represented a series of hastily planned and rather haphazard attempts at reform. M O'Callaghan's, *British High Politics and a Nationalist Ireland* (Cork, 1994) explores how Liberal and Conservative policy on Ireland evolved in different directions. Land purchase, she argues, was anathema to Gladstone, but Balfour, desperate to claw back the ground conceded to Irish Nationalism by the Liberals before and during 1886, found it ideologically acceptable to recognise rural poverty in the west of Ireland and provide state funding for its relief. Of course, agrarian violence had contributed to this Conservative change of heart, a theme developed in C Townshend's, *Political Violence in Ireland: Government and Resistance since 1848* (Oxford, 1983) which claims that, while English politicians rejected the idea that they were only spurred to action in Ireland by the threat of serious violence, the opposite was true in practice. Analysing the rural disorder in 1880-81, he also points out that this occurred not during the time of maximum economic distress, but after the restoration of stability. This leads him to reject the simplistic notion of "a rack-rented, exploited, poor tenantry forced into resistance" as a result of the agricultural depression of 1878-79.

An original interpretation of constructive Unionism is provided by A Gailey's, *Ireland and the Death of Kindness: The Experience of Constructive Unionism 1890-1905* (Cork, 1987). Gailey describes Conservative policy as a mixture of strong government and social amelioration, a policy which pleased both the traditional Tories and Chamberlain's Liberal Unionists. His key argument is that conciliation was not aimed primarily at irreconcilable Irish Nationalists, but at the

Conservatives' political allies, the Liberal Unionists. With Westminster's two party system now structured on the divisions within Irish politics it was vital for the Conservatives to keep Chamberlain in the fold which, of course, allowed the Conservatives to govern for seventeen of the twenty years down to 1905. Gailey judges that constructive Unionism failed because it lacked active proponents at Westminster, where it was often viewed in English terms as an attack on socialism. One consequence of the policy was to undermine Irish Unionism; another was to weaken the IPP. Gailey concludes by arguing that the period of constructive Unionism contributed to the growing polarisation in Irish politics, leading eventually to partition. Sir Horace Plunkett's contribution to Ireland is assessed in Lyons's, *Ireland since the Famine* which stresses his impartiality in politics that at times made him "one of the best-hated men in Ireland". Finally, a brief outline of all the relevant land legislation can be found in M J Winstanley's pamphlet, *Ireland and the Land Question 1800-1922* (London, 1984).

Chapter 3

Nationalism old and new

A ny investigation of the mobilisation of Irish Nationalism must focus on the crucial 1879-82 period, when the forces of agrarianism and Nationalism came together. Earlier, it was true, the Irish peasantry was mobilised under clerical and middle class leadership against the Anglo-Irish gentry class, but O'Connell's Nationalist movement was strangled by the famine. Moreover, the aim of self government had never been clearly spelt out by O'Connell, whose bourgeois followers were just as keen to benefit from the Union as they were to tamper with it. O'Connell's real achievement had been to demonstrate that constitutionalism was a viable political strategy, offering a real alternative to physical force. Indeed, these two strains of Nationalism, constitutional and revolutionary, tended to operate in tandem, and whenever constitutionalism faltered the other would re-emerge. Thus Fenianism, though a military embarrassment, served to re-awaken Irish Nationalism after the famine and provided an early opportunity for the huge, anti-British American diaspora of Irish origin, which had been created by the famine, to make a contribution to Irish Nationalism. It would be wrong, however, to compartmentalise constitutional and revolutionary Nationalism, as they could, and frequently did, overlap. Even the great pacifist, O'Connell, realised the value of sharing a platform with 1798 veterans in helping to popularise his causes. A more obvious example was the victory of the Fenian, Jeremiah O'Donovan Rossa, in the Tipperary by-election of 1869 or, more significantly, the effective mix of physical force and constitutional Nationalism which characterised the Land War. The land agitation was directed by both Fenian activists and Home Rulers, and it was the disciplined mass action, backed up by the threat, or reality, of violence, which was transformed into a national policy.

The economic distress of 1879 was not as bad as earlier crises, but what was remarkable was the response that it provoked from the tenant farmers, which allowed the politicians to adopt the agrarian issue. The land agitation changed the nation's thinking, as the national aim became inextricably linked to the great social issue of the day. It attracted a cross-section of rural Irish support, uniting the strong farmer, smallholder and labourer in a single cause, though this much vaunted unity was not to survive the duration of the Land War. In this respect Nationalism built upon the belief that landlordism was an alien institution, as Parnell realised that the national aim of self government had to be combined with an attack on the landlords to win mass support. Moreover, this attack on landlordism added to Irish Nationalism's powerful anti-British bias which, again, found expression in both constitutional and more militant Nationalism. Yet the land issue did not just provide active participants in the national struggle, because it also gave Nationalism a new moral legitimacy. Landlords not only denied the legitimate rights of the Irish farmer, but they were also a living testament to both past and present English domination and, therefore, in its opposition to landlordism the Land League came to represent the national will. In addition to providing this moral legitimacy, the Land League also laid the foundation for the effective political organisation which bound the Nationalist movement to the most powerful social forces in Ireland. Soon, the League's organisational structure, encouraging grass roots participation at local level, was duplicated by the National League, which relegated the land issue to concentrate on the political aim of Home Rule. The uneasy alliance of agrarian, constitutional and physical force Nationalism, which was Parnellism, was then able to take advantage of the extension of the franchise which, combined with the parliamentary pledge, produced an independent and influential Irish party at Westminster. Thus Irish Nationalism became constitutional, though its character under Parnell can be more accurately labelled as militant constitutionalism. This changed in 1886, when Gladstone opted for Home Rule and Parnell committed the Irish party to the Liberal alliance. The Irish party lost its independence and the days of militant constitutionalism were numbered, as the key task for Irish Nationalism now was to influence English, not Irish, opinion.

A subsequent attempt to make the land issue the cutting edge of Nationalism failed when the Plan of Campaign collapsed in 1890. The Plan, which had targeted some of the worst landlords, could not match the dynamism of the Land League in mobilising the rural Irish for the Nationalist cause. Still, for a few years, the Plan of Campaign again forced the government onto the defensive, providing, as it did, an alternative authority to that government in those areas designated for agitation. However, with the IPP having given priority to the development of its alliance with the Liberals, the militant agrarian component of Irish Nationalism exerted much less influence. While Parnell continued to pay lip-service to the need for further land reforms, he usually did so in moderate tones, preferring to concentrate on the political aim of Home Rule. Yet his National League was a formidable political machine which did not just confine itself to simple electoral tasks. In 1888 it demonstrated its strength when Irish MPs denounced the Papal condemnation of the Plan of Campaign as an impertinence, even though the Catholic Church in Ireland was so closely tied to the IPP. After Gladstone's conversion to Home Rule, the church had endorsed the demand for Home Rule as representing the legitimate demands of the Irish people, and it moved quickly to secure its interests and influence once Home Rule seemed likely. Naturally, such a change bound Irish Nationalism and Catholicism even more closely together, but it may also have contributed to the erosion of the Nationalist movement's radical edge. Another factor which sapped the vitality of the Nationalist movement was the growth of the new propertied farming class, which was evident even before the Parnell split. Such developments emphasised the growing conservatism of Irish Nationalism, a trend which became more pronounced after Parnell's fall, when the church increased its influence.

The disintegration of the Irish Party

The last decade of the nineteenth century was dominated by the bitter internecine feud within the IPP, which had burst open with Parnell's removal from the leadership in December 1890. Moreover, his death in October 1891 had, if anything, deepened the divisions within the party. The moral issue, which had dominated the whole question of Parnell's leadership in Ireland, obscured the fact that a serious political difference had emerged between the two wings of the Irish party. The Parnellites believed that when forced by Gladstone to choose between Parnell and Home Rule, the anti-Parnellites had sacrificed not just Parnell but the independence of the party. John Redmond, the Parnellite leader, constantly reminded his opponents that Home Rule, as Parnell had so ably demonstrated, would only be achieved by an independent Irish party determined to keep the pressure on the Liberals. In response, the anti-Parnellites denied that they had surrendered the party's freedom but, in reality, the prospect of Home Rule now depended totally on the goodwill of the Liberal party. These arguments were played out in two bitter by-elections held soon after Parnell's death, both of which saw Redmond standing for the Parnellites. In the first, Cork City, Redmond lost heavily to the anti-Parnellite candidate, but in the other by-election Redmond secured a narrow victory over Michael Davitt in Waterford. Early in 1892, John Dillon and William O'Brien had tried to move the warring elements towards conciliation but, with a general election imminent, the Parnellites, fired up by their by-election triumph in Waterford City, were not interested in any compromise. Yet when the general election took place in July 1892, the Parnellites could win only nine seats. Redmond blamed clerical influence for the Parnellites' poor showing, but the crucial factor was that the electors saw the Liberal alliance as the best hope of securing Home Rule and, consequently, the anti-Parnellites won 71 seats.

By the autumn of 1892 the split appeared irrevocable. The Parnellites' disappointing performance in the general election failed to reflect the significant level of support which they enjoyed. Outside Ulster, roughly one-third of the electorate backed Parnellite candidates who polled particularly well in urban areas. The Catholic clergy had campaigned aggressively during the election contest, but it was principally in rural Ireland that they were able to impose an anti-Parnellite line. Of course, the split also divided the party organisation. The Irish National League, which had been formed in 1882, remained with the Parnellite wing and was strongest in the counties around Dublin and in Roscommon in the west. Previously, the National League had been well spread, though the most active political areas in Ireland were those counties forming a central spine and stretching southwards from Leitrim to Tipperary. This central area seemed to combine, in just the right proportions, the concerns of the politically conscious middle class of the east and the preoccupation with the agrarian radicalism of the west. Though they had a majority of MPs, the anti-Parnellites were forced to create a new party organisation which they launched in Dublin on 10 March 1891. This was the Irish National Federation and it was soon challenging the National League. In many instances old branches of the League simply changed their allegiance and their title to become new branches of the Federation. Yet despite the interest shown by anti-Parnellite MPs, the Irish National Federation failed to take off. Over the whole country only about one in three parishes had branches of the Federation, and it was only really strong in Laois and Wexford and in the Ulster border counties of Leitrim, Cavan and Monaghan. This lack of interest was indicative of the wholesale political demobilisation which occurred during the 1890s. The truth was that the agrarian-Nationalist movement, which had sprung to life in the 1879-82 period, had now run out of steam and interest in local organisations declined rapidly.

This apathy was only temporarily interrupted by the introduction of the second Home Rule Bill in 1893. Following the Liberals' comprehensive defeat in the 1886 general election Gladstone, despite his age, had refused to resign as party leader. In this final stage of his long political career Gladstone was consumed by the Irish Question, and he was driven by his determination to do justice to Ireland. A string of by-election successes in 1890-91 had convinced him that a substantial Liberal majority could be achieved at the impending general election. This would have allowed the Liberal leader to carry Home Rule by such a clear majority in the Commons that he hoped the House of Lords would be intimidated into waving it through. With this crowning achievement in place Gladstone could then have handed over to a successor. Such a scenario, however, failed to materialise, as the 1892 general election left a new Liberal government dependent on the support of the Irish party to produce a working majority. Undeterred, Gladstone pressed on, fearing that no other Liberal Prime Minister would give Home Rule the priority it deserved. In the event, of course, the Liberals fell well short of the one hundred majority Gladstone had believed would be required to force the Lords' hand. Perhaps surprisingly, the rejection of the second Home Rule Bill by the Upper House caused little stir in Ireland, a further indication of the political stagnation affecting the country in the 1890s.

During the debates on the 1893 bill the divisions within the Irish party were again highlighted, as Redmond, to Gladstone's embarrassment, attacked the bill's limitations, while the anti-Parnellites warmly endorsed the proposals. Yet potentially more serious for the Irish party, were the divisions which existed within the ranks of the anti-Parnellite wing. With the lightweight Justin McCarthy a reluctant and ineffective Chairman, a power struggle soon developed between two of the most powerful figures in the anti-Parnellite group, John Dillon and Tim Healy [30]. Trouble had first erupted when a dispute arose over the control of a new Nationalist newspaper. Following the split in December 1890, the influential *Freeman's Journal* had stayed loyal to Parnell, forcing the Irish party to launch the *National Press* which, under Healy's direction, began a sustained attack on the displaced leader. By September 1891, however, McCarthy and his colleagues succeeded in separating the *Freeman* from the Parnellite camp, and it was then decided to merge the two newspapers. This decision was bitterly opposed by Healy who, as editor of the *National*, had suddenly established a personal power base. When he failed to prevent the merger, Healy fought tenaciously, though without success, to influence the composition of the governing board of the *Freeman's Journal*. Healy realised that control over the main Nationalist organ meant control over Nationalist opinion but, for the remainder of the 1890s, the *Freeman* was generally sympathetic to Dillon. A similar situation had occurred with the Nationalist press in Ulster. Following the divorce scandal, the *Belfast Morning News* had remained loyal to Parnell, but a rival, the *Irish News*, was soon launched by Catholic businessmen supported by the church and within a year it was able to buy out the failing *Morning News*.

It was perhaps inevitable that the removal of Parnell, who had been such an imposing and dominant figure, would unleash a bitter power struggle among his most senior lieutenants, but the quarrel between Dillon and Healy was not simply a clash of personalities, as they each held very different views on the future role of the Irish party. In short, Dillon advocated Parnellism without Parnell. He wanted a united and disciplined party under the control of a strong leadership, arguing that such a development was necessary if the Irish party hoped, once again, to become an effective political force. For Dillon the attainment of Home Rule was of paramount importance, and this explains his commitment to the Liberal alliance. Healy held different opinions. Whereas Dillon wanted the concentration of authority, Healy sought to weaken central party control and devolve more power to the constituencies, particularly in relation to the selection of candidates. Such a diffusion of power would, of course, increase the influence of local priests who were always prominent figures in local constituency branches. Indeed it soon became clear that Healy's intention was to turn the Irish party into a right wing clerical party under the control of a large committee. Both men had substantial followings among the rank and file and, from 1893 to 1898, the Dillonites repeatedly clashed with the Healyites in a struggle for supremacy.

The differences between the two factions were clearly illustrated when Lord Rosebery succeeded Gladstone in March 1894. Almost immediately, Rosebery indicated that the Home Rule issue would no longer receive the priority that it did under Gladstone. This led the Healyites to question the value of the Liberal alliance, as they argued that the Irish party should, henceforward, pursue a more independent line at Westminster. To Dillon, on the other hand, it was crystal clear that only the Liberals, despite Rosebery's lack of enthusiasm, could be expected to deliver Home Rule and, therefore, it was essential that the Liberal alliance be retained. The issue still had to be resolved, when a general election intervened in July 1895. On the surface this election was a bitterly fought contest, which resulted in the return of 70 anti-Parnellites and 11 Parnellites. Yet equally bitter were the series of squabbles, which took place behind the scenes at constituency level, to select the anti-Parnellite candidates. Both the Dillonites and Healyites fought ferociously to have their men selected and, in the end, Dillon's supporters enjoyed a very narrow majority. The 1895 election also highlighted the increasing political apathy in Ireland, as only 42 of the 103 seats were contested, half the number which had been fought in 1892.

Shortly after the election, matters came to a head when a vacancy occurred in the South Kerry constituency. Acting quickly, the local clergy, undoubtedly prompted by Healy, met to endorse William Martin Murphy as candidate. Murphy, a wealthy Dublin businessman, was one of Healy's most influential supporters and, since the late 1880s, he had been closely identified with the Catholic right wing of the party. This was a challenge which Dillon could not shirk, and an 'official' party candidate was nominated to contest the seat, making it an open contest between the Healy and Dillon nominees. After a rough, even by Irish standards, by-election campaign, Dillon's candidate won comfortably and, as a result of what many in the party regarded as Healy's insubordination, a number of prominent Healyites including Healy himself were expelled from the Executive Committee of the National Federation. Although these expulsions strengthened Dillon's position, Healy still retained considerable influence in Nationalist circles and he continued to be a member of the party. Even when Dillon succeeded the ineffective McCarthy as Chairman of the Irish party in February 1896, the ambitious Healy continued to snipe from his position within the party. At the beginning of 1897 Healy, again enjoying clerical support, launched the People's Rights Association to challenge the National Federation and undermine Dillon. By this stage, however, Dillon was clearly in the ascendant, and he used his growing power to re-model the party along Parnellite lines. This resulted in the re-establishment of central authority at the expense of local privilege and renewed emphasis on iron party discipline both inside and outside parliament. Healy remained an MP, but the Healyites, who struggled to make an impact beyond selective counties in Leinster and Ulster, had failed to gain control of the Irish party.

Although Dillon succeeded in imposing his will on the party, thwarting Healy's attempts to create a Catholic party, constitutional Nationalism had been seriously weakened by the long years of faction fighting. The constant bickering between the Healyites, the Dillonites and the Redmondites left many voters bewildered and disenchanted. Parnell continued to cast a long shadow over the Irish party, and though Dillon had fought to re-model the party on Parnellite lines, there was no Parnell present to give it an effective voice both inside and outside parliament. Yet even the great lost leader would have found it difficult to spark a revival of constitutional Nationalism in the circumstances prevailing during the 1890s. Lacking any agrarian impetus and with Home Rule off the political agenda at Westminster, the Irish party had become sterile. It lacked popular appeal and its organisation was practically moribund. Moreover, the policy of constructive Unionism, which was implemented by the Conservatives following their victory in the 1895 general election, presented the Irish party with new problems. While Healy welcomed the improvements, Dillon believed that the Conservative government might succeed in killing Home Rule with kindness, arguing that social and economic reform would undermine the Nationalist movement.

Old Nationalism reunites

The fierce rivalry between Dillon and Healy for control of the party during the 1890s tended to obscure the contributions of other significant personalities who possessed strong claims to be Parnell's successor. Thomas Sexton was the party's best orator and its expert on finance. From 1892 he chaired the board which ran the *Freeman's Journal*, the main voice of Nationalist opinion, but he refused to press his considerable claims to the leadership. Another important figure, William O'Brien, had joined with Dillon to direct the Plan of Campaign, but though he had undoubted political gifts, he preferred to remain an agrarian campaigner. In fact, O'Brien retired from parliament in 1895, disgusted by the party's internal wranglings. Following his retirement O'Brien took up residence in a remote part of County Mayo, but he was soon drawn back into politics. What had forced O'Brien's change of heart was the plight of the Connacht farmers, which he witnessed at first hand. In both 1896 and 1897 the potato crop in the west had been badly hit, and O'Brien believed that the heightening of feeling caused by the poor harvests could lead to a revival of the Land War. Initially, he thought that if a new wave of land agitation was to be successful, it would require a united Irish party to lead it and, during 1897, he made efforts in this direction, hoping that Dillon, his old colleague, could lead a reunified party. However, when he saw his attempts at reunion frustrated, O'Brien turned away from the national leadership and put his faith in the rank and file in Connacht. Accordingly, O'Brien launched the United Irish League (UIL) at a public meeting in Westport on 23 January 1898.

Unlike previous agrarian campaigns, the immediate target of the new agitation was not the Protestant landlord. Rural poverty by itself would not have been sufficient to spark a fresh wave of agrarian unrest, but developments in the west, particularly in County Mayo, combined to create a new set of conditions favourable to agrarian struggle. Mayo had many smallholders whose economic security, perilous even in good years, had been threatened by the poor harvests of 1896-97. Yet existing alongside these uneconomic holdings were many large grazing farms, and the contrast between the poor smallholder and the wealthy grazier was becoming more pronounced. Usually to be considered a grazier, or rancher, a man had to hold over 200 acres, though the typical grazier holding was probably between 400 to 600 acres. Towards the end of the nineteenth century there had been a marked shift from tillage to pasture, a process accelerated by the increased demand for beef from British cities. Moreover, ranching was also viewed as a step up the social ladder, and this created a new source of tension in rural Ireland, because peasant farmers came to regard the graziers as an appendage to the landlord class. Indeed graziers were frequently absentees who lived in neighbouring towns, and a good number of them had added to their holdings by taking over land made vacant by evictions. Many were business or professional men, a large number were publicans, and their herds were looked after by stockmen who lived on the land. By the late 1890s, therefore, circumstances had come together to provide the basis for a new movement of agrarian protest with the grazier as its target. O'Brien's war-cry was "the land for the people", and the UIL campaigned for the break up of the large grazing estates.

While O'Brien's motives were primarily agrarian, he also hoped to use the UIL to reunite the Irish party. Certainly, the agrarian objectives provided new common ground for united action among the various party factions, and though divisions remained at national level, the UIL had instigated reunion at local level by focusing exclusively on rural distress. By the end of 1898 there were nearly one hundred UIL branches in Mayo alone, and it was beginning to spread into other parts of the west. The land question seemed poised, once again, to spark renewed interest in the national question. From the outset, however, serious differences between O'Brien and Dillon, the two former allies, acted as a brake on the regeneration of constitutional Nationalism. Although Dillon attended the inaugural meeting of the League in Westport, he had little enthusiasm for renewed agrarian agitation which, he feared, might distract attention from the Home Rule struggle at Westminster. Still, by the end of 1898, Dillon backed the idea that the UIL should supplant the National Federation as the party's national organisation. Where they continued to disagree was in their views of the UIL's relationship with the party. Either way, it was clear that the early success of the UIL was pushing the party towards reunion. The League had continued to expand during 1899 and its influence was significant in the local government elections of that year. Suddenly, a new and large body of Nationalist representatives owed their position to the League, which now threatened to extend its influence by de-selecting MPs considered to be corrupt or ineffective and replacing them with UIL nominees. Such a prospect drove the Irish MPs towards reunion. Therefore, O'Brien's aim of uniting Dillonites, Healyites and Redmondites was well advanced, though his hopes that they would combine to press the League's agrarian demands were not fulfilled.

Towards the end of 1899 these three principals were manoeuvring to strengthen their political positions, while O'Brien continued, with great energy, to pursue his political and agrarian agenda. Earlier in the year, Dillon had resigned the Chairmanship of the party, the position being left vacant until a new Chairman of a unified party could be selected, and this resignation cleared the way for serious attempts at reunion to begin. Significantly, O'Brien backed Redmond, the leader of the Parnellite rump, in the leadership race, assuming that he could influence Redmond to act in the League's interests. Surprisingly, Healy also supported Redmond's claim, and with a Redmond-Healy alliance threatening his own position, Dillon took the decisive step of outlining a programme on which reunion could be based. Firstly, he suggested that all Nationalist MPs be reunited in one party on the constitution of the old party. Secondly, the reunited party was to pursue an independent line at Westminster. Thirdly, the party's main objective would be to secure Home Rule. Fourthly, the party was to fight for a whole range of social and economic reforms, land and education in particular, which would benefit Ireland. Finally, and crucially, the old anti-Parnellites would agree to support a Parnellite MP as leader of the reunited party. Under these terms the party formally reunited on 30 January 1900. Bowing to pressure from O'Brien, Dillon reluctantly agreed to back Redmond and, at a party meeting on 6 February, he was the unanimous choice to be the new Chairman of the reunited IPP.

It would be wrong, however, to assume the UIL alone had been responsible for the reunification of the Irish party. Two other factors were important. Firstly, the centenary of the 1798 rebellion was marked by various celebrations and commemorative events, all of which gave Nationalism fresh impetus. More significantly, the outbreak of the Boer War in October 1899 had a major influence on Ireland and provided all the Nationalist factions with the perfect opportunity to unite in their opposition to British policy in South Africa. Dillon, in particular, was very pro-Boer, and he led the Irish opposition to the war in the House of Commons [31]. Undoubtedly, both of these factors helped to create the conditions which made reconciliation more likely, but the real driving force behind the reunification of the IPP was O'Brien's UIL. Initially, Dillon had taken a cautious approach to the League, seeing it as a competitor to the party. Healy had distrusted the League, and Redmond was no more than lukewarm in his support. Yet all three men, despite their reticence, acknowledged that the UIL was sweeping the different factions together and, if they did not respond positively, they would be marginalised as constitutional Nationalism sought to reassert itself in the new century.

The IPP under Redmond

Although the reunification of the Irish party was greeted with enthusiasm in Ireland, Redmond was under no illusions about the nature of the union. The rivalry among the old parliamentary factions remained and the question of the party's relationship with the UIL still had to be resolved. Almost immediately after his election to the Chairmanship, Redmond was coming under attack from O'Brien who was questioning the party's attitude to the League. This uncertainty was ended, apparently to O'Brien's satisfaction, when Redmond was compelled to throw in his lot with the League at the Convention held in June 1900, when the UIL was officially accepted as the party's national organisation. The merger was bitterly opposed by Healy who had always distrusted the League, and the second half of 1900 saw open warfare between Healy and the League. When Healy refused to dissolve his own movement, the People's Rights Association, he was formally expelled from the party in December 1900. Although Healy's following was considerably smaller than it had been during his quarrel with Dillon during the 1890s, he was sufficiently powerful, enjoying the loyal support of Murphy's *Independent*, to remain a constant thorn in the side of the reunited party. In fact, Healy had only scraped home in the general election of October 1900, an election which the IPP had fought with great efficiency through the local machinery of the UIL. The general election had also given William O'Brien the opportunity to return to Westminster as one of the party's Cork MPs. On the surface it appeared that his organisation, the UIL, now dominated Nationalist politics and exercised decisive influence on Redmond. The reality, however, was different, as the UIL, despite its growth after 1900, fell between the agrarian and Nationalist stools.

O'Brien was determined to maintain the League's radicalism, but his hope that a reunited Irish party would identify with agrarian militancy was not fulfilled. Publicly, Redmond gave his approval to a new wave of agrarian agitation in 1901-2 which expressed itself in public protest meetings, boycotting of graziers and occasional outbreaks of violence. Not surprisingly, this drew an uncompromising response from the Conservative government and a return to coercion. By the spring of 1902 the counties of Cavan, Leitrim, Sligo, Mayo, Roscommon, Clare, Cork, Tipperary and Waterford had been proclaimed, and a stream of arrests, including a number of MPs, had taken place. Soon, Redmond was urging caution and pressing O'Brien to limit the agitation. O'Brien was aware that the UIL, his real power base, had changed its character since its merger with the party in 1900. Then, he believed that the growth of an active organisation in the country with the goal of land ownership, the only demand which would encourage widespread participation in a new struggle, would force the government at Westminster to listen to the IPP. However, it was in the west that land hunger and agrarian distress were most acute and, when the UIL spread outside the west, as it did successfully in 1900-2, it lost its radical edge. At the time of the merger it had 653 branches and 63,000 members but, within a year, this had shot up to 989 branches with nearly 100,000 members. As the League spread into Munster and Leinster, its agrarian objectives were diluted, and it assumed a political character with electoral, not agrarian, aims. Indeed in many areas the UIL quickly developed into a simple fund-raising organisation for the local MP.

By 1902, therefore, the Irish party had really suffocated the radicalism of the UIL which became synonymous with the party machine. The attitude of the Catholic Church may have contributed to this because, by 1900, the church, which had previously opposed the League, realised that it would have to accept the League as the national organisation and try to work within it. The church was keen to see emigration fall, and this would only be achieved through major land reforms which would lead to the division of the large grazing farms. Yet herein lay another problem for the League. While the grazier was the prime target of UIL agitation, there was nothing to stop the grazier being a good Nationalist. Many of the graziers were strong Nationalists, and it is remarkable to note how many of the UIL leaders at local level were graziers themselves. Certainly, the UIL never achieved rural mobilisation on the same scale as the Land League and was too constitutional to engage in the agrarian violence which had proved so effective during the Land War. The UIL's spread into the other provinces had attracted new members but, outside the west, there was a noticeable lack of enthusiasm for the League's agrarian programme.

Not surprisingly, these developments promoted discord within the agrarian movement, and this was to have serious consequences for the parliamentary movement. The party's lukewarm support for agrarian agitation seems to have convinced O'Brien that a new strategy was necessary and, as a result, he began to advocate co-operation with the progressive landlords who had answered Shawe-Taylor's call for a Land Conference. Moreover, by the summer of 1902 it was clear that the smallholders of the west were becoming weary of the agitation. O'Brien threw himself into the four-man tenants' delegation, and the consultations produced a unanimous report that formed the basis of the 1903 Wyndham Land Act. This crucial piece of legislation, however, brought Nationalist divisions to the surface. O'Brien now believed that the preparations for the 1903 legislation pointed the way ahead, arguing that the process of conciliation, or 'conference plus business', was a panacea for all of Ireland's problems. This view was bitterly opposed by a significant section of the party. Davitt criticised the Land Act and the *Freeman's Journal* ran a series of savage articles denouncing O'Brien, but the most decisive opposition voice belonged to John Dillon. In August 1903, only two weeks after the passage of the Land Act, Dillon told his constituents in Swinford, County Mayo, that the legislation contained serious flaws but, more significantly, he attacked the whole policy of conciliation with the traditional enemy, the Unionist landlords, stating that only sustained agitation would bring concessions from the government at Westminster [32]. The 'Swinford Revolt', as it became known, threw the whole issue of party unity back into the melting pot. Redmond had co-operated with O'Brien in their dialogue with the landlords but, despite constant cajoling, he refused to come out openly against the Dillonite line. Such a refusal increased O'Brien's sense of frustration and contributed to his hasty and unwise decision to resign in November 1903. The party was still intact, but the furore meant that an opportunity was missed to develop co-operation with Lord Dunraven and his enlightened associates on the landlord side, as Redmond sided with Dillon and the other critics of landlordism. On the other hand, a quick survey of the political situation at Westminster, where it looked as if the Liberals would soon take over the reins of government, may have influenced

Redmond in thinking that conciliation with Irish Unionists was not his best option.

Although Redmond had turned his back on co-operation with the landlords, Dunraven was determined to press ahead, believing that the successful resolution of the land problem could be repeated if a similar strategy was used to tackle the political problem. Consequently, the Land Committee, whose members had remained in contact following the Wyndham Act, reconstituted itself as the Irish Reform Association and, in August 1904, it issued a manifesto calling for "the devolution to Ireland of a larger measure of self government than she now possesses". In September the Reform Association made public the details of its devolution proposals, which suggested that a new Irish Financial Council should be given administrative control over Irish expenditure. For the group of progressive Unionist landlords working in tandem with Dunraven the maintenance of the Union was deemed vital, but they felt that a modest scheme of devolution would pose no threat to the Union. The majority of Unionists, however, and particularly those in Ulster, regarded the devolution proposals as a sinister development, which would lead to the implementation of Home Rule by installments. In fact, the detailed devolution proposals had come largely from the pen of Sir Anthony MacDonnell who had served as Under Secretary at Dublin Castle since 1902, a post he had been persuaded to accept by the promise that he would be given a free rein in the Irish administration. Indeed MacDonnell had considerable administrative ability and had enjoyed an outstanding career in the Indian civil service. Yet he lacked political skills, and the fact that he was a Catholic, a self confessed Liberal with a brother in the IPP, had already caused Unionists to be wary of the new Under Secretary. Their suspicions were naturally reinforced, when MacDonnell's role in the preparation of the devolution scheme came to light. Early in 1905, Unionists carried their attack on MacDonnell to the House of Commons, but the revelation that MacDonnell had been given power over policy formulation saw attention shift from Ireland's leading civil servant to the political head of the Irish Office, the Chief Secretary. Although Wyndham dissociated himself from the devolution proposals in a letter to *The Times*, the Unionists increased their attacks on the Chief Secretary, believing that he had colluded with MacDonnell in the preparation of the scheme. This was certainly untrue, but Wyndham's position had become so weak that he had no alternative other than resign, a decision he took in March 1905 [33].

The devolution debacle exposed the limitations of constructive Unionism which had obviously failed to move public opinion in Ireland. Most Unionists felt that the government had gone too far in its attempt to placate Irish Nationalism and, crucially, the conciliation strategy also drew savage criticism from the IPP. Redmond had been in the United States when the devolution proposals were made public and, though initially supportive, the IPP leader was soon having second thoughts. Once again, it was left to Dillon to state the orthodox Nationalist position. He denounced the scheme as a delaying tactic which might threaten national unity and stifle the demand for Home Rule. Redmond had no difficulty in concurring, as thoughts now turned ahead to a general election though, to the IPP's surprise, the Conservative government managed to limp on in office until December 1905. For the last nine months of its life the Balfour government returned to first principles as far as Irish policy was concerned. Nothing would be done which interfered in any way with the

Union and, meanwhile, the imposition of a tough law and order policy in rural Ireland would be given priority. Responsibility for overseeing this change of policy was passed appropriately to Walter Long, a hard-line Unionist, whose appointment as Chief Secretary did much to reassure Irish Unionists who had felt betrayed by the government during the devolution crisis. Certainly, Long frequently sought the advice of influential Irish Unionists and took an uncompromising stance on the issue of agrarian crime, though his retention of MacDonnell as Under Secretary undoubtedly raised a few Unionist eyebrows.

While Irish Nationalists were unhappy with Long's appointment, they were confident that his tenure would be brief. Early in December 1905, Balfour finally resigned and the Liberal leader, Sir Henry Campbell-Bannerman was asked to form a government. Having done this, Campbell-Bannerman opted for a general election in the following month. The general election of January 1906 offered proof of Redmond's success in restoring party discipline. The IPP won 81 seats but, of these, 73 were gained without a contest. On the eve of the election Redmond had struck a deal with O'Brien, ensuring that O'Brien and a number of allies would be returned without a Nationalist challenge, thus allowing the O'Brienites to appear as a minority group within the IPP. The only black spot in the party's triumph was North Louth, which continued to return the maverick Healy as an independent Nationalist. The overall Nationalist total rose to 83 when T P O'Connor again won the Scotland Division of Liverpool. The Westminster picture was more dramatic as the Liberals won a landslide victory, emerging from the general election with a clear overall majority. The Conservatives had polled disastrously, dropping from 369 to only 157 seats. The Liberal victory naturally raised expectations in Nationalist Ireland, but the precise direction of the new government's Irish policy was by no means clear. In mid-November 1905 Redmond along with O'Connor, the IPP's ambassador in London, had a secret meeting with Campbell-Bannerman at which the Liberal leader pledged his support for Home Rule but, realistically, concluded that it would not be possible to pass full Home Rule in the next parliament. This statement of Liberal policy was confirmed when Campbell-Bannerman spoke in Stirling a week later, stressing that any new measure introduced for Ireland should be consistent with and contribute to the long term goal of Home Rule [34]. Immediately, Rosebery denounced the speech, which he knew threatened to reopen old wounds in the Liberal party, but his influence was now on the decline. In effect, the Liberals had groped their way to a new Irish strategy, which involved the taking of short and careful steps towards Home Rule rather than one long and precarious stride.

It seems clear that the Liberal landslide came as a shock to Redmond. He had expected the IPP to hold the balance of power and the manoeuvring undertaken before the election was based on the assumption that his party would tip the scales in the new parliament. Otherwise, the IPP leadership would surely have pressed Campbell-Bannerman to spell out the details of the interim measure, or measures, he had in mind. Still, characteristically, Redmond was optimistic, trusting in Campbell-Bannerman's personal commitment to Home Rule and confident that his government was more than merely sympathetic to the Irish Nationalist position. The Prime Minister appeared to live up to this optimism, when he promised the new parliament that, henceforth, Ireland could expect to be governed "in accordance with

Irish ideas". Of course, this was a vague statement which failed to commit the incoming Liberal government to any decisive step towards Home Rule. What soon became clear was that the new administration was not going to give priority to any interim Home Rule measure, or even to Irish affairs in general, a state of affairs determined by the government's independence of the Irish vote in the new parliament. The Liberals had not been elected to settle the Irish Question, but to implement the great range of social reforms promised in their manifesto. These took precedence during 1906, leaving the IPP with no alternative other than wait patiently until the government had time to consider the details of a new Irish initiative.

Unfortunately, Irish patience quickly wore thin, a development hastened by the impact of the new Liberal Chief Secretary, James Bryce. Though his Home Rule credentials were never in doubt, it soon became clear that Bryce lacked the authority to make significant changes in the day-to-day administration, which could have given encouragement to Nationalists. Worse still, Bryce failed to strike up any kind of friendly relationship with the IPP leaders who found him remote and indecisive. Their exasperation lasted until the end of 1906, when Bryce resigned his post to become British Ambassador in Washington. Yet Irish disappointment with the Liberal administration could not be attributed solely to the ineffective Bryce. Closer examination of the Liberals' radical social programme unsettled a large number of MPs in the Irish party, whose own instincts were a good deal more conservative. More significantly, the delay in producing new Irish proposals led a growing number in the party to question the Liberal government's commitment to Home Rule. It was not unreasonable to conclude that one section of the cabinet regarded Home Rule as an unnecessary risk which could jeopardise the whole Liberal programme of social reform.

This was the situation which confronted Bryce's replacement, Augustine Birrell, who took office in January 1907. In Dublin Castle Birrell found MacDonnell, who had been given a new lease of life by the Liberal election victory, working on a new version of his devolution scheme. What the Liberals had to do was produce a measure which went far enough to satisfy the IPP, but stopped short of incurring the wrath of the House of Lords. Early soundings revealed that this would prove a difficult task, as both Redmond and Dillon dismissed initial draft proposals as inadequate. The government's final modifications were introduced by Birrell as the Irish Council Bill on 7 May 1907. Emphasising the moderate character of the bill which they claimed represented no movement at all towards Home Rule, the Liberals nevertheless hoped that the Nationalists could be persuaded to regard it as genuine, if modest, progress. The bill itself proposed the establishment of a 107 member Irish Council, 82 of whom would be elected on the local government franchise with the remaining 25 to be nominated by the government. To this Council the government would transfer the control of eight key departments of the Irish administration, the most important of which were Education, Local Government and Agriculture. Significantly, the Council would have no powers over taxation or law and order, and decisions taken by the new body could be vetoed by Westminster acting through the Lord Lieutenant. Not surprisingly, the Unionists attacked the measure which they regarded as a replay of the previous devolution scheme, but the crucial factor for the government would be Nationalist reaction to the bill. Initially, Redmond, though critical of the bill's deficiencies, refused to dismiss the measure out of hand. His caution was necessary, as a National Convention was due to meet on 21 May to give its verdict on the new bill. Yet when it became apparent that opinion in Ireland was fiercely hostile to the new measure, Redmond abandoned his previous caution and in his speech to the Convention denounced the Irish Council Bill as "utterly inadequate". Faced by the IPP's rejection of the bill, the government gratefully dropped the measure at the beginning of June [35].

The Irish Council Bill had turned into a disaster for the IPP, as the high hopes that the Liberal alliance would bring substantial gains were dashed. The episode revealed the party's lack of influence at Westminster because, with the Liberals enjoying such a big majority, the IPP found it difficult to bring pressure to bear on the government. It was also apparent, moreover, that many Liberals continued to regard Home Rule as an unnecessary danger. The lesson drawn by Redmond and his colleagues was that the gradualist approach to Home Rule actually diminished its prospects and, consequently, only the undiluted Gladstonian version should be considered. Yet this forced them back to the unpleasant truth that the ultimate success of any Home Rule measure was out of their hands and would only come from the retention of the Liberal alliance. Thus for the Irish Nationalists, Home Rule became the 'English Question', as they sought to translate Liberal goodwill into a specific legislative commitment. The fiasco with the Irish Council Bill had also caused great embarrassment for the IPP at home, where it provoked serious dissension within the party. In reality, the measure had been rejected by the Nationalist public, and the leaders who appeared sympathetic to it were savagely attacked. The *Freeman's Journal* was hostile and the Catholic Church was unequivocal in its opposition to the bill. Moreover, the most radical elements of the UIL were highly critical of those leaders suspected of flirting with the measure. Redmond, in particular, had not ruled out acceptance of the bill choosing to remain non-committal until Nationalist opinion had been ascertained. Yet once he sensed how public opinion was moving, Redmond acted quickly to reject the bill. Even though he had been frustrated by the bill's limitations, Redmond must have been tempted to accept the measure hoping that, if the Irish Council proved successful, more powers would be transferred to Dublin. This might have reassured Irish Unionists and made it easier for the Liberals to move forward steadily in the direction of Home Rule. However, his fear that the acceptance of a measure which fell far short of Irish expectations would expose the party to attacks from more extreme Nationalist opinion, as Dillon constantly warned, convinced Redmond that rejection was the safer option.

By the summer of 1907, therefore, Redmond must have been relieved by the government's decision to introduce a new piece of land legislation which diverted attention away from the embarrassment of the Irish Council Bill. Birrell, who had offered to resign following the bill's withdrawal, was keen to meet one of Dillon's longstanding demands by introducing a new measure for the restoration of evicted tenants. The Evicted Tenants Act, passed in late August 1907, led to 3,500 tenants being either reinstated or given new holdings on some 26,000 acres which had been acquired through compulsory purchase by the Estates Commissioners. Yet, significantly, the legislation fell well short of what Birrell had intended because the bill had been mutilated by the House of Lords. Naturally, this increased the frustrations of Nationalist representatives and reminded them, and the Liberals, that the Lords remained a serious barrier to the prospects for progress on the Irish Question. Birrell enjoyed more success with the 1909 Land Bill which tidied up the loose ends left by the ground-breaking Wyndham Act and introduced a limited element of compulsion. While it was also subjected to amendments in the Upper House, the essential elements demanded by the IPP remained, thus allowing the 1909 Land Act to give fresh impetus to the whole process of land purchase in Ireland.

The most significant piece of Irish legislation during this period, however, was the 1908 Irish Universities Act, which finally met the Nationalist demand for a Catholic University. The new measure gave the Queen's College of Belfast university status and grouped the university colleges of Dublin, Cork and Galway into a National University which, although technically non-denominational, was in effect the Catholic University Nationalist MPs had campaigned for so vociferously. Such an arrangement providing, as it did, one university for northern Protestants and another for southern Catholics was a realistic approach. Previously, the restrictions on students entering Trinity College had been relaxed, but the old university and its links with the Protestant Ascendancy continued to be viewed with great suspicion by the Catholic hierarchy. Nationalists were quick to express their gratitude for the new legislation which offered a much needed reminder of what could be achieved by Irish Nationalists working constructively with the Liberals at Westminster. Moreover, the establishment of the new Catholic University undid some of the damage caused by the Irish Council Bill. The Irish Universities Act also went some way towards repaying the faith in the IPP shown by the Catholic Church which had worked closely with the Nationalists and with the Liberals in the run up to the bill's introduction. In fact, Birrell had been in constant contact with Dr William Walsh, the Roman Catholic Archbishop of Dublin, on the university question [36].

The disappointment over the Irish Council Bill led to a fresh attempt by Nationalists to create a really united IPP, and negotiations began to bring William O'Brien fully back into the fold, a process which was completed by January 1908. This allowed O'Brien and his friends to co-operate with the leadership during the debates on the University Bill. This new spirit of co-operation, however, would not last. O'Brien had stuck doggedly to the belief that the policy of conciliation which had produced the 1903 Land Act was the best course for the party to follow. Pending the introduction of a new Home Rule Bill, O'Brien argued that collaboration with progressive Unionists would produce agreement on new social legislation beneficial to Ireland. He also claimed that the bulk of Nationalist opinion was behind him on this. While this may have been true in 1903, the situation had changed considerably and, by 1908, most of the party shared Dillon's view that co-operation with both the Liberals and the Irish Unionists would be impossible. Moreover, Dillon was still convinced that concessions to Ireland granted by any Westminster government could reduce the demand for a full Home Rule measure. Such tensions were bound, sooner or later, to lead to fresh disagreements. When O'Brien was shouted down as he attempted to explain the virtues of his conciliation policy to the UIL's National Convention in February 1909, he withdrew from the party, this time with Healy in tow, and set about launching a new popular movement, the All-for-Ireland League, which he hoped would repeat the success of the UIL and develop into a moderate centre party capable of challenging the IPP.

In his memoirs O'Brien claimed that the heckling at the 1909 National Convention had been orchestrated by members of the Ancient Order of Hibernians (AOH), a movement which had become a crucial support organisation for the IPP. The AOH was an aggressively Catholic organisation which had its historical roots in the sectarian conflict that had swept Ulster in the late eighteenth century. Its modern roots, however, were to be found in the United States, where it developed as a kind of Catholic freemasonry among the rapidly growing Irish community in the mid-nineteenth century. By the end of the century it had 100,000 members there. Although it generally stayed out of politics, the AOH was broadly Nationalist in sympathy and, following a fund-raising tour of the United States in 1903 by a leading Irish MP, the AOH in America was persuaded to give its backing to the reunited IPP. After two decades of bitter feuding the American and Irish branches of the AOH had come together in 1902. By then the AOH was growing wherever Catholics as a group felt vulnerable and this, of course, included Ireland, particularly Ulster, where the organisation developed as the Orange Order's sectarian rival. Previously, its links with the Ribbon tradition had meant determined opposition from the Catholic Church, which had always frowned upon any secret society but, during the 1890s, the Hibernians in Ireland sought respectability and acceptance by the church. By 1904 the church's formal ban on the AOH as a 'secret society' had been lifted, a move which accelerated its growth all over Ireland. Moreover, the movement acquired greater respectability as it became increasingly linked to the IPP [37].

The political potential of the AOH was first spotted by Joe Devlin, the most gifted newcomer to the Irish party following its reunion in 1900. Devlin had entered parliament as MP for North Kilkenny in 1902 and, in the next year, he was appointed general secretary of the UIL. As a native of Belfast, however, his chief concern in the early stage of his career was the development of northern Nationalism, and he quickly saw how the AOH could provide a powerful local base for the party in Ulster. With the help of the movement he won West Belfast for the IPP at the 1906 general election and, as leader of northern Nationalism with the organisational power of the AOH behind him, Devlin exercised considerable influence on the Nationalist movement as a whole. By 1905 Devlin had become Grand Master of the Board of Erin, the governing body of the AOH which had been established when the movement reunited. With a foot in both the UIL and AOH camps Devlin quickly developed a personal power-base which Redmond could not ignore. At the same time, Devlin was emerging triumphantly from a bitter struggle he had fought with Dr Harry Henry, the Bishop of Down and Connor, who had tried to dominate Nationalist politics in Belfast through his Belfast Catholic Association. Henry's aim was to establish a clerical party in Belfast, a move which Devlin fought against tenaciously, believing that it posed a serious threat to the authority of the IPP.

When Devlin tightened his grip on the AOH in July 1905, the movement framed a new constitution, committing it to the Home Rule policy of the IPP. Thus Devlin controlled the AOH for the benefit of the party, providing it with new organisational strength and an effective instrument for 'getting out' the Nationalist vote at forthcoming elections. Under his direction the AOH expanded rapidly, rising from 10,000 members in 1905 to 60,000 by 1909. It was most successful in Belfast and

County Tyrone, but the Hibernian movement was generally strong throughout Ulster, where it undoubtedly reinvigorated Nationalism. It also managed to spread into Leitrim, Sligo and North Roscommon, and it became a significant force in Dublin City. The movement grew rapidly where it received clerical support, though a number of the hierarchy, particularly Cardinal Michael Logue, remained very hostile to the AOH. Significantly, Devlin's dual role allowed the AOH and UIL to work well together. Where land purchase had taken place following the 1903 act, the AOH smoothly replaced the UIL. Yet, more interestingly, in those areas such as the great grazing ranches of County Roscommon and East Galway where the UIL was still strong, the AOH was able to establish itself in the local market towns, thus ensuring that the two movements worked in tandem. In the towns the AOH provided social facilities, with card-playing a favoured pastime, but it also provided business contacts and quickly developed as a patronage and brokerage machine to ensure that preferential treatment was given to its members in the labour market. Unfortunately, this added to the movement's sectarian image and the IPP, by its association with the AOH in this period, was criticised by both Unionists and more moderate Nationalists for resorting to such an overtly sectarian strategy. Still, with the UIL in decline over much of the country, only the AOH could muster any enthusiasm and provide the party with local organisation. Indeed it was in the political vacuum which characterised the early 1900s that the AOH expanded rapidly.

While it was true that the UIL's appeal to land-hungry peasants made little impact in Ulster, the agrarian movement remained an important force in the west. Evidence of its strength came to light when the UIL took the decision to focus, once again, on agrarian issues following the rejection of the Irish Council Bill in May 1907. In fact, agrarian agitation had surfaced a few months before the Irish Council Bill fiasco, and the starting date for what became known as the Ranch War can be fixed at 14 October 1906. Then Laurence Ginnell advocated the new tactic of cattle-driving to a meeting of young men in his County Westmeath constituency. Ginnell, who was first returned for the county at the 1906 general election, had found a temporary home on the radical agrarian wing of the IPP which, led by Dillon, had routinely condemned the 1903 Land Act, claiming that Irish tenants were being overcharged for their land while Unionist landowners were receiving too large a cash payment. The practice of cattle-driving was taken up enthusiastically in the west with the first such cattle-drive taking place in County Roscommon. Usually, this took the form of cattle being driven off the grazing farms at night and being left to wander along the narrow country roads. The agrarian militants hoped that the targeted graziers would feel so frustrated, and threatened, that they would surrender their lands to avoid further disruption. More incidents followed in the spring of 1907 and the IPP gave its general backing to this new wave of agrarian agitation. The escalation of the agitation in the second half of 1907 saw a total of 292 cattle-drives being reported in the period from August to December, and Birrell came under fire from Irish Unionists who claimed that he was failing to enforce the law. Like all Chief Secretaries, Birrell was faced with the perennial dilemma of striking a balance between letting the agitation blow itself out and demonstrating that the government still possessed the will to rule the country. During the Ranch War Birrell favoured a 'softly, softly' approach, hoping that the country would calm down of its own accord.

In the circumstances this was the best strategy, even though it angered the Unionists, as Birrell knew it was very unlikely that an ordinary jury would convict any offender brought before the courts.

Undoubtedly, Redmond had been embarrassed by the scale of this new wave of agrarian agitation, but his call for caution made little impression on the cattle-drivers. While the old fusion of land and Nationalism had instinctively led the leadership to identify with anti-grazier feeling, Redmond, crucially, would not endorse cattle-driving. In fact, the practice was loudly condemned by a number of senior Catholic clerics, including the influential Archbishop of Tuam and, towards the end of 1907, the militant Ginnell came under pressure from the party to withdraw from the agitation. By the beginning of the following year the practice of cattle-driving had become sporadic, as an increasing number of parliamentarians argued that it was counter-productive and, early in 1910, the agitation fizzled out altogether. Although the Ranch War never reached the levels of previous agitation, it did prove a powerful vehicle for social protest in those areas which were active. Indeed, Unionists claimed that the 1909 Land Act was a surrender to the cattle-drivers. By this stage, however, the divisions within constitutional Nationalism had resurfaced in a manner which made it difficult for agrarian radicals to gain any backing on the land question. O'Brien, who had tried both moderate and extreme strategies, was critical of the 1909 Land Act, arguing that it offered the tenants poor terms, but his defeat on the conciliation programme at the National Convention and his subsequent withdrawal removed him from the equation.

Yet the crucial factor in reducing agrarian agitation in this period had been Wyndham's legislation of 1903, which had enabled the bulk of the tenant farmers to become proprietors. Despite this, the defeat of O'Brien saw the party continuing to pay lip-service to radical agrarianism, even though it could no longer expect those tenants who had become proprietors to support and participate in new land agitation devoid of any relevance for them. While the Ranch War had demonstrated that the lower elements in the rural social strata who had not benefited from the 1903 legislation could still be mobilised, the fact that many of the graziers were prominent figures in the Nationalist movement meant that its potential was always limited. By the beginning of the twentieth century, moreover, land was less of an issue as the rate of urbanisation increased, creating new problems with which constitutional Nationalism had to wrestle. With the land issue fading as a galvanising force for constitutional Nationalism, the party turned to the issue of religion which could also define and organise the Nationalist community. This was achieved through the rapid expansion of the AOH, which became absorbed by the IPP and introduced a new element of Catholic sectarianism to the party. The rise of the AOH allowed northern Nationalists excessive influence on the whole constitutional movement and, not surprisingly, the Hibernians had little time for O'Brien's toleration of Unionism. Thus Devlin, the leader of the Hibernians, and Dillon, the chief opponent of conciliation, became close allies, and together they exercised considerable influence on Redmond who, in spite of his instincts, turned his back on O'Brien's policy of seeking compromise with the progressive elements in the ranks of the Unionist landowners. Yet by persisting with its agrarian rhetoric in the wake of the Wyndham Act, Redmond and the other leaders greatly narrowed the IPP's basis of support in Ireland,

and the party became a vehicle for class and sectional interests.

If the IPP had suffered the loss of its social base, it still retained the clear ideology of Home Rule. This was reinforced after the Irish Council Bill fiasco, when the party again adopted the Dillonite line by concentrating on Home Rule and rejecting interim measures which Dillon had always suspected would suffocate Irish Nationalism and curb the desire for Home Rule. However, the IPP was surely mistaken in this belief, because even the pioneering 1903 Land Act had done nothing to reduce the demand for Home Rule. In addition, Redmond only rejected the Irish Council Bill when he sensed that the Nationalist public was hostile, but the assumption that opinion in the country was more advanced than in the party may have been flawed. While the *Freeman's Journal* and much of the provincial press criticised the bill's inadequacies, this may have proved nothing more than disappointment which could have been overcome by building on the concessions offered by the bill. Yet in adopting the 'Home Rule or nothing' strategy, Redmond ensured that party unity would be maintained, as there was less opportunity for more advanced Nationalists to undermine the IPP's position. Indeed Ireland had entered the twentieth century with a strong parliamentary tradition, and Redmond was trying to develop this by cultivating a more respectable image at Westminster. This helps to explain his opposition to the Ranch War of 1906-10, because he knew that agrarian unrest was frowned upon by his friends in the Liberal party.

It is, nevertheless, too simplistic to describe the IPP as a party of old, conservative, constitutional Nationalists who were being increasingly sucked into the world of Westminster. While it was true that many Irish MPs had first entered politics at the beginning of the Parnell era, when the Land League created Nationalists and gave them a national policy, the fact that the land issue no longer provided Nationalism with the same bedrock of support does not mean that, in the first decade of the twentieth century, old Nationalism was ineffective. Although support for the IPP may have lacked the enthusiasm of the earlier years, Home Rule remained a very popular goal, and even the younger elements that had been attracted to cultural Nationalism continued to give their tacit support to the older generation of Nationalist MPs. The secret in the IPP's success was the ambivalence of the Home Rule idea. For some in the party Home Rule was viewed as a final settlement and the limit of their aspirations, while for others it was simply a stage on the road towards full independence. Encompassing both views was the beauty of the Home Rule ideology and rather than seek to clarify this ambivalence, Redmond's party actively encouraged it. Thus constitutional Nationalism could identify with the enthusiasm which greeted the royal visit in July 1903, and then take a full part in the celebrations, only two months later, to commemorate the Emmet insurrection. For old Nationalism there was no contradiction in this.

The new Nationalism

In the period 1890-1910 the IPP's hegemony was challenged by a new form of Nationalism. The quickening pace of urbanisation, the improvements in education and the general modernisation of society confronted Irish people with a new set of opportunities and problems which sometimes seemed beyond the competence of the

IPP. Previously, its identification with the land question and the support of the Catholic Church were all that was required for the IPP to retain its grip on Nationalist Ireland but, around the turn of the century, an alternative basis for the development of Irish national consciousness emerged. The idea that Ireland had a distinctive cultural identity took hold. Of course, interest in Ireland's language and culture was not new, but what had enabled cultural Nationalism to establish a firm footing in the early 1890s was the collapse of Parnellism. This caused an identity crisis within Irish Nationalism and, for a minority of the more politicised middle classes, the Gaelic revival offered a way ahead. The ousting of Parnell and the bitter feuding and faction fighting which followed led an increasing number to feel disillusioned with mass politics. In turning their backs on what they regarded as the failure of parliamentary agitation, this group was drawn to cultural Nationalism, which not only offered an escape from the discredited methods of the IPP but also provided an opportunity to rise above the often shabby and degrading world of political Nationalism.

Before the 1890s cultural regeneration had been kept in check by Parnell's success, but his fall lifted the block on cultural and literary activity and allowed the younger generation, who had felt shut out by established Nationalism, a chance to express their nationality in a new way. Old Nationalism's insistence that politics had to come before culture was called into question by the apparent failure of parliamentary politics in the early 1890s, and the defeat of the second Home Rule Bill removed the need to postpone all cultural activity until self government had been achieved. The most distinctive feature of this new Nationalism was its emphasis on the revival of the language and, in this, the Irish experience was similar to that of central Europe. Some years earlier in Austria-Hungary, the Magyar, Czech, Serb and Croat languages had all enjoyed a revival and, in each case, the effect had been to raise national consciousness in the relevant parts of the multi-national empire. The language revival caught the IPP off-guard because, while a number of senior figures such as Healy and O'Brien wanted to preserve the language, the party, in general, did not share their interest. Thus the language became another issue in the on-going generational conflict which was a significant feature of contemporary Ireland. Still, it was the successful mobilisation of Irish political Nationalism under Parnell which, in a sense, created the conditions for cultural Nationalism to flourish.

An early indication that something was stirring beneath the surface came with the formation of the Gaelic Athletic Association (GAA) in Thurles, County Tipperary, on 1 November 1884. The aim of this new movement was the promotion of Irish sports, principally hurling, football and handball, which were perceived to be under threat from 'foreign' games such as rugby, cricket, soccer and tennis [38]. The key figure in the formation of the GAA had been Michael Cusack, and he received powerful clerical backing from Dr T W Croke, Archbishop of Cashel. Earlier, Croke had been a notable supporter of the Land League agitation, but it was the GAA which allowed this committed Nationalist a better opportunity to denounce English culture and draw attention to what he regarded as Irish subservience to this culture. Croke became the first patron of the GAA and gave his name to Croke Park, the Dublin headquarters of the movement. Although some of the Catholic clergy were suspicious of the GAA, a potential rival in rural Ireland, the movement did attract a considerable number of conservative clerics, many of whom were concerned about the growing influence of English urban culture on the youth of Ireland. Gaelic games, the clergy believed, provided an effective means of channelling the dangerous passions of youth into harmless physical activity. The GAA also attracted a significant number of Fenians, and at least four of the seven men who attended the inaugural meeting were Fenians. In fact, in these early years, a series of disputes between these republicans and the clergy threatened to tear the movement apart.

As the movement spread throughout the country, its anti-English bias became more evident. It initiated a controversial ban on all English games, which prevented its members from playing or even being associated with such games and, significantly, it excluded from participation policemen, soldiers and other individuals associated with 'Britishness'. The structure of the GAA fostered the development of local patriotism, as neighbouring parishes vied for their own county title and then the thirty-two counties contested the All-Ireland Championships in both hurling and football. Such competition transformed football and hurling from participatory to spectator sports, which benefited from the improvements in railway transport and the increasing prosperity that meant a growing number had the money to spend on such leisure pursuits. This sporting activity had, of course, a powerful political undercurrent and, while it certainly raised local interest and pride, the GAA also made a major contribution to the revival of national feeling in rural Ireland.

A second indication that something was stirring beneath the surface was the launch of the Dublin University Review in 1885. It was established by a group of young Protestants and led by Charles Oldham and T W Rolleston, both recent graduates from Trinity College. Whereas the GAA attracted a very large number of members, the Dublin University Review represented a tiny, elitist, Protestant ginger group which followed a tradition of Anglo-Irish Protestant interest in cultural Nationalism. In the early 1840s Thomas Davis had used *The Nation* to promote interest in Ireland's cultural past, hoping that the discovery of a common heritage might bring the two religions together. Davis provided the Protestant Nationalists of the Dublin University Review with inspiration, and a measured analysis of recent political developments convinced them that Irish Protestants had to be reconciled to the inevitability of an autonomous democratic Ireland and encouraged to play a leading role in this development.

It was the Dublin University Review which gave two of the most prominent figures in Ireland's cultural regeneration, Douglas Hyde and W B Yeats, the opportunity to put across their revivalist message. In December 1891 Yeats and Rolleston founded the Irish Literary Society of London and it was followed, in May 1892, by the establishment of the National Literary Society in Dublin, which held its inaugural lecture on 16 August 1892. The National Literary Society wanted to create a new school of literature based on old Irish myths and legends, and a collection of such folk-tales published by Yeats in 1893, *The Celtic Twilight*, accurately characterised this literary strand of the 'Irish revival'. Interest in such Irish themes had been stirred by the work of another Protestant Irishman, Standish O'Grady, whose *History of Ireland: The Heroic Period*, which appeared in 1878, popularised Celtic mythology. Significantly, it was O'Grady who brought the mythical hero, Cuchulainn, to life, and this heroic view of the Irish past provided the basis for much of the revivalist writing.

Yeats was the dominant figure in this literary revival, and he conceived a national literature free from contemporary English influence and grounded in an idealised vision of Ireland's Gaelic past. Yet the construction of such high culture meant that his ideas had difficulty in breaking out of the elite intellectual circle around him. Moreover, how could he explain the contradiction in a literature steeped in Ireland's Celtic past, but written in English?

The Gaelic League and the Irish Ireland movement

The establishment of the Society for the Preservation of the Irish Language in 1876 gave an indication that interest in the revival of the spoken language remained strong for a committed minority of middle class activists. Yet this group failed miserably to attract popular support, and it was only the failure of parliamentary politics, highlighted by the appalling depths to which old Nationalism sank at the 1892 general election, that encouraged these enthusiasts to press their case for revival of the language. This case was brilliantly articulated in a lecture which Hyde delivered to the National Literary Society in November 1892. The title of his address, 'The Necessity for de-Anglicising Ireland', paraphrased its content. Hyde warned that the distinguishing features of Irish nationality were being steadily eroded by the growing influence of English culture, and he pleaded with all Irishmen, Catholic and Protestant, to abandon everything English before they lost all sense of their separate Irish identity. Although he had worked closely with Yeats and the Anglo-Irish literary movement, Hyde was convinced that it was the revival of the Gaelic language which offered the best protection against English influences [39].

Hyde's lecture had provided a clear and persuasive argument for reviving the language and, on 31 July 1893, he became a co-founder and first President of the Gaelic League. The son of a Church of Ireland rector from Sligo, Douglas Hyde grew up in County Roscommon and learned Irish from the rural peasant community. From these country neighbours Hyde also uncovered an amazing store of myths and legends, and he further broadened his horizons by acquiring a taste for snuff and poteen. His great passion for the language had led to his involvement in a number of organisations and, by 1893, therefore, he was well known among the urban middle class intelligentsia whose interest in the revival of the language he had helped to foster. His famous lecture to the National Literary Society on 'The Necessity for de-Anglicising Ireland', advocating a full-blooded revival of the language as the core of a general return to native civilisation confirmed him as the pre-eminent figure in the whole Gaelic revival movement. Hyde, from the outset, disavowed any political aims, determined that this cultural revival would concentrate on linguistic Nationalism. Despite his extraordinary literary talents, however, he was guilty of political naivety. By insisting that most Irish Nationalists were illogical, as they condemned English domination without seeing the need to preserve the language, the single most important distinguishing feature of Irish separateness, Hyde was making a political statement. Certainly, others who joined him in the Gaelic League had no doubt that the driving force behind the cultural revival was Nationalism.

One of those most influenced by Hyde had been Eoin MacNeill who came from an Ulster Catholic middle class family. Growing up in Glenarm, County Antrim, MacNeill, like Hyde, had not been a native speaker, but he was to learn Irish in a search for his personal roots. While working as a junior civil servant in Dublin, MacNeill carried out extensive research into Ireland's Gaelic past, quickly establishing himself as a leading authority on the subject. Indeed, his academic prowess was recognised when he was appointed as the first Professor of Early and Medieval Irish History at University College Dublin (UCD) in 1908. Still, MacNeill was a man of action, not a stuffy intellectual, and this led to his involvement in the language revival. Inspired by Hyde's famous lecture, MacNeill published 'A Plea and a Plan for the Extension of the Movement to Preserve and Spread the Irish Language' in March 1893 and, shortly afterwards, he made the arrangements to bring together a small number of enthusiasts who formed the Gaelic League. Among the exclusive group summoned to meet in Dublin on 31 July 1893 was Father Eugene O'Growney, Professor of Irish at Maynooth, the Catholic seminary in County Kildare. Both Hyde and MacNeill were well known to O'Growney, and together these three are credited with the formation of the Gaelic League, though Hyde as the organisation's most eloquent propagandist was the key figure. This combination of southern Protestant, southern Catholic and northern Catholic seemed an appropriate leadership for a movement whose constitution declared that "no matter of religion or political difference shall be admitted into the proceedings". It was hoped that the organisation would bring together different cultures sharing the same aim or, in Hyde's words, use "the language as a neutral field upon which all Irishmen might meet". While this was a laudable objective, it proved difficult in practice to divorce the cultural and the political in contemporary Ireland.

As with Hyde, MacNeill's conception of the language movement was non-sectarian, but it had profound political and, indeed, religious implications. In his writings MacNeill drew a distinction between countries like England, which he described as a political nation, and countries like Ireland, which he saw as a cultural nation. His conclusion that Ireland was not only different, but superior, naturally led some cultural Nationalists to consider the option of political separation. In searching for the roots of Irish nationality, MacNeill dismissed the contributions of mainly Protestant Nationalist leaders in the late eighteenth century, instead arguing that these roots were to be found in the remote Gaelic past. He claimed that this Irish nation had been submerged by the Williamite conquest in 1691, but was convinced that it could be reawakened by the Gaelic League. Thus in denouncing the tradition of political Nationalism as established in the late 1700s, MacNeill implicitly undervalued the Protestant contribution to Ireland. Moreover, in his desire to take the language to the masses, he thought that this could only be achieved through working closely with the patriotic elements among the Catholic clergy, whom O'Growney had helped to influence during their training at Maynooth. MacNeill believed that previous attempts to revive the language had been unsuccessful, as they had been too elitist, but he was determined that the Gaelic League should become a mass movement [40].

The task of reviving the language was a daunting one. It had been in decline since the middle of the eighteenth century and, by 1801, it was estimated that only 50 per cent of the population spoke monolingual Irish. Its decline in the nineteenth century, however, was staggering. By 1851 the figure for those speaking only Irish had fallen to 5 per cent, and most of these lived in the poorest and most remote districts in the west of Ireland which, of course, had been devastated by the famine. Where other languages were dying out in three generations, the Irish language was dying within two generations. In the second half of the nineteenth century parents were determined that their children should learn English, a task performed effectively for them by the national school system. But they were equally determined that children should not speak Irish at all. Only by taking such action could parents give their children an opportunity to make progress in a world of increasing literacy. Together, the pressure towards assimilation and the desire of Irish people to survive in a modern world were killing the language. By 1901 the figure for those whose only language was Irish had fallen to 0.5 per cent and, by this stage, the number who were bi-lingual, speaking Irish and English, was down to 14 per cent.

It was against this depressing backdrop that the Gaelic League sought to revive the use of the language. Initially, the League grew very slowly and, by 1897, only 43 branches had been formed. One of its few achievements in the 1890s had been Hyde's successful campaign to force the Post Office to accept parcels and letters addressed in Irish. While this provided useful propaganda, it made little impression in the overall struggle to revive the language, and the League was unable to achieve the ambitious goals it had outlined. In fact, despite its efforts, the Irish-speaking area, or Gaeltacht, continued to reduce in size. In these early years, the organisation failed to realise MacNeill's declared aim of appealing outside the educated strata, or Catholic intelligentsia, directly to the people. Instead, it concentrated on establishing new Gaelic journals, sponsoring weekend literacy camps and publishing Irish literature and school textbooks. Although it did attract the support of a small group of sympathetic Protestants in this formative period, its early membership was predominantly urban, bourgeois, well-educated and Catholic with the clergy often in the vanguard. While these early members were genuinely enthusiastic in their attempts to revive Gaelic culture, their idealism did not translate easily into practical solutions. At the core of Hyde's de-Anglicisation philosophy lay his rejection of an English culture which had been moulded by nineteenth century capitalism. Although this anti-materialism struck a chord with a section of the Catholic intelligentsia, it had little relevance for the bulk of the Irish population who wished to benefit from the process of modernisation that the country was experiencing around the turn of the century.

Interest in the Gaelic League, however, increased sharply around 1900. By then the organisation was able to reap the rewards of all the enthusiastic hard work and boundless energy shown by the leadership during the early years. Still, the most important factor behind the sudden rise in League membership was the war in South Africa. The Boer War, which lasted from October 1899 to May 1902, had the effect of heightening national feeling in Ireland, as all shades of Nationalist opinion had little difficulty in identifying with the Boers who were fighting for their independence against the might of the British Empire. This provoked a powerful anti-imperialist Nationalism which was most easily expressed through simple anti-English feeling. The impact of the Boer War had helped to move the IPP towards reunification, but it also stimulated interest in the new Nationalism which, at the time, was most conspicuously illustrated by the Gaelic League. New branches of the League were established, and the number of new members rose steadily. By 1901 there were around 100 branches, and this doubled during the following year. By 1904 there were 600 branches and a total membership of around 50,000.

A significant number of these new members were former emigrants who had returned to Ireland and were eager to participate in something which offered more potential than the rather dreary IPP. Most of the new members, however, tended to be young people of ambition and talent from the towns, who felt excluded from politics by the established forces of old Nationalism. The Gaelic League also attracted a number of IRB activists who wanted to keep the republican flame alight and felt that the growing League might provide the vehicle for such an objective. New members also came from the ranks of the clergy, as an increasing number of priests believed that the organisation offered the best bulwark against English popular culture which was gaining in influence and threatening to secularise Irish society. In addition, the movement became a home for a small group of enthusiastic social reformers who had been frustrated by the conservatism of the IPP and hoped that the League might advance the cause of social reform in Ireland. Among these reformers were a number of prominent women who sought to advance Irish feminism through the channel of the Gaelic League. Interestingly, this small group first made an impact in Unionist Belfast, where the League managed to attract some Protestant members. There the principal figures were Alice Milligan and Anna Johnston, who wrote under the pen name Ethna Carbery. Together they formed the periodical, *Shan Van Vocht* (The Poor Old Woman) which, during the three years of its existence, published the prose and poetry of leading Nationalist writers [41]. While *Shan Van Vocht* did not disguise its separatist beliefs, a more overtly political group gathered around Maud Gonne, who had connections with the suffragette movement and was the first woman to be associated publicly with the Irish Nationalist cause since the Ladies' Land League had been wound up in 1882. With the help of Countess Markievicz and Frances Sheehy-Skeffington, Maud Gonne founded the Inghinidhe na hÉireann (The Daughters of Ireland), which fully supported Irish separation and opposed the IPP.

The Gaelic League launched its official newspaper, *An Claidheamh Soluis* (The Sword of Light) on 17 March 1899. It had campaigned successfully to have St Patrick's Day recognised as a national holiday and, at the beginning of the new century, the journal led the fight to have Irish introduced to the national school curriculum. The introduction of Irish in the national schools was regarded as vital for the preservation of the language and, by 1904, this objective had been achieved. More publicity was gained in 1909, when the League campaigned successfully to have Irish accepted as a compulsory subject for matriculation to the new National University. The controversy over the place of Irish in the education system had brought the League into conflict with the IPP's deputy leader, John Dillon. The League had led the agitation for Irish to be a requirement for entry to the National University, but it was ironic that Dillon should be in the opposite corner, since he had been one of a small number of Irish MPs with a genuinely strong attachment to the language revival. He disliked any form of compulsion, but the real reason for his opposition to Irish being a compulsory subject for matriculation was his dislike of exclusiveness. He did not want this issue to become an obstacle to the removal of differences between Unionists and Nationalists or Protestants and Catholics, which he saw as the most urgent task facing the Irish nation once Home Rule had been achieved. In the end Dillon lost the argument at the IPP's National Convention in February 1909, as the party moved to reflect the change in attitude to the language among the Catholic middle class [42].

The wishes of the Gaelic League prevailed in this instance, but it would be wrong to assume that the League had become more important than the IPP. Moreover, in view of what happened at Easter 1916, the tendency is to exaggerate the significance of the League at the expense of the IPP. It did become a mass movement, but its membership was still well short of the IPP's, and the party easily remained the dominant force in the 1890-1910 period. Even though the League had made rapid progress, particularly after 1900, it was still tied to the culture of a minority. Nonetheless, the League's prestige had risen to such an extent that Redmond offered Hyde the choice of twenty seats in 1904, but he refused to be tempted by parliamentary Nationalism. For the growing band of young members, however, the League offered self-respect and provided a sense of purpose which had been missing in an Irish society still dominated by the forces of old Nationalism. As it grew, the League took on the appearance of a petty bourgeois movement, attracting civil servants and shop assistants in the larger towns and schoolmasters and the clergy in smaller towns. Indeed, in these smaller towns, the union of priest and schoolmaster was vital to the League's development. The priest was the clerical manager of the local national school and allowed, and frequently encouraged, the use of the building for evening classes which were usually conducted by the resident schoolmaster. The combination of the predominantly urban Gaelic League and the predominantly rural GAA did allow the cultural revival to influence most of the country but, overall, Hyde's wish to revive Irish as a spoken language was not realised. Yet what the League did achieve was to make Irish a widely taught school subject and, by 1909, about one-third of all national schools were teaching Irish as part of the curriculum. Despite his attempts to steer the League clear of politics, Hyde found it impossible to advocate de-Anglicisation without engendering anti-British political feeling. For Hyde, moreover, the fight against modernisation, which was his real motivation, became synonymous with the fight against Anglicisation, and this confusion only increased sectarian divisions and further polarised relations between the Unionist north and Nationalist south. In fact, as the League became more 'political' after 1900, it seems that the number of Protestant members began to decline.

The growing link between Gaelicism and Catholicism was most clearly articulated by D P Moran. Having moved to London in 1888, Moran joined the London branch of the Gaelic League while working as a journalist in the capital. Though he experienced real difficulty in actually learning and speaking Irish, Moran became an active participant in London's Irish revivalist scene. Returning to Ireland in 1898, with the Nationalist celebrations of the 1798 centenary in full swing, Moran was shocked at the level of drunkenness, gambling and immoral literature which, he claimed, were symptoms of demoralisation in society. Immediately, he set about producing a programme for the regeneration of Irish life, promoting it in *The Leader*, the weekly journal which he founded, owned and edited. It made its first appearance on 1 September 1900. While he hoped to foster the language, Moran was wary of the cultural attachment to the misty Gaelic past, arguing that Ireland must have a competitive society, and this would require the practical values of self-reliance, discipline, industry, thrift and sobriety to be instilled in all Irishmen. In particular, Moran denounced publicans and journalists, two groups who figured prominently in the IPP, and argued that much of the corruption in national life could be attributed to the forces of parliamentary Nationalism. Moran was convinced that English culture had permeated Irish life and threatened to suffocate it altogether, a process which he believed the IPP had failed to take account of, never mind reverse. He saw the Gaelic League, with its meetings and social pastimes, as an 'Irish Ireland' alternative to the English music-hall and one which, in the long run, would prevail. In *The Leader*, Moran, a devout Catholic, rejected the desire of so many Nationalists who wanted to rebuild bridges to the Unionist community in Ireland. This, he argued, had perpetuated the weakness of Catholics who now had to assert their claim as a majority. Moran, therefore, really identified Catholicism with Irish nationality, warning that non-Catholics "must recognise that the Irish nation is de facto a Catholic nation" [43].

Moran acknowledged the importance of the language revival in his quest to create a modern Irish nation, which he accepted had its roots in the remote Gaelic past, but he realised that the Gaelic League would not achieve this objective by itself. He placed his hopes for a modern Irish nation on the emerging urban Catholic educated middle class and hoped to link the language revival to the secular aspirations of this class. Thus he hoped that the ideals of the revivalists might be translated into political, social and economic programmes, which would transform Ireland into a modern urban civilisation. Moran's ideas appeared in book form in 1905, and the title, *The Philosophy of Irish Ireland*, was significant, because he had become the leading spokesman for the Irish Ireland movement. In the book, which was based on a series of articles published between 1898 and 1903, Moran developed his concept of Irish Nationalism and blamed Britain as the source of all the evil influences that were, in his opinion, corrupting Irish national values. Irish Ireland was the generic title for the various forms of cultural Nationalism, but its most potent expression was found in the Gaelic League. Not surprisingly, Moran's development of the Irish Ireland ethos led him into conflict with Yeats and his Anglo-Irish literary friends. With the help of Lady Gregory, George Moore and Edward Martyn, Yeats had founded the Anglo-Irish Literary Theatre at the end of 1898, intending to produce plays which would allow creative figures in this literary renaissance to develop 'the Celtic note' in literature and reach a wider audience. Presumably, Yeats also hoped that the theatre would quickly establish itself as an important integral component of the cultural revival, but his group was soon under attack from Moran who described their work as a fraud. Behind Moran's criticism of the Irish Literary Theatre lay his belief that Yeats and his circle belonged to Anglo-Ireland, not Ireland. Matters came to a head in 1907 with the production of J M Synge's play, *The Playboy of the Western World*, in which a youth who kills his domineering father is feted by the young ladies in the locality. The work reflected one of the most powerful themes in Irish rural life, as the older generation sought to exert iron control over the youth. *The Leader* damned the play as pagan, but the real storm erupted when the play opened and was howled down by outraged Irish Irelanders. Such was the bitterness of feeling that the 'Playboy riots' continued for a full week. Anglo-Irish Ireland was now in open conflict with Irish Ireland, but the numbers decided this contest, and Yeats opted to cocoon himself in his circle of aristocratic friends, finally exasperated by what he saw as a squalid, sectarian and narrow-minded Nationalism of the Catholic bourgeoisie and its representatives.

Clashes with Yeats were welcomed by Moran, not just because they provided open criticism and debate, but also because such controversy led to a sharp increase in *The Leader*'s circulation. Unlike many other cultural Nationalists, Moran was blessed with good business sense and he ensured that his project was economically viable. *The Leader* was well marketed and it brought in substantial advertising revenue, with many of the advertisements urging readers to buy Irish goods. He also resented the way in which the best jobs, particularly in the senior ranks of the civil service, were dominated by Protestants, and he used *The Leader* to demand an end to discrimination against Catholics. Under Moran's influence, therefore, many Gaelic Leaguers became exclusive Nationalists, arguing that Irish Nationalism had to develop in a Catholic atmosphere. He won powerful support from the younger clergy but, undoubtedly, this emphasis on the bond between cultural Nationalism and Catholicism caused many Protestants to leave the League, a move which coincided with a more general decline in activity. By the end of 1905 the League had close to 1,000 branches but, thereafter, a steady fall in membership occurred. At this stage, the League was racked by bitter internal wrangling, but the principal reason for its decline was the revival of old Nationalism following the general election victory by the Liberals in 1906. It seems that the prospect of Home Rule led many revivalists to give at least tacit support to the IPP. Indeed even Moran, in spite of his earlier criticisms of the IPP, moved closer to the party after 1906. While he had consistently advocated the need to concentrate on cultural autonomy, leaving political adjustments to follow naturally, Moran had too much practical sense not to be excited by the growing prospect of self government for Ireland. Of course, it should be stressed that the IPP at the time contained several different factions, ranging from moderates like Redmond to more extreme constitutional separatists. Both factions could co-exist amicably under the party umbrella, something which was facilitated by the catch-all ideology of Home Rule. It was with these more extreme elements, a number of whom were active participants in the Irish Ireland movement, that Moran established contact. Two such figures were Richard Hazleton, the MP for North Galway, and John J Horgan, a prominent Nationalist MP in Cork City, both young politicians who contributed to *The Leader*.

Sinn Féin and the IRB

A more direct challenge to the IPP came from Sinn Féin. The key figure in this new group was Arthur Griffith, a printer by trade who had been active in various cultural Nationalist groups before leaving for South Africa in 1897. There he learned, at first hand, of the Boers' struggle against Britain, and he used this experience when he returned to Ireland at the beginning of 1899 to edit a new weekly newspaper the *United Irishman*. This paper enjoyed a more secure financial footing than the similar monthly, *Shan Van Vocht*, whose proprietors Alice Milligan and Anna Johnston were happy to send Griffith their subscription list when they wound up their own publication in March 1899. Griffith's close collaborator, William Rooney, had invited him back, seeing in his old friend the energy and propaganda skills which might pull together the various political and cultural factions engaged in the language revival. Both Griffith and Rooney were dismissive of Hyde's determination to keep the Gaelic League out of politics, arguing that any organisation which sought to promote the idea of a separate Irish identity could not stay out of politics. From the date of its first issue on 4 March 1899, the *United Irishman* banged the separatist drum. Griffith agreed with Moran that cultural regeneration offered a means of mobilising the people to demand an independent modern nation. Like Moran, he was not a native Irish speaker and he too made a determined, if not totally successful, effort to learn the language, appreciating that it was the clearest distinguishing feature of Ireland's separate identity. Yet Griffith had also joined the IRB, remaining a member until 1910, and he gave full vent to his militant Nationalist thinking in the *United Irishman*, consistently advocating self government for Ireland. When Rooney died suddenly in May 1901, Griffith was left to carry the burden of running, and largely writing, the paper by himself.

In these early years the South African influence was crucial to the development of Griffith's thinking. He had been encouraged to go to South Africa by John MacBride, a militant Nationalist friend, who was to remain in the country and take part in the Boer War. MacBride served as second-in-command of an Irish brigade which he had helped to raise. It was drawn from men of Irish origin living in the Transvaal. This helped to arouse interest back in Ireland, where a small group of MacBride's former associates, with Griffith to the fore, came together on 10 October 1899 to form the Irish Transvaal Committee. In February 1900 Griffith and his colleagues on the Irish Transvaal Committee had the opportunity to test the level of popular support for the advanced Nationalist, pro-Boer stance, when a by-election was held in the South Mayo constituency. The vacancy had been caused by Michael Davitt's decision to resign his parliamentary seat as a protest against the war. Griffith and Rooney, who had frequently attacked the IPP and stressed the degenerative effects of parliamentary Nationalism, moved quickly to have MacBride, a native of Westport in Mayo, nominated for the vacant seat. With MacBride still in South Africa the Irish Transvaal Committee ran his campaign against the Irish party's official candidate, but the hope that the popular sympathy for the Boer cause could be translated into solid votes proved unfounded. MacBride polled only 427 votes to the 2,401 cast for the IPP candidate.

This unqualified rejection failed to deter Griffith from establishing a new organisation, Cumann na nGaedheal, which built on the base created by the Irish Transvaal Committee and was officially launched on 30 September 1900. Membership was open to anyone of Irish birth or descent who promised to help restore Ireland to her former position of sovereign independence. This allowed Cumann na nGaedheal to become a rallying point for a number of tiny advanced Nationalist groups which had recently sprung up. The new movement's aims, which emphasised cultural independence and resistance to Anglicisation, were designed to further the cause of national independence and followed a similar pattern to the other groups already in existence. It was a further two years before Griffith was able to outline the basis of a new political strategy. In the interim Cumann na nGaedheal became a magnet for a small number of urban political men and women drawn from the ranks of the petty bourgeoisie, who felt that the ineffective IPP with its limited Home Rule ideology failed to reflect their vision of Irish Nationalism. In October 1902, however, Griffith advocated the new programme which he had borrowed from Hungarian Nationalists. Griffith's 'Hungarian Policy' was based on a form of constitutional separation, advocating the abstention of Irish MPs from the Westminster parliament and the declaration of an Irish state. The method of achievement was to be passive resistance to British rule. These ideas were fleshed out in a pamphlet, *The Resurrection of Hungary, A Parallel for Ireland*, which was published in 1904. The pamphlet, which sold almost 30,000 copies, pushed a reluctant Griffith further into the limelight generated by the new Nationalism. Indeed, by this point, Griffith was seeking to politicise the Gaelic League, using the pages of the *United Irishman* to goad the movement into popular campaigns against particular aspects of British rule [44].

In advocating abstention Griffith was claiming that Irishmen could not expect to have their aspirations met at Westminster. This then was a rejection of the strategy adopted by Parnell and Redmond, both of whom sought to influence English opinion in order to produce a parliamentary majority in favour of Home Rule. Yet despite his temporary membership of the IRB, Griffith was keen to put forward a constitutional solution. As the Irish parliament of the eighteenth century had been bribed into taking its own life, Griffith could argue that the withdrawal of Irish MPs from Westminster and the reconstitution of the Irish parliament was not a revolutionary step, but a return to legality or constitutionality. Here the Hungarian experience seemed to offer an example. Following the crushing of the Hungarian Revolution of 1848-49 the Magyars came to the opinion that they had to find an alternative to armed insurrection if they were to realise their Nationalist aims. This came about when, under the leadership of Francis Deak, the Magyars followed a policy of passive resistance to secure the Ausgleich of 1867, by which Austria-Hungary became a Dual Monarchy. This gave Austria and Hungary a common monarch, but completely separate and autonomous legislatures. The fact that Austria had only conceded these Magyar demands following a humiliating military defeat by Prussia in the previous year was conveniently overlooked by Griffith. While the Hungarian Policy aroused interest in Dublin, it brought Griffith into conflict with Moran who denounced the 'Green Hungarian Band' for its attachment to the Anglo-Irish dominated parliament of the eighteenth century.

While he borrowed political ideas from Hungary, Griffith looked to Germany for economic inspiration. He disliked English liberalism and its attempt to achieve economic hegemony through unfettered capitalism. Moreover, he claimed that England had deliberately reduced Ireland to the level of an agricultural colony when, but for the Act of Union, it could have developed as the co-ruler of the Empire. Griffith was drawn to Friedrich List's idea of autarky, and he believed that Ireland could become a thriving, self sufficient nation. In one of his articles Griffith made the staggering claim that an Irish economy, with new industries protected from competition by high tariffs, could support a population of up to 20 million. Yet such ideas, emphasising self sufficiency and economic independence, aroused further interest in the Hungarian Policy.

Earlier, the question of autarky was not under discussion when, in 1903, members of Cumann na nGaedheal formed the National Council to co-ordinate protests against the royal visit of that year. The Council remained in existence long after the visit and Griffith came to regard it, rather than Cumann na nGaedheal, as the most important Nationalist grouping. Still, for others, neither body seemed capable of making headway, and a breakaway group led by two young Ulstermen, Denis McCullough and Bulmer Hobson, founded the Dungannon Clubs in 1905. While the Dungannon Clubs endorsed most of Griffith's programme, they aimed to establish a republic rather than a Dual Monarchy. All of these groups indicated real interest in advanced Nationalism, but the number of factions, often with overlapping memberships, meant that effort was being wasted. The logical step was to bring these closely related groups together in a new movement which could advance the cause of national independence. Yet it was with great reluctance that Griffith agreed to such a merger. While his associates wanted to create a united movement in order to challenge the IPP, it seems that Griffith was content to concentrate on a small-scale propaganda campaign that would generate interest in his ideas among Dublin intellectuals and gradually permeate other groups including the IPP. Griffith's strategy, therefore, took the long view, but his colleagues did not share his patience.

Seeing the way events were moving, Griffith took the initiative and, at the annual convention of the National Council held in November 1905, he outlined the details of his plans which led ultimately to the formation of a unified movement. The policy, Sinn Féin, meaning simply 'Ourselves', gave the movement its name. In 1906 Griffith's newspaper changed its title to *Sinn Féin*. Nevertheless, the movement towards unity was painfully slow. Most of the activists had been attracted by Griffith's ideas and, naturally, they looked to him for a lead. He, however, was not suited to such a task. He was a very shy, cantankerous and quarrelsome individual who lacked any real political ambition but, despite these limitations, a united movement was eventually established. In April 1907 Cumann na nGaedheal and the Dungannon Clubs amalgamated to form the Sinn Féin League. When the National Council then merged with the League in September 1908, the new body took the name Sinn Féin. It immediately endorsed a new constitution aimed at creating "a prosperous, virile and independent nation". Among its objectives Sinn Féin sought to protect Irish industry, to establish a national bank, to withdraw all voluntary support to the British armed forces and to pursue a policy of non-recognition of the Westminster parliament.

An opportunity for Sinn Féin to test its strength against the IPP had already taken place, as the two had met head-on in the North Leitrim by-election on 24 February 1908. The vacancy had been caused by the resignation of the young sitting Irish party MP, Charles Dolan, in the previous month. This move has been attributed to Dolan's growing interest in Griffith's ideas, but his resignation seems to have been sparked by his disgust at the party's shortcomings during the Irish Council Bill fiasco. Dolan contested the by-election under the Sinn Féin banner, basing his campaign on a promise to abstain from Westminster but, despite frenetic activity on his behalf by IRB activists who visited the constituency, he was unsuccessful. Still, Dolan polled 1,157 votes to the IPP candidate's 3,103 votes, a result which encouraged Griffith and fired a warning to the IPP's leadership that from this point they would have to give serious consideration to this new challenge [45]. Undoubtedly, a good number of the votes cast for Dolan, a gifted orator, would have been personal votes for the former constituency MP. This put Sinn Féin's first venture into national politics in perspective and served as a reminder that the IPP was still the dominant voice of Irish Nationalist opinion.

In fact, the North Leitrim contest marked the high point of Sinn Féin's rise for some years. Soon after, Griffith's attempts to establish a daily evening paper proved to be an expensive failure, and the venture was wound up after five difficult months. Moreover, Sinn Féin was losing members. It had been very much a minority movement with around 100 clubs, but the revival of the Home Rule cause during 1909-10 appeared to sideline Sinn Féin, threatening to consign Griffith's band to a mere footnote in Irish history. Therefore, while Sinn Féin was an important component of the new Nationalism, its impact in the first decade of the twentieth century was negligible. Griffith had given advanced Nationalism a political strategy based on the Hungarian model, and he had aroused interest by making abstention from Westminster a cardinal principle, but Sinn Féin's overall appeal was limited. While differences with its more extreme cousin, the Dungannon Clubs, were smoothed over in the merger of 1907, it was clear that although Griffith was a separatist Nationalist, he was not a republican Nationalist. What he had tried to accomplish was the evolution of an alternative policy which lay between the physical force separatism of the IRB and the constitutional Nationalism of the IPP. Accordingly, Griffith was keen to see Home Rule enacted, though he hoped that it would provide a stepping-stone to an independent Ireland. While Sinn Féin aimed, therefore, to be a broad front for various groups of advanced Nationalists, its membership in reality was Dublin-based, small in number and principally drawn from petty bourgeois critics of old Nationalism.

The final piece in the jigsaw of new Nationalism had much older roots. The interest in cultural Nationalism had given the IRB, established back in 1858, an opportunity to take advantage of the separatist potential present in the myriad of romantic and visionary political movements which had sprung up around the turn of the century. Central to this new Nationalism was an anti-political, or anti-parliamentary, ideology which the IRB hoped to exploit. Operating as a secret society with a distinctly conspiratorial style, the obvious strategy for the IRB to pursue was to infiltrate the various organisations and try to win converts to the cause of physical force separation. The GAA provided an excellent cover for such IRB activity and, from the outset, the IRB worked within the movement spreading the separatist message and recruiting new members to their secret organisation. Indeed, about one half of the GAA's founder members were IRB men and, as the sporting movement grew, the IRB sought to put its men into senior positions at both national and county level. Such was their success that the Catholic Church became alarmed and moved to counter the IRB influence. The result was that much of the early history of the GAA was dominated by a bitter struggle for control of the movement between the IRB and the Catholic Church which, at one point in the 1890s, threatened to destroy the GAA altogether. It was only with the triumph of the Catholic Church, which had always been unsettled by the IRB's conspiratorial efforts, that the GAA overcame these obstacles and began to grow rapidly.

Engaging in bitter disputes was very much part of life for the small numbers involved in the misty world of revolutionary Nationalism. In 1894 a split occurred in

Clan na Gael, the American wing of the IRB which had been established in 1867, and a more radical element joined together to form the Irish National Alliance. Soon, a military wing of the Irish National Alliance appeared, the Irish National Brotherhood and, as it spread in Ireland, it attracted a number of converts from the IRB. For the next few years the IRB quarrelled constantly with the Irish National Brotherhood, and, the bitter feud prevented the IRB from taking full advantage of the favourable circumstances which accompanied the centenary celebrations of 1898. The dispute was ended in 1899 when John Devoy, the senior figure in Clan na Gael, managed to heal the divisions within the republican movement in the United States. Thereafter, the Irish National Brotherhood withered away quickly in Ireland, leaving the IRB to continue with its strategy of infiltrating advanced Nationalist groups in an attempt to influence their direction.

Still, at the beginning of the twentieth century, the IRB was only a shadow of its former self, and its failure to capitalise fully on the Nationalist revival of 1898 led some observers to conclude that the organisation was practically defunct. Its leadership was ageing, and the flow of American dollars had been reduced to a trickle. It was led by three Dublin veterans, P T Daly, Fred Allen and Sean O'Hanlon, all of whom ignored the demands of a younger faction which was keen for the IRB to become more active. In Belfast, nevertheless, a successful purge of the old IRB leadership in the city was mounted by a group of young militants led by Denis McCullough and Bulmer Hobson, the co-founders of the Dungannon Clubs. By 1906 McCullough had been co-opted onto the IRB's ruling Supreme Council, prompting an attempted takeover of the organisation by the militant Ulster group. The old, conservative, traditional leadership, much of whose business was conducted in selected public houses in Dublin, provided a sharp contrast to the young, teetotal militants who were the offspring of the Irish Ireland revival. Soon, McCullough and Hobson were joined by two other figures who were to make a significant contribution to the IRB, Patrick McCartan, who had returned from the USA in 1905 and later became a doctor in his native Carrickmore in County Tyrone, and Sean MacDermott, a Belfast barman who had been born in County Leitrim. Yet, despite their efforts, these 'Young Turks' were failing to make any headway in their attempt to overhaul the organisation.

This was to change, however, with the return of Tom Clarke from the United States in December 1907. Clarke had been born on the Isle of Wight where his father was serving in the British Army. In 1880 Clarke emigrated to America and joined the Clan na Gael movement. By 1883 he was on his way to England on a dynamiting mission, but was arrested by the authorities and sentenced to life imprisonment. Although he was released from Portland prison in September 1898, the harsh treatment he had endured during his fifteen years in jail took a heavy toll on his health. Following his release Clarke returned to the United States where he resumed his clandestine work for the Clan. When he came back to Ireland at the end of 1907, Clarke was determined to revitalise the IRB, and this drew him to the young militants who quickly came to regard him as the father-figure of the movement. Clarke ran a tobacconist's shop in Dublin which became the centre for IRB activity. His rapid elevation to the Supreme Council strengthened the position of the younger elements at the expense of the older generation. Clarke pursued his goal of mounting a future revolutionary strike and in the young militants, whom he attracted like a magnet, Clarke saw the potential for revolutionary action. The clearest indication of their growing influence was in the IRB's decision to establish a Fenian newspaper, a move opposed by the old guard, but Clarke's support for the new venture proved decisive. The paper, *Irish Freedom*, was in circulation from 1910 until its suppression in 1914. It was run by MacDermott, who had established himself as Clarke's lieutenant, Hobson and P S O'Hegarty, a young militant from Cork. *Irish Freedom* aimed to bring a more militant republican viewpoint to the attention of a wider audience. Although the paper was defiantly republican, it adopted a practical approach to the revived interest in the Home Rule cause in 1910, arguing that the IRB could take advantage of either a limited measure of self government for Ireland or the public's anger at Westminster's refusal to pass such a measure. Of more significance to Clarke's circle of young militants in their struggle to win control of the movement was the resignation of the veteran P T Daly as Secretary of the Supreme Council in 1910. This opened the way for MacDermott to become the new Secretary and for Hobson's co-option onto the Supreme Council. The question now was what this militant group would do with its growing influence. The answer came at Easter 1916.

Historiography

Many historians have commented on the importance of the land issue in charting the development of constitutional Nationalism towards the end of the nineteenth century. P Bull's, *Land, Politics and Nationalism: A Study of the Irish Land Question* (Dublin, 1996) offers a sharp analysis of the link between land and Nationalism which, he claims, was forged in the late 1860s and, thereafter, such was the strength of the fusion that the separation of the two issues became impossible in practice. He stresses the importance of the Land League which he views as a political movement that challenged British rule in Ireland, but stresses that the Land War is best understood as running from 1879-1903. In an essay, 'Land and Politics, 1879-1903', which appeared in D G Boyce's (ed), *The Revolution in Ireland, 1879-1903* (London, 1988), Bull insists that the Land League had political as well as agrarian objectives and reminds us that the land issue could be used as a weapon against British rule in general. He claims that Irish Nationalism was given a social base when the national cause was identified, both ideologically and organisationally, with the interests of the tenant farmers. Conversely, W E Vaughan's pamphlet, *Landlords and Tenants in Ireland, 1848-1904* (Dublin, 1984) argues that it is too easy to exaggerate the success of the Land League though, he concludes, there is no doubt that the land question gave Nationalism the opportunity to establish itself in the last two decades of the nineteenth century. In *Land, Politics and Nationalism* Bull returns to look at the importance of the land issue to Nationalism, when he argues that the Plan of Campaign is best regarded as a statement of Dillon's and O'Brien's belief that agrarian agitation was an effective component of an effective Nationalist strategy, rather than an indication that they gave priority to the interests of the tenant farmers.

The IPP's failure to reunite following Parnell's death in October 1891 is examined in F S L Lyons's, *The Irish Parliamentary Party, 1890-1910* (London, 1951) which claims that the question of Parnell's leadership had been so confused with the moral issue that the serious political differences between the Parnellites and the anti-Parnellites were often overlooked. Yet, herein, lay the real reasons for the decade of faction fighting which characterised parliamentary Nationalism during the 1890s. Lyons describes the anti-Parnellite triumph in the 1892 general election as an endorsement of the Liberal alliance, while Foster's, *Modern Ireland* adds that the anti-Parnellite decision to stick with the Liberal alliance rather than return to the militant constitutionalism of the early 1880s was very significant. Lee's, *The Modernisation of Irish Society* qualifies the anti-Parnellite success in 1892 by stressing that Redmond's followers polled well in urban areas, where clerical influence was less crucial. The geography of the IPP split is revealed in T Garvin's, *The Evolution of Irish Nationalist Politics* (Dublin, 1981) which agrees with Lee's claim that, despite the very aggressive nature of the priests' influence at the polls in 1892, there was a strong minority current of popular support for the Parnellite candidates. Garvin also argues that the period of political stagnation which characterised the 1890s was no surprise, because Nationalist organisations were already in decline before the fall of Parnell, an event which undoubtedly accelerated this process. Boyce's, *Nineteenth Century Ireland* emphasises that while Parnell's downfall broke the alliance of IPP, Catholic Church and constitutional Fenianism, Irish Nationalism still retained its central Catholic character and still depended on the Liberal party to deliver Home Rule.

Justin McCarthy's period as Chairman of the party is sympathetically assessed in E J Doyle's, *Justin McCarthy* (Dublin, 1996) which explains how McCarthy won the support of both Dillon and O'Brien for the anti-Parnellite cause. Doyle highlights the difficulties facing McCarthy, when Rosebery succeeded Gladstone as Liberal leader and immediately confirmed his lack of enthusiasm for Home Rule. The conflict between Dillon and Healy is covered in two impressive biographies. F Callanan's, *T M Healy* (Cork, 1996) chronicles Healy's failure to establish a clerical (Catholic) Nationalist party, but also sheds new light on the complex relationship between Catholicism and Nationalism in Ireland. Much earlier, F S L Lyons's, *John Dillon* (London, 1968) stressed his subject's commitment to the Liberal alliance and his belief in the absolute necessity of keeping the party under strong central authority, something which McCarthy's reign as Chairman made very difficult. This, of course, ran counter to Healy's demand for greater powers to be given to the local constituencies, where clerical influence could often prove decisive. Lyons sees the defeat of Healy's candidate in the South Kerry by-election of September 1895 as the turning point in Dillon's struggle with Healy. Thereafter, Dillon held the upper hand and he was determined, when the opportunity arose, to force Healy out of the party. Both Lyons', *The Irish Parliamentary Party* and D G Boyce's, *Nationalism in Ireland* (London, 1982) describe how the years of bitter feuding lowered the party's stock in the country, and Boyce notes the failure of the competing factions — Redmondite, Dillonite or Healyite — to harness the energies of revolutionary Nationalism to the constitutional movement in the way that Parnell had done.

The role of the UIL in facilitating the reunion of the IPP is described in Bull's, *Land, Politics and Nationalism* which highlights O'Brien's role in transforming spasmodic agrarian outrages into a coherent organisation, with the calculated intention of using it in the service of the national cause. P Bew's, *Conflict and Conciliation in Ireland 1890-1910* (Oxford, 1989) charts the growth of the UIL which, he claims, soon established a real unity in the countryside that prepared the base for a reunited party. Bew agrees with Lyons's, *Ireland since the Famine* that the Boer War had a great impact on Ireland, where anti-British/pro-Boer sentiment allowed the various Nationalist factions to combine easily and fight for a popular cause. Lyons's, *Dillon* stresses his subject's interest in South Africa and his very powerful Boer sympathies. He also notes that though Dillon attended the inaugural meeting of the UIL in Westport in January 1898, it was not until the end of that year that he was persuaded the League should become the party's organisation. The details of the reunion are expertly unravelled in Lyons's, *The Irish Parliamentary Party* which details the list of meetings and contacts prior to the reunion. D Gwynn's, *The Life of John Redmond* (London, 1932) argues that Redmond's election to the Chairmanship of the IPP was a bitter pill for Dillon to swallow, as the two men had long disagreed, particularly on their assessment of the government's 'killing Home Rule with kindness' policy. While Dillon believed that Conservative reforms would make it difficult to sustain interest in the Nationalist cause, Redmond argued that the movement would only gather strength as the result of increased prosperity in Ireland. Bew's, *Conflict and Conciliation* suggests that O'Brien had supported Redmond's candidature, thinking that he could manipulate the new leader but, soon, the two men were at odds. In his recent biography, *Redmond* (Dublin, 1996)

Bew makes the point that by 1902 Redmond was taking a tougher line on O'Brien's agrarian militancy. Warwick-Haller's, *William O'Brien and the Irish Land War* concludes that the victories achieved by O'Brien, such as the party reunion of 1900, the acceptance of the UIL as the national organisation and the party's espousal of compulsory land purchase, all came together to undermine his influence.

Bew's, *Conflict and Conciliation* highlights the significance of the 'Swinford Revolt', in which Dillon attacked the O'Brienite policy of conciliation. He draws a distinction between two kinds of contemporary Nationalism, which he calls 'Parnellite' or conciliationist and 'radical agrarian', a thesis which is rejected in Bull's, *Land, Politics and Nationalism*. Bull does not see Dillon as a 'radical agrarian', but as an anti-landed, anti-Anglican, anti-establishment and anti-imperialist political activist. Bew, however, offers a brilliant assessment of the tense relations both within the agrarian movement and within the parliamentary party. In analysing the defeat of the conciliation policy, Bull argues that it was ironic that a crucial role in defeating this policy was played by Devlin's Catholic Nationalists who had little real interest in the land question. Moreover, by continuing with the agrarian rhetoric after the Wyndham Act, the Nationalist leadership doomed the party to a narrowing of its basis of support in Ireland. This strategy also contributed to unnecessary divisions in Irish society and, therefore, must, in Bull's opinion, have contributed to partition.

The details of both the 'devolution crisis' and the fiasco of the Irish Council Bill are recounted in E O'Halpin's, *The Decline of the Union: British Government in Ireland 1892-1920* (Dublin, 1987). O'Halpin describes the contributions of both Sir Anthony MacDonnell and Augustine Birrell in this period and comments on Redmond's relationship with Campbell-Bannerman's Liberal government. The story behind the granting of a Catholic university is described in D W Miller's, *Church, State and Nation in Ireland, 1898-1921* (Dublin, 1973). Initially, the Catholic hierarchy had been apprehensive about the Liberals' attitude to Catholic interests in education, but Birrell played a crucial role in smoothing out potential difficulties and worked closely with Archbishop Walsh to produce the legislation for the new university. The contribution made by Dillon on the university question is clarified in Lyons's biography. A full chapter in A C Hepburn's, *A Past Apart: Studies in the History of Catholic Belfast, 1850-1950* (Belfast, 1996) is devoted to the AOH which, the author shows, grew rapidly at the beginning of the twentieth century, when it became linked to the IPP. Hepburn attributes much of this growth to Devlin's skill and enthusiasm, adding that his dual role in the AOH and in the UIL ensured that there was no rivalry between the two organisations. Devlin's close relationship with Dillon is examined in Lyons's biography, and both Hepburn and Lyons stress the consequences of the sectarian character which the AOH brought to the IPP.

Many of the books which cover the period up to 1910 overlook the revival of agrarian agitation in the Ranch War of 1906-10. One exception is Bew's, *Conflict and Conciliation* which allows the author to return to the issue of class division within Nationalism. In orchestrating the tactic of cattle-driving, Ginnell was fighting for those at the bottom of the agrarian pile but, though it frequently resorted to militant agrarian rhetoric, the IPP was keen to see an end to the Ranch War. Thus Bew concludes that ranching was "more despised in rhetoric than in practice". While its instinct for unity allowed the IPP to overcome the various challenges in the first decade of the twentieth century, Boyce's excellent, *Nationalism in Ireland* argues that the price of this unity meant failure for one of Irish Nationalism's key goals – the creation of a comprehensive Irish nation featuring all creeds and classes of Irishmen.

A vast quantity of literature exists which deals with Nationalism in general, but much of it is of little value. The following are useful and each adds to our understanding of the development of Irish Nationalism. E Gellner's, *Nations and Nationalism* (London, 1983) claims that Nationalism is 'natural', only needing the right conditions to make it compelling. In analysing its link with culture, Gellner stresses the importance of improvements in education. G L Mosse's essay, 'Mass Politics and the Political Liturgy of Nationalism', which appeared in E Kamenka's (ed), *Nationalism: The Nature and Evolution of an Idea* (London, 1976) argues that Nationalism was boosted by mass politics attributable to the spread of democracy. Mosse also claims that historical consciousness formed the basis of all modern Nationalism. One excellent study is E J Hobsbawm's, *Nations and Nationalism since 1780* (Cambridge, 1990) which draws a distinction between the 1830-80 period, when Nationalism was part of liberal ideology and regarded as progressive, and the 1880-1914 period, when Nationalism shifted to the right. Much of this latter variety was 'petty bourgeois' Nationalism, and this referred especially to linguistic Nationalism which was frequently led by teachers, provincial journalists and civil servants. The clearest examples of this, Hobsbawm argues, are to be found in many parts of Austria-Hungary and in Ireland.

An excellent overview of the new Nationalism is provided in Foster's, *Modern Ireland*. Foster begins by stressing that the conflict between old and new Nationalism was closely tied to the generational conflict which was an important feature of contemporary Ireland, though he adds that in terms of numbers the massed ranks of old Nationalism easily dwarfed its new rival. Moreover, if the IPP was to be challenged, it seemed that this would come from movements like the AOH and the UIL, both of which clearly exhibited political energy, rather than "the minority rhetoric of cultural revivalism and revolutionary separatism". Foster describes the Gaelic League as "respectable, suburban and bourgeois", whereas the Anglo-Irish literary avant-garde was closed and elitist. Only Hyde, Foster shows, straddled the two movements, though he qualifies his 'apolitical' description of Hyde by highlighting the influence of 'Fenian-inspired' rhetoric on his thinking. Foster describes the GAA's decision forbidding its members to play English games as a 'cultural boycott', which used the successful weapon of the Land League. More detailed comment on the GAA can be found in W F Mandle's, *The Gaelic Athletic Association and Irish Nationalist Politics* (Dublin, 1987) which argues that the GAA re-created an image of Gaelic culture and made it suit the middle class tastes of Catholic Ireland.

The best account of the Gaelic revival is J Hutchinson's, *The Dynamics of Cultural Nationalism: The Gaelic Revival and the Creation of the Irish Nation State* (London, 1987) which argues that it was impossible for the distinction between cultural and political Nationalism to survive for long in a country where the awareness of nationality was so pervasive. The book contains useful sections on MacNeill, Moran and Griffith and details the great tensions in the revival, as the intellectuals tended to recoil against the Gaelic League's growing identification with sectarian or separatist causes. Hutchinson also comments on the great influence of Edmund Rice's

Christian Brothers Schools which, with their explicitly Nationalist education, may have been more significant than the Gaelic League intellectuals. S O'Tuama's (ed), *The Gaelic League Idea* (Cork, 1972) contains useful material on the establishment of the League. In the opening essay, 'The founding of the Gaelic League', D Greene claims that the radical and revolutionary nature of Hyde's policy of de-Anglicisation has tended to be overlooked because of his disavowal of any political aims. The figures charting the early difficulties and then the surge in interest from around 1900 are contained in B S MacAodha's essay, 'Was this a Social Revolution?' This growth, he argues, was like a successful adult education movement with well trained, full time Organisers or Timiri travelling around the countryside establishing new branches. An illuminating assessment of MacNeill's contribution to the Irish Ireland movement can be seen in D McCartney's essay, 'MacNeill and Irish Ireland', which appears in F X Martin and F J Byrne's (eds), *The Scholar Revolutionary: Eoin MacNeill, 1867-1945 and the Making of the New Ireland* (Shannon, 1973). McCartney focuses on MacNeill's pre-eminence as a Celtic scholar, but also claims that Irish Irelandism grew out of "the Nationalist fermentation" of the previous thirty years, which was, in effect, a combination of Land League agitation, Home Rule agitation and Fenianism. Hutchinson's, *The Dynamics of Cultural Nationalism* contributes to the revisionist debate by suggesting that the Gaelic League and GAA should not be seen as part of a Gaelic revival, but as movements engaged in the invention of traditions for Ireland.

Garvin's, *The Evolution of Irish Nationalist Politics* claims that the Gaelic League attracted talented young men who felt excluded by the forces of old Nationalism and concludes that the League "educated an entire political class". In his stimulating, *Nationalist Revolutionaries in Ireland* Garvin argues that the League was the central institution in the development of a revolutionary elite, and he draws parallels with other European countries, where similar romantic political movements were being dominated by a petty bourgeois, educated class. In an article for *Irish Historical Studies*, 'Priests and Patriots: Irish separation and fear of the modern, 1890-1914', XXV, No 97 (May 1986), Garvin claims that the League, under the guise of cultural revival, was turned into a weapon against all the resented establishments in Ireland except for the Catholic Church, and this allowed it to be both radical and respectable. Boyce's, *Nationalism in Ireland* describes Yeats's movement as 'literary Parnellism', and states that Hyde was either ingenious or dishonest in claiming that the League would not identify with any particular group or organisation.

Other important contributions come from L Curtis's, *The Cause of Ireland* (Belfast, 1994) which chronicles the role played by women in the new Nationalism, while F S L Lyons's, *Culture and Anarchy in Ireland 1890-1939* (Oxford, 1979) claims that Parnell's fall in 1891 left Irishmen bitter and disillusioned, and they turned away from parliamentary politics. An interesting account of Alice Milligan's life and her contribution and commitment to the Gaelic revival is offered in S T Johnston's, *Alice: A Life of Alice Milligan* (Omagh, 1994). Johnston describes Milligan's great difficulty in learning the language, a problem she shared with many of her contemporaries in the revival movement, and then chronicles her hectic schedule in the service of cultural Nationalism. In assessing Moran's contribution to the Irish Ireland movement Lyons stresses Moran's determined pursuit of the objectives of industrial development and the language revival. A brief but impressive biography, P Maume's, *D P Moran* (Dublin, 1995), describes how Moran coined his nickname

'Sourfaces' which he used to describe Irish Protestants. Significantly, Maume emphasises the frustration of Catholic clerical and white-collar workers who experienced discrimination in the labour market, and concludes that this gave Nationalism a powerful appeal for Catholic white-collar workers.

A careful analysis of the early Sinn Féin movement can be located in R Davis's, *Arthur Griffith and non-violent Sinn Féin* (Dublin, 1974), while Griffith's prickly character is brought to life in C Younger's *Arthur Griffith* (Dublin, 1981). A neat precis of Griffith's interpretation of the events leading up to the Act of Union is provided by MacDonagh's, *States of Mind*. Miller's, *Church, State and Nation in Ireland* makes the interesting observation that Dolan's campaign in the North Leitrim by-election of 1908 enjoyed the very active support of the younger clergy in the area. Two essays in F X Martin's (ed), *Leaders and Men of the Easter Rising* (London, 1967) by K B Nowlan, 'Tom Clarke, MacDermott, and the IRB', and Martin's, 'McCullough, Hobson and republican Ulster', describe the struggle between the old guard and the young militants for control of the IRB. Travers's, *'Settlements and Divisions'* also contains a clear account of the IRB revival, but the most comprehensive treatment of the IRB remains L O'Broin's, *Revolutionary Underground: the Story of the Irish Republican Brotherhood 1858-1924* (Dublin, 1976).

Chapter 4
Unionism old and new

In the quarter of a century from 1885 to 1910 Unionism emerged as a powerful force in Irish and British politics. Unlike Nationalism, it had a more distinctive geographical character and, within Unionism, it was possible to distinguish between British Unionism, Southern Unionism and Ulster Unionism. While the common goal of maintaining the Union provided a rallying ground for these different strands of Unionism, each was to rely on different methods and, as the period wore on, each was to develop specific objectives within the overall framework designed for maintenance of the Union. Initially, Irish Unionism was very much part of British Unionism and, therefore, it developed primarily as a parliamentary movement with Westminster as its main sphere of activity. Yet, from the outset, there were significant, if not obvious, differences within Irish Unionism. Unionists in the south of Ireland identified closely with Britain, but they also had a strong sense of their own Irishness, whereas Unionists from the north, while they had a British identity, quickly developed their own regional, or Ulster, identity. More apparent were the differences in numerical strength and the contrast between the social bases of the sister movements.

Unionists made up only 10 per cent of the population in the three southern provinces. Their real strength in the south lay with the landowning class but, naturally, this meant that they were well scattered. Only in a few isolated pockets was there a concentration of Protestants in the south. They were, however, well represented among the business and professional middle class in Cork and, especially, Dublin, and they were fairly numerous in the more fashionable towns just south of the capital such as Bray and Greystones. Unionists in the north, on the other hand, enjoyed a narrow majority in the nine counties of Ulster, though they were much stronger in the six north-eastern counties and particularly concentrated in the four 'plantation' counties of Antrim, Down, Londonderry and Armagh. In the north-east, moreover, they practically formed their own self contained society which included landowners, tenant farmers and landless labourers in rural areas, and a strong middle class of businessmen and professionals together with the full range of skilled and unskilled industrial workers, all of whom could be found in urban areas. Obviously, such a strong geographical base gave Ulster Unionism a powerful regional identity, but the new movement also benefited from the long tradition of Protestant organisation in the north which had been evident since the Ulster plantation in the first half of the seventeenth century [46, 47, 48].

In the 1880s Irish Unionists realised that the involvement and the organisation of Ulster were essential if they were going to form a mass movement which might offer an effective challenge to Parnell's Nationalism. Previously, Irish Protestants tended to be divided between Liberals and Conservatives. Liberalism was weak in the south, but a small number of Conservatives, taking advantage of the restricted franchise, could expect to be elected in any Westminster general election. In Ulster, Liberalism enjoyed greater strength, drawing support from both Catholic and Protestant tenant farmers, while the Conservatives faithfully represented the landlord interest and enjoyed majority support in the province. The 1880 general election saw the return of 18 Conservatives, 9 Liberals and 2 Home Rulers for the province's Westminster seats. This pattern was to be shattered by the two general elections of 1885 and 1886. Initially, the Home Rule party made little impression in Ulster, but a by-election victory by Tim Healy in North Monaghan in June 1883, and the subsequent Nationalist claim that 'the invasion of Ulster' had begun, sent shock waves through Ulster's Protestant community. One immediate consequence was a boost for the revival of Orangeism which had already been stirred into action by the threat of Land League agitation. Yet this by itself failed to bring unity and organisation to the Unionist cause. More significant was the reaction to the extension of the franchise in 1884 and the consequent redistribution of Ireland's Westminster seats early in 1885. Both the 1884 Reform Act and the 1885 Redistribution Act were regarded as being very unfavourable to Irish Conservatives who suddenly had to come to terms with the reality of Catholic electoral strength.

This was very apparent in Ulster, where the Home Rulers increased their tally of seats from 3 to 17 at the 1885 general election, giving them the majority of the province's 33 seats. The 1885 general election, therefore, ushered in a new era in Ulster politics. The election saw a high degree of religious polarisation, and the Liberal party, which had sought support from both the Protestant and Catholic communities, suffered serious, if not yet fatal, damage. The 16 Conservatives, as they were still known, who had been returned for Ulster, spent the next seven months anxiously watching Salisbury's minority administration which seemed to be considering some kind of alliance with Parnellism. By January 1886 a clearly identifiable Unionist group of MPs, still under the wing of the Conservative party, had gathered around Edward Saunderson, the MP for North Armagh, who, therefore, emerged as the first leader of Unionism. Saunderson immediately set about making the arrangements for Lord Randolph Churchill's famous visit to Belfast on 22 February 1886.

Churchill was a senior figure in the Conservative party and he harboured powerful leadership ambitions. He represented the progressive wing of the Conservative party which, at times, drew him into conflict with the reactionary Tory leader, Lord Salisbury. Although Churchill had previously been highly critical of Ulster's Conservative MPs, he saw an opportunity to strengthen the Conservative party, and his own position within it, when Gladstone came out publicly in favour of Home Rule. Now, as he wrote to a close friend, "the Orange card was the one to play". In his carefully stage-managed performance at the Ulster Hall in February 1886, Churchill reassured Ulster Unionists that they could count on the unequivocal support of the Conservative party in their struggle against Home Rule before issuing his famous battle-cry, "Ulster will fight (and) Ulster will be right". Moreover, Salisbury was equally defiant in his support of Unionist interests with his public speeches during the early part of 1886. Obviously, the Conservative leaders recognised the potential in the Home Rule issue, believing that if they came out strongly against the measure, they could divide and discredit their Liberal opponents. Of course, there was more to Conservative opposition to Home Rule than just simple political opportunism. They viewed the whole question of Home Rule for Ireland in an imperial context and feared that the concession of even such a limited measure of freedom would have serious repercussions in the rest of the Empire.

The emergence of Irish Unionism

Reacting to the growing demand for Home Rule from Parnell's Nationalists, a small group of southern landowners and academics met on 1 May 1885 to form the Irish Loyal and Patriotic Union (ILPU). Its aim was to co-ordinate opposition to Home Rule, and it was determined to mount an electoral challenge to Nationalism in the November general election. The ILPU fought 52 seats in the election but, despite polling well in a few constituencies, Southern Unionists failed to win any of the contests. This left the three southern provinces with only two Unionist MPs, the members for Trinity College who were returned unopposed and, therefore, Southern Unionists realised the futility of contesting safe Nationalist seats. On 8 January 1886 a meeting of the ILPU resolved to expand its activities but, despite such intentions, it remained a small, elitist pressure group representing Anglo-Irish opinion. Coincidentally, on the same date, an organisation was founded in Ulster to co-ordinate Unionist resistance to Home Rule over the whole province. The new body, the Ulster Loyalist Anti-Repeal Union (ULARU), was dominated by former Conservatives who immediately sought to establish close relations with both the Orange Order and the Protestant churches. In contrast to the ILPU, the ULARU spread rapidly, organising a series of well-attended meetings throughout the province and taking advantage of the concentration of Protestants in the north-east. It also played a key role in the arrangements for Churchill's visit to the province. Gladstone's introduction of the Home Rule Bill in April 1886 was viewed with dismay by Ulster Unionists and gave a new sense of urgency to the ULARU's activities. The bill also dealt a hammer blow to Ulster Liberals and forced them to make a decision. Very quickly, the majority of Ulster Liberals signalled their intention to break with their party and, on 13 April, this decision was confirmed when they participated in a mass meeting with their former Conservative opponents in the Ulster Hall. Ulster Unionism was rapidly gaining in strength, and its improved organisation allowed the Unionists to win 17 of the 33 Ulster seats in the general election held in July 1886 [49]. The 2 Trinity seats brought the Irish Unionist total in the new parliament to 19.

The defeat of the Home Rule Bill and the return of a Conservative government allowed Unionists to breathe easily, a state of affairs which continued until the early 1890s. Under Saunderson's direction the Irish Unionists continued to operate as an identifiable, if not always united, group within the Conservative fold. Gladstone's decision, despite his age, to continue as Liberal leader, and his determination to introduce another Home Rule measure when his party returned to office, meant that Irish Unionists had to guard against complacency. By 1891 it was clear to these

Unionists that the ageing Liberal leader was absolutely absorbed by the Irish Question, and the prospect of a Liberal general election victory in 1891-92 prompted Unionists in Ulster to organise a display of their outright opposition to any Home Rule scheme which, they hoped, would influence opinion on the mainland. The Ulster Unionist Convention met in Belfast on 17 June 1892 and proved to be an important propaganda strike in the struggle against Home Rule. Tentative proposals for a similar Convention in 1886 had failed to arouse sufficient interest among Ulster Unionists but, in the spring of 1892 with a general election imminent, the idea was taken up eagerly. The driving force behind this decision was Thomas Sinclair, the Chairman of the Ulster Liberal Unionist Association, but Joseph Chamberlain, who through personal contacts was very well informed on Ulster politics, was an enthusiastic supporter.

The Convention assembled at the Botanic Gardens in Belfast, where a special wooden pavilion had been built to accommodate the 12,000 delegates who attended. The construction of the pavilion was completed in only four weeks. The delegates represented a broad cross section of Ulster Protestant society with at least one-third coming from the tenant farming class. All nine Ulster counties were represented, but the 400 strong platform party was dominated by the landed and business classes. One of the province's best known landowners, the Duke of Abercorn, chaired the proceedings, and he concluded his opening address by insisting "Men of the North, once more I say, we will not have Home Rule". Indeed, the speeches and the resolutions indicated that resistance to Home Rule was developing a distinctly Ulster character. While Ulster Unionists were keen to pledge their support for their fellow Unionists in the other three provinces, speakers at the Convention were thinking primarily about Unionists in the north-east. Another interesting feature of the speeches made at the Convention was their moderate tone, suggesting that the enactment of Home Rule would be met, not with violence and disorder, but with passive resistance on a province-wide scale. Any violence, it was assumed, would be contingent on a Dublin parliament's reaction to this passive resistance in Ulster [50].

Immediate reaction to the Convention came from Gladstone who replied to the Unionist demands, arguing that Ulster Unionist claims, which took no account of majority opinion in Ireland, were simply unreasonable. Within a fortnight parliament had been dissolved and the general election brought the Liberals back to power, though Gladstone's high hopes of a commanding majority were not realised. Again, the Liberals were dependent on Irish Nationalist support, and they had to accept that British voters had not provided a ringing endorsement in favour of Home Rule. In Ireland the election was regarded as a triumph by Irish Unionists. They won a total of 23 seats, 19 of which were in Ulster, increasing their tally in the south to 4. In addition to the 2 Trinity seats, the Southern Unionists also won the St. Stephen's Green division of Dublin and South Dublin, where Sir Horace Plunkett was returned. The successful campaign in Ulster was attributed to the assiduous attention paid to the registration of Unionist voters, particularly in marginal seats, in the 1886-92 period. The introduction of the Second Home Rule Bill in February 1893 concentrated Ulster Unionist minds, and a new attempt was made to organise grass roots opinion. Earlier, an Ulster Convention League had emerged from the Convention, but it was supplemented by new groups which were established in 1893.

The first such body, the Unionist Clubs Council, was formed in February, and it undertook propaganda work in both Ireland and Britain. In the following month another new organisation, the Ulster Defence Union, made a more specific attempt to involve a broader cross section of Unionist opinion, organising an elected central assembly of 600 representatives drawn from all over the province. This assembly selected a 40 strong executive council, chaired by Thomas Sinclair, which joined with Ulster Unionist members from both the House of Commons and the House of Lords to co-ordinate future resistance to Home Rule. While there was threatening talk that such resistance would be violent, and there was evidence of rifles being imported, the real significance of these organisations was their involvement in the planning of a wave of demonstrations in the spring and summer of 1893, which became the chief Unionist weapon in the campaign against Home Rule.

With the debate on the Second Home Rule Bill under way, Arthur Balfour crossed to Belfast to outline his opposition to the measure and reassure Unionists that the Conservative party remained steadfast in its support. After watching a four-hour march-past of 100,000 Unionist supporters in Belfast on 4 April, Balfour, one of the most active Home Rule opponents in the Conservative party, addressed 4,000 Unionists in the Ulster Hall in a repeat of Churchill's 1886 visit. He began by arguing that Ulster's economic prosperity depended on the maintenance of the Union, but went on to reject Gladstone's notion that Ireland was 'one nation'. For Balfour, the historical and religious differences, so obvious in the north-east, made the one nation concept a dangerous basis for any attempt to settle the Irish Question. Four days later Balfour was addressing an audience of 5,000 Unionists in Dublin's Leinster House. While he claimed that Ulster Unionists could always fight against the Liberal government's attempt to impose Home Rule, he geared his comments to his southern audience, warning that Home Rule would lead ultimately to full separation. Balfour and other senior Conservatives also spoke at many protest meetings in England and Scotland, and these attracted very large audiences. Following his nephew, Lord Salisbury arrived in the province on 23 May when he was greeted by a large and enthusiastic Unionist crowd in Larne. In his major speech in the Ulster Hall two days later, Salisbury stressed Ulster's importance to the Empire. For leading Conservatives such as Salisbury, Balfour, Chamberlain and the Duke of Devonshire, all of whom were vocal in the campaign against Home Rule, it was deemed essential that Ulster Unionists should not feel deserted. Running in conjunction with these anti-Home Rule demonstrations was a series of protest meetings organised by various Unionist women's groups. The Home Rule crisis had contributed to the political mobilisation of women on the Unionist side, a feature which was mirrored by women's activities in the Nationalist camp, originally with the Ladies' Land League and then with the more advanced groups linked to the new Nationalism. Women's demonstrations in support of the Unionist cause were held all over the province, and a number of petitions, sometimes bearing the signatures of over 100,000 women, were organised and dispatched to Westminster.

The rejection of the second Home Rule Bill by the House of Lords in September 1893 was greeted with the lighting of bonfires all across the province, a traditional form of celebration in Protestant Ulster. Gladstone's retirement in the following year and his successor's determination to avoid controversial Irish legislation brought more good news for Unionists. Moreover, the general election triumph by the Conservatives in 1895 and the return of Salisbury as Prime Minister convinced Unionists that, in the short term at least, the Home Rule danger had passed, and this led to a general slackening of Unionist activity and organisation. The struggle against Gladstonian Home Rule had helped to mould the three strands of Unionism. While British Unionism, Southern Unionism and Ulster Unionism had united in opposition to both the 1886 and 1893 bills, the reasons for their opposition, as outlined in the crucial parliamentary debates, indicated that there were significant differences between them. Following the split in the Liberal party over Home Rule and the defection of Gladstone's opponents to the Conservatives, the Conservative party adopted the title 'Conservative and Unionist', though for convenience the shorter 'Unionist' was frequently used to describe the party until 1922. In general, the key issue for British Unionists was the threat that Home Rule posed to the Empire. They believed that any move, which conferred even a limited measure of political freedom on Ireland, would be followed by similar claims from other parts of the Empire, and imperial unity could not survive such a development. They were also convinced that Home Rule would only whet Nationalist appetites for full independence, a move which could lead to the destruction of the United Kingdom. In addition, Irish Nationalists had been associated with agrarian violence, and Unionists in Britain did not want to see them rewarded with Home Rule. Although they identified strongly with Ulster in 1886 and 1893, British Unionists showed little real concern for Ireland. It was also noticeable that such defiance was reserved for periods when they were out of office. Obviously, this left the leaders of British Unionism open to the charge that the playing of the 'Orange card' smacked of political opportunism. One consequence of Churchill's support for Orangeism was that he helped to transform it from a fringe group outside respectable society into a powerful political organisation. Yet, in spite of their lack of empathy with Ulster Unionism, British Unionists had to ally themselves with Irish Unionism, particularly the Ulster variety, if they were to combat successfully the policy of Home Rule. In effect, Gladstone had created British Unionism, when he introduced the first Home Rule Bill. Then, fighting Home Rule in 1886 and 1893 was to strengthen the bonds between Irish and British Unionism and, even though they only had around 20 MPs, the Irish Unionists exerted significant influence on Conservative politics.

Like British Unionists, Southern Unionists were frequently embarrassed both by the extremism of Orange leaders and, more noticeably, by the wild speeches of Ulster Unionist MPs at Westminster. Southern Unionists were much more tolerant of the Catholic religion than their Ulster counterparts and, consequently, the threat to religious freedom never figured prominently in Southern Unionist objections to Home Rule. Instead, Southern Unionists feared that Home Rule would destroy the traditional pattern of life in Ireland and, more significantly, remove them from their privileged position within Irish society. Coming hard on the heels of the land agitation, which had placed them under serious threat, Southern Unionists could not accept that their future would be dictated by a Home Rule parliament dominated by lower class Catholics, many of whom they viewed with suspicion because of their involvement in the Land League. With their instinctive superiority, Southern Unionists believed that such a Home Rule parliament, lacking enough people of real ability, would soon plunge the country into financial chaos. Their principal fear, however, was that their land would be confiscated, either directly through radical land legislation or indirectly through penal taxation. They claimed, without much justification, that all sections of the community in Ireland had prospered under the Union, and warned that it would be foolish to experiment with a new type of administration in Dublin for which, they argued, there was little genuine support among the wider community. This was a strange assertion considering the existence of a powerful Irish Nationalist party with over 80 MPs, but Southern Unionists dismissed this, claiming that behind the IPP stood the land agitators, the Catholic hierarchy and the anti-British Irish community in the United States, and it was from this quarter only that the demand for Home Rule came.

Gladstone's initiative in 1886 had forced Southern Unionists to take a more pro-Union stance but, while they recognised their limitations, they never felt inferior in relying on Ulster Unionists and British Unionists for support. Supremely confident of their own political worth, Southern Unionists formed a close-knit group, frequently marrying within their own circle, which enabled them to maintain their pre-eminent position in Irish society. Besides, Southern Unionists were much more closely integrated with British Conservatism than their Ulster cousins. They often enjoyed close family ties, and a number of the larger landowners had estates in Britain as well as Ireland, giving them a foot in both the British and the Southern Unionist camps. Moreover, British Unionist leaders, especially Salisbury and Balfour, who came from a landed background, could easily identify with the plight of the landowning class in Ireland, and this further strengthened the links between British and Irish Unionism. Whenever possible, Southern Unionists used their influence to persuade English Conservatives to come out strongly against Home Rule. Such efforts were greatly facilitated by the heavy presence of Southern Unionists among the political elite at Westminster. In 1886, 116 of the 144 peers with Irish interests had Southern Unionist connections and they moved easily in Conservative circles at Westminster. In addition, 17 Southern Unionists were MPs in the House of Commons, representing British constituencies, mainly in the south of England. This gave them significant influence within Conservative ranks [51].

The Parnellite split led to a fresh attempt by Southern Unionists to create a more efficient party organisation in Ireland. A new body, the Irish Unionist Alliance (IUA), which superseded the ILPU, was established in 1891. While its name suggested that Unionists all over Ireland would now work closely together, the IUA represented only Southern Unionists. It was dominated by the landowning class. Southern Protestant businessmen, though they may have sympathised with its aims, generally stayed aloof from the IUA, fearing that open involvement would alienate their Nationalist customers and ruin their businesses. The IUA adopted an ambitious programme, planning to organise constituency branches, each with multiple sub branches, in the southern provinces, but such an unrealistic venture had to be abandoned in 1906. Thereafter, the IUA was content to have county committees reporting back to its Dublin office. More significant was the establishment of a London office, and the IUA came to see its main function as sustaining an effective anti-Home Rule campaign on the mainland. Consequently in 1892-93, marginal seats in Britain were flooded with speakers organised by the IUA and bombarded with propaganda material supplied by the IUA. By this stage it was becoming clear to the IUA that Ulster Unionism was developing its own anti-Home Rule strategy, a trend which seemed to be confirmed by the staging of the Ulster Unionist Convention. Still, Southern Unionists were comfortable with this development, believing that the maintenance of a broad British/Irish Unionist front would safeguard the Union.

An obvious reason for the differences between Ulster Unionists and Southern Unionists was that the former could always expect to win a significant number of parliamentary seats. The simple fact that it frequently engaged in election contests with Nationalists helped to mould Ulster Unionism in a different way. Ulster Unionism had been caught off-guard by the Nationalist advance in 1885, but the replacement of the land question by the Union as the dominant issue in Ulster politics worked to the benefit of the province's Unionists. By 1886 these Unionists had come to terms with the extension of the franchise and the changes to constituency boundaries, and in doing so they were able to take advantage of the intensity of emotion which had been building up in the previous years. Like Southern Unionists, the Ulstermen saw Home Rule as a weak government's response to Nationalist land agitation, and this strengthened their determination to oppose Home Rule. While the 1885-86 period had witnessed a transformation in Ulster politics, the rigid polarisation really reflected demographic reality. Following the example of Ulster Catholic Nationalism, Ulster Protestant Unionism emerged as a united force during these years. Although the differences between the Protestant denominations were not totally eradicated, they were at least submerged in the new movement which, crucially, enabled the landowning class to reassert its leadership [52].

Ulster Unionists cited a variety of reasons for their opposition to Home Rule. They questioned the ability of Nationalists to govern Ireland and pointed to their participation in agrarian unrest as evidence that Nationalists could not be expected to uphold the law. Those with an eye on the political scene at Westminster accused Gladstone of introducing Home Rule to secure the Irish Catholic vote in Britain for his own Liberal party. There was some justification for this, because the return of T P O'Connor, for what should have been a safe Liberal seat in the Scotland division of Liverpool from 1880 on, raised the prospect of Irish Nationalists interfering in other constituencies, where a substantial Irish population existed, at the Liberal party's expense. Yet a similar motive existed on the Conservative side which, with its anti-Home Rule stand, could expect to win Irish Protestant votes on the mainland. Again, Liverpool with its significant Irish Protestant population offered a good example. Ulster Unionists also repeated the argument that Nationalist aspirations would never be satisfied by such a limited measure, and a successful Home Rule campaign would initiate a new drive for complete separation. However, the two dominant themes in their anti-Home Rule campaign were fear of religious persecution, a feature which distinguished them from Southern Unionists, and the threat to Ulster's economic prosperity. Unionists claimed that the Catholic Church would exercise unacceptable influence on a Home Rule parliament and, ignoring the role played by their own church leaders in Unionist politics, they frequently criticised the regular participation of Catholic clerics in Nationalist politics. The claim that Ulster industry would suffer if the Union was broken was consistently stressed. By the end of the nineteenth century it was clear that the province's key industries, linen and shipbuilding, were export-oriented with many of the finished products ending up in Britain itself. This was, for example, very apparent in the purchase of ships by the great White Star Line of Liverpool, which had been built in Belfast.

In their struggle against the two Home Rule Bills Unionists tended to emphasise the religious objection in 1886 and the economic argument in 1893. On both occasions there were dire warnings about armed action, which Liberals and Irish Nationalists refused to take seriously, but it was more likely that the enactment of Home Rule would have signalled the beginning of a coordinated campaign of passive resistance in Ulster. Unionists in the province could not see any contradiction between professing their repeated loyalty to the Sovereign on the one hand, and threatening to resist that Sovereign's government on the other. Thus, one historian has described the Ulster Unionist people's relationship to the British state as 'contractarian'. Unionists had come to Ireland in the seventeenth century to colonise Ulster on England's behalf and, in return, therefore, England must not, as Home Rule threatened to do, hand these Ulster people over to their enemies. If an English government broke this 'contract', the Ulster Unionists would be absolved from any obligation to obey Westminster's laws. This argument has some merits, though it is doubtful if many contemporary Unionists outside the leadership thought in these terms. There is some evidence, however, that the last two decades of the nineteenth century saw at least the partial development of what could be described as Ulster Nationalism. In the 1880s there was a growth of Orange culture as a group of Ulster Protestants sought to define their cultural and historical roots though, as with aspects of the Irish Ireland movement, much of this fell into the 'invention of traditions' bracket. Yet in speeches made by the Unionist leadership there were occasional references to the racial superiority of the Ulster Protestant. Undoubtedly, this was influenced by the discussion of 'Social Darwinism' in Victorian drawing rooms, but leading British Unionists such as Joseph Chamberlain also articulated these sentiments. In one of his speeches during a visit to the province in October 1887 Chamberlain stressed "the northern Protestants' racial economic and religious separation, and superiority to, the rest of Ireland".

Still, in its earliest phase, a much greater influence on the development of Ulster Unionism was the impact of its landed leadership. Landowners dominated the Irish Unionist party at Westminster in 1886, and under Saunderson's leadership the various factions united to fight Home Rule. Saunderson, a County Cavan landowner, regarded Ulster Protestantism as Ireland's bulwark against the agrarian chaos generated initially by the Land League and later by the Plan of Campaign. He led Unionism through the first twenty years of its existence, and he proved himself an uncompromising opponent of Irish Nationalism at Westminster. Yet Saunderson also fought to save Irish landlordism, and this was to give the Unionist movement he led a special flavour. For the new Irish Unionist party and its leader, the House of Commons became the focus of activity. Even though they had only twenty or so MPs, this figure remained constant, giving Irish Unionism at Westminster both a real sense of cohesion and a significant voice within British Unionism. Like his party, Saunderson was really the creation of Parnellism and the Home Rule crisis and, despite his utter condemnation of Irish Nationalism, it was apparent that the political success of the IPP had set an example which Unionism could follow. Hence, Irish Unionists copied the IPP in trying to act as an Irish pressure group at Westminster, which might operate in tandem with one of the two great British parties. Although Saunderson regarded Westminster, and the House of Commons in particular, as the chief battleground in the defence of the Union, he saw the Liberal government's attempt to push through a Home Rule measure as an act of betrayal and one, therefore, which could justify armed resistance. In parliament his combative style proved effective, though this did not conceal the fact that his brand of Unionism was usually expressed in negative and antagonistic terms. This did not always endear him to his Conservative allies, and his starring role in the famous Commons' fracas on 27 July 1893, when the committee stage of the second Home Rule Bill was completed, certainly raised a few British eyebrows.

Indeed, the relationship between British and Ulster Unionism sometimes seemed uneasy, in spite of the high profile Ulster visits by heavyweight Conservative politicians pledging their full support to the Unionist cause. In both 1886 and 1893 British Unionists readily identified with Ulster, but part of the intention in doing so was to give British Unionists greater credibility in their campaign to maintain the Union and protect the Empire. The rather parochial Ulster Unionists never really shared this wider viewpoint and they were wary of placing too much trust on British Unionism. This, at times, led them to take a more exclusive or independent stance on the Union. Increasingly, it appeared that their chief concern was the retention of their Ulster, or regional, identity, though they acknowledged that this could best be preserved under the Union. Moreover, Ulster Unionism shared something of the Anglophobia which is generally associated with contemporary Irish Nationalism. Many Ulster Unionists found it difficult to suppress their anti-English feelings, and the deep conservatism of Ulster Protestants, particularly those in rural areas, made them uncomfortable with the increasingly permissive society of liberal England. Such feelings were, of course, similar to those expressed on behalf of Irish Catholics by D P Moran.

The emergence of a recognisable group of MPs at Westminster, the 'Ulster Party', drew attention to the differences which existed within Irish Unionism. By 1892-93 Ulster Unionism had developed a strong regional identity, a fact which was more apparent when the prospect of extra-parliamentary opposition, or passive resistance, was raised. Yet, while opposition to Home Rule followed a constitutional pattern, as it almost always did, then Ulster Unionism and Southern Unionism could function effectively together as parts of a broader Irish movement. Ulster Unionists provided a solid support base and the great bulk of the party's MPs, leaving Southern Unionists to wage the propaganda war in Britain and foster close relations with the Conservative party. A crucial factor in the maintenance of a united Irish Unionist movement was Saunderson's leadership. As a landowner, Saunderson easily identified with the landowning class in the southern provinces, and the shared concern for the future of landlordism in Ireland was a significant factor in welding Ulster Unionism and Southern Unionism together [53]. Irish Unionists had, of course, good reason to be concerned about the future of the landowning class. The series of land purchase measures, culminating in the 1903 Wyndham Act, had contributed to the decline of landlordism, a development which was reflected in the changing composition of the party at Westminster. In 1886 landlords held more than one-half of the party's Westminster seats, but this figure was to fall to one-third in 1900 and to one-quarter in 1906. Although their numbers were falling, the landlords remained important, if declining, influence in the Unionist party and they always had Lord Salisbury's ear at Westminster. However, his retirement in 1902 brought fresh problems for the landed element within the Unionist movement. In terms of Westminster personnel the landlords were gradually replaced by businessmen and lawyers, and both were to play an increasingly prominent role in the Unionist party. In fact, the Unionists were particularly successful in attracting new commercial wealth, and a number of the great linen barons and shipbuilders became MPs. These changes in personnel could not alter the fact that the occupational composition of the Unionist party had much more in common with the Conservative or Liberal parties than with the Irish Nationalists.

Factions within Unionism

The difficulties which strained Irish Nationalism in the 1890-1910 periods were, to some extent, similar to those facing Irish Unionism. Although the Unionist party never suffered the kind of spectacular split which tore the IPP apart, its unity was threatened by the emergence of various factions which, at times, challenged the authority of the leadership. Certainly, when there was a real threat to the Union, as in 1893 with the second Home Rule Bill or in 1904-5 with the devolution crisis, Irish Unionists closed ranks and effectively marshalled their forces to defend their position. Yet when there was no threat of Home Rule, particularly during the long period of Conservative rule, Irish Unionists at Westminster could, and frequently did, act in a disunited fashion. Party discipline was never as rigidly enforced as with their Nationalist opponents, and this sometimes encouraged independent action by certain MPs. Unionist activity in the House of Commons was chiefly confined to those periods when the Union was in danger and, while their attendance at Westminster was generally good, it was noticeable that most Irish Unionist MPs showed little interest in British affairs. The free rein given to these Unionist MPs allowed individuals such as Horace Plunkett the opportunity to pursue a progressive approach. Plunkett represented South Dublin from 1892 to 1900, and his unorthodox views were treated with great suspicion by Saunderson.

Although Plunkett shared Saunderson's dislike of Home Rule, he advocated a more enlightened, long term strategy which might reconcile the bulk of the population to the Union. He demanded social and economic improvements for the tenant farming class, believing that the development of Irish agriculture would transform the Irish economy and, with it, attitudes to the Union. In the House of Commons Plunkett demonstrated his detailed knowledge on all agricultural matters, and this impressed the Balfour brothers who backed his scheme for a new Department of Agriculture and Technical Instruction. For his part, Plunkett fully endorsed the policy of constructive Unionism, and his efforts in seeking common ground with moderate Nationalists, as he did with the Recess Committee, encouraged the Conservative government to believe that it was possible to kill Home Rule with kindness. In his pursuit of such a liberal strategy Plunkett felt increasingly uncomfortable with the narrow-minded Ulster members of the Unionist party. Their reaction to Plunkett was predictable. Saunderson was particularly angered by Plunkett's repeated attacks on Irish landlordism, but other MPs were concerned with the general effect of Plunkett's progressive style of Unionism, which seemed to be reflected in the government's attempts to conciliate Nationalist opinion at a time when the Unionist leadership was demanding tough action against the United Irish League. Plunkett's views had aroused so much anger that a Unionist candidate ran against him in the 1900 general election. He owed his previous successes in South Dublin to a very effective constituency organisation but, with the Unionist vote split in 1900, the Nationalist candidate secured a comfortable victory. Over the next decade Plunkett's political thinking continued to evolve, culminating in his declaration of support for the principle of Home Rule, a development which did not go unnoticed by his former Unionist colleagues.

As far as Ulster Unionism was concerned, Plunkett's unorthodox views were occasionally embarrassing but, even though many Unionists were unhappy at the way in which he was ousted by his Southern Unionist colleagues, he was generally dismissed as a peripheral figure. The same could not apply to T W Russell, an Ulster Unionist MP who shared some of Plunkett's liberal Unionist beliefs but offered a more direct challenge to Saunderson's leadership. Born in Scotland, Russell had settled in County Tyrone and first came to prominence as a leading activist in the temperance campaign. At the 1886 general election he was returned as MP for South Tyrone, a victory based on the support he enjoyed from the Presbyterian tenant farmers, whose problems he fought hard to overcome for the next twenty years. His outstanding ability was immediately recognised by leading British Unionists, particularly Arthur Balfour and Joseph Chamberlain, and he became a frequent speaker in support of Conservative candidates at British by-elections. In Ulster, Russell's criticism of his Unionist colleagues became much more pronounced in 1894. The defeat of the second Home Rule Bill in the previous year had encouraged Russell to believe that with Home Rule off the agenda class divisions would emerge within Irish Unionism, giving him the opportunity to build on his Presbyterian tenant farmer base. Naturally, this drew him into conflict with Saunderson and the landed element, which could do little to control Russell. The South Tyrone MP attacked what he described as unsympathetic Irish landlords, advocating compulsory land purchase and frequently voting with Irish Nationalists in the House of Commons in favour of progressive land legislation [54]. During the winter of 1894-5 Russell toured rural Ulster in an attempt to win new supporters among the tenant farming class. Certainly, Russell's voice was being heard at Westminster, where the Conservative government's policy of constructive Unionism saw the implementation of many of the progressive measures demanded by Russell. At Chamberlain's suggestion, moreover, Russell had been appointed as a junior minister in the Local Government Board, a position which increased his influence on the Salisbury administration as it moved towards land purchase and local government reform.

However, Russell was only partly constrained by office and, in 1900, he became involved in a new wave of land agitation. Salisbury responded swiftly by dismissing him from the Local Government Board in November 1900, a move which greatly cheered Saunderson and the landed faction in Ulster, but opened the way for Russell to launch an all-out assault on Ulster Unionism's reactionary landed leadership. With great energy Russell renewed his campaign for compulsory land purchase and, in the spring of 1901, he decided to mount an electoral challenge to those Ulster Unionist MPs who refused to back compulsion. Using the Ulster Farmers' and Labourers' Union and Compulsory Purchase Association, which he founded in June 1901, Russell worked hard to rouse support in rural constituencies. He was rewarded in January 1902 and March 1903, when Russellite candidates enjoyed by-election successes in East Down and North Fermanagh respectively. Yet Russell was, to some extent, a victim of his own success. His campaign for compulsory purchase had forced most landlord MPs representing rural constituencies to support compulsion, and this contributed to the decline of landlord influence within Ulster Unionism in spite of Saunderson's efforts. In addition, Salisbury's retirement in June 1902 had been a decisive blow for Irish landlordism. The generous terms of Wyndham's 1903 Land Act, which went a long way to appease all of Ireland's tenant farmers, plunged Russell into trouble. While he supported the measure, his Ulster Farmers' and Labourers' Union organisation denounced the legislation's failure to introduce compulsion. By this stage nearly every Ulster Unionist MP was comfortable with the government's progressive land legislation, leaving Russell with very little room to manoeuvre.

Still, what really undermined Russellism was the breaking of the devolution crisis at the end of 1904 and the revival of Home Rule fears which accompanied it. The belief that the Union was in danger gave Unionist calls for unity fresh resonance and ensured a return to the norm of political polarisation in Ulster. This was significant, because the victories achieved by the Russellite candidates in East Down and North Fermanagh had depended on an alliance of Protestant and Catholic tenant farmer voters. Thus, the electoral success of Russellism depended on the development of class politics in Ulster, but there was little likelihood of any such development in the period after 1905. Although Russellism may have peaked by the end of 1902, it was not yet a spent force. At the 1906 general election a Russellite candidate won North Antrim, but the two previous by-election gains in East Down and North Fermanagh were lost to official Unionist candidates. Russell himself was again returned as an independent Unionist in South Tyrone, though he was forced to concede that he owed his seat to the votes of Catholic tenant farmers. The call for Unionist unity and, to a lesser extent, the government's imaginative response to the land question had eroded Russell's electoral base among the Presbyterian tenant farmers of rural Ulster. Russell recognised the way events had turned against him, and he accepted the Liberal government's invitation to succeed Plunkett as Vice-President of the Department of Agriculture in Dublin, a post he held from 1907 to 1918. In the general election of 1910 Russell, standing as a Liberal and supporting Home Rule, finally lost his South Tyrone seat, but he quickly returned to Westminster by winning North Tyrone at the subsequent general election. He held the seat until 1918.

The challenges mounted by Plunkett and Russell to official Unionism had just about been seen off, when another maverick Unionist, T H Sloan, attacked the party from a different direction [55]. Tom Sloan was a shipyard worker and Belfast Orangeman who had risen to prominence through the Belfast Protestant Association (BPA). The BPA was a working class, anti-Catholic organisation which drew its membership from the city's Orange lodges. The 1890s had witnessed the rapid growth of the Orange Order, and the BPA was strengthened by a new wave of sectarian tension which gripped the city in 1900. Both developments were welcomed by Sloan, but it was his action at the 12 July parade in 1902 which really enhanced his reputation as a defender of Protestant interests. At the Belfast parade Sloan jumped onto the platform to berate Saunderson, the leader of the Unionist party and the Belfast Grand Master, whom he accused of being soft on Catholicism. Only a few days later Sloan was given the chance to test his support in the city. The death of William Johnston, the MP for South Belfast whose rabid sectarian politics had won him a special position in Orange circles, presented Sloan with the opportunity to expose what he saw as the Unionist party's indifference to Protestant interests. Backed by the BPA and a number of Orange lodges, Sloan contested the by-election as an independent and won a comfortable victory over his official Unionist challenger. Almost immediately, he was expelled from the Orange Order because of his antics at the 1902 Belfast rally and his subsequent refusal to dispatch a written apology to Saunderson. This led to the secession of a number of lodges from the Orange Order and, in June 1903, the Independent Orange Order was formed from these dissident lodges. Only eight lodges marched in the Independent Orange Order's first Twelfth demonstration in 1903, but the breakaway Orange movement soon enjoyed significant growth in both Belfast and County Antrim.

Despite their differences Saunderson quickly recognised Sloan's potential as an MP and, for a short period, the fiery Orange populist was integrated into the Unionist party. Yet, at the same time, the growth of the Independent Orange Order was bound to create tension between Sloan and the Ulster Unionists. At the heart of the Independent Orange Order was its opposition to the Unionist party's conservative, commercial and landed interests. The new movement had a strong evangelical Protestant base, but the leadership quickly appreciated that it required a social programme in order to justify its separate existence as an alternative to official Unionism. This challenge was taken up by Lindsay Crawford, a gifted journalist, who had been drawn to the Independent Orange Order on its formation. Earlier Crawford, himself an evangelical Protestant and a prominent lay member of the Church of Ireland, came across in his writings as a sectarian Orange populist in the Sloan mould, but the Independent Orange Order gave him a platform to develop his political ideas. In 1904 Crawford's talents were recognised with his appointment as Imperial Grand Master of the Independent Orange Order and, at that year's Independent Twelfth demonstration in Ballymoney, County Antrim, he was the principal speaker. Indeed, Ballymoney and the North Antrim parliamentary constituency proved fertile ground for opposition to official Unionism. The constituency's Unionist MP, Sir William Moore, had angered the electorate in this rural area by voting against Wyndham's 1903 Land Bill, thus giving Crawford the opportunity to channel Protestant tenant farmer opposition to Moore into the Independent Orange Order. It was clear that Crawford was coming round to the view that the Independent Orange Order could mount a political challenge to the Unionist party and, in June 1905, a sub-committee was established to produce a policy document for the new movement. The document, which was written by Crawford, was first issued at an Independent Orange Order demonstration held at Magheramorne near Larne on 13 July 1905 [56].

The Magheramorne Manifesto, as it became known, offered an incisive critique of contemporary Unionism, denouncing it as the tool of the landowning and capitalist classes. Crawford's long term aim was to build a new force in Irish politics which could attract both Protestant and Catholic voters in support of a progressive social programme. Although he outlined the common problems facing the lower classes of both groups, there were enough references to Protestantism and democracy to obscure some of the manifesto's more controversial claims. Obviously, Crawford was aware that he had to tread carefully if he was to be successful in developing a radical challenge to official Unionism. Despite such caution, however, the Magheramorne Manifesto seemed likely to produce a split in the ranks of the Independent Orange Order. Its appeal had been directed primarily at the Protestant farmers in rural constituencies like North Antrim and, while Sloan had initially endorsed the manifesto, he was to dissociate himself from the most progressive parts of Crawford's document just before the general election in January 1906. Hoping to be returned unopposed for his South Belfast seat, Sloan announced that he intended to work closely with Ulster Unionist MPs in the new parliament, but such assurances failed to prevent the Unionist party running its own candidate. This forced Sloan to return to his supporters in the Independent Orange Order, though their support was only confirmed when he withdrew his earlier offer of support for the Unionist party. In fact, Sloan had only broken with the Unionist party following the release of the Magheramorne Manifesto, but in the contest for his South Belfast seat he returned to his old theme, attacking the party for its failure to uphold Protestant principles. In the poll Sloan retained his seat by winning just over 55 per cent of the vote in a straight fight with his Unionist opponent.

For his election triumph Sloan had relied on his solid support base in Sandy Row, a working class Protestant district in his South Belfast constituency which was the heartland of the Independent Orange Order in the city. He ignored the radical content of the Magheramorne Manifesto, instead concentrating on his simple message of the Unionist party's weakness in the defence of Protestantism. Whereas Crawford regarded the Independent Orange Order as a springboard for his new brand of progressive liberalism, Sloan saw the movement as the expression of his own Orange populism. He attacked official Unionism and the old Orange Order for being soft on Catholicism but, more than this, he was angered by the way in which the Unionist and Orange leadership appeared to take the Belfast working class, the people he represented, for granted. This tension within the Independent Orange Order, essentially a division between its urban and rural lodges, contributed to the movement's failure. Yet immediately after the 1906 general election, the Independent Orange Order appeared to be consolidating its position. Crawford, clearly the dominant figure in the movement, had backed T W Russell, who won South Tyrone, and R G Glendinning, who defeated William Moore in North Antrim. Soon, both of these MPs were to adopt the Liberal tag, but Crawford's attempt to join them ended in failure. Edward Saunderson's death in October 1906 had created a vacancy in the North Armagh constituency and presented Moore with an early opportunity to return to parliament following his shock defeat in the general election. In the by-election, held in November, Moore was challenged by Crawford who stood as a Liberal. The contest was easily won by Moore and proved to be Crawford's only electoral outing. Sloan had supported Crawford during the North Armagh by-election, but the political differences between the two men had increased significantly. Although the number of lodges attending the Independent demonstrations peaked in 1907, its political influence was already on the wane. Crawford, whose Liberal leanings had caused grave concern, was expelled from the Independent Orange Order in May 1908, and his position as Imperial Grand Master was, not surprisingly, filled by Sloan.

In 1910 Crawford emigrated to North America, where he continued to work as a journalist before accepting a position as the Irish government's trade representative in New York in 1922. Earlier, he had become an advocate of Irish Nationalism. Sloan, meanwhile, presided over a declining Independent Orange Order and continued in his capacity as an Independent Unionist MP at Westminster, where he supported much of the Liberal government's radical social programme. In the general election of January 1910 he defended his South Belfast seat, continuing to denounce the Unionist leadership. By this stage, however, Unionism had reorganised and with the Independent Orange Order in retreat Sloan was easily defeated by his official Unionist challenger. He refought the seat in the December general election of 1910, but again lost heavily with his own vote falling by more than 800 since the January contest. Sloan's parliamentary career was over. He continued to play a dominant role in the Independent Orange Order, but failed to arrest its decline. For a few years the Independent Orange Order had posed a threat to the Unionist party's control of Ulster Protestants, but it was unable to sustain its challenge. There were three reasons for this. Firstly, Unionism successfully closed ranks when the Union was perceived to be under threat, as had been the case with the devolution crisis of 1904-5. Secondly, the division within the Independent Orange Order between Crawford's rural liberalism and Sloan's urban populism rendered it incapable of delivering an effective, sustained attack on official Unionism. Thirdly, the Unionist party, which both Crawford and Sloan had ridiculed, swiftly reorganised itself in 1905 to take more account of grass roots opinion and, consequently, easily saw off the narrow sectarian challenge mounted by Sloan in Belfast. This was conclusively demonstrated in the two South Belfast contests held in 1910. In a sense the Unionist party, like its Nationalist counterpart, was able to present itself as a movement above class politics, leaving very little electoral space for any challenger to exploit. Such a strategy was confirmed when the party shed its conservative, landed image in the first decade of the twentieth century.

New Unionism

The challenges posed by Plunkett, Russell and Sloan had all contributed to the erosion of Saunderson's authority as Unionist leader. Official Unionism had been attacked by progressive landowners in the south who sought an accommodation with moderate Nationalism, by Presbyterian farmers in Ulster who favoured more radical land legislation and by working class Protestants in Belfast who wanted both social reform and a tougher stance on Catholicism. Saunderson's conservative instincts and his determination to defend landlord interests blinded him to the need for change but, fortunately for Unionism, his younger lieutenants recognised the danger and set about rescuing the party. An early indication that Unionist supporters were unhappy with Saunderson's leadership came in 1900, when he struggled to retain his North Armagh seat at the general election. Widespread disaffection among the constituency's Protestant tenant farmers, who claimed that they had been neglected by Saunderson, saw the Unionist leader's majority fall to just over 1,000 in a contest with an Independent

Unionist. From this point on, though he continued to lead the party until his death in October 1906, Saunderson was really only a figurehead. Control of the party had passed to younger, middle class Unionist MPs, leaving Saunderson free to indulge his passion for golf and yachting.

These younger members of the 'Ulster Party' had witnessed the drift under Saunderson and were well aware of the way in which dangerous opponents such as Russell and Sloan had exploited the party's growing unpopularity. Led by William Moore, the MP for North Antrim, and Charles Craig, the MP for South Antrim, the Unionists went on the offensive at Westminster, focusing their attacks on Sir Anthony MacDonnell, the Under Secretary in Dublin Castle, whose appointment in 1902 had aroused Unionist suspicion. MacDonnell, of course, was a Catholic whose brother was an Irish Nationalist MP, and he had been given something of a free rein in Irish policy formulation by the Chief Secretary, George Wyndham. Unionist attacks on MacDonnell reached a peak in the early months of 1905 and led directly to fierce criticism of Wyndham who, the Unionists alleged, knew of his Under Secretary's role in framing the Irish Reform Association's devolution proposals. This resulted in Wyndham's resignation at the beginning of March 1905. The militant Ulster Unionist group, led by Moore and Craig, which had hounded MacDonnell and then Wyndham, claimed that they had uncovered a plot to introduce Home Rule by the back door, but this concealed their real anxiety about the general direction of the Conservative government's Irish policy. Unionists in Ulster had begun to question Arthur Balfour's Unionist credentials, believing that he had endangered the Union in his attempts to appease Irish Nationalism. In return, it was clear that senior Conservatives, including Balfour were angered by the bitter vendetta waged against Wyndham. Yet an even greater priority for Moore and Craig was the need to reorganise and reinvigorate Ulster Unionism in order to meet the electoral challenges thrown down by Russell and Sloan. MacDonnell's involvement in the devolution scheme, with or without the Chief Secretary's knowledge, presented these emerging Unionist leaders with the ideal opportunity to restore the party's flagging morale.

The first move in the development of this 'new Unionism' had been a meeting in Belfast on 2 December 1904, when a new central Unionist association was formed. Again, Moore seems to have played the pivotal role in the formation of this new organisation which, in March 1905, became formally recognised as the Ulster Unionist Council [57]. The aim of this body was to transform Ulster Unionism into a more coherent fighting force, which would be in direct contact with grass roots Unionist opinion. Its central council was to consist of 200 members, though arrangements were put in place for the easy enlargement of this number. Of the 200, 50 were drawn from Orange lodges, while 50 more came from the existing group of Unionist MPs and peers. The remaining 100 members of the body represented local Unionist associations and were elected democratically. This, theoretically, gave grass roots activists the opportunity to have their voice heard in what became the central authority directing the Ulster Unionist policy. In practice, however, the Ulster Unionist Council was dominated by prominent middle class Unionists, confirming the Protestant bourgeoisie's takeover of the movement at the expense of the landlords.

If the Ulster Unionist Council failed to achieve its immediate objective, it, nevertheless, provided Unionism with an organisational framework which later directed the struggle against Home Rule in the 1912-14 period. The formation of the Ulster Unionist Council also marked a symbolic break in the alliance between Ulster Unionists and Southern Unionists. In 1905 Ulster Unionism had stepped decisively outside the Irish Unionist fold and, in the process, it became not just more exclusive but more radical. While the new body made little direct impact in the general election in January 1906, official Unionism was to benefit from the general revival into which the formation of the Ulster Unionist Council fell. The devolution crisis had enabled the Ulster Unionists to revive the Home Rule bogey, something which had been missing for more than a decade, and this had the effect of galvanising the party into action. Although the Russellite vote fell only slightly in some constituencies, Unionist candidates benefited from the increased turn-out, leaving the Russellite runners increasingly dependent on the support of Catholic tenant farmers. This enabled the Unionist party to recapture East Down and North Fermanagh, two seats they had lost in by-elections to Russellite candidates in 1902 and 1903 respectively.

The principal reason for the new direction taken by Ulster Unionism in 1905, therefore, was the need to stem the Russellite tide and mount a Unionist counter-attack. The devolution crisis presented the ideal opportunity and, simultaneously, allowed Ulster Unionists to revive Home Rule fears and call on traditional supporters to close ranks in the face of such a threat. The new Unionism also confirmed the increasing marginalisation of Saunderson, a trend which had been under way since the beginning of the century. His leadership had been undermined by the efforts of William Moore, Charles Craig and the prominent businessman, John Brownlee Lonsdale, the party secretary and MP for Mid Armagh. Moore, in particular, was a key figure in the formation of new Unionism, and at least part of his motivation seems to have been the threat he faced from independent-minded Protestant tenant farmers in his own constituency. Indeed, despite his achievements, Moore actually lost his North Antrim seat in the 1906 general election to an Independent Unionist who had received support from both Russell and Sloan. Of course, Moore made a quick return to parliament where he took his place near the top of the newly styled Unionist movement. Ulster Unionists had emerged as a more coherent group with a more powerful regional identity. This new Unionism was less concerned about its southern counterpart and more sceptical about the depth of support it could expect from the Conservative party on the mainland, particularly after the devolution proposals came to light. It was more responsive to local or constituency concerns, and this was reflected in the structure of its new organisation. New Unionism was also more militant. The Orange Order, which had just enjoyed a period of rejuvenation, was given a key role at the heart of the movement's organising body, and this, together with a determination to pursue a more independent line, contributed to the increased militancy of new Unionism.

Although both Russell and Sloan had retained their Westminster seats in 1906, the Unionist movement had turned the corner. The Independent Orange Order faced serious internal divisions and Russell's appeals to the Presbyterian tenant farmers had been undermined by the Westminster government's programme of land purchase. Clearly, Ulster Unionism had also benefited from the overhaul of its organisation, which allowed it to respond to the demands of an increasingly rebellious electorate. The credit for the formation of this new Unionism belonged to younger, active figures in the parliamentary ranks, not to Saunderson. He had been ill when the devolution crisis struck and did not attend the crucial meeting organised by Moore in December 1904 or the inaugural meeting of the Ulster Unionist Council on 3 March 1905. Indeed, later, Saunderson showed little enthusiasm for the new organisation. Yet while he had become an irrelevant figure as far as most Ulster Unionists were concerned, Saunderson still had one important function to perform.

The devolution affair had opened a rift between Ulster Unionism and the Conservative government. Even Arthur Balfour, the Prime Minister and a staunch supporter of Unionism in the past, was distrusted because of his alleged sympathy for devolution. The Conservatives, on the other hand, were genuinely shocked at the level of bitterness shown by Ulster Unionists and many were disgusted by the personal attacks on Wyndham. Yet Balfour appeared to appease militant Unionism by the choice of Walter Long to replace Wyndham at the Irish Office. Long was an English country squire and an MP for Bristol, but he had strong connections with Ireland, where his family owned a large estate in County Wicklow. He identified totally with the Southern Unionist landlord class and found it difficult to hide his contempt for the Catholic Irish. Naturally, Long's appointment did much to reassure many of those Unionists who had been shocked by the devolution revelations. Still, the most outspoken Ulster MPs remained critical of the government's Irish policy and were angered by Long's decision to retain the services of MacDonnell as Under Secretary. It was in these circumstances that Saunderson was to prove his worth. Long and Saunderson shared the same background and interests, and the relationship between the two men became very close during Long's nine months as Chief Secretary. Frequently, Long sought the ageing Unionist leader's advice, a strategy which helped to restore better relations between the Conservative government and the Ulster Unionists. Moreover, his tenure of the Chief Secretaryship was noted for his uncompromising attitude to agrarian crime and his firm application of the law, something which, of course, endeared him to the Unionists. Afterwards, he was hailed by Irish Unionists as the best Chief Secretary since Arthur Balfour.

Yet the reason for his brief stay at the Irish Office was Balfour's decision, despite pleas from Long and other cabinet ministers who wanted the Conservative government to soldier on, to resign on 4 December 1905. Since the summer of 1903, the Conservative government had been deeply divided over the issue of tariff reform. British industry had suffered in the teeth of fierce foreign competition, leaving a group of Conservative MPs convinced that the introduction of tariffs on imported goods was vital. Led by Joe Chamberlain, they formed the Tariff Reform League to campaign for 'imperial preference', an economic doctrine which sought to transform the British Empire into a self contained trading unit protected against foreign competition by tariffs. But within the party there was another powerful lobby in favour of free trade. Open warfare between the free traders and the protectionists followed, and this left Balfour desperately searching for a compromise. Eventually, he decided that the fiscal question was one on which the party could agree to differ. In truth, the Conservative government was in terminal decline from 1903, a trend which Balfour's refusal to offer decisive leadership only confirmed. The party suffered a series of humiliating by-election defeats and, by the summer of 1905, it appeared that the government would collapse in disarray. By then the battle for control of the party was raging out of control, and yet Balfour continued to play down the divisions between the protectionists and the free traders. When the government finally resigned in December 1905, the incoming Liberal prime minister immediately opted for a general election in which the Conservative party was routed. The tariff reform controversy had split the party just as the repeal of the corn laws had done in the 1840s and Europe was to do in the 1990s. In the general election of January 1906 the Conservatives won only 157 seats, leaving the Liberals with a commanding overall majority.

Unionism under Long

The general election had been a catastrophe for the Conservative party, and further embarrassment was caused by the failure of a number of cabinet ministers to retain their seats. Even Balfour lost his Manchester seat, but he was subsequently returned at a by-election and he refused to relinquish the leadership of the party. Walter Long was another casualty, losing his South Bristol seat, but the fact that the election lasted two weeks allowed him to gain the Unionist nomination in South Dublin, Plunkett's old seat, which he won with a majority of over 1,000. For those Conservative members who had survived the election Balfour's leadership became a key issue. Chamberlain expected to replace Balfour as leader, though he was reluctant to challenge him openly, believing that mounting pressure would make it impossible for Balfour to continue. His analysis of the election results convinced Chamberlain that the party had to abandon Balfour's 'wait and see' policy in favour of reuniting on a policy of tariff reform. In July 1906, however, Chamberlain suffered a serious stroke, which left him paralysed, and he was to take no further active part in politics. While Chamberlain's illness ended the prospect of any serious challenge to Balfour's leadership, it did nothing to restore party unity. Chamberlain passed on the tariff reform mantle to his son, Austen, who, though lacking his father's political ambition and inspirational qualities, continued the campaign for protective tariffs.

The continuation of the tariff reform controversy alarmed Long. He had wanted the defence of the Union to remain the most important plank in the Conservative party, fearing that excessive concentration on the tariff reform issue would cause the party's MPs to overlook Irish affairs. Long was determined to cement the alliance between Irish Unionism and British Conservatism, something which he himself seemed to symbolise, and he recognised that Irish Unionists needed to have their confidence restored in their English colleagues. In August 1906, therefore, he suddenly reopened the Wyndham–devolution dispute when, in a speech to the Irish Unionist Alliance in Dublin, he called for the publication of all the material relevant to MacDonnell's appointment as Under Secretary in 1902. This infuriated Balfour, and the correspondence which followed between the two men revealed just how much the Conservative leader had lost touch with the Unionists. While Balfour refused to publish the material, the reopening of the dispute established Long as the chief spokesman for *British Unionism*.

At the same time, Long's standing among Irish Unionists was greatly enhanced following his sustained attack on Balfour. It was no surprise, therefore, when he became Unionist leader on Saunderson's death in October 1906. While he understood the need for a closer alliance between British and Irish Unionism, Long was equally anxious that a closer relationship should be established between Ulster Unionists and Southern Unionists. Long's position at the head of the two principal organisations, he had been chosen as chairman of the Southern Unionist Irish Unionist Alliance in October 1906 and been elected chairman of the Ulster Unionist Council in January 1907, gave him the opportunity to realise this aim. In December 1907 Long succeeded, with Southern Unionist support, in establishing the Joint Committee of Unionist Associations, which intended to facilitate co-operation between Unionists north and south. The new body, which alternated its meetings between Dublin and Belfast, consisted of representatives from the Irish Unionist Alliance and the Ulster Unionist Council, but it suffered from an obvious reluctance on the part of the Ulster Unionists to surrender their separate identity. Although the failure of the two groups to co-operate fully must have been frustrating for Long, there was one area where full co-operation was assured. Propaganda work in Britain was given a high priority, and both Ulster Unionists and Southern Unionists joined together in an effort to make this effective. Consequently, Irish Unionist speakers made frequent visits to England, where they highlighted the Liberal government's failure to uphold the law in Ireland and protect the 'loyal' population. These sentiments were echoed in a host of propaganda leaflets which were widely distributed on the mainland.

In Britain, meanwhile, Long was desperate to reawaken Conservative interest in the Irish Question. He was well aware that MacDonnell was hard at work in Dublin Castle on a variation of his devolution scheme, and he feared that any move to tamper with the Union would expose Conservative apathy. He worked hard, writing to old friends and pleading with Conservative audiences all over the country, to garner support for the Unionist cause and, in February 1907, he succeeded in launching the Union Defence League. When Birrell, the Chief Secretary, introduced the Irish Council Bill in May 1907, Long hoped that his new organisation, which included a number of senior Conservatives in its ranks, would make a significant contribution to the bill's defeat. However, the withdrawal of the measure by the Liberal government in June left the Union Defence League without the kind of target which might have galvanised it into action and made it an effective force on the mainland. Thereafter, with Home Rule again on the back-burner, the Union Defence League contented itself with the dreary work of educating British voters, while the Conservative Party returned to the tariff reform imbroglio. Long continued to press Balfour, who had maintained an elegant, equivocal position on the tariff question, to give more thought to Irish affairs, warning him that Conservative apathy posed the greatest danger to the Union. For much of 1908 Long was ill, and this contributed to his decision to look for a safe seat in the south of England. The South Dublin seat was a marginal, and the Unionist voters in the constituency fully understood his decision not to stand in the next general election. Long was now virtually detached from the Irish Unionists, and he spent the first half of 1909 on holiday in South Africa and Rhodesia, allowing his health to recover.

Long returned to London in June of that year to find Westminster gripped by Lloyd George's budget plans. When Asquith had succeeded Campbell-Bannerman as Liberal Prime Minister in 1908, he chose David Lloyd George to be Chancellor of the Exchequer. The new Chancellor wanted a tax raising budget which would pay for the Liberal social reform programme and increased naval expenditure, and he decided that the brunt of this burden should be carried by the wealthy, particularly the landed class.

He wanted to raise income tax and proposed a new supertax for those with incomes of over £5,000 per annum. Death duties were to rise significantly, and there were to be new land taxes. Almost immediately on his return, Long was asked to become President of the Budget Protest League, a position he used to denounce a set of financial proposals which he claimed were socialist in principle and would ultimately destroy Britain's landowning class. During the summer of 1909 Conservative opposition to the Liberal budget mounted, and the decision was then taken to use the powerful Conservative built-in majority in the House of Lords to throw out the budget. Yet such a course had serious constitutional implications. Parliamentary convention dictated that the Lords would not block any Finance Bill and, since this had been the position for 300 years, any decision to defeat the measure in the House of Lords and plunge the country into uncharted constitutional waters could not have been taken lightly.

The Liberals, for their part, had become increasingly frustrated by the Conservatives' use of the Lords to strangle certain measures during the previous few years. When the Upper House threw out the 1909 budget on 30 November, it was obvious that the Liberals would seize the opportunity to appeal to the people in a general election, demanding an end to a system by which hereditary peers could overturn the wishes of the elected House. Naturally, any move to amend the powers of the House of Lords had particular significance for Ireland. Irish Unionists had relied on the Lords to throw out the Second Home Rule Bill in 1893, and it was possible that the constitutional crisis, sparked by the rejection of the budget, would trigger a chain of events which might see a new Home Rule measure circumventing a much less powerful House of Lords. Now Long's warning that the Union was in danger, a warning that he had voiced consistently, though with little effect, since his assumption of the Unionist leadership in 1906, really did cause some stir on the mainland. His central argument was that the stability of the British Empire rested on the maintenance of the Union. Moreover, Long was convinced that the Conservative party's only hope of victory in the forthcoming general election lay in concentrating on the Home Rule issue. Indeed Balfour and other leading Conservatives used the election campaign to trot out all the old arguments against Home Rule [58].

Voting in the general election began on 15 January 1910, and the results were announced towards the end of the month. Although the Conservatives recovered much of the ground they had lost in 1906, their total of 273 seats confirmed them in opposition. The Liberals had won 275 seats and could count on the support of most of the 82 Irish Nationalists and the 40 Labour MPs to give them a comfortable majority. Included in the Conservative total were the 22 seats won by the Unionists in Ireland. With Long now the sitting MP in London's Strand constituency, the Unionists began the task of finding a successor immediately after the general election. The party secretary, J B Lonsdale, the MP for Mid Armagh and a prominent figure in the development of new Unionism, dispatched an invitation to Sir Edward Carson, a leading barrister and the MP for Trinity College Dublin, asking him to become Unionist leader. After a good deal of soul-searching Carson, who realised that his acceptance of the leadership would probably end his hopes of promotion to either the very top political or legal posts, informed Lonsdale that he would accept the position as leader. On 21 February 1910 he met formally with the members of the Unionist parliamentary party and was unanimously elected their leader.

Carson was a strange choice to lead the Unionist party. His ability was beyond question, but Unionism appeared to be entering new and dangerous territory following the general election of 1910 and the likely consequences that its outcome would have for both the House of Lords and Ireland. Long's defection to a safe English seat, while understood by his Dublin Unionist friends, must have raised eyebrows in Ulster. In truth, although his interest in Irish Unionism never wavered, Long was much less active on behalf of the Unionist cause from 1908. By that stage his efforts to revive British interest in Unionism through bodies such as the Union Defence League had achieved little success, and he had begun to look for a safe seat in the south of England. Although he had been elected chairman of the Ulster Unionist Council in January 1907, Long failed to attend the body's annual meetings in 1908 and 1909. Such an obvious lack of commitment could not have gone unnoticed by Ulster Unionists. Yet Carson, who had first entered parliament in 1892, was another outsider whose lack of devotion to the Unionist cause in the 1906-10 period was all too obvious. During these years Carson concentrated on furthering his exceptional legal career, but it was well known he had only entered politics in order to defend the Union, and his colleagues hoped he would deploy his considerable talents in leading them in the new struggle against Home Rule.

On assuming the leadership Carson quickly recognised that his strategy would have to take account of, and would benefit from, the existence of new Unionism. It had been apparent during the 1906-10 period that Irish Unionists exerted much less influence on the Conservative leadership that they had in previous years. Other issues, principally tariff reform, now dominated the internal debate within British Conservatism, in spite of all the efforts made by Long. It was significant, moreover, that there had been a cooling of relations between the Conservatives and Unionists, a development which had its origins in the devolution affair. Balfour, of course, remained committed to the Union, but his attitude in opposition after 1906, when there was little danger to the Union, led Ulster Unionists to mistake laziness for indifference. This perception was amended following the general election in January 1910, when Balfour responded quickly to the new situation. Still, the years after the devolution debate saw the development of a more flexible relationship between British Conservatives and Irish Unionists, and this contributed to the changing character of Unionism. New Unionism became more Ulster focused and more isolationist, and the formation of the Ulster Unionist Council neatly symbolised this transition. The collapse of trust in their Conservative allies had forced Ulster Unionists to become more self-reliant, a development which was mirrored by their waning confidence in the value of parliamentary opposition. The switch to much greater grass roots activity in the Ulster constituencies, which was again a feature of this new Unionism, provided the foundation for extra-parliamentary resistance to Home Rule. Carson was to use this to great effect during the next few years.

Historiography

O ur understanding of Unionism has benefited greatly from the recent work of two historians in particular. Patrick Buckland's pioneering research in the early 1970s looked at the three related, though distinct, forms of Unionism - British Unionism, Southern Unionism and Ulster Unionism - and uncovered the tensions which existed within each of these forms. His two volume history of Irish Unionism; *Irish Unionism 1: The Anglo-Irish and the new Ireland 1885-1922* (Dublin, 1972) and *Irish Unionism 2: Ulster Unionism and the Origins of Northern Ireland 1886-1922* (Dublin, 1973) provide the best general account of Unionism. In addition, his *Irish Unionism 1885-1923: A Documentary History* (Belfast, 1973) offers an extensive range of documentary sources linked together by a very useful analytical overview. More recently, Alvin Jackson has produced a number of articles and two excellent books which offer a detailed analysis of the changing nature of Unionism, leading to the emergence of a new style of Unionist politics in Ulster. Jackson's, *The Ulster Party: Irish Unionists in the House of Commons 1884-1911* (Oxford, 1989) describes in great detail how Unionism underwent a process of 'Ulsterisation'. Later Jackson's, *Colonel Edward Saunderson: Land and Loyalty in Victorian Ireland* (Oxford, 1995) is an important work which deals with Saunderson's contribution to the development of Unionism, concluding that he was an Irish, not an Ulster, Unionist.

An excellent analysis of Ulster politics during Unionism's formative years can be found in B M Walker's, *Ulster Politics: The Formative Years 1868-86* (Belfast, 1989). Walker stresses the importance of Tim Healy's Monaghan by-election victory in July 1883 in concentrating Ulster Protestant minds, claiming that the feared 'Nationalist invasion of Ulster' was the catalyst for the formation of Ulster Unionism. This was, of course, closely followed by the franchise changes of 1884 and the redistribution of seats in 1885, and all these factors not only helped to mould the early shape of Ulster Unionism but also contributed to the high degree of polarisation which became a feature of Ulster politics. Walker also explores the denominational and class differences within Ulster Unionism which became, at times, the focus of tension within the movement. A different angle on the intensification of religious polarisation in Ulster politics is provided by an interesting Marxist interpretation. P Gibbon's, *The Origins of Ulster Unionism* (Manchester, 1975) points out that it was in the 1880s that discrimination in the workplace became a much more serious issue, as industry became more capital intensive and thus required more skilled labour. Loughlin's, *Gladstone, Home Rule and the Ulster Question* emphasises the surprising ignorance which both Liberals and Nationalists exhibited in their assessment of Ulster Unionism during this crucial formative period.

Southern Unionism is expertly dealt with in Buckland's, *Irish Unionism 1*. Buckland gives details of the various Southern Unionist organisations and an outline of their activities, describing how Southern Unionists came to realise the futility of contesting elections in the south and west of Ireland. He also clarifies the relationship between Southern Unionists and British Conservatives, highlighting the significance of personal and family ties and stressing that the Southern Unionists felt they deserved help from Britain. While their reliance on British goodwill may seem naive, Buckland argues that it was not without justification. Although

Southern Unionists played a crucial role in the early years of Unionism, they found, by the early 1890s, that the Ulstermen were becoming "more exclusive and independent". This theme was developed in his *Irish Unionism II* which shows how a provincial Unionist movement developed out of a broader Irish movement. Significantly, Buckland argues that the Orange revival in the early 1880s actually proved a barrier to the rallying of anti-Nationalist forces in Ulster. This view is endorsed in Gibbon's, *Origins of Ulster Unionism* which states that in rural Ulster, in particular, the Orange Order was not a reliable vehicle of political organisation. Instead he claims the Orange Order only became an "effective agency of rural political mobilisation" following the replacement of the Unionist landed leadership by the bourgeoisie. Moreover, this only occurred after a "protracted political struggle had seen the evolution of a recognised local leadership". Gibbon concludes his book by dismissing the common assumption that Ulster Unionism was formed by the convergence of various social groups in response to the advance of Irish Nationalism. The truth, he argues, was that the movement emerged because the Belfast bourgeoisie had already been successful in establishing its authority over both the urban workers and the rural tenant farmers. The background to this, he emphasises, was Ulster's peculiar pattern of industrialisation.

Details of the Ulster Unionist Convention can be found in G Lucy's, *The Great Convention: The Ulster Unionist Convention of 1892* (Lurgan, 1995). Lucy outlines the religious objections to Home Rule and explains how any attempt to impose Home Rule on Ulster would lead to a coordinated plan of passive resistance being put into operation. Gibbon's, *Origins of Ulster Unionism* claims that the 1892 Convention marked the triumph of the Belfast bourgeoisie in its struggle with the landlord class for leadership of the movement, but Jackson's, *The Ulster Party*, while agreeing that tensions between the two social groups were crucial factors in the development of Ulster Unionism, argues that the collapse of landlord power within Unionism was a much slower process than Gibbon suggests. This argument is supported by his analysis of the social backgrounds of the Ulster Unionist MPs, which reveals that the Edwardian Irish Unionist party was broadly similar in social composition to both of the main British parties. While the landlord element declined from 50 per cent in 1885, it was still as high as 33 per cent in 1900 and 25 per cent in 1906. Jackson also highlights the substantial growth in the number of lawyers who became Unionist MPs.

In tracing the origins of British Unionism, Boyce's, *The Irish Question in British Politics* points out that the Conservative party regarded Home Rule as the destruction of the United Kingdom, and what made this even more unpalatable was that the Irish "were not a loyal people". Together these factors created an alliance between British Conservatives and Irish Unionists. Still, Boyce stresses that very few British Unionists followed the advice of A V Dicey, the celebrated Oxford don who constructed the soundest intellectual defence of the Union, to campaign in Irish constituencies in order to demonstrate that "the United Kingdom is really a common country". Although Boyce considers Balfour a committed Unionist, he notes that the Conservative leader would not "push an Irish policy beyond the limits" he believed British public opinion would accept. A detailed study of Balfour's views on Ireland can be located in Shannon's, *Arthur J Balfour and Ireland*. Shannon observes Balfour's deep commitment to the Union, but records his frequent frustration with what he judged to be the excesses of the extremist Ulstermen. Indeed all of these works stress the uneasy nature of the Conservative-Unionist alliance and, as Buckland argues, it was the Ulster Unionists' reluctance to place too much trust on British goodwill, which became one of the crucial differences between Ulster and Southern Unionism.

Jackson's, *The Ulster Party* examines this idea and describes the factors which led to Ulster Unionism developing such a strong regional identity. The pivotal role played by Saunderson, the County Cavan landowner, in holding both strands of Irish Unionism together is clearly outlined in his biography of the first Unionist leader. Significantly, Jackson concludes that Saunderson can best be described as an Irish Unionist whose instincts were more in tune with the threatened Southern Unionist landlords. In *The Ulster Party* Jackson argues that the differences between Ulster Unionism and Southern Unionism should be primarily understood "as questions of class rather than geography". D W Miller's, *Queen's Rebels: Ulster Loyalism in Historical Perspective* (Dublin, 1978) describes the Ulster Unionist relationship with the British people as 'contractarian', arguing that the Ulstermen felt absolved from any obligation to obey the laws of parliament if that parliament threatened, as Home Rule would do, to hand them over to their enemies. Both Jackson's, *The Ulster Party* and Loughlin's, *Gladstone, Home Rule and the Ulster Question* dismiss Miller's theory, though Jackson remarks that Miller's claim that the British state had drifted towards neutrality between the religions in Ireland, a move which facilitated the development of 'constructive Unionism' around the turn of the century, has obvious merits.

In looking at the factions within the Unionist movement Jackson's, *The Ulster Party* states that the Unionist party did not try to enforce strict discipline, and this gave mavericks such as Plunkett, Russell and Sloan free rein to pursue an independent line and criticise the party leadership. Lyons's, *Ireland since the Famine* describes Plunkett as a Unionist who "sat very loose to his party". Plunkett's vision, Lyons comments, was his desire to uphold the Union by reconciliation with the Nationalists rather than by coercing them. Unfortunately, his drive and progressive ideas, which saw fruition during the period of constructive Unionism, were not matched by his political judgement. Jackson's, *The Ulster Party* deals with Russell's impact on the Unionist party, a topic which he has examined more specifically in an article for *Irish Historical Studies*, 'Irish Unionism and the Russellite Threat 1894-1906', xxv, No 100 (November, 1987). He notes the strong personal support which Russell enjoyed from Joseph Chamberlain and the Liberal Unionist wing of the Conservative party. In Ulster Russell appealed primarily to the Presbyterian tenant farmers, and Russellism peaked in the 1900-02 period when, significantly, Home Rule did not figure on the political agenda. Jackson concludes that his movement was really undermined by the devolution crisis and the revival of the Home Rule bogey which was seized upon by Moore and the other founders of new Unionism in order to take the party in a different direction. Sloan's break with Unionism and the impact of the Independent Orange Order is analysed succinctly in H Patterson's, *Class Conflict and Sectarianism: The Protestant Working Class and the Belfast Labour Movement, 1868-1920* (Belfast, 1980). Patterson argues that the danger in interpreting these events is "to overestimate the fragility of official Unionism in this period" when, in fact, Ulster Unionists responded quickly and effectively to this new challenge, allowing Patterson to conclude that the Independent Orange Order was looking at a very bleak future less than three years after its formation. Sloan, meanwhile, is described as a sectarian populist who was never comfortable with the more liberal Lindsay Crawford's attempts to take the Independent Orange Order out of its narrow sectarian confines. A Morgan's, *Labour and Partition: The Belfast Working Class 1905-23* (London, 1991) describes the Magheramorne Manifesto as a radical "statement of Irish, or Ulster, liberalism" but, fearing the loss of his South Belfast seat, Sloan publicly dissociated himself from the manifesto on 1 January 1906, and this division between the two men contributed to the failure of the independent challenge to official Unionism.

The best account of Unionist reaction to the devolution crisis is Jackson's, *The Ulster Party* which outlines the crucial role played by Moore, Craig and the other 'Young Men' of the 'Radical Right' in the formation of the Ulster Unionist Council. Jackson's central argument is that the Unionists attacked the government's devolution proposals not because they feared Home Rule, but because they desperately needed an issue on which to make a popular stand. Their target was the 'Russellite menace' which Saunderson had failed to counter. The changes they put in place rocked the serene independence of the Ulster Unionist MPs giving grass roots activists more power and laying the foundations for a new form of Unionism which would not be confined to a purely parliamentary strategy. On the specific question of whether Wyndham, the Chief Secretary, knew of MacDonnell's work on the devolution scheme, Jackson concurs with Gailey's judgement that he was aware of MacDonnell's contribution and was supportive.

Walter Long's brief tenure of the Irish Chief Secretaryship is assessed in J Kendle's, *Walter Long, Ireland and the Union, 1905-20* (Dun Laoghaire, 1992) which describes how he set out to restore Unionist confidence in the Conservative administration following the devolution affair. Part of his strategy was to seek Saunderson's advice on a regular basis, and Kendle claims that, by their efforts, the two men prevented the disagreement between British Conservatives and Irish Unionists developing into a dangerous split. During his nine months at the Irish Office, Long sought to keep Ireland at the top of the Conservative party's agenda, but the tariff reform controversy had, by this stage, eclipsed Ireland as the issue dominating debate within the party. In an article for *Irish Historical Studies*, 'The Unionist Party and Ireland, 1906-1910', XVI, No 58 (September, 1966) Ronan Fanning describes how Unionists were drawn into the tariff reform controversy because, with Chamberlain determined to make tariff reform the central policy of the Conservative party, people like Long realised that this would have serious implications for Irish Unionism. Fanning concludes that Long was 'flogging a dead horse' in seeking to revive interest in the Home Rule question in England in the 1906-09 period. Kendle also cites Long's growing frustration with English audiences and describes his impatience with Balfour, whose failure to provide the party with strong, decisive leadership was damaging the Unionist cause. In his period as Irish Unionist leader Kendle emphasises Long's view that imperial unity and Home Rule for Ireland were incompatible, a view which seems to have been reinforced by his extensive travelling throughout the Empire.

A good account, which explains how the question of tariff reform came to split the Conservative party can be found in D Dutton's, *His Majesty's Loyal Opposition: The Unionist Party in Opposition 1905-1915*, (Liverpool, 1992). Dutton dwells on the 'political crisis' of the Edwardian era, claiming that the Conservative party appeared unsuited to this new style of more fluid parliamentary politics. It lacked "a sufficient identity of purpose and sense of direction" to meet the challenges of the twentieth century. The only issue which Conservatives could agree on, noted Dutton, was the defence of the Union, and it was not surprising, therefore, that this issue should become so prominent, particularly after the party's mauling at the 1906 general election. Yet Dutton also argues that the way in which Ireland came to dominate British politics in 1911 "to the almost total exclusion of all other issues" could not have been predicted when the Conservatives first went into opposition in December 1905. He chronicles a long list of Balfour's failings and notes that he remained in power only because his critics failed to unite behind an alternative leader. The most obvious leadership candidate was, of course, Joseph Chamberlain, but his illness left Balfour unchallenged. Shannon's, *Arthur J Balfour and Ireland* points out how the Conservative leader returned to familiar ground by making opposition to Home Rule a key plank in his strategy for the general election of January 1910.

Finally, Jackson's, *The Ulster Party* describes the formation of the Ulster Unionist Council as "a natural climax in a long process of Ulsterisation" which had followed the decline of landlordism as a force within Unionism. This process of Ulsterisation, moreover, reflected "a failing confidence in parliamentary resistance", something which did not become fully apparent until the crisis over the third Home Rule Bill.

Chapter 5
Labour rise and fall

As a small nation with a very narrow industrial base, nineteenth century Ireland did not lend itself to the development of socialism. Only in a few centres had there been any substantial industrial development. The most notable, of course, was Belfast and its immediate hinterland, which had grown from a small town with a population of just under 20,000 in 1800 to become the fastest growing city in the United Kingdom. By 1900 its population was approaching 400,000. In the first half of the century Belfast's industrial growth had been sparked by the boom in textile manufacturing, and this had attracted newcomers from all over Ulster. Initially, cotton was the main textile but, by the second half of the century, linen was dominant, and Belfast became the greatest centre of linen production in the world by the 1860s, employing over 60,000 workers. In this early phase of capitalist development the cyclical nature of the textile industry was very pronounced with rapid booms preceding spectacular downturns. Added to the consequent job insecurity were the poor conditions and low wages suffered by large numbers of women and smaller numbers of men and children who toiled in the mills. Such a degree of exploitation might have offered fertile ground for the growth of trade unionism, but low paid, mainly unskilled employees, most of whom were women and children and were easily replaced, hindered any such development. The organisation of trade unions proved much more suited to the skilled workers in shipbuilding and engineering, both of which really boomed after 1870.

Shipbuilding in Belfast is synonymous with the name of Harland and Wolff, the firm which first began to construct ships on the Queen's Island in the 1850s. The significant economic growth which Britain enjoyed from the 1860s and the consequent increase in the demand for ships provided an excellent business opportunity for any shipbuilding firm prepared to embrace the latest technology. Harland and Wolff proved to be a very innovative shipbuilding concern, and it quickly developed the capability to produce large iron ships with more sophisticated marine engines. This allowed the firm to become the leading producer of large passenger liners, many of which were built for Liverpool's famous White Star Line. By the end of the century Harland and Wolff was the biggest shipyard in the world, employing some 9,000 men, a figure which increased sharply in the run up to the First World War. Another yard Workman and Clark, opened in 1879, and it specialised in smaller vessels. Closely allied to shipbuilding were the engineering firms which had sprung up in the city. Engineering had first developed to meet the textile industry's demands for new machinery but, by the end of the century, these engineering firms were manufacturing steam engines, water turbines and other shipping components. Both shipbuilding and engineering required skilled labour and paid higher wages, factors which aided the growth of trade unionism among their workforces. By the end of the nineteenth century the difference between average wages for skilled and unskilled workers was higher in Belfast than in any other part of the United Kingdom.

Dublin, by contrast, did not share in the rapid industrial expansion in textiles and shipbuilding. By 1900, moreover, it had been outstripped by Belfast in terms of population. Dublin was essentially a commercial and administrative centre, and its main industries were brewing and biscuit making. Here the household names of Guinness' brewery and Jacob's biscuit factory dominated production. Only the Guinness brewery offered a large number of men the chance of permanent well paid employment, while women worked for less wages in the biscuit factory. Many other jobs in Dublin offered 'casual' employment, and this was common in the docks and in the building trade. In general, the Dublin working class also suffered poorer living conditions than their counterparts in Belfast. They lived in decaying city centre tenements with many families confined to a single room. It was in these overcrowded slum dwellings that the militant trade unionism, which was such a feature of the city in the early part of the twentieth century, found its foot soldiers.

Of course, both Dublin's brewery and biscuit making industries had close ties with agriculture which obviously dominated the Irish economy. In the last quarter of the nineteenth century the land question moved centre-stage, as those who worked the land fought to become the owners of the land. This struggle appeared to offer a glimmer of hope for the advance of socialism, and one of the key figures in the Land War, Michael Davitt, argued strongly that the 'feudal system', that he claimed the landlords operated, should be replaced by the nationalisation of the land. Davitt, however, found that very few people in Ireland shared his vision of collective ownership. Instead, they supported the various land purchase schemes favoured by the British government, and these had the effect of creating a new rural bourgeoisie in Ireland. At the top of this new class in rural Ireland were the thousands of small farmers all over the country who had recently become owner occupiers. Another important layer in this growing rural bourgeoisie were the shopkeepers and publicans in the towns and villages. Their businesses largely depended on the prosperity of the surrounding agricultural hinterland, and this explains their involvement in the land question and in local politics. The fusing of the land and national questions gave the IPP a popular social programme, but it also helped to ensure that Ireland's modern social and economic revolution was carried through within strict bourgeois parameters. This meant that the large number of landless labourers, the rural proletariat, were excluded from the benefits of the huge transfer of land ownership which took place around the turn of the century. The new rural bourgeoisie would ensure that this exclusion would continue.

On this crucial issue of land ownership, therefore, Ireland followed the pattern of most European peasant societies. Thus tenant farmers in Ireland or peasants in the Ukraine demanded only those lands to which they believed they had a moral right. The land, it was argued, belonged to those who worked it, and in Ireland's case such claims also had a certain legal justification, as social revolutionaries such as Michael Davitt constantly reminded the poor smallholders of the west that English landlords had only recently seized their land. Davitt failed, however, to convince these Irish tenants that they should demand land on other grounds and, consequently, his demand for land nationalisation attracted few followers. Two contemporary writers who expressed an interest in the Irish question in general and the land problem in particular were Karl Marx and Friedrich Engels. This duo had formulated a theory, based on the premise that all past history was the 'history of class struggles' which, for them at any rate, proved that the triumph of socialism was inevitable. Marx and Engels were generally sympathetic to Irish Nationalism, but they developed their analysis to argue that Britain's ultimate freedom from capitalism was dependent on Ireland's separation from Britain, and the British working class should, therefore, actively pursue a policy which would hasten Irish independence [59]. Together, Marx and Engels produced some 500 pages on Ireland, mostly in the form of notes, articles and letters, though Engels, who made two tours of the country, had begun a *History of Ireland* which was incomplete at the time of his death. Both men regarded Ireland as England's first colony, and they claimed that the landlord system, which the English government had introduced and protected, was the basis of English power in Ireland. Hence they understood that the struggle against landlordism was necessarily bound up with the struggle for political freedom. While both men constantly stressed the need for the proletariat to assume an international character, Marx, and particularly Engels, could make an exception for Ireland in its pursuit of national independence.

A hesitant start

Although Ireland had provided an interesting case study for the two most important socialist thinkers in the nineteenth century, there was little evidence of progress beyond such intellectual theorising. True, Fenianism had exhibited a socialist tinge, a development welcomed by Marx and Engels but, generally, the predominance of the national question restricted the opportunities for an Irish labour movement. This concentration on the national question had, of course, worked against the development of a party system based on class division, as attitudes to the Union became the key factor in determining political allegiance. Social and economic problems were not ignored, but the Nationalist line was that their solution would have to wait until self government had been achieved. The Catholic Church was another powerful force with a vested interest in maintaining Ireland's social conservatism. While the hierarchy could easily endorse, and openly express, Nationalist sentiments, it was anxious to avoid the kind of social changes which the growth of a more urban society had fostered in the rest of Europe.

All of these factors, together with the crucial lack of industrialisation outside the Belfast area, made Ireland appear an unlikely place for the development of a radical, working class movement. Nevertheless, a powerful, though small, labour movement did emerge around the turn of the century, and it was to have a powerful influence on events. Whereas the labour movement in Britain expanded gradually in the most favourable of climates, slowly adding political influence to its newly found economic power, its Irish counterpart developed rapidly and made an immediate impact. Moreover, while the leadership of the British labour movement was characterised by its moderate approach, the Irish movement threw up two leaders whose advanced socialist views quickly seized the attention of contemporary European activists on the left. Trade unions in Ireland had developed in the nineteenth century, but they were conservative organisations whose concern was to protect the interests of skilled workers. Indeed most of these unions were British based and, with the establishment of the Trades Union Congress (TUC) in 1868, Irish workers were content to fall under the management of a large and potentially powerful British organisation. This situation continued for the next quarter of a century, but the increasing focus on the national question together with the growing realisation that Irish labour interests were receiving little attention from the British TUC fuelled the desire for an Irish organisation. A final spur seems to have been the British TUC's decision to hold its 1893 Conference in Belfast because, in the following year, the Irish Trades Union Congress (ITUC) was established. Despite this breakthrough, however, the ITUC modelled itself on the British body and did not see itself as a replacement for the British TUC, declaring that its aim was to complement the work of its larger brother. Yet in the longer term the establishment of the ITUC led to the gradual separation of the two movements. The Irish organisation was actually ignored by the British TUC during the early years of its existence but, in 1900, it was invited to merge with the British movement, an offer which the ITUC declined. By the end of the nineteenth century the number of workers represented by the ITUC had risen to 60,000, but Congress was still dominated by the skilled unions, most of which had their headquarters in Britain. Not surprisingly, therefore, the ITUC initially adopted a moderate, reformist approach, ignoring the radical socialist demands which were emanating form the left in contemporary Europe.

Only slowly then did a labour political movement emerge. Evidence that working class consciousness was growing came with the formation of Trades Councils in various Irish towns and cities in the last two decades of the nineteenth century. These new bodies, which followed the British example, offered a forum for the expression of radical ideas with the views of skilled workers again to the fore. In fact, the two most important Trades Councils in Belfast and Dublin proved to be more in touch with labour feeling in Ireland than the ITUC and, by the end of the century, the Belfast Trades Council was claiming to represent 19,000 workers. Naturally, the work of the Trades Councils pulled the labour movement towards electoral politics. It was in Belfast that labour political development was most significant and, early in 1893, the Independent Labour Party (ILP) was formed in the city. On the national question the Belfast workers were firmly against Home Rule and, consequently, the political complexion of the Belfast labour movement emerged as a cocktail of socialism and Unionism. The leading figure in the development of this 'Labour Unionism' was William Walker, a shipyard carpenter, who had been active in both the Belfast Trades Council and the ITUC. When the Trades Council contested the 1897 municipal elections, Walker was one of six successful candidates. Labour Unionism, or Walkerism, was closely identified with the interests of Belfast's Protestant workers who believed that their economic prosperity depended on the link with Britain. Nationalism, with its clerical and agrarian trappings, was thus seen as a threat by the city's Protestant working class, particularly the artisan class.

Whereas the labour movement in Belfast was hostile to Irish Nationalism, delegates to the Trades Council in Dublin were in broad sympathy with the IPP. Yet labour political aspirations were raised by the 1898 Local Government Act, which ushered in a new era of democratisation in local government. Labour electoral associations were formed in Dublin and in a host of other towns, and in the Dublin municipal elections of 1899 eleven Labour candidates were successful. Further Labour successes were recorded in places as far apart as Dundalk, Waterford, Castlebar and Limerick, but Labour's impact in local government politics was very disappointing. Few constructive changes were made to improve the lives of the working class, and in Dublin where the expectations of the poor were highest, Labour councillors became sucked into the web of corruption common in municipal politics, as many of them became employees of the corporation. Clearly, Labour suffered from poor organisation and a lack of leadership, and Labour candidates were easily defeated in the 1903 local government elections by a reunited IPP. Only in Belfast, where Labour obviously served the interests of, at least, the Protestant skilled workers, did the labour movement prosper. There Walker had led a carpenter's strike which lasted for eight months in 1899-1900, and he was appointed as a full time organiser for the Amalgamated Society of Carpenters and Joiners in 1903. This proved a crucial appointment, as it gave Walker the opportunity to engage in further labour activity and this culminated in his decision to contest one of Belfast's four parliamentary seats on Labour's behalf.

Between 1905 and 1907 Walker fought North Belfast on three occasions - in two by-elections in 1905 and 1907 and at the 1906 general election. In the by-election held in March 1905 Walker faced the Unionist, Sir Daniel Dixon, a former Lord Mayor of Belfast. Dixon was a poor candidate, and he faced allegations of corruption following his involvement in a major land deal which led to the Belfast corporation purchasing development land at a hugely inflated price. Walker, on the other hand, was a very strong candidate who enjoyed the financial backing of his union, and he also had the advantage of having Ramsay MacDonald, later Labour's first Prime Minister, appointed as his election agent. Just when Walker appeared to be on the brink of victory, he made a fatal error only days before polling which was to cost him the seat. Throughout the campaign Walker had emphasised that he was "a Unionist in politics" but, unlike his opponent, he foolishly replied to a Belfast Protestant Association questionnaire circulated to the candidates. Walker's responses confirmed his fiercely anti-Catholic views, and this was seized upon by his Unionist opponents who immediately placed posters detailing Walker's sectarian comments throughout the Catholic wards in the North Belfast constituency. Undoubtedly, this cost Walker Catholic votes and Dixon won the by-election with a majority of 474 votes. Despite this controversy, Walker fought Dixon again for the parliamentary seat in the general election only nine months later. While he maintained his opposition to Home Rule, Walker avoided the overt sectarianism of the by-election campaign. He increased his share of the vote, losing narrowly by only 291 votes, and it seemed likely that the seat was destined to become the first in Ireland to return a Labour MP to Westminster. A by-election in 1907 following Dixon's death, however, shattered this illusion. The new Unionist candidate was the shipyard owner, Sir George Clark, a man with great influence in the constituency and a powerful representative of the new style of Unionism which had emerged with the creation of the UUC in 1905. Clark scored a comfortable 1,800 majority over Walker whose attempts to stress his anti-Nationalist credentials proved ineffective against such a strong opponent. While Walker remained an active trade union leader, the North Belfast by-election marked the end of Walkerism as an effective political force. Earlier that year, all of Labour's seven candidates, including Walker himself, were defeated in the municipal elections. In the end the combination of reformist socialism and Unionism offered by Walker found itself under increasing pressure from a rejuvenated Unionist party and, as tension mounted on the Home Rule front, there was little opportunity for Labour Unionism to make progress.

If Walker's socialism was both moderate and Unionist, there was an alternative in Dublin which was both radical and Nationalist [60]. The Irish Socialist Republican Party (ISRP) had been formed in Dublin in 1896 with the aim, as its name declared, of creating a socialist republic in Ireland. The driving force behind this tiny group was James Connolly. Connolly had been born to Irish parents in an Edinburgh slum, and after a number of jobs the young James falsified his application and joined the British Army at the age of fourteen. During his seven years in the army Connolly served in Ireland and learned more about the country and its politics. On his release from the army Connolly settled in Edinburgh where he worked for the corporation, and it was in the Scottish capital that he came under the influence of John Leslie, an active Marxist and Fenian sympathiser. Quickly, Connolly came to appreciate that socialism and Nationalism, which many Marxists viewed as opposites were, in fact, complementary to each other in the Irish case. Following his defeat as a socialist candidate in an Edinburgh municipal election Connolly, on Leslie's advice, moved to Dublin where he immediately immersed himself in the politics of the radical socialist fringe before launching the ISRP. The party's general aim was the demand for "public ownership by the Irish people of the land and instruments of production, distribution and exchange". This was a common goal shared by many European revolutionary socialist parties, but the original concept introduced by the ISRP was the demand for an Irish socialist republic and, in his early writings, Connolly indicated that Ireland would have to win full freedom from Britain before a socialist society could be established.

Another figure, this time from the past, to have a profound influence on Connolly was James Fintan Lalor, a revolutionary from the 1848 class, who had argued for the destruction of landlordism and its replacement by the common ownership of the land. Working with adherents to the new Nationalism, such as Maud Gonne and Alice Milligan, Connolly produced a stream of newspaper articles and pamphlets in which he applied Marx's 'scientific socialism' to the conditions in Ireland. In an attempt to educate the Dublin working class the ISRP launched a new newspaper, *Workers' Republic*, in 1898, but it suffered from financial insecurity and had to be wound up after only three months in circulation. Undeterred, Connolly continued with the open-air weekly meetings outside the city's Custom House before restarting the newspaper, this time using an old hand press to reduce costs. Yet despite Connolly's commitment and enthusiasm, the ISRP struggled to hold on to its small number of active members. Moreover, the party's electoral fortunes mirrored its failure to win new converts. Between 1899 and 1903 the ISRP fielded nine candidates, with Connolly himself running on two occasions, in the Dublin municipal elections, but the party never came close to having a councillor elected. Connolly's brand of republican socialism failed to win popular support, and it made him an easy target for clerical opponents who denounced him as anti-Catholic. By 1903 it was clear to Connolly that the immediate prospects for a socialist advance in Ireland were hopeless and, with his own financial situation precarious, Connolly took the decision to emigrate with his family to the United States. The *Workers' Republic* had finally folded and the tiny ISRP almost disappeared with his departure. In the United States Connolly again threw himself into labour politics and became embroiled in the usual faction fighting which seemed to plague all embryonic socialist movements. He continued to produce a plethora of socialist literature, and it was in the United States that he wrote his most important work, *Labour in Irish History*, which was published after his return to Ireland in July 1910 [61].

The rise of Labour

Although he had little formal education, Connolly established an international reputation as a leading socialist intellectual. The other great socialist leader thrown up by the Irish working class movement, James Larkin, was less of a theorist, but more of a practical socialist who was influenced by the syndicalist movement which was beginning to assert itself on the continent. Larkin was born in Liverpool in 1876 but, like Connolly, his parents were of Irish origin. In his native city Larkin, starting at the age of eleven, moved through a variety of jobs before finding employment in the docks. Initially, Larkin had not been involved in trade union activity, but he was a committed socialist and was active in the city's fledgling Labour party. He joined the National Union of Dock Labourers (NUDL) in 1901, but it was 1905 before he rose to prominence in the NUDL's ranks. He became an organiser for the NUDL and helped to spread the union's presence beyond its Liverpool headquarters by recruiting members in other ports. Soon, Larkin came to see militant trade union activity as a necessary stepping stone on the road to the socialist transformation of society. Like the syndicalists, Larkin had little time for moderate Labour leaders who sought the gradual reform of the capitalist system. Instead, he favoured 'direct action' in the form of strikes or, more particularly, the general strike to enable the workers to secure the ownership of the means of production. If this was to be achieved, the unskilled workers had to be organised and, to accomplish this, Larkin helped to build on the success of the 'new unionism' which had seen a move to unionise the unskilled workers, with the dockers in the vanguard, in the 1890s.

In January 1907 Larkin arrived in Belfast. His task was to recruit new members for his Liverpool based union and to organise the Belfast dockers. These workers, who were usually a combination of full time and casual labourers, had been a frequent target for exploitation by ruthless employers. Larkin made an immediate impact. A tall, striking figure with abundant energy, Larkin was an inspirational public speaker and had a charismatic hold on his followers and, within four months of his arrival, he had recruited 4,000 members for the NUDL from both wings of the city's sectarian divide. Soon, the union was involved in a major industrial dispute. The Belfast dock strike began in May 1907, when some NUDL men refused to work alongside nonunion dockers. Although Larkin insisted that his union was not operating a 'closed shop' policy and immediately persuaded the men to resume work, the employers took a tough line, sacking the NUDL men involved in the dispute and replacing them with 'blackleg' labour sent from Liverpool. When Larkin's offer of negotiations was refused, he called his dockers out on a strike which was to last for seven months. Joining the dockers were a significant number of carters and coal labourers and, by mid-July, some 2,500 men were involved in the industrial action. The employers responded by refusing to recognise the NUDL's right to speak on behalf of its members, and they raised the stakes considerably by importing more blackleg labour from England. Violent clashes between the striking dockers and their blackleg replacements followed, but the crisis really deepened when, in July 1907, a section of the RIC, which had been brought in to protect the new workers, also took industrial action.

The police sympathised with the striking dockers, but their action was primarily a consequence of a Royal Commission report on RIC grievances, which had failed utterly to address the problems of low wages, long hours and poor conditions in the police service. By the end of July many of the 200 RIC men who had taken industrial action, and had won Larkin's backing for their stand, had been transferred to country stations, but such was the shock to the authorities that Belfast's Lord Mayor, fearing another police mutiny, called in the army to help maintain order. However, the sudden appearance of some 7,000 troops in the city sparked off fierce rioting in the Catholic Falls Road area and, when the army over-reacted in response to rioting youths, two innocent bystanders were shot dead. The use of troops and the response that this induced in Nationalist areas of the city allowed the employers and the Unionist press to castigate Larkin and the dockers' industrial action, claiming that the strike had been a carefully engineered Nationalist plot aimed at undermining Belfast's commercial prosperity. By November 1907 the strike had all but petered out. The strikers' families were having to survive on meagre strike pay, and this was threatening to bankrupt the NUDL which was providing the money. Larkin came under strong pressure from his union's British leadership to end the strike and, with the carters drifting back to work, the solidarity which had been such a feature of the industrial action began to crumble. The strike ended when two senior trade union officials were dispatched from England to negotiate with the employers, and they settled the dispute without reference to those still on strike. Larkin and his striking dockers had been defeated by a group of ruthless employers who were prepared, if necessary, to starve the strikers into submission and, in the end, the workers were forced to return on unfavourable terms.

Larkin had failed but, as his biographer states, "he shook Belfast to its roots". Although his NUDL men were mainly Protestant, Larkin had, for a short time anyway, succeeded in raising working class solidarity and working class consciousness high enough to blot out sectarian differences in what was, of course, a bitterly divided city. This was in marked contrast to the Orange populism of Tom Sloan, and even to the more respectable Labour Unionism of William Walker, both strong features of contemporary Belfast, but Larkin could only look on in dismay as the religious pattern of industrial relations quickly undermined the short-lived solidarity [62]. Still, his experiences in Belfast had a profound effect on Larkin and helped to convince him that only a big Irish based union could look after Irish labour interests.

Larkin had felt betrayed by the failure of the British trade union movement to maintain its support for the Belfast strikers, and he was determined that future industrial action would not fail because too much trust had been placed on British support. A similar failure, though on a much smaller scale, had occurred with striking members of the NUDL in Newry at the end of 1907, and this served to reinforce Larkin's new thinking. In 1908 Larkin continued to organise NUDL branches in other Irish ports, and he was involved in industrial action in both Dublin and Cork. In Dublin, moreover, Larkin was drawn into disputes involving other groups of unskilled workers, particularly carters, in which he fought for the workers' basic rights to belong to a trade union and to engage in collective bargaining. Ever since the Belfast dock strike, Larkin had been at odds with the NUDL's national leadership, and his diversion into these other industrial disputes strained relations further. The irony for Larkin was that just as he was achieving cult status in Dublin as the workers' organiser and defender, the dockers' executive in Liverpool sacked him as a union official in December 1908. The executive had finally reached its decision after a long debate in which Larkin's actions in Dublin were heavily criticised. Yet their real concern seems to have been over the principle of supporting strike action in Ireland with funds contributed by workers on the mainland.

Larkin's dismissal ended his association with the NUDL, but he was determined to remain in Dublin and organise the city's mass of unskilled workers. After some initial hesitation Larkin was persuaded that the way ahead lay with the organisation of an Irish national union and, consequently, the Irish Transport and General Workers' Union (ITGWU) was launched on 29 December 1908. Larkin was appointed general secretary, and the new union drew its membership from dockers, carters and other, mostly unskilled, workers. In fact, many of Larkin's old NUDL branches simply defected en masse to the new union. In his role as general secretary Larkin was frequently a disorganised and inefficient administrator, but his indomitable spirit and spontaneous genius more than compensated for these failings. Under his leadership the ITGWU grew rapidly, but its Nationalist outlook, which Larkin acknowledged as an inevitable development, hindered its growth among Belfast's Protestant workers. In its desperation to create space between itself and the British movement, therefore, the ITGWU adopted a broadly Nationalist position which ultimately limited its potential for a significant working class advance in Ireland. Despite its Nationalist stance, the ITGWU was the first Irish union to adopt a clear socialist programme which demanded the land for the Irish people together with a major commitment to wholesale nationalisation. In its first few years of existence the union was engaged in a whirlwind of industrial action and, though it enjoyed only limited success, it was clear that the ITGWU under Larkin's direction had transformed industrial relations in Ireland.

Not surprisingly, Larkin's style of leadership made him a number of bitter personal enemies. Moreover, old colleagues in the NUDL, who had been subjected to Larkin's vitriolic attacks, were out for revenge and, on 18 August 1909, Larkin was arrested in Dublin and brought before a magistrate. The charge against him, 'conspiracy to defraud', arose out of incidents in Cork, where it was alleged that he had misused funds belonging to the city's NUDL branch. After much delay Larkin was sentenced in June 1910 to a year's hard labour. The evidence against him was flimsy, but his conviction was a foregone conclusion. His sentence unleashed a wave of popular sympathy and support and, following great public pressure, he was released from Mountjoy prison on 1 October. That evening a torchlight procession wound its way through the streets of Dublin en route to a great rally at which Larkin was given a hero's welcome by his working class followers. Yet it was not just the city's employers who had been shaken by 'Larkinism'. The formation of the ITGWU had been savagely denounced by Arthur Griffith's Sinn Féin, and there followed a bitter personal feud between Larkin and Griffith. The latter opened the columns of his newspaper to a variety of Larkin's enemies who were anxious to pour criticism on the 'English strike organiser'.

While Larkin fully realised the potential of his union as it engaged in industrial warfare, he was not a syndicalist in the purest European sense. There the syndicalists viewed political action as worthless and relied on industrial action, principally the general strike, to undermine capitalism, but Larkin believed that political and economic opposition to society's vested interests had to complement each other. Consequently, Larkin worked hard to shift the balance on the Dublin Trades Council sharply to the left, a feat which he had achieved by the early months of 1911. The labour movement's political organisation received a further boost with the return of James Connolly from the United States in July 1910. When he had sailed for the United States in 1903, the tiny ISRP over which he presided quickly folded, but a group of his devotees came together in 1904 to form the Socialist Party of Ireland (SPI). On his return Connolly resumed the task of rebuilding socialism working as an organiser for the SPI, but the party was unable to raise the money necessary to keep him employed. The situation was retrieved in July 1911, when Larkin offered Connolly the position of ITGWU organiser in Belfast. Although the two men had very different personalities and often quarrelled bitterly, they shared a mutual respect for each other and co-operated in their joint desire to strengthen the labour movement's political wing. Whereas Connolly was small in stature and carried the air of a retiring academic, Larkin was a big, outgoing, charismatic personality who was more interested in practical application than socialist theory. Moreover, while Larkin was a practising Catholic, Connolly was a dedicated atheist whose fierce commitment to a socialist republic naturally made the task of developing the ITGWU in Belfast much more difficult.

Not surprisingly, with tension mounting over a likely Home Rule measure, Connolly was drawn into a struggle against the bitter sectarian rivalry under which the city laboured. He was determined that Belfast should have a united labour movement in which working class consciousness overwhelmed religious differences [63]. This meant, of course, that he had to find common ground with William Walker's Labour Unionism, and a conference aimed at establishing socialist unity was held at Easter 1912 in Dublin. The conference resulted in the establishment of the Independent Labour Party of Ireland, though it later adopted the old Socialist Party of Ireland (SPI) label. The new group had clearly defined socialist aims and it supported Home Rule, arguing that its implementation would be a major step towards ending sectarian division among Irish workers. Walker's North Belfast branch, however, had taken no part in the conference, as he stuck rigidly to the principle of working in tandem with the British labour movement. Meanwhile, supporters of Larkin and Connolly had been pressing the ITUC, to which the ITGWU had affiliated in 1910, to establish a new Labour party but, when this looked likely in 1911, Walker used his influence to defeat the move, arguing that there was no reason whatsoever for Irish workers "to divorce themselves from their English and Scottish fellow workers". By the following year Connolly had been elected as an ITUC delegate, and he used his position to campaign vigorously for the formation of a new political movement. This was achieved in 1912, when Congress voted decisively at its annual conference to form a Labour party, though there was a frustrating delay of several months before the new party was actually launched.

For a few years after there was some confusion in labour politics with the small Independent Labour Party of Ireland, or SPI as it was still called, existing alongside the new Irish Trade Union Congress and Labour party, or the Congress party as it was often known. These political developments were encouraged by success in the 1912 local government elections. Six Labour candidates were elected to the Dublin corporation, and there were Labour victories in a number of other towns where the ITGWU was politically active. One of the successful candidates in Dublin had been Larkin, polling over 1,200 votes, but he was removed from office after only one month following a court action which claimed that, as a convicted felon, he had no right to sit in the corporation. The judge eventually debarred him from sitting in the corporation for a term of seven years. Still, the successes by Labour candidates in local government elections and the launch of the new Congress party gave valuable experience to the growing number of talented young activists thrown up by the emerging labour movement. The most prominent of these were William O'Brien, a master-tailor by trade and a senior official in the ITGWU, P T Daly, another senior ITGWU official who also joined Sinn Féin, Thomas Johnson, a native of Liverpool who had served on Larkin's strike committee during the Belfast dock strike of 1907 and M J O'Lehane, the founder of the Drapers' Assistants Association and a dedicated Larkinite. All of them were committed socialists who worked hard for the labour movement on both the industrial and political fronts. In Belfast, meanwhile, Connolly's struggle for socialist unity was becoming increasingly hopeless, as tension mounted with the introduction of the third Home Rule Bill in 1912. Unionist mobilisation in opposition to the threat of Home Rule had left Connolly exposed, making him an easy target for the Unionist press who denounced him as a Home Ruler. By 1913 he had become dismayed at the degree of control which the Belfast bourgeoisie exercised over the city's Protestant workers, but his uphill struggle to establish working class unity ended in August 1913, when he was summoned to Dublin by his union which was about to engage in militant industrial action against the Dublin employers.

Conflict and defeat

While the political efforts of the various socialist parties had aroused interest in a number of Irish towns, it was the industrial struggle which was of paramount importance. Mirroring events in Britain and on the continent, Larkin's union was engaged in a succession of labour disputes, as industrial strife reached a new peak. The numbers in the ITGWU climbed as industrial unrest grew, and the unions secured a number of concessions from the employers. The key to the power of the Transport Union was the workers' solidarity, as Larkin used secondary action to prevent the movement of 'tainted' goods which were produced by any employer in dispute with his union. In 1911 the ITGWU had about 4,000 paid-up members, but this had doubled to 8,000 by the end of 1912 and to 10,000 by the middle of 1913. Larkin had used the *Irish Worker*, a weekly newspaper costing one penny that had first appeared in May 1911, to reflect the growing militancy of the Irish working class, and the paper had exposed a large number of scandals involving the ruthless exploitation of certain workers. The activities of the Transport Union had obviously shaken the employers, and they had resolved in July 1911 to take action against growing industrial militancy. The employers formed the Dublin Employers' Federation which was based on the Dublin Chamber of Commerce and led by William Martin Murphy, a former Nationalist MP and the city's most prominent business tycoon. He owned the *Irish Independent*, then Ireland's largest newspaper, was chairman of the Dublin United Tramway Company, and had a host of other business interests. Murphy was determined to break the ITGWU's hold on Dublin workers, and a clash with Larkin, whom his newspaper constantly denounced, was inevitable **[64]**.

By 1913 'Big Jim', as he was affectionately known by the Dublin working class, was at the height of his powers. He had succeeded in organising the city's unskilled workers in one big union and had done much to raise their spirits. This had not been an easy task, as Dublin then had the worst living conditions for the poor of any city in the United Kingdom. Census returns in 1911 confirmed that 20,000 families lived in one room, all of them in old tenements which were frequently in a dangerous state. The infant mortality rate was shocking as killer diseases such as cholera took an inevitable toll. Thousands of families had to exist on less than £1 per week, and it was for these people that Larkin demanded social justice. Industrial unrest escalated during 1913. In Dublin alone, from January to mid-August, there were 30 strikes, and a major confrontation between Larkin's Transport Union and Murphy's Employers' Federation moved even closer. What really sparked off this conflict was Larkin's move to enroll Murphy's United Tramway men in the ITGWU. Larkin's case had obvious appeal for the workers, as the Dublin tram men earned on average 25 per cent less than their colleagues in Belfast, but Murphy was adamant that his employees would not join the ITGWU.

In August 1913 Murphy demonstrated his resolve by sacking men in both the dispatch department of the *Irish Independent* and the parcel service of the tramway company, when he discovered that they had joined Larkin's union. He also voiced his determination never to negotiate with the ITGWU. Larkin responded by placing union pickets on the newspaper's dispatch department and, on 23 August, the tram men met at Liberty Hall, the union's headquarters, where they voted in favour of a strike. The date of the strike was fixed for Tuesday, 26 August. Just before 10 o'clock that morning 200 drivers and conductors suddenly left their trams on the streets. Larkin's men had walked out without warning, hoping to cause maximum disruption in the city which was then hosting its famous annual Horse Show. Yet the union knew that it needed this element of surprise to cause confusion, as only a minority of the tram men were in the Transport Union. In fact, the strike was only partially effective as Murphy quickly replaced those tram men on strike. Following a mass meeting on the evening of the strike several leading figures in the union, including Larkin, P T Daly and William O'Brien, were arrested and charged with "seditious speaking, seditious conspiracy to hold meetings, and unlawful assembly". They were released on bail after they had indicated that they would not hold any unlawful meetings, and the authorities confirmed this tough approach when a big labour demonstration organised for Sunday, 31 August, was banned. Not surprisingly, Larkin brushed aside this threat and burned a copy of the proclamation banning the demonstration before a cheering crowd in O'Connell Street. Connolly was equally defiant when he addressed the same audience in an effort to rally support for the strikers.

After the O'Connell Street gathering Connolly was arrested, but Larkin managed to slip out of a rear entrance at Liberty Hall, as the Dublin Metropolitan Police (DMP) approached the building to arrest him. With Larkin in hiding the ITGWU faced a dilemma. Some of the leaders, including O'Brien, were anxious to avoid further confrontation with the authorities, and they announced that the Sunday demonstration would be switched from O'Connell Street to Croydon Park, some distance from the city centre. From his secret location, however, Larkin sent word that in spite of the compromise arrangements announced by O'Brien, he personally would hold a meeting in O'Connell Street. On that Sunday a large force of police had taken up positions along the length of O'Connell Street to prevent any meeting taking place. At Liberty Hall, in the meantime, a huge crowd of about 15,000 assembled and were led off in the direction of the new venue at Croydon Park by O'Brien and Daly. Back in O'Connell Street a small crowd of 300 to 400 had gathered close to the General Post Office (GPO) in the hope that Larkin would make a surprise appearance. He did not let them down because, after donning a disguise and slipping into the Imperial Hotel opposite the GPO, he appeared suddenly on an outside balcony in full view of the crowd [65]. In the excitement the crowd surged across the street only to see Larkin being led away by police. In the confusion which followed a police baton charge was ordered and the small crowd found itself trapped between two lines of baton-wielding police. Many of those who fled were chased into the tenements which were then ransacked by those policemen in pursuit. News of the baton charge caused serious rioting in other parts of the city, which lasted into the next day. The result was that 'Bloody Sunday', as it was quickly dubbed, claimed the lives of two workers and caused serious injuries to some 200 policemen and over 400 demonstrators.

The actions of the authorities certainly stiffened the attitude of those on strike, and Larkin was determined to press ahead with industrial action. The employers, meanwhile, had met on 29 August to consider their response to the ITGWU's tram strike, and they heard Murphy argue that the time had come to crush Larkin and his union. At a further meeting on 3 September, attended by 400 employers, there was general support for Murphy's proposal to lock out all their employees who were members of the ITGWU. Thus began the Dublin lockout. A few days earlier, individual employers, notably Jacob's and the Dublin Coal Merchants' Association had locked out union employees, but now this became the employers' key weapon in their struggle against Larkin. Very quickly, a document was prepared and given to thousands of workers who were expected to sign it immediately. Its aim was to force workers to resign from the ITGWU and to withdraw support for the union in any form. Those who refused knew the consequences. The employers' action was biting hard, and more than 20,000 men were out of work by the third week in September. With their families these men were facing starvation but, despite their hopeless position, Murphy's expectation of a crushing early victory for the employers did not materialise.

With both Larkin and Connolly in jail when the lockout began, it was left to O'Brien and Daly to organise the union's initial response. Larkin was released on bail on 12 September and Connolly two days later, but their priority was to secure immediate financial assistance for their locked-out members. Larkin left for England to appeal for support leaving Connolly in charge in Dublin. The plight of the Dublin working class had been brought starkly to light when a tenement building collapsed in early September killing eight people, an event which further exacerbated the workers' sense of social grievance. Larkin hoped that other trade unions in Dublin might join in a general strike but, though he was to be disappointed, these other unions supported the ITGWU by giving funds and by refusing to handle 'tainted' goods. In late September the British TUC gave £5,000 to the lockout fund, and individuals also made generous contributions. Money also poured in from sympathetic Labour newspapers in Britain which had opened subscription lists, and one newspaper alone, the *Glasgow Forward*, raised a total of £3,300 during the course of the lockout. Though many leading figures in the British trade union movement disliked Larkin intensely, they blamed Murphy for the Dublin dispute and interpreted the employers' action as a challenge to a worker's basic right to join a trade union. Yet while they were determined to offer the Dublin men all the indirect help they could, they were reluctant to engage in any direct action which would take the form of a sympathetic strike. This was, of course, what Larkin desperately wanted.

An attempt to end the dispute was made in late September 1913, when a court of inquiry was established to hear the arguments of both sides in the dispute. Larkin represented the trade unions and Murphy's old confident, the Nationalist MP Tim Healy, conducted the case for the employers. While the inquiry criticised the labour movement for its use of the sympathetic strike, it also confirmed that the workers had genuine grievances and condemned the pledge which the employers had tried to force on the workers. Within a fortnight, however, it became clear that there was little likelihood of a compromise, as Murphy was determined to continue the struggle and destroy the ITGWU. Still, the publicity surrounding the court proceedings strengthened the position of the workers, as they won more sympathy, particularly from the English press and, temporarily, from the Archbishop of Dublin, William Walsh, who was disgusted by the merciless response of the employers. Yet Walsh and the Catholic Church were soon looking at the dispute from a different angle. Plans to send some of the strikers' children to homes in England had been made by two well known women social workers, one English and the other American, but, when Walsh heard of the scheme to find foster homes in England, he issued a public statement in which he claimed that those mothers involved had "abandoned their faith" by sending their children to a strange land, where there was no guarantee that they would be sent to Catholic homes. A bizarre sequence of events followed. On 22 October the first batch of children had been dispatched to England but, when a party of 50 tried to leave on the following day, a number of Catholic priests intervened, persuading and cajoling parents and children alike, with the result that only a handful actually boarded the ship at Kingstown. The foster scheme collapsed amidst bitter feuding between Larkin and the clergy. The recriminations which followed in the Catholic press deflected attention from the plight of the strikers and weakened popular support for the Transport Union [66].

Larkin had little time to reflect on the consequences of the foster scheme because, on 27 October, he was brought for trial arising out of incidents on Bloody Sunday. His seven months' sentence for sedition was harsh, and it brought a howl of protest from all shades of political opinion which, in fact, led to his early release. What made Larkin's sentence appear particularly severe was that Edward Carson and other Unionist leaders were constantly defying the Liberal government and preaching treason during this same period without any interference from the authorities. With Larkin again in jail, Connolly was left to run the lockout. Earlier, both men had given serious consideration to the need for a workers' defence force that would offer some protection against the DMP which was continuing to hound the strikers. Here, Carson's Ulster Volunteer Force offered a useful example, and Connolly authorised the establishment of a new defence force in November 1913 [67]. The Irish Citizen Army, as it rather grandly named itself, had been the brainchild of Captain Jack White, a native of County Antrim who had served with distinction in the British Army during the Boer War. Having settled in Dublin, White quickly came to identify with the workers' struggle and, by the end of November, he was drilling two companies which had enrolled in the Irish Citizen Army. Among the first to join were Countess Markievicz, who had been a prominent assistant to Maud Gonne in the women's organisation, Inghinidhe na hÉireann, and Sean O'Casey, soon to achieve fame as a playwright but then a general labourer in Dublin. The Irish Citizen Army was really a vigilante force consisting of only a few hundred workers. It had no weapons and saw little action during the lockout, but it raised the workers' morale and helped to relieve the boredom during the long period without work.

On his release from prison on 13 November 1913 Larkin again called for an immediate general strike in Britain, and he continued to make frequent visits to the mainland in which he denounced British trade union leaders for their caution. Despite this violent criticism, money continued to pour in from Britain, and contributions topped £56,000 by the end of November, which enabled the Transport Union's lockout committee to give the workers 5 shillings (25 pence) strike pay each week. Larkin's appeals to the British labour movement did find some support, and there were a number of isolated incidents which led to unofficial strike action being taken by members of the National Union of Railwaymen (NUR) in South Wales in support of their Dublin comrades. Without official backing from the NUR, however, such action made little impact. Although it had become clear to Larkin that the British TUC would not sanction a sympathetic strike, he was determined to hold out against the employers. The TUC and the British Labour party, meanwhile, were hoping that an agreement between the employers and the ITGWU could be reached, which would bring the dispute to an end. A British delegation led by the Labour MP, Arthur Henderson, arrived in Dublin on 4 December and acted as intermediaries at a peace conference arranged by Archbishop Walsh. With Larkin absent Connolly took the lead for the Transport Union. He offered to abandon the 'sympathetic' strike, to give a month's notice before beginning a strike and to hold a ballot before calling a strike. These were generous concessions but, in return, the workers insisted that all locked-out men had to be reinstated. This the employers would not accept, arguing that it would be unfair to sack the men whom they had taken on as replacements for the strikers. Thus the British labour movement's attempt at arbitration broke down on Sunday, 7 December, with the two sides as far apart as ever.

These negotiations also highlighted the growing tension between the British and Irish trade union movements. This division really came to a head on 9 December 1913, when the British TUC met in London to consider its response to Larkin's demands for direct action. The lockout committee was represented at the meeting by Larkin, Connolly, O'Brien and Tom McPartlin, the President of the Dublin Trades Council. Arthur Henderson was the first to speak, and he launched a bitter attack on those who had suggested that the British delegation in Dublin had sought to negotiate over the heads of Dublin strikers. Yet he also expressed the view that the British labour movement, which was really paying for the dispute, should have more say in how it was resolved. Connolly attempted to calm the situation with a conciliatory speech, but Larkin was unable to control his anger and his speech made an open split between the British and Dublin trade unionists inevitable. A motion calling for the 'blacking' of all Dublin goods until the locked-out workers were reinstated was overwhelmingly defeated and, instead, Congress backed a motion condemning Larkin's attacks and expressing confidence in the TUC's ability to secure a settlement. This division, which Murphy had been keen to promote since the beginning of the lockout, left the strikers in a very vulnerable position. The men were clearly running out of steam, and even those fortunate to receive the 5 shillings strike pay were finding it difficult to support their families. The British TUC officials, moreover, were preparing to negotiate an end to the dispute without reference to the lockout committee, as funds from the mainland were beginning to dry up. By this stage Murphy realised that he would soon have the victory he had so carefully planned, and he continued to offer nothing more than vague assurances on the prospects of reinstatement for the locked-out workers.

In January 1914 men in both the docks and the coal yards began to drift back to work. The strike was collapsing and Larkin blamed the British trade union leadership for the defeat, claiming in a number of highly charged and emotional speeches in both Britain and Ireland that the TUC leaders had betrayed their Irish comrades. Many of the employers reinstated their old workers without acrimony or recrimination, but a number insisted that their workers should take the pledge to turn their backs on the ITGWU by signing the hated 'yellow' contract. Yet the most militant men found no employer in Dublin willing to take them on, and hundreds were forced to apply for assisted places in England and Scotland, which the Transport Union subsidised during the early months of 1914 in spite of its own precarious financial position. The lockout was over and, on 11 February 1914, the British TUC announced that its Dublin Relief Fund was officially closed. The employers celebrated their victory and paid glowing tributes to Murphy who was praised for his courage in standing up to the anarchist tactics used by Larkin and his union. Larkin himself now faced opposition from within the Transport Union, where a number of senior figures had finally become exasperated with his autocratic style of leadership. In mid-June 1914 Larkin suddenly resigned as general secretary of the union, but an emotional meeting of the Dublin ITGWU, at which his letter of resignation was burned on the platform to the sound of enthusiastic cheering, persuaded him to stay on. Yet, clearly, Larkin had suffered great physical and mental strain during the lockout, and his general disillusionment with the Irish labour movement was likely to create further problems. In October he left for a short lecture tour of the United States, but did not return until 1923.

The lockout had lasted for four months and had directly involved some 20,000 workers. British trade unions had sent £100,000, an incredible sum at to-day's valuation, to support the locked-out men, but Larkin was scathing in his criticism of the British movement for its failure to call a strike, or even to support the blacking of all goods bound for Dublin. His highly personalised attacks on the British labour leaders merely stiffened their resolve not to become embroiled in the Irish dispute by waging industrial war in Britain. Larkin, as his biographer points out, had asked the British leadership "to do the impossible" by going down the path of social revolution. While this was regarded as legitimate political action by Larkin, who viewed the problem of industrial relations and the future of socialism in an Irish context only, the British labour movement, looking at the situation from the British perspective, were only interested in the gradualist, reformist and constitutional course which, they assumed, their followers favoured. Yet while he claimed that his men had been betrayed by the British labour movement, Larkin also realised that the lack of political support for the lockout in Ireland had been significant. This was highlighted in January 1914, when the Dublin Labour party nominated eleven candidates, most of whom were closely associated with the lockout, to contest the municipal elections. Although the Labour vote showed a marginal increase, all but two of the candidates were defeated by United Irish League opponents who were representing the IPP. This was a bitter blow for Larkin and Connolly. The *Irish Worker* had dubbed the IPP the 'baton' party, because of its support for both the employers and the strong arm tactics used by the authorities and, consequently, the Dublin electorate was given a clear choice on the lockout issue. The municipal elections demonstrated that the image of Larkin as a dangerous anarchist was one which was held by a majority of Dublin citizens [68].

Such an image was, of course, carefully fostered by Murphy's *Independent*, which constantly traded blows with the *Irish Worker* and helped to paint the misleading picture that the lockout was really a final showdown between Murphy and Larkin. Where Murphy was undoubtedly obsessed with Larkin, he was clever enough to see that the actions of the ITGWU in 1913 offered him the ideal opportunity to deal a crippling blow to the union by exploiting his fellow employers' fears that a social revolution was imminent. Larkin's personal attacks and wild threats merely facilitated his task. Yet, in reality, the prospect of a left wing takeover in Dublin was non-existent. Certainly, the Dublin working class was united and militant, but its interests were predominantly economic, not political. The workers would fight for the rights of their unions, but the vast majority had little time for, or understanding of, the political side of the industrial warfare in which they engaged. Not surprisingly, the suffering endured by the workers and their families and the violence to which they were subjected by the DMP has entered the city's folklore but, neither this, nor the sight of Murphy's trams, which continued to run with scab labour and police protection through Dublin's poorest districts, could force the workers down the path of revolution.

The lockout also confirmed that the IPP, the 'baton' party, was a bourgeois political force [69]. Yet while its roots were in rural Ireland and though it clearly lacked a social conscience, the IPP could still expect, as the local government elections in January 1914 showed, to win a majority of votes in Dublin. Obviously, the trade union element of the Irish labour movement had run well ahead of its political development. Socialism competed unsuccessfully with Nationalism for the political allegiance of workers in the city, where it was too easy for clerical opponents to cast Larkin and Connolly as dangerous social revolutionaries. Nevertheless, the Irish labour movement had not been destroyed by the lockout, but it had been severely wounded. Larkin left for the United States, disenchanted with Ireland and with the prospects for socialism, while Connolly, who succeeded him as the ITGWU's general secretary, was steadily drawn towards revolutionary Nationalism [70]. Still, despite all of Murphy's efforts, the ITGWU remained a significant force in Irish labour politics and, while it never operated with the militancy of 1913, it continued to win concessions for its members.

Historiography

A good introduction to the Irish labour movement is provided by E O'Connor's, *A Labour History of Ireland 1824-1960* (Dublin, 1992) which successfully disentangles the labour movement from the story of Irish Nationalism. O'Connor looks at the formation of the various labour organisations and assesses their impact, and he comments on the development of working class consciousness in Ireland which spawned a number of small political movements. He describes the organisation of Ireland's unskilled labour in the 1890s; firstly, in the half-hearted attempts of the large British based unions to organise in Ireland and, later, with the success of the ITGWU after its launch in December 1908. O'Connor also stresses the conservatism of the ITUC during its early years, noting the care it took to avoid conflict with the much larger British labour movement. Yet in the long term O'Connor believes that the establishment of a separate body in Ireland made an eventual split between the two movements inevitable. In examining the impact of the Trades Councils, particularly in Belfast and Dublin, O'Connor argues that they played a vital role in introducing the labour movement to electoral politics. An excellent supplement to O'Connor's book is A Mitchell's, *Labour in Irish Politics 1890-1930: The Irish Labour Movement in an Age of Revolution* (Dublin, 1974). Mitchell points out that the 1898 Local Government Act greatly encouraged the development of labour political activity, but he also highlights the negative impact made by the early representatives of labour, particularly those serving on the Dublin corporation.

The living conditions in the Dublin tenements are described in C O'Grada's, *Ireland: A New Economic History 1780-1939* (Oxford, 1994). O'Grada points to the sharp contrast between working class housing in Dublin, where dilapidated buildings were bought up by 'house-jobbers' who let them room by room, and Belfast, where the purpose-built 'two-up two-down' houses were vastly superior. The Dublin working class also existed on a poorer diet and suffered from a much higher incidence of typhoid fever and tuberculosis. The industrial boom enjoyed by Belfast in the late nineteenth century is described in P Ollerenshaw's essay, 'Industry, 1820-1914', which appears in L Kennedy and P Ollerenshaw's (eds), *An Economic History of Ulster 1820-1939* (Manchester, 1985). Ollerenshaw shows how the rapid development of Belfast's shipbuilding industry led to the growth of related industries, particularly rope making and marine engineering, which led to an unprecedented demand for highly skilled labour.

The work done by Marx and Engels on Ireland is analysed in Mansergh's, *The Irish Question* which concludes that Engels had a much clearer understanding of Ireland than Marx who really confined his comments to the general role that Ireland might play in furthering the cause of proletarian revolution. Of course, both men were convinced that events in Ireland could hasten the advent of revolution in England. Further useful comments on the Marxist interpretation of Irish history can be found in A Coughlan's essay, 'Ireland's Marxist Historians' which appears in Brady's (ed), *Interpreting Irish History*. Coughlan notes how surprising it is to find how few references there are to the writings of Marx and Engels in view of the fact that "they were among the few non-Irish writers on Irish affairs ... who were sympathetic to nationalist aspirations". Coughlan concludes this section by quoting a comment made by Engels in 1882: "I hold the view that two nations in Europe have not only the right but even the duty to be nationalistic before they become internationalistic: the Irish and the Poles. They are most internationalistic when they are genuinely nationalistic". Finally, Marx's belief that Fenianism contained a powerful socialist and democratic flavour is examined in P Berresford Ellis's, *A History of the Irish Working Class* (London, 1972).

The development of Belfast's labour movement and an analysis of Walker's particular brand of Labour Unionism can be found in Morgan's, *Labour and Partition*. Morgan claims that Walker has, rather unfairly, been written out of the history of the Irish labour movement because of his anti-Nationalist sympathies. Describing him as a moderate trade unionist in the British tradition, Morgan defends his leadership in Belfast and praises his courage in opposing the powerful conservative elements in the city, concluding that Walker was really "a victim of division in Ireland". The most interesting analysis of Walker's contribution to the labour movement appears in Patterson's, *Class Conflict and Sectarianism* which reminds us that Walker saw Irish Nationalism as a reactionary force, and he opposed Home Rule, believing that it would be detrimental to the Belfast workers whom he represented. Patterson states that Connolly's criticism of the Protestant working class, which was easily duped into supporting the bourgeois Unionist party, was an oversimplification. There had been a long tradition of conflict between capital and labour in Ulster, in which Walker had played a major role, but the growing partnership between Irish socialism and Irish Nationalism, which Connolly himself came to symbolise, saw "Belfast Labourism ... squeezed out of the political arena".

A detailed narrative account of the Belfast dock strike is provided by J Gray's, *City in Revolt: James Larkin and the Belfast Dock Strike of 1907* (Belfast, 1985). Gray argues that the dock strike was a key turning point in Irish labour history and really foreshadowed the events of the Dublin lockout. He describes the "spontaneous and non-sectarian mobilisation" of the Belfast working class in sympathy with the strikers, which resulted in up to 10,000 people attending the daily meetings. Gray emphasises the shock which the display of Protestant working class power gave to the city's Unionist employers who, in the circumstances, turned in desperation to play the sectarian card. In doing so the employers found an unlikely ally in the Liberal government which, following the police mutiny, smashed the strike by using overwhelming military force. Gray then concludes by pointing out that the failure of the British labour movement to support the strike made its eventual defeat a likely outcome, something which Larkin should have kept in mind in 1913.

The labour movement's creation of a political party is recorded in Mitchell's, *Labour and Irish Politics* which describes the revival of the movement's electoral fortunes in 1911-1912. Mitchell claims that for Larkin the Labour party's involvement in elections was essentially the extension of the industrial struggle into the political arena. These developments are also outlined in a useful essay by P Collins, 'Irish Labour and Politics in the Late Nineteenth and Early Twentieth Centuries', which appears in P Collins's (ed), *Nationalism and Unionism: Conflict in Ireland, 1885-1921* (Belfast, 1994). Collins describes how labour activists had to overcome determined opposition from Walker and his Belfast clique before they could establish the Irish Trade Union Congress and Labour Party. Like Mitchell, Collins stresses that both the ISRP and its replacement, the SPI, enjoyed influence well in excess of their numerical strength, but the fact that these revolutionary socialist parties only attracted a tiny group of members should be emphasised.

There are numerous books on James Connolly. His own, *Labour in Irish History* (Dublin, 1910) is a remarkable achievement, confirming Connolly's reputation as an original Marxist thinker and the first to apply the Marxist method of analysis to Irish History. Yet as it also attempted to come to terms with the new Nationalism, Connolly argued that the book could be viewed as part of the new literature of the Gaelic revival. An excellent, brief account of Connolly's life can be found in R Dudley Edwards's, *James Connolly* (Dublin, 1981) which claims that Connolly's concept of an Irish socialist republic was original, as it rejected British Marxist thinking by arguing that an Irish republic had to be established before society could be transformed on the socialist model. Dudley Edwards is also good at conveying the tetchy relationship between Connolly and Larkin. The best Marxist treatment of Connolly's life remains C D Greaves's, *The Life and Times of James Connolly* (London, 1961) which describes him as one of the first great working class intellectuals. On the question of religion, so crucial in Ireland, Greaves notes how Connolly campaigned against clerical interference in politics, but vigorously defended the right of a Catholic to be a socialist while remaining a Catholic.

E Larkin's, *James Larkin: Irish Labour Leader 1876-1947* (London, 1965) is an excellent biography which begins by showing how Larkin's difficult experiences in his early working life influenced him. While the author claims that Larkin shook Belfast to its roots in 1907, he concludes that such was the power of the forces ranged against him that Larkin "achieved little of a tangible nature in Belfast". Larkin argues that Jim Larkin applied the ideas of the syndicalist movement to Ireland, particularly in his use of the sympathetic strike, but he was never a syndicalist in the strictest sense and can best be described as a socialist. The author probably overestimates the impact of Larkin's disqualification from public office following his election to the Dublin corporation in 1912 which, he claims, forced him to concentrate on the development of a much more militant form of trade unionism. However, as Mitchell's, *Labour and Irish Politics* argues, his real interest had always been in the industrial struggle, not in the dreary politics of the Dublin corporation.

E Larkin's assessment of the Dublin lockout in which he describes the strikers as a revolutionary working class is challenged by D Keogh's, *The Rise of the Irish Working Class* (Belfast, 1982). Keogh warns that what he describes as trade union militancy should not be confused with "social revolutionary zeal". His starting point is that since the 1890s, there was a great desire among Ireland's working class for organisation to achieve social and political reform. Therefore, he argues, Larkin and Connolly should be seen as the catalysts, not the causes, of this development. He acknowledges Larkin's great gifts as an orator and organiser, but adds that he arrived in Dublin just at the time "the local men were casting around for a leader"f. What had really created the trade union militancy in Dublin was the acute social deprivation which sustained the workers in their struggle. Keogh is excellent in showing how the employers, led by Murphy, sought to demonise Larkin, and he uses a succession of quotations from the *Irish Worker* to show how Larkin, in turn, personalised the conflict with the Employers' Federation. The author also emphasises the brutality of the DMP during the conflict and describes the bitterness which the response by the authorities engendered in Dublin's poorest quarters. Keogh concludes by emphasising his central argument that labour unity in 1913 was based on "a highly-developed trade union consciousness, but that consciousness was not a revolutionary one ... The trade union movement simply did not go through a revolutionary phase". Finally, A Pimley's essay, 'The Working-class Movement and the Irish Revolution, 1896-1923' which appears in Boyce's (ed), *The Revolution in Ireland* provides an excellent overview of the labour movement. In his analysis of the lockout Pimley argues that the Dublin dispute was of great concern to the British working class and that only the outbreak of the First World War prevented such a confrontation in Britain.

Chapter 6

The Ulster crisis

The results of the general election in January 1910 had left Asquith and the Liberals disappointed but not surprised. A 'hung parliament' with the IPP holding the balance of power appeared to put Redmond and the Irish Nationalists in a powerful position, but bringing pressure to bear on the Liberals to ensure the passage of a new Home Rule Bill was not a straightforward task. Redmond may have wanted to tread carefully, but his deputy, John Dillon, favoured a more cavalier approach, and he insisted that the Liberals must be told that if a firm commitment was not given by the government to introduce a measure limiting the veto powers of the House of Lords, then the Irish party would oppose the Lloyd George budget which had originally sparked the constitutional crisis. This demand placed the government in a very difficult position, because both Asquith and the IPP leaders realised that a promise to reduce the veto powers of the Lords was dependent on the King giving the Liberal government a guarantee that he was prepared to intervene, if necessary, to ensure that the Lords accepted its reduced status. Asquith also realised that such a deal with the Nationalist leaders would leave the government open to the charge that it was engaged in some underhand dealing with the Irish. As he was determined not to concede the moral high ground to his Conservative opponents, Asquith persuaded his cabinet colleagues that they should put their proposals on the House of Lords before parliament and inform Redmond that they were not prepared to give the assurances he desired. Yet when Asquith informed the House of Commons in March 1910 of the government's intentions, Balfour and the Conservatives immediately concluded that the Irish Nationalists, through their leaders Redmond and Dillon, were dictating policy to the government. This charge that the Liberals had entered into a 'corrupt bargain' with the Irish was one which the Conservatives repeated constantly over the next four years. While the cabinet did consider amending the budget to appease the Irish, the Conservatives were wrong to accuse Asquith of political opportunism, because he made no formal promises to the Irish. On 13 April 1910, moreover, Asquith wrote to the King who was holidaying in the south of France, stating that "to purchase the Irish vote by such a concession would be a discreditable transaction, which they could not defend".

The IPP had, of course, genuine difficulties with the budget, as it included higher charges for liquor licences and a high tax on spirits, which hit Ireland's distillers and publicans. By April, however, after a difficult impasse, the Irish MPs shelved their opposition to the budget once Asquith had informed parliament about the steps the Liberal government would take if the Lords rejected the veto resolutions. His contingency plan was to meet such a rejection with another general election which, if the Liberals won, would be followed by a request for the King to create the necessary number of Liberal peers to push the veto proposals through the Lords. This was deemed a sufficient guarantee by the Irish party, and more than 60 Nationalist MPs voted with the government as the budget passed its third reading on 27 April. The vote on the budget was significant, because the arithmetic also demonstrated that the Irish party's influence was more apparent than real. While Conservatives claimed that Asquith was dependent on the Irish party to sustain his government, they conveniently overlooked the fact that the 40 Labour MPs consistently supported the government and thus gave the Liberals a comfortable majority, even if all 82 Irish Nationalists abstained.

Naturally, the ultimate prize for these Irish Nationalists was the establishment of a devolved parliament in Dublin, and the government's plans to reduce the powers of the House of Lords promised to remove a major obstacle on the road to a new Home Rule Bill. While it was assumed that a Home Rule Bill would follow the reduction of the Lords' powers, the Irish party had not received a formal assurance from the government that such a measure would inevitably follow. True, on 10 December 1909, Asquith had told a pre-election Albert Hall rally that the only solution to the Irish problem was Home Rule, but few of his colleagues made any reference to Home Rule during the election campaign, as they wished, not surprisingly, to concentrate the voters' minds on the constitutional question [71]. Even the Conservatives had largely ignored the Irish Question during the election campaign. The priority was clearly the constitutional crisis and, in the spring of 1910, Irish MPs knew they had to wait patiently until this issue had been resolved. Still, while they may have felt frustration, they were fairly confident that the Liberal government could hold its nerve in the struggle over the Lords. The sudden death of Edward VII on 7 May 1910 temporarily shook their confidence. Asquith was anxious that the new King, George V, who had little experience or knowledge of such delicate political matters, should be shielded from the constitutional crisis. Soon, rumours were circulating at Westminster that a search for an accommodation between the two main parties was on, a prospect which made the Irish leaders apprehensive, as they believed that any compromise on the constitutional question would have an adverse effect on the prospects for Home Rule. The hope that filled the Irish party in the wake of the January general election was now replaced by uncertainty, as Liberal and Conservative leaders began the search for an agreement on the future of the Lords.

The first such constitutional conference was held on 17 June and, in all, 21 secret sessions were held between then and 10 November. Any compromise was likely, of course, to see some of the Lords' veto powers retained. No one appreciated this more than Redmond and Dillon who spent an anxious five months, with little information on the progress of the meetings, awaiting the outcome. In the end their nervousness proved unjustified, as the conference finally broke down without any agreement being reached [72]. In fact, one of the sticking points had been the Conservatives' insistence that there should be a special constitutional procedure to deal with Home Rule, something which Asquith refused to consider. There was, however, one important consequence which later proved to have a bearing on the impending struggle for Home Rule. The failure of the two main parties to reach a compromise on the constitutional question contributed to the increasing bitterness of political exchanges between the two front benches. In such circumstances the efforts made by a small number of senior figures in both parties during the summer of 1910 to find a common approach on Ireland were unlikely to lead to success. The general election in December 1910, called after the collapse of the constitutional conference, was another acrimonious affair. During the campaign Asquith concentrated on the Lords' issue, reminding the electorate of the obstructive tactics used by the Upper House to prevent the passage of progressive legislation. The Home Rule issue was largely ignored by the Liberal party, but the Conservatives repeatedly warned voters about the twin evils of Home Rule and socialism which would follow the removal of the Lords' veto. This approach by the Conservatives was not surprising, because many of the party's leading figures, including Balfour, felt that they had to fight this second election in 1910 with the tariff reform millstone still around their necks. At least opposition to Home Rule, though it could not have been a vital issue for many British voters, allowed the Conservatives to offer a united front.

Whatever the merits of the arguments during the campaign, the results of the general election, for which polling had begun on 4 December, were remarkably similar to the January figures. Liberals and Conservatives now both held 272 seats, while the IPP had 84 and Labour 42. For the Conservatives the results were a great disappointment. They had made gains in some areas, but these had been outweighed by losses elsewhere, as more than 50 seats changed hands between the two main parties. The depressing statistic of three general election losses in a row and the knowledge that the assured support of the Irish Nationalists and Labour continued to give the Liberals a majority of well over 100 led some Conservatives to question whether their party would ever hold office again. Naturally, this reinforced the determination of many Conservatives to fight all the way in an effort to safeguard the powers of the Conservative dominated House of Lords. The way ahead for the Liberal government was now a good deal less complex than it had been during the summer of 1910, and Asquith pressed ahead with the Parliament Bill which was introduced on 21 February 1911. The bill contained three main clauses. It proposed that the Lords should not be able to reject or amend any Money Bill; that if any other type of bill was rejected by the Lords, it would automatically become law providing not less than two years elapsed between its introduction and third reading in the Commons; and that the maximum duration of a parliament should be cut from seven to five years. The Conservatives in the House of Commons put up every obstacle they could think of, notably in the form of 900 amendments tabled for the committee stage, but the bill was safely through the chamber by 15 May. The Lords did not consider the Parliament Bill until the end of June.

The Conservative party had still to decide on its strategy. The senior Conservative figure in the Lords, the Southern Unionist Lord Lansdowne, continued to hope that the Parliament Bill would only be passed if it was substantially amended but, by mid-July, he was informed that the King had agreed to Asquith's request to create extra Liberal peers if the Lords finally voted against the bill. The Conservatives were now split between the 'hedgers', those who were not prepared to vote against the Parliament Bill in the Lords and risk the creation of a huge number of Liberal peers, and the 'ditchers', those who would fight the bill 'to the last ditch', whatever the consequences. The tariff reform issue had split the party and contributed to its three general election reverses, but the division over the Parliament Bill went even deeper. Among Conservative MPs there was a majority in favour of the hedgers, with Walter Long a very prominent advocate, but there was also a substantial minority, led by Austen Chamberlain, who backed the ditchers. Balfour infuriated both groups by his refusal to be drawn on this crucial issue, leaving the peers to make their own judgement.

When the vote on the Parliament Bill was finally taken on 10 August 1911, the hedgers, led by Lansdowne, abstained, and the bill was passed by 131 to 114. The ditchers, led by Lord Halsbury, were furious at the decision of a group of over 30 Conservative peers, the 'rats', led by Lord Curzon, who voted with the government to ensure the necessary majority, and the recriminations within the party continued for long afterwards. With the Parliament Act on the statute book the way ahead for a new Home Rule Bill seemed clear. The bitterness between the two main parties had reached new heights with the feuding over the Lords' veto. The Conservative party, out of office and still reeling from its third successive general election defeat, was more divided than ever. The Liberals, by contrast, were looking confident and assured, following a clear strategy which they had put into practice with ruthless efficiency.

Carson and Bonar Law

Edward Henry Carson was born into a Dublin bourgeois family in 1854. His career, first at the Irish then the English bar, had brought him considerable fame and fortune. He represented Trinity College Dublin in the House of Commons from 1892 to 1918 and briefly held the post of Irish Solicitor-General in 1892, having caught Arthur Balfour's eye. In 1900 he was appointed Solicitor-General for England, appearing for the Crown in a number of sensational trials which enhanced his already impressive reputation. Carson had come into direct contact with Parnellism, when he acted as counsel to the Attorney-General for Ireland for two years and undertook the prosecutions arising out of the infamous Criminal Law Amendment Act of 1887. This piece of legislation had been introduced to combat the new wave of land agitation sparked by the Plan of Campaign, and William O'Brien was just one of the notable figures he prosecuted. While this legal work drew him to Balfour's attention, it also demonised him in the eyes of Irish Nationalists. The experience he gained in the Irish courts was put to very effective use in his future legal career in England and, later, in his political career. Then, the court room was a mixture of serious legal procedure and entertainment. The leading counsels were cheered on by an excited public as they plied their trade, and Carson, perhaps more than any other, perfected the art of the passionate appeal which convinced judges, juries and the public that right was on his side. When he moved to England in 1892, he quickly established himself as a leading counsel, particularly after his performances in the Oscar Wilde trials, the first of which took place in 1895. By the end of the nineteenth century Carson was earning £20,000 per year in fees, and he and the great Jewish lawyer, Sir Rufus Isaacs, had established themselves as the outstanding advocates working at the English bar.

In politics Carson was a committed Unionist, but colleagues remembered the progressive, even radical, political causes he had identified with in his younger days.

His acceptance of the Unionist leadership in February 1910 could not have surprised Balfour, whom Carson had told on a number of occasions that he had only entered politics for the sake of the Union. He was also, of course, an Irish Unionist. Carson believed passionately that Home Rule posed a serious threat to Ireland, and he was determined to block any future attempt by the Liberal government, which he accused of corrupt dealing with Redmond, to push through a new Home Rule Bill. In spite of all the uncertainties facing Unionists in the summer of 1910, Carson continued to work on his high profile legal cases. In July that year the famous Archer–Shee case came before the court with Carson appearing for the young naval cadet, George Archer–Shee, who had been accused of stealing a postal order from another boy and cashing it at the local post office. Carson displayed great skill in his tussle with the Crown counsel, who just happened to be his great friend and rival, Rufus Isaacs, and the boy was declared to be innocent. The case was later dramatised in a famous play by Sir Terence Rattigan, *The Winslow Boy*.

Returning to his political duties, Carson was incensed to learn that a number of prominent figures in the Conservative party, including F E Smith, a young MP and another talented lawyer, were giving serious consideration to some kind of devolution scheme which would have involved the creation of new parliaments in England, Scotland, Wales and Ireland. Many of these younger Conservative MPs felt that if federalism could solve the Irish Question to the satisfaction of the two main parties, they could then reach an accommodation on the constitutional question which would enable the House of Lords to retain most of its powers. Such a federal solution received powerful backing from a section of the Tory press in the autumn of 1910 but, following the breakdown of the constitutional conference on 10 November, the impetus for finding a bipartisan approach on the Irish Question disappeared. Still, the fact that even a minority within the Conservative party had found the federal proposals attractive greatly alarmed Irish Unionists, and Carson was quick to vent their anger. The new Unionist leader had, therefore, to attune himself to the occasional difficulties in the relationship between his group of Irish Unionists and the Conservative party, which had not fully recovered from the hiatus over the devolution crisis, despite all of Walter Long's efforts during his period as Unionist leader.

Yet this had advantages which Carson was quick to appreciate. The Unionist party he came to lead was more self reliant and did not feel it had to lean on the Conservative party in the way that it had during previous crises. The new style of Unionism which can be traced to the establishment of the Ulster Unionist Council in March 1905 was also more militant, more concentrated in Ulster and less inclined to feel that their opposition to Irish Nationalism should be confined to the Westminster parliament. Thus Carson, on his accession to the leadership, found an energetic, grass roots movement, ready to resist any attempt to impose Home Rule and only requiring direction. In his last two years in charge of the Irish Unionists Long had been little more than a figurehead, as he was frequently ill and had too many other political interests. Carson, by contrast, had openly declared that there was only one political cause, the maintenance of the Union, which he cared about. Significantly, the Unionist party's scepticism about the level of support it could expect from the Conservative party made the prospect of extra-parliamentary opposition to a future Home Rule Bill more likely. The fact that Unionism had been transformed after 1905, moreover, a development which had been accompanied by a revival of interest in the Orange Order, gave Carson the extra-parliamentary option. Indeed contact with arms dealers on the continent and secret plans for arming and drilling were made as early as November 1910, though it was likely that Carson had no direct knowledge of such developments. By the early summer of 1911 Unionist extremists had organised the purchase of 2,000 weapons, and it seems unthinkable that Carson, by this stage, remained in the dark about their intentions [73].

This raises the question of how a leader with such an intricate knowledge and understanding of the law could contemplate armed defiance of the law. Carson was, of course, an extremely complex figure whose character was full of such ambiguities. A robust, healthy man who lived into his 80s, Carson was a desperate hypochondriac whose correspondence contains numerous references to his various 'illnesses'. Supremely confident on any public platform, he suffered bouts of depression and constant crises of confidence in private, which frequently left him in need of reassurance. A man of principle whose 'guiding star' was the Union between Britain and Ireland, he could forsake his principles as his pragmatic side reasserted itself. Perhaps the greatest paradox, however, was the way in which this Irish Unionist fought for Ulster. In this sense Carson was strangely similar to Parnell. Both were outsiders, leading followers very different from themselves, and both men used the same tactic of militant constitutionalism to achieve their objectives. Like Parnell, he led a mass movement outside parliament which he used to pressurise the government into making concessions. While Carson perhaps felt more at home with the Belfast bourgeois leadership, a number of whom were lawyers like himself, which had made rapid headway within Unionist ranks in the Edwardian era, he was, of course, a regional outsider and, interestingly, one who never lost his rich Dublin accent. Yet the key to understanding Carson's political strategy was his effectiveness as a lawyer, because it was really his legal skills which he used to defend Ulster Unionism from the threat of Home Rule.

The passing of the Parliament Bill in August 1911 hardened attitudes among Unionists and made the organisation of a great public campaign against Home Rule imperative. Not surprisingly, Carson now turned to Ulster where support for the Union was strongest. As he had done in countless legal cases, Carson prepared the ground thoroughly. He had only visited Ulster on one occasion many years earlier to conduct some legal business and, to ascertain the mood in Ulster, he relied on Sir James Craig, the Unionist MP for East Down. In both character and appearance Craig was the archetypal Ulster Unionist. A big, powerful figure from a wealthy Belfast family, Craig had shown great courage and coolness when he fought in the Boer War. Later, in the heat of political battle, he displayed the same imperturbability and acted as the perfect foil for Carson. Indeed Craig's real strength was his capacity for organisation, and he was painstaking in the detailed arrangements he made at every stage of the struggle against Home Rule. In the Unionist party Craig was close to the younger group of bourgeois activists who had reinvigorated the movement in 1905. In fact, his brother, Charles Curtis Craig, the MP for South Antrim, had been, with William Moore, one of the principal architects of the new style of Unionism. When the crisis over the Parliament Bill was drawing to a close, Craig urged Carson to come to Ulster and open the anti–Home Rule campaign, indicating that he would take care of all the arrangements. On 29 July 1911 Carson replied by letter to Craig, seeking assurances about the commitment of his followers in Ulster: "What I am very anxious about is to satisfy myself that the people over there really mean to resist. I am not for a mere game of bluff, and, unless men are prepared to make great sacrifices which they clearly understand, the talk of resistance is no use ... Personally I would be prepared to make any sacrifice, my time, business, money, or even my liberty, if I felt assured we would not in the end be abandoned".

Craig's priority now was to convince Carson that his Unionist supporters in Ulster were fully committed to resisting any attempt by the government to impose Home Rule and would back his leadership without hesitation. In order to give Carson this reassurance Craig organised a massive demonstration in the grounds of his own house, Craigavon, on Saturday, 23 September 1911. The rally was attended by 50,000 men, drawn from the province's Orange lodges and Unionist clubs, who heard Carson outline a programme of action which would be used to defeat the Liberal government's "nefarious conspiracy". He concluded: "We must be prepared ... the morning Home Rule passes, ourselves to become responsible for the government of the Protestant Province of Ulster". Two days later a meeting of the Ulster Unionist Council attended by 400 delegates promised the leadership unwavering support in the struggle against Home Rule, and a committee was established to produce a constitution for the Provisional government. At the Craigavon demonstration Carson and his supporters made a good impression on each other. Craig's meticulous preparations and the obvious sincerity of the Unionist rank and file, who listened in reverent silence, had impressed Carson, and he had responded with a moving and passionate speech which illustrated both his great flair for oratory and his feel for high political drama. A powerful bond now existed between Carson and his Ulster followers.

Carson's speech and the plans for a Provisional government caused a storm in Liberal circles, and the Home Secretary, Winston Churchill, told his Dundee constituents on 3 October that the government would introduce a Home Rule Bill in the next parliamentary session and "press it forward with all their strength". There was a danger, of course, that in defending Ulster against Home Rule, Carson would be guilty of ignoring his fellow Irish Unionists in the three southern provinces. The establishment of an Ulster provisional government would have meant some form of exclusion or partition, which would have divided Unionism as well as Ireland, but the reality was that the removal of the Lords' veto had forced Carson to consider a partitionist strategy. Yet his advocacy of exclusion was only tactical. In November 1911 he indicated in private correspondence that north–east Ulster was the key to the Union, believing that if it could resist Home Rule, then the Liberal government could not propose partition as it would be unacceptable to Redmond and the Nationalists. Therefore, Carson remained committed to the Union in its existing form and intended to use Ulster resistance to kill any new Home Rule Bill. Earlier, he had sought to reassure Southern Unionists, when he told a meeting in Dublin on 10 October 1911, "You need fear no action of Ulster which would be in the nature of desertion of the Southern Provinces ... if Ulster succeeds, Home Rule is dead".

Still, there were problems with Carson's Ulster strategy. The 1911 census returns showed that there were 250,000 Protestants living in the three southern provinces, a figure just below 10 per cent of the total population. In the nine counties of Ulster, meanwhile, Protestants outnumbered Catholics by 891,000 (56 per cent) to 691,000 (44 per cent), but they were by no means evenly distributed. The table below shows that Protestants were really concentrated in the four 'plantation' counties of Antrim, Down, Londonderry and Armagh, but there were clear Catholic majorities, some overwhelming, in the remaining five counties.

COUNTY	PROTESTANTS (%)	CATHOLICS (%)
ANTRIM	79.5	20.5
DOWN	68.4	31.6
ARMAGH	54.7	45.3
LONDONDERRY	54.2	45.8
TYRONE	44.6	55.4
FERMANAGH	43.8	56.2
MONAGHAN	25.3	74.7
DONEGAL	21.1	78.9
CAVAN	18.5	81.5

Distribution of population in Ulster counties, 1911

On the ground in Ulster the Belfast bourgeois leadership that had gathered around Carson emphasised the economic arguments against Home Rule, but it was the cry 'Home Rule means Rome Rule', which stirred the rank and file. In their religious objection to Home Rule Unionist propagandists skillfully exploited the famous McCann affair which surfaced in 1910. Alexander McCann, a Belfast Catholic, left his Protestant wife and took all the children of the marriage with him. Unionist MPs later alleged that this had been encouraged by the local Catholic clergy who had assisted in the children's removal from the country, and the case received wide publicity in both Ireland and Britain. A 1908 Papal Decree, known as Ne Temere, ordered that any mixed marriage, specifically between a Catholic and a Protestant, which had not been solemnised by the Catholic Church should be regarded as null and void. To Ulster Protestants, it seemed that all the children of such mixed marriages would be brought up as Catholics, and the McCann affair reinforced this fear. The Unionist publicity machine had been presented with a golden opportunity to highlight the religious persecution which, it was argued, would follow a Home Rule settlement, and the refusal of Redmond and the Nationalist MPs to speak out on the affair gave Unionist propagandists a free run. Underpinning the religious objection to Home Rule was the Ulster Unionist community's sense of superiority which was central to the belief that Irish Catholics were simply not fit to govern in any Home Rule administration. This superior view was, of course, shared by many leading figures in the Conservative party and, indeed, by Carson, even though he did not identify with the naked sectarianism so obvious in many of his followers.

Carson received a boost in November 1911, when Balfour resigned as leader of the Conservative party. His failure to offer decisive leadership, as the party argued violently over the Parliament Bill, was the final straw for many Conservatives who had endured the squabbling over tariff reform in addition to the three successive general election defeats. By the autumn of 1911 the 'Balfour Must Go' campaign, which had been initiated by the tariff reformers, was gaining widespread support within the party. Then as public criticism of his leadership mounted, Balfour resigned suddenly on 8 November 1911. The two obvious rivals for the leadership were Walter Long and Austen Chamberlain, but neither was certain to secure a majority if it came to a vote of the parliamentary party. Long was a rather dull figure associated with the landed element of the party, or 'squire conservatism' as it was known, but he enjoyed solid support on the backbenches. Chamberlain, by contrast, was a much more able parliamentarian who enjoyed the support of the whips and the front bench, but he certainly lacked the ruthless ambition of his father. Further dissension within the party looked inevitable, as relations between the two groups of supporters were extremely hostile. Meanwhile, however, a third candidate was persuaded to throw his hat into the ring and, almost immediately, he was accepted by both Long and Chamberlain as a compromise choice. Both men withdrew from the leadership race and, on 13 November 1911, Andrew Bonar Law became leader of the Conservative party. He had been proposed by Long and seconded by Chamberlain. The new leader offered a sharp contrast to Balfour. Whereas the aristocratic Balfour had been urbane, intellectual, witty and a highly skilled debater, Bonar Law was a successful businessman with little political experience and none of Balfour's great intellectual gifts or easy confidence. But he possessed great energy and real courage. Where Balfour had appeared lazy, Bonar Law was determined to reunite the party and carry the fight to the Liberals.

Quickly, Carson and Bonar Law met to exchange views at Lady Londonderry's home, and the new Tory leader promised to visit Ulster. This was no surprise, because Bonar Law had strong family connections with the province. His father had been a Presbyterian minister, living and working in Coleraine, County Londonderry, before emigrating to Canada in 1845. There, in September 1858, Andrew was born, though he left at the age of twelve to go to Scotland where he was looked after by an aunt. His father's health forced him to return home to Ulster in 1877, and he spent the last years of his life living there. During these years Andrew came over from his home in Scotland to visit his father almost every weekend. Such regular contact with the province, where his brother also practised as a doctor in Coleraine, gave Bonar Law a distinct feel for Ulster, and this undoubtedly influenced him as the crisis over the new Home Rule Bill unfolded. In fact, he once confided to Austen Chamberlain that in politics he cared intensely about only two issues – Ulster and tariff reform. Yet on his accession to the leadership Bonar Law realised that Ulster was the one issue that could unite the party after the succession of internal wranglings which had reduced the Conservatives to such a shambles. This was significant, because Bonar Law had been a passionate believer in tariff reform but now recognised that in the interests of party unity the demand for tariff reform had to be scaled down. Hence, the Conservatives gradually moved to the position which the party formally adopted in January 1913, when its demands for protective tariffs were greatly modified.

Bonar Law's views on defending the Union were eagerly taken up by the rest of the Conservative leadership. Naturally, Long was supportive, while Balfour, who retained considerable influence following his resignation, renewed his commitment to the Union, and Lord Lansdowne, the Conservative leader in the House of Lords, was especially enthusiastic. Indeed Bonar Law almost regarded Lansdowne as co-leader of the party, and the latter with a huge estate in County Kerry, in addition to his lands in England and Scotland, ensured that the defence of the Union would feature prominently in future Conservative strategy. Still, while the Union was of paramount importance to both men, there was a noticeable difference in emphasis. Whereas Bonar Law's primary concern was for Ulster, Lansdowne, identifying with the group of Southern Unionists whose influence he frequently exaggerated, was prepared to take a wider view. Bonar Law made his first important speech on the Home Rule issue on 26 January 1912, when he told an Albert Hall audience that the Liberals were guilty of deceiving the electorate and were now under Redmond's thumb.

By the beginning of 1912 tension was mounting in Ulster and this was, to some extent, boosted by the derogatory comments made by certain Liberal leaders who could not hide their contempt for Carson. Churchill, in particular, was scathing in his description of the Unionist leader's attempts to raise the temperature in Ulster, dismissing his actions as an empty threat. Never one to shirk a challenge, Churchill, who had moved from the Home Office to become First Lord of the Admiralty on 23 October 1911, accepted an invitation from the Ulster Liberal Association to speak at a pro-Home Rule meeting in Belfast along with Redmond and the Ulster Nationalist, Joe Devlin. This would allow Churchill to gauge opinion in Ulster at first hand and demonstrate that he, at least, was unruffled by Carson's dire warnings. It seems likely, however, that Churchill was misled about the strength of the Ulster Liberal Association which consisted mainly of Presbyterians who had kept the Liberal flame flickering in Ulster after Gladstone's conversion to Home Rule. Two of the association's most prominent members were the Rev J B Armour, a Presbyterian minister from Ballymoney, County Antrim, and the engineering genius Lord Pirrie, who was a director of Harland and Wolff. While both of these high profile figures proved very vocal in their support for Home Rule and were a constant source of embarrassment to the Unionist leadership, this could not disguise the fact that support for the Ulster Liberal Association among Protestants was confined to a small number. Still, the association caused a furore with the announcement that it had booked the Ulster Hall in Belfast for the Churchill engagement on 8 February 1912. This outraged Unionists, many of whom could recall Lord Randolph Churchill's famous visit to the Ulster Hall in 1886, when he encouraged Ulster Unionists to 'fight' against Home Rule. Now the fact that his son had crossed over to the enemy and was going to promote Home Rule in this 'sacred' venue proved too much for Belfast Unionists. Consequently, the Ulster Unionist Council announced that steps would be taken to prevent the Home Rule meeting going ahead. The plan was to hire the Ulster Hall for the previous evening and then remain in place to thwart the Home Rulers who were forced to find a new venue. In the end Churchill spoke to a crowd of several thousand Nationalists at Celtic Park in the Catholic sector of the city but, en route to the meeting, a crowd almost overturned his car, and, rather than returning to his hotel afterwards, he was smuggled out of the city and dispatched to the boat at Larne. Carson, who had crossed to Belfast to direct Unionist operations, claimed a great victory.

In the week following Churchill's Belfast visit a new session of parliament opened, and the government confirmed its intention to introduce a new Home Rule Bill. In response the Unionists began planning a monster demonstration which was to be held in Belfast during the Easter holidays. Bonar Law now kept his earlier promise, and he was one of several key speakers who addressed a crowd of 100,000 assembled in the Royal Agricultural Society's show-grounds at Balmoral on Easter Tuesday, 9 April 1912. Again, Craig's meticulous planning was in evidence. Men marched into the grounds, dividing neatly in ranks of four as they passed the platform close to which a giant Union Jack, measuring 48 feet by 25 feet, was unfurled. In his address Bonar Law described Ulster as the key to the Empire, arguing that in fighting to save themselves from Home Rule Unionists would also save the integrity of the Empire. Significantly, a large group of Conservative MPs had accompanied Bonar Law on his visit. Near the end of the proceedings in a carefully stage-managed piece of drama the bond between British Conservatism and Ulster Unionism was symbolised, when Bonar Law and Carson grasped each other's hands in full view of the crowd. In spite of the government's rather dismissive attitude towards Unionist manoeuvrings, therefore, it was clear by the spring of 1912 that the Liberals would face determined opposition, which would include an extra-parliamentary dimension, in their attempt to place a new Home Rule measure on the statute book.

The third Home Rule Bill

On 11 April 1912, two days after the Balmoral demonstration, Asquith introduced the third Home Rule Bill and confirmed that he would adhere to the Gladstonian principle of Home Rule on an all-Ireland basis. In essence the new measure was very similar to the 1893 bill, though Asquith eloquently explained that the 1912 bill could well lead to a wider scheme of devolution. Ulster was not to be given special treatment, as Asquith reminded the House of Commons that four-fifths of the Irish MPs wanted Home Rule and only an "irreconcilable minority" in Ulster, where there were 17 Unionist MPs to 16 Nationalists, opposed this demand. Their wishes, he argued, could not be allowed to deny the majority in Ireland of their rights. Yet Asquith's apparently total rejection of special treatment for Ulster concealed certain misgivings which had been expressed in cabinet by a number senior ministers. Still, Ulster had not featured prominently in the deliberations of the cabinet committee which had been formed in January 1911 to consider the question of Home Rule. Initially, the cabinet committee had been attracted to the idea of 'Home Rule all round', a federal scheme under which the establishment of an Irish parliament could be followed by assemblies for Scotland and Wales, but, when this was rejected by the cabinet, the committee turned back to the original Home Rule concept and concentrated on the financial relationship between Britain and Ireland under Home Rule. Thus, finance, not Ulster, was considered to be the real potential difficulty in any Home Rule scheme, with the government anxious to erect safeguards to ensure that a Dublin parliament would not become a drain on the Westminster exchequer. Throughout 1911 little attention was paid to Ulster, and only Augustine Birrell, the Chief Secretary for Ireland, raised awareness of the difficulties which the province might cause if the government went ahead with Home Rule on an all-Ireland basis. Although Birrell was sympathetic to the Irish Nationalists, he clearly felt that the talk of resistance in Ulster was not bluff and, accordingly, favoured some form of exclusion for at least part of Ulster. However, he failed to press his views on the cabinet.

In fact, it was not until February 1912, when the general framework of the bill had already been decided, that the cabinet focused its attention on Ulster. Birrell remained anxious, but it was the views of two senior ministers, Lloyd George and Churchill, which dominated the cabinet debate. On 6 February 1912 they presented fresh proposals to the cabinet, which called for the exclusion of Ulster from the forthcoming bill, and this seems to have provoked violent argument among the Liberal cabinet ministers with Asquith apparently swaying both ways before finally rejecting exclusion. In the end, as the Prime Minister reported to the King, the cabinet voted in favour of applying the Home Rule Bill to the whole of Ireland but, significantly, a proviso was added. The government would warn Redmond that it might be necessary to make changes to the bill after its introduction, if "fresh evidence of facts, or the pressure of British opinion" dictated, and that this could take the form of special treatment for the Ulster counties. This, it was made clear, could be achieved either by amending the Home Rule Bill or by not pressing on with it under the provisions of the Parliament Act. It was apparent, therefore, that the government did not rule out special treatment for Ulster as a matter of principle, but Asquith preferred to hold back, waiting to see if any compromise was necessary and then seeing if this particular one would be sufficient. He also believed that the government had stated its case, and the onus was now on the Conservative opposition to produce an amendment.

It is easy to see how such a strategy appealed to the Liberal government. A premature concession on Ulster, which would have undermined Redmond and the Nationalists, seemed a foolish option, when there was the possibility that Ulster resistance to Home Rule might blow itself out as the bill made its way through parliament. Yet in considering this eventuality the government was greatly handicapped by its lack of detailed knowledge about the situation in Ulster. On the one hand the government was hearing from Redmond that all talk of Ulster resistance was mere bluff but, on the other, the administration, having initially failed to consider Ulster as a serious difficulty, then failed to garner accurate intelligence about the likelihood of trouble in Ulster if Home Rule was imposed. In this sense the government was badly served by Birrell who, though worried by developments in Ulster, could not reach a definite conclusion about Unionist intentions and thus allowed the matter to pass. Of course, ultimate responsibility rested with Asquith, but his strategy was to ignore Ulster and hope that Carson's dire warnings turned out to be nothing more than empty rhetoric. Naturally, this meant that Asquith conceded the initiative to his Conservative and Unionist opponents, but this style of leadership was very much suited to the Prime Minister's personality. Never one to take the initiative, Asquith preferred to sit on the sidelines, allowing a situation to develop before he intervened, and this strategy had served him well in past crises. Such procrastination, however, derived not just from Asquith's lack of initiative or imagination, but also from the fact that he was by nature a lazy, though very gifted, politician. His famous catch phrase, "We had better wait and see", neatly summed up his counter-attacking style, but it left the way open for Carson and Bonar Law to make the running as the 'Ulster Crisis' unfolded. At certain times Asquith's procrastination also exasperated Lloyd George and Churchill, two ministers who certainly knew how to seize the initiative. While Lloyd George was to turn his attention to other issues for the remainder of 1912, Churchill kept up the pressure in cabinet for some form of Ulster exclusion, failing to understand the logic in Asquith's policy that if any compromise had to be made, it should be delayed as long as possible.

Both sides in the crisis were caught off guard by an amendment to the Home Rule Bill moved by the Liberal backbencher, Thomas Agar-Robartes, the MP for the St Austell constituency in Cornwall, on 11 June 1912, when the committee stage of the bill opened. During the debate on the bill's second reading, which had been passed by over 100 votes on 19 May, Agar-Robartes had called for north-east Ulster to be excluded from the Home Rule settlement, and his amendment specifically provided for the exclusion of the four Ulster counties with Protestant majorities. The Agar-Robartes' amendment embarrassed the government, because it showed publicly that not all Liberals supported the principle of Home Rule on an all-Ireland basis. Yet the amendment also presented Asquith with the opportunity to wrong-foot the opposition by seeking an early compromise based on exclusion, but this course of action was rejected. Some historians regard this as a missed opportunity. To have accepted such an amendment during the bill's first parliamentary circuit would have been to admit that the original bill was seriously flawed, but Asquith's main reason for opposing the amendment was his contention that it would not reduce Unionist opposition to the bill. In the end the amendment was defeated by 69 votes. Another good reason for the government's decision was that acceptance of the amendment would have unnecessarily, at this point anyway, left the Irish Nationalists disaffected. They had reacted angrily to the amendment, insisting that Ireland had to be treated as a separate unit. The Agar-Robartes' amendment had placed the opposition parties in an even greater dilemma. If the Ulster Unionist MPs supported it, they would stand accused of deserting their fellow Unionists in the remaining 28 counties, when their strategy was to reject Home Rule for any part of Ireland. After some debate the Unionists were persuaded by Carson to back the amendment, and they were joined in the division lobby by Conservative MPs who had decided to support the amendment as a 'wrecking device', hoping that it might destroy the entire bill. This was the approach taken by leading Conservative figures, such as Bonar Law and Balfour, who supported the amendment even though they did not like it. For others with strong Southern Unionist connections, such as Walter Long, there was more of a dilemma but, after some hesitation, he too backed the amendment.

By the summer of 1912, therefore, both the government and the opposition had been forced to confront the possibility of a compromise based on the exclusion of parts of Ulster from the Home Rule Bill. At this stage, however, neither side was keen on compromise. The Liberals, though they had privately agreed on a fall-back position if the need arose, were not prepared to disappoint the Nationalists, and

Asquith had decided that any compromise deemed necessary should only be made when the bill was on its third, and final, parliamentary circuit. The Conservatives, on the other hand, were sticking to their strategy of using Ulster to destroy the entire Home Rule scheme. They were, moreover, in no mood to compromise. Their central argument was that the third Home Rule Bill had been the product of an unscrupulous deal, the 'corrupt bargain', between Asquith and the Nationalists, and they claimed that in their lust for power the Liberal party had deliberately hidden Home Rule from the electorate at the two general elections in 1910. Accordingly, Conservatives demanded a fresh election which would allow the voters the opportunity to declare their verdict on Home Rule. Asquith could easily refute this claim, however, by pointing out his party's longstanding commitment to Irish Home Rule and highlighting the fact that the Conservatives certainly had made Home Rule an issue in 1910. Undeterred, both Bonar Law and Balfour explored other avenues in their efforts to thwart the bill. They argued that the appearance of the Parliament Act on the statute book meant that the royal assent could no longer be considered the formality it once was. The suggestion was made that the King might withhold the royal assent from the Home Rule Bill or, perhaps, dismiss the Asquith government and replace it with one which would promise to hold a general election on the issue.

On 27 July 1912 Bonar Law appeared to commit the Conservative party to an extreme course, when he spoke to a large crowd of supporters at Blenheim Palace in Oxfordshire [74]. Tension had been raised by Asquith's historic visit to Dublin on the previous weekend, when he poured scorn on Unionist threats of civil war and delighted his Nationalist audience in the process. Bonar Law's reply before a crowd of 13,000 gathered in the grounds at Blenheim was intended as a swift riposte to the Prime Minister's dismissive remarks. Again stressing the government's refusal to put Home Rule before the voters, he warned that if the Liberals proceeded with the bill, then the Ulstermen "would be justified in resisting by all means in their power, including force ... if the attempt be made under present conditions I can imagine no length of resistance to which Ulster can go in which I should not be prepared to support them". At the Blenheim rally a significant contribution was also made by F E Smith who claimed that the government lacked the necessary resolve to see off the Ulster challenge. Certainly, the Blenheim demonstration confirmed that opposition to Home Rule was now, more than ever, centred on Ulster, but the sentiments expressed, particularly by Bonar Law, who appeared to be encouraging violence, were alarming. Asquith and the Liberal press were suitably shocked by Bonar Law's apparent disregard for the constitutional process, but the use of such strong language only reinforced the views held privately by Churchill and Lloyd George that special provisions would have to be made for Ulster. Still, the question remains: why did Bonar Law commit himself to such an extreme course? There were a number of reasons. In his new role as party leader Bonar Law was anxious to avoid the mistakes made by Balfour whose drift had allowed divisions within the party to become exacerbated. Clearly, the Union was one issue on which the party was united, and taking a tough line and ruling out compromise made it easier to maintain this unity. Moreover, Conservatives saw Ireland as their best opportunity to press the Liberals and, perhaps in the long run, to return to office. There was also a good deal of lingering bitterness from the Parliament Act, and Conservatives were convinced, though with little justification, that the Liberals and their Irish allies had been acting subversively since 1909. Such feelings made any moves towards reaching an accommodation with the Liberals very difficult. Then, on the positive side, the Conservative party had genuine concerns about the impact which Irish Home Rule would have on the Empire, and many of the leaders saw resistance in Ulster on an imperial scale. Finally, Bonar Law's empathy with the Ulster Unionists led him to move his party to a more extreme position behind the Ulster Unionists, as they planned to step up their opposition to the third Home Rule Bill.

Ulster resistance

The introduction of the third Home Rule Bill had raised sectarian tension in Ulster. This was illustrated by events at the end of June – beginning of July 1912, when up to 2,000 Catholic workers in the shipyard were forced to leave their employment. The problem had been sparked by an incident in the small village of Castledawson, County Londonderry, on 29 June. A large party of Presbyterian children, complete with its own band and Union Jacks, had been on a Sunday School excursion from Belfast, and it became involved in a disturbance with a group of Hibernians who were returning from an AOH demonstration in nearby Maghera. In the confusion terrified children ran for cover into the unfamiliar countryside outside the village, as local Protestants joined in the fighting, and it was some time before all the children were recovered. None had been badly injured but, as news of the episode reached Belfast, the wildly exaggerated story of a vile Catholic mob attacking Protestant children quickly gained credence. Some of the children's fathers worked in the shipyard, and sectarian revenge attacks followed at the beginning of July, forcing out the 2,000 Catholic employees. There were further outbreaks of violence, and the situation over the 'Twelfth' holiday was extremely tense. The sectarian disorder continued into September, when there were violent clashes between two sets of supporters at a Belfast football match. These developments alarmed Carson. He realised that Unionist resistance to Home Rule would only be effective if he could marshal a tightly disciplined mass movement, and any indiscriminate attacks, such as those seen in Belfast, only weakened the Unionist case and played into the hands of the Liberals.

What the Unionist leadership needed was some means to control and focus such intense popular feeling and, not surprisingly, it was Craig, Carson's faithful lieutenant, who emerged with the answer. A number of leading Unionists had for some months thought that they should devise an oath which their supporters could take to signal their determination to resist Home Rule. By September 1912 the situation was ripe for such a development and, after some difficulty, Craig drew up an Ulster Solemn League and Covenant, which he wanted all Ulster Unionists to sign. The Covenant was based on the old Scottish Covenant of 1580 and had a strong Old Testament flavour. It allowed the signatories to profess loyalty to the King, but warned His Majesty's government that the men of Ulster, and the reference was to the nine counties of Ulster, would use "all means which may be found necessary to defeat the present conspiracy to set up a home rule parliament in Ireland" [75]. Again, Craig took responsibility for the organisation of the event. Saturday, 28 September 1912, was designated 'Ulster Day', and Carson and the rest of the leaders were to sign the Covenant in the City Hall following another great demonstration in Belfast. This was to be, however, only the climax to more than a week's special campaigning in the province against Home Rule.

Beginning in Enniskillen on 18 September, Carson addressed a crowd of 40,000, describing resistance to Home Rule as not only a right but a 'duty' which had to be carried out by loyal Ulstermen. In all, Carson spoke at six meetings, and the campaign tour took in other venues at which leading Conservatives appeared before enthusiastic crowds. F E Smith spoke at five meetings and, on each occasion, stirred the audiences with his oratory. Leading peers, who were acknowledged to be on the Conservative party's right wing also spoke. These included Lord Salisbury, Lord Willoughby de Broke and Lord Hugh Cecil [76]. On Wednesday, 25 September, the organisers of the Covenant dispatched copies across the province where they were signed, often in local Orange halls, by Unionist supporters. On the Friday evening a great rally was held in the Ulster Hall, and Carson delivered one of his finest speeches with almost every phrase carrying special significance. Outside the Ulster Hall he then carefully unfolded a yellow silk banner before the expectant crowd and shouted, "May this flag ever float over a people that can boast of civil and religious liberty". Next day, a holiday in Belfast, a series of religious services was followed by the procession to the City Hall, where the leading figures signed the Covenant in another moving ceremony before the rank and file entered in carefully organised groups. Carson signed with a special silver pen which had been formally presented to him by Craig.

Ulster Day had been a huge propaganda success. The press were there in force to witness events, and reporters from the leading English newspapers conveyed the scenes of great emotion to their readers. There was also a distinct 'God's chosen people' feel which the press picked up in the deeply religious nature of the day's events. Here were God's people, as they saw themselves, just like the Israelites who had laboured under great injustice in the Old Testament, doing as the Covenant said, "humbly relying on their God". Undoubtedly, this powerful religious atmosphere, together with the presence and participation of so many Protestant clerics, added to the emotion of the day. More than 218,000 men signed the Covenant and more than 228,000 women signed a corresponding Declaration. The grand total, when over 20,000 signatures from people of Ulster birth in England were added, reached 471,414. Carson was by this stage, of course, an honorary Ulsterman. When he left the docks in Belfast on 28 September on board the night-boat to Liverpool, a crowd of 70,000 gave him a rousing send-off. Next morning he was greeted by 150,000 supporters in Liverpool. The Covenant had achieved exactly what he and Craig had intended. A highly disciplined mass movement had engaged in this great stage-managed act of defiance to demonstrate their resolve by taking this solemn pledge to resist Home Rule.

The events of the summer had lifted Conservative and Unionist spirits, and this was evident when the House of Commons reassembled for its autumn session in October 1912. The committee stage of the bill's first circuit now witnessed a number of stormy incidents. Enraged by the government's use of the guillotine to speed the bill's progress, opposition MPs denounced the strategy as tyrannical, and Bonar Law renewed his demand for a fresh general election. On 1 January 1913 Carson moved an amendment to exclude the whole province of Ulster from the bill's operation. This appeared a natural step, building on the commitment laid down in the Covenant, but it was not without risk. Carson still harboured the hope that Ulster resistance could kill the entire bill, and his speech to the Commons made it clear that even if the amendment was accepted, opposition to the bill would continue unabated. Naturally, any proposal for the exclusion of Ulster left Unionists in the three southern provinces uneasy, and they only accepted the amendment on receiving assurances that it was a tactical manoeuvre. On no account, they were told, would they be abandoned. Yet Carson's amendment was also a reflection of the way in which resistance to Home Rule had become predominantly Ulster-based during 1912. Many Unionists now took a more realistic approach to the Home Rule Bill, privately conceding that they would be unable to block the measure. In such circumstances it made sense to save Ulster from Home Rule. When the cabinet met to decide on its approach, Lloyd George and Churchill wanted to use the Carson amendment as a road out of the Ulster impasse, but the majority favoured the 'no compromise' policy and, in the end, the amendment was rejected by 294 to 197, the low turn-out of MPs illustrating the flagging interest. Soon afterwards, the bill received its third reading on 16 January by a 110 majority. Almost immediately, it was thrown out by the Lords.

With the government rejecting exclusion the Unionists felt obliged to demonstrate that they had the capacity to resist any attempt to impose Home Rule against their wishes. Already, Orangemen in various parts of the province had begun to organise drilling, and groups of men could be seen marching in military style on the country roads outside Orange halls. On 31 January 1913 the Ulster Unionist Council announced that these men would come together in a new body, the Ulster Volunteer Force (UVF). A ceiling of 100,000 was planned for the force, and recruitment was to be limited to those men between the ages of 17 and 65 who had signed the Covenant. By the end of the year the UVF had grown to 90,000 members and had a small full time staff of ex-British Army officers who worked from the force's headquarters in Belfast's Old Town Hall. The UVF was organised on a county basis with a varying number of regiments, battalions and sections, depending on the strength of recruitment in each of the nine counties. A striking feature of the force was its cross-class membership. The great landowners often served in the officer section and many allowed their estates to be used for weekend training camps. Businessmen featured prominently in Belfast and in the provincial towns as did manual workers, and small farmers and agricultural labourers were the mainstay of the UVF's rural units. Frequently, drill involved the use of dummy wooden rifles but, if this provided great amusement for their opponents, the UVF was determined to show that it was a viable military machine. This was apparent in the measures taken to attract experienced soldiers onto its full time staff. Unionists sought the advice of Lord Roberts of Kandahar, and the most famous British soldier alive responded enthusiastically. Through Roberts the UVF obtained the services of Lieutenant-General Sir George Richardson who had enjoyed a distinguished career serving with the British Army in India. Richardson took over command of the UVF in July 1913 and immediately began the task of organising the training of the 50,000 men who had, by that stage, joined the force. Quickly, various support units, including a Medical

Corps, a Nursing Corps and the famous Motor Car Corps, were established, and this helped to give the impression of a well organised military force. The one essential ingredient missing, of course, was a large stock of arms. Still, the UVF gave some substance to Carson's increasingly militant rhetoric which he developed during 1913 and, at the same time, imposed the type of discipline which he desperately wanted from his followers.

The search for a solution

With Asquith determined that the Home Rule Bill should be pushed through its second parliamentary circuit using his big Commons' majority, and leaving little time for debate, a general air of gloom descended on the opposition benches. Many of these sessions attracted only a few MPs, and the lack of interest was noticeable on both sides of the House. The bill duly received its third reading in the Commons on 7 July 1913 and was rejected by the Lords on 15 July. In these circumstances the opposition concentrated on resistance outside parliament. In March 1913 Lord Willoughby de Broke, who had assisted in the Covenant campaign, sent a letter to the London newspapers announcing the formation of the 'British League for the Support of Ulster and the Union'. The letter was signed by 100 peers and 120 MPs, and the movement quickly attracted the support of some famous personalities both inside and outside politics, which added to the propaganda effect and heightened awareness of the Ulster crisis in England. The rejection of the Home Rule Bill by the Lords in July 1913 also helped to concentrate minds. Although Asquith was prepared to 'wait and see' how events unfolded, others lacked his coolness. The King, in particular, was becoming nervous, fearing that he would be dragged into the Home Rule controversy if a solution acceptable to all the parties could not be found. Throughout the spring and early summer of 1913 Bonar Law still hoped, and he made repeated public references to this, that the King could be persuaded to dissolve parliament and call a general election. Towards the end of July the King asked the Conservative leaders to clarify their views. He received their response on 31 July 1913 when a lengthy memorandum was dispatched by Bonar Law and Lansdowne. Again, their key argument was that the King should use the royal prerogative to dissolve Parliament before Home Rule was enacted. This could be put into effect, they suggested, by the King withholding the royal assent and then calling for a new government which would put the issue to the voters. The academic, A V Dicey, whose expertise on the British constitution was widely acknowledged, judged that the King would be acting within his powers in adopting such a course.

Nevertheless, other senior Conservatives had reservations about urging what would be, in effect, a royal veto, as this would draw the monarch into party politics. This would set a dangerous precedent which could ultimately threaten the monarchy's role in the constitution. Balfour certainly believed that the King should not withhold the royal assent, though he was adamant that the King could still seek new ministers. He suggested, moreover, that the King could send for an elder statesman and, demonstrating that his resignation from the party leadership had not doused his ambition, offered his own services as a short term solution. With the King being bombarded with such advice, Asquith's reaction was crucial. On 11 August the

King personally handed Asquith a 400 word memorandum which he had composed after considering the Bonar Law - Lansdowne document. The King's memorandum expressed the growing anxiety about the position in which he now found himself, and it suggested an all - party conference to explore the possibility of a settlement. Asquith's reply to the King was unequivocal. Firstly, he made it crystal clear that the King should not depart from constitutional precedent and should not, therefore, contemplate any intervention in the Home Rule crisis. He followed this with an assessment of the Ulster situation. By this stage he acknowledged that when Home Rule became law, the province was likely to experience 'tumult and riot', though he thought that talk of civil war was alarmist. Asquith also stated that an all-party conference was doomed to fail unless the opposition accepted the principle of Irish Home Rule, but then dangled the possibility that a reasonable compromise on Ulster could be found if this principle was acceptable. At this point in the crisis the King's intrusion must have been an unwelcome distraction for Asquith but, if he can be criticised for his handling of some aspects of the Irish Question, the line he took on the royal intervention was exemplary. He knew that the King was under great pressure from senior Conservatives to intervene, but the Prime Minister handled the situation with great tact and, at the same time, left George V in no doubt about his opposition to the use of the royal prerogative.

On the ground in Ulster, meanwhile, resistance to Home Rule was intensifying. The Twelfth celebrations in July 1913 drew large numbers, and Carson attended the main demonstration which was held in the grounds of Craig's home. Both men were delighted that a repeat of the previous year's violence had been avoided, and Carson attributed this to the discipline achieved through the formation of the UVF. In spite of all these political engagements, Carson continued with his legal career. Indeed, his most famous case in 1913 caused great embarrassment to many of his Unionist and Conservative friends. In June Carson and F E Smith appeared on behalf of Lloyd George and Lord Murray of Elibank, the Liberal Chief Whip, both of whom had been caught up in the 'Marconi scandal' and were issuing legal writs for libel against a French newspaper. These cabinet ministers had foolishly bought shares in the American Marconi Company, a subsidiary of the British parent company which later won a big government contract to set up a chain of wireless stations. Carson secured a public apology for the government ministers, but his actions in defending his political enemies, when relations between the two main parties were so hostile, caused disbelief in opposition circles, baffling Bonar Law and angering many of his colleagues. Carson returned to Ulster in September 1913 and indulged in his most militant rhetoric, when he spoke at a number of UVF parades. By this point Carson sensed that the Liberal government's nerve was beginning to fail, and he was determined to press home his advantage. It was at the Belfast review that F E Smith acquired the nickname of 'galloper' as he officiated on horseback in the company of Richardson, the UVF commander. Four days earlier, on 23 September 1913, Carson attended a meeting of the Ulster Unionist Council at which the 500 delegates formally approved plans for the immediate establishment of a Provisional government if Home Rule became law. Even at this stage Carson hoped that Ulster could break the Home Rule scheme, as there was a chance that the Irish Nationalists would prefer a general election to some form of exclusion.

Certainly, the idea of partition was anathema to Redmond. He had articulated this when Carson had proposed the exclusion of a nine county Ulster in January 1913. The line taken by Redmond, since the Home Rule Bill's introduction in April 1912, was that Home Rule had to apply to all of Ireland. He rejected Ulster Unionist demands for self-determination, arguing that they could not deny the Nationalist majority their democratic rights. Crucially, he was slow to address the Ulster issue, and one reason for this was his sincerely held belief that there was no substance in the Unionist arguments against Home Rule. He also assumed that the dire threats issued by Carson were nothing more than bluff and largely depended on the political support Ulster received from a desperate and hysterical Bonar Law. Moreover, the result of a by-election for the Londonderry City constituency in January 1913 appeared to confirm one of Redmond's key arguments that the Unionists were mistaken in assuming that they spoke for the whole of Ulster. The seat had been won narrowly by the Unionists at the previous general election but, in the January by-election, a Liberal candidate, David Hogg, a Scottish-born shirt manufacturer in the city, polled 2,699 votes to the Unionist's 2,642, giving him a majority of 57. Hogg had stood on a clear Home Rule ticket and in his post election address to the press said that he was "proud to have been the standard-bearer of self government for Ireland in one of the most historic elections ever fought in Ireland". The by-election was significant not just because the Unionists had lost the 'maiden City' seat, but because Hogg's victory gave the Home Rulers a majority of Ulster's 33 MPs, leaving the Unionists with just 16. The victory in Derry contributed to Redmond's complacency on the Ulster issue and, for most of 1913, he continued to dismiss Carson's talk of armed resistance as fantasy.

In the IPP Redmond bore the main responsibility and took the most important decisions, but he had three principal lieutenants who stood head and shoulders above the rest of the party. T P O'Connor, who represented a Liverpool constituency and thus had very little contact with Ireland, formed the key link between the IPP and the Liberal party, and he enjoyed a particularly close relationship with Lloyd George. Joe Devlin, the MP for West Belfast, was a powerful performer in parliamentary debates, and he made some of the most telling contributions as the Home Rule Bill was piloted through the House of Commons. His control over the AOH also made him a vital link between the party and the Nationalist rank and file and, as was noted earlier, his rise to prominence on the back of the AOH contributed to the growing sectarian nature of Irish, particularly Ulster, politics, which made compromise more difficult to find. Devlin was very close to John Dillon, Redmond's deputy and former opponent. Dillon had an intricate understanding of grass roots Irish politics and his experience stretched back to the Land War. For much of 1913, when Redmond was frequently in London, Dillon toured Ireland, addressing Nationalist audiences and hammering on the theme that the threat of resistance in Ulster was bluff. This was a view with which Devlin from his ideal vantage point in Belfast concurred.

When the Ulster crisis blew up in the autumn of 1913, therefore, the IPP was alarmingly unprepared. In effect, the IPP had no policy on Ulster outside its insistence that Home Rule had to be on an all-Ireland basis, and Redmond left it to the Liberals not only to make any compromise deemed necessary but also to defend the Nationalist position. Consequently, the IPP relied too much on the Liberals and had no contingency plan in place, if the Liberals retreated from the position outlined by Asquith on the introduction of the third Home Rule Bill in April 1912. This was a critical error, because Redmond had been informed, following the crucial cabinet meeting on 6 February 1912, that the government retained the freedom to offer some form of protection for Ulster if the circumstances dictated. Throughout 1912-13, moreover, the IPP leadership had enough contact with Lloyd George, Churchill and Birrell, all of whom believed that some kind of arrangement for Ulster would be necessary, to sense that the Liberal government might give way on exclusion [77]. Still, Redmond clung to the belief that if the Liberal government stood firm, Ulster Unionist opposition would evaporate. The alternative would have been to take the initiative by offering Ulster some kind of safeguard, possibly some scheme of Home Rule within Home Rule or perhaps a Unionist veto in the new parliament. Although this would probably have been rejected by Carson, it could well have split the opposition forces, thus making an eventual settlement more achievable. Part of the blame for this must be shouldered by Asquith and the Liberals who generally preferred to reassure the Nationalists on their commitment to all-Ireland Home Rule, rather than encourage them to think of possible concessions for Ulster.

Both Asquith and Redmond were caught off guard by the sensation of the Loreburn letter which appeared in *The Times* on 11 September 1913. Lord Loreburn had served as Lord Chancellor in the Liberal government up to June 1912, and he had been one of the staunchest Home Rule supporters in the cabinet. His letter to *The Times* urged the party leaders to go the extra mile in search of a settlement and suggested they meet for direct talks. Failure to secure an agreement would, he thought, result in serious disturbances in Ulster. The Loreburn letter caused a storm of controversy,not because of its content which was rather vague, but simply because it had been written by Loreburn. Although out of office for more than a year, Loreburn still retained considerable influence, and many of the Conservative leaders believed that the inspiration for the letter had come from the cabinet, though this was certainly not the case. While the Loreburn letter opened up a new channel of public debate, there was more significant activity taking place behind the scenes. The venue for this was Balmoral Castle in Scotland, where the King traditionally took his late summer holidays. There, in September and early October 1913, he received visits from many leading politicians in both the main parties. Bonar Law was one of the first guests to arrive, and he repeated his argument in favour of the King using his powers to dissolve parliament. While the King continued to shy away from such a drastic course, he was, nevertheless, prompted to send another memorandum to Asquith, which asked some pertinent questions. Firstly, the King made it clear that in his opinion a general election should be held before Home Rule became law, and then he raised a new point. Would Asquith, he asked, use the British Army to suppress disorder in Ulster, when it was clear that so many of the army's senior personnel were in strong sympathy with the Ulster cause? Although Asquith replied that the troops would follow orders, the King's intervention provided a strong reminder that there was growing disquiet among senior army officers.

Bonar Law's attendance at Balmoral overlapped with Churchill's visit, and the two men had a long discussion on the Home Rule crisis. Churchill was greatly encouraged by the moderate line taken by the Conservative leader in their private talks. Bonar Law did not hide his anxiety about developments in Ulster, and Churchill found him particularly uneasy about Carson's plans to establish a Provisional government if Home Rule was enacted. In their discussions Bonar Law suggested that a compromise based on the exclusion of Ulster would be acceptable, and the rest of Ireland could have Home Rule. After the meeting Bonar Law wrote to Carson informing him of developments at Balmoral and indicating his willingness to pursue some form of partition as a compromise. His only reservation was that such a course of action might be seen as a betrayal by the Unionists living in the other three provinces. Carson's reply on 23 September not only endorsed the Bonar Law line but went on to focus on the area which should be excluded from the bill: "My own view is that the whole of Ulster should be excluded but the minimum would be the six plantation counties, and for that a good case could be made". This correspondence revealed that Bonar Law and Carson were a good deal more moderate in private than their public statements indicated. Carson had closely identified with, even embodied, the spirit of defiance which had become such a feature of Ulster Unionist resistance but, by the autumn of 1913, he was clearly worried about where such defiance might lead if the government pressed ahead with Home Rule. Inside the Unionist movement Craig and the other more extreme leaders were taking up a more aggressive position and were preparing to use the UVF to threaten the government, thus increasing the pressure on Carson to reach a negotiated settlement.

Bonar Law, too, was displaying a good deal more caution away from the public spotlight, an indication of the difficulties he faced within his own party. Ever since his provocative Blenheim speech which delighted many on the backbenches but startled a number of the party's senior figures, including Curzon who had been angered not just by the language used but by the leader's failure to consult his colleagues prior to the demonstration, Bonar Law had maintained his combative public image. Yet his real concern had been to save Ulster from Home Rule and, by the autumn of 1913, he had made the government aware, through Churchill, of his willingness to reach a settlement based on Ulster exclusion. His problem, however, was the powerful element in the Conservative party, notably Lansdowne, Long, Curzon and the Cecils, who regarded such a course as a betrayal of Southern Unionists. It was conceivable that this group could stage a revolt to block any attempt at a solution based on partition. At this point the problem of the Southern Unionists was addressed directly by Carson who met a Southern Unionist delegation in his London home and persuaded them not to oppose Ulster's struggle for exclusion from the bill. News of this meeting reassured Bonar Law, though he remained concerned about Southern Unionist reaction. While Carson's emotional attachment to the Union was still a factor, his pragmatic side had clearly asserted itself, as he switched his strategy from seeking Ulster exclusion as a tactical manoeuvre in order to smash the entire Home Rule scheme to one of saving at least the greater part of Ulster from an unstoppable Home Rule Bill.

Both Carson and Bonar Law were encouraged by a speech made by Churchill in his Dundee constituency on 9 October. Churchill recognised the shift in Unionist strategy and stated that Ulster's "claim for special consideration, if put forward with sincerity, cannot be ignored by a Government depending on the existing House". Surprisingly, among the Nationalist leaders only T P O'Connor showed concern over the Churchill speech. From his base in London O'Connor was frustrated by Redmond's complacency, and he repeatedly urged his leader to communicate his views to the cabinet, particularly to Asquith. The task of replying to Churchill fell to Redmond and in a memorable speech, but one that came back to haunt him, in Limerick on 12 October the IPP leader warned the government against compromise, adding "Irish Nationalists can never by assenting parties to the mutilation of the Irish nation, Ireland is a unit ... The two-nation theory is to us an abomination and a blasphemy". The Irish leader was still convinced that all talk of civil war was gigantic bluff and, in a speech in Navan only a week later, he likened Ulster threats of resistance to the bravado of the drunken man desperately seeking restraint before he 'attacks' his enemy [78,79].

While Asquith must have been irritated by Churchill's Dundee speech, he recognised that it was now time to demonstrate that he was actively pursuing a settlement. On the day before Churchill's speech Asquith had written to Bonar Law, ruling out the formal conference which both the King and Loreburn had been advocating, but offering informal, confidential talks between himself and the Conservative leader. In fact, this led to three such meetings, on 14 October, 6 November and 10 December, which were held at Cherkley Court, the home of Bonar Law's close friend, Sir Max Aiken. The meetings were Asquith's response to pressure from the King and from Churchill and Lloyd George who, along with other members of the cabinet, were beginning to receive alarming reports about UVF activity. Nothing was agreed at the first meeting, but Asquith learned at first hand of Bonar Law's moderation in private and heard that he would accept Home Rule with Ulster's exclusion, though he did not attempt to define 'Ulster'. Asquith also learned of the difficulties facing Bonar Law if he opted for a settlement based on exclusion. Lansdowne, the chief spokesman for the Southern Unionists, was the most uncompromising figure among the Conservative leaders, and he informed Carson that he viewed the Asquith – Bonar Law dialogue with profound mistrust. Yet it was clear that, despite the longstanding hostility between the Liberals and Conservatives, the two leaders were shaping towards a compromise based on the exclusion of Ulster. Obviously there were difficulties, not least securing agreement on the area of 'Ulster', but the first meeting offered the hope of compromise. Significantly, Asquith was the more skilled negotiator, concealing his own problems while drawing from Bonar Law a number of possible concessions which were, of course, contingent on the agreement of his colleagues.

At their second meeting on 6 November the two leaders focused on Ulster. Bonar Law stated that Carson would not accept anything less than six counties, but Asquith countered with the simple argument that both Tyrone and Fermanagh had narrow Nationalist majorities. Clearly, both leaders knew that if a compromise was going to result, it would be the Nationalists who would have to give up most ground. All along, the Conservative and Unionist opposition had criticised Asquith's dependence on the Nationalists, but the reality was that the Nationalists were totally dependent on the Liberals, a situation which had been exacerbated by Redmond's complacency on the Ulster issue. At the end of the meeting Asquith agreed to Bonar Law's request to put the question of the exclusion of 'Ulster' to his colleagues, though the Conservative leader wrongly assumed that Asquith himself would push for the exclusion of at least part of Ulster in cabinet. At the crucial cabinet meeting on 13 November it was, in fact, Lloyd George who took the initiative, suggesting an amendment to the Home Rule Bill which would allow those Ulster counties with a Protestant majority temporary exclusion for a period of five or six years. Lloyd George argued that the time lapse would make it very difficult for the Unionists to mount a campaign of resistance after such a long delay. Despite Lloyd George's forceful persuasion, there were powerful voices in the cabinet, led by Reginald McKenna and Walter Runciman, against special treatment for Ulster, but it was clear that the balance had been tipped in favour of some form of exclusion.

On 17 November 1913 Asquith finally met Redmond for a discussion on the situation, informing him of the Lloyd George scheme to exclude part of Ulster from Home Rule for a fixed period, after which it would automatically come under a Dublin parliament. The Prime Minister also conveyed the impression that the scheme was really a delaying tactic to prevent an immediate outbreak of violence in Ulster. Redmond was alarmed by the proposal, though he conceded that he might consider it if it was put forward by Bonar Law. He followed this up with a memorandum for Asquith in which he forcefully stated the case against partition and argued that the threat of violence in Ulster was being grossly exaggerated. This tough line appeared to bear fruit and, on 26 November, Redmond received an assurance that the cabinet would not bring forward the Lloyd George scheme. Moreover, Asquith apparently ruled out any prospect of a compromise, when he spoke in Leeds on 27 November: "We are not going to be frightened or deflected by menaces of civil war. We are not going to make any surrender of principle. We mean to see the thing through".

Lloyd George, meanwhile, was convinced that the Nationalists could be pressed into accepting some form of exclusion. He met Dillon on 17 November and from their conversation assumed that Dillon had no serious objection to his scheme of temporary exclusion, provided it was delayed until the very last moment when the bill was going through. On 25 November Lloyd George had an interview with Redmond and, after reassuring the Irish leader that the government would not make an early offer to the Unionists, he pressed Redmond to back his temporary exclusion plan. This left Redmond confused and angry. Inside a few days he had heard different interpretations of the government's thinking from Asquith, Birrell and Lloyd George, but it was surely clear to the Irish leader that opinion in the cabinet had shifted in favour of exclusion. He received some respite, however, when Bonar Law flatly rejected the scheme for temporary exclusion at his third and final secret meeting with Asquith on 10 December 1913. Indeed relations had been soured by Asquith's Leeds speech and by the bitter reaction it provoked in Conservative and Unionist circles, and Bonar Law felt that they were as far away from a settlement as ever. The Conservative leader was also in some confusion about Asquith's personal preference for a compromise but was clearly aware that the Prime Minister's procrastination was a deliberate tactic, as he waited for the right moment, when the government could maximise its advantage, to make his move. He expected Asquith would offer Home Rule within Home Rule in the hope that the rejection of this proposal would turn public opinion in Britain against the Conservative party. For his part Asquith was confident that Redmond could be cajoled into accepting such a compromise, as it maintained the integrity of a 32 county Ireland. In delaying any compromise until the last possible moment, moreover, Asquith was able to retain the Nationalists' confidence. Besides, he was convinced that a premature offer from his government would only bring demands for new concessions from the opposition.

After the breakdown of negotiations with Bonar Law Asquith had two meetings with Carson on 16 December 1913 and 2 January 1914. While these meetings were friendlier than the Bonar Law interviews, they were again futile, as Asquith's offer of a variation of Home Rule within Home Rule was rejected outright by Carson. Yet this suited Asquith who was determined to force the opposition to put forward their own detailed proposals for a compromise, and he believed that by making an offer which he knew Carson would reject, the onus would then be on the Unionist leader to make a detailed counter offer. In fact, Carson's response mirrored Bonar Law's approach. Unless the government accepted the principle of Ulster exclusion, he argued, there would be no point in working out detailed proposals specifying how any excluded counties would be administered. During all of these private discussions Asquith failed to keep his cabinet colleagues informed, and it was not until 22 January 1914 that he reported to them on the breakdown of negotiations with Bonar Law and Carson. The prospect of a settlement had receded during the three months of secret talks and, subsequently, both opposition leaders returned to their defiant rhetoric. On 15 January Bonar Law announced to an audience in Cardiff that negotiations had taken place and had failed, and he then dispatched a letter to the King's private secretary, Lord Stamfordham, analysing the situation. He wrote that the government had only two options – "either they must submit their Bill to the judgement of the people or prepare for the consequences of civil war". Compromise had, in Bonar Law's judgement, been tried and failed, but some Conservative leaders still hoped that if the Liberals could be pressed into offering Ulster exclusion, it would be met by a Nationalist rejection which, in turn, would mean the collapse of the entire Home Rule scheme.

With the new session of parliament about to open Asquith and Redmond had a crucial meeting on 2 February 1914. Amazingly in view of the circumstances, this was their first contact since their meeting on 17 November. The Prime Minister's intention, by this stage, was to see how far he could push the Irish leader into making concessions, and to do this Asquith again emphasised the great difficulties facing his government. The Prime Minister was clearly anxious to avoid violent confrontation in Ulster, and the way to achieve this was to draw concessions from the Nationalists. Yet Asquith also set out to deceive Redmond about his government's thinking, when he assured him that his cabinet colleagues were all firmly opposed to the exclusion of Ulster, even on a temporary basis. If this false assurance was meant to assuage Redmond's fears, what followed was a devastating blow for the Nationalists. "My visitor shivered visibly and was a good deal perturbed" was Asquith's own description of Redmond's reaction. After describing the failure of his negotiations with Carson and Bonar Law, Asquith warned Redmond that the King was frightened of civil war and, crucially, he indicated that the deteriorating situation in Ireland could create unprecedented problems for the British Army. Consequently, the Prime Minister insisted that his government had to make some offer to Ulster, namely Home Rule within Home Rule, which would, in all likelihood be rejected, but the rejection of a reasonable compromise would, he thought, seriously undermine the opposition case in Britain. The weakness of Devlin's position was now obvious. He was joined in London by Redmond and Dillon and together they penned a reply to Asquith on 5 February. Again, they stressed that the threat of civil war in Ulster represented a gross exaggeration, and they warned that an early announcement of concessions would cause grave difficulties for the IPP which would be charged with abandoning those Nationalists living in Ulster.

While Asquith refrained from offering concessions when Parliament met after the winter recess on 11 February 1914, he did promise to make an offer to meet Unionist fears. At this point Lloyd George made the decisive move. He recognised that a concession on Ulster had to meet two criteria if it was to prove successful: (1) it must be an offer the rejection of which would put the Unionists in the wrong as far as British public opinion was concerned; and (2) it must not involve any alteration in the scheme of the Home Rule Bill. For Lloyd George the Home Rule within Home Rule option was much less attractive than his original idea, which he had put to Redmond and Dillon in November 1913, of allowing those Ulster counties with a Protestant majority to opt out of Home Rule for a specified period. Accordingly, Asquith, Lloyd George and Birrell met the IPP leaders, Redmond, Dillon, Devlin and O'Connor on 2 March for a discussion of the Lloyd George initiative. After the meeting Redmond drew up a memorandum outlining the solution which the Liberals had pressed his party to accept. Individual counties could, following a plebiscite, opt out of Home Rule for a period of three years, and Redmond agreed with great reluctance to accept the proposal as "the price of peace". Redmond added that this concession, which also gave Belfast and Derry City the opportunity to vote themselves out of Home Rule, was only on offer if it was fully accepted by the Unionists, and he went on to insist that it should be "the last word of the government". Yet within a few days Redmond had been forced to accept an extension of the time delay from three to six years. This was a clever attempt by Asquith to secure Unionist agreement as, under the terms of the Parliament Act, the length of parliaments had been reduced from seven to five years. A six year period meant, therefore, that a general election would be held in the interim, thus offering Unionists the prospect of avoiding automatic inclusion after the moratorium if the Conservatives were returned to office.

Obviously, the Nationalists had made a major concession and, in the process, Redmond had abandoned the 'one Ireland' principle which, he claimed, had been the centre-piece in Nationalist thinking. Several factors were important in persuading Redmond to agree to the county option scheme. Undoubtedly, he had been influenced by a speech which Carson had made in the House of Commons in February. This was Carson at his most statesmanlike, as he appealed to his "Nationalist fellow countrymen" to win over Ulster by persuasion rather than by force. The speech convinced Redmond that it was worth going the extra mile in search of a solution. The Irish leader convinced himself that the exclusion of probably four Ulster counties would be a temporary state of affairs and that time would do a great deal to heal the divisions between the two traditions, which had clearly deepened during the Ulster crisis. Redmond was also a parliamentarian who believed in compromise and constitutional action. He never grasped, nor ever wanted to grasp, the power of extra-parliamentary pressure which Carson had used to such effect. In analysing his reasons for accepting the county option scheme, moreover, it seems that Home Rule for Nationalist Ireland was more important to Redmond than Irish unity. Certainly Devlin, from his Ulster base, had pressed Redmond to stick to the one Ireland principle, but even he was prepared to swallow temporary exclusion if the prize was Home Rule [80].

It was Carson's extra - parliamentary strategy which eventually forced the Liberal government to seek a solution based on the exclusion of parts of Ulster. When it came to the details of such a policy, Asquith found Redmond much easier to shift than Carson and, consequently, it was the Nationalists who gave most ground in March 1914. Asquith announced the government's offer of county option on 9 March, when moving the second reading of the Home Rule Bill on its final parliamentary journey. It had, of course, been Asquith's plan to delay such a compromise until this juncture, but Carson contemptuously dismissed the government offer in one of his most memorable phrases: "We do not want sentence of death with a stay of execution for six years". A week later in another melodramatic parliamentary scene Carson stormed out of the Commons and left for Belfast where, it was assumed, he would set up the Ulster Provisional government. The ball was now clearly in the government's court. If Asquith was going to deliver the assurance given to Redmond that the county option scheme with the six year time limit was the government's final offer, then he would have to use the army to impose Home Rule on Ulster [81].

Civil war?

The formation of the Irish Volunteers in November 1913 was an indication that there was some concern in Nationalist Ireland over Redmond's handling of the Home Rule crisis. The main inspiration behind the Irish Volunteers was Eoin MacNeill, the Gaelic scholar who had combined with Douglas Hyde to launch the Gaelic League in 1893. The movement was formally established at a public meeting in Dublin on 25 November 1913, and the UVF was used as a model [82,83,84]. The rationale behind MacNeill's thinking was that Carson's extra - parliamentary strategy was proving successful and should, therefore, be imitated by Nationalists. Although the Irish Volunteers immediately attracted the interest of the clandestine IRB, many of whose senior figures infiltrated the new movement, there was little early enthusiasm shown by mainstream Nationalists. Certainly, Redmond was not comfortable with the new movement. He did not want to see Nationalists copy tactics that he had repeatedly condemned, and he genuinely distrusted any political movement which was not entirely constitutional.

The Liberal government was also perturbed by the appearance of a second private army in Ireland and, on 5 December 1913, two royal proclamations were issued banning the importation of arms and ammunition into Ireland. This was resented by the Irish Volunteers, as the UVF had been bringing in guns for much of 1913 without, it was assumed, any interference from the authorities. Indeed several hundred rifles and some machine guns had been purchased and brought to Ulster for the UVF by a group of Unionist extremists. The most prominent of these was Fred Crawford, another Belfast businessman. Crawford had some military experience and impressive technical knowledge of guns, which helped him become Director of Ordnance on the UVF Headquarters Staff. Using this position, Crawford urged the Unionist leadership to back his plan for the importation of a huge quantity of arms and ammunition in a single shipment. Such a scheme would, of course, require considerable funding, but support from the Belfast business community, which had already paid for the establishment of the UVF, was guaranteed. Money also came from wealthy patrons in England. The British League for the Support of Ulster and the Union had about 10,000 members by the beginning of 1914, but its profile had been raised by the efforts of Lord Milner and his able lieutenant, the Conservative MP for South Birmingham, Leo Amery. Working with the British League and the Union Defence League, Milner and Amery organised a British Covenant which was signed by nearly 2,000,000 supporters between March and July 1914. Milner did not, however, confine his efforts to the collection of signatures. His most prominent supporters also contributed large sums of money some of which was used to purchase weapons for the UVF. In March 1914 Rudyard Kipling, the great literary figure, sent Milner £30,000, an astronomical sum at today's valuation.

Significantly, Milner was also one of those establishment figures who had sought to influence the attitude of the British Army's officer class to the situation in Ulster. In many instances this was a straightforward task, as a good number of officers were from landed families, and their political instincts were conservative. Many were also of Anglo-Irish stock, while others had strong connections with Unionist families. Although officers were expected to be non-political, many were active in the British League for the Support of Ulster and the Union, and there were rumours circulating that a number of them would resign if the army was issued with orders to exercise force in Ulster. Milner was on friendly terms with the influential Lord Roberts, who had helped the Unionists find a commander for the UVF, and the two men were in frequent contact with serving officers. Moreover, Bonar Law and Carson had by early 1914 given serious consideration to the crucial role the army might play in the Ulster crisis. Obviously, if there was some doubt about the Liberal government's willingness to coerce Ulster Unionists because of the negative effect this would have on the army, then the bargaining position of the Conservative and Unionist opposition would be strengthened. Still, this was insufficient for Bonar Law. At the beginning of 1914 he formed the opinion that the Conservatives should use their majority in the House of Lords to amend the Army (Annual) Bill in such a way as to exclude altogether the use of the British Army in Ulster until after a general election. The Army Act was a strange piece of legislation which had survived since 1689. Its purpose was to prevent the government from depriving any subject of his rights, and its passage had always been routine. Any move to amend the Army Bill before its April deadline would have been a dangerous risk for the Conservatives, and the shadow cabinet deferred a decision when it met to discuss the matter on 4 February 1914. As it happened, a remarkable sequence of events rendered such a decision unnecessary.

Following Carson's rejection of the county option scheme Churchill raised the temperature when he spoke in Bradford on 14 March. Describing the Ulster Provisional government as a "self-elected body . . . engaged in a treasonable conspiracy", Churchill intimated that the army would be deployed in Ulster if the Unionists continued to reject the government's final compromise offer. On the same day Lieutenant-General Sir Arthur Paget, the army's Commander-in-Chief in Ireland, received instructions from the War Office to tighten security at a number of barracks and arms depots in Ulster, which were thought to be potential targets for arms raids by the UVF. The stores at Carrickfergus, Enniskillen, Armagh and Omagh were highlighted as high risk. Four days later, on 18 March, Paget was in London, where he was required to give details of the actions he had taken and receive further instructions. It seems that Churchill, who met Paget, had conceived a plan to intimidate the UVF by an impressive, and sudden, deployment of military strength in carefully selected locations. Churchill's proposal was backed by Colonel J E B Seely, the Secretary of State for War, and Asquith reluctantly approved the plan. Churchill had also arranged for a number of warships to sail for the Ulster coast from Lamlash in the Firth of Clyde to give added effect. In his meeting at the War Office Paget raised the question of how he should deal with any officers who might refuse to carry out orders to march on Ulster because of their sympathies with the Unionist cause. While Seely answered that any officer who refused to obey orders would face immediate dismissal, he added that special consideration would be given to those officers whose homes were in Ulster.

On 20 March Paget returned to the Curragh, the large army base in County Kildare, where he met his senior officers. By this stage, however, the excitable Paget had clearly lost control of the situation. He had no written orders and in his briefing to the seven senior officers he speculated unnecessarily on the impact of the troop movements which, he warned, would leave Ulster ablaze. He also foolishly passed on the news that officers domiciled in Ulster would be exempted from participating in the operations, but all others refusing to follow orders would be dismissed. Paget's clumsy handling of this delicate situation incensed one of those present, Brigadier-General Hubert Gough, who commanded the 3rd Cavalry Brigade. Gough next gathered round his own junior officers at the Curragh, and Paget was subsequently informed that if orders were given which involved using force against Ulster, then 58 officers, including Gough, were prepared to risk dismissal by refusing to march north. When news of this reached the War Office, Gough and three other cavalry officers were summoned to London, where they were interviewed on 22 and 23 March. The interviews soon established that the situation was largely the result of Paget's indiscretion, and Gough and his subordinates were asked to return to duty and ignore what had happened. However, Gough would not co-operate, and he refused to return to the Curragh until he had been given a written guarantee that the army would not be used to coerce Ulster into acceptance of the Home Rule Bill. Such a course had been urged on Gough by Major-General (later Field Marshall) Sir Henry Wilson, a native of County Longford and the Director of Military Operations at the War Office. Wilson was an ardent Unionist, and he had been intriguing with opposition leaders, including Carson and Bonar Law, for months, using his influence to create problems in the army in relation to the possible coercion of Ulster.

In response to Gough's request the cabinet approved a written statement, but Seely subsequently added two short paragraphs without the cabinet's knowledge which, he believed, were necessary to satisfy Gough. The final paragraph stated that the government had no intention of using troops "to crush political opposition to the policy or principles of the Home Rule Bill", but even this Gough found ambiguous and he demanded an absolute guarantee. Using a sheet of official War Office paper, Gough wrote the following statement: "I understand the reading of the last paragraph to be that the troops under our command will not be called upon to enforce the present Home Rule Bill on Ulster, and that we can so assure our officers". He then showed the note to Field Marshall Sir John French, the Chief of Imperial General Staff and another highly placed Unionist sympathiser, who endorsed Gough's interpretation and added his signature. By the time Asquith realised what had happened the 'Curragh incident', as it became known, had done serious damage to the government, greatly limiting any prospect it had of successfully applying pressure in order to force a concession from the Unionists. Still, despite Churchill's eagerness to stage a display of overwhelming force in the hope of intimidating the UVF, it is doubtful if the Liberal government ever seriously considered coercing Ulster Unionists. Asquith would certainly have balked at such action. What was clear was that the government had handled the situation badly and came close to sparking a full scale mutiny in the army. Paget's initial blunder had been compounded by Seely and, not surprisingly, the Curragh incident forced the resignations of both Seely and French. Asquith tried to restore calm by taking over the War Office portfolio in addition to his own responsibilities as Prime Minister. In parliament, meanwhile, the government faced a barrage of criticism, as the opposition claimed that the troop movements formed the core of a carefully designed "plot against Ulster", the intention of which was to provoke the UVF into firing the first shots, thus giving the government the excuse to crush the movement. The evidence suggests, however, that it was a mixture of Churchill's rashness and Seely's ineptitude, rather than the existence of some sinister plot, which lay behind the extraordinary events of March 1914 [85].

Onlookers in Britain and Ireland had scarcely recovered from the Curragh crisis when, on the night of 24–25 April, the UVF successfully landed a huge consignment of arms and ammunition in Ulster, which had been purchased on the continent. In January 1914 the Unionist leaders had finally given their backing to Crawford's plan for one spectacular arms coup. Previously, the fanatical Crawford's ambitious plan had been put on hold, as Unionists had expected that their militant rhetoric would be sufficient to force the government to amend the Home Rule Bill. However, the failure to extract any major concessions from Asquith during the series of abortive secret meetings, which the Prime Minister had conducted with Bonar Law and Carson, forced the Unionist leaders to acknowledge that their political strategy had not succeeded and, consequently, they bowed to the extremist faction within the UVF and sanctioned Crawford's gun-running plan. This was a grave risk, because the importation of a big consignment of guns, which was, of course, illegal, could have had a detrimental effect of British public opinion.

Crawford then travelled to Germany where he purchased the weapons in Hamburg and, following a difficult operation in which the cargo was transferred at sea onto a former coal boat purchased specifically for the gun-running, the weapons were brought ashore. Small quantities of arms and ammunition were dropped off in Bangor and Donaghadee, but the bulk of the cargo was unloaded at the port of Larne. That evening the UVF had taken control of the town which was effectively sealed off without any interference from the RIC. Telephone and telegraph lines were immobilised and the operation to unload the weapons proceeded rapidly. Cars and lorries pulled up on the quayside to be packed with rifles and ammunition, and most of the weapons were distributed throughout the province that night. In total, 24,600 rifles and 3,000,000 rounds of ammunition had been run into Ulster. The gun-running had been a propaganda coup for the Unionists, and it attracted huge coverage in the British press. Meanwhile, both Carson and Bonar Law publicly associated themselves with the gun-running and took full responsibility for the operation. In reply, Asquith described the Larne gun-running as "a grave and unprecedented outrage", and he warned that the government would apply the full force of the law against those who had been engaged in this illegal, and indeed treasonable, action. It was expected that the cabinet would press for criminal charges against Carson and the other leaders, but the intention to have Carson prosecuted was quickly dropped.

Coming hard on the heels of the Curragh incident, the Larne gun-running appeared to give the Unionists a decisive advantage in their quest to wring further concessions from the government. Nationalists, naturally, were outraged by these events, and this led directly to a sudden increase in the membership of the Irish Volunteers. In March 1914 there were an estimated 7,000 Irish Volunteers, but the figure increased dramatically during May, with recruitment being particularly strong in Ulster counties such as Tyrone. Soon the Irish Volunteers had more than 100,000 members and, with many of these new recruits in Ulster, the prospect of civil war moved closer. Nationalists had flocked to the Volunteers not just to provide a counterweight to the UVF, but to act as a powerful force which could insist on the implementation of Home Rule. They did not like the way that the Liberal government had appeared to buckle in the face of Ulster opposition, but their anger rose considerably after Larne. Many Nationalists were convinced that the authorities in Ulster, particularly the police, had connived with the UVF in the organisation of the Larne operation, and the government's subsequent failure to arrest any of the gun-running participants only confirmed this suspicion.

The sudden growth of the Irish Volunteers also placed Redmond in a difficult position. Uncomfortable though he was with the idea of private armies, he appreciated that if the IPP did not move quickly to control the movement, it could become a rival to his own party. Accordingly, on 10 June, Redmond issued a manifesto which demanded that the provisional committee governing the Irish Volunteers should be expanded to give the IPP a controlling interest in the movement. After some initial opposition the Volunteer leaders gave way and Redmond's nominees took their places on the committee. It appeared as though the Nationalist leader had acted swiftly and decisively to take control of a potentially dangerous development, but it soon emerged that the original leaders of the Irish Volunteers were pursuing their own agenda irrespective of Redmond's wishes. Here the initiative was taken by Sir Roger Casement, a former British consular official, who had joined the Irish Volunteers. Working closely with a number of wealthy, advanced Nationalists, such as Alice Stopford Green, Darrell Figgis and Erskine Childers, Casement organised a gun-running operation for the Irish Volunteers without Redmond's knowledge. Childers's yacht, the *Asgard*, had sailed to Hamburg, where 1,500 rifles and 45,000 rounds of ammunition were purchased and then shipped back to Ireland. The *Asgard* arrived at Howth in County Dublin on 26 July

1914, and the Irish Volunteers had organised a fleet of taxis to transport the bulk of the weapons into Dublin.

The parallels with Larne were obvious, even though the Irish Volunteer operation was on a much smaller scale, but the similarities ended when the guns were brought ashore. In this instance the Dublin Metropolitan Police intervened in an attempt to seize some of the arms. They had not sufficient numbers to achieve this, but they requested reinforcements, and a small detachment of troops was ordered to march out towards Howth. On their journey back to Dublin these troops were followed by an angry crowd, taunting them for their failure to disarm the Volunteers. By the time they had reached Bachelor's Walk, one of the quays on the River Liffey, a rowdier element joined the crowd and some stones and bottles were thrown. The inevitable followed, as troops opened fire, killing three civilians and wounding a number of others. Nationalists were outraged. The contrast with Larne was striking, as it was clear that the authorities were applying double standards.

The Irish Volunteer activists who had organised the Howth gun-running had obviously been influenced by the UVF's exploits in April. Moreover, an increasing number of Nationalists were convinced that the illegal Unionist resistance, which they assumed was being orchestrated by Carson, was proving more effective than the strictly constitutional approach favoured by Redmond. Yet the Unionists' extra-parliamentary strategy also had its pitfalls. Larne had given the UVF a decisive military advantage over the Irish Volunteers, but then only just over one in four of its members had a rifle. What surely concerned Carson was that the gun-running increased the likelihood of sectarian violence in the north, something which Carson was determined to avoid because of the negative impact such a development would have on public opinion in Britain. Significantly, Carson's tone in the House of Commons at the end of April 1914 was distinctly moderate, as he, in spite of his deep concerns, expressed the hope that Home Rule would prove a success for the south and west of Ireland, even speculating that it might be in Ulster's interests "to come in under it (Home Rule) and form one unit in relation to Ireland". If Carson was hinting at a settlement, Redmond did not respond. The Curragh incident, the Larne gun-running and the rapid growth of the Irish Volunteers had combined to limit his room for manoeuvre, as he realised that further concessions would expose him to criticism from more advanced Nationalists in Ireland, which might do irreparable damage to the IPP.

On 5 May Asquith had another secret meeting with Bonar Law and Carson. Although the conversation confirmed that a settlement was not on the horizon, the leaders did reach an understanding on procedure. It was agreed that any changes to the Home Rule Bill should be made, not by amendment to the bill, but by a separate amending bill which would receive the royal assent on the same day as the Home Rule Bill itself. What was not agreed, of course, was the content of the amending bill. In fact, when the bill to amend the Home Rule Bill was introduced in the House of Lords on 23 June 1914, it was almost identical to the county option terms which Carson had rejected in March. The Conservative response highlighted the gap which still existed between the two main parties. On 8 July Lansdowne moved an amendment to the government's amending bill which permanently excluded all nine counties of Ulster from Home Rule, and this was passed by the House of Lords on

14 July and then sent down to the Commons. With the Commons certain to throw out the Lords' amendment, the government had reached an impasse. Parliamentary time had almost run out, as the Home Rule Bill, under the terms of the Parliament Act, would be ready for the royal assent within a month.

It was at this point that Asquith finally agreed to the King's persistent requests for a conference at which the party leaders should try to settle the issue. He could have taken up the King's suggestion in the previous March, when the deadlock over the county option scheme first materialised, but he preferred to wait until the last possible moment, believing that negotiations were more likely to succeed when the pressure for a settlement was at its most intense. This was a mistake, because Asquith eventually entered the negotiations with little expectation of a successful outcome. Moreover, the Buckingham Palace Conference, which ran from 21 to 24 July 1914, only highlighted the differences between the parties. Two representatives from each of the four parties attended the conference – Asquith and Lloyd George for the Liberals, Bonar Law and Lansdowne for the Conservatives, Redmond and Dillon for the Nationalists and Carson and Craig for the Unionists. After a brief address by the King, in which he expressed his sincere hope for a settlement, the conference got down to business under the chairmanship of James Lowther, the Speaker of the House of Commons. The two crucial issues under discussion were the area to be excluded from Home Rule and the time limit for that exclusion. In the actual conference area was discussed in great detail, but without agreement being reached, while the time limit was never considered.

At the Buckingham Palace Conference Carson and Redmond, reminiscing about their old days together on the Leinster legal circuit, quickly struck up a warm friendship. Each had genuine respect for the other, but they could not agree on the future of Tyrone and Fermanagh. Carson opened by demanding the exclusion of all nine Ulster counties, arguing that such a generous gesture by the Nationalists would make it more likely that Ulster would, after a "reasonable time", be willing to come into a United Ireland. Bonar Law's notes later claimed that Redmond and Dillon would have been agreeable to this if they had been free agents, but they knew that to have made such a concession would have wiped out their support in Ireland. What is indisputable is that Redmond told the delegates that the exclusion of all of Ulster was "quite impossible". Carson's response was to demand "a clean cut" to exclude six counties on a permanent basis from the operation of the Home Rule Act. This he described as his "irreducible minimum". Of course, both Tyrone and Fermanagh had narrow Nationalist majorities, but the Ulster Volunteers were particularly strong in these counties, and Carson refused to budge on his demand. In rejecting six county exclusion Redmond argued that only those areas with a Unionist majority could be excluded from Home Rule. To support his argument the Nationalist leader produced a series of maps, showing the location of the various Unionist and Nationalist communities. The piebald maps illustrated the complex religious configuration and only highlighted the problems in drawing a border which both sides could find acceptable [86].

In an effort to break the deadlock Asquith suggested that south Tyrone and north Fermanagh could be added to the excluded area, but both Redmond and Carson voiced their rejection. Lloyd George then proposed that the excluded area could be based on the religious division of the Poor Law Union districts, but this was deemed to be impracticable. Soon the conference, in Churchill's famous phrase, ground to a halt along "the muddy byways of Fermanagh and Tyrone". As the negotiations broke up, Redmond and Dillon agreed to give way on the time limit for exclusion, but they could not surrender Tyrone and Fermanagh. Two days later, moreover, the bitter reaction to the Bachelor's Walk killings hardened Nationalist opinion and made it impossible for Redmond to consider any further concession. The amending bill, meanwhile, which was due in the House of Commons, was postponed until 28 July, but at this point the rapidly deteriorating situation on the continent, which was dragging the Great Powers towards a major European war, intervened to force a further postponement. With the new date for the amending bill scheduled for 30 July, Asquith was continuing his hopeless search for a way out of the impasse when, fortunately, Bonar Law and Carson contacted him with the offer of yet another postponement. The opposition leaders felt it important to paper over internal dissension and give the appearance of national unity as the country prepared for war. Asquith, with Redmond's approval, eagerly took advantage of the offer, hoping that it would give him sufficient time to nudge the Nationalists towards the acceptance of six county exclusion, something which, of course, Redmond could not contemplate at this juncture. When the Home Rule Act finally reached the statute book in September 1914, it was accompanied by a Suspensory Act which postponed the operation of the legislation.

At the outbreak of the First World War, therefore, no agreement had been reached on Ulster, but the Nationalists had made significant concessions which would become the starting point for future negotiations. Asquith's policy of delay had built up Nationalist hopes but, even before 1914, it was clear that the Liberal government was unable to fulfil these hopes. Yet Carson had also given ground. His original aim was to use Ulster opposition to kill the Home Rule Bill and thereby keep all of Ireland in the United Kingdom. When this was deemed impracticable, he abandoned the Southern Unionists and opted for the exclusion of Ulster. Then, by the autumn of 1913, he privately acknowledged that six counties was as much as he could reasonably demand. Thus he was prepared to abandon those Unionists in Cavan, Monaghan and Donegal, even though he had pledged to safeguard their future in the Union when he signed the Covenant in 1912. As Redmond was prepared, by March 1914, to give up four counties, the gap between the two Irish parties was not as wide as many assumed. Perhaps a compromise would have been acceptable if the government had moved early in 1912, but both the Liberals and the Irish Nationalists failed to appreciate the strength of Unionist feeling on the Home Rule issue. Of course, this forced Carson to raise the stakes during 1913 in an attempt to convince his opponents that the Unionists were prepared to go to any lengths to oppose Home Rule. Bonar Law's empathy with Ulster Unionists and his endorsement of their extra - parliamentary tactics gave any wavering Unionists the confidence to contemplate violence, or at least the threat of violence. Carson's view was that violence should only be considered as a last resort when all the other options had been exhausted and, in the end, he may well have recoiled from sanctioning UVF resistance against the British Army. This did not, of course, rule out the possibility that Carson could have been jettisoned in favour of a more extreme leader, who would have had few qualms about authorising violence if the Liberal government attempted to impose Home Rule on Ulster. Such a development would have placed Bonar Law in a very delicate position. While he himself would probably have supported armed resistance in Ulster, he would have faced real difficulties in carrying his party with him.

The Curragh incident had removed the possibility of a major UVF confrontation with the British Army, though there was little likelihood that Asquith would have attempted to coerce the Ulster Unionists. Churchill's recklessness may have indicated otherwise, but the thought of coercion ran against the very principles of a Liberal party which regarded dialogue and compromise as the natural way to break political deadlock. There was also disagreement on Ulster within the Liberal cabinet, as Lloyd George, Churchill and Birrell favoured some form of exclusion for, at least, part of Ulster. Still, division also existed within Conservative ranks. Bonar Law wanted to save six counties from Home Rule, but his deputy, Lord Lansdowne, and many other senior Conservatives were much more reluctant to abandon the Southern Unionists. Yet unlike the Liberal party which had been weakened by the Home Rule struggle, the Conservatives had gained distinct political benefits from their association with Ulster Unionist resistance. The party, which had united on the Ulster issue following the bitter internal divisions over tariff reform and the Parliament Act, had clearly strengthened its position by 1914. The Ulster crisis, moreover, had dominated British politics in the 1912-14 period, a factor which also worked to the Conservative party's advantage.

Historiography

The contribution which the Ulster crisis made to the sudden decline of the Liberal party is examined in G Dangerfield's, *The Strange Death of Liberal England* (New York, 1935). Dangerfield's central argument was that Liberalism was in terminal decline by 1909 and, in the years running up to the First World War, the Liberal government then faced four great rebellions which ultimately sapped the party's vitality. In addition to the suffragette movement and the wave of industrial strikes, the Asquith government had to deal with the Conservative party's struggle to preserve the powers of the House of Lords and its opposition to the third Home Rule Bill. Later, a number of historians challenged Dangerfield's thesis, arguing that the Liberal party had coped well with these various rebellions and was, in fact, in a healthy condition when the war broke out.

The Conservative reaction to the constitutional crisis is dealt with in Dutton's, *His Majesty's Loyal Opposition*. He shows how Conservative disagreement over their response to the Parliament Bill exacerbated the deep divisions within a party which was still bedevilled by the tariff reform controversy. Indeed, Dutton considers the split over the Conservative response to the Parliament Bill to have been more serious than the bitter wrangling over tariff reform. He also describes the way in which Balfour's failure to offer clear leadership on the Lords' issue only increased Conservative difficulties. The constitutional crisis, moreover, further polarised British politics, leaving relations between the two main parties at a very low ebb. This point is also illustrated in R Jenkins's, *Asquith* (London, 1964) which describes Lansdowne's attempts to safeguard the Lords' powers on selected controversial issues, notably Home Rule, and concludes that it was Lansdowne who was primarily responsible for the failure of the 1910 constitutional conference. Jenkins goes on to praise Asquith's "masterly display of political nerve and patient determination" which brought the constitutional crisis to a successful conclusion for the Liberals.

Carson's accession to the Unionist leadership is described in H Montgomery Hyde's, *Carson* (London, 1953) with the author suggesting that the decision to accept the leadership was not an easy one. Hyde's treatment of Carson's legal career and his excellent descriptions of his most famous legal battles adds greatly to our understanding of Carson's complex character. The histrionics and the theatrical flourishes, described by Hyde, were subsequently deployed to great effect by the Unionist leader. A very detailed study of Carson's legal and political career appears in I Colvin's, *Life of Lord Carson*. 3 vols (London, 1932-36) – the first volume was written by Edward Marjoribanks – while A T Q Stewart's, *Edward Carson* (Dublin, 1981) provides an excellent, compact synthesis. Jackson's, *The Ulster Party* argues that Ulster Unionism had moved down the extra-parliamentary road before Carson's accession to the leadership. The rejection of conventional constitutional politics which occurred memorably at the great Craigavon demonstration in September 1911 was, in Jackson's view, "the continuation of a process ... dating back at least to 1905". Jackson also stresses the Unionists' lack of trust in their Conservative allies, which the Bonar Law-Carson-Craig alliance tended to conceal. Craig's plan to use the Craigavon demonstration in order to convince Carson of the determination to resist Home Rule among grass roots Unionists is described in

Hyde's, *Carson*. The author quotes extensively from the great volume of correspondence before and after the demonstration to illustrate the impact that the rally made on Carson. Craig's brilliant organisational skills are described in P Buckland's, *James Craig* (Dublin, 1980) which stresses how the Ulster crisis saw the transformation of Craig from a "reliable backbencher" to a "masterly director of operations".

P Bew's, *Ideology and the Irish Question: Ulster Unionism and Irish Nationalism 1912-1916* (Oxford, 1994) analyses the impact of the *Ne Temere* decree on Ulster Unionists, commenting that the IPP, "in theory so voluble in defence of Protestant rights, lapsed into silence on this issue". While Bew claims that the economic argument against Home Rule was a crucial factor for the Belfast bourgeois leadership of Unionism, it was the religious fear which predominated. Early in the book Bew makes the point that historians have generally failed to understand Ulster Unionism, mainly because it has been treated as a simple "negative appendage" to Nationalism. More attention, Bew insists, needs to be given to the interaction of Ulster Unionism and Irish Nationalism. While Bew acknowledges that Redmond believed that the implementation of Home Rule would usher in a new era of harmony and co-operation in Ireland, he did not pursue the conciliatory strategy, favoured by William O'Brien, of trying to win over Irish Unionists to the Home Rule cause. Bew also stresses how Ulster Unionists believed they were misunderstood in Britain, and this contributed to "the profound sense of betrayal" which Unionists felt. Those members of the British power elite who had Ulster family roots, notably Bonar Law, never subscribed to the basic Unionist fear of ill-treatment in a Nationalist-Catholic Ireland. Bew observes that Bonar Law was much more moderate in private than his public speeches indicated. He was never, unlike Walter Long, a serious opponent of Irish self government, as his main concern was to secure some form of exclusion for Ulster. On the question of sectarian violence, Bew emphasises Carson's feeling of embarrassment following the shipyard expulsions in 1912 and highlights his calls for restraint. Later, Bew shows how Carson believed that Asquith had opted for a strategy of delaying concessions in order to test the patience of the Ulster extremists. If they were drawn into violence, Asquith would have had the excuse to use British troops to crush the UVF and, as Bew suggests, this may have encouraged Carson to back the high risk operation of running guns into Ulster. On the suitability of the county option scheme, which he notes also included votes for Belfast and Derry City, Bew speculates that the plan may have worked if Redmond had not demanded a time limit.

Bew offers a fresh assessment of the Nationalist leader's handling of the Home Rule crisis in his brief, *John Redmond* (Dublin, 1996). In Bew's opinion Redmond was not indifferent to Unionist fears which he tried to overcome by arguing that the IPP would quickly wither away once Home Rule had been achieved. Its place would be taken by a new power elite drawn from "the well-heeled upper classes", which obviously would include a significant number of ex-Unionists. Redmond, himself a landowner with strong conservative instincts, would have been happy with such an outcome. Bew agrees with Gwynn's, *The Life of John Redmond* which, though generally sympathetic to Redmond, criticises him for his failure to see how serious the situation had become by the autumn of 1913. In Gwynn's judgement the Curragh incident had greatly damaged the IPP and, henceforward, it compelled the Nationalist movement to look to unconstitutional methods. Redmond had considered the earlier formation of the Irish Volunteers as a nightmare, but Gwynn insisted that his personal influence and prestige reached a peak in June 1914. Kee's, *The Bold Fenian Men* is more critical of Redmond, arguing that in accepting "even as a possibility the principle of permanent exclusion, Redmond can now be seen to have made a disastrous move". He had, in Kee's words, broken the 'one Ireland' principle. Indeed Kee offers the simple criticism, claiming that, from the outset, the great flaw in Redmond's strategy was that he was totally dependent on Liberal goodwill.

A detailed study of Ulster's resistance to Home Rule can be found in A T Q Stewart's, *The Ulster Crisis: Resistance to Home Rule, 1912-14* (London, 1967) which conveys the mood of grim determination among the Unionist rank and file. Stewart also emphasises the discipline of the UVF at a time when sectarian tension was at a peak. While outsiders regarded the activities of the UVF with their dummy wooden rifles as a source of amusement, Stewart recalls the description given by Brigadier-General Gleichen, the senior army commander in Belfast, who wrote that within the province there reigned "a stern and disciplined atmosphere and a serious spirit of unity and organisation". Stewart gives an excellent account of the UVF's formation and the various gun-running operations, and he lays particular stress on the support which the movement received from senior figures in the British establishment, notably Lords Milner and Roberts. The detailed plans for resistance drawn up by the UVF are covered, and Stewart is in no doubt that Carson would have sanctioned, albeit reluctantly, a UVF rebellion if the government had tried to force Home Rule on Ulster. This view is examined by Alvin Jackson in two articles, 'Unionist Myths, 1912-85', *Past and Present,* No 136 (1992) and 'The Larne Gun Running of 1914', *History Ireland,* Vol 1, No 1 (1993). Jackson claims that Carson saw violence in "icily realistic terms; as honourable, but also as suicidal". Larne had, in Jackson's words, turned the UVF from "an unarmed force" into a "badly armed force". After the gun-running Jackson argues that Carson softened his tone, as he searched for a compromise. This line of argument is brilliantly developed in Jackson's, *Sir Edward Carson* (Dublin, 1993) which observes that Carson was ambiguous in private about the use of force. Craig was the inspiration behind the UVF, leaving Carson to conduct the struggle in his main theatre which was the House of Commons. Jackson comments that Carson saw Asquith's government as tyrannical, but he was confident in his belief that this tyranny could be overcome by moral strength. His campaign of 1912-14 was, in his opinion, simply defiance of a dictatorial government. Yet, as Jackson notes shrewdly, he was an unlikely rebel whose chief weakness was that his opponents were fully aware of this. Some 25 years earlier, in his essay on 'Craig and the UVF' which appears in Martin's (ed), *Leaders and Men of the Easter Rising,* A T Q Stewart focuses on Carson's terribly sombre mood as Ulster drifted towards civil war in 1914 and contrasts this with Craig's quiet preparations for a UVF coup to seize control of Ulster. In the same book J C Beckett's essay, 'Carson - Unionist and rebel' reminds us that Carson did not create the movement he led so effectively: "He had come to it from the outside; and though he had given it prestige and cohesion, it still retained an independent force of its own". The role played by the Ulster Women's Unionist Council is touched on in V Kelly's essay, 'Irish Suffragettes at the time of the Home Rule Crisis', *History Ireland,* Vol 4, No 1, (1996). Kelly describes how the women's movement subordinated every women's issue, including the demand for the vote, to the principal task of resisting Home Rule.

In assessing the general histories which deal with the Ulster crisis, some significant points can be highlighted. Lyons's, *Ireland since the Famine* looks at Redmond's reaction to pressure from the Liberal government which wanted him to accept some form of temporary partition at the end of 1913. Redmond's response was to urge the government to stand firm, something which, Lyons judges, "now seems naive in the extreme". Lyons finds it difficult to explain why Carson and the Ulster Unionists would resort to violence, when Home Rule was such a modest measure. Foster's, *Modern Ireland* notes that the Home Rule Bill was presented in Ulster as an issue which "could not legitimately be decided by party votes at Westminster", and this led to the adoption of ludicrously extreme tactics. In Foster's view two points need to be remembered in order to understand the opposition's use of such unconstitutional methods. Firstly, like the Unionists, the Conservatives claimed that the Liberal government was acting unconstitutionally and, secondly, the opposition was convinced that the Liberals were not deeply committed to Home Rule. In his assessment of Unionist tactics, J J Lee's, *Ireland 1912-1985; Politics and Society* (Cambridge, 1989) takes a more controversial view. Lee believes that the Ulster Unionist rejection of Home Rule was based on a sense of racial superiority. He draws a parallel with white South Africans, describing the Ulster Unionists as 'Herrenvolk'. For such people, Lee argues, the fact that a majority in Ireland favoured Home Rule was irrelevant: "Why should a Herrenvolk deign to notice numbers? Why should one Protestant be equated with one Catholic?" Ulster Protestants were convinced that Irish Catholics would behave as "mirror images of themselves" once Home Rule had been achieved. Lee adds that it was precisely because the bulk of Nationalists were not mirror images of Unionists in this respect that "they failed to fully grasp these Protestant fears". In analysing the economic argument against Home Rule, Lee points out that by western European standards Ulster was far from a success story, allowing him to conclude that while the economic argument contributed to the rejection of Irish Nationalism, it was not basic to it. Yet the bourgeois Unionist leadership did not consider Ulster to be a failing economic entity and, besides, the industrial pre-eminence of the north undoubtedly contributed to the essential self confidence of Ulster Unionists, which Lee appears to confuse with the sense of racial superiority. Apart from his assessment of Unionist reasons for opposing Home Rule, Lee has produced an excellent book full of original insights. On Redmond, he points out that the Irish leader failed to grasp the function of force: "He was too much a romantic Commonwealth man, too much a genuine Westminster parliamentarian, to conceive that Ulster Unionists, much less English Tories, ... could really contemplate rebellion".

The biographies of Asquith and Bonar Law by Roy Jenkins and Robert Blake deal in great depth with the Irish policies of the two leaders. Blake's, *The Unknown Prime Minister: The Life and Times of Andrew Bonar Law, 1858-1923* (London, 1955) stresses the importance of Bonar Law's Ulster roots and his frequent visits to the province from his home in Helensburgh. On his accession to the leadership Blake observes that he was a much harsher critic of the Asquith government than the more diplomatic Balfour. He also points out that Asquith's intellectual background and social contacts saw him treat Bonar Law with a touch of condescension, and this may explain why he underestimated Bonar Law. Blake argues that the question of separate treatment for Ulster had never been seriously considered by the Conservatives before the autumn of 1913. Bonar Law, however, had certainly given consideration in private to Ulster exclusion, though the difficulties this created with the rest of the Conservative leadership, particularly Lord Lansdowne, made him cautious. Indeed Blake argues that Bonar Law, who has been regarded as an extremist on the Home Rule issue, was in reality more moderate than many of his colleagues. Yet Blake also notes that Bonar Law was in no doubt that Ulster Unionists would have responded violently if the government had tried to implement Home Rule on an all-Ireland basis. Jenkins's, *Asquith* brilliantly conveys Asquith's general political style of allowing situations to develop before choosing the crucial moment to intervene effectively. Such an approach, Jenkins claims, was perfectly suited to Asquith's character and temperament. His strategy on the Irish Question, therefore, was to press ahead with a full Home Rule measure, refusing to consider possible concessions until the bill was on its final parliamentary circuit. This meant that Asquith ignored Ulster opposition in 1912, a decision which Jenkins defends, claiming that no arrangement for Ulster exclusion in 1912 would have destroyed opposition to the Home Rule Bill. Moreover, the delaying tactics had worked well in the struggle over the Parliament Bill. Jenkins also deals perceptively with the role played by the King in the Ulster crisis, showing how effectively Asquith handled the frequent, unwelcome royal interventions. In his assessment of the Nationalist leader, Jenkins believes that Redmond was too amenable to Liberal pressure and argues that Devlin would have been a much tougher leader.

Jenkins's central argument that Asquith's procrastination was a logical and effective strategy is challenged in P Jalland's, *The Liberals and Ireland: The Ulster Question in British Politics to 1914* (Brighton, 1980). Jalland criticises the Liberal government for its failure to treat the Ulster resistance campaign seriously until the autumn of 1913. By that stage, she believes, it was too late "to avert the growing crisis". In her opinion the government missed a great opportunity to seize the initiative in 1912, when a compromise based on some form of Ulster exclusion may have been possible. Instead, Asquith chose the high risk policy of prevarication and delay which ended in "total failure". Jalland points the finger directly at Asquith, claiming that his "weaknesses as a war-time leader were already foreshadowed in his mismanagement of the Ulster problem". Again, she stresses that the Ulster situation cried out for a courageous initiative in 1912, but Asquith's temperament and inherent caution meant that he preferred the status quo. Only in the autumn of 1913 did Asquith recognise the gravity of the situation in Ulster, though Jalland places some of the blame for this on Birrell's shoulders. The Irish Chief Secretary was guilty of providing too little information on Ulster and minimising the danger of the situation in the province.

A different approach to the Ulster crisis can be found in N Mansergh's, *The Unresolved Question: The Anglo-Irish Settlement and Its Undoing 1912-72* (London, 1991) which offers a classic study of high politics in its examination of the roles of the key players. Mansergh agrees with Blake's contention that Bonar Law, albeit as a last resort, was prepared to back an Ulster rebellion against Home Rule. Thus Mansergh concludes that Bonar Law's accession to the leadership was absolutely crucial to the Unionist campaign of resistance: "It is inconceivable that Long or Chamberlain would have entered into an open-ended commitment to Carson and the Ulster

Unionists, let alone assail the government in such strident tones". In Mansergh's judgement, therefore, it was Bonar Law's commitment rather than the Ulster preparations that "decided how the balance would fall". In an excellent study of the Ulster issue M Laffan's, *The Partition of Ireland 1911-1925* (Dundalk, 1983) casts doubt on the likelihood of the Conservative party supporting a revolt against a Liberal government "so reasonable as to offer the exclusion of those areas where a majority of the population wanted it". If the war had not intervened, Laffan points out that any rebellion led by Carson in 1914 would have had the purpose of imposing exclusion on Tyrone and Fermanagh, since the exclusion of the four plantation counties had already been conceded. Such a rebellion was most unlikely in the summer of 1914.

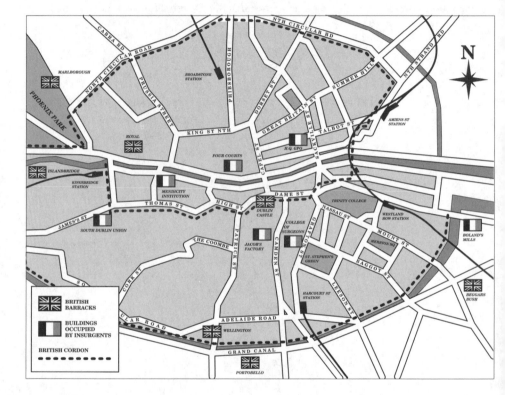

Central Dublin during the Easter Rising

Chapter 7
The Easter Rising

The outbreak of the First World War appeared to place the Home Rule crisis in cold storage. It fell to Sir Edward Grey, the Foreign Secretary, to make the announcement in the House of Commons on 3 August 1914, which warned that Britain was preparing for war with Germany. The Foreign Secretary's sombre tone only lifted when he described Ireland as "the one bright spot in this very dreadful situation". Grey's remark was a reference to the truce which the deteriorating international situation had forced on the respective party leaders. Following Grey's speech Redmond intervened in the debate, pledging Ireland's support for Britain in the war and urging the government to withdraw its troops from the country, leaving it to the Volunteers, both the Irish Volunteers and the Ulster Volunteers, to defend Ireland's coasts [87]. Redmond's decision, which most observers assumed to have been a spontaneous reaction, was something of a political gamble. Certainly, Redmond had to trust his own judgement in reaching his decision. Both Dillon and Devlin were in Ireland and could not be contacted, while T P O' Connor offered the opinion that the bitter feeling aroused during the previous week by the Bachelor's Walk incident, and the subsequent emotional scenes at the funerals, made such a gesture impossible. Still, Redmond's declaration of Irish support for the war effort caused a sensation in the emotionally charged atmosphere of the House of Commons on that Bank Holiday Monday, as his fellow MPs congratulated him for his courageous and magnanimous gesture.

Redmond was fully aware of the great political risk he had taken. Left to Dillon or Devlin, the likelihood was that either would have sought to squeeze concessions from the government before offering Nationalist support in the European conflict. Redmond, however, favoured a unilateral gesture. For him the link between Ireland and Belgium, both small Catholic countries positioned close to powerful neighbours, was a key factor. The Irish leader was also convinced that the war against Germany was right from a moral perspective and, with Britain on the verge of finally doing justice to Ireland, he thought it essential to support the war. Moreover, Redmond genuinely believed that the conflict provided an opportunity to heal the divisions between Unionists and Nationalists, as both groups could co-operate to help Britain win the war [88]. He made reference to this hope in a speech he gave in Maryborough, now Portlaoise, on Sunday, 16 August. This was Redmond's first public speech since his dramatic intervention in the House of Commons, and he appealed to all Volunteers in Ireland, both Unionist and Nationalist, to unite for home defence. In fact, the response in Ireland to Redmond's Commons speech had been more enthusiastic than he had dared to hope. Yet the Nationalist leader knew that he had to press the government to put the Home Rule Bill on the statute book, if he was to maintain this momentum. On the day after his Commons speech he had written to Asquith, emphasising the great risk he had taken before adding, "if I have to go back to Ireland with the enactment of the Home Rule Bill postponed … the result will be disastrous … I would be unable to hold the people". While Redmond pleaded with the Prime Minister to put Home Rule on the statute book, Carson and Bonar Law were insisting that the status quo be maintained, and they painted a bleak picture of the effect any rash move by Asquith would have on the new spirit of cross party co-operation which had been fostered by the European conflict.

On the outbreak of the war Asquith gave up the post of Secretary of State for War, which he had held since Seely's resignation, handing over the responsibility to Lord Kitchener. A few days later, Carson and Craig met Kitchener at the War Office, where they offered to provide at least a division of trained men from the UVF for the British Army. The two Unionist leaders also insisted that the UVF men should be kept together as a fighting unit, and they asked that the title 'Ulster' should be added to the division's official name. Initially, the new Secretary of State for War refused to back these ideas, and the Asquith government delayed reaching a decision on the Unionist offer. By the beginning of September, however, Kitchener had withdrawn his objections to the formation of exclusively Ulster units, as he gratefully accepted Carson's new offer of Ulster Volunteers. The Unionist leader's next move was to cross over to Belfast, where he was to play a significant role in the recruiting campaign which led ultimately to the formation of the 36th (Ulster) Division. The Ulster Division was based on members of the UVF, though it was neither exclusively Protestant nor was it recruited solely in Ulster. Redmond and Dillon, meanwhile, had also been to the War Office in early August, where they had a difficult discussion with Kitchener on the future role of the Irish Volunteers. The War Secretary told the Nationalist leaders that he intended to launch a general recruiting campaign in Ireland to secure new troops for the regular army. Later that month, General Sir Bryan Mahon, who had been sent to Ireland to assess the recruiting potential, asked Redmond what should be done with the Irish Volunteers. His reply was unequivocal. If they were to be used, Redmond argued, they should not be required to take the oath of allegiance to the King and they could only be deployed in Ireland for the purpose of home defence. Mahon's insistence that Britain's fate, and indeed Ireland's, was at that very moment being decided in Flanders failed to change Redmond's opinion that the Irish Volunteers should remain in Ireland. Within a month, however, he had reversed this decision.

It appears that Redmond's thinking had been influenced by Carson's appeal to the Ulster Volunteers to enlist for service overseas, and he was keen to match the Unionist leader's commitment. Another crucial factor in forcing Redmond's change of heart was his feeling of gratitude towards the Liberal government once it had put Home Rule on the statute book. Early in September Asquith had finally decided to put the bill on the statute book, though with a characteristic compromise that it be accompanied by a Suspensory Act which would prevent its operation until after the war. Moreover, Asquith gave an undertaking that the legislation would not come into effect until the question of Ulster had been settled by an amending bill. In spite of this Ulster sweetener added by Asquith, Carson and Bonar Law could scarcely contain their anger when they were informed of the government's intention. The Prime Minister formally announced the news to the House of Commons on 15 September, leaving Bonar Law to reply with a bitter speech which accused the government of betraying the Unionists. The entire opposition marched out of the Commons in protest at the conclusion of his speech. The Home Rule Bill was put on the statute book on 18 September and scenes of great rejoicing followed, as Nationalist MPs celebrated by waving the old green flag with the golden harp in the House of Commons.

The First World War and Ireland

Returning from the celebrations in London to the old shooting lodge at Aughavanagh in County Wicklow, which he had purchased from the Parnell family, Redmond stopped at Woodenbridge on 20 September, where he made an impromptu speech to a group of East Wicklow Volunteers who were holding a Sunday parade. Here Redmond appealed to the Volunteers to serve "not only in Ireland itself, but wherever the firing line extends, in defence of right, of freedom and religion" [89]. This appeal split the Irish Volunteers. In truth the small number of IRB men, Sinn Féiners and other advanced Nationalists within the Volunteers had objected to Redmond's earlier offer of the movement for home defence, but the Woodenbridge speech sharpened this division and brought it into the open. At that point the Volunteers had approximately 170,000 members, and all but 12,000 remained loyal to Redmond. The IPP leader was well aware that his appeal at Woodenbridge would bring him into conflict with these more advanced Nationalists, some of whom had been openly critical of the cautious strategy followed by the Irish party. Immediately, a special meeting of the original committee, which had controlled the Volunteers before Redmond's intervention in June 1914, met to consider his speech and, on 24 September, 20 of its 27 members issued a statement repudiating the new policy [90]. When local Volunteer units throughout Ireland voted on the issue, however, Redmond received overwhelming support for his Woodenbridge stand. This large group, numbering around 160,000, took the name 'National Volunteers', while the much smaller group under Eoin MacNeill continued to be known as the 'Irish Volunteers'. It appeared that Redmond, as he had done on 3 August, had accurately gauged opinion in Ireland.

Although Redmond's policy shift received overwhelming support, with more than 90 per cent of the Volunteers remaining loyal, his Woodenbridge appeal was subsequently criticised as a very serious error of judgement. The raison d'être for the formation of the Volunteers in November 1913 had not been to fight the UVF, but to defend Ireland's rights. By the end of September 1914 a minority of the Volunteers clearly believed that fighting for the British, and hence for the Allies, was not the best way to defend these rights. Within this minority group, moreover, there was yet another minority of IRB activists who, spurred on by the old Fenian maxim, "England's difficulty is Ireland's opportunity", thought that the war might create the right circumstances for a rebellion against Britain. For this tiny group Britain was a much more obvious enemy than Germany. Still, Redmond's support for the war was based on a clear logic. Although it looked certain that Unionists would be offered some form of exclusion at the end of the war, it was equally clear, to Redmond at any rate, that no future British government could renege on the commitment to Nationalist Ireland now that Home Rule was on the statute book. Indeed only by fully supporting the British war effort could Redmond hope to have any influence on the future partition settlement. He still clung to the belief that partnership and co-operation in the war might heal the divisions between Unionists and Nationalists and, significantly, the good relations which quickly developed between Nationalists and Southern Unionists during the early phase of the war demonstrated that this was not merely wishful thinking. It also appears likely that Redmond saw a parallel between Ireland and South Africa, which threw its full weight behind Britain in the war, despite the previous history of conflict between Britain and the Transvaal, and Redmond was impressed by this show of imperial loyalty. He was also fully aware that under the terms of the Home Rule Act decisions on 'peace and war' were the sole responsibility of the Westminster parliament, and Redmond was simply acting, therefore, as if Home Rule was in operation.

In the months following the Woodenbridge speech Redmond's National Volunteers maintained a high level of activity throughout the country. They held a succession of Sunday parades, with the number of participants confirming that enthusiasm for the Volunteers among Redmond's supporters remained high. A new committee was elected with Redmond as President and Colonel Maurice Moore as Inspector-General, and a new weekly newspaper, the *National Volunteer*, began publication. Of course, Redmond renewed his appeal for recruits and, by 1 November 1914, he had been officially informed that nearly 16,500 National Volunteers had enlisted, but many of these were drafted into English regiments. From very early on it was apparent that Ulster Unionists and Irish Nationalists would not receive equal treatment from the War Office. While Kitchener had conceded Carson's demand for the Ulster Volunteers to be allocated their own division, Redmond's request for similar treatment was turned down. He had wanted the National Volunteers to be drafted into a new Irish Brigade, complete with their own officers, emblems and badges but, while Asquith was sympathetic, Redmond found Kitchener obstructive. The War Office insisted on using the existing regular army recruiting system, but this was subsequently amended to ensure that sufficient numbers of Nationalists came forward. The 16th (Irish) Division, which was added to the regular 10th (Irish) Division stationed at the Curragh, was formed following pressure from Redmond, and it became the unit with which Irish Nationalists identified most strongly. Redmond and Devlin helped in raising the 16th Division, but it also included many non-Irish recruits. Inevitably, the cream of the National Volunteers found themselves in the 16th Division or dispersed among various English regiments and, naturally, this contributed to the movement's ultimate decline.

Still, Redmond appeared to be at the peak of his powers during the early phase of the war. Support for the war effort was substantial, and the National Volunteers dwarfed the apparently ineffective Irish Volunteers. However, the uneven split following the Woodenbridge speech masked the potential significance of the minority group. While Redmond enjoyed overwhelming support in rural Ireland, the situation was different in Dublin. There, 2,000 of the city's 6,700 Volunteers supported

MacNeill and, of course, it was principally this group that supplied the manpower for the Easter Rising. In addition, the smaller group under MacNeill was a much more manageable number for the conspiratorial IRB group, which wanted to influence and direct the Irish Volunteers for its own purposes. Such an aim was more achievable within a compact unit, and the fact that the minority group contained more advanced Nationalists was an obvious advantage. Senior IRB figures occupied key positions in the Irish Volunteers, and they worked behind the scenes keeping the vast majority of the 12,000 Volunteers in the dark about their plans. Their goal had been set at a meeting of the IRB's Supreme Council in August 1914, when it was agreed in principle to use the opportunity provided by Britain's distraction with the European conflict to stage a rebellion in Ireland. While IRB men dominated the new General Council which controlled the Irish Volunteers, MacNeill, the Chief of Staff, had neither knowledge of their plans nor of the fact that the IRB exercised a controlling majority.

MacNeill's position, which he shared with the great majority of his followers, was that the Irish Volunteers should maintain a state of readiness to insist on the implementation of Home Rule at the end of the war. When discussion within the General Council touched on the possibility of staging a rising, MacNeill was firmly opposed, arguing that military action could only be contemplated if it was likely to be successful. As there was no prospect of this, MacNeill's rejection of proactive violence was unequivocal. In reality, the only circumstance in which he could have envisaged the Volunteers using violence would have been in retaliation against any attempt by the government to suppress the movement. On the surface, therefore, the majority of the Irish Volunteers were, like their National Volunteer competitors, committed to Home Rule, though MacNeill's group undoubtedly contained many who regarded Home Rule as merely the first installment en route to Irish independence. This latter group was unequally divided between the IRB men who were prepared to use physical force in order to win Irish freedom, and a larger body of constitutional separatists who wanted that same freedom but were against the use of violence. Before the war this group of constitutional separatists had been satisfied by the ideology of Home Rule, the limitations of which they tended to overlook but, as the European conflict dragged on, Redmond's support for Britain had the effect of exposing the very limited nature of freedom which Home Rule would confer.

The Irish Volunteers were just one of a number of groups which became identified with opposition to the war. Redmond's imperialism was attacked in the more advanced Nationalist press, and the Dublin Castle administration showed its concern at the pro - German line being adopted by some of the newspapers. In their reports the British authorities frequently referred to such newspapers as the 'Sinn Féin press', because Sinn Féin was the best known of the more advanced Nationalist groups and was vociferous in its opposition to Irish participation in the war. Soon the Irish Volunteers under MacNeill's command became known as the Sinn Féin Volunteers but, initially, particularly outside Dublin, they struggled to make an impact. The movement lacked clear political direction, and the drift under MacNeill's leadership allowed the minority IRB element to increase its influence. Yet despite their initial failure to arouse public interest, John Dillon, Redmond's deputy who was a shrewd observer of political trends in Nationalist Ireland, concluded that the Sinn

Féin Volunteers represented a potentially serious challenge to constitutional Nationalism. Dillon issued repeated warnings to the authorities in Dublin Castle to ensure that no attempt was made to suppress these advanced Nationalist groups or their newspapers, as this would only expose the IPP to ridicule. He also sensed that the War Office's reluctance to put recruits from Nationalist Ireland on an equal footing with the Ulster recruits was undermining support for the war effort and thereby raising the status of the Sinn Féin Volunteers.

It seems reasonable to assume that the campaign for recruits in Ireland strengthened anti-English feeling. This would have become more pronounced after the early phase, when those with most enthusiasm for the war had actually enlisted. Indeed the figures show that during the first six months of the war just over 50,000 Irishmen joined the British Army, but this number was halved over the next six months and continued to fall steadily thereafter. The steep decline in Irish recruiting is illustrated by the margin between the number who enlisted during the first year of the war and the total for the remaining three years. The number of recruits up to August 1915 was well in excess of the total who subsequently enlisted. During this first fruitful year almost half of the total recruits came from Ulster. Certainly, Redmond's recruitment campaign enjoyed early success, particularly at the beginning of 1915, but recruitment dropped significantly from the autumn of 1915 onwards, though the pro-war Redmondite press tended to ignore the rapidly declining numbers. By the end of 1915 just over 25,000 National Volunteers had enlisted, but more than 7,000 of these were reservists who were mobilised in August 1914. This left the National Volunteers with a 'number' well in excess of 100,000 but, while they continued to parade in 1915, a combination of factors, most notably the increasing unpopularity of the war in Ireland and Redmond's lack of interest in the movement, quickly transformed the National Volunteers into a demoralised and apathetic force [91].

Nationalist Ireland's growing disenchantment with the war, to which Redmond was irrevocably committed, exposed the IPP to attacks form the myriad of more advanced Nationalist groups which had been galvanised and, to some extent, drawn together by their opposition to the war. The IPP, by contrast, had been left in limbo by the government's decision to put Home Rule on the statute book. Soon this was being interpreted as a hollow victory and, besides, its adoption had left the IPP without a programme of action other than its support for an increasingly unpopular war. Many of the party's MPs were ageing figures who had earned their stripes some decades earlier during the various phases of the agrarian struggle and were, by this stage, content to oversee the running of their constituencies. Of course, the resolution of the land problem, which had seen the IPP press successfully for the transfer of land ownership, had weakened the bond between the party and the old tenant farming class. While these new owner - occupiers continued to support the IPP, the removal of the great goal of land ownership quickly dampened the crusading zeal which had previously characterised Nationalist politics in rural Ireland. As the land question faded, the UIL organisation, which had operated as the IPP's political machine, began to crumble.

Despite these obvious difficulties, it is easy, and wrong, to exaggerate the weakness of the IPP at this point. Between the outbreak of the war and the Easter Rising the

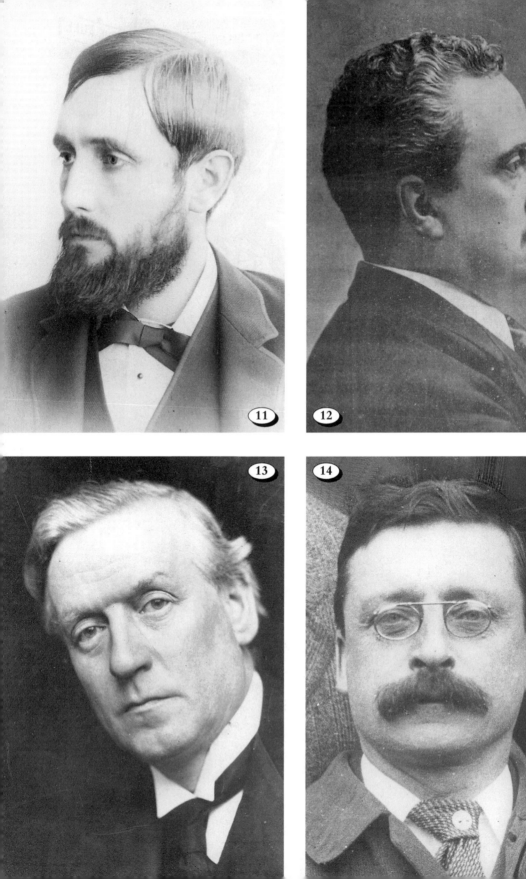

AT THE CROSS ROADS.

Joe (the Cow-boy), "Hoi! – This be your road, measter!"

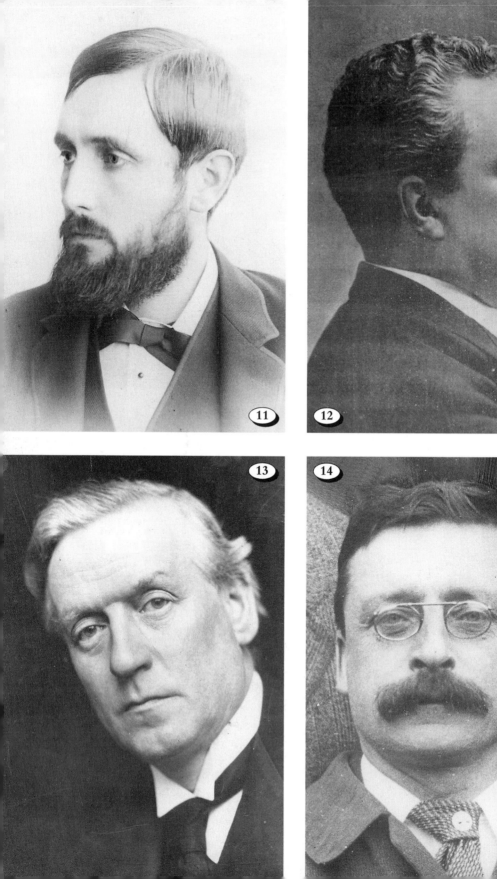

1

2

3

4

5

6

"The creature is formidable, but there is a way of resisting it ... the Devil-fish, in fact, is only vulnerable through the head."

THE IRISH DEVIL-FISH.

Which of 'em will throw it overboard?

THE LIVE SHELL.

15

16

Seagan buide

17

E SECRET OF ENGLANDS GREATNESS

HOLY BIBLE

18

TAX COLLECTOR JOHN:- "But I've come to raise the taxes"!
SIR EDWARD:- "Yes, and I've come to raise you"

BOYCOTT
DAIRIES
FARMING
CAPITAL
SUPERSTITION
GRAIN
INDUSTRY
SYNDICALISM
CATTLE
POVERTY
FOR ULSTER PLUNDER
NATIONALIST CHEQUE DISHONOURED
PROSPERITY
SLOTH

John came to Ulster in
high feather
The Home Rule goal to
score
But Carson caught him in
the nether.
Now, John feels rather sore

Bill Gur

26

27

Ulster Gun Running. "Bravo Ulster."
Discharging the "Fanny," Motor Cars in readiness at Larne Harbo

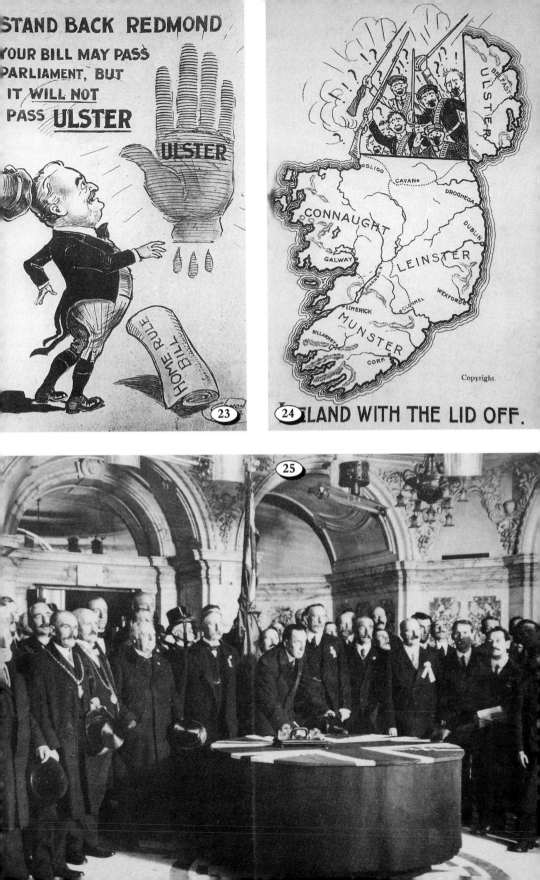

23 STAND BACK REDMOND
YOUR BILL MAY PASS
PARLIAMENT, BUT
IT WILL NOT
PASS ULSTER

ULSTER

HOME RULE BILL

24 IRELAND WITH THE LID OFF.

BELFAST ULSTER

SLIGO
CAVAN
DROGHEDA
CONNAUGHT
DUBLIN
GALWAY
LEINSTER
SHANNON
WEXFORD
LIMERICK
CLONMEL
KILLARNEY
MUNSTER
CORK

Copyright.

25

Ulster Gun Running."Bravo Ulster."
Discharging the "Fanny", Motor Cars in readiness at Larne Harbo[ur]

seagan buide

E SECRET OF ENGLANDS GREATNESS

19

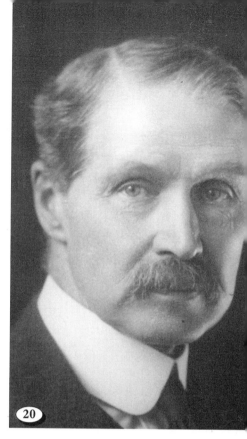

20

21

22

slaiġ na heireann
rish Volunteers.

A

UBLIC MEETING

r the formation of IRISH VOLUNTEERS
and the enrolment of men,

WILL BE HELD IN THE

LARGE CONCERT HALL,

ROTUNDA,

ON

UESDAY, NOV. 25

At 8 p.m.

OIN MacNEILL, B.A., will preside

All able-bodied Irishmen will be
eligible for enrolment.

OD SAVE IRELAND.

CURTIS, PRINTER, 12 TEMPLE LANE, DUBLIN.

28

29

30

48

49

50

44

45

46

47

48

49

50

Left to Right:—
BACK ROW:—Michael Kilroy, T. Kitterick, E. Moane, J. Gibbons, J. Walsh, P. J. Cannon, P. Lambert, J. Kelly, J. Doherty, B. Malone, J. Rush, J.
MIDDLE ROW:—M. Naughton, J. Hogan, J. Hearney, D. Sammon, J. Keane, J. Connolly, R. Joyce, P. McNamara, W. Malone.
FRONT ROW:—Dan Gavin, T. Heavey, J. Duffy, J. McDonagh, P. Kelly, J. Moran, J. Flaherty, B. Cryan, M. Staunton.
IN FRONT:—Dr. J. A. Madden.

42

43

NO CONSCRIPTION
NOW! or AFTER the Harvest.

No Economic Pressure!

Lá na mban.

The Woman's Day,
SUNDAY, JUNE 9th.

FOR HOME & COUNTRY.

IRISHWOMEN,
STAND BY YOUR COUNTRYMEN IN RESISTING CONSCRIPTION.

SIGN THIS PLEDGE AT THE CITY HALL ON
ST. COLMCILLE'S DAY.

"We will not fill the places of men deprived of their work through refusing enforced military service."

"We will do all in our power to help the families of men who suffer through refusing enforced military service."

REFUSE to fill Posts vacated by MEN because of Compulsory Military Service.

All information from Secretary, 18 Kildare Street.

37

38

39

P. Shanahan   S. Etchingham
P. Beasley   R. Barton   P. Galligan
J. McDonagh   J. McEntee
P. Ward   A. McCabe   D. Fitzgerald   J. Sweeney   Dr. Hayes   C. Collins   P. O'Maillie   J. O'Mara   B. O'Higgins   J. Burke   K. O'Higgins
F. McJoney   T. McSwiney   D. Mulcahy   J. O'Doherty   J. O'Mahony   J. Defan   J. McGuinness   P. O'Keefe   M. Staines   J. McGrath   Dr. B. Cusack   L. De Roiste   W. Colivet   Rev. Father O'Fla
L. Ginell   M. Collins   C. Brugha   A. Griffith   E. de Valera   Count Plunkett   E. MacNeill   W. Cosgrave   E. Blythe

laɩʒ na hEIREann
rish Volunteers.

A

UBLIC MEETING

of the formation of IRISH VOLUNTEERS
and the enrolment of men,

WILL BE HELD IN THE

LARGE CONCERT HALL,

ROTUNDA,

ON

UESDAY, NOV. 25

At 8 p.m.

OIN MacNEILL, B.A., will preside

All able-bodied Irishmen will be
eligible for enrolment.

OD SAVE IRELAND.

CURTIS, PRINTER, 12 TEMPLE LANE, DUBLIN.

28

29

30

(31)

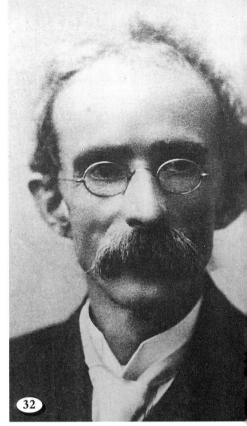

(32)

(33)

IPP comfortably dealt with any electoral challenge mounted by more radical Nationalists. During this period there were eight by-elections in Nationalist constituencies, and three of these, Wicklow West, Galway East and Derry City, were uncontested. Of the remaining five seats three were in rural constituencies, King's County in December 1914, Tipperary North in June 1915 and Louth North in March 1916, and all were won by loyal Redmondites. Only in the last of these, Louth North, did the IPP candidate have to face a radical Nationalist, and the party's nominee, P J Whitby, polled 2,299 votes to the 'Sinn Féiner' Bernard Hamill's 1,810 votes. Although the IPP won all three rural seats, it was clear that the UIL organisation was not in good working order and, consequently, steps were immediately taken to overhaul the UIL machinery throughout the country. The IPP also faced two urban by-election contests. In a very low turnout the party's candidate, J D Nugent, defeated a Labour candidate by 2,445 to 1,816 votes in the College Green division in Dublin in June 1915, a result which emphasised the urban weakness of the IPP. The Labour runner, Thomas Farren, who was backed by James Connolly, was a committed separatist, and he came out strongly against Irish support for the war. In the other city by-election contest in October 1915 the Dublin Harbour seat was easily won by the IPP's official candidate in a three-way fight with two other enthusiastic Redmondites. The separatists had failed to field a candidate in Dublin Harbour. An analysis of these wartime by-elections reveals that Redmond and the IPP still enjoyed the support of a clear majority in Nationalist Ireland. If the charge is made that such support lacked real commitment or enthusiasm, it must also be noted that the more radical strains of Nationalism had failed conclusively in their stuttering attempts to mount any kind of serious challenge to the dominance of the Irish party.

As the European conflict entered its second year, the people's waning enthusiasm for the war effort became more apparent. The most obvious expression of this was in the sharply declining number of troops who enlisted after the summer of 1915. From this point on, moreover, the radical Nationalists, notably Sinn Féin, began to make more impact with their anti-war propaganda. Yet the overall pattern of recruitment was influenced by economic as well as political factors. In the south and west of Ireland the most enthusiastic supporters of the war were the Protestant gentry families whose sons frequently filled the officer ranks in the 10th and 16th Divisions. The carnage on the Western Front took a heavy toll on the gentry class, but their service alongside Nationalist recruits, together with the impression created by Redmond's total commitment to the war effort, did much to heal the old divisions between Irish Nationalists and Southern Unionists. The bulk of the recruits, however, came from the urban working class, particularly Dublin. The prospect of adventure, a break from the drudgery of city life and a decent wage were all powerful incentives for unskilled workers in Dublin, where pay and living conditions were well below standards in the rest of the United Kingdom. In addition, Dublin's economic fortunes were hit hard by the war. Many of the distilleries were forced to close and even Guinness, the one firm where good wages and job security were the norm, moved to half-time working. In many cases, therefore, economic necessity was the primary reason for joining the colours. In their haste to enlist, the Dublin workers ignored the exhortations of James Connolly who appealed in the pages of the *Workers' Republic* for the working class to keep out of this capitalist war. Connolly's frustration with the workers' action was a major factor in convincing him that a rebellion against Britain was now essential.

In rural Ireland, on the other hand, the war brought immediate and significant economic gains. The increased demand for Irish produce and the consequent rise in agricultural prices encouraged Irish farmers to switch to more intensive farming practices. This enabled farmers to employ their younger sons at home, and it quickly emerged that this large group, which the War Office considered to be ideal recruiting material, had no interest in enlisting for foreign service. This was particularly noticeable in the richer agricultural areas of Munster, where farmers' sons in the countryside and the shop assistants of the market towns were increasingly drawn to various separatist movements which had been boosted by the war. Indeed the authorities made frequent references to the reluctance of the 'middling classes', which included clerks and shop assistants in addition to the farmers' sons, to come forward as recruits. It was among these groups that Sinn Féin, with its determined opposition to the war, began to make headway.

The causes of the Rising

The Easter Rising began on Easter Monday, 24 April 1916. It was carried out by approximately 1,600 men and women, the bulk of whom were members of the Irish, or Sinn Féin, Volunteers, with a minority supplied by the Irish Citizen Army. Both of these movements were being secretly manipulated by a small group of men, operating within the IRB, who were determined to organise a rebellion against Britain. Many factors contributed to the Easter Rising. The most obvious point to note is that the rising was staged when British attention was firmly fixed on the war. This gave the IRB revolutionaries the 'opportunity' to strike a blow for Irish freedom when Britain was experiencing the greatest 'difficulty' in her history. While the war may have brought a truce in the Home Rule hostilities between Unionists and Nationalists, it quickly created divisions within Nationalist ranks. Previously, Home Rule had been an umbrella ideology, satisfying both moderate opinion which regarded the third Home Rule Bill as providing a final settlement and the small, but growing, band of constitutional separatists who regarded Home Rule as an important first step in the evolution of Irish freedom. With the outbreak of the war these differences became more pronounced. Home Rule had been placed on the statute book, but its postponement led many Nationalists to focus on the actual limitations of the legislation, and MacNeill's description of Home Rule as a cheque continually post-dated caused many Nationalists to question the wisdom of Irish support for the British war effort. Overall, the war had helped to create a political vacuum in Ireland, which worked simultaneously to the advantage of the separatists and to the disadvantage of constitutional Nationalism. Almost overnight the war enabled the IRB to increase its influence.

Although Redmond's Woodenbridge speech was endorsed by a clear majority in Ireland, it was subsequently regarded as a misjudgement. This was particularly true when it became clear that the war would not be over within a year as most people had anticipated. The War Office's clumsy handling of Nationalist volunteering and the government's refusal to arm the National Volunteers and turn them into a Home Defence Force for Ireland also contributed to Redmond's difficulties, but a more crucial factor was the formation of a Coalition government in May 1915. A series of reverses on the battlefields, most notably the Gallipoli campaign, and major problems with the production of munitions had forced Asquith to bow to pressure for a Coalition government. Although Asquith ensured that the Liberals held all the key positions, the decision to give posts to both Bonar Law and Carson was a serious setback and embarrassment for Redmond. Asquith had tried to persuade Redmond to join the government, but to have done so would have broken the IPP's tradition of independent parliamentary action. While his refusal to join Asquith's Coalition cabinet won the backing of his supporters, one of his most bitter critics, D P Moran, argued in *The Leader* that Redmond had been mistaken in turning down the opportunity to use his influence in government. This contemporary criticism has been echoed by Professor Joe Lee who has argued that Redmond's decision was inconsistent with his support for the war effort. Whatever the views on Redmond's refusal to join the Coalition government, it was strikingly clear to Irish Nationalists that any cabinet with Carson it its ranks was unlikely to implement Home Rule [92]. Undoubtedly, Carson's inclusion in the wartime Coalition gave further encouragement to the separatists who insisted that Redmond's support for the war effort had diluted his Nationalism. The separatists were further boosted by the public's fear of conscription which had been introduced in Britain in January 1916. This fear, which was reinforced by the appalling loss of life on the Western Front, was exploited by the separatists to increase anti-British feeling.

The war undermined constitutional Nationalism in other ways. It curtailed emigration, which had previously acted as a safely valve by removing the most dissatisfied elements in society. This group of men, many of whom were the younger sons of farming stock, were not interested in recruitment, and their opposition to the war and fear of conscription drew them to the more radical Nationalist groups [93]. The war also removed the cream of Redmond's National Volunteers. Immediately after the Woodenbridge split, the National Volunteer movement, which dwarfed MacNeill's group, had demonstrated its strength in an impressive series of parades but, by the spring of 1915 when its most enthusiastic members were in France, it was struggling to retain its influence. The review of National Volunteers at Easter 1915, which saw 27,000 men on parade, was virtually the last occasion that the movement made a significant impression [94]. While all of these problems associated with the war contributed to the growing weakness of Redmond and constitutional Nationalism, they are not, by themselves, sufficient to explain the outbreak of a rebellion in 1916. The war had given a boost to a more radical strain of Nationalism and had generated very visible anti-British feeling. Still, only a very small number of extreme Nationalists were pro-German and actively considering an insurrection. In examining the causes of the rising, therefore, the most crucial aspect of the war was simply that it provided the opportunity for just such an insurrection.

A second cause of the rising was the impact of Ulster resistance to Home Rule. During the Ulster crisis Carson had forced Redmond to play second fiddle and the tactics which the Unionist leader had used further polarised Irish politics. In undermining Redmond and the IPP, Carson had also given a boost to radical

Nationalists, particularly to the old Fenian tradition which was bound to the principle of using force to win Irish freedom. Carson himself had, of course, developed an extra-parliamentary strategy. He had formed a huge private army, obtained 25,000 rifles from Germany and was poised to lead a rebellion against the Asquith government. His actions had inspired the formation of the Irish Volunteers, a body whose early members had been impressed by Carson's use of the threat of armed action to force the British government into granting concessions. Not surprisingly, these men were quick to highlight the ineffectiveness of Redmond's scrupulously constitutional strategy. Thus in forming the Irish Volunteers, MacNeill and his associates were acknowledging, by imitation, the success of the UVF and implicitly criticising Redmondism. MacNeill had taken the initiative with his article, 'The North Began', an action which marked his personal rejection of Redmond's constitutional Nationalism. The subsequent moves to establish the Irish Volunteers were quickly seized on by a number of IRB activists who had been waiting for just such an opportunity. They saw the potential for future revolutionary action in the organisation, if they could gain control, and they regarded MacNeill as the ideal figurehead to lead the new movement. What Carsonism had done, therefore, was to convert a significant number of Home Rulers into radical Nationalists, while simultaneously breathing life into a moribund IRB organisation. This was perfectly encapsulated in the transformation in Patrick Pearse's thinking. Pearse became a central figure in the planning of the rising but, as late as 1912, he was a committed Home Ruler before being influenced by the UVF. He was stirred by the sight of Irishmen with rifles and, by November 1913, he was writing, "Personally I think the Orangeman with a rifle a much less ridiculous figure than the Nationalist without one". Clearly, Carson had brought the gun back into Irish politics.

Still, long before the eruption of the crisis in Ulster men like Pearse had already committed themselves to a romantic vision of a free and Gaelic Ireland which was the goal of the Irish Ireland movement. The new Nationalism, closely associated with the growth of the Gaelic League in the early part of the twentieth century, is another important cause of the Easter Rising. It was the Gaelic League, the key organisation in the quest for cultural regeneration, which brought a generation of young men to Nationalism. The language movement often attracted young men of talent or ambition who felt politically excluded by the established forces of constitutional Nationalism. It was from this group that the Irish revolutionary elite emerged. The revival of the language gave Ireland a claim to nationality, and the Gaelic League classes helped to develop the romantic revolutionary spirit which was so prominent among the leaders of the rising. Pearse made specific reference to this in an essay, 'The Coming Revolution', which appeared only days after MacNeill's article, 'The North Began'. He paid tribute to the vital role which the League had played in the education of a new generation of Irish revolutionaries, claiming that this group had "an ulterior motive in joining the Gaelic League". However, the work and success of the League was, in Pearse's opinion, the great deed of the previous generation. The League had served its purpose, and it was now time for his generation to win the nationhood on which the movement for cultural revival had set its sights. This, he argued, could only be achieved through physical force: "We may make mistakes in the beginning and shoot the wrong people; but bloodshed is a cleansing and sanctifying thing, and the nation which regards it as the final horror has lost its manhood. There are many things more horrible than bloodshed; and slavery is one of them". Subsequent events only increased this desire for bloodshed.

Although Douglas Hyde, the League's President and its original inspiration, had insisted that the movement should stay outside politics, it became increasingly difficult to divorce the desire for cultural Nationalism from the desire for political freedom. From its inception a significant number of its branches, particularly those in Munster, had been infiltrated by the IRB. Matters eventually came to a head in the summer of 1915, when Hyde resigned from the Presidency of the League in protest at the organisation's shift to a more overt political stance. For some time, Tom Clarke and Sean MacDermott, the two most important figures in the IRB, had been exerting pressure on the League to identify with the aim of political freedom. By July 1915 they had achieved success, and the movement's constitution was amended to state that the Gaelic League should also "devote itself to realising the ideal of a free Gaelic-speaking Ireland". It is difficult to measure the contribution of the new Nationalism to the 1916 rising but, undoubtedly, it was a significant, if not a direct, cause. It had boosted the separatist movement and it did produce a number of key leaders, who formulated both a rationale for a rebellion and, crucially, a programme which was summarised in the 1916 Proclamation. Above all, the new Nationalism had created the atmosphere in which a rising might take place, though it required two new factors, Carsonism and the First World War, to bring the rising closer.

Taken together, the new Nationalism, Carsonism and the war are crucial elements in the making of the Easter Rising, but an insurrection in 1916 was, by no means, inevitable. What made it so was the work of the IRB conspirators operating within the clandestine Fenian movement. Here the two most important figures were Clarke and MacDermott. Clarke best typified the indomitable Fenian spirit. He had an abiding hatred of the British, and his fanatical desire to see a new rebellion led him to support the young group of northern militants, principally Bulmer Hobson, Denis McCullough and Sean MacDermott, who were plotting to gain control of the IRB. This had been achieved by 1912, but the IRB remained a weak, marginalised and largely ineffective movement. Then the formation of the Irish Volunteers, in November 1913, gave the IRB the opportunity to use the Volunteers as a front organisation for their own designs, and key IRB figures immediately joined the Volunteers, many of them filling its senior ranks. Of the thirty committee members running the Irish Volunteers, twelve were IRB men and, shortly afterwards, a number of the others, including Patrick Pearse, Joseph Plunkett and Thomas MacDonagh were sworn into the organisation. The IRB's plans were temporarily thrown into confusion by Redmond's swift action in June 1914 to bring the Volunteers under the control of the IPP. This led to a final breach between Clarke and Bulmer Hobson, a fellow member of the ruling Supreme Council and the editor of *Irish Freedom*, the IRB's monthly newspaper. Although Hobson had been the principal organiser of the IRB revival since 1910, his agreement to Redmond's demand for control of the Irish Volunteers ended his friendship with Clarke who never spoke to him again. Hobson subsequently resigned his seat on the Supreme Council and the editorship of *Irish Freedom*, leaving the way clear for the militants, Clarke, the Treasurer, and MacDermott, the Secretary, to direct IRB plans. Together with the President, these three formed the Executive, which acted for the Supreme Council between meetings and thus effectively ran the organisation.

The split in the Volunteers following Redmond's Woodenbridge speech left the IRB holding key positions in MacNeill's minority movement. Pearse was Director of Military Organisation, MacDonagh was Director of Training and Plunkett was Director of Military Operations and, clearly, the IRB had penetrated the ruling body of the Sinn Féin Volunteers and was intent on using the movement for its own purposes now that a decision had been taken, in principle, to stage a rising during the war. MacNeill, the Chief of Staff, and his two closest colleagues on the headquarters staff Hobson, the Quartermaster, and Michael Joseph Rahilly, or The O'Rahilly as he liked to be known, the Director of Arms, were not so naive that they did not suspect the intentions of this IRB inner circle, but they probably underestimated the organisation's ability to bring a rising to fruition. Moreover, many leading IRB men believed that an insurrection should not be launched unless it was likely to attract popular support. Despite such reservations, the Executive of the IRB, consisting of the President, the Treasurer and the Secretary, had decided that a rising would take place irrespective of popular opinion. In fact, James Deakin and Denis McCullough, the successive Presidents of the IRB between 1913 and 1916 discovered that they had little input, as Clarke and MacDermott firmly controlled the reins of power. Even McCullough, who became President towards the end of 1915 and was a close friend of both these men, was kept in the dark about the plans for a rising.

In May 1915 the IRB Executive formally appointed a Military Committee of three to make the detailed plans for a rising. The three chosen were Pearse, Plunkett and Eamonn Ceannt. These young men had previously been enthusiastic members of the Gaelic League and, significantly, all were recent recruits to the IRB. Clarke and MacDermott had turned to this younger generation of Nationalists, convinced that they were fully committed to the need for a rising. The obsession with secrecy meant that the Military Committee liaised only with Clarke and MacDermott, leaving the Supreme Council without any knowledge of their plans. In September 1915 Clarke and MacDermott formally joined the Military Committee which was then renamed the Military Council. The formation of the Military Council was the single most important factor in the planning of the Easter Rising. Yet within this small group a crucial element was at play. This was the fusion of the traditional physical force republican element and the younger romantic revolutionaries, whose sense of nationality had first been stirred by the Gaelic League.

Pearse was the figurehead pushed forward by Clarke, in spite of stiff opposition from many IRB men who disliked him personally and suspected him of political opportunism. Yet Clarke saw in Pearse the qualities necessary for leadership. Not only was he a gifted writer and inspirational speaker, but he was also an idealist and romantic visionary whose clarity of purpose and air of nobility appealed to Clarke. Plunkett was a fellow poet and the chief military strategist in the Military Council. He drew up the military plan which the Volunteers followed during the rising. Ceannt, an employee of the Dublin Corporation, was less well known than his two colleagues. He was an active member of the Irish Volunteers, becoming its Director of Communications in August 1915 and thus tightening the grip which the IRB conspirators had on the Volunteer movement. By late 1915 Clarke was content to sit back, confident that the right men were in place to instigate the rising which had been his life's ambition. This left Sean MacDermott, the key figure among the IRB conspirators planning the rising. It was MacDermott who approved all the important decisions, ensured that strict secrecy was maintained and delighted in the cloak and dagger activity that went into the making of 1916. The crucial decision to go for Easter Sunday was probably taken by the Military Council late in 1915 and, though there were several major hiccups, it was MacDermott who saw that a rising finally went ahead without reference to the Supreme Council.

While the action of the Military Council, prompted by MacDermott, was the main cause of the rising, the roles played by Pearse and James Connolly were also significant. The Easter Rising has been described as a "revolution of the intellectuals", a reference to the influence of the poets and writers who formulated its programme and occupied prominent positions in the revolutionary vanguard. Indeed four of the Proclamation's seven signatories were distinguished writers. While Connolly was the pre-eminent socialist ideologue in Ireland and a major international figure on the left, Pearse, Plunkett and MacDonagh shared a common view moulded, in part, by their involvement in the Gaelic League. Pearse was born in 1879 and brought up in a conventional lower middle class Dublin family. After devoting his early adult life to the Gaelic League, Pearse turned his attention to education, opening his own bilingual school, St Enda's, in September 1908. The school's first pupils came from the best known families in Gaelic revival circles, and the curriculum, which was delivered using the most modern teaching methods, was designed to promote both the Irish language and the study of Ireland's Celtic past. All the boys were introduced to Cuchulainn, the mythical hero, who had died for Ireland and was alleged to have said, "I care not though I were to live but one day and one night, if only my fame and my deeds live after me". This became an important influence in Pearse's life and, later at St Enda's, he became increasingly obsessed with Wolfe Tone and Robert Emmet, two more recent Irish heroes whose names were synonymous with martyrdom in the cause of Ireland. Despite this obsession with two physical force Nationalists, Pearse, like many of his fellow Gaelic revivalists, continued to show deference to Redmond and the IPP, and it was only at the end of 1913 that he fused his desire for a blood sacrifice with the need for violent revolution.

From this point on Pearse's writings displayed a powerful Messianic strain which tied in with this doctrine of blood sacrifice. Like Plunkett and MacDonagh, Pearse was an intensely religious young man who was deeply influenced by Catholic mysticism. He saw Ireland's struggle for redemption in terms of Christ's sacrifice at Calvary. Christ had died on the cross to save men's souls and, he believed, it would take a similar sacrifice to save Ireland's soul and resurrect Irish nationality. This powerful spiritual theme was revealed in Pearse's most famous public utterance, when he gave the oration at the funeral of Jeremiah O'Donovan Rossa on 1 August 1915. The veteran Fenian had died in the United States at the end of June and had been brought home to Dublin for burial, giving the IRB the opportunity to stage a propaganda coup. In his graveside oration, which followed an impressive display by the Sinn Féin Volunteers, Pearse spoke on behalf of "the new generation that has been rebaptised in the Fenian faith". He ended the oration with a mix of religious testimony and the prophecy of impending rebellion: "Life springs from death; and from the graves of patriot men and women spring living nations. The Defenders of this Realm ... think that they have pacified Ireland ...but the fools, the fools, the fools! - they have left us our Fenian dead, and while Ireland holds these graves, Ireland unfree shall never be at peace". What Pearse saw as the noble sacrifices on the battlefields of the Western Front intensified his desire for a blood sacrifice, and his growing obsession with the crucifixion pointed to a rebellion during Holy Week. At Easter he would sacrifice himself for the benefit of his people.

Plunkett and MacDonagh shared this romantic revolutionary zeal and were equally keen to imitate Christ by sacrificing themselves for their country. Indeed Plunkett, who was born in 1887, was most influenced by Catholic mysticism, and the Nationalism which he expounded in his poetry contained powerful religious undertones. In his more practical role as the Military Council's chief strategist Plunkett, who was suffering from terminal tuberculosis, visited Berlin in the spring of 1915 in an unsuccessful attempt to persuade the Germans to support an IRB rising with a strong invasion force. MacDonagh had first met Plunkett in 1910. He had been asked to tutor Plunkett in Irish and, soon, the two were collaborating in various theatre and literary projects. Earlier, MacDonagh had assisted Pearse in the establishment of St Enda's before his appointment to University College, Dublin as an assistant lecturer in English. Of the three writer - revolutionaries MacDonagh was the most intellectually gifted. While his early writings show that he, like his friends, had accepted the need for a blood sacrifice, it was only with his involvement in the Irish Volunteers, where his organisational abilities won him rapid promotion, that he considered the use of violence. He only became a member of the IRB in 1915 and, two weeks before the rising, he became the seventh and final member of the Military Council. Pearse, Plunkett and MacDonagh, all in their late twenties when the rising occurred, were the revolutionary visionaries who gave the rebellion an intellectual dimension. Even when it became apparent that the rising would be a military fiasco, their unwavering devotion to the blood sacrifice doctrine guaranteed their continued support for an insurrection, and this proved vital to MacDermott and Clarke, the hub of the IRB conspiracy.

The final member of the IRB Military Council was James Connolly. He had been travelling down a different road, but his destination was the same blood sacrifice rebellion. Connolly's analysis of Irish history, which focused on the wrongs done to Ireland, firstly by English landowners and then by English capitalists, always had a strong Nationalist flavour. Yet his ultimate dream of a socialist republic bore little relation to the Gaelic republic sought by the bourgeois writer-revolutionaries. They also had very different views on the war. In December 1915 Connolly replied forcefully to a Pearse article which gloried in the carnage of the First World War: "The old heart of the earth needed to be warmed with the red wine of the battlefields". Connolly hated the war and seized on Pearse's misplaced sentimentality, describing him as a 'blithering idiot'. How then did Connolly come to join with the IRB conspirators who were planning the Easter Rising? He had been devastated at the actions of the millions of working class men who had volunteered to fight each other in this capitalist war. In particular, Connolly was frustrated by the sight of thousands of Dublin workers rushing to join the British Army on the outbreak of the war. He threw himself into the anti-recruiting campaign, and the large banner which was displayed on the front of Liberty Hall, the Transport Union's headquarters, publicly proclaimed the labour movement's stance on the war. It read: "We serve neither King nor Kaiser, but Ireland".

Yet Connolly did not intend to be as neutral as the Liberty Hall banner suggested. Early in September 1914, he attended a meeting with senior IRB figures, including Clarke, MacDermott, Pearse, Plunkett, Ceannt and MacDonagh, at which the prospect of a rising was discussed. Connolly was enthusiastic, convincing himself that an Irish revolution would have to be a two-stage process in which the struggle to overthrow capitalism would be preceded by a rebellion to gain independence from Britain. Thus Connolly came to believe that Nationalism and socialism were not antagonistic, but complementary. Here he was deviating from Marxist doctrine which argued that nations were the creation of the bourgeois epoch. Connolly never fully recognised this, believing that the 'nation' had existed through all stages in Irish history, but his analysis was clearly influenced by a strong nationalistic and romantic sentiment. Despite their differences on the need for the battlefields to be sprinkled with the red wine of millions of lives, Connolly's views drew him increasingly towards Pearse. Still, all through 1915, Connolly remained outside the small circle of IRB conspirators, ignorant of the Military Council's activities. This lack of knowledge and the delay in starting the rebellion convinced Connolly that the IRB had taken cold feet and abandoned its plans for an insurrection. By this stage Connolly was very impatient, and he decided to press ahead with his own preparations for a rising, using the 200-strong Irish Citizen Army which had remained in place since the lockout. Although it was small, the Irish Citizen Army was a tightly disciplined and well organised force. Training had been stepped up under Michael Mallin, its Chief of Staff, and weapons practice was carried out on a rifle range which had been installed in Liberty Hall. By the end of 1915 Connolly had become dismissive of the IRB's grand designs and was openly advocating revolutionary action, indicating that the Irish Citizen Army would "advance by itself if needs be".

Connolly's growing impatience alarmed the members of the Military Council who feared that precipitate action by the Irish Citizen Army would lead to the suppression of the Volunteers, thus ruining their own plans for a rebellion. Though he had no knowledge of the Military Council's activities, MacNeill was also anxious that Connolly should be dissuaded from staging an insurrection which might have serious consequences for his own Volunteer movement. With Pearse in attendance, MacNeill met Connolly in mid-January 1916 in an unsuccessful attempt to restrain him from any premature action. In MacNeill's view a rebellion without a realistic chance of success could only be justified if the government tried either to suppress the Volunteers or to impose conscription on Ireland. Significantly, conscription had been introduced in Britain that same month. The Military Council now intervened. From 19-22 January Connolly met secretly with the members of the Military Council who took some time to convince him that a rising would definitely go ahead on Easter Sunday, 23 April 1916. He was then sworn into the IRB, becoming the sixth member of the Military Council, and he was fully involved in the latter stages of the preparations for the rising. Accordingly, Pearse was able to reassure MacNeill that Connolly would not go ahead with an Irish Citizen Army-led rebellion without, of course, informing him that he was now part of the Military Council's operation. In joining the IRB conspirators Connolly had to concede that the rising would not be undertaken in the name of socialism. At this time, moreover, he was coming increasingly under Pearse's influence. Unusually for the rational Connolly, he had been greatly moved by Pearse's oration at the O'Donovan Rossa funeral, and this was to influence his own thinking. This was clearly evident in February 1916, when he published an article in the *Workers' Republic* which argued that Ireland would not enjoy stability and prosperity until she broke free from Britain. It was his generation's responsibility, he added, to make "the supreme act of self-sacrifice – to die if need be that our race might live in freedom". Connolly had identified with the blood sacrifice doctrine advocated by Pearse and the other writer-revolutionaries. Later, the Irish Citizen Army took, in Connolly's words, the "momentous decision" to hoist the Green Flag over Liberty Hall, a significant gesture symbolising the labour movement's links with advanced Nationalism.

In one of his final articles for the *Workers' Republic* he tried to justify his decision to join with the forces of bourgeois Nationalism: "The cause of labour is the cause of Ireland, the cause of Ireland is the cause of labour. They cannot be dissevered". The simple explanation was that Connolly was desperate for an Irish revolution, any Irish revolution. Moreover, he shared the sense of shame which Pearse felt with his generation of Irishmen who had failed to stake a claim to their nationality. While he had not escaped the spell of romantic Nationalism, Connolly had tried to translate this emotional desire for freedom into a practical social programme and, in the process, he had influenced Pearse. Although Pearse had always been sympathetic to the poorest elements in Irish society, the 1916 Proclamation, which he had largely written, offers specific evidence of Connolly's influence. The document contained a brief passage which outlined social and economic goals but, ultimately, the rebellion could not deliver these desired changes. Despite this setback, Pearse and Connolly had together made a significant contribution to the rising. Their determination to stage a rebellion, however hopeless, and their willingness to sacrifice their own lives provided crucial support for MacDermott and Clarke, the two men at the heart of the IRB conspiracy.

Insurrection

Although MacDermott ensured that only a small circle knew the exact plans for the Easter Rising, the British authorities in Dublin Castle were remarkably relaxed in their response to the sedition openly preached during 1915-16 by high profile figures such as Pearse and Connolly. Birrell had continued as Chief Secretary, but he left the day-to-day running of affairs in the hands of his Under Secretary, Sir Matthew Nathan, who had been appointed to the post in October 1914. Soon after his arrival in Dublin Nathan used the monthly RIC reports to compile a long list of Nationalist extremists who were suspected of engaging in subversive activity. The list included most of the men who were to feature prominently in the rising. Nathan also had to decide on what action to take against the anti-British press and, early in December 1914, the most extreme of these newspapers, including *Irish Freedom*, were banned, though they quickly reappeared under different titles. In dealing with radical

Nationalism the new Under Secretary frequently sought the advice of the IPP leadership, and he had a number of meetings with Redmond and Devlin. His main contact, however, was John Dillon who spent more time in Dublin than the other leaders. On their first meeting on 26 November 1914 he had urged Nathan to refrain from banning the seditious press, as this would give succour to the extremists and increase the difficulties facing the IPP. On this occasion, of course, Nathan rejected Dillon's advice and the most extreme newspapers were suppressed [95]. Over the next year the authorities in Dublin took intermittent action against certain seditious publications, and a small number of vocal anti-British agitators were served with deportation orders but, in general, Birrell and Nathan refused to sanction the coercion of radical Nationalist groups demanded by Unionists. Consequently, the Irish Volunteers were allowed to drill and train unmolested, while their leaders continued to enjoy their freedom.

By the end of 1915, however, it was clear that support for the more extreme Nationalist groups, notably Sinn Féin, was on the increase. Both the Irish Citizen Army and the Irish Volunteers were more active and, in a number of rural areas, there were isolated outbreaks of violence, with shots fired in some incidents involving the Volunteers and the RIC. At the same time, rumours of an impending rising were sweeping through Dublin. On St Patrick's Day 1916 the Volunteers staged impressive military manoeuvres in the centre of the city. Most of the Volunteers were armed and traffic was disrupted over a two hour period. A few months before this, Connolly and the Irish Citizen Army had chosen a Sunday to carry out a mock attack on Dublin Castle. Despite such provocation, Birrell and Nathan continued to reject Unionist advice that the Volunteers should be disarmed and not permitted to parade. The army, meanwhile, had been alarmed by the developments of March 1916 and, more specifically, by a report from the Director of Military Intelligence in Britain. It stated that reliable information, most probably from intercepted German code messages, had been received, indicating that a rising with German assistance was being planned for Easter Saturday, 22 April. Some discussion followed between the authorities in Dublin and the army on the need to strengthen the garrison in Ireland, but no decision was reached. Two days later, on 25 March, the Castle authorities arrested Ernest Blythe and Liam Mellowes, both prominent IRB figures, and had them deported to England. By this stage Dillon had become alarmed at the state of the country, and he warned Nathan that tough action by the government was only increasing the tension. At the same time, Nathan was being pressed for his views on the possibility of a rising by senior military personnel in Ireland, who were concerned both by the recent disturbances and by the growing rumours of an insurrection. On 10 April 1916 he gave his assessment of the situation in a letter to the Adjutant General. "Though the Irish Volunteer element has been active of late, especially in Dublin," he wrote, "I do not believe that its leaders mean insurrection or that the Volunteers have sufficient arms if the leaders do mean it".

On the same day the army's senior Intelligence Officer in Ireland sent a report to the Director of Military Intelligence in London with his appraisal of the situation. There had been, he noted, a sharp rise in the level of Volunteer activity and there was no doubt that the Irish, or Sinn Féin Volunteers, as he called them, would stage a rebellion if they were given the opportunity. Still, Nathan's opinion held sway, and he felt that the deportations had helped to restore calm in the country. While rumours of a rebellion were growing almost daily, the lack of specific information coming from government agents within the Volunteer movement only added to the government's complacency. In this sense the Military Council's obsession with secrecy had the desired effect and, where previous Irish rebellions had been scuppered by informers, the 1916 version would at least avoid a similar fate. Even on 17 April, when Nathan received information from the officer in command of the defences at the port of Queenstown on the Cork coast, which suggested that a shipment of arms would be landed somewhere on the south-west coast with a rising following on Easter Saturday, the authorities were sceptical. RIC officers in the neighbouring counties were put on alert, but Nathan remained confident that a rising was not imminent. Subsequent events surprised Nathan, but they unfolded in such a way as to convince the authorities that the danger of a rising had passed.

On Thursday afternoon, 19 April 1916, the *Aud*, a German ship disguised as a Norwegian trawler, sailed into Tralee Bay. In the confusion that followed the insurgents on the shore were unable to make contact with the *Aud* which, crucially, did not have a wireless. The skipper waited for 24 hours before moving off, but he was then intercepted by the Royal Navy and escorted into Queenstown harbour. There he scuttled the ship and with it sank the cargo of 20,000 rifles and any chance of a successful rebellion. On that same Good Friday Sir Roger Casement, the IRB's link with Germany, was put ashore in County Kerry by a German submarine. Within a few hours he had been captured by two alert RIC officers and taken to Tralee jail. Casement had left for Germany in October 1914. His aims were to seek German assistance for the IRB and to form an Irish Brigade from Irish prisoners of war in Germany. When Plunkett visited him in 1915, he discovered just how little progress Casement had made. At that point Casement painted a bleak picture, highlighting German reluctance to support an Irish rebellion, and he informed Plunkett that any rising without German aid would be futile. His attempt to raise an Irish Brigade had also been a fiasco and did nothing for Casement's standing with his German hosts. Indeed his travelling companion, an unscrupulous Norwegian seaman named Adler Christensen, who went as Casement's servant, further undermined his reputation in Germany. Casement's mission was proving a disaster. His health was poor and his lack of progress was exasperating John Devoy, the leading IRB conspirator in the United States, who had been involved in the original decision to send Casement to Germany. The growing disillusionment with Casement, who was more adamant than ever about the need for substantial aid to make any rising a success, saw him being sidelined by the IRB. When Devoy was informed by the Military Council in early February 1916 that the date of the rising had been fixed for Easter, he contacted the Germans through their embassy in Washington, asking for a shipment of arms to be dispatched to the south-west coast of Ireland at some point between Good Friday and Easter Sunday.

Not surprisingly, the problems encountered by the IRB in their communications with the Germans, all of which had to be directed through the United States, added to the general confusion and contributed to the ship's capture and Casement's arrest. In fact, Casement had great difficulty in persuading the Germans to deliver him to the Kerry coast. His intention was to arrive in Ireland in time to dissuade the IRB leaders from starting a rebellion, though he had decided that if he was unsuccessful in this, he would join in the insurrection. His capture, however, meant that he never had the opportunity to present his case to the IRB leaders who were, of course, committed to an insurrection, with or without German help. When news reached the authorities in Dublin that the suspect arrested in Kerry was Roger Casement, they assumed that the plot to stage a rebellion had been foiled. Casement, described by the RIC County Inspector in Tralee as "that lunatic traitor" was regarded as the leader of the insurrectionists, and his arrest and rapid transportation to England via Dublin helped to convince the authorities that a rising had been averted. Nathan knew that the Volunteers were to be mobilised on Easter Sunday, but a notice in the main Sunday newspaper cancelling the manoeuvres scheduled for that afternoon together with the knowledge that they had the 'leader' safely in custody appeared to confirm their view that the danger of a rising had passed.

These late setbacks did not deter the Military Council. Its members were hoping for German assistance and genuinely wanted the rising to have every chance of success, but once the *Aud* was captured they fell back on the blood sacrifice doctrine. Yet they still had to involve sufficient numbers of Irish Volunteers to make the rising feasible, and this might prove to be very difficult if circumstances pointed to a humiliating military defeat. Certainly, MacNeill, Hobson and The O'Rahilly among the Volunteer leadership were very alarmed at the prospect of a rising. In early April, with rumours circulating freely, MacNeill, fearing that the IRB element was about to launch a rebellion persuaded the Volunteer leadership to support his demand that only orders which were countersigned by him could be issued to the Volunteers. MacNeill's nervousness worried the Military Council. They knew that the Volunteer leaders would only support a rising if the government attempted either to suppress the movement or to impose conscription on Ireland. It was against this background that the 'Castle Document' appeared on 19 April. The document, which was almost certainly a forgery organised by MacDermott with help from Plunkett and MacDonagh, contained details of a government plan to suppress the Volunteers. It had the desired effect on MacNeill who issued immediate instructions to the men under his command, warning them to make preparations for resistance. Late on the following day, however, Bulmer Hobson learned that instructions had also been issued by the IRB conspirators to prepare for an insurrection on Easter Sunday. Following this, MacNeill and Hobson drove out to St Enda's to confront Pearse with this latest revelation. There they learned for the first time of the Military Council's plan for the rising on Easter Sunday.

MacNeill reacted angrily to Pearse's admission that he had been deceived by the IRB conspiracy. He intended to countermand the orders issued to the Volunteers for mobilisation on Easter Sunday, but Pearse, MacDonagh and MacDermott managed to persuade him to hold back, arguing that German assistance in the shape of the *Aud's* cargo was expected anytime. Neither the plotters nor MacNeill knew that the ship had sank outside Queenstown harbour earlier that Good Friday. Over the course of the following day, however, MacNeill became aware of the extent of the deception and after consultation with The O'Rahilly and other Volunteer leaders he was convinced that the Castle Document had been a forgery. News of the *Aud's* sinking now reinforced his determination to prevent the rising. Accordingly, orders were dispatched late that Saturday evening which, he assumed, would stop the rising. To avoid confusion he also published his countermanding orders in the *Sunday Independent*, prohibiting all Volunteer movements scheduled for that day. As Chief of Staff, MacNeill must have assumed that his decisive intervention at the eleventh hour had prevented a rising. The IRB conspirators had apparently complied with MacNeill but, unknown to him, they had met at Liberty Hall on Easter Sunday morning and had taken the decision to begin the rising on Easter Monday.

Next morning just under 1,600 insurgents assembled to participate in a rising which the Military Council knew was doomed to fail militarily. The small number was the result of the confusion caused by the sudden changes in instructions and by the secrecy enforced by the planners. Even Denis McCullough, the President of the Supreme Council of the IRB, had only learned about the rising, when he confronted his close friend MacDermott earlier in the week and forced him to reveal the truth. The sight of the insurgents marching through the centre of Dublin that Easter Monday caused little excitement among the city's population, which had become accustomed to the frequent parades and manoeuvres undertaken by both the Volunteers and the Irish Citizen Army. In any case Dublin was relatively quiet on that Easter Monday. Many had journeyed out the short distance to Fairyhouse Racecourse for the traditional holiday race meeting, which also attracted a good number of army officers. The belief that a rebellion had been foiled had given the authorities a false sense of security and the insurgents, therefore, enjoyed the element of surprise. Led off by Pearse, the President of the Provisional Government and the Commandant-General of the forces of the Irish Republic, and Connolly, the Vice-President and Commandant-General of the Dublin division, the insurgents quickly put their military plan into action. It was based on the occupation of the city's key buildings, and the General Post Office (GPO) in O'Connell Street, then known officially as Sackville Street, was chosen as the headquarters. In the GPO Pearse was joined by Connolly, Clarke, MacDermott and Plunkett, the Military Council's chief military strategist whose plan had now been put into operation. However, as Plunkett was really too ill to play any active role, Connolly effectively assumed command. Quickly, two flags were raised above the GPO. One was the old green flag and gold harp, while the other was a tricolour of orange, white and green, a much less well known emblem which marked a link with a previous Irish insurrection.

In his capacity as President, Pearse marched outside the GPO to read the Proclamation from the Provisional Government, signed by all seven members of the Military Council, to a small crowd of bemused onlookers. The Proclamation was full of heroic language [96]. The 1916 insurrectionists wanted to link their action to previous rebellions, emphasising Ireland's right to establish her freedom through force of arms. There was mention of the "six times during the past three hundred years", when Irishmen had fought for their freedom from England. Significantly, the final sentence of the Proclamation also made specific reference to the need for the leaders of the present Irish nation to be ready "to sacrifice themselves for the common good", something which all seven signatories of the Proclamation were fully prepared to accept. The subtext of the Proclamation was the desire to delve into the country's past to recreate a free, Gaelic and egalitarian Ireland, which had been inspired by the various movements of the new Nationalism around the turn of the century. More controversial was the reference to "the gallant allies in Europe" who were, albeit feebly, supporting the rebellion. This ensured that the rising would be viewed by British eyes as a very serious act of treason.

In the initial stages of the rising a unit of the Irish Citizen Army approached the gate at Dublin Castle, shooting dead the policeman on duty and capturing a group of six soldiers. What the Citizen Army men did not realise was that the castle, the centre of British rule in Ireland, could easily have been occupied but, in the confusion, this great propaganda opportunity was spurned, as the insurgents chose to move into some nearby buildings. Apart from the GPO, the other key positions occupied included the Four Courts where Edward Daly was in charge, St Stephen's Green under the command of Michael Mallin, Jacob's biscuit factory where MacDonagh was leading the insurgents and Boland's Flour Mills which was commanded by a young mathematics teacher, Eamon de Valera. The tactics adopted by the insurgents were to hold these defensive positions and wait for government forces to dislodge them, a task they accomplished with the effective use of artillery. During the first few days the poorest elements in the city took advantage of the withdrawal of the Dublin Metropolitan Police from duty to embark on a looting spree, which saw many shops emptied of their contents. As the fighting intensified towards the end of the week, much of O'Connell Street was on fire. Artillery barrages, some of which had been delivered by a gunboat on the Liffey, had forced the insurgents to vacate a number of their positions. By Thursday evening the GPO was in flames and the occupants had to withdraw. Connolly, who had been seriously wounded, had to be stretchered to a house in Moore Street. There, The O'Rahilly was shot down as he led a hopeless charge on a British position. Although he had been deceived by Pearse and the other leaders, The O'Rahilly had felt that it was his duty to fight with his Irish Volunteer comrades.

On Friday the British tightened the cordon around the insurgents and, in order to prevent further loss of life, Pearse and Connolly decided to surrender, a decision which was put into effect on the Saturday afternoon. Instructions to surrender were then sent around the other Volunteer positions, and the rising, which had lasted barely a week, was effectively over by Sunday, 1 May. The ruthless use of artillery had caused great devastation in the city centre and civilian casualties were high. Over 200 civilians had died and, despite their reliance on artillery shells to overcome Volunteer strongholds, more than 100 troops had been killed in the street-fighting. The insurgents, who had lost 64 men, were placed under arrest following their surrender. Among the prisoners were a number of women. About 90 women had taken part in the rising, 60 of whom were members of Cumann na mBan, the women's equivalent of the Volunteers which had been formed in April 1914 and included members from prominent Nationalist families. Most of the Volunteer leaders were reluctant to see women fighting, but Cumann na mBan was welcomed in an auxiliary capacity, with its members serving as cooks, nurses and couriers. Acting as a courier was extremely dangerous, and the women involved displayed great bravery as they took messages and food supplies to the various Volunteer positions. Indeed food frequently had to be commandeered by women who held up vans at the point of a revolver. The remaining 30 women participants were members of the Irish Citizen Army, and they took a more active part in the fighting. True to its socialist principles, the Citizen Army proclaimed the equality of the sexes, and a few of its members played a prominent role. Countess Markievicz, a lieutenant in the Citizen Army, acted as Michael Mallin's second-in-command at St Stephen's Green, and the memory of the flamboyant 48 year old countess in her military uniform with revolver in hand remains one of the most powerful images of the rising.

Outside Dublin there were isolated attacks and some minor successes, but the rising in the provinces lacked the coherence necessary to make a significant impact. The failure to obtain German arms and the false start caused by MacNeill's intervention had proved insurmountable difficulties. In Wexford Volunteers held the town of Enniscorthy for three days, while 1,500 Volunteers commanded by Liam Mellowes held the town of Athenry for a brief period. Mellowes had been deported by the authorities only days earlier but, using a disguise, had made his way back to Ireland to participate in the rising. The most notable success was at Ashbourne in County Meath, where a small unit of Volunteers commanded by Thomas Ashe won a five hour gun battle with an RIC force. Eight officers were killed and a further fifteen wounded, as Ashe's men captured four police barracks and seized a large quantity of arms and ammunition. They were still in control of the area when they received Pearse's order to surrender. Overall, of course, the rising had been a desperate military failure, but both the British authorities and the Irish people, whose failure to support the insurrectionists was particularly noticeable, recognised that a serious attempt had been made to win Irish freedom. The question for the immediate future was how would each of these groups react to Easter 1916?

Historiography

In assessing Redmond's speech to the House of Commons on the outbreak of the war, Gwynn's, *The Life of John Redmond* claims that no other Irish leader would have dared to offer Irish support for the war only a week after the Bachelor's Walk killings. Bew's, *John Redmond* focuses on the Irish leader's sincere belief that involvement in the common struggle would help to heal old Unionist - Nationalist divisions, and he emphasises Redmond's genuine concern for Belgium, another small Catholic country. Gwynn also chronicles Redmond's failure to persuade the War Office to establish an Irish Brigade and contrasts this with Carson's success in winning government approval for a separate Ulster Division. Laffan's, *The Partition of Ireland* regarded the War Office's failure to reciprocate the goodwill shown by Redmond in his recruiting efforts as a significant factor in undermining constitutional Nationalism. D G Boyce's essay, 'Ireland and the First World War' *History Ireland*, Vol 2 No 3 (Autumn 1994) highlights the initial caution shown by both Redmond and Carson before they committed their respective Volunteer forces to the British Army. In addition to exposing some myths about the 36th Division, Boyce argues that the war gave Irish Nationalists "a chance to raise their profile, to place them firmly in the ranks of the white Dominions, Canada, Australia, South Africa, and to get themselves on a level ground with the British and the Unionists". Recruitment figures often appear to be at variance, but the number of just over 200,000 who volunteered for service during the course of the war is a good estimate. This figure includes over 50,000 men who were already serving in the forces at the outbreak of the war.

Mansergh's, *The Unresolved Question* is very critical of Redmond's leadership at the outbreak of the war, arguing that he was "blindly dismissive of what alone could save him, namely, getting his hands on the levers of power". The IPP had not prepared for the transfer of devolved powers and then failed to demand the effective implementation of Home Rule, leaving Mansergh to suggest that the Nationalists would have greatly benefited by the establishment of a "mirror image" Ulster Provisional government in the south. Bew's, *Ideology and the Irish Question* firmly rejects the thesis that Redmond missed a great opportunity in August and September 1914, when he could have exploited Britain's difficulties for political gains. Adopting such an opportunist strategy, Bew argues, would have implied a willingness on Redmond's part "to allow the triumph of German arms in France". At that time, of course, Redmond was about to commit the Volunteers to foreign service against the advice of some of his closest colleagues. While Redmond received general public backing for his Woodenbridge stand, historians differ on their assessment. Foster's, *Modern Ireland* views Woodenbridge as a disastrous miscalculation, suggesting that Redmond's 'misjudgement' can be regarded as a turning-point in Irish history. Lee's, *Ireland 1912-1985* takes a different view, arguing that Redmond was following a logical course of action which was justified "even from a separatist viewpoint". With everyone expecting a short war, British public opinion would realise, and could demonstrate this in a postwar general election, that a Home Rule Ireland posed no threat to British security. Lee speculates that if Redmond had opted to stay neutral, he was sure to reinforce the partitionist mentality. His real mistake, Lee claims, had been made earlier, when he had failed to arm the Irish Volunteers in order to meet the Unionist challenge. The war offered Redmond an opportunity to redress the balance. Lee argues that the return of Irish soldiers, probably in 1915, who were trained and armed, would have given Redmond some 'bargaining power' with both Asquith and Carson. Bew's,

Ideology and the Irish Question goes even farther in Redmond's defence, arguing that he had "no choice but to act as he did", if he hoped to have any influence on a postwar Irish settlement.

O'Broin's, *Revolutionary Underground* describes the anger felt by Tom Clarke and his inner IRB circle at the Volunteers' decision to accept Redmond's takeover bid in June 1914. Clarke never spoke to Hobson again, but the split following the Woodenbridge speech offered a considerable advantage to MacDermott and Clarke who began plotting the rising in September 1914. Foster's, *Modern Ireland* describes the minority Irish Volunteers as representing the "radical, militant IRB-influenced element", noting that they quickly became identified with "Sinn Féin's anti-recruitment campaign and the broad front of Anglophobia that merged inevitably into pro-Germanism". On the other hand, as the year dragged on, enlistment and demoralisation took their toll on Redmond's National Volunteers. Still, Kee's, *The Bold Fenian Men* argues that a description of McNeill's Irish Volunteers as the only active group after Woodenbridge is a "travesty of fact". The National Volunteers were numerous and enthusiastic, and Kee shows that they were an effective and dominant movement for at least the first six months of their existence. On the impact of the war Lyons's, *Ireland since the Famine* notes that while the conflict had boosted the Irish economy, "there was a feeling, widespread if often inarticulate, that the war ... was not Ireland's affair". Bew's, *Ideology and the Irish Question* describes the way in which Redmond's wartime strategy deprived IPP rhetoric of much of its Nationalist bite. Like most writers Lee's, *Ireland 1912 -1985* stresses the significance of the war in bringing about an Irish rebellion against British rule, but wonders why it took so long to stage such a rebellion.

In analysing the causes of the rising Lyons's, *Ireland since the Famine* argues that the background to the Irish revolution is particularly complex, because of the existence of a secret movement, the IRB, operating within the open Nationalist organisation, the Irish Volunteers. The fact that a revolutionary cell, the IRB Military Council, was operating within the secret IRB movement only adds to the difficulties in understanding the background. He then examines the significance of the Gaelic League which he acknowledges created the atmosphere for the rising. Later Lyons's, *Culture and Anarchy in Ireland* takes a more detailed look at the League, noting that most of the young men and women "who brought the old militancy back into politics in the first two decades of the twentieth century had begun their apprenticeship inside the Gaelic League". Lyons suggests that the step from Gaelic League activist to revolutionary leader was a simple one for a man like Pearse, who had already been touched by the Messianic strain "which had appeared in Irish writing repeatedly since the death of Parnell". This is a view shared by B P Murphy's, *Patrick Pearse and the Republican Ideal* (Dublin, 1991) which, agreeing with P O'Farrell's, *Ireland's English Question* (London, 1971), claims that a revolutionary dynamism in Ireland had sprung up in the 1890s. From then, Roman Catholic priests and the language revival were united in "a linkage which swung religious attitudes into sympathetic alignment not only with the contemporary cultural revival, but with major elements in the Irish revolutionary tradition". Tom Garvin's, *The Evolution of Irish Nationalist Politics* argued that the Gaelic League "educated an entire political class:, and noted that the IRB recruited from the League and the GAA. He also discusses how Sinn Féin, with its anti-war stance, made headway in rural Ireland, where it was regarded as "evidence of good sense" to avoid enlistment. Significantly, he points out that in many rural areas the sons of strong farmers viewed the army as a step down socially. In his *Nationalist Revolutionaries in Ireland* Garvin claims that the Gaelic League was the key to the development of the Irish revolutionary elite. It had "profoundly political purposes" and appealed to those who wanted to raise Irish political consciousness. Garvin also claims that the "more military-minded" among the radical Nationalists greatly welcomed Protestant Ulster's threat of armed resistance to Home Rule. While the European war had contributed to the rising, Garvin believes that it was the arming of the north and counter-arming of the south that was "the accelerator of revolution in Ireland". This line was reinforced by Laffan's, *The Partition of Ireland* which argued that the UVF "revived the long-dead Irish tradition of armed, organised and large-scale defiance of governments for political motives". Putting it succinctly, Laffan claimed that Carson "rekindled the fenian flame".

To some extent the list of contributions in F X Martin's (ed), *Leaders and Men of the Easter Rising*, which includes separate essays on Carson and Craig, adds weight to the argument that Carsonism was a major cause of the rising. Martin's own contribution, '1916 – Revolution or Evolution?', describes how the actions of the Ulster Unionists supplied the new dynamism in Irish politics, and notes how the situation was further transformed by the eruption of the European conflict. He also argues that the Gaelic League created the atmosphere for the rising, commenting that "it would be hard to exaggerate the influence" of the League in the rising, but adding that the influence was 'indirect'. He concludes that the Easter Rising only became inevitable when "the seven members of the IRB Military Council led their men at midday on Easter Monday". Martin has written widely on the rising and in his essay, 'The Origins of the Irish Rising of 1916', which appeared in T D Williams's (ed), *The Irish Struggle 1916-1926* (London, 1966), describes the Gaelic League as the greatest single force in "propagating the separatist ideal" among the Irish people. He concludes the essay with the much quoted statistics that despite opposition to British rule in the form of the Gaelic League, the GAA, Sinn Féin, the Irish Volunteers, the IRB and the Citizen Army, less than 1,600 men and women actually participated in the rising. The deception by Clarke and MacDermott of their IRB colleagues is analysed in Maureen Wall's essay, 'The background to the Rising; from 1914 until the issue of the Countermanding Order on Easter Saturday, 1916', which appears in K B Nowlan's (ed), *The Making of 1916: Studies in the history of the Rising* (Dublin, 1969). In her essay for Williams's volume, 'Partition: The Ulster Question (1916-1926)', Wall begins with the perceptive comment that the "Easter rising of 1916 was as much a revolt against the Irish Parliamentary Party as against British rule in Ireland".

David Thornley's essay for Martin's volume, 'Patrick Pearse – the Evolution of a Republican', begins by quoting from L N Le Roux's, *Patrick H Pearse* (Dublin, 1932) which describes Pearse as "possessing all the qualities which go to the making of a saint". This judgement has been savagely reassessed in R Dudley Edwards's, *Patrick Pearse: The Triumph of Failure* (London, 1977) which stresses Pearse's use of Irish history in his writings and his identification with Wolfe Tone and Robert Emmet. She goes on to attack the heroic 'myth' which had built up around Pearse, claiming that his pursuit of martyrdom, and with it the decision to plunge Ireland into an unpopular rebellion, was driven by his failure in life: failure on personal, family and financial grounds. Dudley Edwards's work has subsequently been attacked as 'revisionist iconoclasm' by the anti-revisionist school led by Brendan Bradshaw. This issue was taken up in M Laffan's essay, 'Insular Attitudes: The Revisionists and their Critics', which appeared in M Ni Dhonnchadha and T Dorgan's (eds), *Revising the Rising* (Derry, 1991). Laffan reminds us that for decades "most Irish nationalists regarded the Rising as sacrosanct, immune to criticism or even to serious examination, a model of pure heroism in a world of good and evil",and it was only in the late 1960s that this pattern began to change. This book also contains a very useful essay by Joe Lee, 'In

Search of Patrick Pearse' which attempts a brief reassessment of Pearse's life. Lee claims that Pearse needs to be rescued from both his disciples and detractors, and much of the confusion arises from the contradictions which appear frequently in his writing. He notes that many of the most uncompromising passages may well have been "exercises in reassuring himself". Lee also examines Pearse's doctrine of blood sacrifice, which was less reckless than many have supposed, and argues that he was really working for a military victory in 1916 and desperately hoping for all the arms he could get.

Kee's, *The Bold Fenian Men* offers a good general treatment of the background to the rising, carefully untangling the central role played by the IRB Military Council. He devotes a chapter to the contribution made by Sir Roger Casement, describing Casement's desperate last minute attempt to stop the rising. R McHugh's essay in Martin's volume, 'Casement and German help', describes Casement's success in persuading the Germans to make an official declaration that they would, if victorious in the war, respect Irish independence, but contrasts this with the embarrassing failure to raise an Irish Brigade. A fuller treatment of his life is provided by B Inglis's, *Roger Casement* (Belfast, 1993) which gives a sympathetic, but very moving account, of its subject's life. James Connolly's decision to join the IRB insurrection has been the subject of much historical speculation. Foster's, *Modern Ireland* insists that the Connolly hagiography has failed to explain "how he came round so far and so fast to the theory of nationalist blood sacrifice". Ruth Dudley Edwards's brief biography, *James Connolly* offers as good an explanation as any, claiming that the "retreat of the European socialists, the failure of trade unions to act against a capitalist war, and the success of the Ulster Volunteers in securing partition by threats, all combined to make him despair of achieving without violence the future he had worked for so long".

The response of the British authorities in Dublin in the months and weeks leading up to the rising is examined in L O'Broin's, *Dublin Castle and the 1916 Rising* (London, 1966). He explains in great detail how Nathan, a very able public servant, was caught out by the turn of events. The intelligence system, particularly that of the Dublin Metropolitan Police, had failed to provide accurate information, and this contributed to the complacency shown by the authorities. Politically, Nathan was always ready to listen to Dillon's advice and thus took a cautious approach in his dealings with Sinn Féin. This allowed, O'Broin notes, the Volunteers and the Citizen Army to proceed with their training in spite of strong Unionist pressure to suppress both movements. In particular, Nathan and the Castle authorities seriously underestimated the roles played by Pearse, Plunkett, MacDermott and Ceannt within the IRB movement. Similarly their assessment of Casement as the insurrectionist leader proved a major gaffe. A good account of the role played by women in the Easter rising appears in M Ward's, *Unmanageable Revolutionaries: Women and Irish Nationalism* (London, 1989). Ward notes the differences between the approach of the Citizen Army commanders and the more conservative leadership of the Irish Volunteers in their attitudes to the participation of women, but also highlights the major contributions made by a few formidable female personalities. M Caufield's, *The Easter Rebellion* (Dublin, 1995) gives a detailed description of the events of the rising and quotes the following official figures. These note that 1,351 people had been killed or severely wounded, 179 buildings with a valuation of £2.5 million had been ruined and some 100,000 Dublin citizens, almost one-third of the population, required public relief in the wake of the rebellion.

Chapter 8

The rise of Sinn Féin

The extremely hostile reception which the insurrectionists had received from the citizens of Dublin, as they were being led away by British troops following Pearse's order to surrender, was understandable. Civilians had been killed, property damaged and the lives of Dubliners had been severely disrupted. It can be assumed, moreover, that many of the women who vented their anger on the captured rebels had husbands serving with the British Army on the Western Front. Yet this initial hostile reaction was to change, when the British response to the rising became clear. Martial law had been imposed over the whole country, and Major-General Sir John Maxwell, who had arrived in Ireland just in time to oversee the concluding stages of the rebellion, acted as a Military Governor, suspending indefinitely the powers of the civil authorities. Both Birrell and Nathan resigned, accepting responsibility for the Castle's failure to predict and prevent a rising, but Lord Wimborne, the Lord Lieutenant, was later reinstated after he too had been pressed for his resignation. Maxwell's actions have to be seen in the context of the dire international crisis. Britain was at war, and he was determined to make an example of the ringleaders in an attempt to prevent a further rebellion. Unfortunately, Maxwell was a second rate soldier, whose political judgement and lack of experience in Ireland rendered him manifestly unsuited for what was, in effect, a very delicate task. Ireland's history of suffering at English hands and the general feeling of sympathy for the rank and file who had been led into rebellion by hopelessly misguided, yet patriotic, leaders made the situation delicate. Maxwell's actions, however, showed no understanding of these circumstances.

The British had dubbed the Easter Rising, a 'Sinn Féin Rebellion', obviously unaware of the organisational role played by the IRB. Accordingly, when Maxwell ordered large-scale arrests throughout the country, many of those detained were Sinn Féin activists and sympathisers who had nothing to do with the rising. Although nearly 1,500 of these were released inside a few weeks, nearly 2,000 were shipped to the mainland, where they were held in criminal prisons or in the special internment camp at Frongoch in north Wales. Ironically, it was in these detention centres that less ardent Nationalists came under the influence of more radical comrades who converted them to the principle of resistance to British rule. However, it was Ireland's response to the Dublin courts – martial, established by Maxwell at the conclusion of the rising, which helped to create the conditions for a 'sea-change' in Nationalist opinion. Trials were conducted in secret and executions followed. On 3 May the authorities issued a terse statement announcing that three signatories of the Proclamation, Pearse, Clarke and MacDonagh, had been shot by firing squad at dawn that morning. More such announcements followed over the next nine days. Plunkett, Edward Daly, Willie Pearse and Michael O'Hanrahan were executed on 4 May, and John MacBride met the same fate on the following day. On 8 May Ceannt, Mallin, Con Colbert and Sean Heuston faced the firing squad, and Thomas Kent was executed in Cork. Finally, on 12 May, Connolly and MacDermott were shot in Kilmainham jail. In all, fifteen executions had been carried out and, while all seven signatories had been shot, a number of fairly minor figures, notably Willie Pearse, Patrick's brother, were also executed.

Certainly, the protracted nature of the executions shook Ireland, particularly Dublin, where the secrecy surrounding the trials fuelled wild rumours about the numbers and names of the prisoners who would face the firing squad. The image of blood seeping beneath a closed door exerted a powerful influence on Dublin citizens. A total of 90 prisoners had been sentenced to death, though 75 had their sentences commuted to penal servitude. The most significant of these were Countess Markievicz, whose sentence was reduced because she was a woman, and Eamon de Valera, whose escape from the firing squad was helped by a claim that he was an American citizen. Yet it was British insensitivity and the poignancy of individual cases, which combined to provoke an outpouring of sympathy for the condemned men, as the leaders of the insurrection were transformed into Irish martyrs in the Tone – Emmet tradition. The terminally ill Plunkett was married to Grace Gifford in the prison chapel at Kilmainham on the night before his execution, but the prison authorities refused to allow them to spend any time together. Connolly's execution aroused even more sympathy. Seriously wounded, he had to be stretchered to the execution yard, where he was then strapped to a chair before facing the firing squad. In addition, the authorities were frequently clumsy in their dealings with the clergy who gave Holy Communion to the condemned men. Significantly, all of those executed, with the exception of the fiercely anti-clerical old Fenian, Tom Clarke, received the last rites. Pearse, Plunkett and MacDonagh were, of course, devout Catholics, but even Connolly who had frequently clashed with the Catholic Church also received Holy Communion. Quickly, a cult of the dead leaders developed, which had powerful religious undertones, and there was clearly growing public fascination with the religious piety of those who had nobly faced the firing squad. Requiem Masses attended by large congregations, and frequently followed by emotional processions through the Dublin streets, provided evidence of the change in attitude towards the leaders of the insurrection.

The changing public reaction to the rising also meant difficulties for the IPP. Dillon, who was present in Dublin during the rebellion, had been the first to recognise this. Witnessing the unfolding reaction of Dublin citizens, Dillon, as his biographer notes, had grasped the key political problem, namely, "how to prevent the reaction in favour of the revolutionaries from becoming a reaction against the parliamentarians". While Redmond, who was in London, had been unable to conceal his outrage at the actions of the revolutionaries, but combined this with pleas for clemency, Dillon took a more intransigent line. The uncertainty and tension generated by the extended period of executions led to Dillon's famous intervention in the House of Commons on 11 May 1916 [97]. The speech contained a passionate appeal to the Prime Minister to halt the executions and denounced the secret courts

- martial. He ended by conferring a kind of moral sanction on the insurgents, who had "fought a clean fight, a brave fight, however misguided, and it would have been a damned good thing for you if your soldiers were able to put up as good a fight as did these men in Dublin". Despite Dillon's plea, the executions scheduled for the following day went ahead, but they proved to be the last two. On the night of 11 May Asquith crossed to Ireland and spent a week travelling around the country gauging opinion. Only at this stage did the government urge caution on the military authorities. The cabinet had initially been nervous but had decided on 6 May that Maxwell had to be given discretion in individual cases. His view of the rising was straightforward, namely, that it had been a German inspired plot designed to divert British attention at a critical stage of the war. This inaccurate assessment and the authorities' lack of knowledge about the IRB's role in the planning of the rising had governed Maxwell's thinking.

Dillon's emotional speech in the Commons had also publicly exposed a British atrocity in which Francis Sheehy-Skeffington and two other journalists, Patrick Mackintyre and Thomas Dickson, had been murdered while in custody during the rising. Sheehy-Skeffington, a well known figure in Dublin and a dedicated pacifist, had witnessed the murder of an unarmed Dublin youth by Captain J C Bowen-Colthurst. On the following morning, 26 April, the officer ordered the execution of the three men without any kind of trial, and their bodies were buried in quicklime within the confines of Portobello Barracks. As Sheehy-Skeffington was such a popular figure, the atrocity attracted widespread publicity and triggered a powerful anti-British reaction, especially in Dublin. An inquiry subsequently found Bowen-Colthurst guilty of murder but declared him insane. Even those who had argued for a tough response to the insurrection were embarrassed by the Sheehy-Skeffington case, a fact which Asquith acknowledged during his visit. Certain sections of the British press were also questioning Maxwell's policy of protracted executions, but an open letter sent to the Military Governor by Dr O'Dwyer, the Bishop of Limerick, naturally made more impact in Ireland. O'Dwyer, who had been a ferocious critic of Redmond's wartime support for Britain, was responding to a request from Maxwell to remove priests who had publicly sympathised with the insurrectionists. Describing them as "poor young fellows", O'Dwyer informed Maxwell that the "first intimation we got of their fate was the announcement that they had been shot in cold blood. Personally, I regard your action with horror, and I believe that it has outraged the conscience of the country." This clear indication that a member of the Catholic hierarchy had broken ranks with constitutional Nationalism was significant, but O'Dwyer was the only senior cleric to condone the rising.

There remained one final chapter in the grisly tale of executions. In London at the end of June Casement faced a charge of high treason in a trial which saw the Attorney General, F E Smith, acting as the Crown prosecutor. Smith had, of course, been deeply involved in the extra-parliamentary resistance to Home Rule, an irony which was not lost on Irish Nationalist observers. Casement was found guilty and condemned to death and, despite a powerful campaign to halt his execution, he was hanged in Pentonville jail on 3 August. While Casement had argued during his trial that he had come to Ireland in an effort to prevent the rising, his actions in Germany made his conviction a straightforward task for the Crown. The decision to hang him, however, was a political blunder which further inflamed opinion in Ireland and, significantly, in the United States at a time when the British government was desperately seeking American participation in the war. In Dublin, meanwhile, Asquith had attempted to bring about a return to normality by reintroducing the trappings of civil government. A new Chief Secretary, H E Duke, an undistinguished Conservative lawyer, was appointed on 31 July, while Wimborne resumed his duties as Lord Lieutenant on 9 August, but the administration continued to be dominated by Maxwell. The government's intention was to keep the country quiet, while Britain got on with the war, but Maxwell's presence ensured that anti-British sentiment remained high. Moreover, the failure to determine which prisoners should be granted early release further discredited the administration in Ireland. In short, the continuation of martial law with its consequent arrests, curfews and house-searches, had needlessly embittered Nationalist opinion. Yet from a Westminster perspective the British government's response to the rising had not been draconian. In simple number terms the execution of sixteen Irish revolutionaries, who had conspired with Germany to launch a rebellion, seems insignificant if compared to the decision taken by British authorities to execute 350 of their own troops on the Western Front for alleged cowardice in face of the enemy. The real situation was that there was a strong, but latent, anti-British feeling in Nationalist Ireland, which was ready to surface given the right opportunity. This was revealed in the public's response to the executions. Redmond, whose wartime support for Britain was deeply sincere, could not hope to represent this changing mood. The rising had dealt the IPP a savage blow, as it brought into focus Nationalist Ireland's ambivalence both in its attitude to the war effort and in its support for the wholly constitutional IPP.

The Lloyd George negotiations

On his return from Ireland on 18 May 1916 Asquith decided that a fresh attempt at reaching a political settlement should be made. Clearly, successful negotiations would bolster constitutional Nationalism at the expense of the more radical separatists, but the Prime Minister had an added incentive, knowing that a new political settlement could deflate the fierce international, especially American, criticism which had followed the executions. Lloyd George was selected to conduct the negotiations, because of his Irish experience and his brilliant negotiating skills, and Asquith even suggested that he should become the Chief Secretary. After some hesitation Lloyd George accepted the challenge, but not the Chief Secretaryship, beginning the talks process on 23 May. Mindful of the failure of the round table Buckingham Palace Conference, Lloyd George pursued a different strategy, negotiating separately with the respective Unionist and Nationalist leaders. Lloyd George knew that a settlement would be impossible if Redmond and Carson were brought together. He told Carson, who had resigned from Asquith's Coalition government in October 1915, that Home Rule would be implemented immediately for twenty-six counties, but the remaining six (Antrim, Down, Londonderry, Armagh, Tyrone and Fermanagh) would be excluded. A few days later, on 29 May, Lloyd George wrote to Carson, informing him that the exclusion of these six counties would be permanent. Significantly, Redmond now shifted from the position he had occupied at the Buckingham Palace Conference, as he agreed to the exclusion of the six counties in his discussions with Lloyd George, though this was on the understanding that any such exclusion would be temporary. The Lloyd George negotiations again exposed tensions within the ranks of constitutional Nationalism. Redmond and Dillon had been at odds in their reaction to the rising, and Dillon wanted the IPP to resume open and active opposition at Westminster, rather than pursue the risky option of negotiations, but he was persuaded to suspend his doubts as Redmond staked his political future on the successful outcome of the Lloyd George talks.

Unlike the Buckingham Palace Conference, which had foundered on the question of the area of Ulster to be excluded from Home Rule, Lloyd George had secured agreement on the exclusion of six counties, but the uncertainty over the time limit remained a formidable obstacle. Still, for a few weeks, Lloyd George was able to keep all the balls in the air, leading both Unionists and Nationalists to think that a settlement meeting each of their objectives was possible. His draft proposals, which were contained in a document entitled 'Headings of a settlement as to the government of Ireland' were ambiguous on the question of a time limit, as Lloyd George hoped to leave the crucial decision on whether Ireland was to be permanently or temporarily partitioned to an Imperial Conference at the end of the war. It was against this background that Carson and Redmond sought to win support for the Lloyd George proposals from their respective followings. In addressing a private meeting of the UUC on 6 June Carson gave his backing to the six county partition settlement, arguing that its rejection would do serious damage to the Unionist cause in Britain. Carson had also been influenced by Lloyd George's contention that an Irish political settlement was urgently required to restore harmonious relations with the United States. The British Ambassador in Washington, Sir Cecil Spring-Rice, had informed London on 26 May that the executions had shaken American public opinion. With a Presidential election due in 1916, Westminster feared that Irish-American voters might force a new American government to take a more pro-German line. At the UUC meeting Carson's main opponents were those Unionist representatives from Cavan, Monaghan and Donegal who would be abandoned under the Lloyd George arrangement. These Covenanters had not expected to be sacrificed by a Unionist leadership which had pledged its solidarity in September 1912, and Carson had the unenviable task of meeting them separately. Only then did they give their reluctant approval to six county exclusion. A second meeting of the UUC followed on 12 June and, after several highly emotional speeches, the UUC unanimously authorised Carson to continue the negotiations based on the exclusion of the six counties.

In seeking Nationalist support, Redmond faced an even more difficult task. His chief obstacle was to persuade Ulster Nationalists to back six county exclusion, and to do this he relied on Joe Devlin and his fellow northern Nationalist MP, Jeremiah MacVeagh, who represented South Down. Devlin immediately realised that winning their approval would prove very difficult, as a number of Catholic bishops in Ulster had already stated their implacable opposition to any form of partition. Moreover, Nationalists in Tyrone and Fermanagh, including both lay and clerical elements, had met to co-ordinate resistance to the Lloyd George scheme. As both of these counties had clear Nationalist majorities, the idea of accepting their exclusion from any Home Rule settlement was abhorrent. Still, Devlin enjoyed considerable support among Nationalists in east Ulster where, since 1914, the minority community had partly conditioned itself to the need for temporary exclusion. In the event the issue was to be settled by an Ulster Nationalist conference which met in St Mary's Hall, Belfast on 23 June 1916. The conference was attended by 776 delegates, and Redmond, who chaired the proceedings, had sought the Catholic hierarchy's co-operation to ensure that the IPP leadership would not stand accused of packing the conference with party loyalists. During five hours of bitter debate, in which Redmond struggled to control the rival factions, Dillon was almost shouted down when he rose to speak. Even Redmond, who was received with more respect, could not guarantee a majority for the party line when he issued an ultimatum, warning that if the Lloyd George scheme was rejected, the IPP would be ruined. It took a passionate plea from Devlin to carry the conference, which eventually voted 475 to 265 in favour of the exclusion proposals. He insisted that exclusion would be temporary and during this interim period the twenty-six counties would have a parliament, but the six county area would continue to be controlled by Westminster pending a final settlement [98].

Although Devlin's speech had secured a sizeable majority, he himself knew how bitterly the proposal had been resented. An analysis of the voting figures, moreover, revealed a sharp divergence within northern Nationalism, as the delegates from Tyrone, Fermanagh and Derry City voted overwhelmingly against exclusion. These anti-exclusionists then began to organise opposition to Redmondism in their strongholds west of the Bann. Quickly, this opposition assumed a political character, and the Irish Nation League was launched in Omagh on 5 August 1916. The new movement, which enjoyed widespread support among the Catholic clergy in west Ulster, stood unequivocally against any form of partition. While the Irish Nation League failed to establish itself as a rival political party and was later swallowed up by a rapidly expanding Sinn Féin movement, it did provide a focus for opposition to Redmondism which helped to undermine the IPP in Ulster.

In advocating six county exclusion Redmond had taken a huge political gamble. Although he had secured majority backing at the Ulster Nationalist conference, Redmond's hopes for a successful outcome to the 1916 negotiations were to be dashed, as formidable opposition to the scheme was raised in a different quarter. Lloyd George's manoeuvrings had drawn him into conflict with a number of Conservative ministers in the Coalition government, notably Walter Long, now President of the Local Government Board, and Lord Lansdowne, the Minister without Portfolio. Initially complacent on the direction the negotiations were taking, Long and Lansdowne were to claim, with some justification, that Lloyd George had exceeded his brief by offering Redmond immediate Home Rule for the twenty-six counties. They first voiced their concern at a meeting of a small cabinet committee on 1 June, when they were joined by Asquith, Lloyd George and Lord Crewe, who heard Long argue that the cabinet had never endorsed any proposal which would result in the immediate implementation of Home Rule. At this point Lloyd George raised the problem of the damaging effect which the British response to the Easter Rising had on American opinion. Only an immediate political settlement could, Lloyd George emphasised, guarantee continued American aid to Britain in the form of munitions and other wartime supplies. As the Minister of Munitions, Lloyd George could speak with real authority on this subject, but the argument which stressed the need to placate American opinion did not impress Long. Both Long and Lansdowne had, of course, a particular interest in any future Irish settlement. They had strong links with Southern Unionism and were always prepared to argue the Southern Unionist case at Westminster.

The Easter Rising and the subsequent decision by the British government to seek a fresh political settlement in Ireland had alarmed Southern Unionists, and their concern was expressed to Lloyd George by their chief spokesman, Lord Midleton. On 29 May Lloyd George met Midleton and two other Southern Unionist leaders in an attempt to assuage their fears. Appealing to the patriotism of the Southern Unionists against a worsening international background, Lloyd George insisted that a new Home Rule government for the twenty-six counties would be of a "purely provisional character" until the end of the war. In the interim Southern Unionists would have guaranteed representation in the Home Rule government in addition to the special representation which would be allocated to them in a second chamber. Despite these sweeteners, Midleton remained cautious. He was worried about the provisional nature of the arrangement and correctly guessed that Lloyd George had already promised more in his discussions with Redmond and Carson. Midleton was also greatly concerned by the rise of radical Nationalism in the wake of the rising, but the one development most feared by Southern Unionists was the implementation of a partitionist settlement. By 1916, therefore, Southern Unionists regarded partition as a greater threat than Home Rule, and they were determined to use their considerable influence at Westminster to block any immediate Home Rule settlement based on partition.

Naturally, Midleton also shared his concerns with Long and Lansdowne. Yet while these two were always ready to protect Southern Unionist interests, they were slow to respond positively to the threat contained in the Lloyd George initiative. Lloyd George's strategy for dealing with potential opposition from within the government was to keep the cabinet in the dark during the early stages of the negotiations and then hope to push through the acceptance of immediate Home Rule, when a settlement looked to be within reach. Indeed the failure of Long and Lansdowne to make clear their outright opposition to the proposals at the five-man cabinet committee meeting on 1 June may have encouraged the Minister of Munitions that this was the best strategy, though he was not confident of a successful outcome. It was only after 10 June, when the Lloyd George plan was made public, that Long and Lansdowne launched a sustained attack on the proposals. Long had already been stung by criticism from old Irish colleagues and particularly from HA Gwynne, the editor of the right wing *Morning Post*, all accusing him of betraying the trust of Southern Unionists in complying with the Lloyd George initiative. In a letter to Lloyd George on 11 June, Long acknowledged that he had been slow to see the dangers in the proposals but now warned that he would not give his assent to any agreement which meant the adoption of Home Rule. In his subsequent communications with Lloyd George and other members of the cabinet, Long repeated his contention that Lloyd George had not been authorised to offer immediate Home Rule, a charge he was to make repeatedly. Long was further embarrassed when he received a letter from Carson, which took him to task for his failure to inform the Unionist leader that Lloyd George had made his offer of immediate Home Rule without the cabinet's approval. This sharp rebuke reinforced his determination to undermine the Lloyd George plan.

Long's task was not aided by the discovery that the Conservative members of the Coalition government were not united in opposition to the Lloyd George scheme. Towards the end of June it emerged that they had divided into two camps. While Long and Lansdowne were clearly the principal opponents of the Lloyd George initiative, they enjoyed the solid support of two other ministers, Lord Selborne, the President of the Board of Agriculture, and Lord Robert Cecil, who had just become Minister of Blockade in addition to his duties as deputy Foreign Secretary. In the other camp Bonar Law, Balfour and F E Smith, who had become Attorney General on Carson's resignation, supported the partitionist plan which Lloyd George had outlined to Carson. Another senior Conservative figure in the Coalition government, Austen Chamberlain, sat on the fence, though he was critical of Lloyd George's unnecessarily cavalier approach when the issue was discussed at a cabinet meeting on 21 June. By this stage a serious situation had developed, which threatened danger in a number of quarters. Carson was in an embarrassing position because, having persuaded the UUC to support the permanent exclusion of a six county area, he could not now be seen to block the measure. The Conservative party was in even more difficult straits, as Lloyd George had hatched a scheme with the potential to open a new rift within its ranks. At this critical stage of the war, moreover, Asquith must have feared the resignation of a number of Conservative ministers, which his weak administration might not survive.

With another cabinet meeting scheduled for 27 June, Long and Lansdowne both prepared memoranda which forcefully set out their objections to the immediate implementation of Home Rule. Reading between the lines, it was clear that they believed the Conservative members of the Coalition government had been deliberately kept in the dark and that the proposals were, in effect, a breach of the party truce which had stood since the beginning of the war. They were convinced, moreover, that responsibility for the general state of affairs in Ireland, and the rebellion in particular, rested with the Birrell-led Castle administration, which had been guilty of shocking weakness and criminal neglect. In fact, Long and Lansdowne both gave serious consideration to tendering their resignations, a course which their main supporter in the government, Lord Selborne, had taken on the day before the crucial cabinet meeting. Like Long and Lansdowne, Selborne had been encouraged by Midleton to do everything in his power to thwart the settlement, but his resignation on 26 June, though evidence of his outright personal opposition, did not prove a serious obstacle for the government. Clearly, Long and Lansdowne had the crucial hand to play, and the two refused to dilute their condemnation of the scheme at the cabinet meeting on 27 June. Their opposition, however, was balanced by a Balfour memorandum which argued that the granting of a Home Rule parliament during the war was neither inexpedient nor reckless, but, on the contrary, he urged his colleagues to grasp what he described as a "unique opportunity ... for settling peaceably and permanently the problem of Ulster". Dismissing the concerns expressed by Long and

Lansdowne, Balfour joined with Bonar Law in warning that the rejection of immediate Home Rule would automatically boost radical Nationalism at the expense of the IPP. Bonar Law also reminded his colleagues that the permanent exclusion of a six county 'Ulster' had been the maximum demand made by the Unionists at the Buckingham Palace Conference in July 1914.

With the Conservative party in obvious disarray Asquith, urged on by Lloyd George, seized the opportunity to press ahead with the settlement. He hoped that the establishment of a new cabinet committee, charged with formulating additional safeguards to the Home Rule settlement, which would ensure that law and order was maintained in southern Ireland under British supervision for the duration of the war, would allay Conservative fears. As Lansdowne gave his backing to the committee, it appeared that Long, the main stumbling block to a settlement, could now be isolated. On 5 July Asquith informed the cabinet that Redmond had accepted this condition and, during the discussions which followed, both Long and Lansdowne explained that though they still had many reservations, neither would resign and risk bringing down the government. The Southern Unionists, meanwhile, kept up the pressure, using their contacts in parliament, particularly in the House of Lords, to swing Conservative opinion against the Lloyd George scheme. Although Bonar Law had openly declared his support, a meeting at the Carlton Club on 7 July clearly demonstrated that the party was nervous about the immediate implementation of Home Rule. It was at this point, however, that the ambiguity surrounding Lloyd George's earlier dealings with Redmond and Carson suddenly emerged to create new difficulties. When Asquith informed the House of Commons of the latest developments on 10 July, he seemed to indicate that partition would be temporary. Then, in a speech to the House of Lords on the following day, Lansdowne moved decisively to clarify the issue. Claiming that the proposed legislation would make structural changes to the existing Home Rule Act, Lansdowne stated firmly that the new arrangement would be permanent. He added, moreover, that in order to maintain the rule of law in the twenty-six county area, the government would consider extending the emergency powers given to Maxwell under the Defence of the Realm Act.

Lansdowne's speech killed any hope of a settlement. An outraged Redmond described it as "a gross insult to Ireland", insisting that Nationalists would only consent to partition if they received an absolute guarantee that it would be temporary. It had been on this basis, of course, that Redmond had been participating in the talks. By this point, however, Long, Lansdowne and Midleton all sensed that Conservative opinion was moving decisively in their favour. All of them believed that the government was taking a grave risk by proceeding with such a controversial measure. On 19 July, when the cabinet next met to discuss the issue, it was clear that Long and Lansdowne, both of whom had prepared fresh memoranda for this crucial meeting, were determined to stand firm and thwart the scheme. Both warned against precipitate government action but, in the end, they knew that if they could persuade their colleagues that the exclusion of the six county area should be permanent, then Redmond would break off negotiations. Hence, when Redmond was informed of the cabinet's change of heart, he angrily rejected the new proposal for permanent partition, and the Lloyd George scheme collapsed amid bitter recriminations. The crucial factor had been the opposition campaign mounted by Long and Lansdowne.

Spurred on by their Southern Unionist friends, they managed to exploit the concern within a Conservative party uncomfortable with the prospect of immediate Home Rule, which could be seen as a concession to those who had carried out the rising. Even if the partition problem had been overcome, it was clear that a new political settlement required the endorsement of the Conservative party. To have ignored Conservative fears would, Asquith realised, have caused irreparable damage to the wartime Coalition government.

The collapse of the 1916 negotiations was a disastrous blow for the IPP. Redmond had made further concessions in a desperate attempt to secure the immediate implementation of Home Rule which, he hoped, would rescue constitutional Nationalism and stem the Sinn Féin tide. The failure of the Lloyd George initiative and, more particularly, the circumstances in which the negotiations had broken down demonstrated that Redmond had been, yet again, outmanoeuvred by the Unionists and betrayed by the British government. Clearly, Redmond's influence at Westminster, where they was little appreciation of the risks he had taken, was much weaker than it had been before 1914. Against this background contemporary Nationalists increasingly came to regard Redmond's support for the war, overwhelmingly endorsed after the Woodenbridge speech, as a great mistake. This was a crucial factor in 1916, the year in which the European conflict became a 'total' war. Earlier that year, Britain had been forced to introduce conscription, and there was a growing fear that the government would soon move to extend compulsory military service to Ireland. Indeed, in July 1916, the British Army launched a huge offensive on the Western Front in an attempt to achieve the decisive breakthrough, but the massive infantry attack at the Battle of the Somme only led to enormous casualties. On the first day of the battle, 1 July, the British Army sustained a total of 60,000 casualties, 21,000 of whom died. Significantly, the 36th (Ulster) Division had featured prominently on that fateful day, having 2,000 of its men killed and a further 3,000 wounded. In Ulster, therefore, 1916 marked the year of another blood sacrifice. Unionist propaganda quickly contrasted the Ulster sacrifices on the Somme with the treachery of the German-backed Easter rebels, and this contributed to a hardening of opinion in Britain against Irish Nationalist demands.

The radicalisation of Irish Nationalism

It would be a mistake, however, to write off the IPP as an electoral force. In Nationalist Ireland the five contested by-elections between December 1914 and March 1916 all saw comfortable wins for the party's candidates. Although the UIL machinery no longer worked with its former efficiency, it was clear that Redmond enjoyed majority, if unenthusiastic, support among Irish Nationalists before 1916. The rising and the subsequent debacle of the Lloyd George negotiations dealt the IPP a fatal blow, but the opponents of constitutional Nationalism lacked cohesion and unity of purpose. It was the government's incorrect description of the rising as a 'Sinn Féin rebellion' which began to draw these disparate, and frequently competing, groups together. The rise of Sinn Féin, therefore, was a direct consequence of the Easter

Rising. Still, this was not a simple, quick process, a fact illustrated by the events of the West Cork by-election in November 1916, which saw a victory for the IPP candidate in a three-cornered contest. Previously, the seat had been held by Lawrence Gilhooly, a devotee of William O'Brien's who had remained outside the ranks of the IPP. Although Sinn Féin had benefited from the events of the summer, when separatist feeling had been boosted, firstly, by the sense of betrayal over the Lloyd George negotiations and then by Casement's trial and execution, it was not yet ready to mount an electoral challenge in a constituency where subsequent support for militant Nationalism was to be such a prominent feature.

In the West Cork by-election the IPP candidate, D L O'Leary, was challenged by Frank Healy, an O'Brienite All-for-Ireland League candidate, and an independent, Dr Shipsey, who threw his hat into the ring in protest at the way in which O'Brien had forced the nomination of Healy on the constituency without calling a convention to select a candidate. During the campaign there was savage criticism of Redmond's concession of six counties during the Lloyd George negotiations, while his parliamentary followers were accused of being either "traitors" or a "gang of miserable incompetents". In Healy's words these were "six of the leading business counties that would... help to finance the country", something which Unionists, of course, had long maintained. When the votes were counted the Redmondite, O'Leary, won with a majority of 116 over Healy. O'Brien claimed with some justification that the intervention of Shipsey, the independent candidate who polled 370 votes, had cost the All-for-Ireland League the seat. Although Sinn Féin had not been in a position to field a candidate, newspaper reports claimed that 'the Sinn Féin party' in the constituency was very strong. It was also assumed that O'Brien had nominated Frank Healy specifically to attract the separatist vote in the constituency. Indeed, in September 1916, O'Brien had dismissed the IPP as a political force, predicting that the Irish people would have to look to Sinn Féin for political leadership. The relatively high turnout, with 4,029 of the 5,683 on the register casting their votes, would suggest that O'Brien had achieved his objective of capturing much of the separatist vote. Yet the 1,866 votes polled by O'Leary demonstrated that the IPP could still count on strong party loyalty in spite of all its problems. However, the West Cork by-election threw up another interesting development. On the eve of polling Tomás MacCurtain, the commandant of the Cork Volunteers, who was interned in Reading jail, wrote to the President of the 'Sinn Féiners' in Cork, repudiating the role which Healy had adopted in trying to represent them in the contest. To reinforce this stance the Cork prisoners took out an advertisement in a local newspaper, which stated that "neither Mr Healy nor any of the other candidates for Parliament in West Cork represent the views of either the interned prisoners or Sinn Féin". It is difficult to assess the impact of MacCurtain's intervention but, even though the turnout was high at 71 per cent, the slim margin by which Healy lost could easily have been attributable to a small number of Sinn Féin abstentions. It was also interesting, and a portent for the future, that the interned Volunteers claimed to speak for Sinn Féin [99].

West Cork had illustrated the failure of radical Nationalists to take advantage of the changing public mood and organise a separatist political movement using the Sinn Féin label. A crucial factor in reversing this situation was the release of a large number of prisoners from Frongoch camp and Reading jail in December 1916. Lloyd George had just succeeded Asquith, and one of his first actions as Prime Minister was to order the release of Irish prisoners in time for Christmas. Before this, most of the Sinn Féin activists had been low-ranking members of the Irish Volunteers, but the release of the Frongoch and Reading men, including Arthur Griffith, at last provided the Sinn Féin movement with a semblance of leadership and organisation. Still, when the next by-election took place in early 1917, it was the action of local Sinn Féin activists which proved decisive. The death of J J O'Kelly, the veteran Parnellite, created a vacancy in North Roscommon, a constituency in which separatist feeling ran high. Here, local Sinn Féiners under the direction of the radical priest, Father Michael O'Flanagan, took the decision to run a separatist candidate in the by-election in an attempt to exploit the public's disillusionment with the IPP. When their first choice, Michael Davitt Junior, refused to stand, local Sinn Féiners in the constituency turned to Count George Noble Plunkett, the father of the executed 1916 leader, Joseph Plunkett. This association with the rising undoubtedly helped Plunkett's campaign, though he himself arrived in the constituency only two days before polling. The campaign was amateurish, but it was characterised by the drive and enthusiasm of the Volunteer activists who were working on Plunkett's behalf. Although he stood as an independent without a party label, the voters of North Roscommon were left in no doubt that he represented Sinn Féin [100].

The election took place on 3 February 1917, and Plunkett achieved a convincing victory, winning 3,077 votes to the IPP candidate's 1,708, while a third independent candidate took 687 votes. Plunkett had received support from a coalition of interests including the old Sinn Féin movement, the Irish Nation League and, most prominently, the Volunteers. A number of the men released at the end of 1916, notably Michael Collins, had made their way to the constituency and quickly threw themselves into the campaign, bringing dynamism and energy to the Sinn Féin cause. Indeed the sight of elderly voters being carried through deep snow to the polling booths on the shoulders of youthful Volunteers was one of the most enduring images of the campaign. Another memorable feature was the involvement of the younger clergy who had been mobilised by Fr O'Flanagan to gather support for Plunkett. In terms of policy O'Flanagan ran a largely negative campaign, though he stressed that Plunkett would demand the same freedom for Ireland as those European nations, such as Romania, Czechoslovakia and Serbia, would demand at a postwar Peace Conference. This followed President Woodrow Wilson's speech to Congress on 22 January 1917, which laid down the rights of small nations to self-determination as one of his famous Fourteen Points. From that point an appeal to the Peace Conference for Irish self-determination became a central plank in the Sinn Féin programme.

Plunkett's victory in North Roscommon was crucial to the rise of the new Sinn Féin movement. The by-election had forced the various separatist elements to come together and gave the activists experience in the art of electioneering. Before Roscommon a variety of groups such as the old Sinn Féin, the Gaelic League, the Volunteers, Cumann na mBan and the IRB were all desperately trying to regroup, but they had no clear strategy. Immediately after the by-election victory, however, the leading figures in the separatist movement, including some of those who had just been released, came together in an attempt to secure greater co-operation and agreement on a general programme. The crucial role played by the Volunteers also helped to transform these military men into political figures and, while many of them disliked politics, they realised that it represented the only way forward in 1917. The result was the sudden rise of a radical Nationalist movement, using the existing Sinn Féin organisation, in which Plunkett and Griffith emerged as the leading figures. Although the movement grew quickly, its early progress was hampered by divisions within the leadership. The main problem was Count Plunkett who refused to play the figurehead role envisaged by Griffith, as he worked to become the dominant force in the rapidly expanding Sinn Féin movement. Plunkett's dogmatic, unbending personality first came to light in his quarrel with the Irish Nation League, an organisation which had contributed to his sparkling by-election success. The League's programme was regarded by Plunkett as too moderate and, rather than encourage the Nation Leaguers to unite with the new Sinn Féin movement, he dismissed them as irrelevant. For its part the League disagreed with Plunkett's rigid belief in abstention, because it assumed that the time would soon come when radical Nationalists would have to take their seats at Westminster if they were to mount effective resistance to partition. When he called a convention in April 1917, Plunkett ignored the Irish Nation League because of its stance on abstention [101].

Such an overbearing style alienated many of the bodies which combined to make up the separatist movement. This was clearly illustrated at the April convention in Dublin's Mansion House, which was ignored by many of the separatist delegates invited by Plunkett. By this stage Plunkett was at loggerheads with Griffith, as he attempted to ignore the old Sinn Féin movement, thus repeating his treatment of the Irish Nation League. The two men, who shared an intense personal dislike of each other, disagreed fundamentally on both the character of the emerging separatist movement and the content of its national programme. Plunkett used the convention to announce the formation of an entirely new organisation committed to complete independence, the Liberty League, which would replace the old Sinn Féin network of clubs by operating at grass roots level throughout the country, but Griffith refused to allow his Sinn Féin grouping to be swallowed up by Plunkett's new organisation. A split was only averted when Griffith and O'Flanagan pieced together a compromise which allowed the various Sinn Féin organisations to retain their separate identities, but connected them to a new central body, the 'Mansion House Committee'. This new body, which included supporters of both Plunkett and Griffith, attempted to unite the various factions. Despite this agreement, Plunkett went ahead with the formation of the Liberty League and, for a brief period, Liberty clubs and Sinn Féin clubs vied with each other for supremacy at local parish level. However, this proved to be an unequal struggle and, by the early summer of 1917 the Liberty clubs were swallowed up by the Sinn Féin movement, a fate soon to befall the Irish Nation League, and Plunkett was forced to play second fiddle to Griffith. Sinn Féin had, of course, the advantage of an existing organisation, an efficient central office and two important newspapers [102]. It also enjoyed the crucial advantage of the magical Sinn Féin name, and this proved a significant factor in the separatists' decision to latch on to the old Sinn Féin grouping. Despite the frequent personality clashes among its leaders, the new movement grew rapidly at grass roots level. In July it had 11,000 members and this figure doubled within a month. By October 1917 Sinn Féin claimed to have over 200,000 members in its 1,200 clubs, which indicated that there was a Sinn Féin club in nearly every parish in Ireland. Such a rapid increase can only be attributed to spontaneous local initiative, as the separatist ideal really took hold in Ireland and was translated into practical political organisation.

One of the main factors driving the disparate separatist elements towards unity was the desire to maximise support during elections. A general election would be called immediately after the war but, in the interim, Sinn Féin had further opportunities to demonstrate that it had eclipsed the IPP as the true representatives of Nationalist Ireland. Following North Roscommon a by-election was due in the constituency of South Longford in May 1917. In this contest Sinn Féin decided to run a prisoner who was being held in Lewes jail in the south of England. The nomination of Joe McGuinness was significant, as it demonstrated that the new Sinn Féin umbrella movement would allow the Volunteers to play a prominent role in addition to the larger, but purely political, groupings. However, this was a development which was slow to win the approval of the traditional physical force men who had usually viewed parliamentary politics with contempt. McGuinness, in fact, opposed his nomination, and his view was supported by nearly all his fellow prisoners in Lewes who were, of course, the most senior figures in the Volunteers. Despite this objection, the Sinn Féin organisers, with Collins to the fore, proceeded to canvass for McGuinness, using a poster campaign carrying the slogan "Put him in to get him out", which combined the election contest with the demand for the release of all Irish prisoners. Although McGuinness was a local man, the South Longford by-election on 9 May 1917 was expected to be a closely fought affair.

This was borne out by the result. Following a recount Sinn Féin took the seat with only 37 votes to spare over the IPP candidate. Dillon had taken charge of the IPP campaign, and he made a huge effort to keep the seat in IPP hands. Although Redmond had been shocked by the scale of Plunkett's victory in North Roscommon, he avoided the challenge thrown down by Sinn Féin and left the direction of the by-election campaign to his deputy. Dillon was not helped by the British government's actions, as it had ordered the arrest of prominent Sinn Féin personnel after the North Roscommon contest, a move which increased public sympathy for Sinn Féin. In a memorable attack in the House of Commons on 26 February, Dillon lambasted Lloyd George, accusing his government of "manufacturing Sinn Féiners by tens of thousands" and undermining constitutional Nationalism. If Redmond was complacent, Dillon recognised the importance of the South Longford contest for his party's future. From the constituency he wrote to Redmond: "We have the Bishop, the great majority of the priests, and the mob – and four-fifths of the traders of Longford. And if in the face of that we are beaten, I do not see how you can hope to hold the party in existence". In the event, Dillon's efforts were scuppered by the eleventh hour intervention of Dr William Walsh, the Archbishop of Dublin. On 8 May he issued a statement in the *Irish Independent* which, though it did not specifically endorse McGuinness's candidature, blasted the IPP for its concessions on the partition issue, leaving voters in no doubt about where the cleric's sympathies lay.

Sinn Féin was lucky to win South Longford. The IPP candidate, Patrick MacKenna, had been declared the victor on the first count, but a bundle of uncounted votes was later discovered, which gave McGuinness the seat by 37 votes.

Archbishop Walsh's intervention had been decisive, though some skillful vote rigging by Sinn Féin may have been equally crucial. South Longford was very significant, as it allowed the rapidly expanding Sinn Féin movement to maintain momentum and, simultaneously, it increased enthusiasm among the activists and gave them a greater sense of unity. Again, the South Longford campaign had been notable for the energy and dynamism displayed by Sinn Féin, as a group of Volunteers directed by Collins swooped on the constituency. These by-elections also emphasised the generational gap which had developed in Irish politics. In South Longford it was apparent that most of the younger priests sided with McGuinness, and in the country at large observers noted that the younger men, many of whom had, of course, never voted before and therefore had no party allegiance, followed Sinn Féin. The attractions of a youthful, energetic and dynamic movement as opposed to the older, inactive and unsuccessful IPP were obvious.

After the South Longford victory Sinn Féin received a further boost, when the Lewes prisoners were released and returned to be greeted by an ecstatic Dublin crowd on 18 June 1917. These were the senior surviving figures of the Easter Rising, including Eamon de Valera and Thomas Ashe, and they must have been surprised by the changed mood of the country which was easily discernible. Although many of them were wary of engaging in politics, as had been demonstrated by their opposition to McGuinness's nomination in South Longford, they quickly appreciated that the growing dominance of the Sinn Féin movement in Nationalist Ireland offered a viable alternative to the exclusively physical force struggle for Irish freedom. A new opportunity to develop this strategy appeared immediately after their release from Lewes. A by-election was due in East Clare and Sinn Féin chose de Valera to contest the seat which, ironically, had been held previously by Willie Redmond, the younger brother of the IPP leader, who had been killed in action at Messines on 7 June 1917. De Valera's campaign in East Clare played on his role in the rising and, in order to emphasise this, he campaigned in his Volunteer uniform. His opponent, Patrick Lynch, came from a well known Clare family, and he enjoyed considerable popularity in the constituency. When the polls closed on 11 July, however, de Valera had won the seat by 5,010 votes to 2,035, a stunning victory which surprised even the Sinn Féin election team. As in the two previous by-election successes, Sinn Féin ran a largely negative campaign, short on specifics and aimed at discrediting the IPP. De Valera was portrayed as one of the Easter heroes who, if elected, would refuse to take his seat at Westminster. The most positive note was the Sinn Féin demand for a place at the postwar Peace Conference, where the party would put Ireland's case for independence.

A new slogan, 'self-determination', had replaced Home Rule, and this again featured prominently in another by-election, when W T Cosgrave, another hero of Easter week, easily won the Kilkenny seat in August 1917 in a straight fight with an IPP candidate. During that August the British authorities exacerbated the IPP's difficulties, as they predictably reacted to the growing radicalism of Irish Nationalism with a new wave of repression which led to the arrest of a number of activists. Among those arrested for making seditious speeches was Thomas Ashe, another senior figure in the Volunteers. With a number of other Volunteer prisoners who were being held in Mountjoy jail, Ashe took part in prison protests demanding special category status as 'political prisoners'. Using the old suffragette tactic, Ashe went on hunger strike in an attempt to pressurise the prison authorities into granting special status. The response by the prison authorities to the hunger strike tactic was to keep the prisoners alive by forcible feeding, a very painful operation which involved the use of a long rubber tube to pump liquid food via the prisoner's mouth or nostrils into the stomach. After one such experience Ashe was taken ill and died a few hours later on 25 September. Sinn Féin had a new martyr and Ashe's funeral in Dublin drew a crowd of nearly 40,000. Collins, who delivered the graveside oration, had made the arrangements, and armed Volunteers flanked the coffin before firing a volley of shots at Glasnevin cemetery.

Ashe's death released a new outburst of popular feeling and, by the autumn of 1917, Sinn Féin had clearly established a momentum which threatened to sweep away the IPP completely. This had been achieved by exploiting the public's rejection of the failed Home Rule ideology and the considerable latent anti-British feeling which had surfaced with the authorities' response to the rising. It had taken time for this transformation to assume a political shape, but the release of the second-rank prisoners, including Collins, from Frongoch camp and Reading jail in December 1916 helped the movement to take advantage of the public's shift towards advanced Nationalism. Internal divisions, notably Plunkett's leadership bid and his attempt to create a new separatist organisation, had threatened to disrupt the movement, but Griffith's temporary stewardship and the dynamic growth of Sinn Féin at grass roots level had created a powerful national movement which can accurately be described as a broadly-based popular front. It was at this point that de Valera moved to establish himself as the dominant figure in the movement. Of course, problems remained. Sinn Féin was an umbrella movement and, at times, there was tension between the various coalition groupings some of which were successful in retaining their separate identities. This was certainly true of the Volunteers and the IRB, whose interests occasionally clashed with the more political separatist elements. The four by-election successes and the spectacular growth of Sinn Féin at grass roots level tended to mask the problems facing the fledgling movement. In reality, the by-election victories were unco-ordinated events in which local Sinn Féin activists combined effectively with the Volunteers. By August 1917, however, the Volunteers were becoming restless and were keen to assert their authority. Their leaders met early that month to plan a Volunteer convention. Among those present at that meeting were Eamon de Valera, Thomas Ashe, Michael Collins, Cathal Brugha, Diarmuid O'Hegarty and Diarmuid Lynch, and they decided to hold the convention at the same time as the Sinn Féin convention in October. Before the convention some local Volunteer commanders began to defy the authorities by organising drilling and political meetings. Parades were held, usually after Sunday Mass, and these acts of defiance led to the arrest of a number of Volunteer leaders including Ashe.

The more prominent role undertaken by the Volunteers, therefore, tended to highlight the differences which existed within the separatist movement. Ashe's death, moreover, had a galvanising effect on the Volunteers, making them even more determined to increase their influence within the Sinn Féin popular front. This posed a new threat to Sinn Féin's unity. To consolidate the gains made during the first half of 1917 the leaders recognised that their aims would have to be more clearly defined, and this meant coming to terms with the differences which had emerged within Sinn Féin. On the surface this appeared as a division between the military and political wings of the separatist movement but, more accurately, it was the clash between republicans and non-republicans which threatened to split the movement. Among the republican faction the most prominent leaders were Collins, Brugha, Rory O'Connor and de Valera himself, and they insisted that Sinn Féin must fight for the republic which had been proclaimed by the leaders of the Easter Rising. The key figure on the non-republican wing was Arthur Griffith who continued to advocate support for the old Sinn Féin constitution which was monarchist. Griffith and his supporters wanted a powerful, independent Irish parliament, but they believed that a republic was unobtainable and that to commit Sinn Féin to the goal of a republic was unnecessary and unrealistic.

These differences threatened to disrupt the Sinn Féin convention, or 'Ard-Fheis', which met in Dublin on 25 and 26 October. Yet a few days before the gathering the Sinn Féin executive met to iron out a number of difficulties. One issue had been settled when Griffith agreed to stand down as President of Sinn Féin in favour of de Valera. This was announced publicly at the Ard-Fheis, and de Valera was unanimously elected with Griffith becoming Vice-President. In addition, a new Sinn Féin constitution was drawn up following a series of Sinn Féin executive meetings in the week before the Ard-Fheis. When a split over the terms of the new constitution looked likely, it was de Valera who produced a compromise formula which both moderates and extremists found acceptable. The new constitution contained the following clauses outlining Sinn Féin's aims: "Sinn Féin aims at securing the international recognition of Ireland as an independent Irish Republic. Having achieved that status the Irish people may by referendum freely choose their own form of Government". This amended constitution obviously favoured the republicans, but it was ambiguous enough to hold together all elements of the separatist movement. Indeed de Valera gave an indication of this ambiguity when, in the course of a long presidential address, he told the Ard-Fheis delegates, "We are not doctrinaire Republicans", a phrase which his opponents subsequently used against him. The new leader recognised the importance of maintaining Sinn Féin unity in the struggle for Irish freedom and, following the compromise meetings, the executive was able to present a united front to over 1,000 delegates who had gathered for the convention.

De Valera's search for unity was further enhanced on the day after the Ard-Fheis, when the Volunteer convention met secretly in Dublin on 27 October. In fact, most of the Volunteer delegates had attended the Sinn Féin Ard-Fheis, and they elected de Valera as President of the Volunteers. In his dual role as President of both Sinn Féin and the Volunteers de Valera symbolised the unity of the reconstructed, broadly-based separatist movement. More specifically, de Valera's dual role further fused together the physical force and constitutional elements, and this proved crucial in the struggle for Irish freedom [103]. Not surprisingly, this development increased the movement's ambivalent attitude to the use of the force. While the Volunteers obviously did not rule out the use of force, others in the separatist movement favoured a return to the form of militant constitutionalism which had proved so successful in the Parnell era. De Valera himself was ambiguous on the need for a physical force strategy and frequently made references to the use of 'moral force' in his speeches. Again, this vague approach made political sense. Sinn Féin was trying to win the support of a public which had previously been IPP supporters but had now rejected Redmond's constitutional and parliamentary strategy. The IPP had been severely wounded by a willingness to compromise its Nationalist principles, as it sought to reconcile its differences with both Britain and the Ulster Unionists. Yet while the people identified with the uncompromising and defiant Nationalism adopted by the new Sinn Féin, few were willing to support another attempt at rebellion. The dramatic rise of Sinn Féin in 1917 demonstrated that the people wanted freedom, though the precise constitutional form which this might take was of little general interest [104]. By the end of 1917 it was also evident that de Valera had emerged as the undisputed leader of the separatist movement. Recent revisionist writing has tended to stress Collins's central role at de Valera's expense, but de Valera was unquestionably the dominant figure in the early years of the new Sinn Féin movement. He was a charismatic leader, a fact illustrated by Griffith's out-of-character willingness to stand aside at the October Ard-Fheis, and to the people he was the personification of the whole separatist movement.

The Irish Convention

One extraordinary feature of de Valera's triumphant campaign in East Clare in July 1917 had been the indifferent attitude to the contest displayed by John Redmond. True, he was having to overcome great personal tragedy with the loss of his brother, but his principal reason for ignoring events in Clare was that whatever political energy he had left was now entirely devoted to the Irish Convention which was due to open later that month. The Irish Convention was another Lloyd George initiative to solve the Irish Question. Although he had replaced Asquith as Prime Minister in December 1916, little attention was given to Ireland until March 1917 when the cabinet discussed the formulation of a new Irish policy. While the dislike of partition was apparent, cabinet ministers acknowledged that any attempt to include Ulster in a new Home Rule scheme was bound to end in failure. Accordingly, when the government made a new offer to the respective Unionist and Nationalist leaders in May 1917, a choice was given between immediate Home Rule for Ireland with the exclusion of six counties or the formation of a Convention of Irish representatives which would try to reach an internal settlement. While Redmond predictably rejected the partitionist offer, he agreed to the summoning of a Convention, and Lloyd George promised to give legislative effect to the Convention's recommendations if 'substantial agreement' was reached within the Convention. The British government had an added incentive to make progress on the Irish Question. In April 1917 the USA had entered the war on the Allied side, and Britain was keen to appease Irish-American opinion, which was still seething from the 1916 executions, and prevent any unnecessary damage to Anglo-American wartime relations [105].

Redmond had already suggested the possibility of a Convention to work out a political settlement in private discussions with both party colleagues and certain members of the Coalition government. This guaranteed IPP support for the Convention, but the reaction of Ulster Unionists to the new Lloyd George proposal was less predictable. After some discussion they agreed to participate in the Convention, but only because they were assured that no party would be bound by the Convention's decisions. Carson's personal support for the Convention proved crucial, when the Ulster Unionist Council met to debate the issue on 8 June. He persuaded other Unionists that they should attend the Convention to secure Ulster's position and to fight for safeguards to protect the Southern Unionist minority in the twenty-six counties. The Southern Unionists, for their part, had already expressed a willingness to take part in a Convention provided they were given adequate representation. This decision was reached following a meeting of the Irish Unionist Alliance on 1 June when Midleton, their leader, persuaded his fellow Southern Unionists that they had more to gain then lose by participating in the Convention. Midleton and his closest Southern Unionist supporters were convinced that a radical change in their thinking was essential, and they had been gradually moving to this position since the outbreak of the war. The 'Midletonites' had, by this stage, decided that some form of Irish self government was inevitable and, in such circumstances, 'Realpolitik' dictated that they should use all their influence to get the best deal possible for Southern Unionists. This meant, of course, that they would have to establish common ground with Redmond's constitutional Nationalists, an outcome which might achieve the dual purpose of producing a workable settlement and, simultaneously, undermining the radical Nationalism of Sinn Féin which Southern Unionists regarded as a serious threat. Not all Southern Unionists, however, were ready for such a new departure, as a significant number remained opposed to any tampering with the Union.

After considerable debate on the size and composition of the new body, the Irish Convention held its first meeting in Trinity College Dublin on 25 July 1917. Its total membership was 95 and this was comprised of 52 Nationalists, 26 Ulster Unionists, 9 Southern Unionists, 6 Labour representatives and 2 Liberals. The Convention elected Sir Horace Plunkett, an ex-Unionist MP who had graduated into the ranks of constitutional Nationalism, as its chairman. By virtue of their numbers Nationalists obviously dominated the Convention, and they enjoyed the benefit of a strong team led by Redmond and Devlin. The Southern Unionists, who were to work closely with Redmond's Nationalists, were headed by Midleton, while Hugh Barrie and George Clark, both prominent business figures, led the Ulster Unionist representatives. A crucial drawback, however, was Sinn Féin's refusal to send representatives to the Convention. Griffith had demanded that any such new body should be democratically constituted and have the power to declare Irish independence, conditions which ensured that Sinn Féin would remain outside the Convention, but this did not come as a surprise to the Lloyd George government. Still, among the 52 Nationalists who did attend, two could be described as advanced Nationalists. These two, Edward MacLysaght and George Russell, the poet A E, were known to be sympathetic to Sinn Féin and, while they did not represent the party, it was assumed that through them, though they both subsequently resigned, a line of communication to Sinn Féin might be kept open. The absence of Sinn Féin and the unwillingness of the Ulster Unionists to play a full and constructive part in the proceedings proved to be insurmountable obstacles for the Irish Convention.

During the Convention's early meetings suspicion and a lack of trust were clearly evident between the Ulster Unionists and the Southern Unionists, a development which merely emphasised their growing divergence since 1913. The Ulster Unionists had acted independently in the Home Rule struggle, and they now demanded the clean cut of six counties, arguing that this territory should not be controlled by any parliament in Dublin. In these early debates, moreover, their unconstructive silence exasperated both the Southern Unionists and the Nationalists. The Southern Unionists, by contrast, forcefully raised their objections to partition, while conceding that some form of Irish self government would be acceptable. They realised that the majority of people in Britain regarded Home Rule as a foregone conclusion, but they were primarily motivated by the twin-edged fear of partition and the domination of a southern parliament by Sinn Féin. They had been impressed by Redmond's obvious loyalty and his unswerving commitment to the British war effort, and they recognised that bolstering constitutional Nationalism was their best defence against Sinn Féin. The strategy which Southern Unionists hoped to adopt during the Convention was to play the role of conciliators, maintaining close relations with both the Ulster Unionists and the moderate Nationalists, but such a balancing act proved impossible to sustain. Their co-operation with Nationalists enraged the Ulster Unionists, though it was apparent that even before the Convention met the two Unionist groups were suspicious of each other. The Southern Unionists were ideally suited to playing a constructive role, and Plunkett observed that their attitude had generated considerable goodwill. Evidence of this positive approach appeared in November 1917 when the Convention became bogged down on the contentious issue of fiscal control, but Midleton produced a compromise in an attempt to hold the competing factions together. The Ulster Unionists had wanted Westminster to retain its control over fiscal matters, but Nationalists insisted that fiscal control had to be transferred to a Dublin parliament. Midleton's formula was to give Dublin control of internal taxation while allowing Westminster to retain control over customs duties. Redmond and the more moderate Nationalists seemed willing to accept this compromise and, during December, there was some indication that a settlement was within reach.

The following year, however, proved to be a dismal one for those who had staked so much on the outcome of the Irish Convention's deliberations. The divisions between the two Unionist groups became more pronounced, and this contributed to a subsequent split within Southern Unionism itself. The constitutional Nationalists also became bitterly divided. Many of the Nationalist representatives at the Convention were unhappy with Midleton's fiscal compromise and did not wish to surrender control of customs duties to the imperial parliament. At the beginning of 1918 the Southern Unionist leader decided to seize the initiative as he pressed for an agreed settlement. Accordingly, Midleton travelled to London to meet Lloyd George and received an assurance from the Prime Minister that if the Southern Unionist compromise scheme received widespread support in the Convention, with only the Ulster Unionists dissenting, then the government would act on the agreement and give it legislative effect. The ball was now in Redmond's court. He had to decide whether to throw in his lot with the Southern Unionists and abandon an Irish parliament's right to levy its own customs duties, or to stand firm and hold out for fiscal autonomy. Having committed himself to the politically dangerous Convention process, Redmond favoured making one final concession in a desperate attempt to secure a settlement, even though he must have harboured serious concerns about Lloyd George's guarantee to give such an agreement government backing. Redmond revealed his position in a speech to the Convention on 4 January, when he emphasised the sacrifices Nationalists were willing to make in the search for a settlement and criticised the Ulster Unionists for their negative attitude and policy of obstruction. A brief interlude followed to allow the various groups time for consultation. Redmond, who was unwell, withdrew to County Wicklow and did not have any contact with his colleagues for ten days. When he returned to Dublin for the crucial debate in the Convention on 15 January, he discovered that Devlin and Bishop O'Donnell, two of his closest and most trusted senior colleagues, had decided to oppose the Midleton compromise. Devlin and O'Donnell had consulted with Dillon and together they had agreed that the surrender of fiscal autonomy was one concession too far. Such a move, they argued, would leave the IPP at the mercy of Sinn Féin and, in these circumstances, Lloyd George would not fulfil his promise to support the Convention agreement. When Redmond discovered that Devlin, O'Donnell and the other Catholic bishops in the Convention were against him, he withdrew his support for the compromise.

The episode marked a humiliating personal defeat for Redmond who announced bitterly that he could no longer be of service to the Convention. Without general agreement the Convention was doomed, adding to the list of failed Irish initiatives by various British governments. All the parties now became more intransigent and the debates became more heated. Although Lloyd George made a number of attempts to break the deadlock by holding personal interviews with several of the delegates, the two problems which had dogged the Convention – Ulster and fiscal control – could not be resolved. With the Convention unable to reach agreement, three conflicting reports were finally submitted in April 1918. The majority report, which was approved by 44 to 29 votes, was supported by the Southern Unionists and the more moderate Nationalists. They had achieved consensus by agreeing to postpone a decision on the ultimate control of customs and excise. The 29 delegates who rejected this compromise consisted of 18 Ulster Unionists and 11 Nationalists, and each of these groups submitted their own minority reports. The more advanced Nationalists had included fiscal autonomy in their report, while the Ulster Unionists restated their demand for exclusion.

Unlike the Southern Unionists, the Ulster Unionist delegates attending the Convention kept in close contact with the party's rank and file in the north to ensure that Ulster Unionist unity was maintained. On the other hand, Midleton's support for a new departure and his readiness to embrace Irish self government had placed a considerable strain on Southern Unionist unity. While he was able to hold the Southern Unionist delegates in the Convention together, opposition to Midleton was developing elsewhere. On 20 February a group of irreconcilable Southern Unionists met in the Shelbourne Hotel in Dublin. Here the opinion was voiced that the Union was not a lost cause and that Midleton's acceptance of self government was reckless folly. Those present then formed themselves into a new body known as the Southern Unionist Committee. The members of the Southern Unionist Committee were frequently referred to as 'Callers' following their famous call which appeared in the press on 4 March 1918, demanding that all Unionists should reiterate their conviction that the only hope for Ireland lay in the maintenance of the Union. The Callers tried to persuade the Executive Committee of the Irish Unionist Alliance to block Midleton's Convention policy but, while they failed to achieve this, they later took control of the Irish Unionist Alliance, and a split with the Midletonites followed.

The Southern Unionists had played the dominant role in the proceedings of the Irish Convention. They had tremendous self confidence and a number of their delegates, principally Midleton and Dr John Henry Bernard, the Church of Ireland Archbishop of Dublin possessed undoubted ability. The more imaginative, pragmatic and liberal Southern Unionists had already altered their views on the Home Rule question, and Redmond's attitude to the war greatly eased their traditional fear of Nationalism. The Easter Rising had temporarily shaken many Southern Unionists, but the subsequent rise of Sinn Féin convinced them that some form of self government was inevitable and, in these circumstances, they should make common cause with moderate Nationalists. The 1916 Lloyd George negotiations, moreover, reminded all the interested parties that Southern Unionists feared partition more than Home Rule. It was the establishment of the Irish Convention which gave these liberal Southern Unionists the opportunity to put their new ideas into practice. Yet their willingness to accommodate moderate Nationalism and reach agreement with the IPP on the shape of a new Ireland opened up divisions within the movement which accelerated its decline. The situation was not helped by the actions of the Ulster Unionists who interfered by urging the Southern Unionist irreconcilables to stand firm in the defence of the Union, but later abandoned them to their fate in a Sinn Féin dominated Irish Free State. In general, Midleton's group was primarily made up of those with large British interests, either in business or land, who could accept Home Rule and try to become influential in a new Ireland. If this did not work out to their satisfaction, they could withdraw to the mainland. Their opponents in the Southern Unionist Committee, on the other hand, largely consisted of those whose land and business interests were confined to Ireland. They genuinely feared Home Rule, believing that only the Union could safeguard their future. Therefore, while the Convention demonstrated the influence of Southern Unionism, it also marked a significant stage in the movement's decline. The war had obviously weakened the movement, and many Southern Unionists regarded the Irish Convention as their last real chance to influence the outcome of a lasting Irish political settlement.

Having personally experienced two failures with Westminster-directed attempts to negotiate an Irish settlement, Lloyd George had turned to the idea of a conference of Irishmen in the hope that they might produce an acceptable formula which his government could then turn into legislation. In truth, the Irish Convention never stood much chance of success. The Ulster Unionists remained implacably opposed to any form of Home Rule and refused to play a constructive part in the proceedings. In a desperate attempt to find a solution Redmond was prepared to give up fiscal autonomy, but this drew him into conflict with his closest colleagues in the constitutional Nationalist movement. Redmond was ill, and he died on 6 March 1918, knowing that he had failed to deliver Home Rule. The failure of the Convention, moreover, dealt another savage blow to the reputation of the IPP. Again, Redmond had been prepared to make further concessions for no political gain. Sinn Féin, by contrast, had denounced the Convention as a futile exercise, even claiming that it was the result of a shabby arrangement between Lloyd George and Redmond to con the Irish people. It stood to gain from the Convention's failure to produce workable constitutional proposals. In a sense, therefore, the IPP had been squeezed between uncompromising Ulster Unionists and advanced Nationalists [106].

Sinn Féin triumphant

In rejecting Redmond's concession on the control of customs, Dillon and Devlin had attempted to preserve the IPP for a final showdown with Sinn Féin. On the other hand, the emergence of a united Sinn Féin party gave de Valera the opportunity to supplant the IPP as the sole representatives of Nationalist Ireland. By the end of 1917 Sinn Féin had developed into a powerful national movement with a widespread grass roots following and a coherent, if not very specific, political strategy. Yet this did not guarantee the movement victory at the postwar general election. In spite of all its problems, the IPP could still mount an effective challenge, and this was demonstrated as the old party won three successive by-election victories in the early part of 1918. Admittedly, circumstances in each of these contests favoured the IPP, but their collective impact had a sobering effect on de Valera and temporarily halted the Sinn Féin bandwagon. Two of these by-elections, South Armagh and East Tyrone, were held in February and April 1918 respectively. In these Ulster seats the IPP was still strong and it could rely on the AOH to provide electoral muscle. It was significant, moreover, that both of these constituencies lay within the archdiocese of Cardinal Michael Logue, who had been an outspoken critic of Sinn Féin. In the South Armagh division the IPP's Patrick Donnelly defeated the Sinn Féin candidate, Dr Patrick McCartan, by the comfortable margin of 2,324 to 1,305 votes. Polling had taken place on 1 February. The by-election had been fiercely contested and there were violent clashes between the Hibernians and the Volunteers which demonstrated that in Ulster, at least, the IPP had remained active at grass roots level. A strong organisation had, of course, been essential in order to resist previous aggressive electoral challenges mounted by Unionists. In the East Tyrone contest, for which polling had taken place on 4 April, Sinn Féin's Sean Milroy, an old associate of Griffith's, polled 1,222 votes to the IPP's 1,802 votes. T J S Harbinson was the new MP.

Even though the younger clergy in both constituencies sided with Sinn Féin, Logue's support for the IPP must have acted as a counterweight. More significantly, both contests were dominated by the partition issue, as the constitutional question was pushed aside. The IPP's selection of Harbinson to fight the East Tyrone seat was critical, as he had voted against the Lloyd George partition proposals in June 1916. To Catholic voters in Ulster, moreover, it seemed that on the crucial issue of partition Sinn Féin offered no alternative to the IPP. If anything, the IPP's pledge to carry on the fight against partition at Westminster appeared more attractive than the Sinn Féin policy of abstention which risked allowing the partition argument to go by default. At this point de Valera's personal thinking on Ulster was fairly simplistic. During the South Armagh by-election campaign he had described the Ulster Unionists as "a rock in the road", which might have to be blasted out of Sinn Féin's path. The Ulster

Catholic voters, whose immediate concern was the partition question, were obviously not won over by de Valera's physical force rhetoric, but the Sinn Féin leader's views on the Ulster situation were to evolve considerably over the next few years. The other by-election took place in Waterford on 22 March following the death of John Redmond. In another straight fight with Sinn Féin his son, Captain William Redmond, took the seat by 1,242 to 764 votes. Clearly, the Redmond family still enjoyed substantial loyal support in a constituency which they had represented since 1891. While special circumstances existed in each of these constituencies, the three successive defeats temporarily shook Sinn Féin and offered some encouragement to the IPP.

However, any possibility of an IPP recovery was shattered by the conscription crisis in April 1918. The Germans had launched a massive offensive on the Western Front and this created a sudden shortage of manpower in the British Army. Conscription had existed in Britain since January 1916, and the cabinet now turned to Ireland to produce the 150,000 men it urgently required. Although the Americans had repeatedly warned that the extension of conscription to Ireland would cause grave difficulties, the urgent need for reinforcements forced the cabinet to give serious consideration to the conscription issue at the beginning of April 1918. In cabinet the Conservative and Unionist members were adamant that conscription should be introduced immediately. Lloyd George hesitated momentarily. The authorities in Dublin had informed him that huge numbers of troops would have to be sent to Ireland in order to enforce conscription, but Sir Henry Wilson, the army's Chief of Imperial General Staff, urged the Prime Minister to press ahead. On 10 April he introduced a Military Service Bill which gave the government the power to impose conscription on Ireland by Order in Council without further debate, whenever it was deemed appropriate. At the same time, Lloyd George gave an undertaking that a Home Rule measure would be introduced before conscripts were enrolled in the hope that this would make conscription acceptable to Nationalists. The crisis which followed demonstrated the government's extraordinary naivety and its complete failure to understand the Nationalist psyche.

Parliament dealt rapidly with all stages of the bill and, by 16 April, it was passed by the House of Commons. During the debate Dillon, the new IPP leader warned the government of the consequences, pronouncing that "All Ireland will rise against you", before leading his party from the House. Back in Ireland the IPP joined with Sinn Féin as the old party flung itself into the anti-conscription campaign. On 18 April a conference was held in Dublin's Mansion House at which all shades of Nationalist opinion joined in condemnation of the conscription measure. The Mansion House Conference was attended by Sinn Féin and IPP leaders as well as Labour representatives and William O'Brien, the leader of the dissident Nationalist All-for-Ireland League. The conference delegates supported an anti-conscription pledge, which had been drafted by de Valera, promising "to resist conscription by the most effective means at our disposal". The pledge was signed by huge numbers of supporters outside church doors on the following Sunday and, on 23 April, a one day general strike was called which paralysed economic life everywhere in the county outside Belfast. The strength of feeling on the conscription issue was unmistakable as Nationalist Ireland was energised in a way that even superseded the reaction to the

1916 executions. The clear beneficiary of this development was Sinn Féin. A party truce emerged as leading Sinn Féiners and Nationalist MPs shared public platforms to denounce the government's action. While it was true that Dillon was as vehemently opposed to conscription as de Valera, the public had to weigh Sinn Féin's consistent denunciation of Irish participation in the war against the IPP's earlier support for Britain. In these circumstances the people naturally turned to Sinn Féin for leadership in the battle against conscription [107].

Significantly, in spite of Logue's caution, the Catholic Church was in the vanguard of the anti-conscription campaign, and the bishops, meeting at Maynooth, issued a signed statement in which they claimed that the Irish people had a right to resist conscription "by all means that are consonant with the law of God". The Catholic hierarchy's association with Sinn Féin during the course of the anti-conscription campaign conferred a new respectability on the movement. Unlike the other Nationalist leaders, de Valera never felt in awe of the bishops, and this helped him to establish personal dominance over the all-party anti-conscription campaign. Moreover, this bonding between Sinn Féin and the Catholic hierarchy put an end to claims that Sinn Féin was led by a bunch of dangerous and unpredictable revolutionaries who might plunge Ireland into another open rebellion. Such charges had been causing concern among the Sinn Féin leaders. They were particularly keen to distance themselves from the frequent comparisons with the Bolsheviks who had just seized power in Russia. Their new relationship with the Catholic Church accomplished this. An indication that Sinn Féin was generally accepted to be leading the fight against conscription came when the County Offaly seat became vacant that April. The IPP withdrew its candidate, and Sinn Féin's Patrick McCartan was returned unopposed. Looking at the broader picture, the conscription crisis had unleashed a great sense of anger in Nationalist Ireland which alarmed the government. As a result, Westminster shelved its plans for the early implementation of conscription. Sinn Féin co-ordinated resistance to conscription, articulating the people's feelings and symbolising the public spirit of defiance against British injustice. The anti-conscription campaign, and the partnership between the Catholic Church and the Sinn Féin movement which it produced, removed any lingering questions about Sinn Féin's moral suitability to represent the Irish people. Although the government never implemented compulsory military service in Ireland, the legislation remained in place, allowing Sinn Féin to exploit this background threat of conscription for most of 1918. The conscription crisis, moreover, could not have come at a better time for Sinn Féin. Coming on the back of three successive by-election defeats, the anti-conscription campaign gave Sinn Féin a new lease of life and guaranteed victory over the IPP at the postwar general election [108].

In May the British authorities compounded their error by ordering the arrest of leading Sinn Féin figures. A new Viceroy, Lord French, had replaced Wimborne on 11 May, and he was determined to make his mark with a tough new approach. On the night of 17 May the authorities rounded up the entire Sinn Féin leadership, with the notable exceptions of Brugha and Collins. The latter knew of the authorities' plans to arrest the Sinn Féin leaders and, knowing the publicity value of having Irish political leaders incarcerated unfairly in British prisons, Collins ensured that the individuals concerned would be in locations where the police could expect to find them. On the following morning French issued a statement, claiming that a 'German plot' had been uncovered. Sinn Féin was alleged to be conspiring with Germany, though the authorities never produced any evidence to substantiate their claim that treasonable communication had taken place. In any case 73 Sinn Féin leaders were arrested and deported to England. These included de Valera, Griffith, Plunkett, Cosgrave and Countess Markievicz. The effect of the arrests, and the public's belief that the German plot was a fabrication by the authorities only intensified opposition to British rule and won further sympathy and support for Sinn Féin. Again, Sinn Féin was able to turn this to its electoral advantage. A by-election was due in East Cavan and, though Dillon hoped to avoid a contest, Sinn Féin was determined to run a candidate. The party truce, which had been forged during the conscription crisis, was abandoned in May, as canvassing began in the constituency. Sinn Féin nominated Griffith, still a prisoner in Gloucester jail following the German plot arrests, and the Volunteers worked enthusiastically for his election using the old slogan "Put him in to get him out". When polling took place on 21 June, Griffith was elected by 3,785 to 2,581 votes. Clearly, the conscription crisis and the German plot had worked to Sinn Féin's advantage, and further government crackdowns only consolidated Sinn Féin's supremacy.

On 3 July French issued a proclamation which declared Sinn Féin, the Volunteers, Cumann na mBan and the Gaelic League to be dangerous organisations. Their meetings were declared illegal and the government threatened to prosecute those attending such gatherings. Even hurling matches were banned, as the authorities stepped up their attack on the separatist movement. In spite of political arrests, Sinn Féin continued to expand, attracting new members and organising a campaign of passive resistance to British rule. Public indignation at the government crackdown manifested itself in a variety of ways. Hundreds of public meetings were held that summer and, on one August Sunday, 1,500 hurling matches were played, as Sinn Féin and the GAA defied the government ban. RIC officers frequently turned up at these meetings to record the names of the main participants but, inevitably, they were given a hostile reception. At the same time, the government proclaimed certain counties, particularly in Munster, as it sought to curb the activities of the Volunteers. It was during this period that Michael Collins came to assume a key role within both the military and political movements. With most of the Sinn Féin leadership in English jails, Collins was busy helping to reorganise the Volunteers while playing his part in directing political opposition to Britain, even though he was on the run from the authorities.

However, the Volunteer leaders had to work hard to keep their members focused on purely military matters. In the early months of 1918 the Volunteers had been active participants in a fresh wave of land agitation. There had been food shortages during the winter of 1917-18, and there were rumours of an impending famine if Irish food continued to be exported to England. Sinn Féin now added its weight to the Department of Agriculture's instruction that farmers should till at least ten per cent of their land, and local Sinn Féin clubs divided up grazing land into small units ready for ploughing. This cattle-driving and 'land grabbing' was commonplace in the west, where land hunger remained such a dominant feature of rural society. The Volunteers were prominent in these actions, frequently leading large crowds of interested locals onto grazing ranches which were to be ploughed up in the name of the 'Irish Republic'. The effect of the land grabbing was to win new recruits for Sinn Féin among the rural proletariat, particularly in Mayo, Sligo and Clare where land hunger was so strong. Despite its popularity, Volunteer Headquarters was unhappy at the behaviour of local Volunteers who were acting as social revolutionaries. Land grabbing was deemed to be socially divisive and worked against the separatist movement's desire to represent all sections of Nationalist Ireland. Indeed both the Sinn Féin executive and the Volunteer leadership publicly stated their opposition to land grabbing. On 2 March 1918 Volunteer Headquarters issued an order, forbidding their members to take park in cattle-drives, "as these operations are neither of a national nor a military character" [109].

While the separatist movement rejected social radicalism, it had to contend with the Labour party which threatened to divide the Nationalist vote in a number of constituencies. Labour had demonstrated its power through the stunning success of the one day general strike organised by the ITUC in protest at the conscription threat, but the anti-conscription campaign had also pulled the movement closer to Sinn Féin. De Valera and other Sinn Féin leaders had made various statements, articulating support for improved wages and conditions for workers, but Sinn Féin's social and economic policy clearly lacked working class appeal. In the spring of 1918 the Labour party, encouraged by Thomas Johnson its most able leader, announced its intention to run candidates in the postwar general election. Sinn Féin now turned its fire on the Labour party, but a conference in September confirmed Labour's intention to contest the general election. All through October the Sinn Féin press kept up a sustained attack on Labour's decision. While there was some discussion about an electoral pact which would give Labour a number of Dublin seats, individual Labour leaders were coming under intense pressure to withdraw from the contest. At a special Labour conference on 1 November the party's executive voted by 96 votes to 23 to stand down from the election. This was a surprising decision in view of its earlier pronouncements to participate in the election, and it caused serious long term difficulties for the Irish Labour party. Labour's withdrawal angered the IPP and delighted Sinn Féin which was now able to concentrate its campaign on the national question [110].

Sinn Féin had enjoyed a new burst of energy with the conscription crisis and grew rapidly, particularly in areas where it had not previously been strong. By the end of 1918 Sinn Féin had 1,354 clubs and a burgeoning membership. Yet it was in rural areas that Sinn Féin was strongest, and this gave Labour's decision to withdraw from the general election added significance, as Sinn Féin enjoyed a free run against the IPP in urban constituencies. Clearly, Sinn Féin would enjoy a huge advantage over the IPP in terms of organisational strength. The Volunteers and Sinn Féin clubs provided enthusiastic election workers in contrast to the old UIL organisation which was practically moribund in many constituencies. In such circumstances Dillon had to rely on the press to carry the IPP message, which reminded voters of the many reforms won by the old party and criticised the policy of abstention. Yet even here the IPP was at a disadvantage. A paper shortage restricted the circulation of the *Freeman's Journal*, the party's main organ, to between 20,000 and 25,000 copies, when it could have expected its circulation to be around 50,000. Sinn Féin was also active, selecting candidates for the various constituencies and making detailed preparations for the election. This was in sharp contrast to the apathy and defeatist attitude which characterised the IPP's preparations.

The war ended on 11 November 1918, and polling for the general election was to be held on 14 December. Sinn Féin issued a four-point manifesto [111]. It would abstain from Westminster; it would use "any and every means available to render impotent the power of England to hold Ireland in subjection"; it would establish its own constituent assembly; and finally, it would take Ireland's case for independence to the Peace Conference. The programme had served Sinn Féin well during its period of rapid growth in 1917–18, and it proved irresistible in the general election. When the results were announced on 28 December, Sinn Féin had won 73 seats, the Unionists had captured 26, and the IPP was reduced to only 6 seats. But for an electoral pact in Ulster, the IPP would almost have been obliterated. The parties had agreed on a pact to prevent eight marginal seats from falling into Unionist hands, and Cardinal Logue had the responsibility of allocating the seats. Thus the IPP won North East Tyrone, South Armagh, South Down and East Donegal. The other two IPP victories were in Waterford, where Captain Redmond had a narrow 474 majority over his Sinn Féin opponent, and in the new Falls division of Belfast, where Devlin defeated de Valera by 8,488 votes to 3,245. De Valera had more success in East Mayo, where he defeated Dillon by 8,843 votes to 4,451. In East Clare he was returned unopposed. In fact, Sinn Féin won 25 seats without a contest. Many of these seats were in Munster, but it was a stark illustration of the IPP's low morale that it could not even field candidates in seats which it had previously held.

A crucial factor in the 1918 contest was that it was the first general election held on a universal franchise. For the first time, all men over 21 and all women over 30 had the right to vote, and this increased the Irish electorate from some 700,000 to just under 2,000,000. It seems logical to conclude that many of these first-time voters were attracted to the dynamic Sinn Féin party and cast their votes accordingly. Yet while the extended franchise worked to Sinn Féin's advantage, the party's victory was not just as impressive as the seat returns indicated. In the twenty-six county area Sinn Féin won only 65 per cent of the votes actually cast, though this figure would undoubtedly have been higher if more contests had taken place. Interestingly, many of those who had enjoyed electoral success were languishing in prison, where they had been since the German plot arrests in May 1918. Those arrested, including de Valera who was in Lincoln jail, played no part in the general election campaign which again demonstrated Sinn Féin's organisational strength at local level. One notable Sinn Féin victory came in the St Patrick's division of Dublin, where Countess Markievicz was elected, thus becoming the first woman to win a Westminster seat. Elsewhere Sinn Féin's successful candidates tended to be young men, most of whom were born in the 1880s and 1890s, from fairly successful Catholic middle class families. It was this Sinn Féin elite, together with the Volunteer leadership, which would continue the struggle for independence. The appeal of the mystical idea of an Irish republic had captured the changed public mood.

Historiography

The most interesting assessment of Nationalist Ireland's reaction to the rising can be found in Lee's, *Ireland 1912-85* which challenges the conventional view that the initial response to the rising was almost universally hostile. Using an impressive collection of provincial newspapers, Lee has argued tentatively that public opinion was not reversed, but "simply crystallised by a combination of the executions and better information". Initially, the press saw the rising as a German inspired rebellion or an attempted Bolshevik coup, but perceptions changed quickly once hard news about Easter week began to reach the provinces. This coincided with news of the executions. Historians analysing the reaction in Dublin have, Lee suggests, failed to recognise that much of what passed for 'public opinion' was simply the views of 'articulate' Unionists who "naturally repudiated the rebellion". Lyons's, *Ireland since the Famine* argues that the transformation in Nationalist thinking was due to three factors. Firstly, there was the cult of the dead leaders which was promoted by a succession of religious services. Secondly, the continuation of martial law under Maxwell until November contributed to the growing militant mood. Thirdly, and most significantly, Lyons claims that the continued existence of both the IRB and the Volunteers, both of which had been driven underground, and the formation of new bodies such as the Irish National Aid Association and the Irish Volunteers Dependants Fund provided a "focus for the hatred and bitterness which seemed to grow greater not less as the rising receded into the past". Foster's, *Modern Ireland* highlights the particular significance of the Sheehy-Skeffington murder which, he claims, had an "enormous effect" on the public opinion.

O'Halpin's, *The Decline of the Union* focuses on British political insensitivity in the wake of the rising and notes the damage done to public opinion by the policy of large-scale arrests. Moreover, he claims that many of those interned on the mainland were not at all dangerous, whereas the authorities had granted early release to some well known agitators. In assessing the state of the country in the latter half of 1916, O'Halpin uses RIC reports which described a 'sullen' population, "afraid of conscription, resentful of repression, and dismissive of its parliamentary leaders". Miller's, *Church, State and Nation in Ireland* states that while the Catholic Church was slow to formulate its response to the rising, the public was fascinated by the powerful religious convictions shown by the leaders. Pearse, Ceannt and Plunkett were, he stresses, particularly devout Catholics. A useful analysis of the Catholic Church's role in this period is provided by S Gilley's essay, 'The Catholic Church and Revolution', which appears in Boyce's (ed), *The Revolution in Ireland*. Gilley emphasises that the Easter Rising "confirmed more completely than ever that Irish Nationalism was Catholic". The rising, he argues, had been the outcome of a 'militant Catholicism' in association with Gaelic revivalism. Significantly, Gilley notes that even before the rising, the church was turning against both Irish support for the war and the IPP itself. The most outspoken critic was the Bishop of Limerick, Dr O'Dwyer. Lyons's, *John Dillon* quotes Redmond's reaction to the rising as one of "detestation and horror", and contrasts this with Dillon's more equivocal reaction. He claims that it was Redmond's complete failure to understand the motivation behind the insurrection which was responsible for the gulf between the two men. Dillon was also acutely aware of the disastrous effects which the executions were having and, though he recognised that the 1916 leaders had been misguided, he could not "bring himself to condemn them utterly". Lyons argues forcefully that it was Dillon's background as an agrarian agitator, "very close to the Fenian tradition", which gave him an instinctive sympathy for the insurrectionists. Then, after the rising, he explains how Dillon would have been much happier to swing the IPP onto a path of "open and active opposition" at Westminster, rather than enter into new negotiations.

In his comments on Carson's speech to the UUC on 6 June 1916, when he appealed to Ulster Unionists to support the exclusion of just six counties, D Gwynn's, *The History of Partition (1912-1925)* (Dublin, 1950) describes the Unionist leader's genuine belief that a political settlement was imperative "in the existing war situation". Carson insisted that Unionists had to face hard facts. In the nine counties there were, he said, 900,000 Protestants to 700,000 Catholics, a narrow majority, but, significantly, Unionists held only sixteen seats in Ulster, one less than the Nationalists. Gwynn also examines the opposition of Unionists in the three excluded counties, led by Lord Farnham, and stresses the reluctance with which Unionists reached their decision to opt for a six county settlement, quoting Lord Cushendun's assessment that it was "the saddest hour the Ulster Unionist Council ever spent". An excellent account of Devlin's crucial role in persuading Ulster Nationalists to back the Lloyd George plan can be found in E Pheonix's, *Northern Nationalism: Nationalist Politics, Partition and the Catholic Minority in Northern Ireland 1890-1940* (Belfast, 1994). This is a carefully researched book which provides the definitive account of Ulster Nationalist politics in this period. Pheonix highlights the contrasting strategies pursued by the more pragmatic east Ulster Nationalists and those in west Ulster where the Catholic clergy were particularly active in leading the fight against partition. The formation of the Irish Nation League is also carefully chronicled, though Pheonix notes its failure to spread throughout Ulster, concluding that the League, which only offered "a slightly more aggressive form of constitutionalism", failed to establish itself as a rival Nationalist party.

Long's role in undermining the Lloyd George scheme is analysed in great detail in Kendle's, *Walter Long, Ireland and the Union*. Kendle reveals the tension between Long and Carson, one the previous Unionist leader and the other his successor, and he focuses on the divisions within the Conservative party raised by Lloyd George's offer of partition and immediate Home Rule. The close contacts which both Long and Lansdowne maintained with Midleton and other prominent Southern Unionists are also described. Kendle concludes that Long may have played a crucial role in preventing a split in the Conservative party, but his actions made life more difficult for the moderates in Ireland. In his *Irish Unionism I*, Buckland analyses the reasons for Southern Unionist opposition to the plan, noting that the revival of extreme Nationalism increased their fears. Unlike the Ulster Unionists and the IPP, however, the Southern Unionists, because of their influence within the Conservative party, had a wider range of political manoeuvre, and they used this to great advantage by creating an atmosphere unfavourable to a settlement within the cabinet and by stirring up opposition among the rank and file. The best authority on the 1916 negotiations is George Boyce, and he has written a number of important essays and articles on the topic in addition to various references in his books. Particularly useful are 'How to settle the Irish question: Lloyd George and Ireland, 1916-1921', in A J P Taylor's (ed), *Lloyd George: Twelve Essays* (London, 1971), 'British Politics and the Irish Question, 1912-1922' in Collins's (ed), *Nationalism and Unionism* and, most notably, 'British Conservative Opinion, the Ulster question, and the partition of Ireland, 1912-21' in *Irish Historical Studies*, XVII, No 65 (March, 1970). Boyce describes how Long changed his opinion on the Lloyd George plan after being 'prodded' by Southern Unionists and, thereafter, he was determined to wreck the scheme. He concludes that it was Conservative opposition, not the actions of the Southern Unionists, which ultimately destroyed the settlement plan. Boyce also deals with the influence of the Irish Question in British politics, noting that the failure of the negotiations marked a watershed after which nothing was the same in Anglo-Irish relations. Even during the negotiations, Boyce argues, it was clear that the Conservative party, despite the opposition of its rank and file, had "lost its sharp edge of conviction" in its resistance to Home Rule. In the end, he claims, Asquith chose to force unacceptable terms on Redmond rather than risk the unity of his Coalition government.

The best analysis of the emergence of a united Sinn Féin movement in 1917 can be found in M Laffan's essay, 'The unification of Sinn Féin in 1917' which appeared in *Irish Historical Studies*, XVII, No 67 (March, 1971). Laffan argues that the rise of Sinn Féin falls into three distinct phases. In the first of these, from the Easter Rising to December 1916, the movement lacked real leadership and was unable to take advantage of the new popular mood. This changed with the release of the Frongoch and Reading men in December, and this marks the beginning of a second phase running up to June 1917 when the movement experienced "a dramatic breakthrough", as it finally tapped into the changing popular mood and established itself at grass roots level. In the final phase, from June to October 1917, the Lewes prisoners found "a united, efficient and energetic party awaiting them", and de Valera emerged as the dominant figure in the separatist movement. By late 1917 Laffan claims that Sinn Féin represented "the great bulk of Irish opinion", but unlike other political movements it never faced the task of winning widespread public support, as this had been delivered by the British government. Its main problems, therefore, were internal and this explains the bitter quarrels of the first half of 1917 when the coalition groupings were moulded together. Lee's, *Ireland 1912-1985* describes this unity as "a fragile coalition", which encouraged the leadership to shelve potentially disruptive issues with the inevitable consequence that the social and economic status quo was endorsed.

Garvin's, *Nationalist Revolutionaries in Ireland* draws attention to the impact of generational conflict in Irish Nationalism during this period. In general, young men, particularly farmers' sons, and the younger clergy strongly identified with the political separatist movement, whereas the older generation was slower to turn away from the IPP. A straightforward picture of Nationalist Ireland's conversion to Sinn Féin appears in D Macardle's, *The Irish Republic* (London, 1937). This mammoth book offers a detailed account of the events in the 1916-23 period, but as the author acknowledges that it was inspired by de Valera, who provided the preface, it is not the most objective study of the Irish revolution. Still, it has a wealth of detail and, for this alone, is very useful. An alternative to the de Valera hagiography is provided by T P Coogan's, *De Valera: Long Fellow, Long Shadow* (London, 1993) which casts the revolutionary leader as a Machiavellian figure whose ruthless pursuit of power saw him step over Griffith to become Sinn Féin leader. De Valera had told Griffith that if he challenged him for the leadership, he was certain to lose, but Coogan thinks that this was far from certain. The author is also highly critical of the 'Janus-faced policy' de Valera adopted towards the use of further violence, but this was essential if he was to hold together a separatist movement which had both political and military wings. The story of Ashe's death and an assessment of its impact can be found in R Kee's, *Ourselves Alone* (London, 1976). Describing the funeral, Kee comments on the detailed organisation of the Volunteer units in the presence of the police, adding that a film of the graveside scene was on show in Dublin that same evening. He concludes that the Ashe funeral "testified strikingly to the growing power, both emotional and material, of the new movement".

The most interesting study of this period is D Fitzpatrick's, *Politics and Irish Life 1913-1921: Provincial Experience of War and Revolution* (Dublin, 1977) which discusses the interaction between social experience and political behaviour among a variety of groups. The study focuses on County Clare but, from this, the author can draw generalisations relating to the national movement. Fitzpatrick emphasises the crucial role played by the lower clergy in the rise of the separatist movement, not in the role of leaders but pulled in by local activists to give Sinn Féin the respectability essential to any political movement in rural Ireland. In one sense the movement sought to copy the IPP principle of uniting all Irishmen under one banner. During the East Clare campaign, therefore, de Valera sought votes from all factions, whatever their constitutional views. While he acknowledges that de Valera demonstrated a much keener political sense than Count Plunkett by focusing on the twin policies of abstention and an appeal to the postwar Peace Conference, Fitzpatrick stresses the negative approach of the movement by describing Sinn Féin as "more a mood than an organisation, a repudiation of the old political Nationalism more than a promise to replace it".

R B McDowell's, *The Irish Convention 1917-18* (London, 1970) gives a detailed account of the Convention's birth and life before analysing the reasons for its failure. McDowell argues that Ulster Unionist intransigence and Sinn Féin's non-attendance were major obstacles for any body trying to produce a workable constitutional settlement. The rift which developed between Redmond and his erstwhile loyal colleagues, Devlin and Bishop O'Donnell, is also carefully explained. The Southern Unionist contribution to the Convention is dealt with in Buckland's, *Irish Unionism I* which describes the conciliatory role played by Midleton and his followers in their attempt to reach agreement with the Redmonites. Buckland also shows how Midleton's liberal Convention policy opened up divisions within Southern Unionism itself, and this greatly contributed to the movement's decline. Midleton's opponents, he argues, were drawn from those sections of the landed and business classes whose interests were narrow and centred exclusively in Ireland. Lyons's, *Ireland since the Famine* argues that the Convention had two important consequences. Firstly, it forced Nationalists to realise that Ulster Unionists were not bluffing in their rejection of Home Rule and, secondly, it increased Sinn Féin's advantage over the IPP. Mansergh's, *The Unresolved Question* argues that Southern Unionist influence had waned since the summer of 1916, when the Lloyd George negotiations had broken down, in the author's opinion, on the issue of the future constitutional status of the six county area, which Carson wanted to have permanently excluded but Redmond wanted included in a Home Rule Ireland as soon as possible. The differences between Unionism and Nationalism were again aired at the Convention but, with Sinn Féin hostile on the outside, it was nothing more than a debating forum. Mansergh claims, however, that this partially met Lloyd George's objectives, as it demonstrated to imperial and international interests that the Westminster government was actively pursuing an Irish settlement.

Pheonix's, *Northern Nationalism* looks at the IPP's two by-election victories in South Armagh and East Tyrone during the early part of 1918, concluding that they should not be viewed "as evidence of a major upswing in the fortunes of the Home Rulers". Instead, these by-elections illustrated the significance of the partition issue in the minds of Ulster's Catholic population. Later in the general election, Pheonix records that Devlin apart, the Nationalists had little chance of success in Ulster without a seats arrangement. Sinn Féin's Ulster policy is brilliantly covered in J Bowman's, *De Valera and the Ulster Question 1917-1973* (Oxford, 1982). Noting that both Ulster communities proved "difficult missionary territory" for de Valera, Bowman argues that the Sinn Féin leader initially exhibited "a simplistic perspective on Ulster", which assumed that the Unionist opposition to any form of all-Ireland assembly was really due to British intrigue.

Kee's, *Ourselves Alone* claims that the conscription crisis caused the 'blurring of all Nationalist feeling into a Sinn Féin image', and this view is echoed by Fitzpatrick's, *Politics and Irish Life*. Fitzpatrick also looks at the wave of agrarian agitation which led to cattle-driving and land grabbing in 1917-18. He argues that these activities had genuine socio-economic causes, but then Sinn Féin and the Volunteers decided to hijack the agitation in the way that the IPP used to do. Fitzpatrick notes Sinn Féin's strength at the end of 1918, but qualifies this by arguing that the number of Sinn Féin members in the movement's clubs was not that impressive when compared to the old IPP organisations of the past. The relationship between the Volunteers and Sinn Féin in the period from the Easter Rising to the 1918 general election is described in M G Valiulis's, *Portrait of a Revolutionary: General Richard Mulcahy and the Founding of the Irish Free State* (Dublin, 1992) which reveals how the Volunteer movement was boosted by Ashe's death and stage-managed funeral. Thereafter, Valiulis argues, Sinn Féin and the Volunteers blended or synthesised the constitutional and physical force traditions of Irish Nationalism. She also puts forward an interesting thesis which argues that the importance of the 1916 executions has been exaggerated in explaining the shift in Irish political thinking. It was, Valiulis claims, the actions of Pearse and company, rather than the British reaction to the Easter Rising, which inspired young revolutionaries in the Volunteers such as Richard Mulcahy to fight their "guerrilla war of liberation". Finally, Lyons's, *Ireland since the Famine* analyses the 1918 general election results and concludes that the "lure and glamour of the republic – which, apart from its intrinsic attractions, was the natural focus for the all-prevailing hatred of England – carried everything before it".

Chapter 9
The War of Independence

Sinn Féin's landslide victory proved to be something of an anti-climax. True, the separatist movement had won overwhelming electoral approval for its vision of a free and Gaelic republic, but translating this legal and moral endorsement into practical political change would not be easy. There was to be, of course, an appeal for Irish self-determination at the Peace Conference, but wise heads within the Sinn Féin movement acknowledged that the presence of a British delegation, acting with the authority of one of the senior victorious partners, did not bode well for Irish independence claims. In the period between the announcement of the general election results and the presentation of Ireland's claim at the Peace Conference, moreover, a vacuum developed, allowing the Volunteers, the most active element in the separatist movement, to seize the initiative. Following the rising the Volunteers had been driven underground, and those leaders who were not in prison had the task of reorganising the movement. The leading figure in this development was Cathal Brugha, who had been so badly wounded that he was not put in jail. Mirroring Sinn Féin, the Volunteers enjoyed a boost with the release of the Frongoch internees in December 1916, as the pace of reorganisation was accelerated. Volunteers were particularly active in the 1917 by-election campaigns, and they often provided the inspiration and the initiative in their local areas for many of the Sinn Féin clubs which sprang up that year. Ashe's death in September further galvanised the Volunteers. The Volunteer convention, held in the following month, gave some indication of the movement's intentions, and the elevation of de Valera to the Presidency helped to fuse the political and military wings of the separatist movement. Indeed most of the Volunteers were prominent in Sinn Féin and, though the majority favoured a joint approach by the political and military forces in the quest for Irish freedom, a small minority of Volunteers were unhappy with the movement's political links.

The Volunteer convention also illustrated the extent to which the IRB controlled the military movement. It had been forced to reorganise after the rising but, despite the arrest of its leaders, the clandestine movement managed to retain its influence. At the Volunteer convention in 1917 a number of key IRB personnel were appointed to important new positions in the Volunteers. Most significantly, Michael Collins became Director of Organisation. He had played a crucial role in maintaining the IRB network while in Frongoch, and he was soon to become the President of the IRB's Supreme Council. On the other hand, both de Valera and Brugha, the President and the Chief of Staff of the Volunteers respectively, refused to rejoin the IRB after the rising. De Valera had never been comfortable with the idea of swearing allegiance to a faceless group of men on the IRB executive, and membership of a secret society also ran counter to his strong religious beliefs. Brugha, meanwhile, blamed the IRB's obsession with secrecy for the fiasco of the countermanding orders which had doomed the rising from the outset. Yet in spite of the actions of de Valera and Brugha, real power lay with the IRB men. However, this division between IRB men and non-IRB men among Volunteer personnel sowed the seeds of future strife within the movement.

The growth of the Volunteer movement towards the end of 1917 convinced the Volunteer executive that it should establish a General Headquarters Staff in an attempt to co-ordinate the activities of the various units on a national scale. In March 1918 Richard Mulcahy was put in charge of this new headquarters staff, and he had the task of overseeing the rapid increase in Volunteer membership, which was brought about by the conscription crisis. The threat of conscription had given the Volunteers a new sense of urgency, as the need for a large, trained force to resist the implementation of conscription became paramount. This increased Volunteer activity in the summer of 1918 drew a predictable response from the authorities, and certain districts were proclaimed as 'Special Military Areas' under the Defence of the Realm Act. Soon, parts of Tipperary, Cork and Clare were virtually ungovernable. The Volunteers were becoming more numerous, more confident and more defiant and, in particular areas, they led the opposition to British rule. By imposing military rule in these districts the authorities only increased the local people's sense of alienation. This surge in activity had carried the Volunteers through to the general election in December. Again, with some of Sinn Féin's leaders still in English jails, the Volunteers played a prominent role in the election. Of course, some of the Volunteer leaders had been selected as candidates, and eleven of the twenty members on the Volunteer executive won seats in the election. Naturally, this overlapping of personnel further cemented the political and military wings of the separatist movement, a factor which proved crucial in the struggle for independence.

The opening phase

Training for the Volunteers during 1918 had been along familiar lines, as instructors concentrated on drilling and manoeuvres imitating regular armies. Yet the conflict which developed in 1919 saw the Volunteers switch to the tactic of guerrilla warfare. Concentration on guerrilla warfare was a sensible strategy for the Volunteers to adopt. The defensive tactics and pitched battle formation used during the Easter Rising had proved a military embarrassment, and it would have been foolish for the poorly armed Volunteers to return to such a flawed strategy against, what was clearly, a superior military force. In 1919 the Crown Forces numbered some 38,000 troops in addition to 10,000 armed RIC men spread all over the country. Yet while there had been a good deal of discussion in the jails and internment camps about developing an alternative military strategy which would take account of the military imbalance, Volunteer GHQ was slow to see the merits of guerrilla warfare. Although Sinn Féin's election manifesto had pledged to use "any and every means available to render impotent" British rule in Ireland, Volunteer headquarters did not have a clear plan designed to promote the struggle for independence. Balanced against this, however, was the growing impatience of certain individual Volunteer units whose members were determined to act on their own initiative. This small group of men were keen to engage the Crown Forces and, while they did not initially intend to launch a sustained campaign of guerrilla warfare, this is what emerged as the conflict unfolded.

The first serious action took place at Soloheadbeg in County Tipperary, when local members of the Third Tipperary Brigade led by Seamus Robinson, Dan Breen and Sean Treacy, three men who were destined to play prominent roles in the War of Independence, ambushed two RIC constables escorting a cart carrying gelignite to a local quarry. The Volunteers wanted to seize the policemen's guns and the explosives but, when the RIC men resisted, both were shot dead. The Soloheadbeg ambush is recognised as the opening engagement in the War of Independence, or the Anglo-Irish War as it is sometimes called. From the summer of 1918, however, there had been growing public disorder and frequent Volunteer actions, as members engaged in a series of raids, usually without GHQ sanction, in their attempts to procure weapons. Indeed, in one such incident, an RIC constable lost his life in a scuffle with Volunteers in County Cork. Still, it was the Soloheadbeg ambush which set the precedent for the first phase of the struggle. Uncoordinated and isolated attacks, which were usually staged to acquire arms and ammunition, dominated the opening months of the conflict. The Soloheadbeg attack had not been sanctioned by GHQ which was worried about the impact of such operations on public opinion. True, initial reaction to the Soloheadbeg killings was hostile. Both of the constables were Catholics who had been popular in the district, and their deaths aroused widespread local indignation, with the Catholic Church particularly vocal in its condemnation of the killings. Despite the horror felt locally, the Volunteers involved disappeared, and the reward of £1,000 for help in their capture was never claimed. The government reacted by proclaiming the south riding of Tipperary a Special Military Area, but the coercion of the entire local population was the wrong way to deal with a relatively small number of Volunteer extremists [112].

Although Sinn Féin agitators had been engaged in turning the population against the police, the political mainstream of the separatist movement was uncomfortable with the notion of a campaign of violence directed against the RIC. The politicians feared that incidents such as Soloheadbeg would turn the people against the separatist movement in general. While Volunteer GHQ, to some extent, shared this caution, an early statement of policy on clashes between the Volunteers and the RIC became essential. This appeared in an issue of *An t Óglach*, the Volunteer journal, on 31 January 1919. Describing the Volunteers as the legitimate army of the republic, the article declared that 'a state of war' now existed between England and Ireland and, in that war, "Every Volunteer is entitled, morally and legally ... to use all legitimate methods of warfare against the soldiers and policemen of the English usurper, and to slay them if necessary" [113]. It was clear, therefore, that extremist elements within the Volunteers, who really only operated in parts of Tipperary, Cork and Clare, had seized the initiative and would dictate the direction of the struggle for independence. Rather than controlling local units, Volunteer GHQ frequently found itself running to catch up with events, as local commanders, acting on their own initiative, carried out attacks on the RIC. Yet, while they were occasionally brutal, these operations were few in number and, during the first six months of the conflict, only a handful of policemen were killed.

Still, the campaign against the RIC was taking effect. In April 1919 Dáil Éireann, reviving the old Land League tactic, passed a resolution which called on the Irish people to boycott the RIC. The aim was to prevent new recruits from entering the force while, simultaneously, encouraging existing members to resign. A campaign of social ostracism, supported, when necessary, by Volunteer threats, allowed the people to play some part in the conflict, even though the majority clearly disliked armed attacks on the RIC. The campaign against the RIC became more ruthless with the assassination of District Inspector Hunt in Thurles on 23 June 1919. The attack had taken place on a crowded street in broad daylight and, though there was a public outcry with the church again to the fore, the assailant was never captured. The Thurles attack followed other isolated incidents in which RIC men were killed in Westport, Limerick city and at Knocklong in County Limerick. In August two more constables were killed in County Clare, and the authorities responded by placing the whole county under military rule. This had been their response to each of the earlier incidents, but its effect was counter-productive. Putting large areas in the south and west of the country under military rule did little to hamper the activities of the small number of fanatics who were engaged in the conflict during this initial phase. Moreover, the sense of revulsion which accompanied these early killings rapidly evaporated, as the public found itself suffering under military rule. In Clare, for example, some 7,000 troops were scattered all over the county by the end of August 1919. Fairs and markets were disrupted, houses searched and a curfew imposed, all of which increased the public's sense of oppression while, simultaneously, failing to curb Volunteer activity.

On 7 September another daring Volunteer commander, Liam Lynch, led an assault on an eighteen strong group of soldiers from the Shropshire Light Infantry as they marched to church in Fermoy, County Cork, on a Sunday morning. Most of their rifles were seized and loaded into waiting vehicles but, in the mêlée that followed, one of the soldiers was shot dead. He was the first soldier to be killed in the conflict. At the inquest the jury expressed horror at this outrage but refused to bring a verdict of murder, claiming that the raid had been staged to obtain the rifles and the killing had not been planned. That night infuriated soldiers attacked property in Fermoy, particularly those houses belonging to members of the jury. The publicity given to such acts of indiscipline naturally worked to the advantage of the Volunteers, increasing the level of moral support for their actions. Indeed the publicity given to the operations carried out by a small group of Volunteer extremists helped to increase their control over the population. Another daring, high profile operation took place at Ashtown, County Dublin, on 19 December 1919, when a group of Volunteers ambushed a two-car convoy in broad daylight. Their target was the Viceroy, Lord French, who was fortunate to escape injury. Still, the ambush had a traumatic effect on French who subsequently issued orders for the mass arrest of all known Volunteer leaders and the deportation of those who could not legally be convicted. In all, 57 men were taken into custody, but the Castle authorities did not match this show of firmness. They insisted on strict legal procedures with the result that deportations were delayed while other suspects, much to the military's annoyance, were released.

By the end of 1919 it was clear that cooperation between the police and military was not good. The arrests ordered by French also revealed the astonishing weakness of the RIC's intelligence system. The intelligence at its disposal was often hopelessly out of date, and new information from the public was not forthcoming. Even though the public may not have approved of Volunteer violence, its sympathies were anti-British. The attacks carried out by the Volunteers, moreover, were often excused as the actions of misguided, but patriotic figures, and the tradition, particularly in rural Ireland, of withholding information from the authorities ensured that the guerrilla campaign would not suffer from public opposition. As a last resort, of course, intimidation could be effectively employed to guarantee the public's co-operation. That the Volunteers were winning the intelligence war was due, in no small measure, to the work of Michael Collins, who clearly understood the need to deny the British information if the Volunteers were to have a chance against a much more powerful military force. Collins ensured that the Castle system was infiltrated at every level, but the work of four of his agents in the 'G' (detective) division of the DMP proved crucial to the Volunteers' success in the war of information. These men, Eamonn Broy, James Kavanagh, Patrick MacNamara and David Neligan passed vital information to Collins, identifying those detectives whose work posed a real threat to the activities of the Volunteers [114]. Collins dealt ruthlessly with such figures. He formed an elite assassination unit, the 'Squad', which was composed of a small number of young, dedicated Volunteers whose IRB connections made them fiercely loyal to Collins. The Squad's first victim was Detective Sergeant Harry Smith who was gunned down near his Dublin home on 30 July 1919. A number of other assassinations followed in 1919 and, though they were roundly condemned by the capital's clergy, they achieved Collins's aim of totally disrupting the police's intelligence system.

The second half of 1919 had seen the Volunteers step up their campaign against the police and, during the winter of 1919-20, the RIC abandoned many outlying barracks under increasing pressure from local Volunteer units. While a number of barracks had been vacated during previous periods of tension, notably in the weeks before the 1918 general election, the RIC had returned when the prospect of serious trouble receded. At the beginning of 1920, however, the Volunteers systematically destroyed vacated barracks to ensure that they were not re-occupied. During the first six months of 1920 over 400 such barracks were destroyed. The RIC was becoming a demoralised force, and it was clearly under-strength. New recruits had been attracted in the second half of 1919 due to enhanced pay and conditions, but there were not enough new men to balance the high number of resignations. Significantly, those most reluctant to resign were older men who had served on the force for many years and did not want to lose their pensions. The dangerous nature of the job was rarely cited as a reason for resignation, but it can be assumed that Sinn Féin's political campaign of social ostracism made a considerable impact. Indeed, during 1919, only eighteen policemen were killed in the conflict. The attacks were organised at a local level, sporadic and, apart from the Squad's operations against Dublin detectives, uncoordinated, making it difficult to describe the conflict as a war.

Nevertheless, the campaign mounted by the Volunteers won increasing approval from the general public, as the authorities reacted by placing large areas of the country under military rule. This was, of course, a continuation of the strategy employed in

1918 when public disorder, often arising out of the tension between the Volunteers and the RIC, led to some parts of rural Ireland becoming virtually ungovernable. However, the British approach to the deteriorating situation in Ireland in 1919 was conducted in a haphazard fashion which took little account of prevailing political and security conditions. In general, each Volunteer action was followed by a show of strength which only increased the popular feeling of British oppression. The entire population was being subjected to inconvenience, or a mild form of coercion, which failed to pinpoint the relatively small number of Volunteer extremists engaged in the conflict. Thus the authorities failed to take advantage of the sense of public outrage which followed the killings of RIC men, who were, of course, Irish Catholics, and isolate the extremists. Rather naively, the government viewed the attacks as the work of criminal gangs. A more imaginative political approach, in conjunction with a more surgical security policy, could have drawn the great bulk of the separatists down the constitutional road, leaving the Volunteer activists isolated. Instead the British drifted into a security policy which had no clear military or political objectives.

There were two reasons for this. The general election of December 1918 allowed Lloyd George to continue as head of a Coalition government but, from this point, it was a government dominated by the Conservative party. The Conservatives had won over 330 seats, almost twice as many as Lloyd George's Coalition Liberals. Although the new Chief Secretary, Ian Macpherson, was a Liberal, the cabinet was naturally dominated by Conservatives and included Bonar Law, Curzon and Long, all of whom were to argue in favour of a tough security policy. Differences in cabinet between the Liberals and Conservatives contributed to the drift in Irish policy during 1919. Some Liberal ministers argued that the government should press ahead with Home Rule but, by the time Lloyd George and Bonar Law agreed to the implementation of a new Home Rule scheme in October 1919, neither believed it would be enough to satisfy the Irish. Significantly, it had taken until October for the Coalition partners to agree on the formation of a cabinet committee to consider the Irish Question and recommend the details of a new policy. The second reason for the government's failure to produce a coherent Irish policy in 1919 was its preoccupation with other affairs. Lloyd George and Bonar Law were frequently in Paris attending the Peace Conference and, when he returned to England, the Prime Minister's time was frequently spent dealing with the problems of postwar reconstruction and handling a new wave of industrial strife sweeping the country. There were, moreover, rumblings in other parts of the British Empire, notably in India and Egypt, which demanded government time and pushed Ireland further down the list of priorities. The result was that the government failed to follow a clearly defined strategy and instead relied on mild repression punctured with half-hearted attempts at conciliation. Such a development ensured that unity was maintained between the political and military wings of the separatist movement and, furthermore, it allowed the minority of extremists on the military side to dominate the Sinn Féin movement for the duration of the conflict.

Still, tension did surface within the movement during the War of Independence. Essentially, this was between the political and military elements, though there was also conflict within the military group itself [115]. Disagreement regularly arose over the conduct of the War of Independence, and there was constant friction between the

Volunteers and the Dáil, the constituent assembly established by Sinn Féin in 1919. Coincidentally, the Dáil had its first meeting in the Mansion House on 21 January, the same day as the Soloheadbeg shootings. Most of the proceedings, which lasted for two hours, were conducted in Irish, and only 27 elected Sinn Féin members were present. Another 34 members, including de Valera and Griffith, were in prison, while a further 8 were unavailable for a variety of reasons. A short provisional constitution was adopted, establishing an executive consisting of a Prime Minister (Priomh-Aire) chosen by the Dáil and four other ministers (Finance, Defence, Home Affairs and Foreign Affairs) who were to be selected by the Prime Minister. This was followed by a reading of the Declaration of Independence which linked the Irish Republic ratified by the people at the 1918 general election to the one proclaimed by the 1916 insurrectionists and demanded international recognition of the new Irish state. More idealistic was the unanimous approval given to the 'Democratic Programme', a fairly radical statement of intent on social and economic policy which, it was claimed, was based on Pearse's thinking. It was radical in the sense that it stated, "all rights to private property must be subordinated to the public right", but it was vague on how this aim could be put into practice. In fact, the Democratic Programme had been drafted in its original form by Thomas Johnson, the leader of the Labour party, and then substantially toned down on the eve of the opening Dáil session by a Sinn Féin leadership nervous about its socialist content. It was essentially a document that mirrored other high-minded, idealistic statements which were commonplace in contemporary Europe after the war. The Democratic Programme was not a precursor to an Irish social revolution and, though there was the potential for class conflict in the 1919-21 period based on renewed agrarian agitation, the socially conservative Sinn Féin leadership moved quickly to focus rural Irish minds on the struggle for independence [116].

The other piece of business conducted by the Dáil in this opening session was the selection of a Sinn Féin team, consisting of de Valera, Griffith and Plunkett, to take Ireland's claim for independence to the Paris Peace Conference. Of course, two of those chosen were in jail, and it was left to Sean T O'Kelly, the Dáil's Ceann Comhairle (Speaker), to act as the Irish envoy in Paris. Arriving on 10 February, O'Kelly wrote to the conference leaders informing them that he represented the 'Provisional Government of the Irish Republic', but his letters were ignored. Crucially, President Wilson of the United States considered the future of Ireland to be an internal British problem. In fact, the Irish representatives were snubbed by the conference delegates and, despite all of O'Kelly's desperate efforts through the spring of 1919, it was clear well before the peace treaty was signed that Ireland's claim for self-determination would not be considered in Paris. The appeal to the Peace Conference had been the clearest element of Sinn Féin policy during the 1918 election campaign, and the subsequent failure to have Ireland's case heard in Paris was a serious political setback for Sinn Féin. This forced the leadership to adopt a more militant stance and thus further strengthened the position of the Volunteers.

The political wing of the Sinn Féin movement undoubtedly missed de Valera. When the Dáil first met, de Valera was in Lincoln jail. He had been held there since his arrest for his part in the 'German plot', but he was sprung from prison on 3 February in a daring rescue mission organised by Collins and Harry Boland, a senior

IRB figure who worked closely with Collins. De Valera's escape provided Sinn Féin with a great propaganda coup and, by 20 February, he was back in Dublin, where he informed the movement's leadership of his future political plans. He knew that the initial rejection of Ireland's claims at the Peace Conference had, temporarily at least, blocked that avenue of potential political progress, and he decided, therefore, to go to the United States, where he intended to mobilise Irish-American opinion in support of Ireland's demand for independence. Accordingly, de Valera left for the United States in June 1919 and did not return to Ireland until December 1920, which meant that, for a period of eighteen months during the struggle for independence, the separatist movement had to make do without its leader and most astute political mind. The absence of de Valera for such a prolonged period was yet another factor contributing to the dominance of the Volunteers. He was present at the Mansion House for the second session of Dáil Éireann, which was held on 1–4 April, and he was duly elected Priomh-Aire. Though this was his official title, he soon became known as 'President of the Irish Republic', and this was how he was introduced to American audiences. His first task as President was to appoint a new cabinet, and he immediately raised the number of ministers from four to eight. In addition to himself, de Valera chose Collins (Finance), Brugha (Defence), Griffith (Home Affairs), Plunkett (Foreign Affairs), Cosgrave (Local Government), Markievicz (Labour) and MacNeill (Industries). This second session was attended by 52 members, a figure boosted by the British decision in March to release all prisoners held in English jails and the escape of a number of others from Mountjoy. In this second session de Valera made two important contributions. Firstly, he poured cold water on the Democratic Programme, warning that the priority had to be the overthrow of British rule in Ireland. Secondly, he addressed the growing state of unrest in the country and called for the RIC to be "ostracised socially by the people".

Despite the obvious difficulties, the Dáil cabinet was determined to operate as an underground government and would attempt to construct an effective counter-state. The 1918 general election had given legitimacy to the Dáil's claim to be the *de jure* government of Ireland, but to advance the cause of independence the Sinn Féin leadership realised that it would have to go some way towards establishing itself as the *de facto* government of Ireland. While the Volunteers were edging closer to a strategy of guerrilla warfare, therefore, the political arm of the movement regarded its task in the struggle for independence as the formation of a viable alternative government. Dáil Éireann's third session, which was held on 10–12 April, saw the leadership unveil rather vague plans for resisting British attempts to govern the country. At the same time, there were the usual demands for international, particularly American, support for Ireland's independence claim. Of more practical use was the announcement that the Dáil intended to raise funds in order to carry on the work of the government by issuing bonds for public sale. Initially, a figure of £500,000 was set with the intention that half of this sum would be raised at home with the remainder coming from the United States. Funds were urgently required to pay ministerial salaries, to provide Dáil deputies with expenses, to carry on propaganda work, to finance the Sinn Féin delegation in Paris and to fund the campaign in the United States. As Minister of Finance, Collins took responsibility for the entire organisation of the loan. This included an appearance in a short film about the loan, which was produced by the

Irish Film Company at a cost of £600 and was shown in cinemas all around the country.

Although Dáil Éireann, and de Valera in particular, had created a positive political impression, Sinn Féin had naturally found it difficult to set the wheels of an alternative administration in progress. The aim was to undermine the legitimacy of British rule but, even in April when the Dáil assumed greater significance, the British tended to ignore its activities. Only in September 1919 did the authorities take the decision to suppress the Dáil. When they banned all Dáil meetings, declaring it to be a 'dangerous association', they obviously made it more difficult for Sinn Féin to build an effective, alternative governing body, but they also increased the Irish sense of oppression and made a political settlement less likely. This repeated an earlier government decision of 3 July 1919, when Sinn Féin, the Volunteers and even the Gaelic League were outlawed. Again, this had the effect of weakening the political arm of the separatist movement while, simultaneously, strengthening the military faction. This trend raised questions about Sinn Féin's ability to extend political control over the Volunteers. In theory, the Volunteers were under Cathal Brugha, the Minister of Defence, but there was, in practice, considerable local autonomy with many commanders resentful of political interference. In August 1919 Brugha moved to clarify the relationship between the Dáil and the Volunteers by insisting that every Volunteer had to swear an oath of allegiance to the Dáil. While there was some opposition to the oath, particularly from IRB members, and a good deal of delay before it could be administered in some areas, the oath, in reality, did not achieve Brugha's objective of forcing the Volunteers to accept the authority of the Dáil.

During 1919 Brugha did not play an active role in the conflict, and Collins emerged as the dominant personality in the revolutionary struggle. This was useful, because Collins's dual roles as a Dáil cabinet minister and a member of Volunteer GHQ helped to defuse some of the tension which emerged between the political and military factions. Yet Collins's dominance also created problems. Brugha, his nominal superior, became intensely jealous, and his move, in August 1919, to establish political control over the Volunteers was partly motivated by his desire to limit Collins's influence. He was also furious at the way in which Collins used the IRB to consolidate his power base, and he was determined to reduce the Brotherhood's influence within the Volunteers. While de Valera shared this dislike of the IRB and supported Brugha's plan, they failed to break the IRB stranglehold on the Volunteers. Brugha was further hampered by Richard Mulcahy, his assistant, to whom he delegated much of the responsibility for overseeing the work of the Volunteers. Mulcahy enjoyed a very close relationship with his fellow IRB member, Collins, and both men believed that as the IRB shared the 'aims and methods' of the Volunteers, the activities of the secret Brotherhood could only advance the cause of independence. As Chief of Staff, Mulcahy was realistic enough to acknowledge that Volunteer GHQ exercised little control over the Volunteer units, and he was happy to leave the development of military strategy to those local commanders who were actually engaged in the conflict. Although Volunteer operations were still spasmodic and uncoordinated by the end of 1919, a distinct pattern of guerrilla warfare, organised at local level, had emerged in selected areas of the country.

1920 – year of terror

During 1920 the Volunteers became more commonly known as the Irish Republican Army (IRA). The frequency of operations increased with the focus continuing to be attacks on the RIC. Barracks and police patrols were attacked, leading to gun battles which could last for several hours and, regularly, the trained men of the RIC were successful in repulsing larger numbers of Volunteers. At the same time, the assassination of lone RIC men continued, and this sparked a number of revenge attacks by enraged policemen. All through 1919 police discipline had held firm but, from January 1920, RIC men began to retaliate in a manner which terrorised the local population. The first such reprisal took place in Thurles only hours after an RIC constable had been gunned down. The police took to the streets, firing shots and smashing windows. The houses of local Sinn Féiners were specifically targeted and riddled with bullets, and the offices of the local newspaper, the *Tipperary Star*, had its windows smashed and a hand-grenade thrown through a broken window. Now the Catholic clergy condemned both the IRA operation and the 'orgy of violence' which followed. Thurles had set a pattern of IRA outrages and subsequent police reprisals which changed the nature of the conflict. This handed the IRA the propaganda initiative and extended the movement's control over the population. When police and troops went on the rampage in Cork following the assassination of an RIC District Inspector, their actions were loudly condemned by Tomas MacCurtain, the Lord Mayor and Commandant of the Cork Brigade of the IRA. Then shortly afterwards, in the early hours of 20 March 1920, two men burst into MacCurtain's house, shooting him at point blank range in his bedroom. The local population was in no doubt that responsibility for this atrocity lay with certain officers in the RIC. MacCurtain's funeral drew a huge crowd and was turned into another successful propaganda exercise by the IRA.

In stepping up their campaign the IRA placed an enormous strain on the police. The authorities had already taken steps to find reinforcements in England where recruitment for the force had been under way since December 1919. The first of these new recruits arrived in late March 1920 and by the following month there were 400 on active service in Ireland. As there was a shortage of uniforms, these new recruits wore a combination of police and army uniforms and were, consequently, known universally as the Black and Tans. Most of the Tans were ex-soldiers who had served on the Western Front and were untrained and unsuited for police work. At their peak there were 7,000 Black and Tans serving in Ireland and, significantly, as their strength increased, a growing number of new recruits came from Ulster. A more elite force was also recruited in England during the summer of 1920. By this stage the authorities had serious doubts about the RIC's ability to keep going, but they remained reluctant to send in large numbers of troops, preferring to limit their response to the reinforcement of the police. Accordingly, the Auxiliary Division of the RIC was recruited during the summer, and 500 Auxiliaries were in Ireland by late September. They were ex-officers, who received the generous remuneration of £1 per day, and were, if anything, more ruthless than the Black and Tans. Initially, these recruits were intended to fill the vacancies in the regular RIC but, as the conflict escalated in 1920-

21, an increasing number of these police reinforcements were enrolled.

Both the Black and Tans and the Auxiliaries participated fully in reprisals which had, at least, the tacit support of the authorities. Civilians were shot and property damaged and, as the IRA replied to these acts of retribution with even more terror, the conflict reached new levels of violence. The first major act of indiscipline involving the Black and Tans occurred in Limerick in late April 1920, when they terrorised the city following a drinking spree, firing volleys of shots in the air and assaulting citizens. In the same month a crowd of local people in Miltown Malbay, County Clare, were gathered around a bonfire, celebrating the release of Sinn Féin prisoners, when a joint police and military patrol arrived and began firing shots into the crowd, wounding nine people and killing a further three. By August, creameries, mills and bacon factories were being targeted in a development which caused serious disruption to the local economy. On 22 August one of the largest creameries in Ireland at Knocklong, which is close to Tipperary town but is in County Limerick, was destroyed by RIC men. The city of Limerick suffered again at the end of August when police, angered by the shooting of a District Inspector in the county, damaged property and killed one man. A more notorious incident took place at Balbriggan, County Dublin, in September 1920. A policeman had been shot in the town, and lorry-loads of Black and Tans swept into the town that evening. They terrorised the locals, burning shops and houses and killing two civilians. Only days later similar scenes involving the Black and Tans and Auxiliaries took place in County Clare and County Meath, but the fact that Balbriggan was so close to Dublin focused international attention on the strategy of reprisals [117].

The separatist cause won even more sympathy in international quarters following the death of Terence MacSwiney. He had succeeded the murdered Tomas MacCurtain, both as Lord Mayor of Cork and Commandant of the Cork Brigade of the IRA, and he was arrested in August following a raid by troops on Cork City Hall, where a staff meeting of the Cork IRA was in progress. A number of others arrested, including Liam Lynch, gave false names and, incredibly, were released by the military authorities before they could be interviewed by the RIC. MacSwiney was, however, a well known public figure and, following his arrest, he was sentenced to two years penal servitude and dispatched to Brixton jail in London.

Already, prisoners in Cork jail had gone on hunger strike and MacSwiney began a fast to protest against his sentence. His 74 days on hunger strike gripped the public's attention and the steady decline in his health drew daily comment from the British and international press. The ground swell of sympathy in support of MacSwiney almost caused the cabinet to relent and sanction his release. When he died on 25 October, a wave of public indignation was released both in Britain and Ireland. MacSwiney was another martyr in a now glorious republican tradition, and his funeral in Cork on 31 October was observed as a day of public mourning throughout Ireland. Even more significantly, perhaps, was the display of public grief in London, where thousands lined the streets as the hearse carrying the coffin made its way through the city [118]. MacSwiney was, in a sense, Cork's version of Patrick Pearse, and his noble act of self sacrifice was specifically calculated to serve as an inspiration to the Irish people and to bring international pressure on Britain to force a withdrawal from Ireland. On the day after MacSwiney's funeral Kevin Barry, an eighteen year old medical student, was hanged in Mountjoy prison. He had taken part in a Dublin ambush in which six soldiers had been killed, but had been captured during the engagement. Although there was no evidence that he had been responsible for any of the deaths, a court-martial found him guilty and sentenced him to death. Again, Barry's execution had a profound effect on opinion both in Ireland and Britain, where the Labour party took up the issue in parliament and certain sections of the press attacked the government's policy of repression in Ireland.

These events, however, were quickly overshadowed as the violence surged to new heights in November. This reached a climax on Sunday, 21 November, when Collins, aware that British intelligence agents were closing the net around senior members of the Dublin IRA, sent out assassination units to execute all the agents in one carefully planned operation. Eleven agents were shot dead, as IRA units forced their way into houses and hotel rooms before opening fire on their victims at point blank range. Two Auxiliaries who had been passing one of the houses and had attempted to intervene were also gunned down. Many Dublin citizens were horrified at the callous manner in which the targets had been executed, but any damage done to the IRA's credibility was swiftly cancelled out by the events of that Bloody Sunday afternoon. A gaelic football match was in progress at Croke Park, when Auxiliaries arrived with the declared intention of searching for arms. Undoubtedly, some members of the crowd had handguns in their possession, and a commotion developed in which the Auxiliaries fired recklessly into the crowd. Worse, RIC cadets had been hurriedly dispatched from their Pheonix Park training camp, and these cadets, many of whom were from Ulster Unionist backgrounds, also fired on the crowd. In the end twelve people were killed and a further sixty wounded. That same Sunday night, moreover, two leaders of the Dublin IRA, Dick McKee and Peadar Clancy, both of whom had worked with Collins in the organisation and planning of the Bloody Sunday shootings but had been arrested on the eve of the operation, were, with a third prisoner, shot dead by Auxiliaries in Dublin Castle. The authorities later claimed that the men had been shot while trying to escape, but Dubliners were in no doubt that the killings had taken place following the men's refusal to give the names of those involved in the shooting of the British agents.

The sheer brutality of Bloody Sunday shocked opinion in Ireland and Britain. Yet before the end of November, there was another notorious incident which led to considerable loss of life. At Kilmichael, near Macroom in County Cork, a special IRA unit of 36 men led by Tom Barry staged an ambush on a motorised Auxiliary patrol. After a fierce engagement three members of the IRA column and seventeen of the Auxiliaries lay dead or dying. In his recollection of the event Barry claimed that the Auxiliaries had used the 'false surrender' tactic, whereby the Auxiliaries feigned surrender but then suddenly opened fire on their attackers. The first British officer on the scene noted that a number of corpses had been mutilated by bayonets, a fact confirmed by the doctor at the inquest. Only one Auxiliary survived and, though severely wounded, he made a full recovery [119]. The killings in November 1920 marked the beginning of the final phase of the conflict. The cycle of violence became more intense, as each side responded to the other's actions with even greater brutality. A fortnight after Kilmichael Auxiliaries poured into Cork city centre on the night of 11 December. With a curfew in operation and the streets empty, the Auxiliaries, who had obtained a liberal supply of petrol, set fire to buildings along Patrick Street. Daylight revealed that a sector of the city centre, which included the City Hall, had been destroyed. The burning of Cork was the most spectacular reprisal of the War of Independence and, following a military inquiry, the Auxiliaries were expelled from the city of Cork. A few days after the reprisal the citizens of County Cork were enraged by the murder of two people outside Dunmanway which is in the west of the county. An Auxiliary cadet named Harte had shot dead a young man and a seventy-year-old priest and, though he was found to be insane, the murders caused a wave of revulsion in the county.

The burning of Cork and the Harte murders brought tension between the military and the police to breaking point. General Neville Macready, the General Officer Commanding (GOC) in Ireland, refused to take responsibility for the RIC, the Black and Tans or the Auxiliaries and openly condemned their acts of indiscipline. This friction between the military and the police was a major factor in Britain's failure to implement an effective security policy during 1920. Lloyd George maintained that the Irish situation was a 'policeman's job', arguing that IRA attacks were carried out by criminal elements which he described as 'murder gangs' [120]. This murder gang mentality, together with the cabinet's refusal to recognise that a small war was going on in Ireland, led to the decision to reinforce the police rather than make full use of the army. During 1920, however, the police became increasingly independent and proved difficult to control, and the deployment of the Black and Tans and Auxiliaries greatly exacerbated this problem. When Macready issued instructions to troops forbidding any form of retaliation, Major-General Hugh Tudor, the Chief of Police, refused to issue parallel instructions, arguing that such a course would have a very negative influence on police morale. Tudor had been appointed in May 1920, and Macready had hoped that, with his military background, he would impose strict discipline on his expanding police force. He failed to do so and, instead, with the connivance of both Lloyd George and Winston Churchill, he allowed the policy of 'unauthorised' reprisals to be implemented during the summer of 1920. Clearly, Tudor subscribed to the 'murder gang' theory and, unlike Macready, he showed no political sensitivity, a factor which made a crucial contribution to the failure of Britain's Irish policy in 1920. Tudor overlooked and excused serious acts of indiscipline, arguing that to do otherwise would only increase the level of demoralisation within the police.

The policy of reprisals associated with Tudor was a response to the development of the IRA's guerrilla war strategy in the summer of 1920. At that time special IRA units known as 'flying columns' were established. Each flying column consisted of twenty to thirty full-time guerrilla fighters though, on occasion, they could be much larger. Flying columns were soon operating in Cork, Tipperary, Clare and Limerick, where they moved around familiar territory, billeting on local farms. They staged carefully planned ambushes, such as the Kilmichael attack carried out by Tom Barry's West Cork flying column. To some extent the formation of the flying columns had been forced on the IRA, as the authorities increased their efforts to arrest known Volunteers. This led targeted IRA men to go 'on the run' and, in their eagerness to carry on the conflict and avoid arrest, they grouped together in these flying columns. Only a minority of Volunteers were members of flying columns. The majority continued to be part-timers who worked on their farms and were occasionally mobilised by their local commander. The main tactic employed by the flying columns was the ambush, and it was in response to ambushes that the police carried out reprisals. In theory, the flying columns should have presented the police and the military with a specific target, but the IRA's knowledge of the local terrain gave it an advantage as the flying columns simply melted into the countryside after an operation. The failure of the Crown Forces to come to terms with this new departure saw them rely increasingly on reprisals. While the cabinet disliked the burning of property, certain ministers were prepared to support the shooting of 'suspects'. Of course, this campaign of police counter-terror only increased the public's sense of suffering under intolerable British oppression and turned opinion in Britain against the government's security policy.

Politically, the Lloyd George government was faring no better. The 1920 Government of Ireland Act gave Ireland Home Rule, though this was packaged with partition, but it was clearly too little, too late. The act had emerged from the deliberations of a cabinet committee which had been established in October 1919. Before that the cabinet admitted privately that it did not have an Irish policy, and the 1920 legislation illustrated just how far out of touch the government was with opinion in Ireland. By 1920 Sinn Féin regarded Home Rule as an irrelevance which was not even worth considering as an opening shot in any future political negotiations. The choice of Walter Long, the old Unionist and the cabinet's recognised 'Irish expert', as chairman of the committee ensured that there would be no imaginative, fresh approach. In addition, Sinn Féin's policy of abstention from Westminster meant that, from an Irish perspective, the debate on the Government of Ireland Bill was dominated by the Ulster Unionists. Yet the government believed that constitutional Nationalism remained a powerful force in Ireland, and the offer of Home Rule, with the prospect of an early end to partition, could win a good measure of popular support. Central to this argument was the belief that the vast majority of Irish people were firmly opposed to the IRA's military campaign, and this was the view that guided the Chief Secretary's thinking, as he hoped to marginalise what he considered to be a relatively small number of extremists and then deal with them. Sir Hamar Greenwood had succeeded Macpherson as Chief Secretary in April 1920. Greenwood was certainly not lacking in determination, but he frequently allowed his optimism to cloud reality. When, in July 1920, The Times warned that republicans would use the Government of Ireland Act to strengthen their claim to be the legitimate government of Ireland, as Sinn Féin was "all-powerful, and ... virtually synonymous with the Irish people", Greenwood simply dismissed this view noting that it was too pessimistic. He was convinced that 'respectable Irishmen' were opposed to the IRA and welcomed the presence of the British Army.

Greenwood also became associated with the policy of reprisals, and he constantly voiced his support for Tudor and the police. On his appointment Greenwood appeared to favour toning down coercion, but his attitude hardened in the summer of 1920 as he witnessed the repeated failure of the courts to bring guilty verdicts against captured IRA men. The government's response was to rush through new legislation in August, though it met fierce resistance from the Labour party and some Liberal MPs. The Restoration of Order in Ireland Act (ROIA) introduced new regulations which allowed most offences to be tried by courts-martial. This enabled the authorities to overcome the problem of finding juries which would convict fellow Irishmen, an irony which was not lost on Sinn Féin. On the one hand, the government insisted that the IRA attacks were the work of criminal murder gangs but, on the other, it now resorted to trying these 'civilians' in military courts and abandoned the normal criminal justice system. Only in cases where the death penalty was a likely outcome, moreover, was there to be a proper legal officer present. In such circumstances there were bound to be wrongful convictions and thus more ammunition was given to Sinn Féin's propaganda machine. Although the ROIA gave wide powers to Macready, the military commander, the cabinet stopped short of introducing martial law for the whole country. While martial law was favoured by Macready and had the support of some members of the cabinet, Liberal ministers were reluctant to declare martial law. The legislation gave the authorities the power to arrest and detain anyone suspected of being associated with Sinn Féin and then to try prisoners by courts-martial. Of course, this meant that the bulk of the population were suspects. Public anger at the new regulations was increased by the authorities' use of the Black and Tans and Auxiliaries to seek out and arrest suspects.

Despite all the evidence to the contrary, Greenwood continued to insist that Irish opinion could be won over by the authorities. This ignored the results of the local government elections held in 1920. Elections for urban and municipal councils were held in January while those for the county councils took place in June. The government had delayed giving the go-ahead for the elections and had switched the electoral system from the traditional first-past-the-post method to proportional representation in a calculated attempt to limit Sinn Féin's advantage. The Sinn Féin election campaign in January was also disrupted by the authorities, but the party still managed to poll heavily. In terms of votes Sinn Féin won 87,311, the Unionists 85,932, Labour 57,626 and the Home Rulers 47,102. More impressive was the overall result which left Sinn Féin in control of 9 of the 11 corporations and 62 of the 99 urban councils. Of course, Sinn Féin's real electoral strength lay in rural Ireland and in the June elections the party won control of 29 of the 33 county councils (Tipperary was divided into two ridings). These successes strengthened Sinn Féin's electoral mandate and further weakened British administration in Ireland. The Dáil's Minister of Local Government, W T Cosgrave, instructed councils to impede the Castle administration and to follow the Dáil's direction.

With the help of his deputy, Kevin O'Higgins, Cosgrave worked feverishly to establish an alternative system of local government in the face of determined British opposition. Following the local government elections Greenwood announced in July 1920 that he was withdrawing the annual grants paid to local authorities if the councils refused to recognise the authority of the British government. This action put the entire bill for the damage done by both sides in the War of Independence onto the local ratepayers. Consequently, property owners faced steep rises in their rates bills, a development which drove these generally conservative, wealthier families into the arms of the IRA. Not surprisingly, Cosgrave and O'Higgins faced serious difficulties with local government finance. They tried to levy their own rates but, while this was partially successful in the more prosperous eastern counties, it met stiff resistance in the west where traditional opposition to any form of taxation was strong.

The Ministry of Local government's response was to implement a number of economy measures, all of which made good sense in rural areas where the population was declining. Workhouses were phased out and local cottage hospitals, most of which were half-empty and overstaffed, were closed down and patients transferred to county hospitals. Under Cosgrave's direction, therefore, local government became more efficient and cost effective.

In terms of influencing the daily lives of ordinary people, an equally significant move on Sinn Féin's part was the establishment of the Dáil courts. In an attempt to create an alternative court system Dáil ministers had frequently discussed the advantages of establishing a new justice system which would operate throughout the country, but their grandiose plans were not translated into practical achievements. The Dáil actually passed a decree in August 1919 to set up 'National Arbitration Courts', but they were largely ineffective. Yet from March 1920 republican courts, established by local initiative, began to spring up all over the country, and they immediately won public confidence. Many of these courts went beyond simple arbitration, which was the limit of their powers sanctioned by the Dáil, as they assumed civil and criminal authority. The Dáil desperately tried to catch up with this spontaneous development and, on 29 June, it decided that the new courts could try civil cases. In addition, the Ministry of Home Affairs under the direction of Austin Stack, was given the powers to establish courts having a criminal jurisdiction. Despite the Dáil's eagerness to bring these revolutionary courts under its direction, Stack, who as Minister of Home Affairs had responsibility for justice, proved to be a very poor administrator and an ineffective minister. Thus many of the new courts continued to operate independently with little reference to the Dáil. This was particularly true in the west, where agrarian disputes dominated the legal proceedings, and the courts built on the tradition of the Land League tribunals. Cattle-driving, the division of ranches among landless men and quarrels between neighbouring farmers became subjects for the new courts to settle, and decisions were enforced by the local IRA. By coincidence, some of these disputes in the west indirectly involved the RIC, as one of the force's many duties was to guard cattle owned by graziers who expected to be the target of a cattle-drive. The authority of the courts gained wide acceptance, because they discharged their functions fairly, a fact emphasised by the willingness of Unionist landlords to have cases heard by the Dáil courts. Judges were often drawn from local solicitors or the Catholic clergy, but they ensured that justice was dispensed in an even handed fashion.

Of course, the IRA had a crucial role to play in the new justice system. The campaign against the RIC had led to the withdrawal of the police in many areas, and this created a void which the IRA had to fill. In those towns and villages where a police presence was maintained, bread, beef, butter, milk and fuel had to be commandeered, actions which only increased the hostility of the local population who regarded the RIC as an alien force. Those working as cooks or having any kind of association with the force were intimidated, while women who were friendly with policemen frequently had their hair sheared by local Volunteers. With the pressure on the police mounting, crime was on the increase, and the local population who felt threatened by this trend looked to the IRA to apprehend wrongdoers and deter others from engaging in crime. In June 1920 Mulcahy ordered the IRA to form a police force and it won immediate public approval. In addition to the detection of crime, the republican police took responsibility for the regulation of hours kept by public houses and clamped down on illicit whiskey distilling, a practice which had increased sharply with the absence of the police in many rural areas. Republican police also provided the stewarding at race meetings and Gaelic football matches.

The Dáil had, therefore, achieved notable successes in building an effective counter-state, a development made all the more remarkable by the fact that it was conducted against a background of constant harrying by the police and military. Sinn Féin and the IRA had demonstrated that they could be efficient administrators, not just revolutionaries. This was an important element in the movement's constant struggle to maintain a psychological hold over the people. While the actions of the Black and Tans and Auxiliaries had obviously been counter-productive, Sinn Féin and the IRA could not rely on the unconditional support of the population. The longing for peace and a return to normality exerted a powerful influence in Nationalist Ireland, and Sinn Féin had to work hard to ensure that it maintained its advantage over the British in the propaganda battle. In order to achieve this the Dáil established the *Irish Bulletin*. Making its first appearance on 11 November 1919, the *Irish Bulletin* was issued several times each week and circulated secretly in spite of numerous obstacles. Initially, under Frank Gallagher's editorship, the *Bulletin* concentrated on documenting British acts of aggression, and the wave of reprisals carried out in the second half of 1920 provided the Sinn Féin propaganda machine with plenty of ammunition. Significantly, the influence of the *Irish Bulletin* was also felt in Britain, where excerpts from the news-sheet began to appear in a number of British newspapers including *The Times*. In November 1920 copies of the *Bulletin* were actually circulated in the House of Commons, and such actions helped to turn public opinion in Britain against the Coalition government's Irish policy. By February 1921 Erskine Childers had assumed overall control of Sinn Féin publicity, and the *Irish Bulletin* put more emphasis on challenging government claims that the IRA was nothing more than a 'murder gang'. Thereafter, articles described the IRA as the army of the Irish Republic, which was engaged in a legitimate war against British aggressors.

The final phase

During the final phase of the conflict in 1921 the violence escalated sharply, as both the IRA and Crown Forces suffered increasing losses. Civilian casualties also rose significantly. The figures show that up to December 1920, 177 policemen and 54 soldiers had been killed, while civilian dead, which included IRA personnel, numbered 42. From 1 January 1921 to the truce in July, however, a further 228 policemen and 96 soldiers were killed. The number of civilians killed in the same period was 154. This last figure included IRA men killed in the conflict and those civilians shot either intentionally or accidentally by the Crown Forces. It also included a significant number alleged to have been 'spies', who were shot by the IRA. Clearly, as the figures illustrate, the fighting intensified during 1921. More ambushes, in which the IRA used greater numbers of men, were mounted by the flying columns, as they perfected the art of guerrilla warfare. Major attacks on the Crown Forces took place in Leitrim, Limerick, Longford, Cork, Galway, Kerry, and Mayo, as the IRA extended its operations outside those parts of Munster where it had previously been most active. The British had responded to this upsurge in violence by deploying troops in those rural areas where flying columns were operating. This was partially successful. Large numbers of weapons were uncovered in carefully planned searches, and the flying columns came under severe pressure, frequently having to withdraw to very remote areas. Again, this closer contact between the IRA and the military contributed to the escalation of the conflict.

The city of Dublin also witnessed increasing violence during 1921. Street ambushes on soldiers and policemen averaged about one per day in the first six months of the year, and these were widely reported in both the British and Irish press. Some of the clashes developed into running gun battles in which civilians, including women and children, were caught in the crossfire. Outside the capital civilians were targeted by both sides. Reprisal shootings by Auxiliaries and Black and Tans became an everyday occurrence and an increasing number of civilians were shot by the IRA. As the Crown Forces enjoyed some measure of success during the early months of 1921, the IRA responded with increased ruthlessness. Anyone suspected of colluding in any way with the police or military became a target. A number of businessmen who supplied the Crown Forces were killed but, more often, 'spies' were shot when they were alleged to have passed on information about the IRA to the police authorities. In each case a message was placed on the bodies as a warning to others. Most of those killed as 'spies' had not actually given information to the Crown Forces and were condemned either by 'talk' or by their refusal to co-operate with the IRA. In parts of Munster, moreover, a significant number of those who were shot as 'spies' were killed primarily because they were Unionists. The fact that many of them had been neutral or passive during the hostilities was not enough to save them when the conflict became more brutal during 1921. To some extent, of course, this sectarian development was a reaction to the violence in the north where the Nationalist minority was consistently targeted by both paramilitary and government forces in the 1920-22 period.

Although the IRA had stepped up its operations during the early part of 1921, it stuck to the pattern of guerrilla warfare making the security forces its specific target. The Dublin Brigade of the IRA, however, had given serious consideration to staging more ambitious attacks and, while a number of such operations had been planned, they had to be abandoned due to unforeseen circumstances. On one occasion in February 1921 an attempt was made to lure the security forces into an ambush at the city's Amiens Street railway station where over 160 IRA men were waiting, but the caution shown by the force of Auxiliaries who responded led to the withdrawal of the IRA contingent. De Valera had returned from the United States in December 1920, and he favoured a switch in strategy to a smaller number of more spectacular attacks which, he argued, would give a decisive advantage in the propaganda battle with the British. On 25 May he had his wish granted, when a force of over 100 IRA men entered the Dublin Custom House, the headquarters of local government administration in Ireland, forcing staff to flee from the building. While the Custom House was systematically set ablaze, other units delayed the attendance of the Dublin

Fire Brigade. The eighteenth century building was destroyed, but the IRA force was surrounded by troops and Auxiliaries before they had a chance to escape. In the gun battle which followed six IRA men were killed, twelve were wounded and about seventy had to surrender. The Custom House attack attracted huge publicity, as de Valera had predicted, but the loss to the IRA was a serious blow to morale. Collins was furious that de Valera had used his influence to persuade officers in the Dublin Brigade to mount this high profile attack which had ended in military disaster. The fact that many of the men involved in the Custom House operation had only a few rounds of ammunition enraged Collins who, along with Mulcahy, did not hide his contempt for de Valera's failure to understand the realities of guerrilla warfare.

By the beginning of 1921 much of the south and west of Ireland was under martial law. This put pressure on the IRA, but it also increased the sense of British oppression felt by the population. Proclamations issued in Macready's name warned that anyone found with arms or explosives would face a court-martial and the death penalty. In many localities the use of Sinn Féin prisoners handcuffed to security vehicles in order to deter ambushes became a common sight. With the application of martial law official reprisals were sanctioned, and this usually took the form of burning the property of those suspected of complicity in an ambush. During the first five months of 1921 these official reprisals were carried out at the rate of one per day. In response individual IRA commanders ordered their units to engage in counter-reprisals, warning that for every house burned by the Crown Forces they would burn two Unionist houses in reply. Naturally, this led to a further escalation of the conflict, but the army was enjoying some success in the martial law area. A new system of military intelligence had been established which led to significant arms finds, and the use of foot patrols in rural areas was effective in putting pressure on IRA flying columns. While this pleased Macready, he was still complaining about the police's capacity for independent action in the martial law area and, during 1921, he became increasingly frustrated by police indiscipline. In December 1920, just after the Kilmichael ambush, Auxiliaries stationed at Macroom Castle had issued a 'New Police Order' which warned all male inhabitants of Macroom or those passing through Macroom, that they must not "appear in public with their hands in their pockets". The inference was that such men could quickly produce a pistol and fire on the Crown Forces, and the order ended by stating "Any male infringing this order is liable to be shot on sight".

This kind of proclamation was, of course, a public relations disaster but, during 1921, the authorities were relying on ever increasing numbers of Black and Tans and Auxiliaries to supplement the RIC, and serious breaches of discipline became commonplace. In February 1921 a party of Auxiliaries, while searching a shop near Trim in County Meath, stole £325 worth of food and liquor from the grocery store which they subsequently burned. When Crozier, the commander of the Auxiliaries, arrived in Trim to investigate the incident, he quickly dismissed twenty-one of the Auxiliary Cadets in the local company and placed a further five under arrest to await court-martial. Astonishingly, Tudor, the RIC chief who had overall control, re-instated the men pending a full enquiry. A bitter Crozier resigned a few days later, alleging that the men had only been reinstated when they threatened to make public a catalogue of atrocities carried out by the police in Ireland. Crozier's resignation focused unwelcome attention on the government's policy of repression, and there were loud calls for Greenwood's resignation in the British press. Lloyd George himself did not escape criticism. Only in the previous November he claimed that the Crown Forces had "murder by the throat" in Ireland, as he forecast that by meeting terror with terror, the IRA would quickly be overcome. By the spring of 1921, however, he was forced to reassess this verdict.

The dramatic escalation of the conflict made it necessary for the government to clarify its position on Ireland, and it became increasingly clear that public opinion in Britain was turning against the government's Irish policy. Bonar Law's retirement from the cabinet through ill health in March 1921 certainly allowed Lloyd George to be more flexible in his thinking, and the possibility of bringing hostilities to an end was discussed. Nevertheless, Greenwood remained optimistic, urging his colleagues to finish the job in Ireland. Even more significant, at this point, was the government's commitment to the 1920 Government of Ireland Act which was due to come into effect in the early summer of 1921. Elections for the two parliaments would have to take place and, with Sinn Féin refusing to work the legislation, it seemed that coercion was the only viable policy. This was the depressing background against which the cabinet once again considered the situation in Ireland on 24 May. Although a number of ministers were clearly unhappy at the violence of the coercive approach, the cabinet took the decision to apply martial law throughout the twenty-six counties.

Additional troops were to be dispatched, and it was planned that this extended martial law would take effect from 14 July. Macready had given his opinion that if martial law was to succeed at all, it would have to be ruthlessly applied. Yet the Commander-in-Chief was ambiguous with his assessment. He had earlier revealed his personal belief to a number of cabinet ministers and officials, when he stated that coercion was unlikely to succeed in Ireland. In his memorandum for the cabinet, moreover, he had insisted that the troops under his command could not be expected to endure another winter in Ireland, and this led him to conclude that October 1921 should be the deadline for the achievement of a military victory. Although the cabinet confirmed its backing for full martial law in the twenty-six county area at the beginning of June, there was an obvious lack of enthusiasm and little real conviction. Indeed both Lloyd George and Churchill showed a reluctance to embrace the new security strategy, as they repeated their earlier pronouncements that the Irish problem was 'a policeman's job'.

Yet the crucial factor in determining British policy in the summer of 1921 was the clear shift in public opinion in England against the government's reliance on coercion. The violence had reached an unacceptable level and criticism of the government was mounting. Writers and intellectuals loudly condemned reprisals, and the press denounced the government's failure in Ireland. Only the right wing Morning Post stood firm, as it called for an all out assault on the IRA, but this brought little comfort to the beleaguered Coalition government. The Labour party established its own commission which travelled to Ireland to investigate the situation, and its report, published on 29 December 1920, was scathing in its criticism of the government. Asquith and his Liberal followers, meanwhile, pressed the government to seek a political settlement by offering Sinn Féin dominion status, but Lloyd George remained opposed to conciliation. By early 1921, however, the worsening state of affairs in Ireland made Coalition Liberal MPs very uneasy, and a growing number withdrew support for the government. Outside parliament two pressure groups, the non-party Peace with Ireland Council and the Trades Union Congress, demanded reconciliation with Ireland and turned the moral screw on the Coalition government. On 6 April a letter from the Church of England bishops was published in *The Times*, deploring indiscriminate reprisals and urging the government to conclude hostilities and reach a negotiated settlement with Sinn Féin [121].

While the necessary military preparations were under way, the cabinet was, by mid-June, anxious about both the public and parliamentary reaction to the extension of martial law. Although the Conservative members of the Coalition government were generally opposed to negotiations and in favour of continuing with repression, Lloyd George was hesitant, but he sniffed an opportunity created by the intervention of Jan Smuts, the South African Prime Minister who had arrived in London in June 1921 to attend the Imperial Conference. The influential Smuts saw the deteriorating situation in Ireland as a threat to the British Empire, and he urged the government to abandon coercion and take a more positive approach by considering a new political settlement for the twenty-six counties. He argued that the establishment of the Northern Ireland parliament gave the government a pretext for such a change in direction, and he proposed that the King should use the occasion of his speech at the opening of the Belfast parliament on 22 June to issue a plea for peace. Lloyd George had repeatedly stated his unwillingness to negotiate with Sinn Féin, but these past assurances were now outweighed as he considered the imminent prospect of draconian martial law which, his military advisers had warned, could not guarantee victory. Clearly, the political will to carry on with coercion was evaporating and, in these circumstances, the Prime Minister judged that the time was right for negotiations. Moreover, the British public's very favourable reaction to the King's Belfast speech was also significant, as it allowed Lloyd George to open negotiations without the appearance of a personal climbdown [122].

The King's gesture had drawn the British side towards a truce, but there was no guarantee that Sinn Féin would follow suit. Despite the government's public stance, peace 'feelers' had been emanating from London since the end of 1920, but the Sinn Féin leadership was wary of the government's proposals and refused to consider either the surrender of weapons or the dilution of the demand for a republic, both of which had been suggested by the British. De Valera's return from the United States on 23 December 1920 appeared to present an opportunity for the ending of hostilities. He had played no part in the development of the IRA campaign, and this led progressive elements in Britain to view him as a political rather than a military leader. While de Valera wanted to take charge of any negotiating process involving Sinn Féin, he had other more immediate problems to tackle. Towards the end of 1920 the administration of the Sinn Féin counter-state had clearly been losing vitality, as the British stepped up their campaign of repression. The Dáil's Ministry of Home Affairs was much less influential, and this was best illustrated by the decline of the Dáil courts. In other areas the Department of Local Government was suffering huge financial difficulties which greatly reduced its effectiveness. De Valera worked hard to halt this trend and, though he gave the underground government a new focus, the Dáil clearly suffered from the growing British security presence. This was apparent from the numbers attending the sittings of the Dáil. Although the Dáil met only infrequently, it was often attended by just over twenty deputies with the remainder either in prison or on the run.

Obviously, this increased security presence also disrupted the IRA's campaign. More rigorous application of emergency legislation saw the number of suspects interned rise from about 1,500 in January 1921 to just under 4,500 by the following July. While mounting British repression had a predictable effect on the Irish population, the IRA was also being forced to adopt more ruthless tactics which attracted serious condemnation from a number of different quarters. Indeed, some of this criticism came from within Sinn Féin ranks. Roger Sweetman, the Sinn Féin deputy from Wexford, was deeply shocked by the brutality of Bloody Sunday and he made his feelings public. From the beginning of the conflict Sweetman had been an outspoken opponent of violence but, by the beginning of December 1920, he was openly denouncing the IRA's methods of warfare and calling for peace talks. If Sweetman represented the feelings of a section of opinion within Sinn Féin, it was not apparent. He was bitterly attacked for his suggestion of a peace conference and resigned his seat in the Dáil. Further trouble arose following criticism from the Catholic hierarchy, which had become louder in the early part of 1921. While the bishops consistently denounced British repression, a number of them were equally vociferous in their condemnation of the IRA. Cardinal Logue, Dr Gilmartin, Archbishop of Tuam, and Dr Cohalan, Bishop of Cork, all criticised the IRA's terror campaign and, in December 1920, Cohalan actually excommunicated all Catholics in his diocese who had been engaged in acts of murder. In spite of this opposition, it was clear that these clerics were out of touch with popular opinion, and Sinn Féin was usually able to ignore such criticism. What the republican movement could not ignore, however, was the growing war weariness which was easily discernible among the ordinary population in the final phase of the conflict. The commandeering of food and other supplies by the IRA was increasingly resented by local people whose lives had been severely disrupted by the conflict. As the War of Independence entered its final phase, the yearning for peace among rural people, particularly the strong farmers who had helped to sustain the guerrilla campaign, became more noticeable. These difficulties were exacerbated by the IRA's tactics in 1921, when they destroyed roads, bridges and other communications. While this made it difficult for the security forces, it also placed a further unwelcome burden on the population.

The IRA commanders in the field recognised that they needed popular support in order to survive. In the first half of 1921, however, some of them were reporting increasing public hostility towards the IRA in a number of areas. This raised questions among the IRA leadership about how long they could remain a viable force. Moreover, the use of martial law in the south and west had placed a growing strain on the flying columns, and commanders noted the drop in morale which followed. With such difficulties in mind the leadership of Sinn Féin became more interested in the prospect of a peace conference. In April 1921 Lord Derby, sporting a ridiculous disguise, arrived in Ireland as an emissary of the British government. On his visit he first met Cardinal Logue and then de Valera, who clearly did not enjoy his position as number two in the running order, and, though Derby failed in his mission, he did not damage the prospect of future negotiations between Sinn Féin and the British government. Earlier peace initiatives by the Australian Archbishop of Perth, Patrick Clune, and Father O'Flanagan, the Sinn Féin priest, had never really got off the ground, but this did not deter a number of senior officials in the Castle administration who favoured negotiations. The most prominent of these was Alfred ('Andy') Cope who had established lines of communication with the Sinn Féin leadership and worked tirelessly to promote negotiations. Still, Lloyd George hesitated, reluctant to offer the concessions that would be necessary for a truce. He had listened to Greenwood and some of his military advisers who had assured him that the IRA was being 'hit hard'. Although preparations were under way for the extension of martial law by the end of May, Lloyd George was having second thoughts. Gloomy predictions by Macready and the clear shift in British public opinion against coercion was changing his mind, and he expressed an interest in negotiations if Sinn Féin would drop its insistence on a republic.

This shift in public opinion, which had been highlighted by the reaction to the King's speech in Belfast on 22 June, also had some influence on Sinn Féin. With public opinion clearly in favour of a negotiated settlement the Sinn Féin leadership was aware that any rejection of a reasonable truce offer would alienate public sympathy. Yet Sinn Féin was really travelling on its own road towards a truce, and there were good military reasons for this. By the summer of 1921 the IRA was increasingly hard pressed. It had an estimated 3,000 men on active service, facing a combined police and military force in excess of 40,000. The establishment of a proper intelligence system and the greater flexibility shown by the army, which included the use of aircraft to attack flying columns, had put the IRA under severe pressure. Collins was greatly concerned by the deteriorating situation, and the prospect of the rigorous application of martial law over the twenty-six counties and the deployment of thousands of extra troops only increased his anxiety. After the truce had been signed Collins was to suggest that the IRA could only have survived for another three weeks. Tom Barry, on the other hand, has estimated that he could keep his flying column in the field for another five years. Both men were exaggerating. However, Collins's increased concerns about the IRA's ability to sustain its military campaign surely influenced de Valera as he groped his way towards a truce. The Sinn Féin leader knew that he had to carry the gunmen with him, thus avoiding a split in the republican movement, as he tried to negotiate Irish independence, and to achieve this Collins's collaboration would be vital.

While de Valera was not averse to the idea of peace talks, it would be up to the British to make the decisive move. This came in a letter from Lloyd George on 24 June, inviting de Valera to a conference in London in order to explore the possibility of a settlement. Only two days earlier, on the same day as the King's address at the opening of the Northern Ireland parliament, de Valera had been arrested after troops had swooped on his rented Blackrock home, but Cope intervened to secure his release. Next day he was surely shocked by the arrival of the conference offer. Although British ministers and officials had been discussing the possibility of negotiations, the Lloyd George peace move represented a sudden change of policy. Clearly, de Valera was taken by surprise and it was some days before Sinn Féin was in a position to make a response to the British offer. On 4 July he met with Midleton and other Southern Unionist representatives and on the following day he entertained

Smuts in Dublin, and they used their influence to press the case for a conference. Midleton also journeyed to London to secure Lloyd George's consent to a truce, which de Valera had demanded as a prerequisite for any conference. Finally, on 8 July, Lloyd George received de Valera's response stating that he was ready to come to London to begin negotiations. The truce, which came into operation at noon on Monday 11 July, was signed by Macready in the Mansion House [123]. The violence continued right down to the deadline. During the last week of hostilities the IRA killed three civilians and three soldiers, while the Black and Tans shot a prominent local figure in Cork and, on the final morning of the War of Independence, two long serving RIC men were killed in separate incidents. This brought the total killed during the conflict to 751. British security policy had been a disaster, as the government had allowed the situation in Ireland to drift out of control. The militarisation of the police in 1920 poured petrol onto a flickering flame and guaranteed popular support for the IRA. Yet the IRA was running out of steam by the summer of 1921, leaving both sides grateful that an opportunity for a cessation of hostilities had presented itself.

Historiography

A number of books on the War of Independence or Anglo-Irish War have been written by participants on the IRA side. The most notable are T Barry's, *Guerrilla Days in Ireland* (Dublin, 1962), D Breen's, *My Fight for Irish Freedom* (Dublin, 1964) and E O'Malley's, *On Another Man's Wound* (Dublin, 1979). Each of them gives an insight into the IRA's guerrilla campaign, describing in detail daring operations carried out by men under their command and providing snippets of useful information. For example, Breen describes how Volunteers regularly disguised themselves as priests, claiming that RIC men probably suspected many of them, but, as staunch Catholics, would not put them under arrest. This changed in 1920 with the arrival of the Black and Tans whom, he states, murdered three priests – one in Galway and two in Cork. Barry gives his account of the Kilmichael ambush, alleging that the Auxiliaries had used the false surrender tactic which caused the IRA to concentrate their fire on those Auxiliaries who were still alive. Afterwards, Barry claims that he had to drill his men for five minutes among the dead bodies and blazing lorries to enable them to regain their composure. This version of events has recently been challenged by P Hart's, *The IRA and its Enemies* (Oxford, 1998) which uses new documentary evidence, in the shape of a secret account written by Barry just after the event, to prove that Barry had invented his story. Hart states that wounded Auxiliaries were killed after the battle with bayonets, or shot with revolvers at close range. O'Malley's book, which is the best literary account, is very good at conveying the friction which surfaced regularly between local IRA commanders and GHQ in Dublin. He often represented GHQ, and he describes the difficulties he encountered in trying to persuade local commanders, who were very young, impatient and headstrong, to mount a more coordinated campaign. Together these memoirs offer useful detailed accounts of IRA operations, but they can create a false picture.

The most useful books for this topic are C Townshend's, *The British Campaign in Ireland 1919-1921: The Development of Political and Military Policies* (Oxford, 1975), D Fitzpatrick's, *Politics and Irish Life*, A Mitchell's, *Revolutionary Government in Ireland: Dáil Éireann 1919-22* (Dublin, 1995) and Tom Garvin's two books, *Nationalist Revolutionaries in Ireland* and *The Evolution of Irish Nationalist Politics*. Townshend has analysed the reasons for Britain's inability to govern Ireland in this period. He emphasises the government's failure to define British objectives in Ireland and, consequently, the cabinet did not follow a clear policy. Indeed, as Townshend asserts, for much of the War of Independence the British government had no policy whatsoever. He claims that the British response to the IRA campaign was 'instinctive' and, moreover, some of the Conservatives in the cabinet regarded the suppression of Irish separatism as a natural defence of British interests. For their part the Liberals had no constructive ideas on Ireland and thus tended to acquiesce in the decisions to militarise the police and conduct reprisals. On the security front Townshend points to the appalling lack of co-operation between the police and military and puts much of the blame on Tudor for this failing. While he criticises the policy of coercion, Townshend also notes that it was not sustained as the government drifted between repression and attempts at conciliation. Instead he describes it as 'mild' coercion, suggesting that it was "repression too weak to root out opposition, but provocative enough to nurture it". He then analyses the IRA's strategy, a theme he returned to in his *Political Violence in Ireland*, concluding that "by matching its operations to its means it (the IRA) could ensure its survival for long enough to achieve psychological victory out of military stalemate".

Mitchell's, *Revolutionary Government in Ireland* offers the best account of the attempt to establish a 'counter-state', a term he borrows from Townshend. He analyses the impact of the Dáil administration and notes its early successes in establishing a rival court system, financing the administration, winning control of local government and taking responsibility for law and order. However, he also explains that these successes did not continue into 1921, declaring that by this stage the administration of the counter-state had lost its 'vitality'. Mitchell provides a detailed account of the actions of the Sinn Féin delegation at the Paris Peace Conference, stressing that many within Sinn Féin knew that there was little likelihood of progress in Paris. He quotes O'Kelly who regarded the whole Paris mission as a 'concession' made by Sinn Féin extremists to the moderates who urged that "every possible instrument of peaceful negotiation should at least be tried". On the boycott of the RIC Mitchell notes that it won almost universal public support within weeks of its inauguration in April 1919. He then quotes a policeman who had resigned and claimed that there would have been wholesale resignations if alternative employment could have been arranged, something which Sinn Féin had considered but only in a half-hearted way. Mitchell deals comprehensively with the success of Sinn Féin's publicity machine which, though run on a shoestring budget, was very effective in swaying both Irish and international opinion. He then analyses the impact of Sinn Féin's success in the 1920 local elections, using the voting returns to demonstrate that, particularly in urban areas, the party's victory was not as sweeping as might have been expected. He argues, moreover, that many of the new Sinn Féin councillors continued to communicate and co-operate with the British Local Government Board. A detailed analysis of the impact of the Dáil courts can be found in M Kotsonouris's, *Retreat from Revolution: The Dáil Courts, 1920-24* (Dublin, 1994) which emphasises that the Dáil courts were not established by the Dáil but by the spontaneous actions of local communities.

In both his *Nationalist Revolutionaries in Ireland* and *The Evolution of Irish Nationalist Politics* Garvin examines the socio-economic backgrounds of the IRA leadership, noting that the bulk of them were middle class, which corresponded to revolutionary leaders in other countries. More specifically, as many as half of them had parents who were well-off farmers, though the majority of these sons had moved off the farms. Significantly, he adds that over 40 per cent of these leaders had lived outside Ireland, usually in Britain or the United States, for considerable periods. Looking at the revolutionary elite's geographical background, Garvin emphasises the importance of central Munster, stating that one-sixth of the leadership came from Cork city and county. This leads him to argue that it was the influence of the prosperous Munster farming class which turned Sinn Féin away from involvement in social revolution, as the idea of a "stabilized, conservative Irish Republic dominated by the yeoman farmer made direct sense in Munster". Bew's essay, 'Sinn Féin, Agrarian Radicalism and the War of Independence, 1919-21', which appears in Boyce's (ed), *The Revolution in Ireland* develops this argument. He claims that the very restrained contribution of Connacht to the conflict can be attributed to the revolutionary leadership's refusal to sanction land seizures in the summer of 1920. Land hunger remained a powerful force in Connacht which had previously, of course, provided the inspiration and the manpower for various bursts of land agitation. Fitzpatrick's, *Politics and Irish Life* also focuses on the problems which the "land-hungry westerners" posed for the Dáil administration, noting the fear of the Sinn Féin leadership that agrarian unrest would "divert the attention of the people from the national struggle". He argues that Sinn

Féin failed initially to establish an alternative government, but claims that the situation was transformed in the summer and autumn of 1920. In his analysis of the IRA campaign Fitzpatrick describes how the formation of Michael Brennan's flying column did not follow orders from GHQ, but was "a purely spontaneous development which arose directly from the prevailing conditions". The development of the flying column system, he argues, made it even more difficult for GHQ to influence local units and, significantly, fierce local resentment, suspicion and personal rivalries between these local units became a prominent feature. Fitzpatrick also highlights the growing hostility of the Clare population to the IRA units in the spring of 1921, claiming that "the Irish Revolution had come to an uneasy military standstill by mid-1921".

Both Lyons's, *Ireland since the Famine* and Kee's, *Ourselves Alone* argue that the conflict can be divided into three distinct phases. The first, from January 1919 to the beginning of March 1920, was characterised by a relatively small number of sporadic attacks on individual policemen. The second phase, from March 1920 to October 1920, saw growing lawlessness, a process accelerated by the arrival of the Black and Tans and the Auxiliaries though, as Kee emphasises, there were only 1,500 Black and Tans and 500 Auxiliaries in Ireland by October 1920. In the final phase, from November 1920 to July 1921, these numbers of special police reinforcements rose rapidly as the conflict entered its most brutal phase. Kee also assesses the impact of the fighting on the Irish population, conveying something of the fear and real terror created by the 'Tans' and 'Auxies'. A useful, succinct analysis of the War of Independence is provided by K Jeffrey's essay, 'British Security Policy in Ireland 1919-21', which appears in Collins's (ed), *Nationalism and Unionism*. Jeffrey argues that there was a "muddle between a civilian security strategy and a military one", a problem exacerbated by the government's preoccupation with other "bigger problems" and, moreover, Ireland was only one of a number of countries within the British Empire, where Nationalist forces were challenging British rule. In his comments on the Tans and Auxiliaries Jeffrey emphasises the shocking lack of training which the men in these forces had, and he blames Tudor for failing to deal with woeful police indiscipline. Finally, he suggests that the truce let both the British government and the IRA off the hook.

S Lawlor's, *Britain and Ireland 1914-23* (Dublin, 1983) clearly explains the reasons behind the government's U-turn in agreeing to a truce in July 1921. As Lawlor indicates, Lloyd George was prepared to consider a truce as early as December 1920, and yet, at the same time, the cabinet was authorising the use of martial law over most of Munster. In the early part of 1921, however, Lloyd George, with Greenwood's optimistic assurances of an early military victory ringing in his ears, thought that it was not the right time for conciliation. Instead there was the faint hope that the 1920 Government of Ireland Act, which was, of course, unrealistic, might break the deadlock. While the Conservatives in the cabinet favoured the continuation of coercion, Lawlor points out that the government's decision to offer truce terms was determined by the weight of public opinion which was, by the spring of 1921, clearly outraged by the policy of repression in Ireland. D G Boyce's, *Englishmen and Irish Troubles: British Public Opinion and the Making of Irish Policy 1918-22* (London, 1972) also notes that "British public opinion was instrumental in producing the government's offer of 24 June". He records the growing press campaign for peace in Ireland and emphasises the significant contribution of two pressure groups, the Trades Union Congress and the Peace with Ireland Council. The latter organisation was particularly effective, Boyce argues, because its membership was almost exclusively English and cross-party, which enabled it to influence a wide section of English opinion. The key role played by Smuts in the run up to the truce is analysed in Mansergh's, *The Unresolved Question*. No one, Mansergh argues, was better fitted "to extol the virtues of dominion status", but it is wrong to suggest that he persuaded Lloyd George of these virtues, and thus no offer of dominion status was made in the King's speech at the opening of the Northern Ireland parliament. In Mansergh's opinion this had a "significant bearing" on the negotiations that followed.

The crucial personal contribution made in the War of Independence by Collins is examined in Coogan's, *Michael Collins*. Coogan is good at illustrating the tremendous devotion and loyalty with which Collins was revered by many of his comrades. This was particularly true of the Squad, and Coogan offers a detailed account of its birth and a comprehensive guide to its operations. In this book and in even more detail in his later, *De Valera: Long Fellow, Long Shadow* Coogan goes on to relate his analysis of the bitter personal battles which became, particularly in his view, such a significant feature of the revolutionary struggle. Coogan finds de Valera's absence in the United States for a period of eighteen months, as his republic battled for its survival, inexcusable. When he returned on 23 December 1920, he was completely out of touch with the situation on the ground and was, more significantly, shocked and disturbed by the dominance which Collins had achieved. In Coogan's view he was soon plotting Collins's downfall. The hostility between Collins and Cathal Brugha, his apparent superior, is also analysed fully in these two books. Valiulis's, *Portrait of a Revolutionary* deals perceptively with these internal personal battles, but she also has attempted to reassess the role of the IRA's headquarters staff. She argues that the common assumption, made by both historians and the participants, that GHQ was ineffective is a 'misconception'. When one considers the practical difficulties facing the headquarters of a guerrilla army, Valiulis claims, the IRA's GHQ was "effective and over time, grew even more effective". Mulcahy and his staff adapted quickly to the needs of guerrilla warfare, encouraging local commanders to engage in 'small actions' as this took account of the IRA's strengths and weaknesses. Moreover, she argues that GHQ successfully used its influence to ensure that the conflict retained its focus and did not "degenerate into wanton violence, sectarian conflict or personal vengeance".

Chapter 10
The Anglo-Irish Treaty

The truce opened the way for negotiations between Sinn Féin and the British government, and de Valera arrived in London on 14 July 1921 to discuss the basis upon which a conference between the two sides might take place. At this first meeting Lloyd George met de Valera face to face, and he used the occasion to give a theatrical performance, pointing to the empty chairs around the conference table in 10 Downing Street which, only days earlier, had been occupied by the dominion leaders. Turning to de Valera he then asked Ireland to take her place in this family or Commonwealth of 'free nations'. In all, the two leaders met on four occasions between 14 and 21 July. On his London mission de Valera was accompanied by a number of leading figures in the Sinn Féin movement, including Griffith, Stack and Childers, but he left an angry and bitter Collins behind. In these preliminary discussions de Valera tried to let Lloyd George do most of the talking. The Prime Minister made it clear that whatever new constitutional arrangement was designed, Ireland would have to remain in the Empire. De Valera wanted to avoid dealing with the question of Ireland's future relationship with Britain, but, at the same time, he did not want to be seen to compromise on Sinn Féin's demand for a republic. The Irish leader was determined to keep Sinn Féin united, and he was afraid that an early concession on Ireland's future status would result in extremists within the movement breaking away. This explains his concentration on the partition issue, and he criticised the British government for its indefensible and immoral decision to establish a statelet in the six county area. This early sparring was further complicated by Craig's interference. Now established as Northern Ireland's first Prime Minister, Craig arrived in London as a physical reminder of Northern Ireland's existence, and his presence was an obstacle for the Lloyd George government. Ignoring the appeals of the Prime Minister, Craig refused to participate in the discussions, and he took every opportunity to inform the press that de Valera's claim to speak for the whole of Ireland was an outrageous impertinence. The Unionist leader's strategy was simple: he would sit on his 'Ulster rock' and defend Northern Ireland's position.

These initial discussions did not fill de Valera with optimism. From London he wrote to Collins, warning him to prepare for an early resumption of hostilities. His real problem was that he realised a compromise on republican status was inevitable, but he was reluctant to commit himself on this, knowing that any dilution of the demand for a republic would have serious consequences for Sinn Féin unity. This left Lloyd George confused about the Irish leader's real thinking. Although Lloyd George realised that de Valera was not entirely his own master, it was apparent that he wanted negotiations to proceed. On 20 July Lloyd George declared his hand to his cabinet colleagues, adding that no consideration would be given to Sinn Féin's demand for a republic. He would offer Ireland dominion status, but only if she agreed to special undertakings on defence, trade and finance, while partition was to remain in force until the people in Northern Ireland decided otherwise. When de Valera discussed these proposals with Lloyd George on the following day, he pointed out that no other dominion was subject to such constraints. Even leaving this aside, de Valera found the proposals totally unacceptable, declaring that he could not recommend anything in the document to the Dáil or his people. Lloyd George countered by warning de Valera that the outright rejection of the proposals would bring the truce to an end, a suggestion which, though not a surprise, left de Valera in a dilemma. He left Downing Street without the British proposals but, after a suitable interlude, sent a messenger to fetch them. De Valera then returned to Dublin with the proposals, where they were considered by the Dáil cabinet. Before this Smuts called on de Valera to urge acceptance of the dominion offer, claiming that if Dublin made a success of self government, partition would end with Northern Ireland voluntarily throwing in her lot with the south.

The debate within the Dáil cabinet reflected the wide range of opinion within Sinn Féin on Ireland's future constitutional status. While Griffith was encouraged by the British offer, an angry Brugha argued that it should not even be considered by a Dáil cabinet which claimed to be the government of the 'Republic'. De Valera's delayed reply to the British on 10 August should be regarded as an attempt to hold Sinn Féin together rather than a serious counter offer. On the crucial question of status the Irish suggested 'external association', though precisely what this meant was not made clear. External association was de Valera's ingenious suggestion to appease republican hard-liners in the cabinet, notably Cathal Brugha and Austin Stack. The crux of the idea was that Ireland could enjoy the freedom of an independent state but be externally associated with the British Commonwealth. Of course, such a proposal was unacceptable to the British and, over the course of the next few weeks, an exchange of telegrams and letters took place, but no progress was made in bridging the gap between the British offer of limited dominion status and the rather vague Irish notion of external association. A frustrated Lloyd George had given serious consideration to breaking off the truce, and this was discussed at a cabinet meeting held in Inverness Town Hall on 7 September. Lloyd George was enjoying his summer holiday, and his cabinet colleagues were summoned to Inverness for this crucial meeting which considered the prospects for negotiations. Ministers reaffirmed the decision to insist that the Irish must accept the Crown and Empire as preconditions for a conference, but, while this was conveyed to the Irish, there was a narrow majority against sending Sinn Féin an ultimatum. The Irish reply, delivered in person to the Highlands by Harry Boland and Joseph McGrath, insisted on Ireland's right to be recognised as an independent state. A fuming Lloyd George dismissed the two emissaries and later informed de Valera that a conference was impossible. More talks about talks followed, but there was no indication that the deadlock would be broken. Then, on 29 September, Lloyd George moved to break the impasse. His letter restated the government's position that Ireland would have to remain in the Empire, but coupled this with a fresh invitation to a conference which ignored all previous correspondence.

The Dáil cabinet gratefully accepted Lloyd George's new offer and arranged to send a delegation to the London conference. While de Valera could put a favourable spin on this decision, stressing that he had agreed to a conference without preconditions, realists within the cabinet recognised that in accepting this new offer Sinn Féin had already made a crucial compromise. A republic was not on offer, and it was on this basis that substantive negotiations would proceed. Still, the Lloyd George invitation of 29 September appeared to leave significant room for manoeuvre, as it stated that a conference would ascertain "how the association of Ireland with the community of nations known as the British Empire may best be reconciled with Irish national aspirations" [124].

Decisions on the make-up of the Irish delegation which would attend the London conference had already been taken. Crucially, de Valera had indicated that he did not want to attend the conference and, when the Dáil cabinet voted on the issue, he used his casting vote to decide the result. Griffith, Collins and Cosgrave supported him going, but de Valera backed Brugha, Stack and Barton who were against his attendance. This decision infuriated Collins, and he argued forcefully that in refusing to go de Valera was abdicating his responsibilities. Later, on 14 September, Cosgrave again raised the issue in cabinet, outlining the arguments in favour of his going and concluding that it was like playing a vital match with their "ablest player in reserve". Again, the decision to keep him at home was reaffirmed. De Valera's key argument was that as 'President of the Republic', a position which had only been created on 26 August, he was now the 'symbol' of the republic and, as such, his office as head of state should not be compromised "by any arrangements" which the Irish delegation might have to agree to in London. Other reasons for de Valera's refusal to attend were subsequently advanced. He knew that Brugha and Stack would create mayhem if concessions on status were made, and de Valera thought that his presence in Dublin could keep such potential opposition under control. Moreover, any Treaty would have to be ratified by the Dáil, and he could intervene in that forum to raise any objections which might be necessary. Yet it is hard to escape the conclusion that de Valera would not go, because he knew from first-hand experience that a significant compromise on Ireland's status was inevitable, and he did not want to be associated personally with that compromise. A number of historians have stressed that by sitting on the sidelines and insisting on Collins's participation, he was taking a decisive advantage over Collins in his rivalry for the leadership. In his defence, however, it is necessary to point out that Collins's acceptance of any compromise would be a crucial factor in determining the IRA's response, and de Valera recognised that any settlement approved by Collins had a better chance of being accepted in Ireland.

The President's absence left Griffith leading the Irish delegation, but de Valera had been careful to ensure that the delegation would reflect the divergent viewpoints expressed within the cabinet. Collins was very unhappy at his selection for the delegation, arguing that he was a soldier and it was not "his place". De Valera had left him behind when he went to London in July, but he had now decided that Collins should join Griffith on the Irish team. In the end he relied on Collins's sense of duty and the persuasive powers of Batt O'Connor, a close friend of Collins, whom de Valera had asked to talk Collins into going. De Valera assumed that Collins and Griffith would work closely together and would be prepared to make concessions on national status. To balance them Robert Barton, the Dáil's Minister of Economic Affairs, was added to the team. He was to collaborate with his friend and relative, Erskine Childers, who acted as secretary to the delegation. Two other Dáil deputies, George Gavan Duffy and Eamon Duggan, both of whom were lawyers, completed the five-man delegation, though Childers, acting as the delegation's secretary, was to play a much more prominent role than these last two delegates. He was the most doctrinaire republican among the Irish representatives in London and, as de Valera correctly assumed, would urge the delegation to reject dominion status. This division within the Irish delegation proved a crucial weakness when the negotiations got under way, and the problem was exacerbated by the intense personal bitterness which existed between some of the delegates. Griffith and Childers were particularly hostile towards each other, and Collins did not trust Childers whom he suspected was in secret communication with de Valera. A further weakness was caused by the Dáil cabinet's failure to ensure that the delegation was fully prepared. The limits of any concessions they might offer were not clarified, and the delegates set out with Griffith and Childers far apart on the crucial question of national status. De Valera was fully aware of this, but he was content with this state of affairs. The Irish were to negotiate for external association, something which neither Griffith nor Collins fully understood, and, if the conference broke down, they would try to ensure that the break would come on Ulster. This would be favourable to the Irish and cause most problems for the British.

Finally, confusion was caused by the ambiguous status of, and instructions given to, the Irish delegation. They were to be 'plenipotentiaries' (envoys with full powers), but these powers were to be limited. While de Valera was not prepared to lead the delegation in London, this did not stop his attempt to direct events from Dublin. Accordingly, he drew up the following document which he circulated to the plenipotentiaries:

1) The plenipotentiaries have full powers as defined in their credentials.

2) It is understood before decisions are finally reached on a main question, that a dispatch notifying the intention to make these decisions will be sent to members of the Cabinet in Dublin, and that a reply will be awaited by the plenipotentiaries before final decision is made.

3) It is also understood that the complete text of the draft treaty about to besigned will be similarly submitted to Dublin and a reply awaited.

4) It is understood that the Cabinet in Dublin will be kept regularly informed of the progress of the negotiations.

Having set out to contain Griffith and Collins by balancing the delegation with more uncompromising republicans, de Valera clearly intended that these instructions, particularly clauses 2 and 3, would enable him to veto any draft document which he considered unacceptable. Griffith and Collins, for their part, were unhappy with the limitations and, when the crunch came, they chose to ignore these instructions.

Despite the divisions, which were immediately obvious to the British, the Irish delegation was a formidable team. Griffith was experienced, able and determined, and in Collins he had a very skillful colleague who could easily hold his own in negotiation. Although he had undoubted ability, Collins suffered from something of an inferiority complex, as he thought of himself first and foremost as a soldier who did not have the necessary qualifications for politics. However, Collins was open-minded and pragmatic. While the republic was a 'sacred cow' for the Sinn Féin extremists, Collins was more interested in securing practical changes which would give Ireland considerable freedom and enable her to extend that freedom. Crucially, he did not favour a return to war with the British, because he was certain that this would result in defeat for the IRA. This left him in the opposite corner to Brugha who had accepted de Valera's idea of external association as a final compromise and wanted to end the truce if the delegation failed to win 'republican' status in the negotiations. Collins considered such a course suicidal. The selection of the Irish delegation and the subsequent negotiations in London increased the hostility between Collins and Brugha. Collins had good reason to be suspicious of Brugha whom he believed was constantly plotting in Dublin to undermine the work of the delegation in London. Brugha was continually pressing de Valera to curb Collins's powers, and he remained bitter about the role of the Collins-directed IRB within the army. This was, indeed, another factor for Collins to consider, and he held regular meetings with the IRB leadership before and during the Treaty discussions in order to keep the movement informed about the progress of the negotiations and gauge reaction to the developments. Collins made no secret of the IRB's role. While the rest of the Irish delegation stayed at Hans Place, Collins stayed at Cadogan Gardens where he had his own staff who were, not surprisingly, colleagues in the IRB.

The Irish delegation was able but divided. The British delegation, by contrast, was superbly talented and united in its determination to make Sinn Féin accept the Crown and Empire. The delegation was led by Lloyd George, a brilliant politician with a very forceful personality, who had a wealth of experience in dealing with Ireland. He was joined by the two senior Conservatives in the Coalition government, Austen Chamberlain and Lord Birkenhead. Chamberlain may not have possessed the ruthlessness of his father, which might have enabled him to become Prime Minister, but he was, nevertheless, an outstanding politician who enjoyed the full respect of his colleagues. Birkenhead was a charismatic figure who had played a memorable role in support of Carson during the Ulster crisis. He was also a tough negotiator and one of the foremost constitutional experts in the country. The fourth member of the British delegation was Winston Churchill. Again, he had a wealth of experience in Anglo-Irish relations and was the British team's expert on defence. This talented quartet were joined by Hamar Greenwood, the Chief Secretary for Ireland, Laming Worthington-Evans, the Secretary of State for War, and Gordon Hewart, the Attorney-General. Tom Jones, another expert in Anglo-Irish affairs who had worked closely with Lloyd George, acted as secretary to the British delegation, and he was to make an important contribution to the negotiations.

Despite this array of talent, it was Lloyd George, the 'Welsh wizard', who dominated the British delegation. Even before the negotiations began he had won back public support for his Irish policy. His offer of a conference seemed fair and generous, and this was reflected on the pages of the main newspapers which had been so critical of the government's coercion policy earlier in the year. Even more significant, however, was the expectation in the minds of the British public that at the end of the negotiations Ireland would still be in the British Empire and Britain's defensive requirements would be met. Thus public opinion was firmly behind Lloyd

George as he pressed the Irish delegation to accept dominion status, and, moreover, he could expect the British public to support the reopening of hostilities if the negotiations broke down on Sinn Féin's refusal to come into the Empire. All through the negotiations Lloyd George used this to his advantage, and the prospect of a resumption of the war was kept firmly before the Irish delegation. Yet this advantage was in danger of being outweighed by the problem of Ulster. The British knew that they were vulnerable to attacks on partition, and they fully expected the Irish to exploit this weakness [125].

If the conference broke down on a refusal by the British to end partition, Lloyd George and his colleagues sensed that the British public would not support a return to war in order to maintain the existing border. Lloyd George also realised that the Unionists in Belfast were unlikely to be flexible and accommodating by making any gesture which might assist the Prime Minister in his dealings with Sinn Féin. With his Coalition government wholly dependent on continuing Conservative support, and with Bonar Law looking on from the sidelines, the coercion of Ulster was never an option and this left Lloyd George with little room for manoeuvre on the partition question. Yet, ultimately, the crux of the matter for the Conservative leaders in the Coalition was that the negotiations must secure an agreement by the Irish to accept the Crown and remain within the Empire. To achieve this Lloyd George had to keep Birkenhead and Chamberlain on board and content with the direction of the conference, if his rocky Coalition government was to survive.

The Treaty negotiations

The negotiations in London lasted from 11 October until 6 December 1921. On the opening day the Irish were presented with the British proposals which were based on the document rejected by de Valera on 20 July. The crucial element in the paper was the insistence on dominion status and, in firing this opening shot, the British had set strict parameters outside which they were not prepared to venture. This development was facilitated by the inexplicable failure of the Irish delegation to table their counter proposals until 24 October. Griffith wrote to de Valera, urging him to forward their alternative Treaty proposals, as he had allowed the delegation to leave Dublin with their draft document incomplete. In fact, the Irish document was based on the idea of external association, which required Britain and the dominions to recognise Ireland as a sovereign independent state, while, in return, Ireland would become 'associated' with the Commonwealth for matters of common concern. The delay, however, enabled Lloyd George to dismiss the Irish proposals as being outside the scope of the discussions. The Irish had allowed the Prime Minister to seize the initiative and he was not to relinquish it.

In the early plenary sessions the British proved willing to make concessions on finance and trade, but their insistence on defence facilities in Ireland provoked disagreement, with Childers commenting that Ireland must have the right to remain neutral in any future conflict involving Britain. Still, it seemed as though problems relating to trade, finance and even defence could be overcome without great difficulty, leaving only the questions of status and Ulster as areas of contention. It was these two issues, therefore, which dominated the Treaty negotiations. The British wanted dominion status with allegiance to the Crown, but this, as Childers constantly reminded all the delegates, ignored Ireland's right to proclaim her separate nationality. Whenever possible, Griffith, who was the least hostile to dominion status, sought to move the negotiations onto the question of Ulster. The fourth plenary session was dominated by Ulster, and the Irish delegation must have been surprised at the genuine dislike of partition expressed by their British counterparts. Both Griffith and Collins focused on the plight of the Nationalist community in Northern Ireland, which had been forced to accept an artificial state and an unnatural border that failed to take account of the wishes of the Nationalist majorities living in Tyrone and Fermanagh. Lloyd George offered the opinion that Northern Ireland could be persuaded to come into a reunified Ireland of her own accord, but Griffith wanted the British government to put pressure on the Unionists to go down the road of a united Ireland. Perhaps surprisingly, he found Lloyd George eager to apply this pressure. In the seventh plenary session on 24 October the Irish finally submitted their counter proposals, 'Draft Treaty A', which, Griffith explained, would involve 'association with' rather than 'membership of' the British Empire. Ireland had given up the title 'Republic' and she would agree to be associated with the Empire. When the British pointed to the degree of freedom enjoyed by dominions such as Canada and New Zealand, it drew a blank reaction from the Irish.

As the negotiations progressed, the British delegates found Childers prickly and unreasonable and, following this seventh plenary session, the principals on the two delegations agreed that more progress might be made if the plenary sessions were replaced by sub-conferences. This suited the British as it sidelined Childers, but it also suited Griffith and Collins, and it was these two who first suggested that subsequent discussions should take place in sub-conference. A fortnight into the negotiations, it was clear to both that they would have to outflank the inflexible and dogmatic Childers if an agreement was to be reached. Childers, his cousin, Barton, and Duffy had been acting in unison but, henceforth, the use of sub-conferences excluded them from the key discussions. The two principals in the Irish delegation were also experiencing problems with Dublin. De Valera had intervened following an exchange of telegrams between King George V and Pope Benedict, in which the King had replied to the Pope's good wishes for success in the negotiations by stating that he too hoped that the conference would "initiate a new era of peace and happiness for my people". De Valera then sent his own telegram to the Pope, a copy of which he issued to the press on 21 October, stressing that his Holiness must not be confused into thinking that the Irish people were the King's subjects [126]. This snub for the King infuriated Lloyd George who regarded it as a deliberate attempt by the Irish leader to break up the conference. Worse was to follow. After the seventh plenary session Griffith reported to de Valera the content of a frank discussion he had alone with Lloyd George and Chamberlain, in which they had pressed him to recommend the acceptance of the Crown, but Griffith had taken the line that this would only be accepted if the British could guarantee the 'essential unity' of Ireland. This drew a hostile response from de Valera who warned that there could be no question of Irish people becoming British subjects and then added, "If war is the alternative, we can only face it, and I think the sooner the other side is made to realise it the better".

When they received de Valera's letter, Griffith and Collins were furious, viewing de Valera's remarks as an attempt to curb their powers as plenipotentiaries. Both men threatened to walk out of the conference, and calm was only restored when a letter repudiating de Valera's attempts to impose new restrictions on the plenipotentiaries was signed by all the delegates and sent to Dublin. De Valera now sought to reduce the tension by sending a fresh letter in which he claimed that there was no question of seeking to limit the powers of the Irish delegates, adding that he was only trying to keep them informed on the views of the Dáil cabinet. Griffith and Collins needed no such information, and Collins told the others that Brugha and Stack, with de Valera's assistance, were deliberately laying a trap for him.

By the time the negotiations reached the sub-conference stage a clear pattern had emerged. The Irish would make provisional concessions on status which would be contingent on the government guaranteeing the essential unity of Ireland. This appeared to be a clever strategy because, if the conference failed, it should have been possible for the Irish delegation to engineer a break on Ulster. On the other hand, the linking of national status and Ulster muddied the waters, and Lloyd George caused further ripples when he drew the Irish into having an interest in the survival of his government. On 30 October Lloyd George met Griffith. The Prime Minister was preparing a speech for the following day when his government faced a censure motion. The Diehards, right wing Conservatives who opposed the Coalition, had tabled a motion in the Commons which expressed "grave apprehension" at the government's action in entering negotiations with Sinn Féin, and Lloyd George had made it a vote of confidence in his government [127]. He asked Griffith for personal assurances on the Crown, free partnership with the Empire and naval facilities for the British in Ireland and, in return, promised to crush the Diehards and fight on the Ulster matter to secure the essential unity of Ireland. In the end Griffith gave the desired assurances and Lloyd George led the government to victory in the vote of confidence. On 1 November Griffith made a further concession when Lloyd George requested some kind of documentary evidence expressing Ireland's willingness to come into the Empire, which could be used to defend the government at the Conservative party conference in Liverpool in mid-November. The Conservative members of the Coalition government expected to come under attack for their involvement in the negotiations, and Griffith penned a letter to Lloyd George stating that he would "recommend free partnership with the British Commonwealth", if he could be satisfied on Irish unity. Before it was sent, however, this was amended, on the insistence of Childers, Barton and Duffy, to "recommend free partnership of Ireland with the other States associated within the British Commonwealth". This form of words left ample room for future discussion, but the word *within* was a crucial pointer to the final agreement.

Childers, in particular, had been angered by the switch to the sub-conference method of negotiation, and he tried to persuade de Valera to intervene and order a return to the plenary sessions. The sub-conferences usually involved Griffith and Collins facing Lloyd George and Chamberlain but, on occasion, Chamberlain was replaced by Birkenhead and, less frequently, by Churchill. These discussions were more open with each side outlining their own difficulties. The sub-conferences also enabled the extraordinary personal rapport between Collins and Birkenhead to develop. These two charismatic, but pragmatic, figures shared a good deal in common, and Birkenhead, because he best understood Irish difficulties, quickly won Collins's confidence. It was clear to Collins, moreover, that Birkenhead wanted the talks to succeed and did not want a return to war.

For the British the assurances given by Griffith were a clear indication that the Irish would accept allegiance to the Crown if they received satisfactory guarantees on unity. It was now time for Lloyd George to put pressure on the Unionists in Belfast. He had told Griffith that if Ulster was unreasonable, he would resign and, while this pledge delighted Griffith, it was to have serious repercussions for the Irish delegation. The British delegation had been rebuffed, and Jones, the secretary to the British delegation, passed on this news when he met Griffith and Collins informally at the Grosvenor Hotel on 8 November. Craig, who was constantly in touch with senior Conservatives outside the government such as Bonar Law and Balfour, was of the opinion that the British negotiators could come to any arrangement they wished, but he was staying out of it and holding on to his six counties. Jones then stated that Lloyd George would make one final effort to persuade the Ulster Unionists to accept an all-Ireland parliament and, if they refused, he would resign. This would, Jones suggested, lead to the collapse of the Coalition government with its likely replacement being a Conservative government under Bonar Law, which would be hostile to Sinn Féin. It was at this point that Jones proposed the Boundary Commission as a possible way forward if Craig refused to accept an all-Ireland parliament. Griffith's understanding of this was that Northern Ireland would lose a large chunk of her territory with the rump eventually falling under Dublin rule. Griffith and Collins were clearly encouraged by the Boundary Commission proposal, but they did not yet commit themselves and dutifully reported the content of the conversation to Dublin. De Valera's reply congratulated Griffith on the Ulster negotiations, but warned him to hold his ground on the Crown and Empire if the British tried to tempt him with further moves on unity. Nevertheless, Jones, directed by Lloyd George, had seen and heard enough to sense that the Prime Minister could escape from his pledge to resign if he failed to secure an all-Ireland parliament. Griffith wanted Lloyd George, whom Jones portrayed as Sinn Féin's friend, to remain in office and, at a further meeting on 9 November, he decided that it did not matter if Craig refused an all-Ireland parliament, because the Boundary Commission would take care of the Ulster problem. This was a crucial error. Although Ulster had often exasperated Lloyd George and appeared as an insurmountable obstacle for the British delegation, it turned out to be very useful, because it kept Sinn Féin moving towards the British position on the fundamental issue of status [128].

As promised, Lloyd George renewed his attempts to cajole the Unionists. On 10 November he wrote to Craig, urging the Unionists to accept an all-Ireland parliament, as this would enable the Coalition government to reach agreement with Sinn Féin on allegiance to the Crown and inclusion in the Empire. In this same letter, moreover, the Prime Minister sought to apply economic pressure to force a Unionist change of heart, stressing that taxation under the United Kingdom parliament would be much higher than taxation rates under an all-Ireland parliament. This was no idle threat because taxation rates in the United Kingdom were particularly high in the early postwar years, and Lloyd George hoped that the bourgeois leaders of Ulster

Unionism would be swayed by their wallets. This pressure, coming from the same Coalition government which had established the Northern Ireland state, worried Craig who reaffirmed the Unionist view that the 1920 Government of Ireland Act was, for Unionists, the 'supreme sacrifice', and they would not buckle under pressure from the government. There is some evidence that Craig was personally willing to make some concessions in order to help the Coalition government in its dealings with Sinn Féin, but his colleagues clearly did not share his wider imperial concerns. Lloyd George had failed in his bid to shift the Unionist government, but the idea of a Boundary Commission had compensated adequately for this failure. On 12 November the Prime Minister had an important meeting with Griffith, and it was here that Griffith formally committed himself to the Boundary Commission, failing to realise that in taking this course he was greatly limiting Sinn Féin's option of breaking on Ulster. Lloyd George instructed Tom Jones to draw up a memorandum on these proposals which was shown to Griffith on the following day. After a brief glance at the memorandum Griffith agreed to its contents, and Lloyd George retained the document for future use.

On 16 November the British presented the Irish delegation with a draft Treaty which contained the Boundary Commission proposals. These would come into effect if Ulster opted out of an all-Ireland parliament. In considering their response a row broke out among the Irish delegates. Duffy returned to Dublin to see the other members of the Dáil cabinet and to complain about the way Griffith and Collins were negotiating by sub-conference, but de Valera refused to order a halt to the sub-conferences, arguing that the delegates could not sign any Treaty without first submitting it to his cabinet for approval. In London, meanwhile, Childers and Barton presented a document, an amended version of which was dispatched to the British on 22 November. This memorandum argued that legislative and executive authority in Ireland should have an exclusively Irish derivation, but Ireland would be associated with the Commonwealth and would recognise the Crown as "symbol and accepted head of the association". The British delegation did not hide its disappointment with this document and made various references to the conference breaking down. However, another sub-conference was arranged for 24 November, which made it clear to Griffith and Collins that the British could not touch external association. There followed a good deal of discussion on symbolism, which was important to both sides, and together they agreed that the title Irish Free State, a less controversial translation of Saorstat Eireann, would be used in the Treaty. Birkenhead had also suggested that the Irish delegates should be accompanied to this meeting by a constitutional lawyer and, therefore, John Chartres, the second secretary to the Irish delegation, was in attendance. Again, Childers was bypassed, as Chartres and Birkenhead discussed the Crown. Birkenhead assured the Irish that it would be no more than a symbol just as it was in Canada, and there would be no question of a future British government trying to influence Ireland against her will. Yet as a symbol, the Crown was of vital importance to the British, because it bound together in voluntary union all the members of the Commonwealth. Chartres put the Irish viewpoint which emphasised that Ireland was not like Canada or any other dominion. Ireland's proximity to Britain and her history of conflict with Britain would, in his opinion, mean that a future British government would interfere in

Ireland, using those constitutional powers which the British delegation was insisting were essential.

The issue of the Crown was discussed in detail at a Dáil cabinet meeting on 25 November, when it was decided that they could recognise the Crown for the purposes of association, as symbol and accepted head of the combination of associated states. While the Irish were sticking fast on external association, they had moved slightly in recognition of the Crown, and this was a significant compromise for Brugha and Stack. Of course, the cabinet stopped short of accepting allegiance to the Crown, claiming that the existence of the Crown within Ireland would mean in practice that, for the historical and geographical reasons already outlined by Chartres, Ireland would be denied the freedom which the dominions undoubtedly possessed. In replying to Griffith the British offered him the chance to word any phrase which would ensure that the position of the Crown in Ireland would be no more 'in practice' than it was in any other dominion. The Irish found it very difficult to counter this move. When the British presented their final proposals on 1 December, it was apparent that they had made minor concessions on defence but, in reality, they had not strayed far from the original dominion status offer made by Lloyd George to de Valera on 20 July.

The Irish delegation then returned home for a crucial meeting of the Dáil cabinet on Saturday, 3 December. Griffith left on the early boat from Holyhead on the Friday morning, but Collins, Childers and Duffy, who had loose ends to tie up at the Treasury, returned on the night mailboat. Drama now unfolded. The mailboat was in collision with a fishing smack in the Irish Sea and had to return to Holyhead. By the time it finally berthed in Dun Laoghaire it was 10.15 am. This was not the best preparation for the cabinet meeting which was due to begin at 11 am that morning. Moreover, Collins was unable to attend an early morning meeting of the IRB Supreme Council, and a copy of the Treaty proposals had to be sent to his IRB colleagues together with Collins's request for an opinion on the document by lunchtime. When he met an IRB representative during a cabinet adjournment, he was informed of the IRB's objections to the oath, but they supplied Collins with an alternative form of words which would be acceptable.

Back in the Mansion House, where the Dáil cabinet was meeting, the Irish delegates gave their opinions on the British proposals. Griffith, supported by Duggan, judged that this was Britain's final offer and no further concessions could be gained. Barton and Duffy disagreed, convinced that more could be wrung out of the British. The cabinet sat for a total of seven hours, and much of the time was taken up by acrimonious personal bickering. The worst scene occurred when Brugha stated that the British had "selected their men" in opting to negotiate by sub-conference, clearly implying that Griffith and Collins were weak on the fundamental question of Ireland's future relationship with Britain. Griffith reacted angrily and, following a stormy exchange, Brugha instructed the cabinet secretary to withdraw his remarks. Collins had suggested that if Brugha was so dissatisfied with the work of the delegation, he should select a new team to go to London. Though he made little contribution to the debate, it was clear that Collins was in substantial agreement with Griffith, but he expressed his concern about the wording of the oath of allegiance. De Valera struggled to find a new form of wording which would be acceptable to both wings of the cabinet, but the various records of this crucial meeting do not agree on the precise words he used. The official record claimed that he had suggested:

> I ... do solemnly swear true faith and allegiance to the constitution of the Irish Free State, to the Treaty of Association and to recognise the King of Great Britain as Head of the Associated States.

De Valera subsequently offered two different versions of what he had said, but Childers noted that he had used the term 'King of the Associated States'. Certainly, Collins was convinced that de Valera would accept a slightly modified oath, but the President was unwilling to give a clear lead and returned to the idea of external association which he wanted the delegation to put forward again. Barton appealed to de Valera to join the delegation in London, arguing that it was unfair to ask Griffith to press for these terms, which could only be successful if the Irish threatened war, when he was not prepared to go to war. The issue was only settled when Griffith said he would not sign the Treaty, but would bring it back to Dublin and submit it to the Dáil. This assumed that the British would grant this extra time without threatening war. In the end the Irish delegates returned to London confused about the instructions they had been given.

On their arrival Childers, Barton and Duffy quickly produced yet another draft based on the external association concept, but Collins did not accompany them to Downing Street for what he regarded as a hopeless mission. Griffith led the team for the conference on 4 December, and he argued vigorously and with considerable skill for the Irish alternative. Amid all the confusion the only clear instruction given to the plenipotentiaries by the Dáil cabinet was to reject the oath in its existing form, and then, if the conference was heading for a breakdown, try to ensure that the break would come on Ulster. Griffith was sticking to this plan in the discussions, but a careless remark by Duffy was seized on by the British team and in another moment of high drama, which may well have been rehearsed, they collected their papers before striding out of the conference. Duffy had said that they wanted "to be as closely associated with you in large matters as the Dominions, and in the matter of defence still more so, but our difficulty is coming into the Empire". At that Chamberlain jumped to his feet, crying "That ends it", and the British team followed him out of the room. The British would send their final proposals on the following day and Craig was to be informed that the conference had broken down. Later that night, Jones visited Griffith at Hans Place in an attempt to resurrect the negotiations. Griffith said that they needed some concession on Ulster, however small, if they were to push the Treaty through the Dáil, and he suggested that Lloyd George should see Collins on the following morning. Collins duly arrived at Downing Street on the morning of 5 December, and he discussed both the dominion status clauses and the Boundary Commission with the Prime Minister. Enough was said to restart the conference, and Griffith, Collins and Barton returned to Downing Street that afternoon. Birkenhead and Collins had worked on a revised form of wording for the oath, which moved closer to the IRB's recommendation, but the conference inevitably moved on to the question of status.

Griffith stuck to the cabinet's line, arguing that the Irish delegation's provisional concessions on status had been contingent on the satisfactory conclusion of the Ulster issue and refusing to sign any Treaty until they had Craig's decision on the acceptance of unity.It was at this point that Lloyd George left the room to seek out the memorandum on the Boundary Commission proposals which Griffith had assented to in the previous month. Neither Collins nor Barton had any knowledge of this document, but Lloyd George insisted that if the Irish now tried to break on Ulster, they would be guilty of a serious breach of faith. Griffith reacted angrily, but stated that he would sign the Treaty. His protest that the other two were not party to this agreement and, therefore, should not be expected to sign any Treaty until word had been received from Craig, was ignored by Lloyd George. In another piece of high drama Lloyd George produced two letters, claiming that he had promised to let Craig know the outcome of the negotiations. One would inform the Unionist leader that a Treaty had been signed and peace restored, while the other would say that the conference had broken down and war would be resumed. Brandishing both letters Lloyd George warned that those who were not for peace must take "full responsibility for the war that would immediately follow refusal by any delegate to sign". As Griffith had already pledged his signature, and the British were confident that Collins would sign, Lloyd George's remarks were really addressed to Barton. Lloyd George had issued the Irish with an ultimatum, and Barton was shocked when, in the car on the way back to Hans Place, Collins announced that he would sign the Treaty. Duggan, who had worked closely with the two principals during the negotiations was also willing to sign, but Barton and Duffy held out for an agonising few hours. Duffy finally relented following an emotional plea by Duggan, which recalled vividly the sight of young Volunteers being hanged in Mountjoy prison. This left only Barton and, though pressed by Childers to stand firm on this point of principle, he too gave in, and the Anglo-Irish Treaty, known formally as the 'Articles of Agreement for a Treaty between Great Britain and Ireland', was signed by both delegations at 2.30 am on 6 December 1921. In the final exchanges Lloyd George had dropped the British demand for free trade and given the new Irish Free State fiscal autonomy [129].

Reaction to the Treaty

It had been of paramount importance for Lloyd George in his negotiations with the Irish plenipotentiaries to secure the backing of the Conservative party. Already in 1921, the Coalition government had been declining in popularity with its Conservative supporters who feared that Lloyd George's attempts to break the existing party system might succeed and, consequently, destroy the identity of the Conservative party. Fortunately, the party had shed its fanatical obsession with the Irish Question, which had been such a feature of the immediate prewar period. The Irish Question had changed since 1914, and it was recognised that this new question demanded a new solution. In the past the Conservative party had viewed its support for the Unionists as a natural defence of the Empire, but the situation had changed to such an extent that many Conservatives regarded Unionist intransigence, when pressed for concessions in November 1921, as a greater threat to the Empire. This was the line taken by most of the British press which attacked the Unionist government in Belfast for taking such a narrow, self-interested view. Lloyd George's demand that the Ulster Unionists should accept legislative subordination to a new all-Ireland parliament while retaining their existing devolved powers, appeared reasonable to British public opinion. The Coalition government did put pressure on the Unionists, but it was Bonar Law who came to their rescue. Following his resignation from the government in March 1921 Bonar Law had made a political comeback, pledging his continuing support for the Unionists. Accordingly, any thoughts Lloyd George might have harboured about coercing Ulster were abandoned and, from mid-November 1921, he began to squeeze Sinn Féin. Nevertheless, the commitment to establish a Boundary Commission in the Articles of Agreement could not be ignored, but Bonar Law surprised many of his followers when he gave his backing to the Treaty in the parliamentary debate which opened in both Houses on 14 December. In his opinion the Boundary Commission would make only very minor adjustments to the border and, so long as Ulster was safeguarded, Bonar Law had no problems with the other parts of the Treaty. Indeed British public opinion acclaimed the Coalition government for its success in concluding the Treaty. The end product represented a stunning volte-face for a government which had been committed to a policy of coercion only six months earlier, but it was also a stunning success for Lloyd George who, at a stroke, had taken a giant stride in removing the Irish Question from British politics.

Of course, not all Conservatives welcomed the Treaty. The Diehards, a rump of extreme Conservatives who opposed the government on a range of issues, were savage in their criticism of the Treaty. With a strength of about 50 in the House of Commons, the Diehards had made two attempts to thwart the negotiations by tabling a censure motion on 31 October and in attacking Chamberlain and Birkenhead at the Conservative party conference in mid-November. Both attempts were easily overcome, but fresh attacks were expected in the debates which followed the signing of the Treaty. When the time came, the Diehards denounced the government's actions in negotiating with 'murderers' and then poured scorn on the terms of the Treaty which, they claimed, were humiliating for Britain and would do lasting damage to the Empire. In these debates the Diehards were bolstered by Carson who delivered a memorable speech, full of vitriol, in the House of Lords. Earlier in the year, Carson had accepted a position as Lord of Appeal, and the Treaty debate on 14 December was to be the occasion of Carson's maiden speech in the House of Lords. Describing the Treaty as shameful, concluded "with a revolver pointed at your head", Carson berated the government for having neither the resolve to deal with criminals in Ireland nor the 'pluck' to rule over the Empire. He was scathing in his condemnation of the Conservative party, but he then turned his fire on his old political ally, Lord Birkenhead, who had signed the Covenant in 1912 and had now signed the Treaty, describing those "who will sell their friends for the purpose of conciliating their enemies" as "loathsome". Birkenhead responded with another powerful speech, and an ugly scene followed when he was interrupted by Carson. In the end, however, only 47 peers voted against the government when the Upper House divided. Carson's bitter attack on the Coalition government was a testament to his Irish Unionist past. He had, of course, fought for Ulster, but he cared passionately about all of Ireland and could not hide his feelings now that the Union had been irrevocably broken [130].

In the Commons the Treaty was endorsed by an overwhelming majority with only the Diehards and the Ulster Unionist MPs in opposition. Craig's brother, Charles, was particularly bitter during the debate in the Commons. He expressed revulsion at the Boundary Commission clause and accused the government of betrayal. Sir James also thought that Lloyd George was guilty of duplicity and on the next day he sent a letter to Chamberlain, which expressed Unionist anger and ended with a warning that if the Treaty was not modified, the government should withdraw British troops and "allow us to fight it ourselves". Not surprisingly, the Treaty was also a source of concern for Southern Unionists. During the negotiations they had hoped that the government would look after their interests and, indeed, arrangements had been made to ensure that Southern Unionist views would be available to the British delegation. However, without the protection of Long or Lansdowne, both of whom had left the government, the Southern Unionists found that the new Conservative leaders, Chamberlain and Birkenhead, were unwilling to jeopardise the negotiations in the defence of Southern Unionist interests. They had to be content with personal assurances from Griffith who promised to consider Southern Unionist claims, particularly with regard to representation in the new state. Thus Midleton and his followers in the Lords did not vote against the Treaty, as they waited to lobby the Provisional Government of the Irish Free State on possible safeguards which might be included in the new constitution.

While Birkenhead believed that in signing the Treaty he had risked his political life, Collins wrote to a friend that he had signed his actual 'death warrant'. Both Griffith and Collins knew that Sinn Féin would be split on the Treaty, but they were prepared to argue the document's merits in the Dáil. For his part, de Valera was shocked that the delegates had not, as promised, consulted him before signing the Treaty, describing their decision as an "act of disloyalty". To those around him it appeared that he was more annoyed by this personal snub than by the actual terms of the Treaty. His initial plan was to sack the three members of the Dáil cabinet, Griffith, Collins and Barton, who had signed the Treaty, and he convened a meeting of the other three cabinet ministers in Dublin to inform them of his intentions. Brugha and Stack, he assumed, would support this action, but he was stunned by Cosgrave's objection to the sackings. De Valera had come to regard Cosgrave as his most devoted cabinet colleague, and he was astonished by his disciple's independence of thought. His next move was to summon a full meeting of the cabinet for 8 December, and he published the notification for this meeting in a manner which publicly declared his opposition to the Treaty. At the cabinet meeting the old arguments were again played out, but when a vote was taken in favour of referring the Treaty to the Dáil, it was passed by a 4:3 majority. Griffith, Collins, Barton and Cosgrave were in favour; de Valera, Brugha and Stack were in opposition. De Valera had denounced the delegates for their breach of faith in failing to consult him before signing, but Barton countered by insisting that the real problem had been caused by de Valera's refusal to attend the conference. Before the Dáil could meet de Valera acted somewhat irresponsibly by issuing a proclamation, outlining the cabinet split and stating that he could not recommend acceptance of the Treaty to either the Dáil or the Irish people. De Valera had gambled in not going to London, but this mistake was compounded by his refusal to offer whatever decisive leadership he could from Dublin. This allowed Griffith and Collins to present him with a fait accompli which, he was stunned to learn, was acceptable to a majority of the Dáil cabinet. He had known since July that compromise was inevitable but, as one historian has suggested, rejected the Treaty because it was not his compromise.

The Dáil debate on the Treaty opened on 14 December 1921, but any attempt to maintain Sinn Féin unity had already been abandoned. Although de Valera had been very adept at preserving unity within both the cabinet and the Dáil during the early stages of the negotiations, his subsequent actions, particularly after 6 December, only served to increase the uncertainty, the confusion and the division. Recently, a number of historians have judged that he deliberately set out to attract extremist support in order to wreck the Treaty and destroy his political rivals, notably Collins. Others, however, argue that this view ignores de Valera's sincerity in pursuit of his external association idea and his genuine, but unsuccessful, attempt to distance himself from the military opposition to the Treaty. From the outset he recognised that a referendum on the Treaty would have produced a majority in favour of acceptance, but he now wanted the Dáil to reject the Treaty and allow the cabinet to table new proposals based on external association. Undoubtedly, de Valera's reputation was tarnished, and with good reason, by his attitude and actions in the immediate post-Treaty period.

The opening day of the Dáil debate was wasted arguing about the precise instructions, or lack of them, which had been issued to the Irish delegates, and it was not until the secret session of 15 and 16 December that the debate focused on the fundamental issue of national status. De Valera dominated the debates, and in the course of these long and frequently acrimonious discussions, he produced his alternative to the Treaty, which became known as 'Document No 2' [131]. It was based on the idea of external association and, therefore, had rewritten all the clauses dealing with dominion status. Crucial to the debate was the discussion on the oath which de Valera found unacceptable. Article 4 of the Treaty contained the oath which Griffith defended as honourable:

> I ... do solemnly swear true faith and allegiance to the constitution of the Irish Free State as by law established and that I will be faithful to H.M. George V, his heirs and successors by law, in virtue of the common citizenship of Ireland with Great Britain and her adherence to and membership of the group of nations forming the British Commonwealth of Nations.

It was this oath of allegiance which most exercised the minds of the Treaty's republican opponents. Document No 2 made no mention of an oath, stating that "for purposes of common concern, Ireland shall be associated with the States of the British Commonwealth". However, Griffith also pointed out that Document No 2 made no mention of the word 'republic'. Indeed in proposing the motion that the Dáil should accept the Treaty Griffith put great emphasis on the fact that the Irish delegation had not negotiated for a republic. He also reminded de Valera that, while they had all taken an oath to the Irish Republic, the President himself had gone on record to state that this was only an undertaking to do the best he could for Ireland. In Griffith's view, which ran close to his old 'Hungarian policy', the Treaty merited support, because it gave Ireland equality with England. While he acknowledged that the Treaty was not the "ideal thing", the simple fact that it had been signed proved a compelling argument in its favour.

In opposing the Treaty de Valera dwelt on symbolism, arguing that the oath acknowledged the King as "the direct monarch of Ireland (and) the source of executive authority in Ireland". De Valera's discourse on semantics left many deputies bewildered, and his attack on the Treaty lacked the clarity of some of his anti-Treaty supporters. Part of his problem was that Document No 2 was only in rough draft form, and the discussion of its content was restricted to the private session. Before Christmas his opponents had tried to bring these proposals into the public domain in order to highlight the fact that de Valera's alternative was not a republic, but external association. For de Valera the difference between dominion status and external association remained fundamental, but the real logic of his argument was that these differences were sufficiently narrow to prevent a return to war by the British. In the debates de Valera's anti-Treaty stand was supported by Brugha, Stack and Childers and by most of the women deputies, for whom the principle, or perhaps the romantic vision of an Irish Republic, remained a powerful emotion [132]. These included Mary MacSwiney, Kathleen Clarke, Margaret Pearse and Countess Markievicz. Perhaps the most powerful speech opposing the Treaty had come from Childers who analysed in detail the defects of the agreement. In his opinion it was not an honourable settlement as he argued that it gave Ireland less real freedom than other dominions such as Canada. Other anti-Treaty speakers did not follow this analytical, subtle approach. For Austin Stack 'full Canadian powers' fell well short of Ireland's legitimate demands, and he gave the Dáil a pledge that he would fight in the Fenian tradition to destroy the oath of allegiance.

The most important contribution in favour of acceptance came from Collins. He emphasised that Ireland had compromised on the republic by agreeing to participate in the London conference, but he was convinced that the agreement gave Ireland freedom, "not the ultimate freedom that all nations aspire and develop to, but the freedom to achieve it". The speech made a powerful impression both inside and outside the Dáil. Of course, Collins also used his influence to rally support for the Treaty from within the IRB and the IRA. The Supreme Council of the IRB, of which Collins was President, had endorsed the Treaty, and many IRA commanders added their support on the basis that if it was acceptable to Collins, it would be acceptable to them [133]. In the Dáil debates Collins received powerful backing from Kevin O'Higgins who spoke immediately after Childers. He acknowledged that the Treaty had its defects, but its acceptance was the only practical and sensible course. He claimed that it granted "a broad measure of liberty for the Irish people" and, in a remarkably prophetic statement, declared that the evolution of the British Commonwealth would see a natural and inevitable progression towards increased freedom for the various nations and 'equality of status'. O'Higgins warned the Treaty's opponents that they should not vote against its ratification, unless they could demonstrate clearly how more concessions could be won in practice. This ruled out, in his opinion, any irrelevant discussion of a return to war which was sure to end in military disaster. After this the debates became more acrimonious, and a number of the leading figures, notably Collins, were subjected to a torrent of personal abuse.

By the time the Dáil adjourned for the Christmas break on 22 December, all the main arguments had been heard. The long Christmas recess worked in favour of the pro-Treaty side, as deputies who had returned to their constituencies were generally exposed to the people's pro-Treaty sentiments. A string of resolutions from a variety of bodies advocating acceptance of the Treaty reflected public opinion. The press was overwhelmingly pro-Treaty, the Catholic hierarchy had added its support and 24 county councils had declared in favour of the Treaty [134]. This more than outweighed the personal pressure which de Valera had applied to individual Dáil deputies in his efforts to defeat the Treaty. Still, the Dáil's support for the Treaty was by no means a foregone conclusion, as many of those who had been nominated for the second Dáil in May 1921 were militant republicans. When the Dáil reassembled on 3 January, Collins advocated a way forward which might prevent the split on the Treaty becoming more pronounced. He suggested that those opposed to the Treaty should abstain on the vote, thereby upholding their principles, and allow the formation of a Provisional Government which, as outlined in the Treaty, would draft a new constitution. This new constitution would derive its authority from the Irish people, not from the Crown, and this would allow the anti-Treaty deputies to take the oath safe in the knowledge that they would no longer be swearing allegiance to the Crown but to the constitution of the Irish Free State. However, de Valera rejected this offer. Instead, he intended to introduce his own alternative, Document No 2, which he had revised during the Christmas recess, and have the Dáil vote on it as an amendment to Griffith's motion that the Treaty be accepted. Such a course would have prolonged the debates as countless new amendments could then have been tabled, but Griffith brought matters to a head when he released Document No 2 to the press in its original pre-Christmas form. This undermined de Valera's position but, in spite of numerous pleas from many deputies to pull back from the brink and prevent a dangerous split, de Valera raised the temperature with another bitter speech on 6 January. The decision on the Treaty was finally reached on the following day, when the Dáil accepted it by 64 votes to 57. De Valera duly resigned as President, but then stood against Griffith in the hope that he would be re-elected, thus enabling him to sack pro-Treaty cabinet members and open up a fresh attack on the Treaty. The vote was 60 to 58 in Griffith's favour. The new President quickly put together a new cabinet, but real power now rested with the Provisional Government which was formed on 14 January and led by Collins. He carried the responsibility for implementing the Treaty.

The Dáil debates were significant for the lack of attention which was paid to Ulster. Only one deputy, Sean MacEntee who was a native of Belfast, opposed the Treaty because it perpetuated partition, and only Collins among the key players seems to have been genuinely concerned with Ulster [135]. Indeed there were only very minor differences in the clauses relating to partition between the Treaty and Document No 2. The real issue for the Dáil was allegiance and thus most of the speeches focused on the oath. Yet in his speech endorsing the Treaty Lloyd George had told the House of Commons that the agreement gave the Irish the freedom "to work out their own national destiny". The Treaty divide had created an open split in the Sinn Féin popular front. In terms of numbers the split in the Dáil was very even with only a narrow majority on the pro-Treaty side. This did not reflect opinion in the country where there was a substantial pro-Treaty majority. The opponents of the

Treaty, moreover, included varying shades of 'republicans'. De Valera himself, and those who thought like him, were still advocating external association, essentially a compromise between British imperial and Irish republican aspirations, but there was also a group of militant republicans for whom external association was anathema. They wanted a republic and would settle for nothing less. Indeed during the debate militants such as Rory O'Connor and Liam Mellowes left deputies in no doubt about their attitude, and O'Connor even berated Brugha for being contaminated with politics. This was an important factor, because many of those on the anti-Treaty side were irreconcilable zealots who had no regard for democratic niceties such as majority opinion. Yet what gave the anti-Treaty side real political credibility was not the stand of these doctrinaire republicans, but de Valera's enormous prestige. This was to be a crucial factor in the civil war which followed.

Historiography

Three general commentaries, Foster's, *Modern Ireland*, Lee's, *Ireland 1912-1985* and Lyons's, *Ireland since the Famine* all make perceptive judgements on the Anglo-Irish Treaty. Foster stresses the importance of liberal and international opinion in driving Britain to the conference table, but comments that Lloyd George then had to conduct the negotiations within Conservative parameters. While they were ready to accept a special oath of allegiance for Ireland, external association was out of the question. He is of the opinion, moreover, that the Treaty was only possible because partition had already been implemented. From the Irish perspective he judges that the plan to break off negotiations on the Ulster issue was the correct tactic, but he then states that both pro and anti-Treaty factions became diverted by their "Anglophobic obsession with the Crown". Lee focuses on de Valera's genuine concern with Sinn Féin unity, but he criticises his refusal to attend the negotiations and his equally determined insistence that Collins should go. Still, Lee argues that it was very unlikely that he could have secured better terms, and his real mistake was to overestimate his support in the Dáil cabinet. Lyons also considers de Valera's non-appearance in London, concluding that his presence in Dublin would ensure that the Treaty would have to be referred to him before any vital decisions were taken. If this was the case, however, Lyons views the failure to issue clear instructions to the Irish delegates as "inexcusable".

A number of books are fiercely critical of de Valera's actions immediately before the negotiations, during the conference itself and in the subsequent Dáil debates on the Treaty. Chief among these are Coogan's, *De Valera: Long Fellow, Long Shadow* and his, *Michael Collins,* and T Ryle Dwyer's, *Michael Collins and the Treaty: His Differences with de Valera* (Dublin, 1981), *De Valera's Darkest Hour 1919-32* (Cork, 1982) and his brief biography, *Eamon de Valera* (Dublin, 1980). Dwyer alleges that de Valera tried to portray a moderate image in public but was more extreme in private, while Collins tended to do the opposite. In his opinion events during this period were dominated by the power struggle between de Valera and Collins, and de Valera is presented as a scheming Machiavellian figure out to destroy his chief political rival. Coogan endorses this view in his two very detailed biographies. He claims that de Valera had little grasp of British political realities and no understanding of Lloyd George's precarious position. In his early jousts with Lloyd George Coogan declares that de Valera's pride meant that he could not compromise without losing faith, and this influenced his decision to remain in Dublin. The author also emphasises how much effort de Valera put into ensuring that history would record his actions in the most favourable light, but Coogan is convinced that de Valera knew exactly what lay ahead and selected suitable 'scapegoats' to make the crucial compromise. He concludes that Griffith and Collins were "Unsupported by Dublin and deeply mistrustful of Lloyd George" and, therefore, whenever the opportunity arose for Ireland's 'freedom to achieve freedom', they took it. In both books Coogan describes the acrimonious bickering and the utter confusion which characterised the famous meeting of the Dáil cabinet on 3 December 1921, and again takes de Valera to task for his attempt to ensure that it was his version of events which was left for posterity. The manner in which he rejected the Treaty is described as "arrogant and destructive", compared, by Coogan, to Parnell's refusal to accept his removal as leader of the IPP. Like Parnell, moreover, in rejecting the Treaty de Valera was deliberately setting out to attract extremist support.

The most detailed study of the Treaty negotiations remains Lord Longford's, *Peace by Ordeal* (London, 1935). Generally, Longford is sympathetic to de Valera and very critical of Lloyd George's 'duplicity'. He begins by discussing the huge transition in the Coalition government's thinking which, in a matter of weeks, changed from viewing the Irish as a 'murder gang' to negotiating with them as 'equals'. Longford deals in detail with the tension and differences of opinion within the Irish delegation, which were reflected in the Sinn Féin movement as a whole. He argues that of all the negotiators involved none attended the conference with a more open mind than Collins. Yet while Collins clearly recognised the difference between external association and dominion status, this was not, as it was for de Valera, fundamental. In analysing the British position Longford stresses that they had one decisive advantage which the Irish could not match. This was the threat of war, and Lloyd George played this card with devastating effect. Longford also discusses the very significant role played by Tom Jones who consistently portrayed Lloyd George as Sinn Féin's friend, thereby drawing the Irish delegation, and Griffith in particular, into attempts to ensure the Prime Minister's political survival. Thirty years later, Longford revised some of his judgements in an essay, 'The Treaty Negotiations', which appeared in Williams's (ed), *The Irish Struggle*. He suggests that it should have been possible to reach such a settlement in July 1921 and this, in his opinion, would have averted the civil war. He acknowledges, moreover, that Lloyd George's political position was much weaker than he had suggested in the book. The book had stressed the importance of Griffith's error on 12 and 13 November which prevented the Irish delegation breaking on Ulster but, on reflection, Longford feels that the 'break on Ulster' strategy had severe limitations, and the British could simply have issued an alternative ultimatum: "join the Commonwealth or else". It needs to be emphasised, therefore, that Griffith signed the Treaty not under duress, but because he regarded it as an honourable agreement, and Collins only signed when he was convinced that the Boundary Commission would deliver Irish unity.

Longford's book also raises the question about the failure of the Irish delegation to telephone Dublin during the final hours of the negotiations, suggesting that they had come under Lloyd George's spell, but Mansergh's, *The Unresolved Question* poses a further query: "Who was to be telephoned?" De Valera was probably in Ennis, and only Stack was in Dublin. In addition, the telephone line was sure to have been tapped. Mansergh has analysed the Treaty in some detail. He judges that Lloyd George got the better of the early exchanges with de Valera, as he refused to discuss the problem of Ireland's future status outside the context of intra-Commonwealth relations, whereas de Valera failed to win "explicit affirmation of the existence of a republic" before accepting the invitation to negotiations. Mansergh then discusses the significance of the Irish failure to have their proposals on the table at the opening of the conference on 11 October. Only the British paper was there for the early sessions, and he states that "the basic paper at any conference is apt to determine the parameters of subsequent discussions". On the Ulster issue Mansergh points out that Irish views on how to attain unity underwent a change during the conference. By accepting a Boundary Commission Griffith released the British from their obligation to establish an all-Ireland parliament by persuading himself that the Boundary Commission would achieve the same result. On the oath Mansergh claims that the wording was as far away from the concept of traditional allegiance as one could go, but it was the 'existence' of the oath which raised objections.

A British insider's guide to the negotiations can be found in T Jones's, *Whitehall Diary, Vol III, Ireland 1918-25* (Oxford, 1971) which contains the recollections of an important figure at the conference and sheds new light on some of the events. For example, Jones records that the request for sub-conference negotiations came from the Irish and not, as Griffith later insisted, from the British. Lawlor's, *Britain and Ireland* looks at Lloyd George's July meetings with de Valera, commenting that he found it very difficult to say precisely what the Irish leader wanted. His own strategy was clear, as Lawlor describes how he set out to obtain assurances from the Irish on the essentials, allegiance and the Empire, in return for Irish unity. She also draws attention to the difficulties which Bonar Law created for Lloyd George in November 1921. These were more serious because Lloyd George was unsure whether Bonar Law was solely motivated by Ulster, or whether he suddenly saw an opportunity to become Prime Minister. Lawlor ends this section by suggesting that Lloyd George had not given serious consideration to the resumption of war in early December. Unlike de Valera, he had been involved in the negotiations, and a breakdown would, therefore, be regarded as a personal failure on his part. War might have followed the failure of the conference but, in Lawlor's opinion, it was more likely to have been "war under Bonar Law, rather than under Lloyd George".

The influence which public opinion had on Lloyd George is skillfully examined in Boyce's, *Englishmen and Irish Troubles.* The decision to publish, on 15 August, details of the offer made by Lloyd George to de Valera and the Irish reply rallied public opinion behind the Coalition government, as Boyce notes that the press saw the British proposals as a fair and generous offer which Sinn Féin could reasonably be expected to accept. Moreover, in accepting the British invitation to a conference, Boyce is clear that public opinion in Britain assumed that "the limitations which had been laid down by Lloyd George on 20 July still applied". The Irish were further hampered in his opinion by their failure to state clearly what their "limits of concession were". He also focuses on the role of the Conservative party which, he argues, had clearly loosened its connections with Ulster from the prewar period and now wanted Ulster to 'co-operate' in a new settlement. The role of the Conservative party is also touched on in P Canning's, *British Policy towards Ireland 1921-1941* (Oxford, 1985). Canning claims that from July to November 1921 Lloyd George conducted the negotiations with two options in mind. He could either work with the Conservatives in giving Ireland much more autonomy than Home Rule, but, if they proved obstructive, he could force an election on the old programme of "maintaining Irish unity against Ulster and Conservative intransigents", though the latter option may have been just a tactic to blackmail the Conservatives. One other brilliant study of contemporary high politics deserves mention, as it also deals with the Irish Question. M Cowling's, *The Impact of Labour 1920-1924: The Beginning of Modern British Politics* (Cambridge, 1971) argues that in dealing with Ireland Lloyd George "made almost total capitulation to the Conservative, if not to the Ulster, position". However, he did come very close to persuading the Conservative members of his cabinet to bring moral and financial pressure on Ulster to accept an all-Ireland parliament, but Bonar Law intervened to scupper this idea. In Cowling's view Lloyd George, at some point between 12 and 23 November, switched his fire to press the Irish delegation, not Craig. The book is excellent in putting the Treaty negotiations into the general background of British politics, where Lloyd George was working to smash the existing party system and was using the Irish Question in this context.

Chapter 11
The Irish Civil War

One of the first duties Collins had to perform as Chairman of the Provisional Government was to preside at the ceremony on 16 January 1922, when the British formally surrendered control of Dublin Castle, the old seat of British rule in Ireland. Behind the occasion's symbolic importance there was the reality that the Treaty had given the new state considerable powers. In the background Collins was in constant contact with the British, working out the fine details on the transfer of powers to Dublin. British troops were withdrawn and the RIC was disbanded but, in spite of this visible demonstration of Britain's disengagement, the Provisional Government still faced determined opposition to the Treaty. There was also confusion about the best way forward with some advocating decisive action against anti-Treaty elements, while others considered various ways to unite the two factions. What was clear, however, was that the Dáil could not fulfil this function. Instead it was to become an obstacle to unity and tended to magnify the political divisions. This meant that the attitude of the IRA assumed crucial importance.

Both Brugha, the outgoing Minister of Defence, and Mulcahy, the new Minister of Defence, had given assurances that the "Army would remain the Army of the Irish Republic", but there was obviously a question mark over its ability to remain united and its willingness to accept civilian authority. In fact, the IRA was clearly divided on the Treaty. A majority of GHQ staff were pro-Treaty, but many of the units in the south and west of the country, which had borne the brunt of the fighting in the War of Independence, were solidly anti-Treaty. Sometimes, local officers determined the reaction of the IRA members under their command, but others were influenced by the most prominent figures in the army, such as Michael Collins and Richard Mulcahy who were pro-Treaty and Liam Lynch and Ernie O'Malley who were anti-Treaty. In some areas, moreover, attitudes to the Treaty were dictated by personal rivalry and family feuds. In general, the IRA's response to the Treaty was confused, and in one sense this was a continuation of the indiscipline and internal wrangling which had plagued the IRA in the truce period.

Added to this turmoil was the deteriorating situation in Northern Ireland, where news of the Boundary Commission proposals had inflamed an already tense situation. At this point Churchill intervened and brought Craig and Collins together for a meeting at the Colonial Office in London in an attempt to halt the violence in the north. The result was the Craig-Collins pact signed on 21 January 1922. Craig promised to use his influence to prevent the further persecution of Northern Ireland's Nationalist minority, and Collins agreed to end the Belfast boycott which had been imposed by the Dáil as an economic sanction against the north. Within days, however, the pact had collapsed. Craig had raised the temperature with a defiant speech in which he pledged his government's opposition to any future attempt by the Boundary Commission to make anything more than very minor alterations to the border, and Collins replied with an emphatic statement outlining his expectation that the Boundary Commission would recommend the transfer of large areas to the Irish Free State. The two men met again on 2 February in an attempt to heal the rift, but no progress was made. This was followed by an escalation of the violence in the north, where 30 people were killed in Belfast in a one-week period in mid-February. Still, Churchill showed uncharacteristic patience and, on 30 March, he brought the two leaders together again at the Colonial Office in a fresh attempt to reconcile their differences. This led to a second Craig-Collins pact which, at Churchill's insistence, contained the opening clause: "Peace is today declared". The pact included more specific promises relating to the treatment of the Catholic minority, and Collins gave an undertaking to use his authority to end the IRA campaign in the north. The two leaders also agreed to a future conference with a view to settling the border question without recourse to the Boundary Commission [136]. In spite of the optimism generated by this second accord, the pact collapsed and the violence in the north intensified. In these circumstances the IRA renewed its campaign, and Collins and Lynch were involved in ensuring that both pro and anti-Treaty IRA units co-operated in a joint offensive. It was essential, of course, that this collusion was carried out in secret to prevent the British charging the Provisional Government with a very serious breach of the Treaty. IRA personnel were sent north to assist local units, but the offensive, which they launched in the spring of 1922, proved a dismal failure. The IRA was weak in the north and the leadership in the south failed to develop a coherent strategy.

The need for joint action in the north should have been a powerful incentive to maintain army unity but, like the politicians, the soldiers of the republic were more disturbed by the oath of allegiance than by partition. Real problems would only arise, however, if the army attempted to force their opinions on the Dáil. During the debates in the Dáil the Cork IRA had threatened to shoot any deputy from their area who supported the Treaty. On 11 January anti-Treaty IRA officers wrote to Mulcahy requesting an army convention to consider the formation of an executive which would have supreme control over the army. If such a resolution was passed the danger to the Provisional Government was obvious. Mulcahy was not against a convention, but he wanted to delay it in the hope that the image of British troops being sent home would convince the doubters that the Treaty had brought real advantages. There would be, of course, a number of extremists who could never be reconciled, but Collins, Mulcahy and the other leaders of the Provisional Government hoped to persuade the more moderate elements among the IRA anti-Treaty officers not to oppose the Treaty. Yet time was not on their side, and Mulcahy knew that if he delayed too long dissident elements would organise their own convention thereby making one section of the army unaccountable to civilian control. In the end it was agreed that an army convention would not meet until the new constitution had been drafted. If this could move Ireland closer to a republic under the Treaty, it would prevent an irrevocable split in the army.

As the British withdrew, their military barracks were occupied by local units of the IRA irrespective of their attitude to the Treaty. Obviously, this left anti-Treaty IRA units in control of certain areas, but it was a price the Provisional Government was willing to pay in order to contain the military split. Problems occurred in Limerick, however, when the Provisional Government departed from this policy in an attempt to prevent the city falling under the control of local IRA units which were solidly anti-Treaty. Limerick's strategic importance had caused a GHQ rethink, and Michael Brennan's 1st Western Division, which was based in Clare, was ordered to occupy the city's barracks. The anti-Treaty IRA reacted by moving men into the city and they were reinforced by O'Malley's 2nd Southern Division. Soon every available building, in addition to the barracks, was occupied, and a clash between pro and anti-Treaty troops looked unavoidable. What prevented a confrontation was the great reluctance of both sides to fire on their old comrades and, by early March, a compromise was reached as units from outside the city were withdrawn, leaving the local anti-Treaty force in control. This looked like a climbdown on the part of the Provisional Government, and it angered Griffith who had demanded a military strike against the anti-Treaty troops in Limerick. Though he was President, Griffith was not a member of the Provisional Government, the body which exercised real power. Mulcahy had a crucial role to play as Minister of Defence, and it was his determination to avoid confrontation which led to the compromise deal brokered with Liam Lynch.

Lynch and Mulcahy were in regular contact in their efforts to prevent a slide into civil war. The mutual respect they had for each other was strengthened by their IRB background, and Mulcahy desperately needed Lynch's support with the approach of the army convention. The convention was scheduled for 26 March and IRA units from all over the country were electing delegates to attend the convention. As the date approached, however, the Provisional Government became increasingly concerned about the outcome of the convention. Most likely, it would establish its own executive independent of the Dáil, and this raised the prospect of the new IRA body acting as a military dictatorship. At the eleventh hour the Provisional Government banned the convention, but Mulcahy was unable to prevent dissident elements ignoring the ban and holding their own convention which was attended by 22 anti-Treaty delegates. Still, Mulcahy retained the hope that army unity might somehow be preserved, and he met Lynch and other anti-Treaty officers on 20 March, but any prospect of a rapprochement ended when the militant republicans within the anti-Treaty IRA asserted their authority. First, Rory O'Connor held a press conference on 22 March in which he indicated that his section of the IRA would ignore the Dáil and act as a military junta. Second, the delegates attending the convention on 26 March reaffirmed their allegiance to the republic and declared that the army would be brought under the complete control of a newly elected, sixteen-man executive. Despite all the attempts at reconciliation, it was now clear to everyone that the IRA had split irrevocably and this increased the likelihood of open confrontation. For weeks the Provisional Government had been building up its own army dominated by officers whose pro-Treaty credentials were beyond question. On the other side, however, the anti-Treaty troops were not united. Lynch had been selected as chief of staff, but there was a more radical faction led by O'Connor which resented any notion of normal democratic practice and threatened civil war.

The slide into Civil War

The anti-Treaty military factions held a second meeting of their rump convention on 9 April, and the general tenor of the meeting indicated that Ireland's independence could not be trusted to the politicians. On 14 April a section of their forces led by O'Connor seized the Four Courts building in Dublin and established a new military headquarters. Other buildings were then occupied and, in a replay of 1916, these were quickly transformed into defensive military positions. This was a direct challenge to the Provisional Government and an open invitation to all IRA men who were unhappy with the Treaty to follow the new executive. While there was an obvious reluctance by both sides to open fire on the opposition, there was an increasing number of incidents involving the competing armies which, by early May, had resulted in the deaths of eight men. These skirmishes increased the tension and there were growing calls from a variety of groups including the church and the press to halt the slide into anarchy. Yet the best placed body to broker an agreement was the IRB. It established a six-man committee which included Lynch and was equally divided between pro and anti-Treaty elements. Four meetings were held, but Lynch's insistence that the army must remain the army of the Irish Republic and be under the control of an independent army executive led to the collapse of the negotiations. Still, other avenues remained open. Early in May 1922, a group of army officers, all but one of whom opposed the Treaty, presented compromise proposals following a series of meetings they had with Collins. Their spokesman, Sean Hegarty, even addressed the Dáil and made a passionate appeal for reconciliation. The officers hoped that the Treaty could be accepted as the basis for a reunification of the army, and this would be followed by an uncontested election. A new coalition government could then proceed to draft a republican constitution ignoring British demands to adhere strictly to the terms of the Treaty. The officers' appeal was denounced by the Four Courts leaders, but Hegarty had logic on his side when he argued that a civil war would not produce a republic and would only give the British an excuse for military intervention [137].

Although the officers' intervention had been criticised by the Four Courts militants, it did lead directly to a truce. Even O'Connor and his two irreconcilable colleagues in the new anti-Treaty headquarters, Liam Mellowes and Ernie O'Malley, were anxious to prevent the sporadic violence degenerating into full-scale civil war, but there was to be no agreement between the pro and anti-Treaty military leaders. This development did, however, allow negotiations to reopen between the pro and anti-Treaty political factions, and Collins met de Valera in a new effort to map out some common ground. De Valera had formed a new political movement, Cumann na Poblachta (League of the Republic), which was really a forum for his supporters in the Treaty debates, but both he and his new party had been quickly overtaken by events. While his hard-line rhetoric may have contributed to the growing instability, de Valera was privately seeking reconciliation, but O'Connor and the radicals had moved the goalposts by seizing the initiative. The country's drift into anarchy was not helped by the complex and overlapping political structures. In effect there were now three 'governments', in addition to the Unionist administration in Belfast, operating in Ireland. Collins's Provisional Government was to remain in existence until the formal establishment of the Irish Free State in December 1922. Griffith's Dáil administration was even more 'provisional', as it was scheduled to dissolve with the election of a new parliament. Finally, O'Connor's army executive, while it had no legal status, based its authority on the claim that the Dáil had acted wrongly in voting away Ireland's independence. This division of authority only added to the background of uneasiness and confusion against which the competing factions operated. Meanwhile, the growing state of lawlessness in the country, much of which was caused by a wave of bank and post office raids carried out by anti-Treaty troops to finance their activities, demanded positive action from the Provisional Government. By refusing to move against the anti-Treaty troops Collins had angered some of his colleagues. Naturally, he was reluctant to order military action against his former comrades, many of whom were close personal friends, and he also needed the anti-Treaty IRA's assistance to conduct an offensive in the north. However, he shocked many of his supporters when he reached agreement with de Valera and signed an electoral pact on 20 May [138].

The Collins-de Valera pact was concluded after three days of intensive negotiations between the two men, and Collins had struck a deal without consulting his cabinet colleagues. Griffith, in particular, was furious at the contents of the pact, and this ended the close relationship which had developed during the second half of 1921 and had carried the Irish delegation through the Treaty negotiations. The electoral pact was designed to prevent a popular division on the Treaty and to create a unity government which would preserve peace. Indeed the pact made no mention of the Treaty. A national Sinn Féin panel of candidates was agreed upon for the forthcoming election with the proportion of pro and anti-Treaty candidates mirroring the then strength of the two factions in the Dáil. The pact also dealt with the creation of a unity government after the election, which would include a Minister of Defence and five pro-Treaty ministers and four anti-Treaty ministers. Collins had been very reluctant to accept these terms, but he was persuaded by his old IRB associate, Harry Boland, who impressed on him the desire for unity. In entering into an electoral pact with de Valera Collins had made all the concessions, and it looked as if he was on the point of repudiating the Treaty. The pact was endorsed by a special Sinn Féin Ard Fheis on 21 May when Collins offered a blunt assessment of the development: "Unity at home was more important than any Treaty with the foreigner, and if unity could only be got at the expense of the Treaty - the Treaty would have to go". On the one hand Collins's actions were reminiscent of his old conspiratorial days. Even his response to the Treaty which he expected to use as a 'stepping stone' to a republic revealed something of the conspirator as well as the pragmatist. Yet on the other hand it was clear that only such a pact could enable the promised election to take place in a peaceful atmosphere. Otherwise, an election was a recipe for widespread intimidation and disruption, particularly in those areas where anti-Treaty troops were in control. Of course, Collins was also desperate to avoid a conflict with his former comrades and he retained the hope that the new constitution, which was close to completion, could reconcile many of the republican dissidents.

The British government was more than an interested spectator as events unfolded in Dublin. As the Colonial Office had taken over many of the duties previously administered by the Irish Office, it was Churchill, the Colonial Secretary, who was supervising Irish affairs. He had been very disappointed with the Provisional Government's failure to deal positively with the anti-Treaty faction, particularly after O'Connor and his men had occupied the Four Courts. Initially, he was convinced that, despite the political furore in Dublin, Griffith and Collins were men of good faith who could be relied upon to implement the Treaty, and he had no hesitation in supplying the Provisional Government with weapons for the new Free State army. Yet subsequently, Collins's reluctance to dislodge the Four Courts garrison and then his collaboration with de Valera over the election left Churchill dismayed. He was, moreover, under intense pressure from Conservatives, both the mainstream and the Diehard variety, who demanded that the government should force Dublin to take tough action against the republican militants. Following the pact announcement Churchill summoned Griffith and Collins to London, where they were joined by Lionel Curtis, the constitutional expert who had acted as an adviser to the British delegation during the Treaty negotiations. Although Curtis pointed out that the electoral pact was technically not a breach of the Treaty, it was clear that the British no longer trusted Collins to adhere to the spirit of the Treaty, as he had obviously surrendered to the republican faction [139].

This feeling of disappointment and anger with the Provisional Government increased when Griffith and Collins arrived back in London on 27 May with the draft Free State constitution. That there should have been any scope for disagreement was a consequence of the way that the Treaty left crucial facets of Anglo-Irish relations open to future negotiation. Article 1 defined Ireland's constitutional status as that of a dominion, but Article 17 dealt with the administration of the Irish Free State in the period before a constitution came into effect. This constitution was to be framed by the Provisional Government and was, of course, to be consistent with the Treaty. Despite this stipulation, Collins believed that this left the Provisional Government considerable latitude and he, therefore, moved the constitution in a republican direction. Accordingly, the draft constitution he took to London made no mention of the oath of allegiance and virtually dismissed any role for the Crown. The Irish draft also ignored the 1920 Government of Ireland Act and was, not surprisingly, dismissed by the British as an evasion of the Treaty. At a second meeting with the British on 1 June Lloyd George indicated that the situation was now very grave, while Churchill threatened military intervention if the Irish did not meet their Treaty obligations. This infuriated Collins who attacked the British for their failure to protect the Nationalist minority in the north, where there had been a further escalation of the conflict in May. On the following day the Irish recognised that their proposals were not acceptable, and a new constitution was agreed which met British requirements on the oath and status. They agreed, moreover, that the Treaty should have more authority than the constitution. This meant that subsequent amendments to the constitution which were deemed to be inconsistent with the Treaty would be rendered null and void. Still, as Kevin O'Higgins was to argue forcefully, the Crown's role in the new constitution was clearly symbolic, leaving "the real power in the hands of the people".

Due to the inevitable delay in publication the details of the new constitution only became available to the public on the morning of 16 June which, by coincidence, was polling day for the election to the Third Dáil. The Irish capitulation on the constitution had placed an intolerable strain on the Collins–de Valera pact. Two days before the election Collins made a speech in Cork when he called on voters to choose the candidates they considered best, irrespective of whether they were on the panel or not. This is often seen as a deliberate attempt by Collins to break the pact but, in truth, he recognised that the pact could not survive his failure to win acceptance of his 'republican' constitution. In any case the pact was completely shattered by other pro-Treaty leaders, particularly Eoin O'Duffy and Ernest Blythe, who were urging voters to give their third preference votes to other parties and independents, rather than anti-Treaty Sinn Féin runners. The use of proportional representation in the June election was significant, as it allowed the electorate to express preferences between pro and anti-Treaty candidates. While there was a Sinn Féin panel of candidates, newspapers had left voters in no doubt about where each candidate stood on the Treaty issue. Outside the panel, moreover, there was an array of other parties and independents all of whom were pro-Treaty. When the results were declared, it was clear that the Treaty had received an overwhelming endorsement from the people. Of the 620,283 votes cast only 133,864 were won by anti-Treaty Sinn Féin candidates. Pro-Treaty panel candidates won 239,193 votes, and the remaining 247,276 votes were divided among the independents and other parties. In terms of seats pro-Treaty Sinn Féin won 58, anti-Treaty Sinn Féin won 35, Labour won 17, the Farmers' party won 7, Independents won 4 and the Unionists won 4. Undoubtedly, the anti-Treaty faction owed a good number of its seats to the existence of a panel. Anti-Treaty candidates polled well in Connacht, reasonably well in Munster, but very poorly in Leinster where they won only 5 out of 44 seats. In total they won less than 22 per cent of the first-preference votes. Perhaps the most striking feature of the election, however, was the large number of votes won by non-Sinn Féin candidates. Labour won over 29 per cent of the vote, and it certainly missed the opportunity to win more seats by not running enough candidates. Elsewhere, particular interest groups polled well, and the Farmers' party won seats in all but one of the constituencies which it contested.

The people were not to have the final say on the Treaty. Indeed the republican militants did not wait for the announcement of the results on 24 June. On 18 June they summoned an army convention which led to a further split within the ranks of the anti-Treaty IRA with a majority, the 'Four Courts executive', supporting a motion proposed by Tom Barry to declare war on Britain. The militants then retired to the Four Courts building having deposed Lynch as chief of staff. Lynch, in turn, withdrew to the Clarence Hotel in Dublin where he established new headquarters. He still retained the faint hope that unity in the army could be achieved. Events took a further twist with the assassination of Sir Henry Wilson in London on 22 June. Wilson, now a Unionist MP in Northern Ireland, had been acting as a security adviser to the Belfast government and was, in Collins's opinion, responsible for many of the attacks which were carried out against the minority community in the north. Various suggestions have been made about the decision to assassinate Wilson. Hard evidence is missing because Wilson's two assailants, Reginald Dunne and Joseph O'Sullivan, whose wooden leg made an escape problematic, were apprehended and executed, but they steadfastly refused to reveal the source from which the order had emanated. The most likely answer was that the attack was ordered by Collins in response to the treatment of northern Catholics. Of course, none of this was suspected at the time, and the Provisional Government issued a swift condemnation of the killing. The British government was outraged by the Wilson murder, and they blamed the anti-Treaty IRA group housed in the Four Courts. Accordingly, the government in London ordered the military to make the necessary preparations for an attack on the Four Courts occupants. If the Provisional Government was not prepared to dislodge the republican extremists, the British government would assume responsibility.

On the day after Wilson's assassination the Lloyd George government put in place plans for unilateral action against the Four Courts but then postponed its attack at the eleventh hour. Macready, who had remained in command of the troops in Ireland, was concerned about the possible consequences of British military intervention. Such an operation could have the effect of unifying the IRA, and the British might then be sucked into another protracted conflict. A decision was taken, therefore, to step up the pressure on the Provisional Government to take action against the Four Courts executive. This had been their strategy since mid-April, and Wilson's assassination had given the British fresh ammunition as they attempted to force the Provisional Government's hand. At the same time, the Provisional Government was feeling the pressure, and an uncompromising speech by Churchill in the House of Commons on 26 June was widely regarded as a thinly veiled ultimatum to Collins [140]. By this stage, however, the Provisional Government had virtually decided to break the deadlock, and the kidnapping by the Four Courts men of J J O'Connell, a popular pro-Treaty senior officer, in retaliation for the arrest of one of their officers, finally tipped the balance. Another factor which Collins considered in taking the decision to attack the Four Courts was the knowledge that the anti-Treaty ranks were split, though he was unaware that attempts to heal this division were ongoing. Still, it was with great reluctance that Collins arrived at this painful decision. He had made great efforts to find a compromise and in the process had exasperated both the British authorities and his political colleagues. Griffith and O'Higgins had consistently argued that military action would be necessary to establish democratic authority, but the political faction had to wait on Collins. In the end it was Rory O'Connor's stubborn refusal to vacate the Four Courts which gave Collins no room for manoeuvre. O'Connor had hoped to provoke the British into staging an attack, but this was a development which Collins knew he had to prevent. An ultimatum calling on the Four Courts occupants to surrender was delivered at 3.40 am on 28 June 1922. Within half an hour the attack on the Four Courts by Free State troops had begun.

Irish fighting Irish

Churchill's delight on hearing that hostilities had begun was tempered by news that the bombardment carried out by young and inexperienced Free State troops was having little effect. The new troops showed little enthusiasm for the conflict, and it was only the leadership and courage displayed by officers such as Emmet Dalton which maintained morale. Churchill even considered deploying British gunners to complete the operation, but the Provisional Government knew that it would be a fatal mistake to ask for British assistance. By 30 June the situation was under control as the Four Courts garrison marched out of a blazing building to surrender. Anti-Treaty units, or the 'Irregulars' as they became known, had also occupied key buildings along O'Connell Street. Again, this made no military sense, and the occupants were easily dislodged by Free State troops who were now gaining in confidence. It was from one of these buildings that Cathal Brugha, after ordering his men to surrender, ran onto the street brandishing a gun and was immediately shot down. He died later that evening. One week into July the Irregulars had evacuated the city. Some of their leaders, notably O'Connor and Mellowes, were in jail, and there was considerable disagreement on future tactics. In the Dublin fighting 65 had been killed and the damage to property was estimated at £4 million.

For six months the country had been sliding towards civil war. Confusion and general lawlessness had increased since April, but the shelling in Dublin quickly clarified the situation. The fighting united anti-Treaty elements. The political opponents of the Treaty led by de Valera rallied to the Irregulars, and de Valera condemned the attack on the Four Courts, describing O'Connor and his men as "the best and bravest of our nation" and appealing for the people's support in the struggle to save the republic. More significantly, the attack on the Four Courts had ended Lynch's caution. Although he and his close colleague, Liam Deasy, had been arrested, they had been released on Mulcahy's orders in the forlorn hope that they would dissuade their followers from taking up arms against the Provisional Government. Lynch and Deasy travelled south to link up with their 1st Southern Division, and Lynch became commander of the Irregulars . At the outbreak of the civil war the Irregulars controlled the south and west of the country, and their relatively well armed troops enjoyed an initial numerical advantage. The Provisional Government's forces were concentrated in Dublin and, though they did not yet have enough trained men to mount an offensive campaign in the provinces, the swelling of their ranks and the delivery of arms by the British would give them a decisive advantage. While the Irregulars benefited by operating in their own localities, this was more than outweighed by the generally hostile attitude of the public to the republican troops. Taken together, these factors indicated that if the Irregulars were to achieve a military victory, it would have to come quickly. The situation demanded that they strike an early and decisive blow before the inevitable strengthening of the Free State army. From the outset, however, the Irregulars suffered from their failure to adopt a coherent military strategy.

The outcome of the civil war was decided during the first two months of the conflict, when the Irregulars passed up the opportunity to seize the initiative. Instead they found themselves trying to defend the areas they controlled, but, when they were threatened with attack, they evacuated their positions after burning their barracks. It was in this manner that the Irregulars abandoned the important towns of Clonmel, Waterford, Sligo and Castlebar. Republican forces remained in control of Cork and Limerick, and these became obvious targets for the Free State army. Although Collins did not like the thought of further bloodshed and wanted to retain lines of communication with the Irregulars, the conflict had established a momentum of its own. By early August an extensive recruitment campaign, which was conducted against a favourable background of high unemployment, had pushed up the number of regular troops in the Free State army to 14,000. Collins had become commander in chief and had resigned from his ministerial positions, leaving Cosgrave in charge of the Provisional Government. A determined assault was launched on republican strongholds in Munster, and troops were sometimes transported by sea to overcome problems with road and rail communications. Strategically, Limerick was of crucial importance. If the Irregulars controlled Limerick, they would have effectively cut off Michael Brennan's forces in Clare and Sean MacEoin's forces based in Athlone, and these were the only real pro-Treaty strongholds outside Dublin. Yet though the republican forces in Limerick were particularly strong, they evacuated the city soon after the Free State troops began their offensive. In mid-August Cork fell to Dalton's troops, as they advanced on the city following a daring mission which landed a large Free State army contingent on the south coast. The Irregulars in Cork put up even less resistance than the Limerick garrison, and the retreat was a hasty, disorganised affair which damaged morale. These early weeks also witnessed serious skirmishing in a number of counties, particularly in the west, and, though they controlled most of South Tipperary, Kerry, West Galway, Mayo and Sligo, their failure to hold any large town or city was a major blow for the Irregulars [141].

The month of August also saw the deaths of Arthur Griffith and Michael Collins. Griffith, who had been suffering from exhaustion for some time, died of a brain haemorrhage on 12 August in a Dublin nursing home. On 22 August Collins died from a gunshot wound to the head following an ambush at Beal na mBlath in his native County Cork. He was in a motor column, accompanied by Emmet Dalton, which was returning to the city of Cork after a day spent touring Free State positions in the area. There were also strong rumours that Collins was hoping to make contact with republican leaders in an attempt to secure a cease-fire. It seemed foolhardy in the extreme for Collins to have ventured into such an Irregular stronghold without such a motive. What strengthened these rumours was de Valera's presence in the immediate locality, where he had arrived to urge Deasy to open peace negotiations. If the Irregulars intended to surrender, they would have expected to obtain better terms from Collins than from the Provisional Government in Dublin, but there is no evidence that Collins intended to meet de Valera. That aside, the suspicious circumstances surrounding Collins's death have spawned a number of conspiracy theories which suggest that he may have been killed by one of his own party acting at the behest of either the British secret service or the republicans. Neither suggestion holds up, and Collins's tragic death at the age of 31 was attributable to his foolish bravado under fire when escape was the only sensible option. Of course, the manner of his death was less important than the fact that he was killed. The loss of Collins was a major blow for the Provisional Government which momentarily lost its way. He had been the dominant figure in both the army and the government, but Cosgrave and O'Higgins moved quickly to fill his political shoes, leaving Mulcahy to take control of the army. Mulcahy issued an address to the army appealing for discipline and calm, and, while he acknowledged that no one could match Collins's personal appeal, he reaffirmed the army's determination to finish the job which Collins had so reluctantly begun.

Despite the loss of Collins, the outcome of the civil war had already been determined by events during the first six weeks of fighting. The failure of the Irregulars to mount an offensive when circumstances were most favourable had been the decisive factor. This was partly due to their reluctance to mount attacks against their old comrades, though this quickly disappeared once the conflict was under way. It was also true that republican forces had failed to make preparations for such a conflict. What developed was a haphazard, confused and incoherent campaign with little attempt made to establish any form of centralised control. While the Irregulars had in their numbers many of the best fighting men from the key areas in the War of Independence, their experience and undoubted courage would not be enough to stave off certain defeat in these changed circumstances. There were, moreover, other notable commanders who, though they opposed the Treaty, refused to link up with the Irregulars. Men like Sean Hegarty and Florrie O'Donoghue preferred to remain neutral, and this was a blow to the republican forces. As they were driven out of the larger towns and cities, the Irregulars returned to the old style of guerrilla warfare which they knew best. Yet this type of campaign relied on the support of the local population, and this was generally not forthcoming during the civil war. Lack of finance forced republican troops to commandeer food and other supplies, and this increased public hostility, particularly during a period when most people were trying to recover from the social and economic disruption caused by the War of Independence. In some cases Irregulars engaged in looting to obtain supplies with a predictable effect on the local population. The Irregulars also lacked an effective intelligence system, a feature which is essential in guerrilla warfare. All of these problems were compounded by Lynch's indecision and by his failure to establish unity of command. This latter failing may have been impossible to overcome with the forces at his disposal. It was very difficult to instill discipline in many of the Irregular units and almost impossible to guarantee effective co-operation between these units. Communication between divisions was a serious problem and was usually left to the women of Cumann na mBan, but, in most cases, individual commanders preferred to operate on their own initiative. In addition, neighbouring forces were often very suspicious of each other, and this added to the difficulty of developing a coherent military strategy.

Republican forces were also very suspicious of political leaders, and this contributed to their failure to develop a viable political alternative which may have attracted some popular support. Certainly, Lynch was very cool towards de Valera whom he suspected of seeking peace terms. Lynch saw peace initiatives and the pursuit of political objectives as a diversion from the military campaign. Nothing else, in his opinion, should be allowed to interfere with the military struggle, and, despite the early reverses, he remained very enthusiastic about the outcome. De Valera, however, was not prepared to accept such constraints, and he sought a meeting with Mulcahy which took place on 6 September. Mulcahy's agreement to de Valera's request had ruffled his cabinet colleagues, whom he had failed to consult, but the meeting was unsuccessful and finally put paid to any hope of a compromise. The failure of the Mulcahy-de Valera discussions reinforced Mulcahy's determination to crush those elements whose aim, he insisted, was to spread anarchy and chaos. On

15 September 1922 he asked the cabinet to extend the army's powers in its struggle with the Irregulars. Accordingly, a Public Safety Bill was introduced in the Dáil on 27 September, proposing the establishment of military courts which would be given very wide powers. These included execution for a variety of offences such as possession of arms, commandeering of property, looting and arson. Following the June election the Third Dáil had held its opening session on 5 September and, as de Valera's followers refused to attend, the Public Safety Bill was guaranteed to become law. Still, many doubts were expressed. The Labour opposition attacked the bill, claiming that it was akin to the introduction of a military dictatorship, and a number of pro-Treaty deputies expressed concern about giving the army such wide ranging powers. In response to such criticism Mulcahy was at pains to point out that the army would always be subject to political authority. To mollify the opposition it was announced on 3 October that there would be a general amnesty for all republican troops who handed in their weapons and accepted the government's authority. The government also received powerful backing from the Catholic bishops who issued a joint pastoral on 10 October condemning the actions of the Irregulars as unjust and immoral. The Public Safety Bill came into force on 15 October and executions began within five weeks.

De Valera, who was furious at the bishops' stance, had earlier persuaded his Cumann na Poblachta followers not to attend the Dáil. He intended to establish a republican government, but this depended on the attitude of the republican army. Ernie O'Malley had been pressing for the formation of a new government and his demand was supported by some of those who were in prison. One of those in jail, Liam Mellowes, advocated the need for a new republican government to revive the Democratic Programme, but Lynch was highly sceptical about the need for any political initiative. In due course, however, he relented and following a meeting of his army executive on 16 and 17 October, it was decided to form a republican government with de Valera as its president, even though all of those involved appreciated that their new creation would exist on paper only. The natural choice as Minister for Publicity in de Valera's shadow government was Erskine Childers, and he was asked to make his way back to Dublin. Since mid-August Childers had been on the run in Cork and Kerry, relying on a pony and trap to cart around his printing press which he was using to produce propaganda material. On his journey to Dublin he was arrested by Free State troops on 10 November near the Barton family home in County Wicklow. He had in his possession a revolver which may have been given to him by Collins, but under the new emergency legislation this was a capital offence. The fact that some of the Irish and English press painted Childers as the mastermind behind the Irregulars' campaign would not help his cause. Neither would the Provisional Government's belief that he was one of the anti–Treaty leaders who had done most to lead others astray, and he was personally disliked by some government ministers, particularly O'Higgins. It was no surprise when a military court found him guilty, and he was executed on 24 November 1922.

Childers had not been the first to face execution. On 17 November four young men who had guns in their possession when they were arrested in Dublin were executed. The country was stunned by these early executions, and Labour deputies were loud in their condemnation. Mulcahy, however, defended the government's firm action warning that the army had a 'responsibility' to save the country in this very grave situation. In response, Lynch issued a general order at the end of November, instructing his troops to shoot deputies who had voted for the emergency legislation and other categories supporting the Provisional Government [142]. There was great reluctance to carry out such a threat but, on 7 December, Sean Hales was killed and Padraic O'Maille wounded, as they travelled to a meeting of the Dáil. Hales had been a courageous soldier who had won fame in the War of Independence, and his killing shocked the nation and drew an immediate response from the Provisional Government. On the evening of 7 December, four senior prisoners who had been in jail since the surrender of the Four Courts were informed that they would be executed as a reprisal for the killing of Hales. The four men, Rory O'Connor, Liam Mellowes, Joseph McKelvey and Richard Barrett, one from each of the four provinces, were executed on the morning of 8 December. It was likely that Mulcahy had taken the initiative in the cabinet, but O'Higgins took some time to convince. O'Connor had been best man at his wedding, but Mulcahy was determined to deter future assassination attempts. The executions had the desired effect. There were no further assassinations and the morale of republican troops was severely shaken, but this had been achieved at a terrible price. Labour deputies in the Dáil, which was not informed of the executions until after they had been carried out, denounced the government, claiming that the executions were really murders.

Although no further assassinations took place, the Irregulars began the systematic destruction of property belonging to prominent government supporters in December. In the early months of 1923, Unionist property became a target, and this led to the burning of some of Ireland's finest country houses. More successful in terms of its military effectiveness was the attack on the railway system. As early as August 1922 all rail routes to the south and west had been affected, and the government was forced to establish a Railroad Protection and Maintenance Corps to carry out repairs. The Railroad Corps did sterling work, but many local lines in Cork and Kerry were only reopened after the conflict. By the end of 1922 a clear pattern of guerrilla warfare was identifiable. Indeed one of the first casualties of the guerrilla style ambushes had been Michael Collins, but Lynch was generally disappointed by the failure of the Irregulars to mount an effective campaign in those parts of Tipperary and Cork which had been so active in the War of Independence. In these areas local particularism rendered close co-operation between neighbouring units impossible, though it was also true that the local population, having borne the brunt of the fighting against the British, wanted a return to peace. It was noticeable that the most active areas in the civil war, such as Kerry, Galway and Mayo, had experienced very little fighting during the War of Independence. Of course, the remote areas in South Kerry, West Mayo and Connemara provided the ideal terrain for guerrilla warfare. In West Mayo and West Connemara the Irregulars were brilliantly led by Michael Kilroy who, until his capture at the end of November 1922, was to prove a very effective local commander and a real thorn in the Free State army's side. In these poor western regions there was solid republican support. Government troops in these areas were notoriously unpopular, and there was a long tradition of opposition to and suspicion of central government. Support for the Irregulars in the south and west also had a socio-economic basis. The continuing hunger for land was a powerful factor which was translated into opposition to the Provisional Government. However, despite the appeals of Liam Mellowes, both the anti-Treaty political and military factions failed to harness this agrarian support. By the end of 1922 local Irregular units in some very poor regions such as West Connemara were complaining that the local population simply did not have the means to support them.

The Free State government stepped up its offensive at the beginning of 1923 as it predicted the early defeat of the Irregulars. In January alone 34 executions took place, and this had a demoralising effect on the Irregulars. The Free State army had grown significantly and in March it passed the 50,000 mark. It was only Lynch's intransigence and his refusal to accept the hopelessness of the republican position which kept the conflict going into the spring of 1923. There were growing calls on the republican side for peace negotiations and, though Tom Barry made a concerted effort to secure a peace deal in February 1923, Lynch emphatically rejected all peace proposals, insisting, without any evidence, that better times for the republican forces were just around the corner. The capture of one senior Irregular leader, Liam Deasy, who acted as Lynch's deputy, had a devastating effect on republican morale. Deasy too had been interested in peace, but he was arrested on 18 January, and the authorities ruthlessly exploited his desire for peace. Threatened with execution Deasy appealed to his comrades to end the fighting, arguing that this was the best course for the republican cause in the longer term. Although all the recipients of the 'Deasy letter' turned down his call for peace negotiations and Lynch issued a statement to all officers denouncing any talk of compromise, the appeal had a very damaging effect. Even Lynch was rattled by Deasy's change of heart [143].

It is perhaps surprising that the Free State army took so long to finish the job in 1923. Of course, it had been hastily recruited, and troops were often dispatched to the provinces with only a modicum of training. In cabinet O'Higgins demanded sterner measures and constantly attacked Mulcahy whom he held responsible for the army's weak performance. Undoubtedly, O'Higgins exaggerated the army's failure to deal with a whole range of crimes perpetrated by the Irregulars and its inability to protect the population. Really O'Higgins was using the situation in parts of Kerry to generalise about most of the south and west. The civil war was more bitterly fought in Kerry than in any other Irish county. This was particularly true in Mid and South Kerry, where ambushes of Free State troops travelling in convoy along main roads became a regular occurrence. At the same time, Irregulars moved around openly in large flying columns cutting communications and generally disrupting the social and economic life of the country. The Free State army occupied the large barrack towns of Listowel, Tralee, Castleisland and Killarney, leaving the Irregulars in control of the surrounding hills. While the Irregulars were incapable of mounting large-scale attacks, they adopted a holding strategy and proved very difficult to dislodge. Free State troops were forced to divide into columns and conduct large sweeps of the countryside in their attempts to flush out the enemy. In January 1923 General Paddy Daly who led the Dublin Guard, the crack regiment which had been created by Collins, arrived in Kerry to take command of the Free State troops. These men were very unpopular with the local population, and this only added to the already considerable support which the Irregulars enjoyed. Their behaviour and indiscipline frequently caused offence, and there were many rumours concerning the ill-treatment, and sometimes torture, of prisoners. Daly himself had been one of Collins's Squad which had operated to such effect in the destruction of the British intelligence system during 1919-21, and many of his Dublin Guard were battle-hardened veterans of the War of Independence. They had been fiercely loyal to Collins and quickly established a fearsome reputation for their ruthlessness. With local Irregular units displaying equal fanaticism, the conflict in Kerry had the potential to dissolve into a bloody vendetta.

It was ironic that in March 1923 just as the conflict was on the point of petering out elsewhere, it should erupt in Kerry in a series of atrocities and reprisals which left a legacy of terrible bitterness. Interwoven with the wider conflict in Kerry was a distinct layer of family feuding which added to the intensity of feeling. On the night of 5 March 1923 three officers and two soldiers in the Free State army died when a trap mine exploded at Knocknagoshel, which is in the north-east of the county close to Castleisland. Subsequently, the Irregulars claimed that their target was a Lieutenant O'Connor who was alleged to have participated in the torture of republican prisoners. Certainly, Daly's men were outraged by O'Connor's death, and an order was issued by Daly stating that republican prisoners should be removed from the jails and used to clear barricades suspected of containing trap mines. In the next few days seventeen Irregular prisoners died when explosions occurred in barricades which they were clearing. On the night of 6 March nine prisoners were taken from their cells in Tralee and ordered to clear a barricade at Ballyseedy near Castleisland. The men were tied together and the mine was allegedly detonated by Free State soldiers. Amazingly, one of the prisoners, Stephen Fuller, survived the blast and made his way to a safe house. He went on to become a Fianna Fail deputy in North Kerry, and he later gave his version of the events at Ballyseedy in a television interview with Robert Kee. On the same night as the Ballyseedy incident, four prisoners died while clearing an obstruction at Countess Bridge in Killarney, and a further five died when a mine exploded outside Cahirciveen. An army enquiry chaired by Daly was hastily arranged. It claimed that all the mines had been laid by Irregulars and firmly denied that the prisoners had been killed as a reprisal for the Knocknagoshel explosion. Mulcahy defended the army's actions in the Dáil, though he promised that in future more careful checks would be undertaken to detect the presence of mines before prisoners were sent in to clear obstructions. A different version, however, was presented by Fuller, the Knocknagoshel survivor. He claimed that prisoners were removed from their cells and deliberately led to their deaths by Free State troops, though disputes still run over who laid the mine at Ballyseedy [144].

The four trap mine incidents did not end the killing in Kerry. Following a republican attack on Cahirciveen, Free State reinforcements arrived by sea and in a follow-up operation five Irregulars were killed. Another five who had been taken prisoner were executed on 28 March. Further clashes led to more republican losses, and there was fresh controversy. Irregulars hiding in the cave system north of Kerry Head were surrounded and, after a siege lasting several days, a number were killed while trying to surrender. Again, more executions of those captured were to follow. At the same time, however, a more significant loss occurred on the slopes of the Knockmealdown mountains in neighbouring County Limerick when Lynch was killed. The republican will to carry on the conflict indefinitely died with Lynch. Frank Aiken, his successor as chief of staff, favoured negotiations, and de Valera tried to secure a ceasefire on favourable terms at the beginning of May. When the government dismissed de Valera's proposals, Aiken issued the order to dump arms. On 24 May 1923, the day that Aiken's order was published, de Valera issued his famous proclamation to the republican forces:

> Soldiers of Liberty! Legion of the rearguard! The Republic can no longer be defended successfully by your arms. Further sacrifices on your part would now be in vain, and continuance of the struggle in arms unwise in the national interest. Military victory must be allowed to rest for the moment with those who have destroyed the Republic.

Republican forces, therefore, had not recognised the legitimacy of the Free State, and they refused to hand over their weapons. But the civil war was over [145].

Estimates vary on the number of casualties during the conflict, but a total figure of just under 3,000 seems reasonable. The nearest comparison to contemporary Ireland was Finland which had also achieved independence. It experienced a bloody civil war in 1918 which claimed over 25,000 lives out of a total population of 4,000,000. Moreover, the total of 77 executions carried out by the Cosgrave-led government, which left such a bitter legacy in Ireland, appears insignificant when set beside the 8,300 executions in Finland. By contrast, therefore, the Irish civil war was a relatively small affair, but it imposed a very heavy financial burden on the embryonic Free State and its psychological impact acted as a millstone around the new state's neck. On the surface the civil war was fought over the differences between the Treaty and Document No 2 or, more particularly, over the oath. The real cause of the civil war, however, was the split in the IRA which was separate from Sinn Féin. The immediate trigger had been the pressure applied by the British to clear the Four Courts following Wilson's assassination. One historian of the civil war, Michael Hopkinson, has argued that military confrontation was inevitable once rival IRA units had taken over empty barracks following the Treaty. On a more general level the revolutionaries of 1916-21 had to make the transition from revolutionaries to politicians. In some cases the transition was difficult, in others it proved impossible. This latter group would not accept the people's verdict when it was at odds with their own. They justified their actions by placing themselves in the Irish revolutionary tradition of 1916, which saw Pearse and company winning almost immediate retrospective legitimacy for their military action. De Valera's position on the fringe of the irreconcilable faction added substance to this view. While he was not responsible for the civil war, he had given political credibility to the republican forces when, in 1922, he declared that the people have no right to do wrong. Yet the conflict was decided by military, not political, factors. Solid support for the republican cause had prolonged the conflict in selected areas, such as South Kerry, South Galway and West Mayo, which had escaped the fighting during the War of Independence, but the overall outcome was not in doubt following the Irregulars' failure to strike an early military blow at the beginning of hostilities when the Free State was most vulnerable.

Consolidation

The preoccupation with the civil war had deflected attention from the partition question. The conflict had not spilled into Northern Ireland, and the most active IRA units in the north made their way across the border where some of them participated in the civil war. The republican side had not made the border an issue in the civil war. On the other hand, the attacks on the north's Catholic minority had made partition an issue for Collins. During the first half of 1922 he had sought the co-operation of both pro and anti-Treaty factions in launching a joint offensive in the north, but this had not been successful. With the outbreak of the civil war his energies were devoted to the new Free State army of which he was commander in chief, but he did meet northern IRA leaders in Dublin at the beginning of 1922. Collins supported the non-recognition of the state by northern Nationalists, though he acknowledged that the IRA, without support from the south, could do no more than try to protect the Catholic community. He did reassure his audience that support would be forthcoming, but nothing definite was arranged. Meanwhile, the Provisional Government had formed a committee to draw up a northern policy. A memorandum submitted on 9 August 1922 by Ernest Blythe, an Ulster Presbyterian and a key member of this five-man committee, set the scene for a shift in policy. Blythe rejected the use of either military coercion or economic sanctions, both of which had been tried, to restore Irish unity. Instead he thought that the policy of non-recognition should be allowed to fizzle out, and the aggressive posturing towards the new Northern Ireland state should be ended. Ten days later, the Provisional Government endorsed Blythe's views, favouring a policy of conciliation regarding the north. This coincided with the death of Collins. He was the one leader in the Provisional Government who was really concerned about partition and the treatment of the minority, and his death meant that the north quickly slipped down the Provisional Government's list of priorities.

Clearly, the civil war had entrenched partition and consolidated the Unionist government's position. Cosgrave wanted to improve relations with the north and argued against interference in northern affairs. His government's overriding concern was the successful prosecution of the civil war and the north was regarded as an unwelcome distraction. This feeling persisted in the period immediately after the civil war, as the Cosgrave government wrestled with the huge difficulties of rebuilding the country's infrastructure. Again, there were more pressing problems than partition. The conflict had postponed the establishment of the Boundary Commission promised in the Treaty, and it was without enthusiasm or expectation that Cosgrave requested its establishment in July 1923. Obstructionist tactics by the Unionist government in Belfast resulted in the Boundary Commission's first meeting being delayed until November 1924. The commission then deliberated for much of 1925 but, in the end, recommended only very minor changes. In the confusion a weak Cosgrave government opted to sign a tripartite agreement with London and Belfast in December 1925, which revoked the powers of the Boundary Commission, recognised the existing border and, in return, released the Free State from its liability for some of Britain's public debt. Cosgrave's republican opponents were furious at what they regarded as the surrender of the north, but he had little real alternative.

One reason for the Free State government's weaknesses was the financial drain on the public purse caused by the civil war. The conflict had cost some £17 million and damage to infrastructure was put at £30 million. The government also faced considerable compensation bills for property losses and personal injuries. With the budget in deficit, and expenditure still high after the cease-fire owing to the existence of a large Free State army, the government had to implement austerity measures and place much of the financial burden for the civil war on the taxpayer. This contributed to the caution and financial conservatism of the early Free State administrations. Ireland also suffered from an economic depression in 1923, which caused particular difficulties for the farming population, and this had some influence on the outcome of the election held on 27 August. Under the terms of the constitution which the Dáil had accepted on 6 December 1922, fresh elections were to be held within a year, and Cosgrave opted for a surprise election in August 1923. In March of that year Cosgrave had formed a new political party from his pro-Treaty supporters, Cumann na nGaedheal, and he confidently expected his new party to secure a comfortable overall majority in the new Dáil which had been enlarged from 128 to 153 seats. The results were a disappointment for Cosgrave. While Cumann na nGaedheal emerged as the largest party with 39 per cent of the first preference votes and 63 seats, Sinn Féin won 27.6 per cent of the vote and 44 seats. De Valera had abandoned the Cumann na Poblachta label and chose to run his anti-Treaty followers under the Sinn Féin banner which retained something of its former aura. Of the other parties, Labour was disappointed with its return of 15 seats, the Farmers' Union won 15 seats and the remaining 16 were shared between independent candidates. After the election Cosgrave formed the first Cumann na nGaedheal government with himself officially in the role as President of the Executive Council. The other members of the Executive Council were Kevin O'Higgins (Home Affairs), Ernest Blythe (Finance), Joseph McGrath (Industry and Commerce), Eoin MacNeill (Education), Desmond Fitzgerald (External Affairs) and Richard Mulcahy (Defence).

Although the election results had been a shock, Cosgrave's government enjoyed a comfortable Dáil majority. Sinn Féin had refused to recognise the Dáil and the party's deputies adopted a policy of abstention. The legacy of the civil war, the substantial vote for Sinn Féin and the prospect of renewed violence ensured that the task of establishing a stable government would be fraught with difficulty. Both Cosgrave and O'Higgins had regarded civil war as necessary if democracy was to be established in Ireland. As Minister of Home Affairs, O'Higgins was directly responsible for law and order, and he was determined to re-establish the rule of law and stamp out the anarchy which, he believed, was at the root of republican violence during the civil war. Immediately after the war, O'Higgins pushed through his Public Safety Bill which allowed the government to arrest and intern suspects without trial. These powers were widely used during 1923-24, a period in which violence, arson, robbery and general lawlessness continued to pose a real threat to the new state. Democracy, of course, had to be forced on a substantial minority, now led by de Valera, which continued to deny the legitimacy of the new state. The election of August 1923 had been a violent affair, and riots, arrests and intimidation all featured prominently during the campaign. De Valera had been arrested a fortnight before polling and was not released until July 1924, but the election demonstrated that both he and republicanism were to have an enduring appeal. In addition, there is enough evidence to suggest that the Cumann na nGaedheal vote in the 1923 election was hit by the public's concern at the brutality used, particularly the 77 executions, in pursuit of victory.

The 1923 election also confirmed that attitudes to the Treaty would define political allegiance for the next generation. On the one side, the pro-Treaty Cumann na nGaedheal, led by the solid but uninspiring Cosgrave, was intent on establishing a conservative administration, closely based on the British model, while treating the Catholic Church with due deference. Beyond the twenty-six counties the Cumann na nGaedheal government recognised the reality of partition and sought to play a leading role in the evolution of the British Commonwealth. On the other side stood Sinn Féin, led by the charismatic but self-righteous de Valera, which sought the creation of an independent, united Ireland from outside the Dáil. Yet this Treaty division also masked something of a class division which existed between the two parties. Cosgrave's party was the dominant force in central and eastern Ireland where there were larger farms and more prosperous farmers. Sinn Féin polled well among the poor smallholders of the west where it was able to exploit the traditional resentment of authority. Yet in spite of these differences between east and west Irish rural society was relatively stable. The land question which was the dominant theme in the last quarter of the nineteenth century had been solved by successive Westminster governments, and the Cosgrave administration completed their work with the 1923 Land Act. This transferred those remaining landlord holdings to the tenants. Overall, the Ireland of the 1920s enjoyed a relatively high standard of living, certainly on a par with the rest of western Europe, and this helped Cumann na nGaedheal to promote stability. A strong education system was an added bonus. Blythe's budgets were cautious, and he steadily reduced government expenditure during the 1920s. In their further attempts to develop a stable and legitimate public order the state-builders of Cumann na nGaedheal benefited from the existence of a relatively homogeneous Irish nation which was almost exclusively Catholic. This degree of uniformity was missing in some new, contemporary European states. In this sense partition was an advantage, as it removed the obvious potential problems which might have resulted from the inclusion of one million irreconciled Ulster Protestants.

While the new state gradually succeeded in establishing its authority, it had to acknowledge that there was a lingering contempt for the democratic process among that section of society which had lost out in the civil war. Yet the greatest immediate danger to the new state after the civil war was not to come from de Valera's Sinn Féin, but from its own Free State army. Following the civil war the government had to reorganise its army which had grown to over 50,000, of whom over 3,000 were officers. The aim was to reduce the army's overall strength to 20,000 men, of whom 1,400 would be officers. Financial pressure on the new state meant that demobilisation would have to proceed quickly. There was also the more difficult problem of ridding the army of political influences. Matters almost came to a head in July 1923 when a group of officers who had been in the 'old IRA' openly criticised Mulcahy. They complained, with some justification, that Mulcahy was favouring officers who were in the IRB, and they convinced O'Higgins that the IRB controlled the army. Meanwhile, Joseph McGrath, the Minister for Industry and Commerce, backed the old IRA officers who were reported to be planning some kind of coup in January 1924. Tension had been raised by the demobilisation of 1,000 officers in the previous month, but the crisis really broke on 6 March 1924, when a group of old IRA officers led by General Liam Tobin and Colonel C F Dalton presented Cosgrave with an ultimatum, demanding the sacking of Mulcahy and his three colleagues on the Army Council. These old IRA officers had taken this action on the day before another list of 1,000 officers due for demobilisation was to be published. The problems in the army stretched back to the War of Independence, when Collins had encouraged men of action who could lay ambushes and carry out raids. These loose cannons, who had stayed loyal to Collins after the Treaty, became officers in the Free State army, but they were uncomfortable with the organisation and discipline which any regular army must have.

The 'army mutiny' of March 1924 presented the Cumann na nGaedheal government with a direct challenge. If the mutineers' demands, which included the suspension of demobilisation, were rejected, there was the threat of a military takeover. The situation demanded resolute action by the government and, while Cosgrave dithered, O'Higgins made the decisive move. He was a committed constitutionalist who had dedicated his political life to the principle of civilian government and had no time for either the old IRA officers or the IRB clique. The ringleaders of the mutiny were arrested and McGrath, their chief supporter in the government, resigned. A much more unfortunate casualty was Mulcahy. For some time he had been at loggerheads with O'Higgins who had accused him of failing to impose strict discipline on the army. O'Higgins also harboured the suspicion that Mulcahy was not a sound democrat and posed a militarist threat to the civilian government. If this had been the case, Mulcahy might have used his support in the army to challenge the government and expose O'Higgins's witch-hunt tactics. Retaining all his dignity, Mulcahy tendered his resignation as Minister of Defence, though Cosgrave brought him back to the Cumann na nGaedheal front bench in 1927 as Minister for Local Government. Within days of his return, his great rival and the real strong man in the government, Kevin O'Higgins, was assassinated on 10 July 1927, as he walked to Mass at a church near his Blackrock home. Republicans were suspected, but there was no evidence to link them to the murder. De Valera was unequivocal in his condemnation of the killers. In 1926 he had split with Sinn Féin on the issue of abstention from the Dáil and had formed Fianna Fail. In August 1927, one month after O'Higgins's death he led the Fianna Fail deputies into the Dáil to become the official opposition to the Cumann na nGaedheal government. Within a few years Fianna Fail was in power, and de Valera found himself vindicating Collins's central argument that the 1921 Treaty had given Ireland the freedom to achieve freedom.

Historiography

The British response to the Provisional Government's early attempts to implement the Treaty is fully analysed in Canning's, *British Policy towards Ireland*. The key figures in this phase were Lloyd George and Churchill. Both had developed a sympathy for the Irish leaders during the Treaty negotiations and they fully expected Griffith and Collins to keep faith. Canning notes that the pressure put on the Coalition Conservatives by the Diehards greatly limited the government's freedom on its Irish policy during the first half of 1922. At that time the British government was pursuing two objectives in Ireland. Firstly, it wanted to see free elections in the Irish Free State and the formation of a stable government which could establish its authority. Secondly, it wanted to ensure the survival of the Northern Ireland government. For Churchill, Canning points out, these two objectives went hand in hand. Despite his disappointment with the outcome of the Craig-Collins pacts and with the prevarication over the constitution by Collins's Provisional Government, Churchill showed great patience and understanding in his handling of the Irish situation, though the Collins–de Valera electoral pact and Wilson's assassination caused him great concern. Coogan's, *Michael Collins* looks closely at Collins's reasons for agreeing to the pact and emphasises the impact of Harry Boland's powers of persuasion. Collins, however, had his own reasons. Coogan argues that only such an arrangement could have secured an intimidation-free election, but, more significantly, he judges that the pact placed Collins "more in the light of a conspirator than a statesman", because he needed the pact to launch the joint IRA offensive in the north. Details of the preparations for the offensive are examined in Pheonix's, *Northern Nationalism* which shows that Collins had kept his plans secret from Sinn Féin's political leaders in the north. He goes on to analyse the impact of the IRA's northern campaign in May 1922 which had come as a 'severe shock' to the Craig government, but resulted in a vicious sectarian backlash against the north's minority population. Pheonix stresses the significance of Collins's death in reinforcing partition, but demonstrates in detail that a change in the Provisional Government's northern policy was already taking shape even before Collins's death.

De Valera's actions in the run up to the civil war are examined in Coogan's, *De Valera: Long Fellow, Long Shadow*. Coogan accuses de Valera of deliberately cultivating extremist support prior to the civil war and thus rejects the 'official' line that de Valera had been dragged along by Rory O'Connor and the extremists. He had issued a press statement,following an abortive meeting with Griffith, Collins and Brugha on 29 April 1922 designed to avert a civil war, which said: "Republicans maintain that there are rights which a minority may justly uphold, even by arms, against a majority". Coogan is highly critical of de Valera's failure to use his influence to bring the civil war to an early conclusion, particularly when it became clear that defeat was inevitable. This was certainly the case when he rejected the Deasy peace initiative which was published on 8 February 1923. J M Curran's, *The Birth of the Irish Free State 1921-1923* (Alabama, 1980) stresses that the civil war took a long time to get under way due to the "evident unwillingness of some IRA officers to defy the people's will", and this had given Collins real hope that a conflict might be averted. For Collins, Curran argues that the electoral pact of May 1922 represented the surest way to save the Treaty, but, for de Valera, it was a huge gamble, because it meant the acceptance of the people's vote as the final decision on the Treaty. The author claims that de Valera took such a risk, because his desire to avert a civil war was as strong as Collins's. Curran also notes the strain which the pact and the proposed constitution placed on the Lloyd George Coalition, and he focuses on Chamberlain's unhappiness with these developments which had shocked his own Conservative party. At the same time, while under fierce pressure from the British for his agreement to the pact, Collins, though genuinely very concerned, exploited the pogroms against Ulster Catholics for maximum political advantage. A more focused treatment of British concerns in this period can be found in J McColgan's essay, 'Implementing the 1921 treaty: Lionel Curtis and constitutional procedure' which appeared in *Irish Historical Studies*, XX, No 79 (March, 1977). McColgan shows how the British government reached agreement with the Provisional Government on the practical application of the controversial clauses dealt with in Articles 17 and 18 of the Treaty, emphasising the concentration on the symbols – the oath, the crown, the empire – rather than practical autonomy.

By far the best scholarly account of the civil war is M Hopkinson's, *Green against Green: The Irish Civil War* (Dublin, 1988). Hopkinson highlights the significance of the split in the IRA which he regards as the single main cause of the civil war. He comments on the failure of the Provisional Government to influence the occupation of barracks vacated by the military, noting that in Munster only Listowel and Skibbereen were in the hands of pro-Treaty forces. Hopkinson describes the reluctance of even the most intransigent anti-Treaty IRA leaders such as O'Connor and Mellowes to begin a civil war. He sees the electoral pact as an attempt by de Valera to re-establish both the position of Sinn Féin and his own leadership, but Sinn Féin without the pro-Treaty faction was, in Hopkinson's view, already doomed. On the military side he discusses the absence of a coherent strategy among the various anti-Treaty units and points to the wide range of opinion existing within the leadership. This lack of preparation manifested itself once the conflict was under way, and the indecision and lack of a clear military strategy, particularly when the Irregulars failed to seize the initiative at the outset, doomed the anti-Treaty faction to defeat. On the other hand, Hopkinson describes the many weaknesses of the Free State army, particularly the poor calibre of officers at its disposal. Yet this new army would be strong enough to deal with republican troops who were largely ineffective outside their own areas. By the end of August, notes the author, the Irregulars had opened the guerrilla phase of their campaign which was partially successful in isolated areas such as West Mayo and South Kerry, where there was substantial popular support for the republican cause. He states that the executions shocked opinion in Ireland and England but judges that they weakened morale and reduced military activity by the Irregulars. On the geography of the civil war Hopkinson shows how it was those areas which had been quiet during the War of Independence, such as Mayo and Kerry, that were most active in the civil war. Other potentially active areas such as Cork and South Tipperary were relatively quiet, because the Irregulars in these counties ran up against the local population's desire for peace and were also hampered by what Hopkinson describes as "local particularism". Indeed large areas of the country were really unaffected by the conflict. He concludes by suggesting that the conflict may have been necessary for the Provisional Government to establish effective political authority.

There are a number of other useful accounts which deal directly with the civil war. The best account by one of the participants is E O'Malley's, *The Singing Flame* (Dublin, 1978). O'Malley fought on the anti-Treaty side, and his account shows something of the confusion which dominated the struggle. During the conflict he was captured and later severely wounded following his escape, and much of the book is his description of his time in prison and prison hospitals. E Neeson's, *The Civil War 1922-23* (Dublin, 1989) brings out the real bitterness of the conflict, describing how individual families were often divided by the civil war. He also describes the economic impact of the fighting in rural areas, noting that the 'bourgeois element' stubbornly resisted anti-Treaty IRA attempts to collect income tax in the Cork area. Another narrative account of the conflict can be found in C Younger's, *Ireland's Civil War* (London, 1970) which, in addition to meticulous presentation of the facts, highlights the efforts of the women of Cumann na mBan in those parts of the country where republican troops were most active. Macardle's, *The Irish Republic* also covers the civil war period in great detail, treating sympathetically the attempts by the Irregulars to keep the Free State army at bay. The book includes details of the Kerry atrocities of March 1923.

An interesting book which casts its net over the civil war period is T Garvin's, *1922: The Birth of Irish Democracy* (Dublin, 1996). This book puts the Irish experience in its European context, illustrating how democracy was forced on a section of Irish political opinion against the vicious background of the civil war. The establishment of a democratic state and the creation of order and stability were each due to the successes of the Provisional Government in 1922. Garvin argues forcefully that militant republicanism always lacked popular legitimacy, and he notes, moreover, that there was popular indifference to the "entire Free State versus Republic issue". In truth, he claims, the civil war was fought over issues that "most people saw, accurately, as pointless and unreal". Garvin also stresses that the transformation from revolutionary to politician was a painful process for many of the key figures involved in the civil war period. Some, such as Tom Barry, made no apology for his desire to see a military dictatorship put in place, whereas others, notably Cosgrave and Mulcahy, both of whom he regards as "profoundly underrated" in their contribution to the Irish Free State, were always willing to rely on the people's judgement. Both of these men, together with O'Higgins, viewed the civil war as necessary in establishing Irish democracy. On the other side, anti-Treaty IRA leaders showed a "fear and contempt" of democracy. Another excellent biography which overlaps the civil war is Valiulis's, *Portrait of a Revolutionary*. The book chronicles Mulcahy's exhaustive attempts to patch up some kind of workable compromise in the army prior to the outbreak of hostilities. He was optimistic that an agreement could be reached with Lynch, refusing to blame the militant IRA officers who had provoked the crisis. Instead Mulcahy blamed the political leaders, particularly de Valera, whom he held responsible for the civil war. When the civil war began, both Mulcahy and Collins assumed that they would have to fight the Four Courts occupants, and both were surprised when Lynch and his 1st Southern Division took up arms. Collins's death left Mulcahy increasingly isolated in the cabinet, and O'Higgins, who had actually favoured him over Cosgrave for the leadership position, became a determined opponent. This rivalry saw O'Higgins seize the opportunity to oust Mulcahy during the 'army mutiny' in March 1924. Part of Mulcahy's problem was that he distrusted politicians and did not keep them fully informed during the civil war. This allowed anti-military sentiment to build up in the cabinet, and it was forcefully expressed by O'Higgins. Valiulis concludes that Mulcahy, who was "never at ease" as a politician, did not fit into either the Cosgrave or the de Valera camp, and, while he had made a huge contribution to the struggle for independence, his reputation was tarnished by the civil war.

Of the general histories which deal with the civil war J A Murphy's, *Ireland in the Twentieth Century* (Dublin, 1975) offers a succinct analysis of the important political developments. D Keogh's, *Twentieth-Century Ireland; Nation and State* (Dublin, 1994) looks in some detail at the crisis in the army in 1924, concluding that Mulcahy and his most senior colleagues had been unfairly treated. Earlier, he notes the unfortunate failure to halt the civil war when the opportunity existed in September 1922. This would have prevented the subsequent atrocities on both sides, though Keogh's judgement is that, compared to other civil wars, the Free State army was usually "kept strictly under civilian discipline". Lyons's, *Ireland since the Famine* argues that during the conflict the Irregulars "lacked the sinews of war" and quickly alienated the people by their behaviour. He goes on to stress that the end of the civil war had done nothing to heal the divisions which had caused it, but in very unfavourable circumstances the Cosgrave government's success in establishing a sound administration with a sensible legislative programme was an "astonishing performance". Perceptive comments on the civil war period can also be found in R Fanning's, *Independent Ireland* (Dublin, 1983). Fanning stresses the importance of the Provisional Government's relationship with the Catholic Church which certainly augmented the new state's authority. The timing of the bishops' joint pastoral in October 1922, coming only a week after the government's offer of an amnesty to all those who would surrender their arms is considered significant. When the amnesty expired just days after the publication of the pastoral, the government's moral authority to put into practice its executions policy was greatly strengthened by the church's support. On Northern Ireland Fanning claimed that Collins's death "removed the last obstacle" to a major policy shift on the north. Under Blythe's guidance a more pragmatic, conciliatory approach to the north was implemented, though this had been in preparation for some months. In examining the legacies of the civil war Fanning points out that the prospect of a "monolithic, one-party state" representing Irish Nationalists, which Unionists had always dreaded, never became a reality. Finally, he notes that the great majority of the politicians who were to enjoy office under Cumann na nGaedheal were not 'old soldiers' of the Collins variety, but were lawyers, such as O'Higgins, or academics, such as Patrick Hogan who was to prove an excellent Minister for Agriculture.

Lee's, *Ireland 1912-1985* also deals in detail with the civil war period. Commenting on the Dáil elections in June 1922 which endorsed the Treaty, Lee notes that O'Connor and Mellowes were "as contemptuous as any Black and Tan of the opinion of the mere Irish as recorded in the election result". He sums up the civil war by noting that "the Treaty was the mere occasion, not the cause, of the war. The cause was the basic conflict in nationalist doctrine between majority right and divine right". The real choice for the Irish people lay between "democracy and dictatorship". Although the conflict was extremely bitter and "bequeathed so poisonous a legacy", Lee puts it into perspective by describing the Finnish experience of 1918 which was a much more brutal affair. In his assessment of the post civil war administration Lee analyses the advantages enjoyed by the new rulers as they embarked on the task of state-building, and he claims that the legacy of British rule was a factor in contributing to political stability. Finally, the social geography of republicanism is examined in E Rumpf and A C Hepburn's, *Nationalism and Socialism in twentieth century Ireland* (Liverpool, 1977) which argues it was the poor farmers of the west, "with their more primitive subsistence economy and traditional Irish culture", who were "less open to practical economic considerations, and adhered rigidly to the ideal of a republic". These were the people who supported the Irregulars in Mayo and Kerry. It was, of course, in just these areas that the continuing commitment to republicanism was demonstrated in the Dáil elections of August 1923. Yet, as the authors note, republicanism did not embrace radical social goals and deliberately tried to keep above simple economic questions, as their leaders pursued the mystical or 'spiritual' republic.

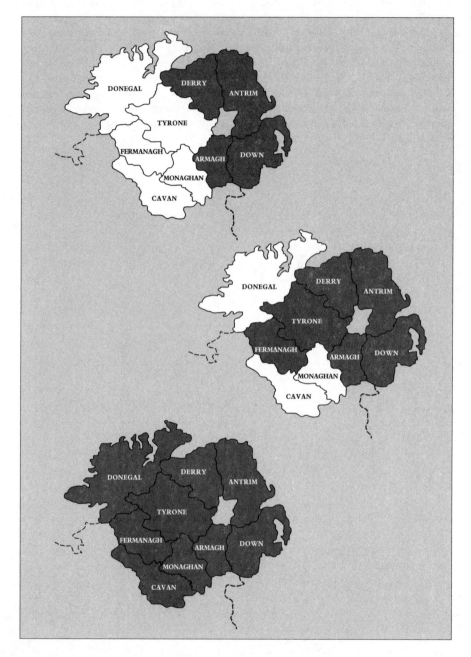

Ulster showing three different options for partition.

Chapter 12
The establishment of the Northern Ireland state

The existence of the new Northern Ireland state had considerably reduced Lloyd George's room for manoeuvre during the 1921 Treaty negotiations. He had pressed Craig to make concessions on territory, but the new Northern Ireland premier, supported by Bonar Law, famously stood his ground indicating his determination to hold on to every inch of the six counties. Clearly, Lloyd George did not like partition, but his government's Irish policy had to reflect the views of Conservative backbenchers on whose support the survival of the Coalition government depended. Indeed, after the Treaty, the government found itself for the last ten months of its life defending Northern Ireland's position against challenges from the Provisional Government in Dublin. Yet for most Conservatives the key British objectives during the negotiations with Sinn Féin had been to keep Ireland in the Empire and to safeguard British defence interests. Ulster was of secondary importance. This should not be surprising, as it was imperial concerns that had first stirred Conservative interest in the Unionist cause.

Unionism emerged as a distinctive ideology in 1885 in response to intensifying Nationalist pressure. The initial impetus for the new movement had come from Dublin Protestants but, once Conservative-Liberal divisions had been overcome in Ulster, Unionism began to organise in the North. While it was a provincial movement, Unionism in Ulster clearly sheltered under the broader Irish umbrella. Thereafter, Irish Unionism developed as a counter to Parnellism, though it was in Ulster that Unionism naturally enjoyed greatest success in mobilising mass opinion while, at times, imitating its Nationalist rivals. Consequently, Ulster became the principal electoral battleground in Ireland. Of crucial importance for the Unionists in their struggle against the 1886 and 1893 Home Rule Bills was the support of the Conservative party in Britain. Conservatives were not motivated by concerns over Ulster, but by their strong links with the landed gentry in the three southern provinces. While leaders such as Lord Randolph Churchill could exploit Ulster opposition to Home Rule for selfish personal and party reasons, many Conservatives were embarrassed by the overt sectarianism of Ulster Unionism. Ulster Unionists placed great stress on the religious objections to Home Rule, and they made full use of the Orange Order in their attempts to broaden the Unionist base. This further highlighted the differences between landlord-dominated Southern Unionism with its powerful British Conservative connections and the more self reliant Ulster Unionism with its powerful grass roots support. Still, both wings shared the common objective of defending the Union, and the broader Unionist movement had little trouble in maintaining a united front during the first twenty years of its existence. Yet outside the periods of crisis in 1886 and 1892-3, Unionist organisation suffered from complacency, and the return of the Conservatives to power in 1895 led to a further decline in interest.

This changed in 1904 when the Conservative administration flirted with the idea of devolution. Ulster Unionists, in particular, were outraged, and they mounted a determined campaign against those individuals whom they held responsible for the devolution experiment. Yet changes were already under way within Unionism, as the movement made the transition from a nineteenth century, part-time landlord party to a modern political force. A younger group of more professional politicians, drawn from the ranks of the Protestant bourgeoisie and more in touch with the electorate, had revitalised Ulster Unionism and steered it in a new direction following the period of drift under Saunderson. It was this group which was behind the formation of the UUC in 1905. The UUC gave Ulster Unionism a more democratic flavour, and its formation helped Ulster Unionists to become the driving force within Irish Unionism. The creation of the new movement was, moreover, a defining moment on the road to the evolution of an exclusively Ulster movement, and it was an expanded UUC which played a pivotal role in the direction of Ulster resistance to Home Rule in the 1912-14 period. Under its principally Belfast bourgeois leadership the UUC gave Ulster Unionism a new organisational framework which permitted effective grass roots participation, while its now formal links with the Orange Order contributed to a more militant style of politics. This strengthened the regional identity of Ulster Unionism. The other crucial lesson drawn from the devolution crisis was that Unionism might not always be able to count on unequivocal Conservative support in the battle against Home Rule, and this fostered the development of a more self reliant brand of Unionism in Ulster.

However, Walter Long's brief reign as Unionist leader from 1906 to 1910 helped to bridge the gap that was developing between Southern and Ulster Unionism, while his English connections did much to restore Conservative-Unionist relations which had been damaged by the devolution crisis. On the surface it appeared that his successor as Unionist leader, Edward Carson, who also enjoyed a Southern Unionist background and strong English contacts, would further cement Conservative-Unionist relations and prevent the regional division of Unionism. While the former was achieved, the latter objective met with failure. During the Home Rule crisis of 1912-14 the Conservative party drew much closer to Unionism, though it did so in a way which exposed the regional differences within Unionism. Desperate for an issue to reunite the party following three disastrous general election defeats, the Conservatives chose outright opposition to Asquith's Home Rule policy. Of crucial importance was the emergence of Andrew Bonar Law as leader in November 1911, because his major political concern was to save Ulster from Home Rule. Carson did not share this narrow view but, over the course of the Home Rule crisis, he became the leader of a more localised, partitionist and militant Ulster movement. This had not been his intention when he assumed the mantle of leader in 1910. Carson did not identify with the religious fanaticism at the core of Ulster Unionism, and he did not believe that there were two nations in Ireland. His aim was to save all Ireland from the Home Rule threat, using Ulster resistance to thwart the Liberal government. Yet in launching this campaign of resistance within his overall Irish Unionist strategy,

Carson himself had helped to create a situation in which Ulster Unionism quickly established itself as a confident, dominant and destructive force separate from Southern Unionism. Carson had given an early indication of this when he told followers at Craigavon in September 1911 that if Home Rule was enacted, then Unionists must take the necessary steps to govern Ulster by themselves. Although he subsequently reassured Southern Unionists that they would not be deserted, Carson was set on a course which pointed in the direction of partition. The Ulster nature of Home Rule resistance, which revealed itself in the shape of mass demonstrations, the formation of the UVF and propaganda events such as the Covenant, ensured that serious long term divisions would open up within Unionism. By 1913 Carson, realising the logic of his own position, switched from using Ulster exclusion as a tactical ploy to making it the ultimate objective.

Carson's 1912 strategy of using Ulster to defeat the entire Home Rule scheme was called into question by the amendment unsuccessfully moved by Agar-Robartes to exclude the four Ulster counties with Protestant majorities form the Home Rule Bill. While the Ulster Unionists had supported the amendment for purely tactical reasons, they had by their action increased the prospect of partition becoming accepted as a workable, if not very attractive, compromise. By the beginning of 1913 Unionists themselves were endorsing their own partition scheme, having abandoned their Southern Unionist brothers, as the only way to break the Home Rule deadlock. At that stage they were thinking in nine county terms, as indicated in the Solemn League and Covenant, but, by September 1913, Carson was informing Bonar Law privately that a six county area would be his bottom line in negotiations over Ulster's future. This was to be his exact approach at the Buckingham Palace Conference in July 1914. Of course, other key contributors to the final outcome were the Liberal government and the IPP. While the government publicly, and sometimes privately, assured Irish Nationalists that they were committed to Home Rule on an all-Ireland basis, the strength of this commitment was in doubt from the outset. When the cabinet discussed Home Rule in February 1912, two key ministers, Lloyd George and Churchill, voiced the opinion that Ulster should be left out of the forthcoming bill. Although Asquith decided against this, the cabinet did not rule out a retreat on Ulster if circumstances demanded. Indeed, in October 1913, at the first of three secret meetings he had with Bonar Law, Asquith discussed Ulster exclusion, thus giving the opposition a clear indication that the government was seriously contemplating partition but was unsure of the actual area to be excluded. As the crisis entered its crucial phase, Redmond came under strong pressure to compromise on exclusion, finally relenting in March 1914 when he accepted Lloyd George's county option proposals. This was a very significant milestone on the road to partition. Thereafter, the IPP found that negotiations on the Ulster matter were based on the acceptance of the principle of partition, leaving only the questions of area and time open for discussion. This was very clear at the Buckingham Palace Conference. Although the conference collapsed without reaching agreement, some form of partition now appeared to be the only compromise acceptable to all the main British and Irish parties.

The outbreak of the First World War shifted attention from the Ulster problem. In September 1914 Asquith had moved to put Home Rule on the statute book, but

Ulster's future remained undecided. Redmond's Irish Volunteers and Carson's Ulster Volunteers joined the British Army in large numbers, both eager to demonstrate their loyalty to the Empire and hopeful of influencing any postwar Irish settlement. Yet events unfolded in a way which clearly favoured the Ulster Unionists. Firstly, the war undermined the Liberal party and it never recovered its prewar strength. Then, by May 1915, a Coalition government was in place, and the presence of Bonar Law and Carson in the cabinet ensured that Ulster interests would be safeguarded. In short, the war had strengthened Ulster Unionism and Conservatism, while weakening Liberalism and Irish Nationalism. Next, in part due to the war, the IRB launched the Easter Rising, one consequence of which was the reinforcement of the partitionist mentality. In his attempt to resolve the Irish Question immediately after the rising, Lloyd George persuaded both Carson and Redmond to accept six county exclusion, albeit on contradictory terms. In view of what eventually transpired the Lloyd George peace initiative was another significant milestone on the road to partition. Redmond had angered Nationalists in Tyrone and Fermanagh, both of which had Nationalist majorities, while Carson had to overcome determined opposition from Unionists in Cavan, Monaghan and Donegal, many of whom had signed the Covenant and now found themselves abandoned in the numbers game. Of course, the major concession had been Redmond's surrender of Tyrone and Fermanagh in his desperation to obtain a settlement. While the principle of partition had already been accepted, the area to be excluded had now taken a more definite shape. In the end the Lloyd George proposals were never implemented, partly because Southern Unionists who were more afraid of partition than Home Rule used their influence to scupper the plan. His subsequent attempt to find a settlement saw Lloyd George leave the negotiations to the Irish themselves. The Irish Convention sat for nine months and, though Southern Unionists and moderate Nationalists reached agreement, Sinn Féin on the outside and the Ulster Unionists from the inside blocked any progress.

The war had also seen the IPP displaced as the representatives of Irish Nationalism by Sinn Féin, and this had implications for partition. In fact, much of Sinn Féin's fire directed at the IPP had been based on Redmond's willingness to accept partition. While he subsequently moderated his views, de Valera argued forcefully in 1917-18 that the IPP had been misguided in its attempts to appease Unionism, implying that Ulster would have to be coerced into acceptance of an all-Ireland legislative body. Not surprisingly, the rise of Sinn Féin strengthened the determination of Ulster Unionists to resist inclusion in any new all-Ireland arrangement. They were, moreover, angry at Sinn Féin's opposition to the war and fiercely critical of the Catholic Church's central role in the anti-conscription campaign which, they argued, justified their claim that the Catholic hierarchy would constantly interfere in the political affairs of any new Dublin administration. Clearly, the gap between Unionism and Nationalism was wider in 1918 than it had been at the outbreak of the First World War when civil war looked a real possibility. With little prospect of compromise between Ulster Unionists and Sinn Féin, the attitude of the Coalition government would prove decisive. In the quarter of a century up to 1914 the Irish Question had been the great issue dividing the two main British parties, but the survival instinct which drew the Liberals and Conservatives together in their desperation to defeat Germany radically changed attitudes towards Ireland. Initially, both parties shared a common interest in keeping the potentially divisive Irish Question off the political agenda. When circumstances, particularly the Easter Rising, demanded British intervention, it was Conservative views which dominated the Coalition government's 'bipartisan' approach. While both main parties had quickly grown tired of the Irish Question, Conservative commitment to the Ulster Unionists easily outweighed Liberal commitment to the Irish Nationalists. The exclusion of Ulster from a future Irish political settlement was assured. Some sense of the disillusionment felt by British politicians for the Irish Question in general and the Ulster problem in particular, can be gauged from Churchill's memorable speech in which he referred to the "dreary steeples of Fermanagh and Tyrone emerging once again". Although the war had changed the face of Europe, Churchill judged that the "integrity of their quarrel remained unaltered". Sooner or later, the postwar Coalition government would have to address this issue.

The Government of Ireland Act

In view of the Coalition government's wartime boredom with Irish affairs, it was not surprising that the postwar administration had a number of priorities which it deemed more important than Ireland. Chief among these was the Paris Peace Conference, and both Lloyd George and Bonar Law spent considerable time in the French capital deciding the future shape of Europe. Still, the actions of the Irish Volunteers from January 1919 onwards ensured that the government would have to overcome its reluctance to become embroiled yet again in Irish affairs. One member of the government whose sustained interest in Ireland was never in question was Walter Long, an ex-Unionist leader and now First Lord of the Admiralty, and colleagues frequently deferred to Long's expertise in Irish affairs. From the opening shots in the War of Independence Long urged the adoption of a tough security policy, claiming that only when order had been established through coercion, would the government be in a position to seek a political settlement. Another concern for the government was the fact that the Home Rule Act was on the statute book and was due to come into effect when the last of the European peace treaties was signed. In its election manifesto for the general election in December 1918 the Coalition government had claimed to possess an open mind on a future Irish settlement, though it did add two strict provisos. One was that Ireland must remain within the Empire; the other was that 'the six counties of Ulster' could not be forced into an all-Ireland parliament against her will. Indeed Ulster's position was further strengthened by the outcome of the general election. Following a redistribution of seats which gave urban areas more representation, Unionists were victorious in 22 of the 37 Ulster constituencies, thus adding weight to their demand for the permanent exclusion of the six county area. Carson's decision not to contest his Trinity College seat and his return for the new Belfast constituency of Duncairn marked a final symbolic breach between Ulster and Southern Unionism.

The government eventually took up the Irish Question when a cabinet committee was appointed on 7 October 1919 to draft a fourth Home Rule Bill. Known formally as the Irish Situation Committee the five-strong team was under the chairmanship and guidance of Walter Long. Unionists must have been relieved to see Long heading the committee, because they recognised that their former Conservative allies were not as supportive of the Ulster cause as they had been in pre-war days. The committee's first report on 4 November recommended that special treatment for Ulster should be at the heart of the new settlement, though questions over area, time and the precise constitutional arrangements remained open for debate. For some months before the appointment of the committee Long had been arguing that a new federal system should be adopted for the whole of the United Kingdom, suggesting that this could include two parliaments in Ireland, one in Belfast and one in Dublin. The report to the cabinet on 4 November was consistent with Long's federalist leanings. It had considered and then rejected an all-Ireland parliament as unworkable, arguing, moreover, that an Ulster committee to protect Unionist interests was not feasible. It also dismissed county option, thereby endorsing Long's personal opposition to plebiscites in Ireland. In short, the Long committee's first report proposed the establishment of two Home Rule parliaments in Ireland, but it also favoured the establishment of a north-south joint council to promote the eventual reunification of Ireland. Partition was to be the basis of a settlement, but the government wanted, with international opinion in mind, to take such steps as would facilitate reunification. For this purpose the exclusion of a more evenly balanced nine county Ulster was favoured. When it fully considered the Long committee's report on 11 November, the cabinet expressed its concern that Sinn Féin would use the proposed southern parliament to declare an independent republic. Indeed for some Conservative members of the cabinet the situation in the south was a crucial factor. A number of them were unhappy that their actions might be construed as making concessions to violence, and Birkenhead only gave his backing because he was convinced that Sinn Féin would reject what American and Dominion opinion would regard as a reasonable offer. Long, meanwhile, was proceeding on the basis that order would have to be restored in advance of any political offer, and he became a vociferous exponent of a tough security policy in cabinet.

Conservative ministers also assumed, wrongly as it turned out, that Ulster Unionists would be opposed to the creation of a Belfast parliament, believing that they would demand the continuation of Westminster rule over the excluded area. The cabinet, in general, was opposed to direct rule over any area of Ulster, as this gave the impression that partition was the government's aim in both the medium and long term. However, majority opinion in the cabinet, and this included most of the Conservative ministers, viewed the creation of an all-Ireland parliament bound as closely as possible to Westminster as the favoured course. By mid-November Craig, who had replaced Carson as the key Unionist voice, had informed the government that his strong preference was for a six county cut but, significantly, added that he was sympathetic to the idea of a new Belfast parliament. On 17 November the committee produced a second report which concentrated on the need to press ahead with legislation as soon as possible. Two further reports followed in quick succession, one dealing with financial considerations and the other looking at possible arrangements for the transfer of powers to the new devolved administrations. The cabinet discussed all these issues at two meetings on 3 and 10 December. It was clear from the discussions that nearly all ministers regarded partition as a temporary expedient.

Again, the cabinet expressed a preference for the excluded area to consist of the historic nine county province, noting that such a cut would prove more defensible against criticism from both inside and outside parliament. It would also prove more temporary. However, one senior Conservative minister objected to these proposals. Arthur Balfour firmly supported Craig's view that a six county unit was preferable, and he hoped that partition would be permanent.

In a progress report for the House of Commons on 22 December 1919 Lloyd George laid out the government's new Irish strategy, stating that his ultimate objective was to create a devolved all-Ireland parliament under Westminster's authority [146]. The area to be excluded in the short term was not specified, but *The Times* in commenting on Lloyd George's address to the Commons declared itself in favour of a nine county unit, stating that "the ancient province of Ulster should remain a unit in any scheme of Irish self-government". The article went on to explain that "the existence of a strong nationalist minority in Ulster would not merely be a guarantee of the protection of the rights and interests of that minority, and of a certain harmony of development between the two Irish States, but that it would also prove a powerful force working in the direction of union".

While the bill was being drafted, Craig mounted a sustained campaign to have the proposed excluded area reduced to six counties. Unionists in the north-east warned that their control over a nine county Ulster would be too precarious, and a number predicted that the higher Catholic birth rate would condemn Unionists to accept Dublin rule. Although the new bill had been carefully revised by February 1920, the area to be excluded had not been settled. Another issue to be resolved was the possible transfer of customs and excise powers either to the two new parliaments, or on the occasion of their union. These problems were discussed at a meeting of the Irish Situation Committee on 17 February. At Lloyd George's request, Bonar Law presided over the meeting. No agreement was reached on the financial issues which were left to the cabinet for a settlement. On the crucial question of area Long reported the Ulster Unionists' earnest desire for a six county bloc, but the committee went back to its original proposal and recommended a nine county Ulster as this was more likely to lead to future reunification. The decision naturally angered Ulster Unionists who were also concerned at the committee's support for an all-Ireland judiciary.

A bizarre sequence of events followed. Ulster Unionists made it known that they would oppose the bill unless it was altered. Long called the committee together again on 18 February, and they unanimously agreed to drop the idea of a single judiciary. His next move was to meet the Ulster Unionist leaders who reaffirmed their demand for a six county bloc in which they would have a commanding majority. The cabinet then met on 24 February and, following an appeal by Long, decided to ignore the committee's recommendations and opt for a six county parliament. Balfour had also used his influence to push the cabinet in this direction. A hastily redrafted bill received its first reading on the following day, while it was carried on its second reading on 31 March by a margin of 348 to 94. Having been appeased on the excluded area, Ulster Unionists decided not to oppose the bill during the three-day debate. In fact, with Sinn Féin abstaining, the Government of Ireland Bill went through with little difficulty. Only Joe Devlin raised effective Nationalist objections to the bill which, he claimed, would condemn Ulster Catholics to the status of a permanent and ill-treated minority in a ridiculous statelet [147]. The most significant contribution from the Unionists in the parliamentary debate came from Captain Charles Craig, James's brother and the MP for South Antrim. On 29 March 1920 he explained to the House that Ulster Unionists would have preferred their territory to remain under direct rule from Westminster, but Craig went on to suggest that a Belfast parliament would have obvious advantages for Ulster Unionists. He told MPs that "once a parliament is set up and working well ... we feel that we would then be in a position of absolute security". In his reference to security, Craig was thinking of potential threats not from Irish Nationalists, but from future Westminster governments which might favour Irish unity. For Unionists, therefore, an Ulster parliament provided a bulwark against potential Westminster threats and, despite the arrangements for a Council of Ireland to promote eventual reunification, they assumed that partition would be permanent.

The success enjoyed by Ulster Unionists in establishing a six county bloc could not hide the bitterness within Unionist ranks which almost split the UUC. In his quest for Unionist supremacy, James Craig had sacrificed his fellow Unionists in Cavan, Monaghan and Donegal. Matters came to a head at a meeting of the UUC on 10 March 1920. Bitter argument ensued between those Unionists who favoured a nine county Ulster as the Covenant had stipulated and those who wanted a six county bloc as the leadership had advocated in 1916. There were some 70,000 Unionists in the three abandoned counties which contained approximately 260,000 Nationalists, and no Unionist had been returned for any constituency in the three counties in the recent general election. While it was likely that some Unionist success could be expected in the first election for a new regional parliament, which would use the PR system, the leadership argued that a nine county parliament would leave them with only a narrow majority and the very real prospect of defeat in the longer term. Unionists from the three county area urged the UUC to maintain the spirit of the Covenant, and they moved a resolution at the March meeting proposing the expansion of the area defined in the Government of Ireland Bill. Although their amendment was defeated, Unionists in the six county area were acutely embarrassed by the proceedings and a second meeting of the UUC had to be held on 27 May to confirm the decision. In the meantime, the excluded Unionists continued their struggle, and they published a pamphlet in April entitled *No Partition of Ulster*. It set out historical, geographic and economic reasons in favour of a nine county parliament, adding that the creation of a six county parliament with a commanding Unionist majority would create the wrong impression [148]. The pamphlet also highlighted the anomalies produced by the partition proposals. While recognising that Unionists were in a clear minority in the three excluded counties, the pamphlet suggested that this alone could not be the basis for exclusion. Tyrone, Fermanagh and Derry city all had clear Nationalist majorities, and the same was true in South Armagh and South Down. Indeed North Monaghan, which was approximately 35 per cent Unionist, and East Donegal, with a 40 per cent Unionist population, both had greater concentrations of Unionists than some areas within the six county bloc. Despite such arguments, Unionist leaders refused to reverse their earlier decision. At the meeting on 27 May only 80 of the 390 delegates present supported the nine county option.

If anything, the violence which erupted in the north in the summer of 1920 hardened Ulster Unionist opinion. At the same time, the Lloyd George government had to consider the implications of the escalating conflict in the south for the new legislation. Unless order could be restored, there was no prospect of the bill operating for a southern parliament. In the circumstances the government had little alternative but to delay the bill in the hope that the situation in the south could be brought under control. There was some speculation that the bill could be altered to give the south dominion Home Rule, but the government, with Long particularly defiant, refused to make any concessions to Sinn Féin. Towards the end of 1920 it was clear that the new legislation would have to come into effect, but it would only apply to the new state of Northern Ireland, where, in spite of the government's efforts, the Unionists would enjoy a permanent majority. In truth, there had been little real conviction behind the government's wish for a nine county parliament, but the crucial element in the decision was the government's dependence on the Ulster Unionists to make the bill work. This left the Ulstermen with a strong hand to play, and the price of Craig's co-operation was a six county area.

There was also a lack of conviction on the part of the government with regard to the future reunification of Ireland. Clearly, a majority in the cabinet wanted the Government of Ireland Bill to facilitate ultimate unity, but this was more an aspiration than a firm commitment. As Charles Craig had indicated to the House of Commons, Unionists did not see partition as a temporary feature and they planned to ignore the Council of Ireland. Indeed the entire Council of Ireland concept calls into question the strength of the British desire for eventual unity. The council was to be drawn from representatives of both parliaments, and it was to be given very modest powers dealing with non-controversial issues, though it was hoped that these could be extended with the full backing of northern and southern representatives. This meant that the envisaged development of the Council of Ireland depended on Unionist consent, something which was unlikely to be forthcoming. Although they were a minority in Ireland, Unionists were to enjoy equal representation on the Council of Ireland and this, in effect, handed them a veto over future progress towards unity. While the British were to create partition in a formal sense through the 1920 legislation, it merely recognised the existing political divisions within Ireland. Austen Chamberlain was correct in suggesting that reunification could only come about through agreement between north and south and could not be imposed by a British government. That said, however, Westminster failed to lay the necessary foundations which might have facilitated future reunification. A nine county parliament and a Council of Ireland with real teeth might have accomplished this. In the event, the British government's keenness to tie up the Ulster problem, if not the Irish Question, and the continuing influence of the Ulster Unionists at Westminster together with the government's dependence on them to work the new legislation, determined the outcome.

Although a number of Southern Unionists in the House of Lords mounted a bitter campaign against the bill, it made its way through parliament without any significant amendments and received the royal assent on 23 December 1920. The new legislation included a number of clauses designed to limit the powers of the devolved parliaments. Section 5 of the act prohibited both parliaments from making laws interfering with religious liberty or equality. Obviously, this would prevent a Unionist government in Belfast enacting legislation which disadvantaged the Catholic minority. Section 75 of the act decreed that in all cases the regional parliaments would be subordinate to Westminster. In theory, therefore, any law passed by the Belfast parliament could be annulled by Westminster instructing the Governor, the King's representative, to withhold the royal assent. More restrictions applied to the range of services over which the regional parliaments could exercise control, and the financial constraints placed on the devolved administrations were particularly severe. The act came into operation on 3 May 1921 and elections for the two parliaments were held three weeks later. In the south, of course, Sinn Féin refused to recognise the new assembly and used the election to establish the Second Dáil. The Lloyd George government was now forced to recognise reality. The Government of Ireland Act only dealt with the Ulster problem. In the north Unionists surprised themselves in winning 40 of the 52 seats, with the remaining 12 being equally divided between Sinn Féin and Devlin's Nationalists. Craig, the new Prime Minister of Northern Ireland, then selected a cabinet team drawn from the group of Unionist leaders who had earned their spurs in the struggle against the third Home Rule Bill. The men chosen were Hugh McDowell Pollock (Finance), Sir Richard Dawson Bates (Home Affairs), J M Andrews (Labour), Lord Londonderry (Education) and Edward Archdale (Agriculture and Commerce).

Early problems for the new state

The Unionists achieved a major success in the early establishment of a separate administration with all the necessary bureaucratic paraphernalia. From the outset they seemed to have recognised that the creation of institutions and the effective day-to-day functioning of an administration would give partition an air of permanence. Ulster Unionists had used their influence to ensure that, as far as possible, there would be a complete division of those powers transferred from the Irish executive. This left the Council of Ireland with very few administrative functions. The key for Unionists was the 'partition' of those services transferred to the regional parliaments under the Government of Ireland Act, as this meant that Northern Ireland would be virtually independent form the rest of Ireland. Although the British were to provide all the machinery for reunification, this was really a cosmetic exercise. Before partition was enacted British civil servants, notably Sir Ernest Clark, the assistant under-secretary in Belfast, were in consultation with leading Ulster Unionists to advise them on the necessary administrative foundations for the new state. By the summer of 1921 the Unionist government had the assistance of nearly 20 administrative experts form Westminster departments. While Lloyd George's negotiations with Sinn Féin delayed the final transfer of services to Northern Ireland, this took place before the end of 1921 and a total of 300 civil service volunteers were moved from Dublin to new posts in Belfast. The northern administration was now functioning and ready to tackle the problems facing the new state. The successful establishment of a new state apparatus was important, because the fledgling Unionist government felt itself under threat from a number of quarters. The 1921 Treaty recognised the unity of Ireland and provided for the operation of a Boundary Commission if the Northern Ireland parliament opted out of an all-Ireland assembly. With the future of Northern Ireland's border open to question the solid foundation work in setting up the new state proved to be very significant.

When the Northern Ireland parliament was opened on 22 June 1921, Craig looked to the future with real optimism as he promised fair treatment for all the citizens of Northern Ireland. Such a lofty ideal, however, was never put into practice as the state struggled for survival during the early years of its existence. Its most immediate problem was dealing with the existing divisions in Ulster society which had resulted in a fresh outbreak of sectarian violence in June 1920. 'The Troubles', as this period became known, lasted into June 1922, and the Unionist government's handling of the situation only served to exacerbate divisions between the two communities There had been sporadic violence as the War of Independence occasionally spilled over into the six county area, but serious confrontation took place in Derry, where IRA units and the police attacked each other in June 1920. The violence led to the mobilisation of former UVF groups and they quickly became engaged in the violence. Tension rose further with the annual Twelfth demonstrations and then an incident in the War of Independence sparked off bitter sectarian fighting in Belfast and a number of other northern towns. On 17 July Colonel G F Smyth, the RIC Divisional Commissioner in Munster, was shot dead in Cork. Smyth came from Banbridge and on the day of his funeral violence erupted in the shipyard as Catholic workers came under a sustained assault. Catholics working in the city's large engineering firms were also expelled from their workplaces. The violence spread quickly to Banbridge and Dromore where Catholic families were driven from their homes by angry mobs. An uneasy calm was restored, but this was shattered by the shooting of District Inspector Swanzy in Lisburn on 22 August 1920. Earlier, Swanzy had been named at an inquest on the murder of Tomas MacCurtain, the Lord Mayor of Cork, and, soon after his death, serious trouble flared in Lisburn [149]. Catholic homes and businesses came under fierce attack and many of the town's Catholic population fled to Dundalk to escape the violence.

The Protestant response to the upsurge in violence led to the revival of the UVF. The UUC had decided to revive the force at the end of June, but even before this Protestant vigilante groups had been organised to deal with growing disorder in a number of counties. The most prominent of these was Sir Basil Brooke's loyalist vigilantes in County Fermanagh. Brooke had served as an officer in the First World War and was to become Prime Minister of Northern Ireland in 1943, and he wanted his vigilante force to be recognised by the government as special constables. Other Unionist leaders added their weight to a growing campaign to have a revived UVF reconstituted as a special constabulary which could assist the police. The violence of the summer of 1920 strengthened this demand. In addition to his desire to respond to the IRA, Craig realised that the establishment of an official force could help to curb Protestant violence, the naked sectarian nature of which was damaging the Unionist cause at Westminster. Although the British government was nervous about the creation of an official armed Protestant force charged with maintaining the rule of law, a precedent had been set in the south where Black and Tans and Auxiliaries were both operational by the autumn of 1920. Without significant planning the government gave way to Unionist pressure, and the formation of an Ulster Special Constabulary (USC) was announced on 22 October 1920. The new force was divided into three classes. 'A' Specials were full-time, paid constables who could be used in any trouble spot to assist the RIC. 'B' Specials were part-time constables who received an allowance and operated in their own localities, while 'C' Specials were an unpaid reserve of usually older men available in serious emergencies. By the end of 1920 the USC consisted of 3,500 A Specials and 16,000 B Specials. As expected, the bulk of the force's recruits were ex-UVF men and, though it enjoyed considerable success in combating the IRA, its sectarian character and the fact that some of its members undoubtedly engaged in attacks on Catholics easily outweighed whatever effectiveness the force may have had on the security front.

While Ulster largely escaped the effects of the War of Independence, sporadic violence continued to dog the north during the winter of 1920-21. April 1921 witnessed a number of killings in Belfast and more regular IRA activity in the new border areas. Craig did make an astonishing attempt to promote peace, when he travelled south for a meeting with de Valera which took place on 5 May at a secret location outside Dublin. While Craig had demonstrated real courage in agreeing to such a meeting, the discussion between the two leaders only emphasised their differences and no agreement was possible. The cool reception which Craig received from Unionist supporters on his return from the de Valera summit was an indication that the future Northern Ireland premier would have very little room for manoeuvre in his dealings with either Dublin or London. Of course, Northern Ireland interests were soon subordinated to the greater need of Anglo-Irish relations, as the Lloyd George Coalition government and Sinn Féin agreed to a truce and then opened negotiations which the British hoped would lead to a final resolution of the Irish Question. During the negotiations the Irish delegation played on the British government's embarrassment with partition. As Westminster retained control over security and policing in Northern Ireland until the transfer of these powers on 22 November 1921, a decision was taken to reduce the security presence following the truce signed in July. This involved the immobilisation of the USC and the withdrawal of the army from peace-keeping activities. The Unionist government, which had not been consulted on the decision to immobilise the USC, was furious. Its concerns had been increased by an upsurge of violence between July and September 1921 in which loyalist vigilantes took the law into their own hands. Craig blamed the Westminster government for the suspension of the USC which he regarded as a safety valve for Protestant aggression. The sight of the IRA regrouping and openly drilling in the north under the protection of the truce enraged Unionists who demanded the remobilisation of the Special Constabulary. At the end of September following another burst of violence the authorities finally relented, but they stipulated that the B Specials could only be used to protect Protestant areas, leaving the regular police to patrol Catholic districts.

The transfer of security powers to the new Northern Ireland government took place in a week when 27 lives were lost in sectarian fighting. Further clashes in December brought to over 100 the number killed in Belfast during 1921. The Unionist government, therefore, had inherited an explosive security situation. The new state faced a ruthless challenge from the IRA and, in addition, Craig found himself struggling to keep Unionist extremism under control. His answer to both of these problems was to strengthen the USC and fresh recruits began enrolling in the force before the end of 1921. The problem of paying for the force now that it was the Northern Ireland government's responsibility was conveniently overlooked. The first six months of 1922 witnessed very serious violence which claimed the lives of 236 people, with Catholic losses outnumbering Protestant losses by two to one. Attempts by Craig and Collins to defuse the situation failed, as the pacts of January and March collapsed. The initial spark for this new wave of violence had been the arrest of eleven members of the Monaghan gaelic football team on 14 January, which was travelling to an away fixture with Derry. The players arrested included a number of senior IRA men. In retaliation IRA units kidnapped 42 prominent loyalists in Tyrone and Fermanagh on 8 February. Three days later, a party of Special Constables travelling by rail from Newtownards to Enniskillen was ambushed when the train drew up at Clones station in County Monaghan. In the ensuing gun battle the IRA leader and four of the Specials were killed. This led to more violence in Belfast and in a three day period, 13–15 February, a total of 31 people were killed in bitter sectarian clashes, with Catholics again bearing the brunt of the violence. Another 60 lives were lost in the city during March, and this included the infamous attack on the McMahon family in which the police were alleged to have been involved [150]. Five members of this prominent Nationalist family were gunned down in their home, and the youngest child only escaped by hiding under the parlour table. In the following week a bomb was thrown into a Protestant home killing the male occupant and his two young sons. It was this sickening spate of violence which had prompted Churchill to bring Craig and Collins together again at the end of March. In the previous month Sir Henry Wilson, now a Unionist MP, had been appointed as security adviser to the Northern Ireland government, and Collins held him responsible, without any justification, for the persecution of northern Catholics.

Unionists reacted to the rising tide of violence by rushing through the Civil Authorities (Special Powers) Bill which became law on 7 April 1922. This was regarded as emergency legislation which would operate for one year, but it was set to become permanent. The Special Powers Act conferred draconian powers on the Belfast government and allowed the Minister of Home Affairs, or any policeman acting on his behalf, to arrest and detain suspects without trial. Special courts were also empowered to hand out a variety of punishments including penal servitude and the death sentence, though the authorities initially hesitated to apply the full force of the new legislation. Obviously, the act was extremely controversial and serious objections were raised in both London and Dublin. It was clear, however, that the Coalition government was relieved to be rid of the Ulster problem, preferring to leave contentious issues such as security to the new administration in Belfast. Craig also played a vital role in smoothing over difficulties and, in his frequent visits to London, explaining how desperate measures were required to overcome the grave difficulties facing his government. While Craig was to prove a very effective London ambassador for the Unionist government, his calm leadership was sorely missed during this critical formative period and, too often, important decisions were left to hard-liners such as Bates. A new burst of violence in May 1922 led to the government making full use of the powers contained in the Special Powers Act. On 22 May W J Twaddell, a local Unionist MP, was shot dead in Belfast, and the government responded by imposing internment. A few days after the Twaddell shooting the authorities made over 200 arrests, virtually all of them Catholics, and those arrested were held on an old ship, the *Argenta*, which was moored on Belfast Lough but then moved to Larne harbour. The internment strategy which was aimed at the Catholic population was indefensible, because the 66 people killed in Belfast during May consisted of 44 Catholics and 22 Protestants, but this religious balance was not reflected in the arrests. Between May 1922 and Christmas 1924, when internment was suspended, the vast majority of those brought before the special courts were Catholics.

The government was justified in its attempts to deal with IRA activity in the north, but its failure to tackle Protestant violence only increased the suspicion and distrust already felt by the minority community. Such views were repeatedly put to the British government, but its only response was to send an official, Stephen Tallents, to Belfast at the end of June 1921. His brief was to furnish Churchill with a report to explain the breakdown of the second Craig-Collins pact. While Tallents was critical of Bates, he blamed the IRA for the violence in the north and generally overlooked the sectarian attacks carried out by Protestant gangs. His advice was that there was no need to hold a judicial enquiry into the violence in the north and this view was endorsed by the British government which was anxious to stay out of Ulster affairs [151].

At the end of May the Unionist government faced a direct challenge when IRA columns invaded the north and seized control of the Belleek-Pettigo triangle, an area of approximately 30 square miles close to the border with County Donegal. Collins had been outraged by the British government's failure to protect the Catholic minority, particularly in Belfast, and he had been instrumental in the formation of a united IRA northern policy following the 'Monaghan Footballers' crisis. The incursion into this vulnerable triangle of territory, which was cut off from the rest of County Fermanagh by Lough Erne, was the most visible demonstration of this strategy. The IRA's action created a state of panic among Protestants living close to the border. While the British government, with one eye on the impending conflict in the south, did not want to become directly involved, Churchill took the initiative and dispatched troops to the area with the intention of dislodging the IRA force and securing the border. This was quickly accomplished by the use of artillery to remove the IRA from their defensive positions in the two villages of Belleek and Pettigo. Thereafter, there were isolated incidents along the border, but the outbreak of civil war in the south at the end of June 1922 took the pressure off the Unionist government's security forces. Although Belfast continued to witness occasional outrages, the worst of the violence had passed. The Northern Ireland state had survived, but the price of survival had been high. The Unionist administration had relied on a sectarian security strategy which took little account of Protestant violence. During the two years of The Troubles 428 lives were lost, the majority Catholic, but the government was reluctant to use the full rigour of the law against Protestants. Consequently, members of the Ulster Protestant Association (UPA), a loyalist terror group responsible for some of the worst sectarian outrages, were not brought to justice. Instead the government tried to curb their activities by enrolling them in the Special Constabulary. The last murder committed by the UPA took place on 5 October 1922, and the group drifted out of existence soon afterwards.

Closely related to the security problem was the financial crisis which dogged the state during its formative years. The cost of security placed a severe strain on the province's stretched finances. Yet an even greater problem lay in the limitations and constraints imposed by the financial provisions of the Government of Ireland Act. Under the terms of the legislation Northern Ireland had to pay an annual 'imperial contribution' which was set against the cost of imperial services, but it was fixed at such a high level, initially at nearly £8 million, that it threatened the province with bankruptcy. The Unionist government was constantly seeking a reduction of its contribution toward the cost of imperial services, but it found the Treasury in London unsympathetic. Northern Ireland's staple industries, linen and shipbuilding, suffered badly in the postwar slump, and this drove up unemployment towards the 100,000 mark. The Unionist administration, meanwhile, was fully committed to a 'step-by-step' policy which involved keeping pace with Britain in the provision of major cash social services. As the province was much less prosperous than most other regions in the United Kingdom, the commitment to this policy created financial difficulties for the Northern Ireland government, particularly in unemployment insurance where Craig and his colleagues had decided that benefits would be identical to those offered in Great Britain. This policy, however, proved financially disastrous in a small country with such a high level of unemployment, and the Minister of Finance, Hugh McDowell Pollock, had to admit towards the end of 1923 that Northern Ireland's Unemployment Fund was insolvent. Still, the Unionist government's desperate pleas for a complete revision of the province's financial relations with Westminster were consistently rebuffed by the Treasury. One answer would have been to fix unemployment benefit at a lower level in Northern Ireland, but such a move would be politically dangerous as it threatened the Unionist party with the loss of Protestant working class support in Belfast [152]. Some improvement in the province's financial condition came with the Colwyn Award in 1925. Under this arrangement the British government agreed that domestic expenditure on Northern Ireland services, rather than the imperial contribution, would be the first charge on the province's income. This brought a few years of financial stability, but severe problems reoccurred with the great economic recession of the 1930s, leading to further clashes between the Belfast government and the Treasury.

When the Unionist government assumed responsibility for law and order in November 1921, the Special Constabulary became its primary peace-keeping force. As the violence intensified during the first half of 1922, the cost of the USC rose sharply. Craig demanded that the British should pay for the force, but Treasury officials argued that security was the devolved government's responsibility and it should find the money to finance the USC. Despite the Treasury's hostility, the government soon agreed to provide generous financial backing for the force. Much of the credit for this was due to Craig's quiet persuasion, but Westminster was at fault in not making more use of the financial pressure it had at its disposal to influence the Unionist government in its handling of sensitive issues affecting the Catholic minority. Another financial problem for the new state was the 'Belfast Boycott'. In January 1921 the Dáil endorsed an embargo on Ulster goods which had earlier been imposed by Sinn Féin local councils. This action was taken in retaliation for the expulsion of Catholic workers from the shipyard in the summer of 1920, and the Dáil hoped that the application of economic pressure would force the Unionists to end discrimination and would also act as a barrier to partition. The boycott hit the north's economy very hard, and most of the trade which was previously conducted with the south was lost. In the early months of 1922 the two Craig-Collins pacts addressed the boycott issue, but nothing was achieved. Although it had created serious economic difficulties for the north, the embargo was unsuccessful in bringing about the reinstatement of Catholic workers and, if anything, the distinction it drew between the two separate economic units only served to reinforce partition.

Of course, in addition to opposition from the south, the Craig government had to cope with a disaffected Catholic minority in the north. All shades of Nationalism in the north had been opposed to partition, and the representatives of both the IPP and Sinn Féin refused to attend the new Northern Ireland parliament. Subsequent actions by the government, particularly in relation to law and order and the administration of justice, intensified Nationalist disaffection. Discrimination, internment, the use of the Special Powers Act and the role of the B Specials deepened divisions and strengthened the minority's determination to withhold their allegiance to the new state. Both the Belfast and London governments hoped that the Royal Ulster Constabulary (RUC) which took over policing from 1 June 1922 would operate as an impartial force, thereby gaining the confidence of the Nationalist population. It was intended that the RUC would eventually have an establishment of 3,000, one-third of whom would be Catholics. Preference in recruiting was given to ex-RIC members, but the new force failed to attract Catholics in sufficient numbers. This policy of non-recognition which the minority adopted in the early 1920s was embarrassing for the Unionist government. Parliament, with only Unionist MPs in attendance, had an unreal atmosphere, but the situation at local government level was much more serious. Following the 1920 local government elections a combination of Nationalists and Sinn Féiners had won control of Derry city council and both the Tyrone and Fermanagh county councils. When partition was established these Nationalist councils, together with a number of other local authorities under Nationalist control, refused to recognise the Unionist government and instead gave their allegiance to the Dáil. Unionists were determined to overcome this problem and, consequently, the Local Government Bill was pushed through the Northern Ireland parliament in the summer of 1922. Its main feature was the abolition of PR for local government elections. The clear intention was to use the simple majoritarian system and the necessary redrawing of local government electoral areas to give the Unionist party an advantage at the polls.

Nationalists in the north were outraged by these new proposals and Collins made strong representations to the British government, claiming that the changes would not only discriminate against northern Catholics but would also cause serious problems in Anglo-Irish relations. The 1922 Local Government Bill had been passed by the Belfast parliament on 5 July, but it did not receive the royal assent until 11 September. In the interim Westminster had delayed giving the royal assent in an attempt to pressurise the Unionist government into dropping the measure [153]. The authorities in London were clearly concerned about the bill's implications and they were embarrassed by the whole issue. While Craig understood their concerns, he shared his government's determination to force the matter. Angered by Westminster's decision to withhold the royal assent, Craig threatened to resign and call an election on the issue. The challenge was enough to force a change of mind at Westminster. The prospect of a new constitutional crisis with the Ulster problem being catapulted back into the arena of British politics was not welcomed by the Coalition government, and the decision to authorise the royal assent to the Local Government Bill was taken with some relief. The outcome of the crisis had an important bearing on future relations between London and Belfast. Although the Government of Ireland Act had given legislative effect to Westminster's sovereignty, there was really little that Westminster could do to influence the Unionist government. This was, of course, partly through choice. Westminster did not want to become embroiled in Northern Ireland affairs and was happy to leave such problems to the Unionist administration. Financial muscle could have been used to greater effect but, ultimately, it was clear that Westminster was wholly dependent on the Ulster Unionists to work the Government of Ireland Act. It was also true, moreover, that if Craig did resign, he would, in all likelihood, be replaced by a more extreme leader. The authorities at Westminster might have had reservations about Craig but, in the circumstances, he offered the best prospect for political stability in the north.

The 1922 Local Government Act had the desired effect for the Unionist party as local government electoral areas were redrawn to maximise the Unionist vote. This gerrymandering enabled Unionists to win control of Tyrone and Fermanagh county councils and, most famously, Derry city council [154]. Yet in other areas the Unionist government had made an effort to act impartially. The 1923 Education Act attempted to break the clerical control of schooling and create a non-denominational education system under local control. Indeed the first Minister of Education, Lord Londonderry, had never shared the narrow sectarian views expressed by some of his colleagues, and he was determined to remove sectarianism from the education system. Initially, he had to face opposition from Catholic teachers in Catholic schools who refused to recognise the authority of the Northern Ireland Ministry of Education. This action was supported by the Provisional Government in Dublin which took responsibility for the payment of Catholic teachers' salaries from the beginning of 1922. Thus, for ten months from January to October 1922, approximately 800 teachers in 270 Northern Ireland schools refused to accept their salaries from the Northern Ireland government and were paid from Dublin. By the end of October 1922, however, the cost of this action, which was running at some £18,000 per month, was depleting the Provisional Government's hard pressed finances, and a decision was taken to discontinue the payments. Thereafter, Londonderry concentrated on the preparation of his Education Bill. Much of the groundwork for the legislation had been completed by the Lynn committee which had been appointed in September 1921 to examine the whole education system. The Catholic Church had no input, because the hierarchy had boycotted the Lynn committee. Later, the bishops recorded their opposition to the 1923 Education Act and demanded a return to clerical control. These sentiments were endorsed by the three main Protestant churches which enlisted the help of the Orange Order in pressing for changes to the Londonderry act. Protestant opposition was meticulously organised and, by March 1925, Craig had agreed in principle that the 1923 Education Act should be amended to meet the concerns of the Protestant churches. The resulting 1925 Education Act fractured Londonderry's vision of a non-denominational system and he resigned as Minister of Education in January 1926. Following further pressure from both the Protestant churches and the Catholic hierarchy the government introduced a new Education Bill in 1930 which firmly established a dual education system [155].

Despite his misgivings, Craig quickly surrendered to pressure from the Protestant churches. His main interest at the time was to present a united front to Protestant voters in the approach to the Northern Ireland general election in April 1925. Craig had called the election as the Boundary Commission was preparing to begin work in order to demonstrate to both London and Dublin that Unionists were unwilling to surrender any part of the six counties [156]. The Unionist government had already demonstrated its opposition to the Boundary Commission by refusing to nominate a commissioner to represent Northern Ireland. In October 1924 the Westminster government amended the Treaty and appointed J R Fisher, a former newspaper editor and prominent Unionist, as the north's representative. Fisher worked with Eoin MacNeill, the Free State's representative and Justice Feetham, a South African judge whom the British had chosen as its representative. The Nationalist minority were optimistic, but Craig made it clear that his government would resist any move to transfer even a small area of territory from Northern Ireland. Of course, when its work was complete, the Boundary Commission's final report, leaked to the press on 7 November, proposed only minor transfers of territory on each side of the border. MacNeill resigned in protest, but the Cosgrave government which had requested the establishment of the Boundary Commission had no contingency plan. In the circumstances a decision was taken to suppress the report and, on 3 December 1925, a tripartite agreement was signed between London, Dublin and Belfast, which confirmed the existing border and also scrapped the Treaty provision for the Council of Ireland [157]. The Northern Ireland state looked to have cleared the last hurdle. It had survived internal and external challenges and could now look forward to a longer period of stability. Yet Catholic disaffection with the new state remained strong, as the policies which the Unionist government had deemed necessary for survival further alienated the minority. Craig's instinct was in favour of conciliation, but he took the easy option in these formative years, and he allowed Bates and other leading figures in the party to institutionalise Unionist supremacy. Discrimination, particularly in public service employment, a sectarian security policy and the abolition of PR in local government elections were all grounds for continuing Catholic opposition to the new state. In the late 1920s Devlin, the northern Nationalist leader, did move tentatively towards full participation in the state, but he received little encouragement from the Unionists. By 1929, moreover, PR had been abolished for elections to the Northern Ireland parliament. Unionists knew that it was in their own interests to suffocate political alternatives and to maintain the old sectarian division in politics, as this gave them a permanent advantage in the numbers game. The Unionist government, therefore, was to perpetuate and deepen the divisions which had always existed in Ulster society.

Historiography

A good starting point for any discussion of partition can be found in Laffan's, *The Partition of Ireland* which begins by stating that all Irishmen in 1911 "would have been amazed" if they could have foreseen partition. He argues that the immediate causes of partition were "the beliefs and actions of a few British and Irish politicians to the impact of developments as varied as the threat of civil war in 1914, the reality of rebellion in 1916, the effects of the world war, and a fundamental change in the political balance of power in both Britain and nationalist Ireland". Immediately after the war, he notes that British politicians did not regard Ulster as a priority and, in any case, the Conservative party was much less enthusiastic for the Ulster Unionist cause. Boyce's essay, 'British conservative opinion, the Ulster question, and the partition of Ireland, 1912-21' in *Irish Historical Studies* suggests that Conservatives were caught in two minds about Ulster. While they agreed that Ulster Unionists "had a claim on their gratitude", it was clear that British interests were of greater concern. It is Boyce's view that this led to the failure of Lloyd George's 1916 partition proposals. Mansergh's, *The Unresolved Question* argues that if there was "one crucial moment on the road to partition", it was Bonar Law's selection as Conservative party leader in November 1911. When Lloyd George, in his role as Prime Minister, took up the Irish Question in 1917, he contemplated a solution based on the exclusion of six counties in "quasi-permanent terms", but Mansergh judges that his mind was not fixed on partition. Buckland's, *Irish Unionism 2* shows how the Irish Convention represented a threat to Ulster Unionism, but concludes that by adopting an inflexible attitude the Ulster Unionists "successfully defended their own claim for exclusion". Jackson's essay, 'Irish Unionism, 1905-21' in Collins's (ed), *Nationalism and Unionism* emphasises that despite the public unity of Conservatives and Unionists in the 1912-14 period, Ulster Unionists were "pursuing an independent and local political strategy". He develops this idea that partition was taking shape during the Home Rule crisis by stating that from the moment Unionists backed Agar-Robartes's amendment in June 1912, partition became "a probable component of a Home Rule settlement". Bowman's, *De Valera and the Ulster Question* analyses the impact which the sudden rise of Sinn Féin had on the likelihood of partition, arguing that more militant Nationalist rhetoric naturally strengthened Ulster Unionist claims for exclusion.

There are a number of useful accounts which deal with the work of the Long committee and examine the key influences on the Coalition government in the drafting of the Government of Ireland Bill. R Murphy's article, 'Walter Long and the making of the Government of Ireland Act', *Irish Historical Studies*, XXV, No 97 (May, 1986) notes how the choice of Long reassured Ulster Unionists and guaranteed the acquiescence of Conservative backbenchers. From the outset, Murphy argues, the Long committee worked on the basis that there should be two separate parliaments and a council to promote ultimate reunification. Significantly, Murphy judges that the Government of Ireland Bill was not a concession to IRA violence, but was introduced in the mistaken belief that it "could be turned against Sinn Féin". Long himself favoured a six county parliament, but a majority of his committee wanted nine. In the end, he states that it was the need to secure Unionist support for the bill which led the cabinet to back down. At the same time, Long was influential in the cabinet's decision to adopt tougher security measures in mid-1920. Murphy's conclusion is that partition was "the only way out of an otherwise insoluble problem". Kendle's, *Walter Long, Ireland and the Union* also looks closely at Long's contribution to the 1920 act, suggesting that he wanted to preserve the Union "while removing an overweening British presence from Irish affairs". In general, Long believed that a 'quasi-federal structure' offered the best solution to the Irish problem. Disagreeing with Murphy, Kendle argues that Long favoured a nine county parliament, and the cabinet initially supported him in this and rejected Balfour's argument for the exclusion of six counties. By February 1920, however, Long recognised that a six county bloc was necessary if the bill was to be successful, though he was "naturally reluctant to open the door for a permanent partition". Interestingly, Kendle notes that the Government of Ireland Bill aroused very little interest among British MPs as it made its way through parliament. Shannon's, *Arthur J Balfour and Ireland* stresses Balfour's role in the decision to opt for a six county bloc, noting that the Long committee, despite its knowledge of Ulster Unionist opposition, had decided on 17 February 1920 to recommend the exclusion of nine counties. Shannon concludes that Balfour's subsequent intervention was 'crucial' in reversing this decision.

An excellent overview of Anglo-Irish relations in this period can be found in R Fanning's article, 'Anglo-Irish Relations: Partition and the British Dimension in Historical Perspective', *Irish Studies in International Affairs*, Vol 2, No 1 (1985) which emphasises the shift in the political balance of power at Westminster. This was caused by the collapse of the Liberal government and its replacement by a Coalition government and by Asquith's removal in favour of Lloyd George. During the war, he argues, it became necessary "to placate Conservative opinion in the interests of bipartisanship". Then with the general election in December 1918, the Conservative 'stranglehold' on the Coalition government's Irish policy "tightened immeasurably". Fanning uses the term 'Ulstercentricity' to describe the influence behind the 1920 act which was, in his opinion, "not so much a sincere attempt to settle the Irish question as a sincere attempt to settle the Ulster question". By embracing this 'Ulstercentric' initiative Lloyd George kept his rocky Coalition government together. In his assessment of the 1920 act Lee's, *Ireland 1912-1985* argues that "Partition had long existed in the mind. Now it existed on the map". He then goes on to describe the anomalies created by the new border, claiming that it was chosen explicitly to give Unionists "as much territory as they could safely control" and to ensure "Protestant supremacy over Catholics". Foster's, *Modern Ireland* stresses the importance of partition in clearing the way for the Anglo-Irish Treaty. He argues that the inducements to unity contained in the act were simply 'window-dressing', but most British politicians were reluctant to admit this.

Many of the arguments advanced by Gwynn's, *The History of Partition* have subsequently been challenged. Gwynn describes the Ulster Unionists as being "entirely isolated" in their opposition to Home Rule at the end of the war. This view exaggerates their isolation and fails to appreciate that it was a six county bloc which the Ulster Unionists wanted. Gwynn gives too much focus to Carson's judgement and does not take Craig's views into consideration, thus concluding that Ulster Unionists did not welcome the 1920 act. This analysis is challenged by Mansergh's, *The Unresolved Question* which argues that during the cabinet discussions on the impending bill in December 1919, the "general trend of Cabinet opinion" remained in favour of legislation which would lead ultimately to a single all-Ireland parliament. Yet he claims that once it had been decided to create a separate parliament in the excluded area, the most likely outcome was a six county Northern Ireland. A subordinate parliament such as this depended on Ulster Unionist co-operation, and, consequently, the cabinet had to drop its own preference for a nine county Ulster which would have facilitated future reunification. Mansergh illustrates the advantages of the 1920 act to Ulster Unionism, recalling the government's view that "Irishmen had self-determined their own division and only they could end it". He also endorses many of the claims made in J McColgan's, *British Policy and the Irish Administration 1920-22* (London, 1983) which argues convincingly that administrative partition was already in place by the time the Government of Ireland Act was in operation. McColgan emphasises the influence which Ulster Unionists, notably Craig, exercised in the drafting of the Government of Ireland Bill. He shows that Unionists had no intention of participating in the Council of Ireland, noting that the legislation could not compel Unionist participation. With the intentions of the Ulster Unionists so obvious, McColgan judges that it was "remarkable that the British should continue to place so much faith in the pretence that their Bill would motivate North and South to co-operate with a view to eventual union". He also chronicles the preparation which civil servants had made for partition, declaring that the Unionist leaders had shown great foresight in understanding the advantages to be gained from having an administrative machine in place. Laffan's, *The Partition of Ireland* comments on the debate over the area of a new northern state with references to similar decisions which were being made in contemporary Europe. This created a dilemma for the Long committee, because plebiscites were the obvious way to decide the issue, but in opting for nine counties, or even six, British politicians were left open to the charge that they were ignoring the principle of self-determination.

There are numerous accounts which deal with Northern Ireland in its formative period. An excellent starting point is D Harkness's, *Northern Ireland since 1920* (Dublin, 1983) which demonstrates the vital role played by Craig in the period surrounding the implementation of partition. In September 1920, when he was a junior minister in the Lloyd George Coalition government, Craig had been a key influence in the establishment of the USC. Later, in his capacity as Prime Minister, Craig used his extensive network of contacts at Westminster to smooth over potential difficulties for his fledgling administration. Harkness argues that continuing support from Bonar Law was important for the Unionist government, particularly when it came under intense pressure from Lloyd George during the Treaty negotiations. Lloyd George, whom Unionists regarded as unreliable, had tried to bribe Craig with the prospect of lower taxation and, though the Unionists stood firm, they had to acknowledge that the Treaty recognised the unity of Ireland. Harkness judges that Protestant fears on the security issue were genuine and this contributed to the 'siege mentality' which Unionists developed, but the civil war let Unionists off the hook and had, in Harkness's opinion, a profound impact on the prospects for unity. The Troubles are vividly described in Bardon's, *A History of Ulster* which states that Unionists did not trust the RIC in the summer of 1920, because of its predominantly Catholic membership, and this increased their demands for a Protestant force based on a revived UVF. In his assessment of the first Northern Ireland government Bardon quotes the views of James Lichfield, a senior civil servant seconded to Northern Ireland. Lichfield regarded Craig as the only worthwhile member of the Unionist government and, though Bardon rejects this as too sweeping a verdict, he does acknowledge that other members of the cabinet, the products of 'defensive' Unionism, were unlikely to prove imaginative or innovative. The most comprehensive treatment of Ulster Unionism in the immediate post-partition era is P Buckland's, *The Factory of Grievances: Devolved Government in Northern Ireland* (Dublin, 1979), with many of the main arguments repeated in the same author's, *A History of Northern Ireland* (Dublin, 1981). Buckland's general claim is that the performance of the Unionist government during these early years remains a powerful argument against the whole concept of parliamentary devolution. Still, Buckland does examine the Unionist government's responses to the problems it faced with considerable understanding. It was not surprising that facing violent internal and external opposition, a siege mentality should take hold. Indeed the sectarian security policy pursued by the Unionist government emerged almost by accident, as the new state reacted to the violence which was threatening its existence. In other areas, the Unionist government deliberately set out to discriminate against the minority. Nationalist rhetoric emanating from Dublin and Westminster's unwillingness to become involved in the province's affairs contributed to this development. Buckland concludes by describing Westminster's unsuccessful attempt to frustrate the 1922 Local Government Act which abolished PR in local government elections. With Westminster reluctant to intervene directly, it "could do little to supervise the conduct of government in Northern Ireland".

Two books fiercely critical of the Unionist government's early performance are M Farrell's, *Northern Ireland: The Orange State* (London, 1976) and his, *Arming the Protestants: The Formation of the Ulster Special Constabulary and the Royal Ulster Constabulary 1920-27* (London, 1983). Farrell dismisses the idea that the new state was under siege and describes this formative period as a bloody pogrom against the Catholic population in Belfast, which had the support of the Unionist leadership. He also describes the activities of the UPA, a loyalist terror group whose aim, in the words of one senior police officer, was "the extermination of Catholics by any and every means". In his assessment of the USC, Farrell attacks the Unionist government for its use of the force to defend "the Protestant supremacy', and he criticises successive governments at Westminster which established and financed a force with such an extreme sectarian character. He also argues that attempts by Nationalists to redress these grievances were consistently rebuffed by the Unionist leadership. A more complete analysis of the political aims of northern Nationalism in this period is found in Pheonix's, *Northern Nationalism* which outlines the divisions within Nationalism. In general, Pheonix claims that Devlin and Nationalists in the east of the province were, by the end of 1922, looking for a formula which would enable them to recognise, and then participate in, the Northern Ireland parliament. Border Nationalists, on the other hand, took a more uncompromising line. Significantly, the growing indifference of the Dublin government to the plight of northern Nationalists reinforced Devlin's determination to enter the Belfast parliament. In 1925 Devlin finally led his followers into parliament where, with the support of the Catholic hierarchy, they aired minority grievances, particularly in relation to education. They were joined in the summer of 1927 by the border Nationalist MPs.

Perhaps the most interesting account of this period is P Bew, P Gibbon and H

Patterson's, *The State in Northern Ireland 1921-72: Political Forces and Social Classes* (Manchester, 1979) which provides a subtle critique of Farrell's hostile commentary. This book stresses the importance of class relations within the Protestant community, arguing that Craig had to retain the support and confidence of the Protestant masses if his government was to survive. The outbreak of civil war in the south represented a huge stroke of luck for Craig, as one of its consequences was the removal of Westminster pressure on the Belfast administration. The authors examine the political and economic implications of the expulsions of Catholic workers in 1920 which, they argue, "marked a critical phase of class relations within the Unionist bloc, a crisis which permitted the development of the B Specials and gave the Unionist state apparatuses a particularly repressive aspect from the Catholic point of view". The British authorities failed to prevent this and full Catholic recognition of the new state which, they claim, was 'negotiable' in the first instance, became impossible. Thereafter, the authors analyse the struggle which developed within the Unionist leadership between 'populists' led by Craig and 'anti-populists' led by Pollock, the Minister of Finance. Craig's group triumphed with the result that no effort was made to build a consensus, in which the minority would be fully involved, and, instead, a 'Protestant state' was allowed to develop.

Chapter 13
Conclusion

The rise of Irish Nationalism posed a new challenge for successive Westminster governments during the nineteenth century. Under O'Connell's direction Nationalism evolved as a mass movement and, both as a cause and a consequence of this, it developed as Catholic Nationalism. Yet it was in the second quarter of the nineteenth century that Irish Nationalism put down firm liberal foundations which kept it wedded to the democratic tradition for much of the nineteenth and early twentieth centuries. This was, of course, punctuated by isolated bursts of activity, as revolutionary Nationalism, or 'Fenianism', building on the inspiration of 1798, tried unsuccessfully to end British rule in Ireland by the use of force. Then in the late 1870s Nationalism underwent a crucial metamorphosis when the socio-economic grievances of the dominant tenant farming class became bound up with the political objective of Irish Home Rule. With Parnell taking the helm Nationalism adopted a strategy of militant constitutionalism, based on sustained land agitation in Ireland and an independent, united approach by the Irish party at Westminster, which drew a series of concessions from the British. This combined approach had forced Ireland onto the political agenda at Westminster. The Conservative party's response was to introduce land legislation which, in a very short period, enabled tenants to become owners of their farms, believing that a solution to the land problem would deflate Irish Nationalism and negate the demand for Home Rule. For a brief period in the mid-1880s Parnell's Irish party held the balance of power at Westminster and this state of affairs contributed to Gladstone's decision to opt for Home Rule. The Liberal leader's conversion to Home Rule had significant ramifications for British politics. A number of Liberal dissidents broke ranks and joined the Conservative party though, in the long run, this was to prove more detrimental to the Conservatives.

Parnell's strategy of militant constitutionalism had obviously brought substantial gains to Irish Nationalism, but there was a limit to what 80 - something Irish MPs could achieve at Westminster. His fall from grace tore the Irish party apart and it never fully recovered from this upheaval. Crucially, it was not in strong enough shape to take advantage of the potential gains which might have come from Unionist-Nationalist consensus, the 'conference plus business' policy urged by William O'Brien around the turn of the century, and an opportunity to square the Unionist-Nationalist circle was missed. Under Redmond the IPP became increasingly wedded to the Liberal party and its fortunes became, to some extent, bound up with those of the Liberals. As the Liberal party declined, the IPP was dragged down with it. The Liberals took up the Home Rule cause in 1912 with little enthusiasm or conviction. If either had been present in any quantity, Home Rule would have been introduced after the 1906 general election when the Liberals enjoyed an overwhelming majority. In such circumstances a bill commanding a huge majority in the Commons would either have been waved through by a protesting House of Lords or, if rejected, would have given the Liberals the opportunity to strangle the Upper House and thus cleared the path for the government's radical social programme.

The Irish Question dominated British politics in the immediate prewar years, as an increasingly desperate Conservative party strayed well outside the boundaries of conventional political opposition. Bonar Law, with his Ulster connections, undoubtedly strengthened the Conservative commitment to the Unionist cause. For their part the Ulster Unionists were remarkably successful in mobilising the Protestant population of the north-east in support of their resistance campaign though, behind this facade of determined and united opposition, there was a good deal of uncertainty and division. Carson's attempts to find a political escape from the Home Rule deadlock, while he maintained his 'No Surrender' public posture, is further evidence of this. In the end partition was unavoidable. Certainly, some form of psychological partition existed well before 1921, or even 1912, but its final shape could have been very different. The inclusion of Tyrone and Fermanagh in the new Northern Ireland state was indefensible, and much of the blame for this mistake can be attributed to the IPP's decision to accept six county exclusion in the summer of 1916. Still, the obvious point that Sinn Féin and de Valera fared no better on the Ulster problem than the IPP and Redmond needs to be emphasised.

The militant constitutionalism and mobilisation of grass roots opinion associated with Parnell was, to some extent, copied by Carson and the Ulster Unionists in the 1911-14 period. Yet much of the enthusiasm for Parnellism was based on land agitation, and Ulster Unionism had no comparable socio-economic motor. Simple opposition to Home Rule had galvanised opinion in Ulster, and this led Unionism to develop both an increasingly negative or defensive character and a powerful religious undercurrent. It was true, moreover, that the IPP under Redmond lacked the vigour of the Parnell era. The removal of agrarian discontent was the primary reason and, though it enjoyed overwhelming, essentially unchallenged, electoral support, there was not the same popular enthusiasm for the party under Redmond. In this new phase it could only offer Home Rule and its failure to deliver on this quickly eroded support for constitutional Nationalism. Discontent with old Nationalism was already evident among the educated Catholic middle class in the early years of the twentieth century. It was this group, feeling itself frustrated both by the inherent corruption and limitations of local Nationalist politics and by the British presence in Ireland, which developed a new form of Nationalism. This first found expression through the cultural pursuits of the Gaelic League, though it inevitably took on a more political character and, consequently, laid an important foundation-stone for the 1916 rising. While it attracted considerable attention, partly through its own successful propaganda efforts, this more advanced Nationalism, with its heavy cultural baggage, only stirred a minority of the population. Still, it was from this minority that a revolutionary generation emerged which eventually supplanted the IPP. The IRB activists, led by Clarke, saw the potential in this development and, using the distraction of the First World War, launched their rebellion. No effort was made to make the rising a popular rebellion. It was, rather, an attempt by a revolutionary elite to drag an unwilling population in its wake.

The war had provided the backdrop to the rising. The conflict had diluted Redmond's Nationalism, and the British tendency to take Irish support for granted had generated anti-war feeling, particularly in rural Ireland, and this was quickly translated and articulated as anti-British feeling. Latent anti-British feeling was, of course, a common feature of Irish rural life, but it took the rising and the subsequent executions to unleash this sentiment on a large scale. Sinn Féin, a broad banner for all those alienated by British rule or frustrated by constitutional Nationalism, was the beneficiary of this development. In one sense the rise of Sinn Féin was a signal that Irish Nationalism, as Pearse had wished, had finally caught up with Ulster Unionism. Yet, more significantly, Ireland shared in the common European experience which saw political opinion radicalised across the continent. While Benes and Masaryk would have been content with Home Rule for Czechoslovakia in 1914, they were demanding independence in 1919. De Valera and Sinn Féin echoed this demand in Ireland. The notion of a national war of independence against British rule is a myth. The War of Independence was a low-key affair in which the IRA improvised to overcome its shortage of men and equipment. The British security response was counter-productive, but many IRA commanders were concerned about the lack of popular support at local level. While there was a common enemy, however, it had been possible to bury the divisions within the broad 'republican' front, but the British withdrawal allowed these differences to surface. The result was a needless civil war which did lasting political and economic damage to the Irish Free State. The defeat of the republicans in the civil war was not a counter revolution. Even though workers had set up soviets and the landless had seized the land, there was little real desire to change Ireland's social or economic structure. This was not surprising in a society where Westminster's progressive land legislation had created a new dominant landowning farmer class, and the instincts of this class were clearly conservative. This was reflected in Sinn Féin's social outlook.

Therefore, the state which survived the civil war was characterised by its caution and conservatism, though it did a fine job in laying solid foundations for an independent Ireland. As expected, Southern Unionists did not enjoy a position of power in the new state. Their numbers and influence dwindled, but this process was already under way once they had been abandoned by their British and Ulster colleagues. The Nationalist minority in the north did not follow a parallel path. They had also been abandoned by their fellow Nationalists in the south, but their numbers were much more significant. Generally, northern Nationalists did not recognise the new Northern Ireland state, and their sense of alienation increased as they experienced life under Unionist rule. Circumstances in the 1920-22 period made it difficult for Ulster Unionists to seek an accommodation with Nationalists, but the Unionist leadership failed to recognise that it was in their long term interests to encourage Nationalist participation in the new state. Successive Westminster governments, which were ultimately responsible for Northern Ireland, also failed to appreciate that the Unionists' failure to create a fair and stable society in the north would force them, once again, to confront the Irish Question.

Index of people

Index of historians

General index